APPLIED
BUSINESS
STATISTICS

Fadil H. Zuwaylif

California State University, Northridge

APPLIED
BUSINESS
STATISTICS

ADDISON-WESLEY PUBLISHING COMPANY
Reading, Massachusetts
Menlo Park, California • London
Amsterdam • Don Mills, Ontario • Sydney

Sponsoring editor: *Cindy Johnson*
Production manager: *Herbert Nolan*
Production editor: *Stephanie Argeros-Magean*
Text designer: *Margaret Ong Tsao*
Cover designers: *Margaret Ong Tsao and Vanessa Pineiro*
Art editor: *Joseph K. Vetere*
Copy editor: *Barbara G. Flanagan*
Illustrator: *ANCO/Boston*
Cover photographer: *George Glod, Four by Five*
Manufacturing supervisor: *Hugh J. Crawford*

To my loving wife, Sabah

Library of Congress Cataloging in Publication Data

Zuwaylif, Fadil H., 1932–
 Applied business statistics.

 Includes index.
 1. Commercial statistics. 2. Statistics. I. Title.
HF1017.Z88 1984   519.5'024658   83-11928
ISBN 0-201-09627-7

PREFACE

Having taught statistics for years in a number of university business schools, I observed that most students entered such classes thoroughly convinced that the subject would be difficult, indeed, incomprehensible. *Applied Business Statistics* is designed to show that statistics can be understood by students whose mathematical background is limited to a basic course in algebra. The first edition of the text has been consistently praised for its ability to communicate the basic concepts of statistics—concepts important to anyone who will need to make decisions in an increasingly competitive business environment.

FEATURES

There are many elements that make this book effective, the foremost being its *simplicity* and *organization*. The concepts basic to a solid foundation in statistics are logically and lucidly developed, without the distraction of unnecessary detail. A clear distinction between a population and a sample is made at the beginning of Chapter 1, and this distinction is maintained throughout the text. Chapter 2 is devoted to the treatment of population parameters. A general survey of probability is presented in Chapters 3 and 4, with an expanded treatment of the distinction between objective and subjective probabilities. Sampling is the subject of Chapter 5. Since the book deals primarily with statistical inference concerning the arithmetic mean and the proportion, Chapters 6, 7, and 8 are devoted to the problems of estimating the mean and testing hypotheses concerning the mean. Statistical inference concerning the proportion is the subject of Chapters 9 and 10. The first ten chapters thus provide a solid foundation in the basics of descriptive and inferential statistics and probability, which is critical to the interpretation of statistical results that all managers must deal with. Further study will build on these basic concepts.

The second half of the book is designed to provide *maximum flexibility* for the instructor. Chapter 11 presents an elementary treatment of simple linear regression and correlation. Two new chapters—Inference in Regression (Chapter 12) and Multiple Regression and Correlation (Chapter 13)—expand the subject for instructors who wish to go into greater depth. Chapter 13 includes the use of STATPAK and MINITAB for performing multiple regression. Chapters 14 and 15 deal with the analysis of time series. After a concise treatment of linear and semilogarithmic trend measurement and seasonal index construction, the use of these tools in forecasting is thoroughly discussed. Chapter 16 presents index numbers and Chapter 17 is devoted to nonparametric statistical techniques. Chapters 18 and 19 deal with Bayesian Decision Theory and use the discrete case (binomial distribution) to illustrate the prior and posterior analysis of a decision problem. If the instructor wishes, index numbers, nonparametrics, or decision theory can be studied immediately after Chapter 10, and times series after Chapter 11, since these units are independent of one another.

For many students, the *extensive use of practical examples and exercises* will be the most important feature of the book. Concepts are introduced through a business-related example, then carefully developed and illustrated in this practical vein. A wealth of worked-out examples reinforces the applied nature of statistics for the student.

Cumulative review exercises test the student's ability to integrate the material covered in previous chapters. The three Cumulative Reviews, which follow Chapters 4, 8, and 10, recap and reinforce the basic concepts contained in the first half of the text.

Useful end-of-chapter study aids are also provided—a *summary of formulas* presented in the chapter and *a glossary of key terms*.

The book ends with a *table* section, the *answers* to exercises, and a combined glossary/index.

SUPPLEMENTS

The *Study Guide* that accompanies the text was prepared by Kevin Miller. For each chapter in the text there are chapter objectives, a summary of main points, self-evaluation exercises, a posttest, partially solved problems, additional problems, and exercises and projects for more in-depth practice. A complete *Solutions Manual* for text exercises is available for the instructor.

ACKNOWLEDGMENTS

I would like to thank the following individuals for their helpful comments on the new edition: Professors Jorge Andre, St. Francis College; Roger Gledhill, Eastern Michigan University; Harold Hackett, SUNY Agricultural and Technical College–Alfred; Albert Kinderman, California State University, Northridge; Russell Lebo, Northampton County Area Community College; R. Burt Madden, University of Arkansas at Little Rock; David Murphy, Boston College; William Weiss, Seattle University; and Richard Westfall, Cabrillo College. In addition, I wish to express my appreciation to Pam Gresham, Nancy Meadows, and Judy Wolgamott for their tireless typing. My sincerest thanks to James Robertson, Dean of the School of Business Administration and Economics, California State University, Northridge, for his continued encouragement and support. My love and gratitude to my daughter, Samara, for her many efforts in editing the new chapters, in formulating new exercises, and for her patience in the tedious task of proofreading the galleys. And finally, I would like to thank my editor Cindy Johnson for her help and encouragement throughout the revision of the text. Also, my deep and sincere thanks to Stephanie Argeros-Magean for her patience and relentless efforts in producing the book.

Northridge, California   F.H.Z.
November 1983

CONTENTS

APPLIED
BUSINESS
STATISTICS

INTRODUCTION TO STATISTICS

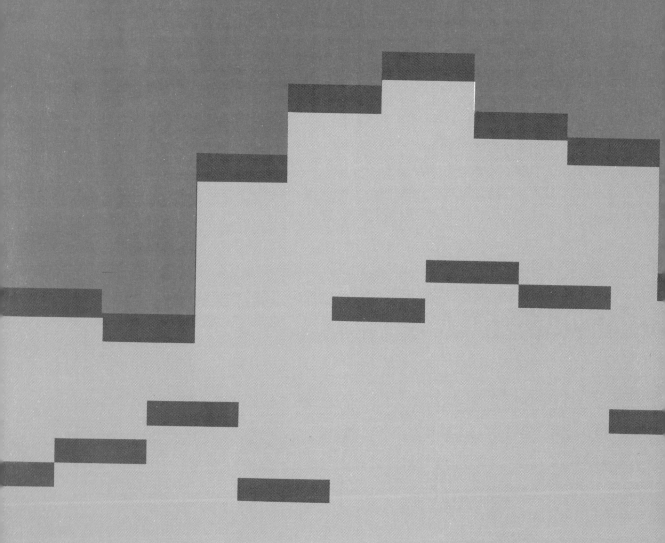

1

Many business students view statistics as a difficult subject that can be understood and used only by a mathematician or a specialist. In this chapter we present the general nature of the subject in such a manner as to alleviate the reader's apprehensions. More important, we show that statistics can provide the businessperson with some proven tools to solve everyday business problems. Specifically, we present definitions of basic statistical concepts and terms utilizing simple and familiar examples.

As purchasing manager for the Pocket Radio Corporation you must decide between two brands of 9-volt batteries that are available locally in ample supply. The wholesale prices of the two brands, A and B, are identical. The choice must therefore be based on the comparative quality of the two products.

There are various measures for quality, but you have chosen the average life of a battery as the most important measure. You wish to purchase the brand with the highest average life.

To make your choice, you test 100 batteries of each brand. Brand A shows an average life of 48 hours and brand B, 47 hours. Concluding that A has a longer life than B, you purchase A.

Are you *absolutely* sure that A is superior to B? The answer clearly is no. Most probably brand A is superior to B. However, the possibility exists that the two brands are of the same quality. It is also possible that brand B is superior to A, although this possibility is less probable.

How, then, can we compare the average lives of the two brands if we desire our conclusion to be absolutely correct? We must examine not only 100 batteries, not even 1000 batteries, but all the batteries that are made and will be made of the two brands.

If the life of every battery of brand A is measured (this is an impossible task indeed, since more and more batteries are produced every day), we obtain what is called the **statistical population** of brand A. The statistical population of brand A, therefore, consists of thousands and thousands of numbers, where each number measures the life of an individual battery. A statistical population is complete data. If such complete data are available, the average life of a brand A battery can be determined with absolute certainty.

In the same manner, the statistical population of brand B consists of very many numbers, each describing the life of a particular battery of brand B.

The statistical populations of the two brands are infinite, and complete data are impossible to obtain. Therefore, the average life of each brand must be determined from a given number of batteries, say 100. These 100 batteries represent a part or a **sample** of the complete population. A sample is a part of a population.

When we compare the average lives of the two brands of batteries, our conclusion will be based only on a sample selected from each brand. But any conclusion based on a sample rather than on complete population data may be erroneous because the sample may not be representative of the population from which it was selected.

It is true that the risk of incorrect conclusions is always present unless we obtain data on the entire population. However, conclusions based on sample data can be evaluated by various statistical methods and techniques. Knowledge of statistics enables us to attach certain confidence to our conclusions. We may be able to state, for example, that there is .95 or .99 confidence that brand A is superior to brand B. It must be emphasized again that absolute certainty is obtained only when complete population data are examined.

Statistics, therefore, is a field of knowledge that enables the investigator to derive and evaluate conclusions about a population from sample data. Specifically, statistics deals with theorems, tools, methods, and techniques to be used in

1. gathering, selecting, and classifying data;
2. interpreting and analyzing data; and
3. deriving and evaluating the reliability of conclusions based on sample data.

STATISTICAL POPULATIONS

The distinction between a sample and a population must be made clear at the outset. A set of data is a population if decisions and conclusions based on these data can be made with absolute certainty. In other words, if population data are available, the risk of arriving at incorrect decisions is completely eliminated. In contrast, a sample is only a part of a population, and conclusions based on any part of a population could be erroneous indeed.

The data of which a statistical population consists are either measured or described characteristics of certain objects. These objects are called the **elementary units** of the population. We will give some examples of statistical populations to clarify these concepts.

1. Suppose we wish to determine the average annual family income in a community of 10,000 families. Then our population consists of 10,000 numbers ($5273, $4000, $10,500, . . .), each number representing the income of a particular family. The elementary unit is a family living in that community, and the characteristic to be measured is a family's annual income.

2. We wish to determine the average age of a student attending San Francisco State University, where total enrollment is 15,000 students. Then our statistical population consists of 15,000 numbers (18, 23, 22, . . .), each indicating the age of a particular student. The elementary unit is a student attending San Francisco State University, and the characteristic to be measured is a student's age.

3. Not all characteristics can be measured; some can only be described. We want to determine the vacancy rate in Northridge, California, where there are 20,000 dwelling units. Our population of interest consists of 20,000 terms (occupied, occupied, occupied, vacant, occupied, . . .), each term

describing the occupancy status of a particular dwelling unit in North-ridge.

Thus, a statistical population is a set of measured or described observations made on each and every elementary unit. Measurable observations are called **quantitative observations.** The annual income of a family, the age of a student, the life of an electric bulb, and the shearing strength of a weld are all measurable and are, therefore, quantitative observations. In comparison, the vacancy status of a dwelling unit, the marital status of a person, the make of the car we drive, and the brand of coffee we drink cannot be measured; they can only be described. Such nonmeasurable observations are called **qualitative observations.**

The values assumed by quantitative observations are called *variates.* Thus, if the annual income of a family is $15,320.17, the number $15,320.17 is called a variate. Similarly, if the life of an electric bulb is 852 hours, the number 852 is called a variate.

Quantitative observations are further classified as either discrete variates or continuous variates. A **discrete variate** can assume only a limited number of values on a measuring scale. The number of students in a statistics class, for example, can be 25 or 26, but it certainly cannot be 25.3 or 25.712. Similarly, the size of a family can be 1, 2, 3, 4, . . . , but it cannot be 2.37 or 4.15. The number of students in a statistics class and the size of a family are thus considered discrete because each can assume only a limited number of values on a measuring scale.

Some quantitative observations, on the other hand, can assume an infinite' number of values on a measuring scale. These quantitative observations are called **continuous variates.** The age of a student in this class, for example, can be 18 or 19 years; but it can also be, at least theoretically, one of an infinite number of values between 18 and 19, such as 18.31 or 18.813 years. In the same manner, a pineapple can weigh 3 or 4 pounds as well as an infinite number of other values between 3 and 4 pounds, such as 3.178 pounds. The age of a student and the weight of a pineapple are thus considered continuous quantitative observations because each can assume an infinite number of values on a measuring scale.

Qualitative observations cannot be measured; they can only be described. The vacancy status of a dwelling unit, for example, can be described by the term occupied or vacant. These terms are called **attributes.** Similarly, the marital status of a person can be described by such terms as single, married, divorced, and widowed. These terms are also called attributes.

The distinction between a population of variates (a set of *measured observations*) and a population of attributes (a set of *described observations*) is important. Since variates are measurable, their arithmetic mean or simple average can be calculated. The average age of a student, the average family income, the average life of an electric bulb, and the average shearing strength of a weld can be and most often are calculated.

Ratios or percentages, on the other hand, are calculated for attributes. The percentage of vacant dwelling units, the percentage of defective articles in a given lot, and the percentage of seniors in a college are usually calculated from data that consist of attributes.

In conclusion, it must be emphasized that although the decision in a given problem depends on such information as the value of the average variate in the population, such an average value is seldom calculated using the entire population data. The value of the average variate is usually estimated from a carefully selected sample.

In many problems, the statistical population is infinite, and therefore complete data are impossible to obtain. Even when population data can be obtained, the cost and time involved in collecting and analyzing such data would be prohibitive. Information is therefore obtained from sample data, and decisions based on sample information constitute the hard core of statistics.

FREQUENCY DISTRIBUTION

Statistical data may consist of a very large number of observations. The larger the number of observations, the greater the need to present the data in a summarized form that may omit some details but that reveals the general nature of a mass of data. A **frequency distribution** is a summary of a large number of observations. Table 1.1 summarizes the ages of 1,763,000 unemployed males in the United States in a certain month.

Although the frequency distribution in Table 1.1 does not list the age of every unemployed male, it certainly presents a better general picture of the

TABLE 1.1   UNEMPLOYED MALES LOOKING FOR FULL- OR PART-TIME WORK, BY AGE, DURING ONE MONTH

Age	Number of Unemployed Males
14 to 19 years	218,000
20 to 24 years	313,000
25 to 55 years	977,000
55 years and over	255,000
Total	1,763,000

TABLE 1.2   MAJOR FIELDS OF STUDY OF STUDENTS AT SCHOOL OF BUSINESS, CALIFORNIA STATE UNIVERSITY, NORTHRIDGE, FALL 1984

Major Field	Number of Students
Accounting	472
Business education	42
Economics	88
Finance	224
Marketing	163
Office administration	50
Personnel	73
Production	39
Quantitative methods	34
Undecided	116
Total	1301

ages of unemployed males than would a list of 1,763,000 individual numbers occupying hundreds of pages.

Table 1.2 summarizes the major fields of study of 1301 students attending the School of Business at California State University, Northridge, during the fall of 1984.

Table 1.1 shows a frequency distribution of variates, because the age of an unemployed person can be measured in years. Table 1.2, on the other hand, is a frequency distribution of attributes. A student's major field cannot be measured but can only be described as accounting, marketing, finance, and so on.

Frequency Distribution of Attributes

The construction of a frequency distribution of attributes is a simple task indeed. One simply lists the various attributes together with the frequency of their occurrence.

Example   Twenty students in a business statistics class reported their major fields as follows:

Accounting, Accounting, Marketing, Management, Management, Marketing, Accounting, Management, Finance, Accounting, Marketing, Finance, Accounting, Finance, Finance, Accounting, Marketing, Marketing, Accounting, Accounting.

TABLE 1.3 FREQUENCY DISTRIBUTION OF STUDENTS' FIELDS OF STUDY

Major Field	Number of Students
Accounting	8
Finance	4
Management	3
Marketing	5
Total	20

The set of attributes can be summarized in the frequency distribution shown in Table 1.3.

A frequency distribution of attributes can also be represented graphically by a bar chart, in which the length of each bar is determined by the frequency of the attribute it represents. The bars should have the same width, and the space between them should be uniform. See Fig. 1.1.

Frequency Distribution of Variates

Summarizing a large number of variates by a frequency distribution is in general more difficult than summarizing a set of attributes because of the very many different values of the variates. A ledger of accounts receivable, for example,

Figure 1.1 Major fields of 20 students in business statistics class.

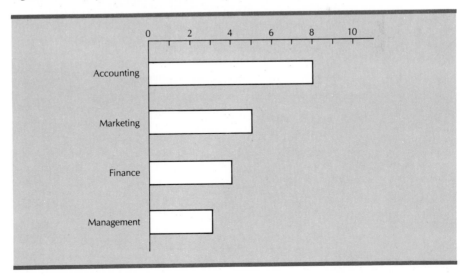

may list amounts of $20.24, $83.17, $9.92, and so on. Thus a list of all the values of the accounts receivable in the ledger, together with the frequency of their occurrence, may lead exactly nowhere if no two accounts in the ledger have the same value. Even when some accounts have the same value, the resulting summary may be as detailed as, and no more useful than, the original unsummarized data.

The difficulty of summarizing a set of variates, however, can be overcome by grouping the variates into a limited number of classes called *class intervals.* A concrete example will best explain the construction of class intervals.

Example   The following are the balances (in dollars) of 100 accounts receivable taken from the ledger of the XYZ Store.

31,	38,	41,	52,	59,	46,	74,	69,	39,	60,
69,	83,	78,	74,	77,	35,	79,	80,	71,	65,
56,	69,	34,	33,	92,	37,	60,	43,	51,	61,
74,	68,	83,	49,	34,	71,	58,	83,	94,	66,
78,	48,	34,	50,	68,	65,	64,	95,	92,	81,
77,	84,	41,	40,	38,	38,	60,	67,	50,	86,
76,	99,	38,	94,	48,	70,	80,	95,	98,	42,
55,	49,	54,	60,	62,	70,	88,	94,	85,	51,
59,	68,	51,	87,	53,	57,	54,	46,	46,	76,
69,	64,	61,	63,	78,	55,	66,	73,	75,	64

These accounts are summarized in the distribution given in Table 1.4.

In constructing the frequency distribution in Table 1.4, we group the 100 accounts into seven class intervals: 30–39, 40–49, 50–59, 60–69, 70–79, 80–89, and 90–99. Each of the seven classes has a lower and an upper limit. The lower limit of a class is the smallest number that falls into the class, and the

TABLE 1.4   FREQUENCY DISTRIBUTION OF ACCOUNTS RECEIVABLE, XYZ STORE

Class Dollars	Number of Accounts
30–39	11
40–49	12
50–59	16
60–69	23
70–79	17
80–89	11
90–99	10
Total	100

TABLE 1.5

Class Interval	Lower Boundary	Upper Boundary	Class Mark	Frequency
30–39	29.5	39.5	34.5	11
40–49	39.5	49.5	44.5	12
50–59	49.5	59.5	54.5	16
60–69	59.5	69.5	64.5	23
70–79	69.5	79.5	74.5	17
80–89	79.5	89.5	84.5	11
90–99	89.5	99.5	94.5	10

upper limit is the largest number that falls into the same class. The first class interval, 30–39, has a lower limit of 30 and an upper limit of 39. The lower limit of the second class is 40.

Overlapping class limits (for example, first class interval 30–40, second class interval 40–50) should be avoided to eliminate confusion as to which class an individual amount belongs to.

Once again, the upper limit of the first class interval is 39 and the lower limit of the second class interval is 40. The midpoint between these two successive class limits is 39.5. This midpoint is called the *upper boundary* for the first class interval and the *lower boundary* for the second class interval. Similarly, the point 49.5 is the upper boundary for the second class interval and the lower boundary for the third class interval. All variates in a given class must be greater than the lower boundary and smaller than the upper boundary of the class. Class boundaries must be carried to *one more decimal place* than the variates to be grouped, to avoid ambiguous assignments of variates.

To continue our definitions, the difference between the upper and lower boundaries of a class is called *class width*. The width of the first class is $10.0 ($39.5 − $29.5), and the width of the second class is also $10.0 ($49.5 − $39.5). All class intervals in a given frequency distribution must have the same width.

The midpoint between the two limits (or boundaries) of a given class is called the *class mark*. The class mark for the first class interval is

$$\left(\frac{30 + 39}{2}\right) \quad \text{or} \quad \left(\frac{29.5 + 39.5}{2}\right) = 34.5.$$

Finally, the number of variates falling in a given class interval is called the *frequency* of that class. Table 1.5 shows the class intervals, class boundaries, class mark, and frequency of each class interval in the frequency distribution of the 100 accounts receivable for the XYZ Store.

How to Construct a Frequency Distribution of Variates

In constructing a frequency distribution of variates, we must first decide how many classes there are to be. In general, the number of classes to be used in constructing a frequency distribution of variates depends to a large extent on the nature of the data to be summarized as well as on the purpose for summarizing the data. However, some guidelines may be helpful. First, the number of classes should not be too small or too large. A small number of classes may conceal the general nature of the data, and a large number of classes may be too detailed to reveal any useful information. As a rule, it is recommended that the number of classes be between 5 and 20. Sturges' rule, furthermore, may provide a convenient approximation to the number of classes. According to this rule,

$$\text{Number of classes} = 1 + 3.3 \log N,$$

where N is the number of observations to be summarized. Applying Sturges' rule to the 100 accounts receivable of the XYZ Store, we find that

$$\text{Number of classes} = 1 + 3.3 \log 100$$

$$= 1 + (3.3)2$$

$$= 7.6 \text{ classes.}$$

Thus, according to Sturges' rule, we should have about 7 or 8 classes summarizing our accounts receivable. In constructing our frequency of these accounts we have used 7 classes.

Once the number of classes has been determined, we must decide on the class width. All class intervals must have the same class width. In such a case, the class width can be approximated as follows:

$$\text{Class width} = \frac{\text{Highest variate} - \text{Lowest variate}}{\text{Number of classes}}.$$

Referring to the 100 accounts receivable, we have

$$\text{Class width} = \frac{\$99 - \$31}{7} = \$9.7.$$

For ease of computing, we use $10 rather than $9.7 as a class width.

Having determined the approximate number of classes (7) and the width of each class ($10), we now choose the bottom limit (the lower limit of the first class). Since the smallest account receivable is $31, the bottom limit should be $31 or less. Here, again because of convenience, we choose a bottom limit of $30.

Having determined that the lower class limit for the first class interval is 30, our next step is to establish the lower class boundary for this first class interval. Since our accounts receivable are rounded to the nearest dollar, and since class boundaries must be carried out to one more decimal place than the accounts receivable, the lower class boundary for the first class interval must be established as 29.5. (This lower boundary would be 29.995 had the accounts receivable been given to the nearest cent.)

The upper class boundary for the first class interval can now be obtained by adding the class width, 10, to the lower boundary.

$$\text{Upper boundary} = \text{Lower boundary} + \text{Class width}$$

$$= \quad 29.5 \quad + \quad 10$$

$$= \quad 39.5.$$

Consequently, the upper limit for the first class interval is 39.

Class Interval	Lower Boundary	Upper Boundary	Class Width
30–39	29.5	39.5	10

The successive class limits and boundaries can now be obtained by adding the class width, 10, to the preceding limits and boundaries (see Table 1.6). Once the appropriate class intervals have been constructed, the number of

TABLE 1.6

Class Interval	Lower Boundary	Upper Boundary	Class Width
30–39	29.5	39.5	10
40–49	39.5	49.5	10
50–59	49.5	59.5	10
60–69	59.5	69.5	10
70–79	69.5	79.5	10
80–89	79.5	89.5	10
90–99	89.5	99.5	10

TABLE 1.7 FREQUENCY DISTRIBUTION OF ACCOUNTS RECEIVABLE, XYZ STORE

Class Interval	Frequency
30–39	11
40–49	12
50–59	16
60–69	23
70–79	17
80–89	11
90–99	10
Total	100

accounts receivable falling in any given class is counted, and that number is regarded as the frequency of that class. The resulting frequency distribution is shown in Table 1.7.

A frequency distribution of variates can also be represented graphically by a *histogram.* In constructing such a diagram, class boundaries are marked off along the horizontal axis of the graph, and a rectangle is drawn to represent

Figure 1.2   Distribution of 100 accounts receivable, XYZ Store

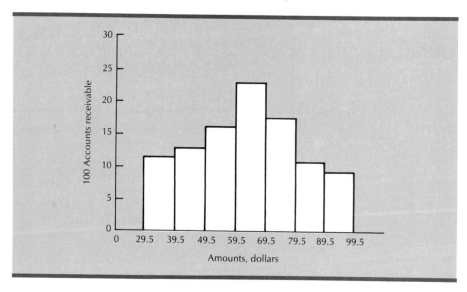

each class. The base of the rectangle corresponds to the class width, and the height of the rectangle corresponds to the frequency of the class. (See Fig. 1.2.)

1.1 Determine the class boundaries, the class width, and the class mark for the class intervals 10–14, 15–19, 20–24, 25–29.

1.2 The lifetimes in hours of sixty 100-watt electric bulbs are

807,	811,	620,	650,	817,	732,	747,	823,	844,	907,
660,	753,	1050,	918,	857,	867,	675,	880,	878,	890,
881,	872,	869,	841,	847,	833,	829,	827,	822,	811,
766,	787,	923,	792,	803,	933,	947,	717,	817,	753,
1056,	1076,	958,	970,	776,	828,	831,	781,	1088,	1082,
832,	863,	852,	788,	980,	889,	1030,	897,	755,	891.

a) Construct a frequency distribution of the lifetimes of these 60 electric bulbs (use equal class widths).

b) Draw a histogram of the frequency distribution.

1.3 Draw a bar chart to represent the following frequency distribution of attributes.

Surgical Operations Performed in Dillingham Memorial Hospital, 1984	
Type of Operation	*Number of Cases*
General surgery	98
Thoracic surgery	20
Abdominal surgery	112
Proctologic surgery	67
Urologic surgery	79
Eye, ear, nose, and throat surgery	56
Neurosurgery	25
Operations on bones and joints	44

1.4   The annual sales of 80 branches of McCarthy Department Stores (in millions of dollars) are as follows.

38	30	36	32	33	27	38	45
43	21	24	45	33	49	41	36
28	32	43	24	36	47	33	24
35	38	36	44	24	39	21	26
20	42	30	42	43	46	41	46
27	34	32	23	27	34	32	23
25	23	21	44	35	34	33	28
21	24	44	44	23	28	36	30
24	27	25	29	36	47	42	40
27	31	46	48	20	23	48	21

a) Construct a frequency distribution of the annual sales for these 80 branches.

b) Draw a histogram of the frequency distribution.

1.5   Draw a bar chart to represent the following frequency distribution of attributes.

Wholesale Trade by Type of Operation, 1984

Type of Operation	Establishments (thousands)
Merchant wholesalers	200
Manufacturers' sales branches and offices	50
Petroleum bulk plants and terminals	60
Merchandise agents and brokers	55
Assemblers of farm products	130

KEY TERMS

statistical population   The collection of measured or described observations made on every elementary unit of interest to an investigator.

sample   A portion of a statistical population.

statistics   A field of knowledge that enables an investigator to derive and evaluate conclusions about a population from sample data.

elementary unit   An object belonging to a statistical population.

quantitative observation   An observation that results in a measurement of an elementary unit.

qualitative observation   An observation that results in a description of an elementary unit.

discrete variate   A quantitative measurement that can have only a limited number of values.

continuous variate   A quantitative measurement that can have an infinite number of values.

attribute   A term that describes a qualitative observation.

frequency distribution   A summary of a large number of observations showing how many observations fall into various categories or classes.

POPULATION
PARAMETERS

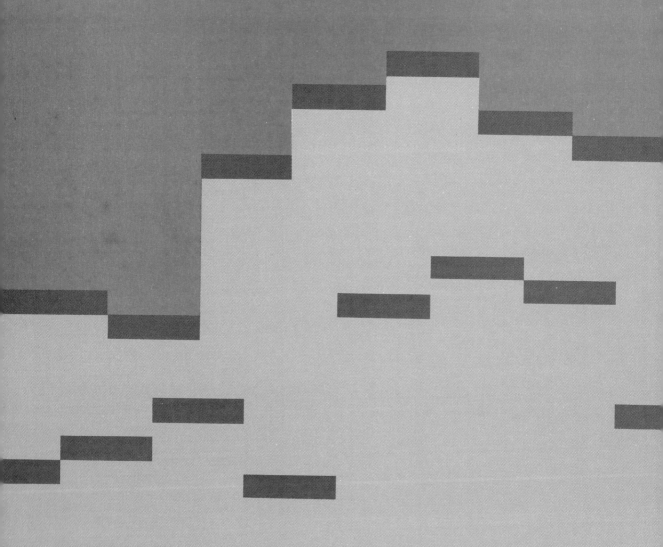

2

Although statistics deals with the analysis and evaluation of sample data, we will for the moment set aside the problem of sampling and pretend that decisions and conclusions are to be based on complete population data. In other words, we assume that population data are available and that decisions, therefore, are made with complete certainty. Although this assumption is unrealistic, it is nevertheless a useful and convenient step in the development of our topic.

But if population data are available, how can such data be utilized in solving specific problems? This chapter deals with the organization and summarization of population data into a form that enables us to make decisions and derive conclusions.

PARAMETERS

Decisions and conclusions can often be made with absolute certainty if a single value (or values) that describes a certain aspect of a population is determined. For example, to determine whether to accept or reject a lot of 1000 articles received from a supplier, one must know the percentage of defective articles in the entire lot. To determine whether families in Los Angeles or Chicago are economically more prosperous, one must know the average family income in each city. A single value such as the percentage of defective articles in a lot or the average family income in Los Angeles is called a **parameter.** Thus a parameter is a single number that describes one aspect of an entire population; to determine its value, one must utilize complete population data.

For any given population, a wide variety of parameters can be computed. This chapter, however, deals with the parameters that are most frequently used in statistical analysis. The meaning, significance, properties, and method of computation of each parameter are thoroughly examined. The usefulness of individual parameters in solving specific problems is also discussed.

Aggregate

The **aggregate** is a parameter that can be computed only for a population of variates. Denoted by A, the aggregate is the sum of the values of all variates in the population.

Example Let our population of interest consist of the ages of five houses:

$$X_1 = 2 \text{ years}, \qquad X_2 = 2 \text{ years},$$
$$X_3 = 4 \text{ years}, \qquad X_4 = 5 \text{ years},$$
$$X_5 = 2 \text{ years},$$

where X_1 is the age of the first house in the population, X_2 is the age of the second house in the population, and so on. The aggregate, A, is the sum of the ages of the five houses:

$$A = 2 + 2 + 4 + 5 + 2 = 15 \text{ years}.$$

In more general form,

$$A = X_1 + X_2 + X_3 + X_4 + X_5,$$

or, in shorthand notation,

$$A = \sum_{i=1}^{5} X_i.$$

The Greek letter sigma, $\sum$, indicates the summation of variates. Since we have only five variates, i goes from 1 to 5. For the sake of completing the notion of notation, the aggregate of 7 terms would be written as

$$\sum_{i=1}^{7} X_i = X_1 + X_2 + X_3 + X_4 + X_5 + X_6 + X_7,$$

and that of 89 terms as

$$\sum_{i=1}^{89} X_i = X_1 + X_2 + \cdots + X_{89}.$$

Finally,

$$\sum_{i=1}^{N} X_i = X_1 + X_2 + \cdots + X_N,$$

where there are N variates in the population.

It must be emphasized that an aggregate can be computed only for a population of variates because the population consists of measurable observations whose values can be added. A population of attributes, on the other hand, consists of nonmeasurable observations that cannot be summed. The aggregate as the sum of the values of all variates in a population must not be confused with the population size, N, which refers to the number of observations in the population.

The preceding example dealt with the computation of an aggregate for a population of variates. The question now arises: For what type of problem do we compute the aggregate and utilize it as an end in itself? The aggregate is calculated whenever the decision in a given problem depends on the aggregate value. The following example illustrates a situation in which the aggregate serves as a basis for decision.

Example In 1985 city X needs an additional revenue of 50 million dollars; the existing sales-tax rate of 4% therefore must be increased. The increase depends on the anticipated aggregate retail sales in 1985. Thus, if the aggregate sales are $10,000 million, the needed increase in tax rate would be

$$\frac{50}{10,000} \cdot 100 = \frac{1}{2}\%.$$

If, on the other hand, aggregate sales are $5000 million, the needed increase in tax rate is

$$\frac{50}{5000} \cdot 100 = 1\%.$$

Proportion

Proportion, denoted by π, refers to a fraction of the population that possesses a certain characteristic. In the example of the population of five houses, the proportion of houses more than two years old is .40.

$$\pi = \frac{2}{5}, \qquad \pi = .40.$$

In a population of 1000 articles, 82 of which are defective, the proportion of defective items in the population is .082.

$$\pi = \frac{82}{1000}, \qquad \pi = .082.$$

The proportion is the parameter used most often in describing a population of attributes. Its use as a basis for decision can be illustrated with the following example.

Example A television manufacturer can purchase electronic components in lots of 100 components from two different suppliers: A and B. Because the cost of purchasing a lot is the same from either supplier, the manufacturer wishes to purchase the lot with the smaller proportion of defective components.

MEAN, MEDIAN, AND MODE

When the population consists of observations of variates, the investigator is often interested in finding a value that can best describe the average or typical variate in the population. The investigator may wish to know, for example, the typical family income in Los Angeles, the typical life of a certain brand of tire, or the typical tensile strength of a particular fiber. The arithmetic mean, the median, and the mode are parameters that represent the typical variate.* But why three different measures?

Each of these three parameters is calculated in a different way, and this difference in calculation may render one of the parameters a better representative of the typical variate in a given problem.

Arithmetic Mean

The arithmetic **mean,** denoted by μ, is simply the familiar average. It is obtained by dividing the sum of all variates in the population by the number of variates. Symbolically,

$$\mu = \frac{\sum\limits_{i=1}^{N} X_i}{N}, \qquad \text{or} \qquad \mu = \frac{A}{N}.$$

---

*Other parameters that describe the typical variate are the geometric and harmonic means. Because of their limited use, however, these two measures are not treated here.

The arithmetic mean of the ages of the five houses in the earlier example is

$$\mu = \frac{X_1 + X_2 + X_3 + X_4 + X_5}{5},$$

$$\mu = \frac{2 + 2 + 4 + 5 + 2}{5}, \qquad \mu = \frac{15}{5}, \qquad \mu = 3 \text{ years.}$$

The arithmetic mean has an interesting property. The sum of the deviations of the individual variates from their arithmetic mean is always equal to zero. Thus, in the example of the houses, if we subtract the mean, 3, from the age of each house, the resulting five deviations will add up to zero:

X_i	$(X_i - \mu)$ $(X_i - 3)$
2	−1
2	−1
4	1
5	2
2	−1
$\sum X = 15$	$\sum (X - \mu) = 0$
$\mu = 3$	

The arithmetic mean is used much more often than the median or the mode to describe the typical variate in the population. It best describes such values as the average life of an electric bulb, the average nicotine content of a certain brand of cigarettes, the average tensile strength of a fiber, the average carbohydrate content of a grain of wheat, and the average corn yield per acre of a given farm. It often serves as a basis for decision making in a great variety of problems. A few examples illustrate this point.

Example An agronomist wishes to compare the effectiveness of two different types of fertilizer mixes used in wheat production. She decides to use the average yield per acre as a measure of effectiveness. The average yield is the arithmetic mean.

Example A manufacturer of a certain brand of cake mix packages his product in boxes of one pound net weight. As a representative of the Fair Trade Commission you must decide whether the manufacturer's operation is satisfactory. The average weight per package as determined by the arithmetic mean can be used as a basis for your decision.

Median

Like the arithmetic mean, the **median** describes the typical variate in the population. The method of computing the median, however, differs from that used in computing the mean. To compute the median for a population of variates, the variates must be arranged in an increasing or decreasing order. The median is the middle variate if the number of the variates, N, is odd. If N is even, the median is the arithmetic mean of the two middle variates. The median of the five variates 3, 3, 7, 11, 19, for example, is 7, and the median of the six variates 3, 3, 7, 11, 19, 22 is

$$\frac{7 + 11}{2}, \quad \text{or } 9.$$

The median divides the variates in the population into two equal or approximately equal halves. Half of the variates are less than or equal to the median, while the other half are greater than or equal to the median. Thus, if the median income in Los Angeles is $16,000, then 50% of all Los Angeles families have annual earnings of $16,000 or less, and 50% of all families have an annual income of $16,000 or more.

Unlike the arithmetic mean, the median generally is not affected by the existence of either extremely high or extremely low variates in the population. The mean and median of the set (4, 5, 6, 7, 8) are the same, namely 6. However, the mean of the set (4, 5, 6, 7, 198) is 44 and the median is 6. While the median continues to represent most of the variates in the set, the mean does not represent any of the variates. Thus, in a population having variates with extreme values, the median describes the typical or average variate more accurately than the arithmetic mean does. For example, such populations of variates as family income in Chicago, hourly earnings at Lockheed Corporation, and retail sales in Los Angeles are likely to contain a few extremely high variates. The arithmetic mean will be more extreme than the median, which can therefore be considered the better "average."

Mode

The **mode** is another parameter that describes the typical variate. The mode is the most frequently occurring variate or attribute in the population. In the population of the ages of five houses (2, 2, 4, 5, 2), the mode is 2 years. Similarly, the modal annual family income in Los Angeles is $14,800 in 1985 if more families earned $14,800 than earned any other amount in that year. The following example illustrates the use of the mode as a basis for decisions.

Example A clothing manufacturer wishes to market three standard sizes of the Hollywood Flair sport jacket: large, medium, and small. She must decide on a sleeve length for each of the standard models. Her decision is based on the modal sleeve length (mode) of the potential buyers of each size.

Selecting the Appropriate Measure

To determine how to select the appropriate measure, let us consider the following characteristics of a group of 12 people.

Age (in years): 22, 24, 25, 26, 27, 28,
28, 29, 30, 31, 33, 34

Annual income: $8000, $8200, $9000, $10,000, $11,000, $12,000,
$12,300, $12,500, $13,000, $13,500, $86,000, $97,000

Shoe size: 8½, 9, 9½, 9½, 9½, 9½,
10, 10, 10½, 10½, 11, 11½

What is the typical age, typical annual income, and typical shoe size for this group of 12 people?

The typical age may well be described by the arithmetic mean. Although the median and mode can also describe the typical age, we have, in this case, chosen the arithmetic mean for two reasons. First, more people are familiar with the arithmetic mean than with either the median or the mode. Second, there is no advantage to choosing the median or mode when the values of the three measures are almost the same (mean = 28.1, median = 28, mode = 28).

Examining annual incomes, we see that the annual incomes of two members of the group are extremely high. We know that extreme values affect the arithmetic mean much more than they affect the median: the mean annual income is $24,375, the median is $12,150. Thus the median represents the majority of the variates, while the arithmetic mean represents none of the variates. The median is therefore the better measure for income.

As to shoe size, both the mean and the median are somewhat meaningless (mean = 9.92, median = 9.75); in fact, neither of these two measures represents any actual shoe size. The mode, on the other hand, represents the actual shoe size of four members in the group. Thus the mode is the better measure for shoe size.

There is no doubt that the preceding illustration is oversimplified in that the choice of measure is rather obvious. However, it does emphasize that the choice among the three measures depends on the purpose for which the data are selected as well as on the nature of the data gathered.

In many statistical problems, the choice among mean, median, and mode may not be obvious. Thus some general comments concerning the advantages and disadvantages of the three measures may be helpful.

First, we must recognize that of the three measures the arithmetic mean is most easily understood by the general public. Second, but all-important, the arithmetic mean lends itself much more readily to further statistical analysis. It is for these two reasons that most statistical studies report the arithmetic mean as the typical value.

The arithmetic mean has the disadvantage, however, of being more affected by extreme values than either the median or the mode. Thus, whenever there are either extremely high variates or extremely low variates, the median or the mode is preferred over the arithmetic mean.

MEASURES OF VARIATION

While such parameters as the mean, median, and mode describe the typical variate, other parameters, namely the range, the standard deviation, and the average deviation, measure the dispersion among values of the various variates making up a population. These parameters, called *measures of variation*, indicate the degree of uniformity among variates.

A population of variates has no variation when all the variates have the same value. In a population of five variates 3, 3, 3, 3, 3, each variate, as well as the arithmetic mean, is the same, and the population therefore has no variation. The set (1, 3, 3, 3, 5), on the other hand, has some variation because some of the variates have different values. The variation among variates can be measured by the range, the average deviation, or the standard deviation.

Range

The **range,** denoted by R, is the difference between the highest and lowest variate:

$$R = \text{maximum variate} - \text{minimum variate}.$$

The range of the five variates 1, 3, 3, 3, 5 is 4:

$$R = 5 - 1$$
$$= 4.$$

The range as a measure of variation is deficient because it considers only the highest and lowest values and neglects the variation among the remaining values. The two sets of variates

$$1, 3, 3, 3, 5 \quad \text{and} \quad 1, 1, 4, 4, 5$$

have the same range, 4, although there is less variation in the first set than in the second.

Average Deviation

The **average deviation** is the average absolute deviation of each variate from the arithmetic mean. (When the sign, plus or minus, is ignored, the deviation is called *absolute* and is designated by two vertical bars | |.) Symbolically,

$$AD = \frac{\sum_{i=1}^{N} |X_i - \mu|}{N} \, .$$

For a population of five houses 2, 2, 4, 5, and 2 years old, the average deviation is 1.2 years, as shown in the following table.

X_i	$\begin{array}{c} \|X_i - \mu\| \\ \|X_i - 3\| \end{array}$
2	1
2	1
4	1
5	2
2	1
	$\sum |X - \mu| = 6$

$$AD = \frac{\sum |X - \mu|}{N}$$

$$AD = \tfrac{6}{5} = 1.2 \text{ years}$$

Thus the age of each house is different from the mean of the population by an average of 1.2 years. It must be emphasized that the average deviation is measured in the same unit as the variate itself. In this example, both are measured in years.

Standard Deviation

The **standard deviation,** denoted by σ, is the most important measure of variation. In a broad sense, it measures the average deviation of each variate from the arithmetic mean. Symbolically,

$$\sigma = \sqrt{\frac{\sum_{i=1}^{N} (X_i - \mu)^2}{N}} \, .$$

In words, the standard deviation is the square root of the average square deviation of each variate from the arithmetic mean.

For the population of five houses aged 2, 2, 4, 5, and 2 years, the standard deviation is 1.26 years, as shown in the following table.

X_i	$(X_i - \mu)$	$(X_i - \mu)^2$
2	-1	1
2	-1	1
4	1	1
5	2	4
2	-1	1
		$\Sigma (X - \mu)^2 = 8$

$$\sigma = \sqrt{\frac{\Sigma(X - \mu)^2}{N}}$$

$$\sigma = \sqrt{\frac{8}{5}} = \sqrt{1.6} = 1.26 \text{ years}$$

Thus, on the average, the age of each house differs from the arithmetic mean of the population by 1.26 years. (Incidentally, the square of the standard deviation is called *variance* and is denoted by σ^2.)

Both the average deviation and the standard deviation are good measures of the average deviation of each variate from the arithmetic mean. However, the standard deviation is the more relevant measure because only the standard deviation lends itself to further statistical analysis and treatment.

In addition to its basic role in the development of the theory of statistics, the standard deviation has some important practical applications, two examples of which are given below.

Example   A food processor markets his instant coffee in 16-ounce jars. He considers that his filling operation performs satisfactorily if the average weight of all jars is 16.2 ounces and the standard deviation is .04 ounces. (You will understand later that if the average weight of a jar is 16.2 ounces and the standard deviation is .04 ounce, then virtually no jar will contain less than 16.0 ounces of coffee.)

Example   A machine shop accepts an order for 10,000 ball bearings of 2-inch diameter. The size specification of the product can be maintained only when the average diameter is 2 inches and the standard deviation is very small.

EXERCISES

2.1   A population consists of the weights, in pounds, of five babies born on August 28, 1985, in West Valley Hospital. The weights are 11, 5, 9, 11, and 4.

a) Compute the mean, mode, and median weights. Compare their values.

b) Compute the range, the average deviation, and the standard deviation.

2.2 On December 31, 1984, 10 babies were born in West Valley Hospital. Their weights, in pounds, were 7, 8, 8, 6, 4, 9, 10, 11, 8, 9. Compute the mean, median, and mode. Compare their values.

2.3 Is it possible for the standard deviation to be larger than the arithmetic mean?

2.4 The blood pressures of 10 men were measured before and after smoking. The changes were +10, −5, +7, −4, +2, +3, −4, −5, −3, +9. Compute the mean change and the standard deviation, and compare their values.

2.5 The annual salaries of the 12 faculty members in the Department of Economics at Bradford College are $17,200, $17,200, $17,200, $17,500, $17,500, $17,800, $18,100, $18,100, $18,400, $18,400, $19,000, $26,800. Compute the mean and the median annual salary. Which is a better "average" and why?

2.6 The Department of English at Bradford College, reporting on the annual salaries of its faculty members, states that $\mu = \$18,000$, and $\sigma = 0$. What is the median annual salary? What is the mode?

2.7 An agronomist reporting on the weight of a new variety of apples states that $\mu = 8$ ounces, and $\sigma = 2$ inches. What is wrong?

2.8 The 10 members of the Play Toy Club have the following characteristics:

Annual income: $32,000, $31,000, $105,000, $34,000, $32,000, $33,000, $35,000, $33,000, $30,000, $32,500,

I.Q.: 102, 97, 103, 137, 105, 108, 107, 102, 96, 111

Weight (pounds): 150, 157, 162, 170, 155, 163, 167, 172, 165, 173

Hat size (inches): 6⅝, 6⅞, 7¼, 6⅞, 6¾, 6⅞, 6⅞, 7½, 6⅞, 6⅞

What is the appropriate average for each of the above characteristics of the members of the Play Toy Club?

2.9 The Sullivan and the O'Connor families have 5 children each. The ages of the Sullivan children show a mean of 11 years, a standard deviation of 3.16 years, and a median of 10 years. The O'Connor children, on the other hand, have a mean age of 9 years, a standard deviation of 3.16 years, and a median of 10 years. Explain how the mean ages of the children in the two families are not the same, while the medians and standard deviations are the same.

2.10 Consider the following two populations of variates.

Population A: 8, 9, 10, 11, 17
Population B: 3, 9, 10, 11, 12

a) Compute the mean, median, and standard deviation for each population.

b) Compare the results for the two populations and explain the differences, if any.

2.11   Compare the means, the ranges, and the standard deviations of the following two populations. Explain the differences, if any.

$$\text{Population A:}\quad 1, 4, 5, 6, 9$$
$$\text{Population B:}\quad 1, 2, 5, 8, 9$$

2.12   A population of variates has a mean of 10 and a standard deviation of 3.

a) If each variate is increased by 2, what are the new mean and standard deviation of the population?

b) If each variate is multiplied by 2, what are the new mean and standard deviation of the population?

2.13   The final examination grades of 20 students in an elementary statistics class are

$$50,\quad 55,\quad 61,\quad 60,\quad 71,\quad 73,\quad 53,\quad 54,\quad 67,\quad 67,$$
$$54,\quad 77,\quad 72,\quad 76,\quad 81,\quad 83,\quad 87,\quad 44,\quad 48,\quad 67.$$

Determine the percentage of grades that fall in the interval (a) $\mu \pm 1\sigma$, (b) $\mu \pm 2\sigma$, (c) $\mu \pm 3\sigma$.

2.14   On receiving your accounting degree from the university, you are offered a junior accountant position by two public accounting firms: A and B. Your starting salary in both firms would be $14,000 per year. Further investigation reveals that for those accountants who have been employed by firm A for five years, the mean annual salary is $20,000 with a standard deviation of $5000. Similar accountants with firm B earn a mean salary of $20,000 but with a standard deviation of only $2000. Assuming that all other employment conditions in both firms are the same, which offer do you prefer? Explain.

2.15   The annual sales, in millions of dollars, for the 25 department stores in Santa Barbara, California, are as follows.

38	35	43	27	24
40	38	21	34	27
35	36	24	33	25
33	44	45	23	33
33	24	33	27	25

a) Compute the mean, median, and modal sales.

b) Compute the range, average deviation, and standard deviation.

c) Determine the percentage of sales that fall in the interval (1) $\mu \pm 1\sigma$, (2) $\mu \pm 2\sigma$, (3) $\mu \pm 3\sigma$.

KEY TERMS ━━━━━━

parameter A single number that describes some aspect of an entire population.

aggregate (A) The sum of all the variates in a population.

proportion (π) The fraction of the population that possesses a characteristic of interest.

mean (μ) The average value of all the variates in a population.

median The middle value when a population of variates is arranged in increasing or decreasing order.

mode The most frequently occurring variate or attribute in a population.

range (R) The difference between the highest and the lowest variates in a population.

average deviation (AD) The average of the absolute values of the deviations of the variates from the mean μ in a population.

standard deviation (σ) The square root of the average square deviation of each variate from the mean in a population; a measure of the distance a typical variate is from the mean.

**SUMMARY
OF FORMULAS** ━━━━━━

aggregate

$$A = \sum_{i=1}^{N} X_i$$

mean

$$\mu = \frac{A}{N} = \frac{\sum_{i=1}^{N} X_i}{N}$$

average deviation

$$AD = \frac{1}{N} \sum_{i=1}^{N} |X_i - \mu|$$

standard deviation

$$\sigma = \sqrt{\frac{\sum_{i=1}^{N} (X_i - \mu)^2}{N}}$$

PROBABILITY

3

We have already learned that statistics consists of tools and methods that enable us to evaluate the reliability of conclusions derived from sample data. Of all the tools of statistics, the concept of probability is most important. Modern statistics may, indeed, be regarded as an application of the theory of probability. It is for this reason that two chapters are devoted exclusively to probability.

OBJECTIVE AND SUBJECTIVE PROBABILITIES

The concept of probability can be approached in two ways: objectively and subjectively. In the objective approach, the *probability* of an event is defined as the relative frequency of its occurrence in the long run. To clarify this notion, we can assume that a balanced coin is tossed 50 times and the event "heads," appears 23 times. The relative frequency of the event "heads," denoted by $RF(H)$, is

$$RF(H) = {}^{23}\!/_{50} = .46.$$

The probability of the event H, denoted by $P(H)$, is the limit of its relative frequency as the coin is tossed an infinite number of times. Since the relative frequency of the event "heads" approaches .5 as the number of tosses approaches infinity, we may conclude that the probability of getting heads on a single toss of a balanced coin is .5. Similarly, we can conclude that the probability of getting a 4 in a single throw of a fair die is $\frac{1}{6}$.

Initially, probability theory was developed in connection with games of chance; and in that connection the objective approach to probability is most appropriate indeed. In contrast, we can consider some other situations, such as business, where the objective interpretation of probability may no longer be possible. We can state, for example, that the probability of having a recession next year is .3 or that the probability that the price of a given stock will rise tomorrow is .9. Clearly, these probabilities can hardly be viewed as relative frequencies. Rather, these probabilities measure the degree of belief we attach to the occurrence of such events. Hence, in contrast to the objective approach, which defines probability as a relative frequency of an event, a subjective or a personal approach to probability defines the probability of an event as a measure of the degree of belief an individual attaches to the occurrence of that event.

Subjective probabilities are individualistic. An individual assesses the probability of an event based on whatever information (past and current) is available together with his or her personal biases, experience, judgment, and expectations. Subjective probabilities are also personal probabilities in the sense that two individuals may assign different probabilities to the same event owing to differences in their attitudes, experiences, and outlooks.

Note that all probabilities, whether objective or subjective, must satisfy the same theorems and obey identical rules.

SETS

Your understanding of probability will be greatly enhanced if you first understand some elementary notions of sets.

A **set** *is a collection of objects.* Our 50 states constitute a set, the positive integers 1, 2, 3, 4, . . . form a set, and the students in a college are a set. A set is a well-defined collection of objects, and those objects are called *elements* or *members* of the set. Thus the state of California is a member of the set of the 50 states and the integer 4 is an element of the set of positive integers.

A set may contain a limited or an infinite number of elements. The set of states in the United States, for example, contains only 50 elements. The set of positive integers contains an infinite number of elements. In this context, a set of particular interest is the *null* or *empty set*. Denoted by $\emptyset$, the null set contains no elements. The set of all people with 22 fingers, for example, is a null set. We will have more to say about the null set later.

A set is usually denoted by a capital letter—*A*, *B*, *C*. A member of the set is denoted by a lower-case letter—*a*, *b*, *c*. When the object *x* is a member of set *A*, we write

$$x \in A,$$

which we read "*x* is an element of *A*." We also write

$$y \notin A$$

to mean that the element *y* is not a member of set *A*.

A set can be described by listing all its elements. The set *A* consisting of the first seven positive integers can be described as

$$A = \{1, 2, 3, 4, 5, 6, 7\}.$$

Note that the elements of a set are separated by commas and enclosed in braces. Similarly, the set *B* consisting of a student, a book, and a pen can be described as

$$B = \{\text{student, book, pen}\}.$$

In some cases, it is either impossible or inconvenient to describe a set by listing all its elements. It is impossible, for example, to list the elements of the set of all positive integers. Such a set may alternatively be described by a statement that specifies the elements that make up the set. Thus the set of all positive integers, denoted by *C*, can be described as

$$C = \{x \mid x \text{ is a positive integer}\},$$

which we read "the set *C* is the set of all *x* such that *x* is a positive integer." Note that the vertical bar is read "such that." Similarly, the set *D* consisting of all families in New York City can be described as

$$D = \{x \mid x \text{ is a family in New York City}\}.$$

Subsets

Let us consider the set $A = \{x, y, z\}$. The set $B = \{x, y\}$ is a subset of *A*. This can be written as $B \subset A$, which we read "*B* is contained in *A*." Similarly, if $S = \{x \mid x$ is a family in Los Angeles County$\}$, and $S_1 = \{x \mid x$ is a family in Los Angeles

County with annual income exceeding \$10,000}, then the set S_1 is a subset of S. In general, the set S_1 is a subset of set S if every element in S_1 is also an element in S. According to this general definition of a subset we may also conclude that $S \subset S$, and $\emptyset \subset S$. In other words, every set is a subset of itself, and the null set $\emptyset$ is a subset of every set.

In a set of n elements, there are 2^n subsets. Thus, a set of three elements contains 2^3, or 8, subsets. The set $S = \{x, y, z\}$, for example, contains the following eight subsets.

$$
\begin{array}{ll}
S = \{x, y, z\} & D = \{x\} \\
A = \{x, y\} & E = \{y\} \\
B = \{x, z\} & F = \{z\} \\
C = \{y, z\} & \emptyset
\end{array}
$$

Note that the first subset is the set itself, and the last subset is the null set.

The Universal Set U

We have already learned that in many statistical problems the investigator is interested in studying some characteristic of a population. For example, he or she may be interested in determining the average age of the students in a given college. The set that consists of the ages of *all* students is our population. This set is called the *universal set* and is denoted by U. Similarly, if we wish to determine the average annual family income in Los Angeles, then our statistical population is the universal set U, where

$$U = \{x \mid x \text{ is the annual income of a family in Los Angeles}\}.$$

The set

$$
\begin{aligned}
A = \{x \mid & x \text{ is the annual income of a Los Angeles family} \\
& \text{earning \$10,000 or more}\}
\end{aligned}
$$

is a subset of the universal set U. In the same manner, the set

$$
\begin{aligned}
B = \{x \mid & x \text{ is the annual income of a Los Angeles family} \\
& \text{earning less than \$5000}\}
\end{aligned}
$$

is a subset of the universal set U.

It is sometimes convenient to represent sets and subsets by diagrams. In these diagrams, known as *Venn diagrams,* the universal set U is represented by a rectangle, and subsets are represented by circles inside the rectangle. In Fig. 3.1, A and B are subsets of the universal set U. Furthermore, A and B have no elements in common.

Equality of Two Sets

Sets A and B are equal only when both sets contain exactly the same elements. Sets $A = \{3, 4\}$ and $B = \{4, 3\}$ are equal. Note that these two sets are considered to be equal although the order of the elements in the two sets is not the same.

Operations with Sets

Let us consider the two sets A and B, where $A = \{1, 2, 3\}$ and $B = \{3, 4\}$. These two sets may be considered subsets of a universal set $U = \{1, 2, 3, 4, 5\}$. Several other new sets can be formed by certain manipulation of the two sets A and B. Some of these new sets are the following.

1. The set $\{1, 2, 3, 4\}$, which is obtained by combining the elements of the two sets A and B, is called the *union* of A and B.
2. The set $\{3\}$, which is composed of the elements common to sets A and B, is called the *intersection* or *product* of A and B.
3. The set $\{4, 5\}$ is composed of all the elements of the universal set U that are not elements of set A. This set is called the *complement of A.*

There are many other sets that can be obtained by manipulating, or by performing certain operations on, sets A and B. The set $\{1, 2\}$, for example, consists of all the elements in set A that are not elements of set B. This set is called the *difference* between A and B. Of all these new sets, however, we will discuss in detail only the union, the intersection, and the complement.

Union of *A* and *B*

The **union** of A and B, denoted by $A \cup B$, is the set of elements that belong to either A or B or both. Thus, if $A = \{2, 7, 8, 5\}$ and $B = \{7, 8, 11\}$, then the union of A and B is the set $A \cup B = \{2, 7, 8, 5, 11\}$. The union of A and B is shown by the shaded area in Fig. 3.2.

Figure 3.1 *A and B, subsets of U*

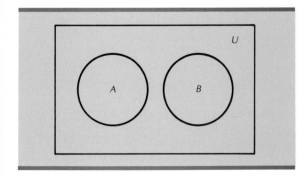

Figure 3.2 Union of *A* and *B*, $A \cup B$

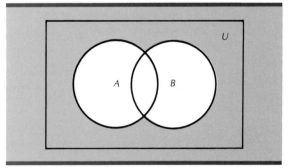

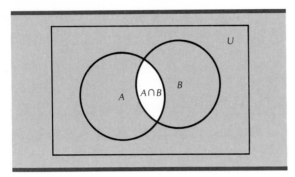

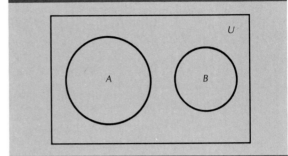

Figure 3.3 $A \cap B$, intersection of A and B **Figure 3.4**   Mutually exclusive sets

Intersection of *A* and *B*

The **intersection** of sets A and B, denoted by $A \cap B$, is the set of elements that belong to both A and B. Thus, if $A = \{2, 7, 8, 5\}$ and $B = \{7, 8, 11\}$, then the intersection of A and B is the set $A \cap B = \{7, 8\}$. The intersection of A and B is shown by the shaded area in Fig. 3.3. If the sets A and B have no elements in common, then the intersection of A and B is the empty set, or null set: $A \cap B = \varnothing$.

Two sets that have no elements in common are called **mutually exclusive.** The two mutually exclusive sets A and B are shown in Fig. 3.4.

Complement of Set *A*

The **complement** of set A, denoted by A', is the set of elements of the universal set U that do not belong to set A. Thus, if $A = \{1, 2, 3\}$ and $U = \{1, 2, 3, 4, 5\}$, then the complement of set A is $A' = \{4, 5\}$. The complement of set A is shown by the shaded area in Fig. 3.5. We can even speak of a complement to the set $A \cup B$. The complement to the set $A \cup B$, denoted by $(A \cup B)'$, is shown by the shaded area in Fig. 3.6.

We will now elaborate on the union, intersection, and complement by presenting a few examples.

Example   **Given:** $U = \{1, 2, 3, 4, 5, 6, 7\}$, $A = \{2, 3, 4\}$, $B = \{3, 4, 5, 6\}$.

Find: The sets (a) $A \cup B$, (b) $A \cap B$, (c) A', (d) B'.

Solution:

a) $A \cup B = \{2, 3, 4, 5, 6\}$,
b) $A \cap B = \{3, 4\}$,
c) $A' = \{1, 5, 6, 7\}$,
d) $B' = \{1, 2, 7\}$.

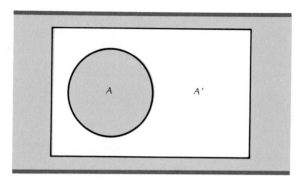

Figure 3.5 *A′ the complement of A*

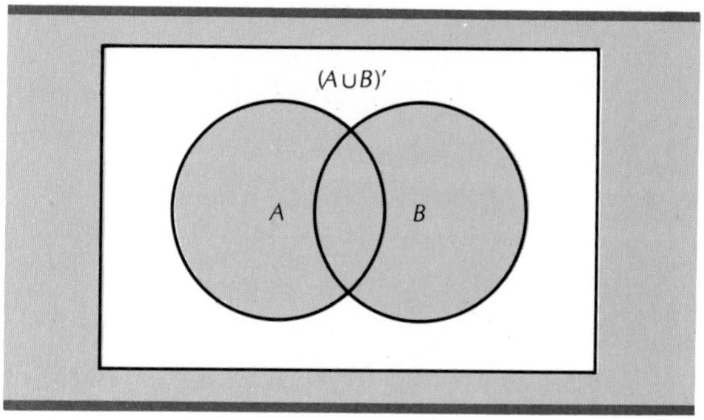

Figure 3.6 *(A ∪ B)′, the complement of A ∪ B*

Example ***Given:*** $U = \{1, 2, 3, 4, 5\}, A = \{2, 3\}, B = \{3, 5, 4\}$.

Find: The sets (a) $(A \cup B)'$, (b) $(A \cap B)'$.

Solution:

a) To determine the set $(A \cup B)'$, we must first determine the union of A and B:

$$A \cup B = \{2, 3, 5, 4\}.$$

The complement of $A \cup B$ is the elements of the universal set $\{1, 2, 3, 4, 5\}$ that do not belong to $A \cup B$. Accordingly, $(A \cup B)' = \{1\}$.

b) Similarly, to determine $(A \cap B)'$, we must first determine the set $A \cap B$. Since $A \cap B = \{3\}$, it follows that

$$(A \cap B)' = \{1, 2, 4, 5\}.$$

Example ***Given:*** $U = \{a, b, c, d, e, f\}, A = \{a, b\}, B = \{c, d, e, f\}$.

Find: The set $(A \cup B)'$.

Solution:

$$A \cup B = \{a, b, c, d, e, f\}.$$

Therefore,

$$(A \cup B)' = \varnothing.$$

Example ***Given:***

$$A = \{x \mid x \text{ is an integer, and } 10 < x < 14\},$$
$$B = \{y \mid y \text{ is an integer, and } 12 < y < 16\}.$$

Find: $A \cap B$.

Solution: Since set A consists of all integers that are greater than 10 but less than 14, $A = \{11, 12, 13\}$. Similarly, set B consists of all integers that are greater than 12 but less than 16. Consequently, $B = \{13, 14, 15\}$, and $A \cap B = \{13\}$.

Example   **Given:**

$$A = \{x \mid x \text{ is an integer and } 2 \leq x \leq 5\},$$

$$B = \{y \mid y \text{ is an integer greater than 3}\}.$$

Find: $A \cap B$.

Solution:

$$A = \{2, 3, 4, 5\},$$
$$B = \{4, 5, 6, 7, \ldots, \infty\},$$
$$A \cap B = \{4, 5\}.$$

Example   **Given:** $A = \{x \mid 10 < x < 14\}, B = \{y \mid 12 < y < 16\}.$

Find: $A \cup B$.

Solution: Set A consists of an infinite number of elements that are greater than 10 but less than 14, such as 10.02, 10.717, 13.9897, and so on.

Set B also consists of an infinite number of elements. The elements of B, however, are greater than 12 but less than 16. Some of these elements are 12.001, 12.97, 15.76, and so on. The union $A \cup B$ is, therefore, an infinite set, and $A \cup B = \{z \mid 10 < z < 16\}.$

Example   **Given:** $A = \{x \mid x^2 + x - 12 = 0\}, B = \{x \mid 2x - 6 = 0\}.$

Find: $A \cap B$.

Solution: To determine the elements of set A, we must solve the quadratic equation

$$x^2 + x - 12 = 0$$
$$(x + 4)(x - 3) = 0$$
$$x + 4 = 0$$
$$x = -4,$$

or

$$x - 3 = 0$$
$$x = 3.$$

Therefore,

$$A = \{-4, 3\}.$$

Similarly, to determine the elements of set B, we must solve the equation

$$2x - 6 = 0$$
$$2x = 6$$
$$x = 3.$$

Therefore,

$$B = \{3\} \quad \text{and} \quad A \cap B = \{3\}.$$

EXERCISES

3.1 List the elements of each of the following sets.

a) Set of integers between 9 and 13

b) Set of positive integers less than 9

c) Set of integers between 1 and 20 divisible by 3

3.2 List the elements of each of the following sets.

a) Set $A = \{x \mid x$ is an integer and $9 \le x < 13\}$

b) Set $B = \{x \mid x$ is an integer and $9 < x \le 13\}$

c) Set $C = \{x \mid x + 2 = 0\}$

d) Set $D = \{y \mid y^2 + 3y = 28\}$

3.3 Let $U = \{x, y, 3\}$. List all subsets of U.

3.4 Let $U = \{$man, woman, baby, home$\}$. List all subsets of U.

3.5 *Given:* $U = \{10, 11, 12, 13, 14, 15\}$, $A = \{10, 11, 12, 13\}$, $B = \{12, 13, 14\}$.
Find: (a) $A \cup B$, (b) $A \cap B$, (c) A'.

3.6 *Given:* $U = \{20, 22, 24, 26\}$, $A = \{20, 22\}$, $B = \{22, 24\}$.
Find: (a) $A \cup B$, (b) $(A \cup B)'$, (c) $(A \cap B)$, (d) $(A \cap B)'$.

3.7 *Given:* $U = \{v, w, x, y, z\}$, $A = \{v, w, x\}$, $B = \{y, z\}$.
Find: (a) $A \cup B$, (b) $(A \cup B)'$, (c) $A \cap B$, (d) $(A \cap B)'$.

3.8 *Given:*

$$A = \{x \mid x \text{ is an integer and } 12 < x < 20\},$$
$$B = \{x \mid x \text{ is an integer and } x > 17\}.$$

Find: $A \cap B$.

3.9 *Given:* $A = \{x \mid x^2 - 7x = 8\}$, $B = \{x \mid 2x - 16 = 0\}$.
Find: $A \cap B$.

3.10 *Given:* $X = \{x \mid 2x^2 + 4x - 16 = 0\}$, $Y = \{y \mid y^2 = 4\}$.
Find: (a) $X \cup Y$, (b) $X \cap Y$.

3.11 Let

$$U = \{x \mid x \text{ is a UCLA student}\},$$
$$A = \{x \mid x \text{ is a UCLA student 20 years of age or older}\},$$
$$B = \{y \mid y \text{ is a UCLA student under 20 years of age}\}.$$

Find: (a) $A \cup B$, (b) $(A \cup B)'$, (c) $A \cap B$.

EXPERIMENT, SAMPLE SPACE, AND EVENT

Experiment

The term **experiment** is used in statistics in a much broader sense than in chemistry or physics. The tossing of a coin, for example, is considered a statistical experiment. Other examples of statistical experiments are rolling a die, selecting one fuse from a lot and observing whether the fuse is defective, and sending a manned vehicle to Mars.

Although those experiments seem dissimilar, they have two properties in common. One is that each experiment has several possible outcomes that can be specified in advance.

Experiment	Possible Outcomes
1. Tossing a coin	Heads, tails
2. Rolling a die	1, 2, 3, 4, 5, 6
3. Selecting a fuse	Defective, not defective
4. Sending a manned vehicle to Mars	Success, failure

The second is that we are uncertain about the outcome of each experiment. In tossing a coin, for example, we are not certain whether the outcome will be heads or tails. Similarly, we are uncertain whether the fuse selected from the lot will be defective or not defective. Finally, in sending a manned vehicle to Mars, we are uncertain whether the venture will be a failure or a success.

Sample Space

The set S consisting of all possible outcomes of an experiment is called a **sample space.** Each element of a sample space is called a *sample point.* When we toss a coin, for example, our sample space is $S = \{H, T\}$, and each of the elements H and T is a sample point. Similarly, when we roll a die, our sample space is $S = \{1, 2, 3, 4, 5, 6\}$, and the element 1 or 4 is a sample point. We will illustrate the concept of sample space with some additional examples.

Example Two coins are to be tossed once. The four possible outcomes of this experiment are shown below.

Coin 1	Coin 2	
	H	T
H	HH	HT
T	TH	TT

The sample space of this experiment is $S = \{HH, HT, TH, TT\}$.

Example A pair of dice is to be cast once. The 36 possible outcomes of this experiment are shown in the following table.

Outcome of One Die	Outcome of Other Die					
	1	2	3	4	5	6
1	(1, 1)	(1, 2)	(1, 3)	(1, 4)	(1, 5)	(1, 6)
2	(2, 1)	(2, 2)	(2, 3)	(2, 4)	(2, 5)	(2, 6)
3	(3, 1)	(3, 2)	(3, 3)	(3, 4)	(3, 5)	(3, 6)
4	(4, 1)	(4, 2)	(4, 3)	(4, 4)	(4, 5)	(4, 6)
5	(5, 1)	(5, 2)	(5, 3)	(5, 4)	(5, 5)	(5, 6)
6	(6, 1)	(6, 2)	(6, 3)	(6, 4)	(6, 5)	(6, 6)

The sample space of this experiment is

$$S = \{(1, 1), \quad (1, 2), \quad (1, 3), \quad (1, 4), \quad (1, 5), \quad (1, 6),$$
$$(2, 1), \quad (2, 2), \quad (2, 3), \quad (2, 4), \quad (2, 5), \quad (2, 6),$$
$$(3, 1), \quad (3, 2), \quad (3, 3), \quad (3, 4), \quad (3, 5), \quad (3, 6),$$
$$(4, 1), \quad (4, 2), \quad (4, 3), \quad (4, 4), \quad (4, 5), \quad (4, 6),$$
$$(5, 1), \quad (5, 2), \quad (5, 3), \quad (5, 4), \quad (5, 5), \quad (5, 6),$$
$$(6, 1), \quad (6, 2), \quad (6, 3), \quad (6, 4), \quad (6, 5), \quad (6, 6)\}.$$

Example Three coins are tossed once. The eight possible outcomes of this experiment can best be displayed by a tree diagram. Such a diagram, describing all the possible outcomes of this experiment, is shown in Fig. 3.7.

Note that each of the two possible outcomes of tossing the first coin is represented by a branch. The two branches are labeled H and T. Each branch of the first coin sprouts two branches that represent the two possible outcomes of tossing the second coin. Thus we associate four branches with the second coin. Similarly, each branch of the second coin sprouts two branches representing the two possible outcomes of tossing the third coin. The eight possible outcomes of the experiment are then represented by the eight possible paths

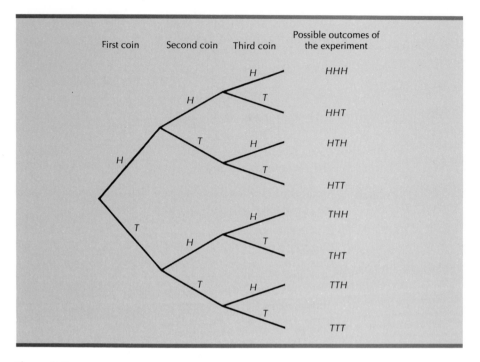

First coin   Second coin   Third coin   Possible outcomes of
                                               the experiment

Figure 3.7

of the diagram. The first of these eight paths (or outcomes) is *HHH*, the second path is *HHT*, and the last path is *TTT*. The sample space or the set of all possible outcomes of this experiment is

$$S = \{HHH, HHT, HTH, HTT, THH, THT, TTH, TTT\}.$$

Example   Four registered voters chosen at random are asked whether they prefer gubernatorial candidate X. List the elements of the sample space *S*.

Solution: Let *Y* stand for yes and *N* stand for no. Figure 3.8 shows the tree diagram representing the various possible outcomes of this experiment. The sample space of this experiment is

$$S = \{YYYY, YYYN, YYNY, YYNN, YNYY, YNYN, YNNY, YNNN,$$
$$NYYY, NYYN, NYNY, NYNN, NNYY, NNYN, NNNY, NNNN\}.$$

Event

We know that when three coins are tossed once, the sample space of the experiment is

$$S = \{HHH, HHT, HTH, HTT, THH, THT, TTH, TTT\}.$$

Let us now assume that we are interested in the outcomes in which the number of heads is exactly 2. These outcomes constitute the subset $A = \{HHT, HTH,$ $THH\}$. Next we are interested in the outcomes in which the number of heads is exactly 3. There is only one outcome in which the number of heads is exactly 3, and the subset $B = \{HHH\}$ represents this outcome.

A subset of a sample space is called an **event.** The subset $A = \{HHT, HTH,$ $THH\}$, for example, is the event that exactly two heads appear when three coins are tossed once. The subset $B = \{HHH\}$ is the event that exactly three heads appear when three coins are tossed once.

Example A pair of dice is to be rolled once. The sample space of this experiment is

$$S = \{(1, 1), \quad (1, 2), \quad (1, 3), \quad (1, 4), \quad (1, 5), \quad (1, 6),$$
$$(2, 1), \quad (2, 2), \quad (2, 3), \quad (2, 4), \quad (2, 5), \quad (2, 6),$$
$$(3, 1), \quad (3, 2), \quad (3, 3), \quad (3, 4), \quad (3, 5), \quad (3, 6),$$
$$(4, 1), \quad (4, 2), \quad (4, 3), \quad (4, 4), \quad (4, 5), \quad (4, 6),$$
$$(5, 1), \quad (5, 2), \quad (5, 3), \quad (5, 4), \quad (5, 5), \quad (5, 6),$$
$$(6, 1), \quad (6, 2), \quad (6, 3), \quad (6, 4), \quad (6, 5), \quad (6, 6)\}.$$

Figure 3.8

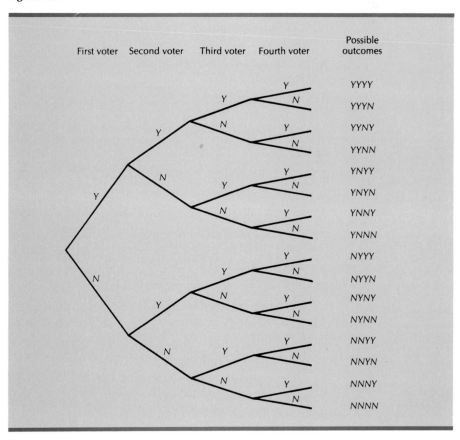

We may now consider the following events.

a) The event that the sum of the two faces is 7; that is, the subset

$$A = \{(1, 6), (2, 5), (3, 4), (4, 3), (5, 2), (6, 1)\}$$

b) The event that the sum of the two faces is 11; that is, the subset

$$B = \{(5, 6), (6, 5)\}.$$

c) The event that the sum of the two faces is either 7 or 11; that is, the union of sets A and B or the subset

$$A \cup B = \{(1, 6), (2, 5), (3, 4), (4, 3), (5, 2), (6, 1), (5, 6), (6, 5)\}.$$

EXERCISES

3.12 A die is to be tossed once.

a) List all the elements of the sample space S.

b) List the elements of S contained in the event that the outcome is even.

c) List the elements of S contained in the event that the outcome is greater than 4.

3.13 An experiment consists of tossing two coins once.

a) List the elements of the sample space S.

b) List the elements of S contained in the event that there is exactly one heads.

c) List the elements of S contained in the event that there is at least one heads.

3.14 A pair of dice is to be cast once.

a) List the elements of the sample space S.

b) List the elements of S contained in the event that the sum is 9.

c) List the elements of S contained in the event that the sum is either 4 or 5.

3.15 An experiment consists of selecting three parts from a manufacturing process and observing whether each part is defective.

a) Denoting a defective part by D and a nondefective part by D', list all elements of the sample space S of this experiment.

b) List the elements of S contained in the event that the number of defective parts is exactly zero.

c) How do you define event $A = \{DDD', DD'D, D'DD\}$?

3.16 An experiment involves tossing a coin and casting a die at the same time. List the 12 elements of the sample space S.

ASSIGNMENT OF PROBABILITIES

Each sample point (each possible outcome of an experiment) is assigned a weight that measures the likelihood of its occurrence. This weight is called the **probability** of the sample point.

In assigning weights or probabilities to various sample points, statisticians have agreed on two rules:

1. The probability assigned to any sample point ranges from 0 to 1.

2. The sum of probabilities assigned to *all* sample points in a sample space must be equal to 1.

A weight or probability close to 0 is assigned to an outcome (sample point) that is not likely to occur. A probability closer to 1 is assigned to an outcome that is likely to occur.

In many games of chance, the various possible outcomes or sample points are equally likely to occur. Consequently, the probability assigned to each sample point is the same. In tossing a balanced coin, for example, we assign a probability of $\frac{1}{2}$ to each sample point in the sample space $S = \{H, T\}$. Similarly, when a fair die is rolled, we assign a probability of $\frac{1}{6}$ to each sample point in the sample space $S = \{1, 2, 3, 4, 5, 6\}$.

The above examples are in the realm of objective probability. How can we assign probabilities that are subjective? Suppose, for example, a firm is planning to market a new product. The two possible outcomes of this experiment are success and failure. That is, $S = \{$success, failure$\}$. How can we assign a probability to each of these sample points? One way is to utilize the firm's past experience in marketing similar products. For example, if 90% of all similar products that have been marketed in the past were successful, it would seem reasonable to assign a probability of .90 to the point "success" and a probability of .10 to the point "failure."

Probability of an Event

The probability of event A, denoted by $P(A)$, is the sum of the probabilities of all sample points in A. This definition is illustrated by the following two examples.

Example   What is the probability of getting *exactly* two heads when three balanced coins are tossed once?

Solution: The sample space of this experiment is

$$S = \{HHH, HHT, HTH, HTT, THH, THT, TTH, TTT\},$$

and the probability of each sample point is $\frac{1}{8}$. Since the event "getting exactly two heads" is the subset $A = \{HHT, HTH, THH\}$, the probability of getting exactly two heads is

$$P(A) = \frac{1}{8} + \frac{1}{8} + \frac{1}{8} = \frac{3}{8}.$$

Example   What is the probability of getting a 7 when a fair pair of dice is rolled once?

Solution: The sample space of this experiment consists of 36 sample points, and the probability of each sample point is $\frac{1}{36}$. Since the event rolling a 7 is the subset

$$A = \{(1, 6), (2, 5,) (3, 4), (4, 3), (5, 2), (6, 1)\},$$

the probability of getting a 7 is therefore

$$P(A) = \frac{1}{36} + \frac{1}{36} + \frac{1}{36} + \frac{1}{36} + \frac{1}{36} + \frac{1}{36} = \frac{1}{6}.$$

Adhering to the two rules that the probability of a sample point ranges from 0 to 1 and that the sum of probabilities assigned to all sample points in a sample space must be 1, according to our definition of the probability of an event, we now arrive at several important conclusions:

1. $P(S) = 1$. This is because a sample space is an event that contains *all* sample points.

2. $P(\phi) = 0$. This is because the null set is an event that contains no sample point.

3. $P(A') = 1 - P(A)$. The probability that event A will not occur, denoted by $P(A')$, is equal to 1 minus the probability that A will occur. Thus, if the probability of getting a 5 on one roll of a die is $\frac{1}{6}$, then the probability of not getting a five is $(1 - \frac{1}{6})$, or $\frac{5}{6}$. Similarly, if the probability that it will rain on a certain day is $\frac{1}{4}$, then the probability that it *will not* rain on that day is $(1 - \frac{1}{4})$, or $\frac{3}{4}$.

RULES OF PROBABILITY

The solutions to many problems involving probabilities require a thorough understanding of some basic rules that govern the manipulation of probabilities. In general, these rules enable us to determine the probability of an event once the probabilities of some other related events are known. Most important of these basic rules are the rule of addition, rule of multiplication, and Bayes' theorem. We will discuss the three rules in great detail.

Rule of Addition

Let us consider a game in which a card is to be selected from an ordinary deck of playing cards. We will win $10 if the card selected is either black or a king. What is the probability of winning in this game?

First, we must define the sample space of the experiment. Since there are 52 cards in an ordinary deck, the sample space of this experiment consists of 52 sample points, with a probability of $\frac{1}{52}$ assigned to each point. Next, we must determine the number of sample points contained in the event "black, or king, or both."

An ordinary deck of cards contains 26 black cards and 4 cards that are kings. However, the two black kings are counted both as black cards and as kings. Hence, to determine the number of sample points in the event "black, or king, or both," we cannot simply add the number of black cards and kings in the deck $(26 + 4 = 30)$. If we did, the two black kings would be counted twice. To prevent this double counting, we must subtract 2 from the sum $(26 + 4)$. Thus in the event "black, or king, or both,"

$$\text{Number of sample points} = \begin{array}{c} \text{Number of} \\ \text{black cards} \end{array} + \begin{array}{c} \text{Number of} \\ \text{kings} \end{array} - \begin{array}{c} \text{Number of} \\ \text{black kings} \end{array}$$
$$= 26 \qquad + \quad 4 \quad - \quad 2$$
$$= 28.$$

Since the event "black, or king, or both" contains 28 sample points with a probability of $\frac{1}{52}$ assigned to each point, the probability of winning $10 in our game is $\frac{28}{52}$.

Letting B = black and K = king, we can summarize and restate our solution in a more rigorous fashion:

$$P(B \cup K) = P(B) + P(K) - P(B \cap K)$$
$$= \frac{26}{52} + \frac{4}{52} - \frac{2}{52} = \frac{28}{52}.$$

The solution to our game can now be generalized into the *rule of addition*, which states that if A and B are events belonging to the sample space S, then

$$P(A \cup B) = P(A) + P(B) - P(A \cap B).$$

In words, the rule of addition states that the probability of event A, or B, or both occurring is equal to the probability that A occurs plus the probability that B occurs, minus the probability that both event A and B occur together.

Example A fair die is to be rolled once. You win $5 if the outcome is either even or divisible by 3. What is the probability of winning the game?

Solution: Let A = the event that the outcome is even and B = the event that the outcome is divisible by 3. To determine the probability of winning, we describe the following events:

$$S = \{1, 2, 3, 4, 5, 6\}, \qquad A = \{2, 4, 6\},$$
$$B = \{3, 6\}, \qquad A \cap B = \{6\}.$$

Then, according to the rule of addition, the probability of the event $A \cup B$ is

$$P(A \cup B) = P(A) + P(B) - P(A \cap B)$$
$$= \tfrac{3}{6} + \tfrac{2}{6} - \tfrac{1}{6}$$
$$= \tfrac{2}{3} \text{ probability of winning the game.}$$

Example A customer enters a supermarket. The probability that the customer buys bread is .60; milk, .50; and both bread and milk, .30. What is the probability that the customer will buy bread, or milk, or both?

Solution: Let B = the event that the customer buys bread, M = the event that the customer buys milk. Then, according to the rule of addition, we have

$$P(B \cup M) = P(B) + P(M) - P(B \cap M)$$
$$= .60 + .50 - .30 = .80.$$

Rule of Addition for Mutually Exclusive Events

We have described events A and B as mutually exclusive when $A \cap B = \varnothing$. Consequently

$$P(A \cap B) = P(\varnothing) = 0.$$

Thus, when events A and B are mutually exclusive (in the sense that they cannot occur at the same time), the rule of addition becomes

$$P(A \cup B) = P(A) + P(B).$$

A few illustrations are now in order.

1. When one card is drawn from an ordinary deck of cards, the card cannot be *both* an ace and a king. Thus the event "ace," denoted by A, and the event "king," denoted by K, are mutually exclusive. Furthermore,

    $$P(A) = \tfrac{4}{52} \quad \text{and} \quad P(K) = \tfrac{4}{52},$$

    since there are 4 aces and 4 kings in the deck. Now, if one card is drawn from the deck, what is the probability that the card drawn will be either an ace or a king? According to the rule of addition for mutually exclusive events,

    $$P(A \cup K) = P(A) + P(K)$$
    $$= \tfrac{4}{52} + \tfrac{4}{52} = \tfrac{8}{52}.$$

    Thus, the probability that the card drawn is either an ace or a king is $\tfrac{8}{52}$.

2. Let us determine the probability of getting either a 4 or a 5 when a die is rolled once. Getting a 4 and getting a 5 in one roll of a die are mutually exclusive because a die cannot show a 4 and a 5 in one roll. According to

the rule of addition, therefore,

$$P(4 \cup 5) = P(4) + P(5)$$
$$= \frac{1}{6} + \frac{1}{6} = \frac{1}{3}.$$

Thus the probability of getting either a 4 or a 5 on one roll of a die is $\frac{1}{3}$.

The rule of addition also applies to more than two events.* Thus, if A, B, and C are mutually exclusive, the probability that A, or B, or C will take place is equal to the sum of their respective probabilities. Symbolically,

$$P(A \cap B \cap C) = P(A) + P(B) + P(C).$$

EXERCISES

3.17 A fair die is to be cast once. What is the probability of getting a) an odd number, b) a number greater than 3?

3.18 Two fair coins are to be tossed once. What is the probability of getting a) exactly one heads, b) at least one heads?

3.19 A fair pair of dice is to be cast once. What is the probability of getting a) 7, b) 11, c) 7 or 11, d) a sum divisible by 3?

3.20 One card is selected from an ordinary deck of playing cards. What is the probability of getting a) a queen, b) a jack, c) either a queen or a jack, d) a queen or a red card, e) a face card?

3.21 The probability that on July 4 it will rain is .10; it will thunder, .05; and it will rain and thunder, .03. What is the probability that it will either rain or thunder on that day?

3.22 In a certain community, the probability that a family has a television set is .80; a washing machine, .50; both a television set and a washing machine, .45. What is the probability that a family has either a television set or a washing machine or both?

3.23 The probability that a car salesperson will sell at least 3 cars in a day is .20. What is the probability that he or she will sell 0, or 1, or 2 cars in a day? [*Hint*: $P(S) = 1$.]

3.24 The probability that a student will receive at most 5 telephone calls a day is .20; at least 9 telephone calls a day, .50. What is the probability that the student will receive 6, or 7, or 8 calls a day?

3.25 A box contains 100 television tubes. The probability that there is at least 1 defective tube in the box is .05. The probability that there are at least 2

---

*The rule of addition can also be generalized for events that are not mutually exclusive. The general rule, however, is beyond the scope of this text.

defective tubes in the box is .01. What is the probability

a) that the box will contain no defective tubes? [*Hint:* $P(S) = 1$.]
b) that the box will contain exactly 1 defective tube?
c) that the box will contain at most 1 defective tube?

Conditional Probability

A box contains black and white balls. Each ball is labeled either *A* or *Z*. The composition of the box is shown in the following table.

	B (black)	W (white)	Total
A	5	3	8
Z	1	2	3
Total	6	5	11

Let us now assume that a ball is to be selected at random from the box. We can then speak of the following probabilities:

1. $P(B)$ = probability of getting a black ball = $6/11$. There are 6 black balls among a total of 11 balls.

2. $P(B|A)$ = probability of getting a black *assuming* that the ball selected is labeled A = $5/8$. $P(B|A)$ (read "probability of *B* given *A*") is called **conditional probability** because it refers to the probability of getting a black ball subject to the condition that the ball selected is labeled *A*. This conditional probability is $5/8$ because there are only 8 balls labeled *A* and 5 of these balls are black.

3. $P(A)$ = probability of getting a ball labeled A = $8/11$. There are 8 balls labeled *A* among a total of 11 balls.

4. $P(A \cap B)$ = probability of getting a ball that is *both* labeled A and black = $5/11$. There are 5 balls that are both labeled *A* and black among a total of 11 balls.

Now let us summarize some of these findings.

$$P(B|A) = 5/8, \qquad P(A) = 8/11, \qquad P(A \cap B) = 5/11.$$

Using these results, we can show that

$$P(B|A) = \frac{P(A \cap B)}{P(A)}$$

$$= \frac{5/11}{8/11} = 5/8,$$

which is exactly the same result as that obtained earlier in number 2. We now introduce a general definition of *conditional probability:* If events A and B belong to the sample space S, and if $P(A) \neq 0$, then the conditional probability of B relative to A, denoted by $P(B \mid A)$, is defined as

$$P(B \mid A) = \frac{P(A \cap B)}{P(A)}.$$

Example   A fair die is to be rolled once. Given that the outcome is even, what is the probability of getting a number greater than 3?

Solution: Let us first define the following sets:

$$S = \{1, 2, 3, 4, 5, 6\}: \quad \text{Sample space}$$
$$A = \{2, 4, 6\}: \quad \text{Set of even outcomes}$$
$$B = \{4, 5, 6\}: \quad \text{Set of numbers greater than 3}$$
$$A \cap B = \{4, 6\}: \quad \text{Set of even numbers greater than 3}$$

Since the die is fair, we assign a probability of $\frac{1}{6}$ to each sample point. Consequently,

$$P(A) = \frac{3}{6}, \qquad P(A \cap B) = \frac{2}{6}.$$

Using the definition of conditional probability, we can now determine the probability of getting a number greater than 3 given that the outcome is even:

$$P(B \mid A) = \frac{P(A \cap B)}{P(A)}$$

$$= \frac{\frac{2}{6}}{\frac{3}{6}} = \frac{2}{3}.$$

This result can be verified by the fact that out of three even outcomes $\{2, 4, 6\}$ only two are greater than 3.

Example   In Honolulu, the probability that it will rain on the first day of December is .50. The probability that it will rain on both the first and second days of December is .40. Given that December 1 is a rainy day in Honolulu, what is the probability of rain on December 2?

Solution: *Given:* $P(R_1) = .50$, $P(R_1 \cap R_2) = .40$. Using our definition of conditional probability, we have

$$P(R_2 \mid R_1) = \frac{P(R_1 \cap R_2)}{P(R_1)}$$

$$= \frac{.40}{.50} = .80.$$

Rule of Multiplication

We begin with the definition of conditional probability:

$$P(B \mid A) = \frac{P(A \cap B)}{P(A)}.$$

If we multiply both sides of the preceding equation by $P(A)$, the resulting equation,

$$P(A \cap B) = P(A)P(B \mid A),$$

is called the *rule of multiplication*. In words, the rule of multiplication states that the probability that both events A and B occur is equal to the probability that A occurs multiplied by the probability that B occurs, given that event A has taken place.

Example   Two cards are to be drawn without replacement from an ordinary deck of playing cards. What is the probability that both of the cards drawn are aces?

Solution: Let A_1 be the event that the first card drawn is an ace and let A_2 be the event that the second card is an ace. Then, according to the rule of multiplication, the probability of the event $A_1 \cap A_2$ is equal to the probability of obtaining an ace on the first draw multiplied by the probability of obtaining an ace on the second draw, given that an ace was obtained on the first draw. Symbolically,

$$P(A_1 \cap A_2) = P(A_1)P(A_2 \mid A_1).$$

The probability of obtaining an ace on the first draw, or $P(A_1)$, is $\frac{4}{52}$ since there are 4 aces in a deck of 52 cards. The probability of getting an ace on the second draw, given that an ace was obtained on the first draw, or $P(A_2 \mid A_1)$, is $\frac{3}{51}$ since of the remaining 51 cards in the deck only 3 are aces. Thus,

$$P(A_1 \cap A_2) = P(A_1)P(A_2 \mid A_1)$$
$$= \tfrac{4}{52} \cdot \tfrac{3}{51} = \tfrac{12}{2652}.$$

Once again, the general rule of multiplication states

$$P(A \cap B) = P(A) \cdot P(B \mid A).$$

$P(A \cap B)$ is called the joint probability of A and B; $P(A)$ is called the marginal probability of A, and $P(B \mid A)$ is the conditional probability of B with respect to A.

Rule of Multiplication for Independent Events

Events A and B are considered to be **independent** when the occurrence of one does not influence the probability of the occurrence of the other. This means that regardless of whether event A has or has not happened, the probability assigned to B is going to be the same. Stated differently, when A and B are independent, the conditional probability of B relative to A is the same as the unconditional probability of B, that is, $P(B \mid A) = P(B)$. If this is the case, the rule of multiplication for independent events becomes

$$P(A \cap B) = P(A) \cdot P(B).$$

To illustrate this rule, let us determine the probability of obtaining two heads in two successive tosses of a balanced coin:

$$P(H_1 \cap H_2) = P(H_1) \cdot P(H_2)$$
$$= \tfrac{1}{2} \cdot \tfrac{1}{2} = \tfrac{1}{4}.$$

As an alternative illustration, let us determine the probability of getting a 6 and a 5 in succession when a die is rolled twice. Since the two events are independent, it follows that

$$P(6 \cap 5) = P(6) \cdot P(5)$$
$$= \tfrac{1}{6} \cdot \tfrac{1}{6} = \tfrac{1}{36}.$$

The multiplication rule, whether for dependent or for independent events, can be extended to cover the case of more than two events. Although we will not state the extended rules rigorously, we will treat them informally in some of the examples that follow. These problems are meant to illustrate the various characteristics and rules of probability studied so far.

Example   An urn contains 6 white and 4 black marbles. Two marbles are to be selected in succession and without replacement from this urn.
  a) What is the probability that the two marbles selected are white?
  b) What is the probability that the first marble is white and the second marble is black?
  c) What is the probability that the first marble is black and the second marble is white?
  d) What is the probability that the two marbles selected are black?

Solution:
  a) $P(W_1 \cap W_2) = P(W_1) \cdot P(W_2 \mid W_1)$
$$= \tfrac{6}{10} \cdot \tfrac{5}{9} = \tfrac{30}{90}$$
  b) $P(W_1 \cap B_2) = P(W_1) \cdot P(B_2 \mid W_1)$
$$= \tfrac{6}{10} \cdot \tfrac{4}{9} = \tfrac{24}{90}$$
  c) $P(B_1 \cap W_2) = P(B_1) \cdot P(W_2 \mid B_1)$
$$= \tfrac{4}{10} \cdot \tfrac{6}{9} = \tfrac{24}{90}$$
  d) $P(B_1 \cap B_2) = P(B_1) \cdot P(B_2 \mid B_1)$
$$= \tfrac{4}{10} \cdot \tfrac{3}{9} = \tfrac{12}{90}$$

In this example, we have actually considered all possible outcomes of our experiment. Furthermore, we have used the general rule of multiplication to determine the probability of each of these possible outcomes. We can summarize our results in the following table.

Possible Outcome	Marginal Probability $P(A)$	Conditional Probability $P(B\mid A)$	Joint Probability = Marg. Prob. · Cond. Prob. $P(A \cap B) = P(A) \cdot P(B\mid A)$
$W_1) \cap W_2$	$P(W_1) = {}^6\!/_{10}$	$P(W_2\mid W_1) = {}^5\!/_9$	${}^6\!/_{10} \cdot {}^5\!/_9 = {}^{30}\!/_{90}$
$W_1 \cap B_2$	$P(W_1) = {}^6\!/_{10}$	$P(B_2\mid W_1) = {}^4\!/_9$	${}^6\!/_{10} \cdot {}^4\!/_9 = {}^{24}\!/_{90}$
$B_1 \cap W_2$	$P(B_1) = {}^4\!/_{10}$	$P(W_2\mid B_1) = {}^6\!/_9$	${}^4\!/_{10} \cdot {}^6\!/_9 = {}^{24}\!/_{90}$
$B_1 \cap B_2$	$P(B_1) = {}^4\!/_{10}$	$P(B_2\mid B_1) = {}^3\!/_9$	${}^4\!/_{10} \cdot {}^3\!/_9 = {}^{12}\!/_{90}$

The same results are also displayed in a tree diagram in Fig. 3.9.

Example Urn A contains 6 white (W) and 4 red (R) marbles. Urn B contains 3 white and 7 red marbles. Two marbles are to be selected, one from A and one from B. What is the probability that the two marbles selected are of the same color?

Solution:

$$
\begin{aligned}
P(\text{same color}) &= P(\text{both white}) + P(\text{both red}) \\
&= P(W_1 \cap W_2) + P(R_1 \cap R_2) \\
&= P(W_1) \cdot P(W_2) + P(R_1) \cdot P(R_2) \\
&\quad {}^6\!/_{10} \cdot {}^3\!/_{10} + {}^4\!/_{10} \cdot {}^7\!/_{10} = {}^{18}\!/_{100} + {}^{28}\!/_{100} = {}^{46}\!/_{100}.
\end{aligned}
$$

Example An assembly consists of three independent components A, B, and C. The assembly is considered defective if one or more of its components are

Figure 3.9

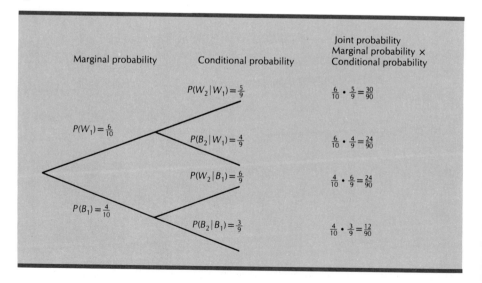

defective. The probability that component A is defective is .01; that component B is defective, .02; and that component C is defective, .10.

a) What is the probability that the assembly is defective?

b) What is the probability of a defective assembly because of the failure of only component C?

Solution:

a) Let

$$P(A) = \text{Probability that component } A \text{ is defective,}$$
$$P(A') = \text{Probability that component } A \text{ is not defective,}$$
$$P(B) = \text{Probability that component } B \text{ is defective,}$$
$$P(B') = \text{Probability that component } B \text{ is not defective,}$$
$$P(C) = \text{Probability that component } C \text{ is defective,}$$
$$P(C') = \text{Probability that component } C \text{ is not defective.}$$

Now let us calculate $P(A')$, $P(B')$, and $P(C')$.

$$
\begin{array}{lll}
P(A') = 1 - P(A) & P(B') = 1 - P(B) & P(C') = 1 - P(C) \\
\quad = 1 - .01 & \quad = 1 - .02 & \quad = 1 - .10 \\
\quad = .99 & \quad = .98 & \quad = .90
\end{array}
$$

The assembly is in good order only if all the components are in good order. Thus

$$
\begin{aligned}
P(\text{good assembly}) &= P(A' \cap B' \cap C') \\
&= P(A') \cdot P(B') \cdot P(C') \\
&= .99 \cdot .98 \cdot .90 = .87318.
\end{aligned}
$$

But

$$
\begin{aligned}
P(\text{defective assembly}) &= 1 - P(\text{good assembly}) \\
&= 1 - .87318 = .12682.
\end{aligned}
$$

b) The probability of a defective assembly because of failure of only component C is

$$
\begin{aligned}
P(A' \cap B' \cap C) &= P(A') \cdot P(B') \cdot P(C) \\
&= .99 \cdot .98 \cdot .10 = .09702.
\end{aligned}
$$

Example   An aircraft is equipped with three engines that operate independently. The probability of an engine failure is .01. What is the probability of a successful flight if only one engine is needed for the successful operation of the aircraft?

Solution: Let

$$P(S) = \text{Probability of a successful flight,}$$
$$P(S') = \text{Probability of an unsuccessful flight,}$$
$$P(F) = \text{Probability of an engine failure.}$$

Since the flight is unsuccessful only when all three engines fail, the probability of unsuccessful flight is

$$P(S') = P(F_1 \cap F_2 \cap F_3)$$
$$= .01 \cdot .01 \cdot .01 = .01^3.$$

But

$$P(S) = 1 - P(S')$$
$$= 1 - .01^3 = 1 - .000001 = .999999.$$

Example Five cards are to be drawn in succession and without replacement from an ordinary deck of playing cards.

a) What is the probability that there will be no ace among the five cards drawn?

b) What is the probability that the first three cards are aces and the last two cards are kings?

c) What is the probability that only the first three cards are aces?

d) What is the probability that an ace will appear only on the fifth draw?

Solution:

a) Denoting the probability of getting an ace by $P(A)$ and the probability of not getting an ace by $P(A')$, we find that the probability that there will be no ace among the five cards drawn is

$$P(A'_1 \cap A'_2 \cap A'_3 \cap A'_4 \cap A'_5) = \tfrac{48}{52} \cdot \tfrac{47}{51} \cdot \tfrac{46}{50} \cdot \tfrac{45}{49} \cdot \tfrac{44}{48}$$

$$= \frac{205,476,480}{311,875,200}.$$

b) Denoting the probability of getting a king by $P(K)$, we find that the probability that the first three cards are aces and the last two are kings is

$$P(A_1 \cap A_2 \cap A_3 \cap K_1 \cap K_2) = \tfrac{4}{52} \cdot \tfrac{3}{51} \cdot \tfrac{2}{50} \cdot \tfrac{4}{49} \cdot \tfrac{3}{48} = \frac{288}{311,875,200}.$$

c) The probability that only the first three cards are aces is

$$P(A_1 \cap A_2 \cap A_3 \cap A'_1 \cap A'_2) = \tfrac{4}{52} \cdot \tfrac{3}{51} \cdot \tfrac{2}{50} \cdot \tfrac{48}{49} \cdot \tfrac{47}{48}$$

$$= \frac{54,144}{311,875,200}.$$

d) The probability that an ace will appear only on the fifth draw is

$$P(A_1' \cap A_2' \cap A_3' \cap A_4' \cap A_5) = {}^{48}\!/_{52} \cdot {}^{47}\!/_{51} \cdot {}^{46}\!/_{50} \cdot {}^{45}\!/_{49} \cdot {}^{4}\!/_{48}$$

$$= \frac{18{,}679{,}680}{311{,}875{,}200}.$$

EXERCISES

3.26 Given that $P(K) = .50$ and $P(K \cap L) = .30$, find $P(L \mid K)$.

3.27 Of all students attending a given college, 40% are males and 4% are males majoring in art. A student is to be selected at random. Given that the selected student is male, what is the probability that he is an art major?

3.28 An urn contains 4 white and 3 red marbles.

a) If two marbles are selected without replacement from the urn, what is the probability that the two marbles selected are white?

b) If two marbles are selected *with* replacement from the urn, what is the probability that the two marbles selected are white?

3.29 Urn A contains 4 white and 3 red marbles and urn B contains 2 white and 5 red marbles. A marble is to be selected from urn A and another marble is to be selected from urn B. What is the probability that the two marbles selected are white?

3.30 Urn A contains 4 white and 3 red marbles, urn B contains 2 white and 5 red marbles, and urn C contains 3 white and 6 red marbles. A marble is to be selected from each of the three urns. What is the probability that the three marbles selected are of the same color?

3.31 Two cards are to be drawn without replacement from an ordinary deck of playing cards. What is the probability

a) that the first card to be drawn is a queen and the second card a king?

b) of drawing a combination of queen and king?

c) that neither of the two cards will be a queen?

d) that neither of the two cards will be a queen or a king?

3.32 Two cards are to be drawn without replacement from a deck of playing cards from which the face cards have been removed. What is the probability that the sum of the two cards drawn will be 19?

3.33 Five cards are to be drawn without replacement from an ordinary deck of playing cards. What is the probability

a) that the first three cards are queens and the last two cards are kings?

b) that only the first three cards are queens?

c) that the first three cards are queens?

3.34 Cards are to be drawn in succession and without replacement from an ordinary deck of playing cards. What is the probability

a) that the first queen will appear on the third draw?

b) that a queen will appear on the third draw?

3.35 Three cards are to be drawn without replacement from an ordinary deck of playing cards. What is the probability of getting at least one king among the three cards drawn?

3.36 A die is cast three times. What is the probability

a) of not getting three 6's in succession?

b) that the same number appears three times?

3.37 One face of a die is colored red, two faces are colored green, and the other three faces are colored black. The die is thrown four times. What is the probability

a) that the first three throws are red and the last throw is green?

b) that only the first three throws are red?

c) that the first three throws are red?

3.38 A die is thrown three times. What is the probability

a) that the sum of the three faces shown is either 3 or 4?

b) that the sum of the three faces shown is greater than 4?

3.39 A hunter fires 7 consecutive bullets at an angry tiger. If the probability that 1 bullet will kill is 0.6, what is the probability that the *hunter* is still alive?

3.40 Ms. Ho boards a 6-engine aircraft to attend a summit meeting in Paris. The probability of an engine failure is .10, and each engine operates independently of the others. If at least one operating engine is needed on each side of the aircraft, what is the probability that Ms. Ho will be absent from the summit meeting because her aircraft crashes?

3.41 A lot of 100 fuses is known to contain 2 defective fuses. If the fuses are tested one at a time, what is the probability that the last defective fuse is found on the third test?

3.42 Marbles are drawn one at a time and without replacement from an urn that contains 6 black marbles and 8 white marbles. The drawing is terminated as soon as marbles of both colors are obtained.

a) What is the probability that the drawing is terminated by the fourth draw?

b) What is the probability that exactly three drawings are needed to terminate the selection?

3.43 A person fires one rifle shot at a time at a given target, until the target is hit twice. The probability that any single shot hits the target is .2.

a) What is the probability that *exactly* three shots are needed to terminate the firing?

b) What is the probability that the firing is terminated by the third shot?

3.44 A box contains 4 fuses, 2 of which are known to be defective. Two fuses are selected at random and without replacement from the box.

a) What is the probability that the 2 defective fuses are selected?

b) What is the probability that there is at least 1 defective fuse among the 2 fuses selected?

3.45 A voucher must be approved by two members of the purchasing department before payment is made. The probability that an erroneous voucher is approved by the first member is .01. Given that an erroneous voucher is approved by the first member, the probability that it is approved by the second member is .20. What is the probability that a payment is made on an erroneous voucher?

3.46 Twenty students in a business statistics class are categorized according to age and sex as follows:

	Male	Female
Under 21 years	4	2
21 years or older	11	3

Assume that two students are selected at random from this class.

a) What is the probability that both students are male?

b) What is the probability that both students are under 21 years?

c) What is the probability that the two students selected are of the same sex?

3.47 Phil E. Buster, the budget analyst in Flat-brook, California, estimates his city's revenues and expenditures for the next fiscal year as follows.

Revenues (billions of dollars)	Probability	Expenditures (billions of dollars)	Probability
50	$\frac{1}{4}$	60	$\frac{1}{6}$
60	$\frac{1}{2}$	70	$\frac{3}{6}$
70	$\frac{1}{4}$	80	$\frac{2}{6}$

a) What is the probability of a balanced budget?

b) What is the probability of a $10 billion budget surplus?

3.48 Bank of America, Westwood Branch, reports that 50% of all UCLA students maintain a checking account with the branch. In addition, 25% of the students have savings accounts, and 10% have both checking accounts and savings accounts. One student is selected at random from UCLA.

a) What is the probability that the student has a checking account with this bank branch?

b) What is the probability that the student has either a checking account or a savings account?

c) Given that the student selected has a checking account, what is the probability that the student has a savings account?

3.49 Referring to the preceding problem, suppose that 3 students are to be selected from UCLA.

a) What is the probability that all 3 students have checking accounts?

b) What is the probability that at least one of the students has any account with the bank branch?

3.50 Jane Dough applies for admission to Harvard, Princeton, Columbia, and Yale. The probability that she is admitted to the 4 universities is .2, .5, .8, .7, respectively.

a) What is the probability that Jane is admitted to exactly 3 of the schools?

b) What is the probability that Jane is admitted to at least 1 of the schools?

3.51 A precinct consists of 400 registered voters. Voters are classified as follows:

	Democrats	Republicans	Independents
Men	120	90	10
Women	80	60	40

Two voters are selected at random and without replacement.

a) What is the probability that the first voter selected is
   1) a Democrat?
   2) a female Democrat?

b) What is the probability that the two voters selected
   1) are Democrats?
   2) belong to the same party?

Bayes' Theorem

Consider the following game. We have two urns. The first, denoted A_1 contains 8 black (B) and 2 white (W) marbles; the second, A_2, contains 3 black and 7

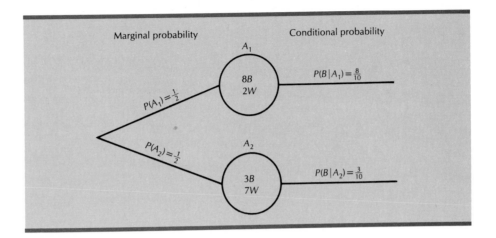

Figure 3.10

white marbles. One of the urns is to be selected at random and a marble is to be drawn from that urn. We win a sum of $10 if the marble drawn is black. What is the probability of winning in this game?

There are two ways of winning in the game (each is represented by a path in Fig. 3.10). First, we will win if we choose urn A_1 and draw a black marble from it. The probability of winning along this path is

$$P(A_1 \cap B) = P(A_1)P(B \mid A_1)$$
$$= \tfrac{1}{2} \cdot \tfrac{8}{10} = \tfrac{8}{20}.$$

We also win if we choose urn A_2 and draw a black marble from it. The probability of winning along this second path is

$$P(A_2 \cap B) = P(A_2)P(B \mid A_2)$$
$$= \tfrac{1}{2} \cdot \tfrac{3}{10} = \tfrac{3}{20}.$$

Thus we win when either of two events occurs: (1) when we select A_1 and draw a black marble from it; (2) when we select A_2 and draw a black marble from it. These two events are mutually exclusive. According to the rule of addition, the probability of winning, or the probability of drawing a black marble regardless of its origin, is equal to the sum of the probabilities of the two events (see Fig. 3.11):

$$P(B) = P(A_1 \cap B) + P(A_2 \cap B)$$
$$= P(A_1)P(B \mid A_1) + P(A_2)P(B \mid A_2)$$
$$= \tfrac{1}{2} \cdot \tfrac{8}{10} + \tfrac{1}{2} \cdot \tfrac{3}{10} = \tfrac{8}{20} + \tfrac{3}{20} = \tfrac{11}{20}.$$

Now let us assume that we played the game once and that we have won the game. What is the probability that we selected urn A_1?

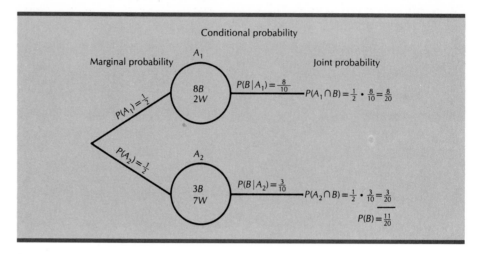

Figure 3.11

First, since the probability contribution of the upper path in Fig. 3.11 is $8/20$ while the probability contribution of the second path is only $3/20$, it is only reasonable to assume that the selection of A_1 is more likely than the selection of A_2. Second, it also seems reasonable to conclude that the probability that A_1 is chosen is

$$8/20 \div 11/20 = 8/11,$$

while the probability that A_2 is selected is

$$3/20 \div 11/20 = 3/11.$$

We can now formally approach this intuitive solution to the problem of determining the probability of selecting each urn after the game has been won. According to the definition of conditional probability, the probability that A_1 is chosen given that the marble selected is black is

$$P(A_1 \mid B) = \frac{P(A_1 \cap B)}{P(B)} .$$

But since we have already shown that

$$P(B) = P(A_1 \cap B) + P(A_2 \cap B),$$

it follows that

$$P(A_1 \mid B) = \frac{P(A_1 \cap B)}{P(A_1 \cap B) + P(A_2 \cap B)}$$

$$= \frac{8/20}{8/20 + 3/20} = 8/11.$$

Similarly, the probability that A_2 is chosen given that the marble selected is black is

$$P(A_2 \mid B) = \frac{P(A_2 \cap B)}{P(B)}$$

$$= \frac{P(A_2 \cap B)}{P(A_1 \cap B) + P(A_2 \cap B)}$$

$$= \frac{3/20}{8/20 + 3/20} = 3/11.$$

Example   Urn A_1 contains 8 black (B) and 2 white marbles (W) marbles. Urn A_2 contains 3 black and 7 white marbles, and urn A_3 contains 5 white and 5 black marbles. A fair die is to be cast. If the die turns up 1, 2, or 3, then a marble will be selected from A_1. If the die turns up 4 or 5, a marble will be selected from A_2. Finally, a marble will be selected from A_3 if the die turns up 6. Given that the marble selected is black, what is the probability that the marble was chosen from A_2?

Solution: We refer to Fig. 3.12 and assume that the marble selected is black.

Figure 3.12

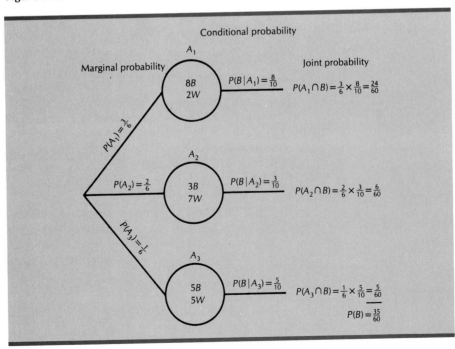

Conditional probability

A_1

Marginal probability

Joint probability

$8B$
$2W$

$P(B \mid A_1) = \frac{8}{10}$

$P(A_1 \cap B) = \frac{3}{6} \times \frac{8}{10} = \frac{24}{60}$

$P(A_1) = \frac{3}{6}$

A_2

$P(A_2) = \frac{2}{6}$

$3B$
$7W$

$P(B \mid A_2) = \frac{3}{10}$

$P(A_2 \cap B) = \frac{2}{6} \times \frac{3}{10} = \frac{6}{60}$

$P(A_3) = \frac{1}{6}$

A_3

$5B$
$5W$

$P(B \mid A_3) = \frac{5}{10}$

$P(A_3 \cap B) = \frac{1}{6} \times \frac{5}{10} = \frac{5}{60}$

$P(B) = \frac{35}{60}$

Then we find the probability that the marble was chosen from urn A_2 is

$$P(A_2 \mid B) = \frac{P(A_2 \cap B)}{P(B)}$$

$$= \frac{P(A_2 \cap B)}{P(A_1 \cap B) + P(A_2 \cap B) + P(A_3 \cap B)}$$

$$= \frac{P(A_2)P(B \mid A_2)}{P(A_1)P(B \mid A_1) + P(A_2)P(B \mid A_2) + P(A_3)P(B \mid A_3)}$$

$$= \frac{\frac{2}{6} \cdot \frac{3}{10}}{(\frac{3}{6} \cdot \frac{8}{10}) + (\frac{2}{6} \cdot \frac{3}{10}) + (\frac{1}{6} \cdot \frac{5}{10})}$$

$$= \frac{\frac{6}{60}}{\frac{24}{60} + \frac{6}{60} + \frac{5}{60}} = \frac{\frac{6}{60}}{\frac{35}{60}} = \frac{6}{35}.$$

We will generalize the foregoing solution, obtaining Bayes' theorem.

Let $A_1, A_2, \ldots, A_k$ be mutually exclusive events that occupy the entire sample space S. If each of these events has nonzero probability and one of them must occur, then for any event B in the sample space S,

$$P(A_1 \mid B) = \frac{P(A_1)P(B \mid A_1)}{P(A_1)P(B \mid A_1) + P(A_2)P(B \mid A_2) + \cdots + P(A_k)P(B \mid A_k)}.$$

$$P(A_2 \mid B) = \frac{P(A_2)P(B \mid A_2)}{P(A_1)P(B \mid A_1) + P(A_2)P(B \mid A_2) + \cdots + P(A_k)P(B \mid A_k)}.$$

and, finally,

$$P(A_k \mid B) = \frac{P(A_k)P(B \mid A_k)}{P(A_1)P(B \mid A_1) + P(A_2)P(B \mid A_2) + \cdots + P(A_k)P(B \mid A_k)}.$$

Example Urn A contains 6 green and 4 red marbles, and urn B contains 2 green and 7 red marbles. A marble is to be selected at random from A and placed in B. One marble is then selected from B. Given that the marble selected from B is green, what is the probability that the marble selected from A was also green?

Solution: Refer to Fig. 3.13. Let

$P(G_1) =$ probability that the marble moved from A is green,
$P(R_1) =$ probability that the marble moved from A is red,
$P(G_2) =$ probability that the marble selected from B is green.

Then, according to Bayes' theorem,

$$P(G_1 \mid G_2) = \frac{P(G_1)P(G_2 \mid G_1)}{P(G_1)P(G_2 \mid G_1) + P(R_1)P(G_2 \mid R_1)}$$

$$= \frac{\frac{6}{10} \cdot \frac{3}{10}}{(\frac{6}{10} \cdot \frac{3}{10}) + (\frac{4}{10} \cdot \frac{2}{10})} = \frac{\frac{18}{100}}{\frac{18}{100} + \frac{8}{100}} = \frac{\frac{18}{100}}{\frac{26}{100}} = \frac{18}{26}.$$

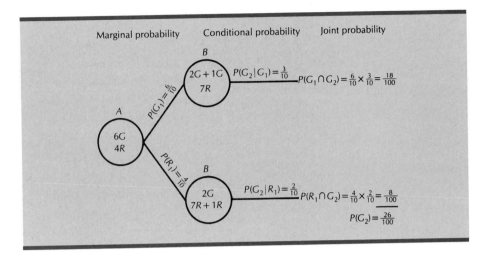

Figure 3.13

Example   The ABC Company is considering the marketing of an electronic printing calculator. According to the market research director, the probability that the product will succeed is .80 if a foreign competing firm does not introduce the same product into the market. However, the probability of success is only .30 if the foreign firm markets the same product. The company further believes that the probability is .40 that the competing firm will market the electronic printing calculator. Given that the ABC Company product is successful, what is the probability that the foreign firm has marketed its electronic printing calculator?

Solution: Refer to Fig. 3.14. Let

$P(M)$ = Probability that the foreign firm markets the same product,
$P(M')$ = Probability that the foreign firm does not market the same product,

Figure 3.14

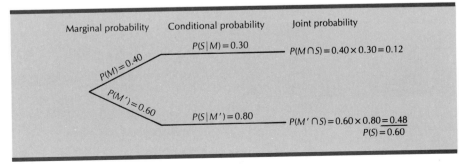

$P(S)$ = Probability that the ABC Company succeeds in marketing its electronic calculator.

Then, according to Bayes' theorem.

$$P(M \mid S) = \frac{P(M)P(S \mid M)}{P(M)P(S \mid M) + P(M')P(S \mid M')}$$

$$= \frac{.40 \cdot .30}{(.40 \cdot .30) + (.60 \cdot .80)} = \frac{.12}{.12 + .48} = \frac{12}{60} = .20.$$

Example A manufacturer is considering the purchase of a lot of 10,000 parts from a supplier. The manufacturer estimates the proportion of defective parts in the lot as follows:

Proportion of Defective Parts (π)	Probability $P(\pi)$
$\pi_1 = .10$	$P(\pi_1) = .20$
$\pi_2 = .15$	$P(\pi_2) = .30$
$\pi_3 = .25$	$P(\pi_3) = .50$

This means that the manufacturer is not certain about the proportion of defective parts in the lot. However, based on past experience, he personally believes there is .20 chance that the lot contains 10% defective parts; there is .30 chance that the lot contains 15% defective parts; and there is .50 chance that the lot contains 25% defective parts.

a) Assuming that one part is selected at random from the lot, what is the probability of selecting a defective part?

b) Assuming that the selected part is defective, what is the probability that the lot contains 25% defective parts?

Solution:

a) There are three possible ways of obtaining a defective part from the lot (each is represented by a path in Fig. 3.15):

1. $P(\pi_1 \cap D) = P(\pi_1) \cdot P(D \mid \pi_1) = .20 \cdot .10 = .0200.$
2. $P(\pi_2 \cap D) = P(\pi_2) \cdot P(D \mid \pi_2) = .30 \cdot .15 = .0450.$
3. $P(\pi_3 \cap D) = P(\pi_3) \cdot P(D \mid \pi_3) = .50 \cdot .25 = .125.$

Hence, the probability of getting a defective part, regardless of whether the lot contains 10, 15, or 25% defective parts, is

$$P(D) = P(\pi_1 \cap D) + P(\pi_2 \cap D) + P(\pi_3 \cap D)$$
$$= .0200 + .0450 + .1250 = .19.$$

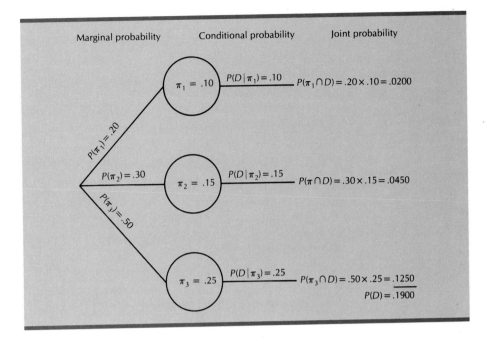

Figure 3.15

b) According to Bayes' theorem, the probability that the lot contains 25% defective parts, given that the selected part was defective, is

$$P(\pi_3 \mid D) = \frac{P(\pi_3 \cap D)}{P(D)} = \frac{.1250}{.1900} = .6579.$$

EXERCISES

3.52 Urn A contains 4 white and 3 red marbles, and urn B contains 2 white and 5 red marbles. One of the urns is to be chosen at random and a marble is to be selected from the chosen urn.

a) What is the probability of drawing a white marble?

b) Given that the marble drawn was white, what is the probability that urn A was selected?

3.53 Urn A contains 4 white and 3 red marbles, and urn B contains 2 white and 5 red marbles. A fair die is to be cast once. If the die turns up 1 or 2, then two marbles will be selected without replacement from urn A. If the die turns up 3, 4, 5, or 6, then two marbles will be selected without replacement from urn B.

a) What is the probability that the two marbles selected are white?

b) Given that the two marbles selected were white, what is the probability that urn A was selected?

3.54 Urn A contains 4 white and 3 red marbles, and urn B contains 2 white and 3 red marbles. A marble is to be selected from A and placed in B. Two marbles are then to be selected from B.

a) What is the probability that the two marbles selected from urn B are white?

b) Given that the two marbles selected from B were white, what is the probability that the marble selected from urn A was also white?

3.55 Twenty percent of all students at UCLA are graduates and 80% are undergraduates. The probability that a graduate student is married is .50 and the probability that an undergraduate student is married is .10. One student is selected at random from UCLA.

a) What is the probability that the student selected is married?

b) Given that the student selected is married, what is the probability that the student is a graduate student?

3.56 The probability that Judith will study for her final examination in economics is .20. If she studies, the probability is .80 that she will pass her finals. If she does not study, the probability of passing the finals is only .50.

a) What is the probability that Judith will pass her economics finals?

b) Given that Judith passed her final examination in economics, what is the probability that she studied for the finals?

3.57 Every night Sam arrives home late, and the porch light is always on. The probability that Sam arrives home after midnight is .60. If he arrives home after midnight, the probability is .90 that he forgets to turn the porch light off. If Sam arrives home before midnight, the probability is only .05 that he forgets to turn the light off.

a) What is the probability that Sam will turn the porch light off on a given night?

b) Given that Sam turned the porch light off on a certain night, what is the probability that he arrived home after midnight?

3.58 A real estate development company is considering the possibility of building a shopping center in a Los Angeles suburb. A proposed freeway route linking the suburb to the Los Angeles central freeway system is a vital element in the company's consideration of the project. The probability that the real estate company will build the shopping center is .90 if the state Department of Public Works approves the proposed freeway route. If the new route is not approved, the probability is only .20 that the company will build the shopping center. Based on all available information, the president of the company believes there is .60 chance that the proposed freeway route will be approved.

a) What is the probability that the real estate company will build the shopping center?

b) Given that the shopping center was built, what is the probability that the state Department of Public Works approved the new freeway route?

3.59 Irving Aircraft has submitted a bid on a contract to build one hundred F-13 planes for the United States Air Corps. The probability that Irving Aircraft will get the contract is .90 if a competing firm, Helga Aircraft, does not submit a bid on the same contract. However, the probability is only .20 that Irving Aircraft will get the contract if Helga Aircraft submits a bid. The president of Irving Aircraft personally believes there is .80 chance that Helga Aircraft will bid against Irving.

a) What is the probability that Irving Aircraft will get the contract?

b) Given that Irving Aircraft got the contract to build the F-13 planes, what is the probability that Helga Aircraft submitted a bid on the same contract?

3.60 The general manager of a nationally franchised neighborhood food store chain estimates the proportion of her stores that will achieve a million dollars in annual sales as follows:

Proportion of Stores (π)	Probability $P(\pi)$
.60	.2
.70	.5
.80	.3

Two stores are to be selected at random from all stores.

a) What is the probability that both stores that are selected have achieved a million dollars in annual sales?

b) Given that both stores achieved a million dollars in annual sales, what is the probability that 80% of all the stores achieved a million dollars in annual sales?

3.61 The ABC Company undertakes a market survey to assess the profitability of each of its newly developed products. Past surveys indicated that 90% of the new products would be profitable. Subsequent analysis of the reliability of such surveys has shown, however, that only 70% of the products predicted to be profitable yielded any profit. By contrast, of those products predicted to be unprofitable by a survey, 20% produced some profit when marketed. The company has marketed a newly developed product called X. Given that product X was actually profitable, what is the probability that the market survey predicted failure for product X?

3.62   Bob drives his automobile to work 40% of the time. He takes the city bus 50% of the time, and he hitchhikes to work 10% of the time. The probability that he will arrive on time to work is .9 if he drives his automobile, .6 if he takes the bus, and .3 if he hitchhikes. Given that Bob arrived late to work on a given day, what is the probability that he took the bus?

3.63   Richard knows only two women: Pat and Jan. He asks Pat for a date ¾ of the time and he asks Jan ¼ of the time. The probability that Pat will accept his invitation to a show is .2, and the probability that Jan will accept is .3. Given that Richard and one of the two girls were at a show last night, what is the probability that Richard was accompanied by Pat? What is the probability that he was accompanied by Jan?

3.64   The Dixon Detective Agency specializes in solving burglary cases. The agency employs two detectives: Holman and Ericman. Holman is assigned 60% of all cases, and he solves 10% of the cases assigned to him. Ericman is assigned 40% of all cases, and he solves 20% of the cases assigned to him. If a burglary case has just been solved by the Dixon Agency, what is the probability that the case was solved by Ericman?

3.65   Johnny Carlson engages one of three comedy writers, Tom, Dick, and Jerry, to write his nightly TV monologue. Tom is assigned the task 50% of the time, Dick 5% of the time, and Jerry 45% of the time. The probability of writing a successful monologue is .20, .10, and .15 for Tom, Dick, and Jerry, respectively. Last night's monologue bombed. What is the probability that the monologue was written by Tom?

3.66   Millionaire oilman Ty Coon has purchased the petroleum rights on a piece of property. Ty's initial estimate is that there is only a .05 chance of oil being present. Ty is thinking about having a seismic survey done. From past experience Ty knows that if oil is on the land, the seismic survey will show a reservoir 90% of the time. Also, if no oil is present, the seismic survey will indicate a reservoir 20% of the time. Suppose that the survey was made and a reservoir was found; find the probability that oil is present.

3.67   Henry finishes writing a college text entitled *The Art of Secrecy and Deception in Foreign Policy* and submits the text to a publishing company for possible publication. The publishing company's past records indicate that only 30% of similar texts were successful when published. To decide whether to publish a new text, the publishing company submits a proposed text to a review board. Past company records indicate that 90% of successful texts published received favorable reviews and that 20% of the unsuccessful texts published also received favorable reviews.

a) What is the probability that the proposed text will receive a favorable prepublication review?

b) Given that Henry's text received favorable prepublication reviews, what is the probability that the text was successful?

RANDOM VARIABLES

Consider the possible number of heads that can appear when 3 balanced coins are tossed once. The 8 possible outcomes of this experiment, together with the number of heads associated with each outcome, are listed in the following table.

Outcome	Number of Heads
TTT	0
HTT	1
THT	1
TTH	1
THH	2
HTH	2
HHT	2
HHH	3

We have assigned a value (0, 1, 2, or 3) to each of the 8 possible outcomes or sample points. The value assigned to any sample point refers to the number of heads associated with that sample point. Thus, we have assigned the value 0 to the sample point TTT (no heads) and the value 2 to the sample points THH, HTH, HHT (each of which has exactly 2 heads).

Let the variable X represent the number of heads in this experiment. Depending on the outcome of the experiment, the variable X can assume any of the values 0, 1, 2, and 3. When the numerical value of a variable is determined by the outcome of an experiment, the variable is called a **random variable.** Thus the variable X, which represents the number of heads when three balanced coins are tossed, is a random variable.

It is useful to distinguish between the random variable itself and the numerical values it can assume. The random variable is designated by the capital letter X, and any value assumed by the random variable is designated by the lowercase letter x.

MATHEMATICAL EXPECTATION

Consider again the possible number of heads that can appear when three coins are tossed once. The eight possible outcomes of this experiment are listed in the table at the left below. Denoting each of the possible number of heads by x, and its probability of occurrence by $P(x)$, we list, in the table at the right, all possible numbers of heads, together with their respective .probabilities of occurrence.

Outcome	Number of Heads	Probability	x (Number of Heads)	P(x)
TTT	0	$\frac{1}{8}$	0	$\frac{1}{8}$
HTT	1	$\frac{1}{8}$	1	$\frac{3}{8}$
THT	1	$\frac{1}{8}$	2	$\frac{3}{8}$
TTH	1	$\frac{1}{8}$	3	$\frac{1}{8}$
THH	2	$\frac{1}{8}$		
HTH	2	$\frac{1}{8}$		
HHT	2	$\frac{1}{8}$		
HHH	3	$\frac{1}{8}$		

Thus, when three coins are tossed once, we obtain 0, 1, 2, or 3 heads. Furthermore, we are more likely to obtain 1 or 2 heads than we are to obtain 0 or 3 heads.

Now let us assume that the three coins are to be tossed an infinite number of times. Although the number of heads that can appear in any of the trials is 0, 1, 2, or 3, in this infinite number of trials we expect to obtain an average of 1.5 heads per toss. This long-run average of 1.5 heads per toss is called the **mathematical expectation.**

Although we intuitively derived the mathematical expectation of the number of heads in a toss of three balanced coins, there is a systematic procedure for determining it. To determine the mathematical expectation of the random variable X, first multiply each possible value of X by its probability of occurrence. The mathematical expectation of X, denoted by $E(X)$, is the sum of all these cross-products. This procedure is illustrated in the following table.

1 x (Number of Heads)	2 P(x)	3 xP(x)
0	$\frac{1}{8}$	0
1	$\frac{3}{8}$	$\frac{3}{8}$
2	$\frac{3}{8}$	$\frac{6}{8}$
3	$\frac{1}{8}$	$\frac{3}{8}$
		$\sum xP(x) = \frac{12}{8}$

$$E(X) = \sum xP(x)$$
$$= \frac{12}{8}$$
$$= 1.5 \text{ heads}$$

Column 1 lists all possible values of the random variable X, and column 2 lists the probability of occurrence of each value. Each possible value of X in column 1 is multiplied by its corresponding probability from column 2, and the resulting cross-product is listed in column 3. The sum of all the cross-products in column 3 is the mathematical expectation of X, or $E(X)$.

The following examples illustrate the application of the mathematical expectation concept.

Example   A box contains 3 black and 7 white marbles. One marble is to be selected from this box. We get $2 if the marble we select is black and we lose $1 if the marble we select is white. What is the mathematical expectation of this game?

Denoting any possible gain or loss by x, and denoting its probability of occurrence by $P(x)$, we calculate the mathematical expectation as follows:

x (Amount of Gain or Loss)	$P(x)$	$xP(x)$
+$2	$3/10$	$6/10$
−$1	$7/10$	$-7/10$
		$E(X) = -1/10 = -\$.10$

Thus the mathematical expectation of this game is a loss of $.10.

Assume that we are to play the game several thousand times. At any one play we will either win $2 or lose $1. However, in all these thousand plays, we can expect an average loss of $.10 per play.

Example   A box contains 4 red, 6 black, and 8 green marbles. One marble is to be selected from this box. If the marble selected is red, we get $3, and if it is black, we get $2. How much should we pay if the marble we select is green, to ensure an equitable game?

A game is considered equitable whenever its mathematical expectation is zero. To make our game equitable, we must determine the loss that is to be associated with drawing a green marble if the mathematical expectation of the game is to be zero. Denoting the loss associated with drawing a green marble by L, we calculate the mathematical expectation of the game as follows.

x (Amount of Gain or Loss)	$P(x)$	$xP(x)$
$3	$4/18$	$12/18$
$2	$6/18$	$12/18$
$L	$8/18$	$8L/18$
		$E(X) = \sum xP(x)$
		$= 8L/18 + 24/18$

We solve for L now by setting the mathematical expectation equal to zero:

$$8L/18 + 24/18 = 0,$$
$$8L = -24,$$
$$L = -24/8 = -\$3.$$

Thus, if we pay $3 when we select a green ball, the mathematical expectation of the game becomes zero, and the game is equitable.

Example The hourly sales of a cigarette vending machine at the Rendezvous Room are 20, 21, and 22 packs, with probabilities of .3, .5, and .2, respectively. What are the expected hourly sales of this vending machine?

x (Number of Packs Sold)	P(x)	xP(x)
20	.3	6.0
21	.5	10.5
22	.2	4.4
		$E(X) = 20.9$ packs

Example A florist estimates his daily sales of carnations as follows.

Estimated Daily Sales (Dozens)	Probability of Estimated Sales
10	.60
11	.30
12	.10

The florist must order the carnations one day in advance. Any carnations left unsold at the end of the day are worthless. If the cost of carnations is $1 per dozen and the selling price is $3 per dozen, how many dozen should the florist order to maximize his expected daily profit?

Solution: The florist could order 10, 11, or 12 dozen a day. The profit from each order depends on the number of dozens sold. The following table shows all possible levels of profit that the florist can make.

Possible Sales per Day	Number of Dozens Ordered		
	10	11	12
10 dozen	$20 (1)	$19 (4)	$18 (7)
11 dozen	$20 (2)	$22 (5)	$21 (8)
12 dozen	$20 (3)	$22 (6)	$24 (9)

The nine entries in the table are interpreted as follows: The first entry, $20, is the profit obtained when the florist orders 10 dozen and sells 10 dozen the same day. The second entry is also $20 because the florist orders only 10 dozen, although he could have sold 11 dozen; and similarly for entry 3.

The fourth entry in the table, $19, is the profit obtained by stocking 11 dozen and selling only 10 dozen. This profit is computed as follows.

$$\text{Profit} = \text{Total revenue} - \text{Total cost}$$
$$= (10 \cdot \$3) - (11 \cdot \$1) = \$19.$$

All other entries in the table are determined in the same manner. The seventh entry, $18, is the profit obtained by stocking 12 dozen and selling only 10 dozen:

$$\text{Profit} = \text{Total revenue} - \text{Total cost}$$
$$= (10 \cdot \$3) - (12 \cdot \$1) = \$18.$$

Before proceeding with the next step in the solution, we summarize the results of our previous computations. The following table lists all possible levels of profit.

Probability	Order 10	Order 11	Order 12
.60	$20	$19	$18
.30	$20	$22	$21
.10	$20	$22	$24

The expected profit of each of the three levels (10, 11 and 12) is the sum of the cross-products obtained by multiplying each possible profit by its corresponding probability of occurrence. The computations are carried out below.

Order 10		Order 11	Order 12	
$20 \cdot .60 =$	12.00	$19 \cdot .60 = 11.40$	$18 \cdot .60 =$	10.80
$20 \cdot .30 =$	6.00	$22 \cdot .30 = 6.60$	$21 \cdot .30 =$	6.30
$20 \cdot .10 =$	2.00	$22 \cdot .10 = 2.20$	$24 \cdot .10 =$	2.40
Expected profit	$20.00	$20.20		$19.50

Thus the expected profit is maximized by ordering 11 dozen per day.

Example   A radio manufacturer receives shipments of tubes in lots of 20. The receiving department uses the following rule of inspection. Two tubes are tested from each lot. If neither of those tubes is defective, no further inspection is made on the remaining tubes in the lot. If any of the tubes examined is defective, the entire lot is inspected. What is the expected number of tubes examined per lot if each lot contains exactly 25% defective tubes (5 defective tubes per lot).

Solution: A lot is partially inspected if both tubes selected are not defective. Denoting a defective tube by D and a nondefective tube by D', we find that the probability of a partial inspection is

$$P(D'_1 \cap D'_2) = P(D'_1) \cdot P(D'_2 \mid D'_1)$$
$$= {}^{15}\!/_{20} \cdot {}^{14}\!/_{19} = {}^{210}\!/_{380} = {}^{21}\!/_{38}.$$

In all other circumstances, the entire lot is inspected. The probability of complete inspection is therefore $1 - {}^{21}\!/_{38} = {}^{17}\!/_{38}$. Thus there is a ${}^{21}\!/_{38}$ chance that only two tubes will be inspected and a ${}^{17}\!/_{38}$ chance that all 20 tubes will be examined. Denoting the number of inspected tubes from a lot by X, we compute the expected number of tubes examined per lot, or $E(X)$, as follows.

x	$P(x)$	$xP(x)$
2	${}^{21}\!/_{38}$	${}^{42}\!/_{38}$
20	${}^{17}\!/_{38}$	${}^{340}\!/_{38}$
	$E(X) =$	${}^{382}\!/_{38}$
	$=$	10.05 tubes per lot

EXERCISES

3.68 One face of a die is red, 2 faces are green, and the remaining 3 faces are black. The die is to be rolled once. You get $2 if red is thrown and $.50 if green is thrown. How much should you pay when black is thrown, to make the game equitable?

3.69 One face of a die is red, 2 faces are green, and the remaining 3 faces are black. The die is to be rolled twice. If the same color appears on both rolls, you get $11; otherwise you lose $7. What is the expected value of this game?

3.70 An urn contains 4 red and 6 blue marbles. Three marbles are to be drawn in succession and *with* replacement. If you get $2 for each red marble and $1 for each blue marble, how much should you pay for the right to play, to make the game equitable?

3.71 An urn contains 4 red and 6 blue marbles. Three marbles are to be drawn in succession and *without* replacement. If you get $2 for each red marble and $1 for each blue marble, how much should you pay for the right to play, to make the game equitable?

3.72 A radio manufacturer receives tubes in boxes, each box containing 100 tubes. The receiving department uses the following rule of inspection. Four tubes are tested from each box. If none of the tubes examined is defective, no further inspection is made on the remaining tubes in that box. If any of the tubes examined is defective, the entire content of the box is inspected. Determine the expected number of tubes examined per box if each box contains exactly 10% defectives.

3.73 The Geneva Weaving Company wants to purchase 10 specialized machines to be used in its weaving process. The company has previously purchased such machines from two different manufacturers. Based on experience, the company can estimate the useful lives of the two brands of machines as follows.

Machine A

Estimated Useful Life (Hours)	Probability of Useful Life
2000	.60
3000	.30
4000	.10

Machine B

Estimated Useful Life (Hours)	Probability of Useful Life
2000	.50
3000	.45
4000	.05

Which brand should the Geneva Weaving Company purchase if the cost of the two brands is the same?

3.74 A television manufacturer uses a special type of electronic component in assembling color television sets. Each television set requires 6 such components. A defective component cannot be detected until a television set has been completely assembled. The cost of detecting, repairing, and replacing a defective component is $15. The television manufacturer has been purchasing these components in lots of 100 from two different suppliers. The cost of purchasing a lot from supplier A is $100, while the cost of a lot from supplier B is $120. Based on past experience, the manufacturers can compare qualities of the lots purchased from the two suppliers, as follows.

Supplier A

Estimated Number of Defective Components per Lot	Probability of Number of Defective Components
1	.30
2	.25
3	.20
4	.15
5	.10

Supplier B

Estimated Number of Defective Components per Lot	Probability of Number of Defective Components
1	.60
2	.30
3	.10

From which supplier should the television manufacturer purchase the electronic components, to minimize the cost?

3.75 The Land Investor Corporation owns a 10-acre lot in a Los Angeles suburb. The corporation has petitioned the city Planning Commission for rezoning the lot from "agricultural" to "multiple dwellings." If the rézoning permit is granted, the lot is worth $1 million. If the rezoning permit is denied, the lot is worth only $200,000. Prior to the commission's decision on rezoning, a large real estate developer offered to buy the lot for $500,000 outright.

a) Should the Land Investor Corporation sell the lot to the real estate developer if the probability of approving the request for rezoning is ½?

b) For the Land Investor Company to have no preference for one of the two alternatives (selling the lot outright or waiting for the decision on rezoning), what probability must be assigned to the chance of rezoning approval?

3.76 A grocer estimates daily sales of Slim & Trim bread as follows.

Estimated Daily Sales (Loaves)	Probability of Estimated Sales
4	.50
5	.40
6	.10

The cost per loaf is $.25 and the selling price is $.50 per loaf. The bread must be ordered one day in advance, and any bread left unsold at the end of the day is turned over to the thrift bakery for a salvage price of $.10 per loaf. How many loaves of this bread should the grocer order every day to maximize the expected daily profit?

3.77 The Associated Students are planning a concert on campus. Using records from similar concerts given on the same campus, they estimate attendance as follows.

Number of Persons Attending (x)	Probability P(x)
2000	.2
3000	.5
4000	.3

If the total cost of the concert is $2000 and the price of admission is set at $1 per person, what is the expected profit (or loss) from the concert?

3.78 A manufacturer is considering the production of a seasonal novelty, with demand estimated as follows.

Number of Units Demanded (x)	Probability P(x)
1000	$\frac{1}{4}$
2000	$\frac{1}{2}$
3000	$\frac{1}{4}$

The cost of producing and marketing the novelty consists of a fixed cost of $5000 and a variable cost of $1 per unit. If the selling price of the novelty is $5 per unit, what is the manufacturer's expected profit?

3.79 Susannah sells used cars. For each car she sells, she receives a commission of either $200 or $100, with a probability of .2 and .8, respectively. The following is a probability distribution of the number of automobiles sold by Susannah on any given day.

Number of Cars Sold	Probability
0	.20
1	.60
2	.15
3	.05

a) What is the expected number of cars sold by Susannah each day?
b) What is her expected commission *per car?*
c) What is her expected *daily* sales commission?
d) What is the probability that Susannah sells two cars each day on two consecutive days?

3.80 A florist estimates his daily demand for carnations as follows.

Number of Dozen Demanded	Probability
10	.3
11	.6
12	.1

a) What is the probability that the florist will sell 12 dozen carnations on three consecutive days?

b) Find the expected number of dozens of carnations sold per day.

3.81 The ABC Company is considering producing and marketing a new product. The company marketing manager estimates the new product's sales as follows.

Sales (Thousands)	Probability
200	.3
300	.5
400	.2

The total cost of producing and marketing the product is estimated as follows.

Total Cost (Thousands)	Probability
300	.6
350	.3
400	.1

a) What is expected sales for the new product?

b) What is the expected total cost?

c) What is the expected profit or loss for the new product?

d) What is the probability that the ABC Company breaks even in producing and marketing the new product?

KEY TERMS

set A collection of objects.

union The union of two sets A and B is the set containing all the elements that are in either A or B or both.

intersection   The intersection of two sets A and B is the set containing only those elements that are in both A and B.

mutually exclusive   Two sets are mutually exclusive if they have no elements in common.

complement   The complement of a set A is the set of all elements that do not belong to A.

experiment   A process that has several specified possible outcomes, of which the particular outcome to be observed is uncertain in advance.

sample space   The set of all possible outcomes of an experiment.

event   A subset of a sample space.

probability   A number that measures the likelihood of an event.

conditional probability   The probability of an event B given that an event A has occurred.

independent events   Two events are independent when the occurrence of one does not influence the occurrence of the other.

random variable (X)   A numerical value (x) determined by the outcome of an experiment.

mathematical expectation $E(X)$, the mean (average) value of the random variable X.

SUMMARY OF FORMULAS

probability of a complement	$P(A') = 1 - P(A)$
rule of addition	$P(A \cup B) = P(A) + P(B) - P(A \cap B)$ $P(A \cup B) = P(A) + P(B)$, if $A \cap B = \varnothing$
conditional probability	$P(B \mid A) = \dfrac{P(A \cap B)}{P(A)}$, if $P(A) \neq 0$
rule of multiplication	$P(A \cap B) = P(A)P(B \mid A)$ $P(A \cap B) = P(A) \cdot P(B)$, if A and B are independent
Bayes' theorem	$P(A_1 \mid B) = \dfrac{P(A_1 \cap B)}{P(B)}$ $= \dfrac{P(A_1)P(B \mid A_1)}{P(A_1)P(B \mid A_1) + \cdots + P(A_k)P(B \mid A_k)}$, where $A_1, \ldots, A_k$ are mutually exclusive events whose union is the sample space
expected value	$E(X) = \sum x P(x)$

PROBABILITY DISTRIBUTIONS

4

Chapter 3 was an introduction to basic probability concepts, rules, and theorems. In this chapter, we deal with some specific probability distributions, which are widely used in subsequent chapters.

The last section of Chapter 3 dealt with the mathematical expectation of a random variable. In computing the mathematical expectation, we listed the various values that can be assumed by the random variable X, together with the probabilities of their occurrence. A table that lists all the possible values of a random variable together with the respective probabilities is called a **probability distribution.**

This chapter presents several theoretical models of probability distributions. To understand certain probability distribution models, you must be familiar with some formal rules of counting. Such rules enable us to determine the number of sample points in a sample space or in a given event.

RULES OF COUNTING

Rule 1.   If operation A can be performed in n number of ways, and operation B in m number of ways, then the two operations can be performed together in $n \cdot m$ ways.

To illustrate Rule 1, let us determine the number of arrangements in which a man can wear a suit and a tie if he has three suits and five ties. The man can choose one of three suits and, with each chosen suit, he may wear any of the five ties. According to Rule 1, he can therefore come up with suit and tie combinations in

$$3 \cdot 5 = 15 \text{ ways.}$$

Example   A coin is thrown and a die is cast. Determine the number of sample points in the sample space of this experiment.

Solution: The coin can land in two different ways (H, T), and the die can land in six different ways (1, 2, 3, 4, 5, 6). The two operations can therefore be performed in $2 \cdot 6 = 12$ ways. Thus, our sample space consists of 12 points.

This rule can be extended to cover the case where there are more than two operations, as illustrated by the following examples.

Example   A die is tossed three times. Determine the number of sample points in the sample space of this experiment.

Solution:

$$6 \cdot 6 \cdot 6 = 216 \text{ sample points.}$$

Example   How many three-digit numbers can be formed from the numbers 2, 4, 6, 7, and 9?

Solution: There are three positions to be filled in a three-digit number, and in this experiment each position can be filled in five different ways. Thus, the three positions can be filled in

$$5 \cdot 5 \cdot 5 = 125 \text{ ways.}$$

Now, how many *even* three-digit numbers can be formed from the numbers 2, 4, 6, 7, and 9? The unit position can now be filled in only three different ways (2, 4, 6), but each of the remaining two positions can be filled in five different ways. Thus we can form

$$3 \cdot 5 \cdot 5 = 75 \text{ even three-digit numbers.}$$

Rule 2. The number of permutations of *n* distinct objects is *n*!.

To illustrate Rule 2, let us consider three distinct objects *A*, *B*, and *C*. These objects can be arranged in a variety of ways: *ABC*, *BCA*, *ACB*, ... Each arrangement of the three letters is called a **permutation.**

How many possible arrangements or permutations can be formed? According to Rule 2, there are 3! possible permutations; that is,

$$3! = 3 \cdot 2 \cdot 1 = 6 \text{ permutations.}$$

This result can be justified as follows. In arranging three distinct objects, we must fill three positions. The first position can be filled by any one of the three objects (see Fig. 4.1).

Having filled the first position with a certain object, we can fill the second position by any one of the other two objects (see Fig. 4.2).

When the first and second positions are filled with two of the objects, the third position can be occupied only by the remaining third object. The six possible paths in the tree diagram of Fig. 4.3 represent the six possible permutations or arrangements of the three letters *A*, *B*, and *C*. Thus the number of possible permutations of the three distinct objects is $3 \cdot 2 \cdot 1$, or 3!.

Figure 4.1

Figure 4.2

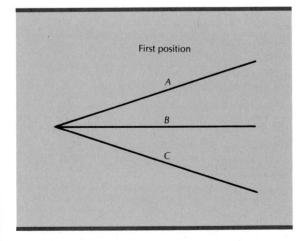

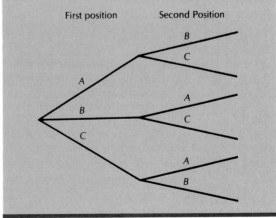

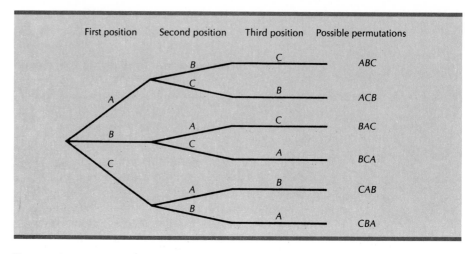

Figure 4.3

Example   The number of possible permutations of the four letters *A, B, C,* and *D* is

$$4! = 4 \cdot 3 \cdot 2 \cdot 1$$
$$= 24.$$

Example   In how many ways can six different books be arranged on a shelf?

Solution:

$$6! = 6 \cdot 5 \cdot 4 \cdot 3 \cdot 2 \cdot 1$$
$$= 720 \text{ ways.}$$

Rule 3.   The number of permutations of *r* objects taken from *n* distinct objects, denoted by $_nP_r$, is $n!/(n - r)!$.

To illustrate Rule 3, let us determine the number of possible permutations of three objects taken from the five objects *A, B, C, D, E* ($r = 3, n = 5$).

According to Rule 3, the number of possible permutations is

$$_nP_r = \frac{n!}{(n - r)!}$$

So

$$_5P_3 = \frac{5!}{(5 - 3)!} = \frac{5!}{2!}$$
$$= \frac{5 \cdot 4 \cdot 3 \cdot 2 \cdot 1}{2 \cdot 1}$$
$$= 5 \cdot 4 \cdot 3 = 60 \text{ permutations.}$$

This result can be justified as follows. There are three positions to be filled. The first position can be filled by any of the five objects. Once the first position is occupied by one object, the second position can be filled by any of the remaining four objects. Finally, with the first and second positions occupied by two objects, the third position can be occupied by any of the remaining three objects. Consequently, the three positions can be filled in $5 \cdot 4 \cdot 3 = 60$ ways.

Example   How many four-digit numbers can be formed from the digits 1, 2, 3, 4, 5, and 6 if each digit *cannot* appear more than once in each number?

Solution:

$$_nP_r = \frac{n!}{(n-r)!}$$

$$_6P_4 = \frac{6!}{(6-4)!} = \frac{6!}{2!}$$

$$= \frac{6 \cdot 5 \cdot 4 \cdot 3 \cdot 2 \cdot 1}{2 \cdot 1}$$

$$= 360 \text{ four-digit numbers.}$$

Rule 4.   The number of combinations in which r objects can be selected from n distinct objects is

$$\binom{n}{r} = \frac{n!}{(n-r)!r!}.$$

To illustrate Rule 4, let us determine the number of three-member committees that can be selected from a total of four people *A, B, C,* and *D* ($r = 3, n = 4$). According to Rule 4, the number of possible committees or combinations is

$$\binom{n}{r} = \frac{n!}{(n-r)!r!}$$

$$\binom{4}{3} = \frac{4!}{(4-3)!3!} = \frac{4!}{1!3!}$$

$$= 4 \text{ committees.}$$

The four possible committees, or combinations, are

$$A \; B \; C,$$
$$A \; B \; D,$$
$$A \; C \; D,$$
$$B \; C \; D.$$

Rule 4 is derived as follows. According to Rule 3, the number of permutations of three objects taken from the four objects A, B, C, and D is

$$_nP_r = \frac{n!}{(n-r)!}$$

$$_4P_3 = \frac{4!}{(4-3)!} = \frac{4!}{1!}$$

$$= 24 \text{ permutations.}$$

These 24 permutations are given in the following four columns.

ABC	ABD	ACD	BCD
ACB	ADB	ADC	BDC
BAC	BAD	CAD	CBD
BCA	BDA	CDA	CDB
CAB	DAB	DAC	DBC
CBA	DBA	DCA	DCB

You may have observed that the six permutations listed in the first column represent the same committee (ABC). Stated differently, there are $3! = 6$ possible arrangements or permutations of the objects A, B, and C. However, all six permutations represent one and the same committee, or combination. A **combination** is a collection of objects that disregards the order of selection. Similarly, the six permutations of the second column represent the combination ABD, the six permutations of the third column represent the combination ACD, and the six permutations of the fourth column represent combination BCD.

Since we have reduced each group of $3! = 6$ permutations into one committee, or combination, we may now generalize and say that each group of $r!$ permutations is reduced to one combination. In other words, the number of combinations of r objects that can be selected from n distinct objects is equal to the number of permutations of the r objects divided by $r!$. Symbolically, we can write

$$\binom{r}{n} = {_nP_r} \div r!$$

$$= \frac{n!}{(n-r)!} \div r!$$

$$= \frac{n!}{(n-r)!\,r!}.$$

Example In how many ways can a five-woman basketball team be selected from seven women?

Solution:

$$\binom{n}{r} = \frac{n!}{(n - r)!r!}$$

$$\binom{7}{5} = \frac{7!}{(7 - 5)!} = \frac{7!}{2!5!}$$

$$= 21 \text{ possible ways.}$$

Rule 5. The number of permutations of n objects of which r are of one kind and $n - r$ are of a second kind is

$$\frac{n!}{r!(n - r)!}.$$

To illustrate Rule 5, let us determine the number of permutations of the five objects

$$\underbrace{A,\ A,\ A,}_{r}\ \underbrace{B,\ B.}_{n - r}$$

Given:

$$n = 5: \quad A,\ A,\ A,\ B,\ B;$$
$$r = 3: \quad A,\ A,\ A;$$
$$n - r = 2: \quad B,\ B.$$

According to Rule 5, the number of permutations of the objects A, A, A, B, B is

$$\frac{n!}{r!(n - r)!} = \frac{5!}{3!(5 - 3)!}$$

$$= \frac{5!}{3!\ 2!} = 10.$$

These ten permutations are the following.

A A A B B	A B A A B
A A B B A	A A B A B
A B B A A	A B A B A
B B A A A	B A A B A
B A A A B	B A B A A

To see how Rule 5 is derived, let us assume that we have n objects A, A, A, B, B, where r of these objects are of one kind,

$$\underbrace{A,\ A,\ A,}_{r}\ B,\ B,$$

and $n - r$ of these objects are of a second kind,

$$A, A, A, \underbrace{B, B.}_{n - r}$$

Let us assume further that the n objects can be arranged in X number of ways (ten possible arrangements in this case).

Next let us observe what happens to the number of possible arrangements X when instead of r objects of the same kind we have r objects that are different from one another. To be specific, let us see what happens to the ten possible arrangements of the objects A, A, A, B, and B when we replace the three like objects A, A, and A by K, L, and M. The first of these ten permutations, $A\ A\ A\ B\ B$, will become $K\ L\ M\ B\ B$. From this permutation we can now generate $3! = 6$ distinct permutations by simply changing the positions of K, L, and M:

$K\ L\ M\ B\ B$	$L\ K\ M\ B\ B$	$M\ K\ L\ B\ B$
$K\ M\ L\ B\ B$	$L\ M\ K\ B\ B$	$M\ L\ K\ B\ B$

Similarly, when the three like objects A, A, and A are replaced by K, L, and M, the second of the ten permutations, $A\ A\ B\ B\ A$, becomes $K\ L\ B\ B\ M$. From this permutation we can again generate $3! = 6$ distinct permutations by simply changing the positions of K, L, and M:

$K\ L\ B\ B\ M$	$L\ K\ B\ B\ M$	$M\ K\ B\ B\ L$
$K\ M\ B\ B\ L$	$L\ M\ B\ B\ K$	$M\ L\ B\ B\ K$

Thus from each of the ten original permutations of the objects A, A, A, B, and B we can generate $3! = 6$ distinct permutations by replacing the three like objects A, A, and A by the three distinct objects K, L, and M. In other words, when the three like objects are made different, the number of possible permutations will be $3! = 6$ times as large as before.

Returning to the general case of n objects of which r are alike and $n - r$ are alike (but different from r), we can thus say that when the r like objects are replaced by r distinct objects, the number of possible arrangements or permutations will be $r!$ times as large as the number of permutations before replacement. In other words, when instead of r like objects we have r objects that differ from one another, the number of previous arrangements, X, will increase to $Xr!$.

Similarly, when the $n - r$ like objects are replaced by $n - r$ distinct objects, then from *each* arrangement or permutation before the change we can now generate $(n - r)!$ permutations, and the total number of arrangements will be $(n - r)!$ times are large as the previous number of arrangements.

Thus we may conclude that once the r like objects (A, A, A) as well as the $n - r$ like objects (B, B) are made to differ from one another, the total number of possible permutations will be $r!(n - r)!$ times as large as the number of permutations before the change. In other words, when all like objects are made distinct, then the number of original arrangements, X, will be increased to $Xr!(n - r)!$.

But if all n objects become distinct, then, according to Rule 2, the number of permutations of these n distinct objects is $n!$. Equating our two results, we obtain

$$Xr!(n - r)! = n! \qquad \text{or} \qquad X = \frac{n!}{r!(n - r)!}$$

as the number of permutations of n objects of which r are alike and $n - r$ are alike but different from r.

Example   In how many possible orders can two boys and three girls be born to a family having five children?

Solution: Let $n = 5, r = 3, n - r = 2$.

$$\frac{n!}{r!(n - r)!} = \frac{5!}{3!\,2!} = 10 \text{ ways.}$$

This rule can now be extended to cover the case where the n objects consist of r_1 objects of one kind, r_2 objects of a second kind, r_3 objects of a third kind, and so on. The number of possible arrangements or permutations of these n objects is

$$\frac{n!}{r_1!\,r_2!\,r_3! \cdots}.$$

Example   How many possible permutations can be formed from the word SUCCESS?

Solution: Let

$$
\begin{aligned}
n &= 7: \quad \text{S U C C E S S;} \\
r_1 &= 3: \quad \text{S S S;} \\
r_2 &= 1: \quad \text{U;} \\
r_3 &= 2: \quad \text{C C;} \\
r_4 &= 1: \quad \text{E.}
\end{aligned}
$$

The number of distinct permutations that can be formed from the word SUCCESS is

$$\frac{n!}{r_1!\,r_2!\,r_3!\,r_4!} = \frac{7!}{3!\,1!\,2!\,1!}$$

$$= 420 \text{ distinct permutations.}$$

EXERCISES ■■

4.1   In how many ways can a customer order a sandwich and a drink if there are five sandwiches and four drinks on a menu?

4.2   A coin is tossed four times. Determine the number of sample points in the sample space of this experiment.

4.3   How many possible permutations can be formed from the word HISTORY?

4.4   How many possible permutations can be formed from the word SUCCESSIVE?

4.5   How many four-member committees can be formed from a group of seven people?

4.6   How many three-letter license plates can be formed

a) if a letter can appear more than once?

b) if a letter cannot appear more than once?

4.7   How many two-digit numbers can be formed from the digits 4, 6, 8, and 2? How many odd two-digit numbers can be formed from the same digits?

4.8   The Department of Economics at Pacific Hope University has the following faculty members: Adams, Baker, Campbell, Daniel, and Edwards.

a) How many three-member committees can be formed from the faculty of this department?

b) How many three-member committees can be formed if Adams and Baker cannot serve on the same committee?

4.9   How many five-member committees can be formed from a group of 5 Republicans and 4 Democrats

a) if no restriction is imposed on the composition of the committee?

b) if the committee must contain two Democrats?

4.10   In how many different ways can five people be seated at a round table?

THE BINOMIAL FORMULA

The basic rules of addition and multiplication used in determining probabilities are supplemented by many specialized formulas, the most important of which is the binomial formula.

To develop the binomial formula, consider the following problem: Assuming that the probability of a "success" on any single trial is $\frac{1}{4}$, what is the probability of getting *exactly* two successes in five consecutive trials?

There are ten possible ways of getting exactly two successes in a series of five trials. Denoting the outcome "success" by S and the outcome "failure" by F, we find the ten possible ways or permutations are as listed in the following table.

Permutation	Probability
$S_1 \cap S_2 \cap F_3 \cap F_4 \cap F_5$	$\frac{1}{4} \cdot \frac{1}{4} \cdot \frac{3}{4} \cdot \frac{3}{4} \cdot \frac{3}{4} = (\frac{1}{4})^2(\frac{3}{4})^3$
$S_1 \cap F_2 \cap S_3 \cap F_4 \cap F_5$	$\frac{1}{4} \cdot \frac{3}{4} \cdot \frac{1}{4} \cdot \frac{3}{4} \cdot \frac{3}{4} = (\frac{1}{4})^2(\frac{3}{4})^3$
$S_1 \cap F_2 \cap F_3 \cap S_4 \cap F_5$	$\frac{1}{4} \cdot \frac{3}{4} \cdot \frac{3}{4} \cdot \frac{1}{4} \cdot \frac{3}{4} = (\frac{1}{4})^2(\frac{3}{4})^3$
$S_1 \cap F_2 \cap F_3 \cap F_4 \cap S_5$	$\frac{1}{4} \cdot \frac{3}{4} \cdot \frac{3}{4} \cdot \frac{3}{4} \cdot \frac{1}{4} = (\frac{1}{4})^2(\frac{3}{4})^3$
$F_1 \cap S_2 \cap S_3 \cap F_4 \cap F_5$	$\frac{3}{4} \cdot \frac{1}{4} \cdot \frac{1}{4} \cdot \frac{3}{4} \cdot \frac{3}{4} = (\frac{1}{4})^2(\frac{3}{4})^3$
$F_1 \cap S_2 \cap F_3 \cap S_4 \cap F_5$	$\frac{3}{4} \cdot \frac{1}{4} \cdot \frac{3}{4} \cdot \frac{1}{4} \cdot \frac{3}{4} = (\frac{1}{4})^2(\frac{3}{4})^3$
$F_1 \cap S_2 \cap F_3 \cap F_4 \cap S_5$	$\frac{3}{4} \cdot \frac{1}{4} \cdot \frac{3}{4} \cdot \frac{3}{4} \cdot \frac{1}{4} = (\frac{1}{4})^2(\frac{3}{4})^3$
$F_1 \cap F_2 \cap S_3 \cap S_4 \cap F_5$	$\frac{3}{4} \cdot \frac{3}{4} \cdot \frac{1}{4} \cdot \frac{1}{4} \cdot \frac{3}{4} = (\frac{1}{4})^2(\frac{3}{4})^3$
$F_1 \cap F_2 \cap S_3 \cap F_4 \cap S_5$	$\frac{3}{4} \cdot \frac{3}{4} \cdot \frac{1}{4} \cdot \frac{3}{4} \cdot \frac{1}{4} = (\frac{1}{4})^2(\frac{3}{4})^3$
$F_1 \cap F_2 \cap F_3 \cap S_4 \cap S_5$	$\frac{3}{4} \cdot \frac{3}{4} \cdot \frac{3}{4} \cdot \frac{1}{4} \cdot \frac{1}{4} = (\frac{1}{4})^2(\frac{3}{4})^3$

Each of the ten permutations in the table represents a way of getting exactly two successes in five trials. The probability of each permutation is $(\frac{1}{4})^2(\frac{3}{4})^3$. The ten permutations, furthermore, are mutually exclusive. Hence, the probability of getting exactly two successes in five trials is the sum of the probabilities of all ten permutations, or ten times the probability of any one permutation:

$$P(\text{exactly 2 successes in 5 trails}) = 10(\tfrac{1}{4})^2(\tfrac{3}{4})^3$$
$$= {}^{270}\!/_{1024}.$$

Now we can develop a general formula to solve our problem. We begin by defining the following symbols:

$$\pi = \text{probability of success on any single trial,}$$
$$(1 - \pi) = \text{probability of failure on any single trial,}$$
$$n = \text{number of trials,}$$
$$x = \text{number of successes,}$$
$$(n - x) = \text{number of failures.}$$

The probability of any permutation is

$$\pi^x(1 - \pi)^{(n-x)} = (\tfrac{1}{4})^2(\tfrac{3}{4})^3.$$

The number of possible permutations is

$$\frac{n!}{x!(n-x)!} = \frac{5!}{2!(5-2)!} = \frac{5!}{2!\,3!}$$

$$\frac{5\cdot 4\cdot 3\cdot 2\cdot 1}{(2\cdot 1)(3\cdot 2\cdot 1)} = 10.^*$$

The probability of getting *exactly* x successes in n trials, denoted by $P(X = x)$ is equal to the product obtained by multiplying the probability of any permutation by the number of possible permutations:

$$P(X = x) = \frac{n!}{x!(n-x)!}\,\pi^x(1-\pi)^{n-x}$$

$$P(X = 2) = \frac{5!}{2!\,3!}\left(\frac{1}{4}\right)^2\left(\frac{3}{4}\right)^3$$

$$= 10\left(\frac{1}{4}\right)^2\left(\frac{3}{4}\right)^3 = \frac{270}{1024}.$$

Similarly, assuming that the probability of success on any given trial is ¼, the probability of getting three successes in seven consecutive trials is

$$P(X = x) = \frac{n!}{x!(n-x)!}\,\pi^x(1-\pi)^{n-x}$$

$$P(X = 3) = \frac{7!}{3!\,4!}\left(\frac{1}{4}\right)^3\left(\frac{3}{4}\right)^4$$

$$= \frac{7\cdot 6\cdot 5\cdot 4\cdot 3\cdot 2\cdot 1}{(3\cdot 2\cdot 1)(4\cdot 3\cdot 2\cdot 1)}\left(\frac{1}{4}\right)^3\left(\frac{3}{4}\right)^4$$

$$= 35\left(\frac{1}{4}\right)^3\left(\frac{3}{4}\right)^4 = \frac{2835}{16384}.$$

The formula

$$P(X = x) = \frac{n!}{x!(n-x)!}\,\pi^x(1-\pi)^{n-x},$$

called the *binomial formula,* is an important tool used in determining the probabilities of certain events. The following examples illustrate some of its applications.

Example   What is the probability of getting exactly 3 heads in 5 flips of a balanced coin?

---

*According to the rule of permutations, this is the number of distinct permutations of n objects of which x are alike (successes) and n − x are alike but different from x (failures).

Solution: Let

$$\pi = \tfrac{1}{2}: \quad \text{probability of obtaining heads,}$$
$$n = 5: \quad \text{number of flips,}$$
$$x = 3: \quad \text{number of required heads.}$$

According to the binomial formula,

$$P(X = x) = \frac{n!}{x!(n-x)!} \pi^x (1-\pi)^{n-x}$$

$$P(X = 3) = \frac{5!}{3! \, 2!} \left(\frac{1}{2}\right)^3 \left(\frac{1}{2}\right)^2$$

$$= \frac{5 \cdot 4 \cdot 3 \cdot 2 \cdot 1}{(3 \cdot 2 \cdot 1)(2 \cdot 1)} \left(\frac{1}{2}\right)^5 = 10 \left(\frac{1}{2}\right)^5 = \frac{10}{32}.$$

Example   What is the probability of getting exactly 4 sixes when a die is rolled 7 times?

Solution: Let

$$\pi = \tfrac{1}{6}: \quad \text{probability of getting a six,}$$
$$n = 7: \quad \text{number of times the die is rolled,}$$
$$x = 4: \quad \text{number of required sixes.}$$

According to the binomial formula,

$$P(X = x) = \frac{n!}{x!(n-x)!} \pi^x (1-\pi)^{n-x}$$

$$P(X = 4) = \frac{7!}{4! \, 3!} \left(\frac{1}{6}\right)^4 \left(\frac{5}{6}\right)^3 = 35 \left(\frac{1}{6}\right)^4 \left(\frac{5}{6}\right)^3 = \frac{4375}{279{,}936}.$$

Example   In a family of four children, what is the probability that there will be exactly two boys?

Solution: Let

$$\pi = \tfrac{1}{2}: \quad \text{probability that a child is a boy,}$$
$$n = 4: \quad \text{number of children,}$$
$$x = 2: \quad \text{required number of boys.}$$

According to the binomial formula,

$$P(X = x) = \frac{n!}{x!(n-x)!} \pi^x (1-\pi)^{n-x}$$

$$P(X = 2) = \frac{4!}{2! \, 2!} \left(\frac{1}{2}\right)^2 \left(\frac{1}{2}\right)^2 = 6 \left(\frac{1}{2}\right)^4 = \frac{6}{16}.$$

After examining the preceding examples, we can observe the following common characteristics:

1. The experiment in each example consists of a series of repeated trials.
2. Each trial has only two possible outcomes. The two outcomes are generally referred to as a "success" and a "failure."
3. The probability of a success, denoted by π, is the same on each trial. The probability of a failure, $1 - \pi$, is also constant.
4. The consecutive trials are independent, that is, the outcome of any trial in the series is independent of the outcome of the preceding trials.

In a toss of a balanced coin, for example, the two possible outcomes of a toss are a heads or a tails. In a series of repeated tosses, furthermore, the outcome of each toss is independent of the outcomes of the preceding trials. In the same manner, when a die is rolled several times, the outcome of each roll can be either a six or not a six, and the probability of getting a six in any roll is independent of the outcomes of the preceding rolls (it is always $\frac{1}{6}$). Finally, a child can be either a boy or a girl, and the probability that a baby will be a boy is independent of the sex of previous children.

We can also examine the applicability of the binomial formula to the general problem of sample selection. The processes of selecting a sample of n elements from a given population can be viewed as an experiment consisting of n repeated trials (a series of n selections). The binomial formula is applicable to this sampling process only when the outcome of each selection is independent of the outcome of preceding selections. The series of n independent selections are considered independent, and hence the binomial formula is applicable under two situations:

1. The sample elements are selected with or without replacement from an infinite population.
2. The sample elements are selected with replacement from a finite population.

In the real world, a sample is often selected without replacement from a finite population, a situation in which the assumption of independent selections is clearly violated, and the binomial formula appears to be not applicable. However, when the sample size is small relative to the population size (the sample size is 10% or less of the population size), the binomial formula can still be used and the results obtained are reasonably accurate.* The following example is an illustration of this case.

Example   A sample of 4 fuses is selected without replacement from a lot consisting of 5000 fuses. Assuming that 20% of the fuses in the lot are known to be

---

*Assuming that the value of π is not very close to zero or 1.

defective, what is the probability that the sample contains exactly 2 defective fuses?

Solution: Since the sample is a small fraction of the population, the probability of getting a defective fuse, π, is approximately the same on each selection, that is, $\pi = .20$. Using the binomial formula we obtain

$$P(X = x) = \frac{n!}{x!(n - x)!}\, \pi^x(1 - \pi)^{n-x}$$

$$P(X = 2) = \frac{4!}{2!\,2!}\, (.20)^2(.80)^2 = .1536.$$

EXERCISES

4.11   A machine is producing parts, of which, on the average, 5% are defective. In a random sample of 5 such parts, what is the probability

a) of getting exactly 1 defective part?

b) of obtaining *at least* 1 defective part?

4.12   Two-thirds of the registered voters in a certain congressional district are Democrats. What is the probability that in a random sample of six registered voters from this district there will be exactly five Democrats?

4.13   It is known that 60% of all students attending XYU college are smokers. In a random sample of four students from the college, what is the probability

a) that there are exactly two smokers?

b) that *only* the first two students interviewed are smokers?

4.14   What is the probability that the sum 9 will appear exactly twice when a pair of dice is rolled four times?

4.15   Five marbles are to be drawn with replacement from an urn that contains 4 white, 4 green, and 12 black marbles. What is the probability of drawing exactly 3 marbles that are not white?

4.16   Machine A and machine B produce, on the average, 5% and 10% defective parts, respectively. A random sample of four parts is to be selected from the output of each machine. What is the probability that the sample selected from A's output will contain exactly one defective part and that the sample selected from B's output will contain exactly two defective parts?

4.17   A bookkeeping firm employs two part-time file clerks: Jan and Jane. Jan works on Monday, Wednesday, and Friday, and Jane works on Tuesday and Thursday. Jan misfiles one out of every four documents and Jane misfiles one out of every five documents. A day of the week is selected at random, and a random sample of four documents from those filed on that day is examined.

a) What is the probability that the sample shows exactly two misfiled documents?

b) Given that the sample shows two misfiled documents, what is the probability that the two documents were filed by Jan?

4.18 Cards are drawn with replacement from a well-shuffled deck of 52 playing cards.

a) What is the probability of getting at least one black card when two cards are drawn?

b) What is the probability of drawing at least two black cards when four cards are drawn?

4.19 It is known that 40% of all students attending a particular university are enrolled in the School of Business. Four students are selected at random. What is the probability that the sample contains

a) exactly two business students?

b) at least four business students?

c) at least one business student?

4.20 The University Pub serves wine and beer exclusively. The probability that a customer will buy wine is $\frac{1}{5}$; the probability that a customer buys beer is $\frac{4}{5}$. For the next four customers, what is the probability

a) that all four customers will buy wine?

b) that the first two customers will buy wine?

c) that exactly two customers will buy wine?

d) that at least one of the four customers will buy wine?

THE BINOMIAL DISTRIBUTION

A balanced coin is tossed four times. On these four tosses, heads could come up 0, 1, 2, 3, or 4 times. The binomial formula can be used to determine the probability of each possible outcome. Table 4.1 gives a probability distribution of the number of heads in four tosses of a balanced coin.

Table 4.2 shows the probability distribution of the number of boys in a family of four children. The family can have 0, 1, 2, 3, or 4 boys, and the binomial formula has been used to determine the probability of each possible outcome.

You may already have noticed that the probability distribution of the number of heads in four tosses of a balanced coin and the probability distribution of the number of boys in a family of four children are the same. This is by no means a coincidence. Both are **binomial distributions** with $\pi = \frac{1}{2}$ and $n = 4$.

TABLE 4.1   THE PROBABILITY DISTRIBUTION OF THE NUMBER OF HEADS IN FOUR TOSSES OF A BALANCED COIN

x (Number of Heads)	$P(X = x)$
0	$\dfrac{4!}{0!\,4!}\left(\dfrac{1}{2}\right)^0\left(\dfrac{1}{2}\right)^4 = \dfrac{1}{16}$
1	$\dfrac{4!}{1!\,3!}\left(\dfrac{1}{2}\right)^1\left(\dfrac{1}{2}\right)^3 = \dfrac{4}{16}$
2	$\dfrac{4!}{2!\,2!}\left(\dfrac{1}{2}\right)^2\left(\dfrac{1}{2}\right)^2 = \dfrac{6}{16}$
3	$\dfrac{4!}{3!\,1!}\left(\dfrac{1}{2}\right)^3\left(\dfrac{1}{2}\right)^1 = \dfrac{4}{16}$
4	$\dfrac{4!}{4!\,0!}\left(\dfrac{1}{2}\right)^4\left(\dfrac{1}{2}\right)^0 = \dfrac{1}{16}$

TABLE 4.2   THE PROBABILITY DISTRIBUTION OF THE NUMBER OF BOYS IN A FAMILY OF FOUR CHILDREN

x (Number of Boys)	$P(X = x)$
0	$\dfrac{4!}{0!\,4!}\left(\dfrac{1}{2}\right)^0\left(\dfrac{1}{2}\right)^4 = \dfrac{1}{16}$
1	$\dfrac{4!}{1!\,3!}\left(\dfrac{1}{2}\right)^1\left(\dfrac{1}{2}\right)^3 = \dfrac{4}{16}$
2	$\dfrac{4!}{2!\,2!}\left(\dfrac{1}{2}\right)^2\left(\dfrac{1}{2}\right)^2 = \dfrac{6}{16}$
3	$\dfrac{4!}{3!\,1!}\left(\dfrac{1}{2}\right)^3\left(\dfrac{1}{2}\right)^1 = \dfrac{4}{16}$
4	$\dfrac{4!}{4!\,0!}\left(\dfrac{1}{2}\right)^4\left(\dfrac{1}{2}\right)^0 = \dfrac{1}{16}$

Let us consider another binomial distribution with $\pi = \frac{1}{4}$ and $n = 3$, shown in Table 4.3 The possible values of X in this distribution are 0, 1, 2, and 3.

The binomial distribution in Table 4.3 can be the probability distribution of the number of spade cards when three cards are drawn with replacement from an ordinary deck of playing cards. It can also be the probability distribution of the number of defective parts in a sample of three parts produced by a machine whose output contains, on the average, 25% defective parts. Each of these two distributions is a binomial distribution with $\pi = \frac{1}{4}$ and $n = 3$.

TABLE 4.3   BINOMIAL DISTRIBUTION ($\pi = \frac{1}{4}$, $n = 3$)

x	$P(X = x)$
0	$\dfrac{3!}{0!\,3!}\left(\dfrac{1}{4}\right)^0\left(\dfrac{3}{4}\right)^3 = \dfrac{27}{64}$
1	$\dfrac{3!}{1!\,2!}\left(\dfrac{1}{4}\right)^1\left(\dfrac{3}{4}\right)^2 = \dfrac{27}{64}$
2	$\dfrac{3!}{2!\,1!}\left(\dfrac{1}{4}\right)^2\left(\dfrac{3}{4}\right)^1 = \dfrac{9}{64}$
3	$\dfrac{3!}{3!\,0!}\left(\dfrac{1}{4}\right)^3\left(\dfrac{3}{4}\right)^0 = \dfrac{1}{64}$

TABLE 4.4 BINOMIAL DISTRIBUTION
$(\pi = \frac{1}{6}, n = 5)$

x	$P(X = x)$
0	$\dfrac{5!}{0!\,5!}\left(\dfrac{1}{6}\right)^0\left(\dfrac{5}{6}\right)^5 = \dfrac{3125}{7776}$
1	$\dfrac{5!}{1!\,4!}\left(\dfrac{1}{6}\right)^1\left(\dfrac{5}{6}\right)^4 = \dfrac{3125}{7776}$
2	$\dfrac{5!}{2!\,3!}\left(\dfrac{1}{6}\right)^2\left(\dfrac{5}{6}\right)^3 = \dfrac{1250}{7776}$
3	$\dfrac{5!}{3!\,2!}\left(\dfrac{1}{6}\right)^3\left(\dfrac{5}{6}\right)^2 = \dfrac{250}{7776}$
4	$\dfrac{5!}{4!\,1!}\left(\dfrac{1}{6}\right)^4\left(\dfrac{5}{6}\right)^1 = \dfrac{25}{7776}$
5	$\dfrac{5!}{5!\,0!}\left(\dfrac{1}{6}\right)^5\left(\dfrac{5}{6}\right)^0 = \dfrac{1}{7776}$

Finally, let us consider the binomial distribution with $\pi = \frac{1}{6}$ and $n = 5$, as shown in Table 4.4. This binomial distribution can be interpreted as the probability distribution of the number of sixes that occur on five rolls of a die.

The Mean and the Standard Deviation of the Binomial Distribution

The binomial distribution with $\pi = \frac{1}{2}$ and $n = 4$ can very well be the probability distribution of the number of heads occurring in a toss of four balanced coins.

x	0	1	2	3	4
$P(X = x)$	$\frac{1}{16}$	$\frac{4}{16}$	$\frac{6}{16}$	$\frac{4}{16}$	$\frac{1}{16}$

To determine the mean of the distribution in the table, we must first multiply each possible value of x by its respective probability. The mean of the distribution, denoted by the Greek letter μ, is the sum of the cross-products. Symbolically, $\mu = \sum xP(x)$.*

---

*To simplify the formulas in this section, the symbol $P(X = x)$ is written simply as $P(x)$.

TABLE 4.5   MEAN OF BINOMIAL DISTRIBUTION
$(\pi = \frac{1}{2}, n = 4)$

x	$P(x)$	$xP(x)$
0	$\frac{1}{16}$	0
1	$\frac{4}{16}$	$\frac{4}{16}$
2	$\frac{6}{16}$	$\frac{12}{16}$
3	$\frac{4}{16}$	$\frac{12}{16}$
4	$\frac{1}{16}$	$\frac{4}{16}$
		$\sum xP(x) = \frac{32}{16}$

$$\mu = \sum xP(x) = \frac{32}{16} = 2 \text{ heads}$$

The mean of the binomial distribution, as shown in Table 4.5, is two heads, that is, although we may get 0, 1, 2, 3, or 4 heads when four balanced coins are tossed, we expect an average of two heads per toss if the binomial experiment is repeated an infinite number of times.

The binomial distribution $(\pi = \frac{1}{2}, n = 4)$ has a mean 2. The standard deviation of this distribution, denoted by σ, is defined as

$$\sigma = \sqrt{\sum (x - \mu)^2 P(x)}.$$

The computations are carried out in Table 4.6.

Thus the binomial distribution $(\pi = \frac{1}{2}, n = 4)$ has a mean 2 and a standard deviation 1. This means that although we may get either 0, 1, 2, 3, or 4 heads

TABLE 4.6   STANDARD DEVIATION OF BINOMIAL DISTRIBUTION
$(\pi = \frac{1}{2}, n = 4)$

x	$P(x)$	$(x - 2)$ $(x - \mu)$	$(x - \mu)^2$	$(x - \mu)^2 P(x)$
0	$\frac{1}{16}$	-2	4	$\frac{4}{16}$
1	$\frac{4}{16}$	-1	1	$\frac{4}{16}$
2	$\frac{6}{16}$	0	0	0
3	$\frac{4}{16}$	$+1$	1	$\frac{4}{16}$
4	$\frac{1}{16}$	$+2$	4	$\frac{4}{16}$
				$\sum (x - \mu)^2 P(x) = \frac{16}{16}$

$$\sigma = \sqrt{\sum (x - \mu)^2 P(x)} = \sqrt{\frac{16}{16}} = 1 \text{ head}$$

when four balanced coins are tossed, we expect an average of two heads if the experiment is repeated an infinite number of times. Furthermore, since the standard deviation is 1, we expect the number of heads in each experiment to differ from the mean, on the average, by 1 head.

Statisticians have found that they can determine the mean and the standard deviation of a binomial distribution without having to calculate the entire distribution, that is, without having to list all possible values of X and their probabilities. The mean and the standard deviation of a binomial distribution can indeed be determined from the values of π and n, using the following two formulas:

$$\mu = n\pi, \qquad \sigma = \sqrt{n\pi(1 - \pi)}.$$

Thus in our experiment of tossing four balanced coins where $\pi = \frac{1}{2}$ and $n = 4$, we have

$$\mu = n\pi$$
$$= 4(\tfrac{1}{2}) = 2 \text{ heads}$$

and

$$\sigma = \sqrt{n\pi(1 - \pi)}$$
$$= \sqrt{4(\tfrac{1}{2})(\tfrac{1}{2})} = 1 \text{ heads}.$$

Example   A die is to be rolled 180 times. Determine the mean and the standard deviation of the number of sixes in this experiment.

Solution: This is a binomial distribution with $\pi = \frac{1}{6}$ and $n = 180$. Therefore,

$$\mu = n\pi$$
$$= 180(\tfrac{1}{6}) = 30$$

and

$$\sigma = \sqrt{n\pi(1 - \pi)}$$
$$= \sqrt{180(\tfrac{1}{6})(\tfrac{5}{6})} = 5.$$

Thus, when a die is rolled 180 times, we may get 0, 1, 2, . . . , or 180 sixes. However, if the experiment is repeated an infinite number of times, we expect an average of 30 sixes per trial. Moreover, the number of sixes in each trial is expected to differ from 30, on the average, by 5.

EXERCISES

4.21   Given the binomial distribution with $\pi = \frac{1}{3}$ and $n = 2$.

a) Compute the entire binomial distribution.

b) Determine the mean and the standard deviation of the distribution, using the data obtained in part a.

c) Verify the results obtained in part b by using the appropriate shortcut formula for determining the mean and the standard deviation of a binomial distribution.

4.22 Compute the mean and the standard deviation of each of the following binomial distributions.

a) $\pi = \frac{1}{2}$, $n = 1600$

b) $\pi = .10$, $n = 900$

c) $\pi = .64$, $n = 400$

4.23 A pair of dice is rolled 180 times. Determine the expected number of times in which the sum 5 appears. Determine the standard deviation.

4.24 If the probability of a defective rivet is .01, what is the expected number of defective rivets in an airplane that has 10,000 such rivets?

CUMULATIVE BINOMIAL DISTRIBUTION

Once again, let us consider the probability distribution of the number of heads appearing in four tosses of a balanced coin. This distribution is a binomial distribution with $n = 4$ and $\pi = .50$. Table 4.7 shows the probability of getting exactly zero heads, exactly one heads, exactly two heads, and so on. The probability of getting exactly two heads is .3750.

Let us find the probability of getting two or more heads. In contrast to the probability of getting exactly two heads, which is $P(X = 2)$, the probability of getting two or more heads is $P(X \geq 2)$, where

$$P(X \geq 2) = P(X = 2) + P(X = 3) + P(X = 4)$$
$$= .3750 + .2500 + .0625$$
$$= .6875.$$

TABLE 4.7 BINOMIAL
DISTRIBUTION
($n = 4$, $\pi = .50$)

x	$P(X = x)$
0	.0625
1	.2500
2	.3750
3	.2500
4	.0625

Similarly, the probability of getting three or more heads is

$$P(X \geq 3) = P(X = 3) + P(X = 4)$$
$$= .2500 + .0625$$
$$= .3125.$$

Both $P(X \geq 2)$ and $P(X \geq 3)$ are called *cumulative probabilities.* Similar cumulative probabilities for other values of X are computed in the same fashion, as shown in the last column of Table 4.8.

Let us find the probability of getting two or fewer heads. The probability of getting two or fewer heads, denoted by $P(X \leq 2)$, is determined as follows:

$$P(X \leq 2) = P(X = 2) + P(X = 1) + P(X = 0)$$
$$= .3750 + .2500 + .0625$$
$$= .6875.$$

Similarly, the probability of obtaining 3 or fewer heads is

$$P(X \leq 3) = P(X = 3) + P(X = 2) + P(X = 1) + P(X = 0)$$
$$= .2500 + .3750 + .2500 + .0625$$
$$= .9375.$$

$P(X \geq 2)$ and $P(X \leq 2)$ are both examples of cumulative probability. $P(X \geq 2)$ is a cumulative probability of the "equal to or greater than" type, and $P(X \leq 2)$ is a cumulative probability of the "equal to or less than" type. Table 4.9 shows three different probabilities for each value of X.

The entries in the second column of Table 4.9 refer to the probabilities of getting exactly zero heads, exactly one heads, exactly 2 heads, and so on. The

TABLE 4.8 **BINOMIAL DISTRIBUTION WITH CUMULATIVE PROBABILITIES**
($n = 4$, $\pi = .50$)

x	$P(X = x)$	$P(X \geq x)$
0	.0625	1.0000
1	.2500	.9375
2	.3750	.6875
3	.2500	.3125
4	.0625	.0625

TABLE 4.9   BINOMIAL DISTRIBUTION WITH CUMULATIVE PROBABILITIES
$(n = 4, \pi = .50)$

x	$P(X = x)$	$P(X \geq x)$	$P(X \leq x)$
0	.0625	1.0000	.0625
1	.2500	.9375	.3125
2	.3750	.6875	.6875
3	.2500	.3125	.9375
4	.0625	.0625	1.0000

entries in the third column refer to the probabilities of getting zero or more heads, one or more heads, two or more heads, and so on, and the entries in the last column refer to the probabilities of getting zero or fewer heads, one or fewer heads, two or fewer heads, and so on.

It is important to note that the probabilities recorded in the second column of Table 4.9, that is, $P(X = x)$, can be indirectly obtained from the cumulative probabilities in the third or fourth column. For example, the probability of getting exactly two heads, .3750, is obtained from the cumulative probabilities in the third column as follows:

$$P(X \geq 2) = P(X = 2) + P(X = 3) + P(X = 4), \tag{A}$$

$$P(X \geq 3) = \qquad\qquad P(X = 3) + P(X = 4). \tag{B}$$

Subtracting Eq. (B) from Eq. (A), we obtain

$$P(X \geq 2) - P(X \geq 3) = P(X = 2).$$

Hence,

$$P(X = 2) = P(X \geq 2) - P(X \geq 3)$$
$$= .6875 - .3125$$
$$= .3750.$$

The probability of getting exactly two heads can also be obtained from the cumulative probabilities of the fourth column, as follows:

$$P(X \leq 2) = P(X = 2) + P(X = 1) + P(X = 0), \tag{C}$$

$$P(X \leq 1) = \qquad\qquad P(X = 1) + P(X = 0). \tag{D}$$

Subtracting Eq. (D) from Eq. (C), we obtain

$$P(X = 2) = P(X \leq 2) - P(X \leq 1)$$
$$= .6875 - .3125$$
$$= .3750.$$

Example Given the cumulative binomial distribution in the following table, find (a) $P(X = 1)$, (b) $P(X = 4)$, (c) $P(X = 5)$.

$(n = 5, \pi = .31)$	
x	$P(X \geq x)$
0	1.0000
1	.8436
2	.4923
3	.1766
4	.0347
5	.0029

Solution:

a) $P(X = 1) = P(X \geq 1) - P(X \geq 2)$
$$= .8436 - .4923$$
$$= .3513$$

b) $P(X = 4) = P(X \geq 4) - P(X \geq 5)$
$$= .0347 - .0029$$
$$= .0318$$

c) $P(X = 5) = P(X \geq 5) = .0029$

Example Given the binomial distribution in the following table, find (a) $P(X = 4)$, (b) $P(X = 1)$, (c) $P(X = 0)$.

$(n = 5, \pi = .69)$	
x	$P(X \leq x)$
0	.0029
1	.0347
2	.1766
3	.4923
4	.8436
5	1.0000

Solution:

a) $P(X = 4) = P(X \le 4) - P(X \le 3)$

$= .8436 - .4923$

$= .3513$

b) $P(X = 1) = P(X \le 1) - P(X \le 0)$

$= .0347 - .0029$

$= .0318$

c) $P(X = 0) = P(X \le 0) = .0029$

You may have noticed that the two preceding examples have the same solutions. The similarity between the two answers can be easily explained if the binomial formula is used to solve both. In the first example, where $n = 5$ and $\pi = .31$,

$$P(X = 1) = \frac{5!}{1!\,4!}(.31)^1(.69)^4 = .3513.$$

In the second example, where $n = 5$ and $\pi = .69$,

$$P(X = 4) = \frac{5!}{4!\,1!}(.69)^4(.31)^1 = .3513.$$

Hence, the answer to part a of both examples, is the same, as are the answers to parts b and c.

The reason for this is that if one person counts the number of successes with probability $\pi = .31$ at each trial and finds one success out of five trials, another person, counting the number of failures with probability $\pi = .69$ of failure at each trial, will find four failures out of five trials.

Cumulative Binomial Tables

Let us determine the probability of getting 47 or more heads in 100 tosses of a balanced coin. Since this is a binomial distribution with $n = 100$ and $\pi = .50$, we can use the binomial formula to determine the probability of getting 47, 48, 49, . . . , 100 heads. The probability of getting 47 or more heads is the sum of the individual probabilities:

$$P(X \ge 47) = P(X = 47) + P(X = 48) + \cdots + P(X = 100)$$

$$= \frac{100!}{47!\,53!}(0.5)^{47}(0.5)^{53} + \cdots + \frac{100!}{100!\,0!}(0.5)^{100}(0.5)^0.$$

But as you may already have noticed, the use of the binomial formula in this case involves many computations—but we can call on the electronic computer for help.

TABLE 4.10   CUMULATIVE BINOMIAL PROBABILITIES ($n = 4$)

Left $P(X \geq x)$												Right $P(X \leq x)$
x	$\pi =$	.01	.02	.03	.04	.05	.06	.07	.08	.09	.10	
1		.0394	.0776	.1147	.1507	.1855	.2193	.2519	.2836	.3143	.3439	3
2		.0006	.0023	.0052	.0091	.0140	.0199	.0267	.0344	.0430	.0523	2
3				.0001	.0002	.0005	.0008	.0013	.0019	.0027	.0037	1
4										.0001	.0001	0
x		.99	.98	.97	.96	.95	.94	.93	.92	.91	.90	$= \pi$ x

$n = 4$

x	$\pi =$	.11	.12	.13	.14	.15	.16	.17	.18	.19	.20	
1		.3726	.4003	.4271	.4530	.4780	.5021	.5254	.5479	.5695	.5904	3
2		.0624	.0732	.0847	.0968	.1095	.1228	.1366	.1509	.1656	.1808	2
3		.0049	.0063	.0079	.0098	.0120	.0144	.1071	.0202	.0235	.0272	1
4		.0001	.0002	.0003	.0004	.0005	.0007	.0008	.0010	.0013	.0016	0
x		.89	.88	.87	.86	.85	.84	.83	.82	.81	.80	$= \pi$ x

$n = 4$

x	$\pi =$	.21	.22	.23	.24	.25	.26	.27	.28	.29	.30	
1		.6105	.6298	.6485	.6664	.6836	.7001	.7160	.7313	.7459	.7599	3
2		.1963	.2122	.2285	.2450	.2617	.2787	.2959	.3132	.3307	.3483	2
3		.0312	.0356	.0403	.0453	.0508	.0566	.0628	.0694	.0763	.0837	1
4		.0019	.0023	.0028	.0033	.0039	.0046	.0053	.0061	.0071	.0081	0
x		.79	.78	.77	.76	.75	.74	.73	.72	.71	.70	$= \pi$ x

$n = 4$

x	$\pi =$	.31	.32	.33	.34	.35	.36	.37	.38	.39	.40	
1		.7733	.7862	.7985	.8103	.8215	.8322	.8425	.8522	.8615	.8704	3
2		.3660	.3837	.4015	.4193	.4370	.4547	.4724	.4900	.5075	.5248	2
3		.0915	.0996	.1082	.1171	.1265	.1362	.1464	.1596	.1679	.1792	1
4		.0092	.0105	.0119	.0134	.0150	.0168	.0187	.0209	.0231	.0256	0
x		.69	.68	.67	.66	.65	.64	.63	.62	.61	.60	$= \pi$ x

$n = 4$

x	$\pi =$	.41	.42	.43	.44	.45	.46	.47	.48	.49	.50	
1		.8788	.8868	.8944	.9017	.9085	.9150	.9211	.9269	.9323	.9375	3
2		.5420	.5590	.5759	.5926	.6090	.6252	.6412	.6569	.6724	.6875	2
3		.1909	.2030	.2155	.2283	.2415	.2550	.2689	.2831	.2977	.3125	1
4		.0283	.0311	.0342	.0375	.0410	.0448	.0488	.0531	.0576	.0625	0
x		.59	.58	.57	.56	.55	.54	.53	.52	.51	.50	$= \pi$ x

Using a computer, cumulative probabilities have been computed and tabulated for selected values of n and for values of π ranging from .01 to .99. (See Table G at the end of the book.) To facilitate the present discussion, we have reproduced in Table 4.10 the cumulative binomial probabilities for $n = 4$ and values of π ranging from .01 to .99. The table is used in two different ways, depending on whether $\pi \leq .50$ or $\pi \geq .50$. The two methods are discussed in turn.

Case I ($\pi \leq .50$).   When $\pi \leq .50$, the value of π is found at the head of the column, and the values of X are located in the far left column of the table. The probability in any section in the table is the probability of getting *x or more,* that is, $P(X \geq x)$.

Example   For $n = 4$ and $\pi = .23$, find (a) $P(X \geq 2)$, (b) $P(X = 2)$.

Solution: Using Table 4.10,

a) $P(X \geq 2) = .2285$.
b) $P(X = 2) = P(X \geq 2) - P(X \geq 3)$

$\qquad\qquad = .2285 - .0403$

$\qquad\qquad = .1882$.

Case II ($\pi \geq .50$).   When $\pi \geq .50$, the value of π is found at the bottom of the column, and the values of X are listed (in decreasing order) in the far right column of the table. The probability in each section is the probability of getting *x or less,* that is, $P(X \leq x)$.

Example   For $n = 4$ and $\pi = .73$, find (a) $P(X \leq 2)$, (b) $P(X = 2)$.

Solution: Using Table 4.10,

a) $P(X \leq 2) = .2959$.
b) $P(X = 2) = P(X \leq 2) - P(X \leq 1)$

$\qquad\qquad = .2959 - .0628$

$\qquad\qquad = .2331$.

EXERCISES

4.25   Given the binomial distribution with $\pi = .26$ and $n = 7$, use the cumulative binomial table to determine the following:
(a) $P(X \geq 2)$; (b) $P(X = 2)$; (c) $P(X \geq 4)$; (d) $P(X = 4)$.

4.26 Given the binomial distribution with $\pi = .84$ and $n = 9$, use the cumulative binomial table to determine the following:
(a) $P(X \leq 7)$; (b) $P(X = 7)$; (c) $P(X \leq 5)$; (d) $P(X = 5)$.

4.27 Given the binomial distribution with $\pi = .37$ and $n = 8$, use the cumulative binomial table to determine the following:
(a) $P(X = 0)$; (b) $P(X = 3)$; (c) $P(X < 3)$; (d) $P(X \leq 3)$.

4.28 Given the binomial distribution with $\pi = .70$ and $n = .20$, use the cumulative binomial table to determine the following:
(a) $P(X = 0)$; (b) $P(X = 12)$; (c) $P(X > 12)$; (d) $P(X \geq 12)$.

THE HYPERGEOMETRIC DISTRIBUTION

We have already stated, in connection with the use of the binomial formula, that the selection of n elements from a given population may be viewed as an experiment consisting of n repeated trials (a series of n selections). The binomial formula is applicable to this sampling process only when the outcome of each selection is independent of the outcome of preceding selections, that is, when the sample elements are selected with or without replacement from an infinite population or when the sample elements are selected *with* replacement from a finite population.

When a sample is selected without replacement from a finite population, the binomial formula is not applicable because the probability of success depends on the previous outcomes and changes from trial to trial as elements are removed from the population. In such a situation, when the probability of success is not constant, an alternative distribution, called the **hypergeometric distribution,** can be used instead of the binomial distribution.

Example Let us consider the following game. We have an urn containing 6 red and 4 blue marbles. A sample of 3 marbles is to be selected without replacement. We win $10 if the sample drawn consists of 2 red marbles and 1 blue marble. What is the probability of winning in this game?

Solution: As an initial step in the solution to the game, let us first determine the number of all possible outcomes. This is the same as finding the number of all possible samples of 3 marbles that can be selected from a population of 10 marbles. According to Rule 4 of counting, the number of combinations in which 3 objects can be selected from 10 distinct objects is

$$\binom{10}{3} = \frac{10!}{3!(10-3)!} = \frac{10!}{3!\,7!}$$

$$= 120 \text{ combinations.}$$

Thus there are 120 equally likely outcomes for our game. Of these 120 combinations, only combinations consisting of 2 red and 1 blue marble are winning combinations. Hence, our next step in the solution is to determine the number of winning combinations.

The number of winning combinations is determined in two steps. First, we must count the number of ways in which 2 red marbles can be selected from a total of 6 red marbles. Using Rule 4 of counting, we find that there are

$$\binom{6}{2} = \frac{6!}{2!\,4!} = 15 \text{ ways.}$$

Second, we must count the number of ways in which 1 blue marble can be selected from a total of 4 blue marbles:

$$\binom{4}{1} = \frac{4!}{1!\,3!} = 4 \text{ ways.}$$

To get a winning combination we need 2 red and 1 blue marble, so the number of winning outcomes is equal to the product

$$\binom{6}{2}\binom{4}{1} = 15 \cdot 4$$

$$= 60 \text{ winning outcomes.}$$

We have so far found that there are 120 possible outcomes to our game, of which only 60 are winning outcomes. Hence the probability of winning the game is

$$P(\text{win}) = \frac{\text{Number of favorable outcomes}}{\text{Total number of outcomes}}$$

$$= \frac{\binom{6}{2}\binom{4}{1}}{\binom{10}{3}}$$

$$= \frac{15 \cdot 4}{120} = \frac{60}{120}.$$

To generalize these results, let a represent the number of red marbles in the population ($a = 6$) and let b represent the number of blue marbles ($b = 4$). The total population consists of $a + b$ objects, 10 in this case. If $n = 3$ objects are selected without replacement from such a population, the probability that the sample selected will contain $x = 2$ red marbles can be determined as follows:

$$\frac{\binom{a}{x}\binom{b}{n-x}}{\binom{a+b}{n}} = \frac{\binom{6}{2}\binom{4}{1}}{\binom{10}{3}}$$

$$= \frac{15 \cdot 4}{120} = \frac{60}{120}.$$

Utilizing binomial distribution terminology, we can call the objects a "successes" and the objects b "failures." The probability of getting exactly x successes in a random sample of n objects can be denoted by $P(X = x)$ and determined by using the formula

$$P(X = x) = \frac{\binom{a}{x}\binom{b}{n-x}}{\binom{a+b}{n}}.$$

This is the general formula for the hypergeometric distribution. It is obvious that we must assume that the number of successes x in the sample cannot exceed a, and the number of failures $(n - x)$ in the sample, cannot exceed b.

Example Once again an urn contains 6 red and 4 blue marbles. A sample of 3 marbles is to be selected. What is the probability that all the marbles will be red?

Solution: Let

$a = 6$: number of red marbles (successes),

$b = 4$: number of blue marbles (failures),

$n = 3$: sample size,

$x = 3$: number of red marbles required in the sample.

Substituting these values into the hypergeometric formula, we obtain

$$P(X = x) = \frac{\binom{a}{x}\binom{b}{n-x}}{\binom{a+b}{n}}$$

$$P(X = 3) = \frac{\binom{6}{3}\binom{4}{0}}{\binom{10}{3}}$$

$$= \frac{20 \cdot 1}{120} = \frac{20}{120} = \frac{1}{6}.$$

There is an alternative procedure—the rule of multiplication—that confirms the solution to this problem. According to the rule of multiplication, the probability of drawing 3 red marbles without replacement from an urn containing 6 red and 4 blue marbles is

$$P(R_1 \cap R_2 \cap R_3) = \frac{6}{10} \cdot \frac{5}{9} \cdot \frac{4}{8}$$

$$= \frac{120}{720} = \frac{1}{6}.$$

This result is the same as that obtained using the hypergeometric formula.

Example   The government of Zaire has 12 loans payable, 10 of which are overdue. If a representative of the International Monetary Fund randomly selects 4 loans, what is the probability that the representative will find exactly 3 overdue loans?

Solution: Let

$$a = 10: \quad \text{number of overdue loans,}$$

$$b = 2: \quad \text{number of loans not overdue,}$$

$$n = 4: \quad \text{sample size.}$$

According to the hypergeometric distribution formula, the probability of finding exactly 3 overdue loans in a random sample of 4 is

$$P(X = x) = \frac{\binom{a}{x}\binom{b}{n-x}}{\binom{a+b}{n}}$$

$$P(X = 3) = \frac{\binom{10}{3}\binom{2}{1}}{\binom{12}{4}} = \frac{120 \cdot 2}{495} = \frac{240}{495}.$$

Example A manufacturer receives certain parts in lots of 20. The manufacturer has adopted the following rule to help decide whether to accept or reject a lot: Four parts are randomly selected and tested from each lot, and the entire lot is accepted if the samples contain no more than 1 defective part. What is the probability that the manufacturer will accept a lot that actually contains 6 defective parts?

Solution: Let

$$a = 6: \quad \text{number of defective parts,}$$
$$b = 14: \quad \text{number of nondefective parts,}$$
$$n = 4: \quad \text{sample size.}$$

According to the manufacturer's rule, the lot is accepted when the number of defective parts in the sample is either 0 or 1. Hence, the probability of accepting a lot is

$$P(\text{accept}) = P(X = 0) + P(X = 1)$$

$$= \frac{\binom{6}{0}\binom{14}{4}}{\binom{20}{4}} + \frac{\binom{6}{1}\binom{14}{3}}{\binom{20}{4}}$$

$$= \frac{1 \cdot 1001}{4845} + \frac{6 \cdot 364}{4845} = \frac{3185}{4845}.$$

EXERCISES

4.29 An accounts receivable ledger contains 20 accounts, of which 5 are erroneous. An auditor randomly selects 4 accounts from the ledger. What is the probability of the auditor's finding exactly 1 erroneous account among the 4 accounts selected?

4.30 The U.S. Senate Foreign Relations Committee consists of 7 Democrats and 5 Republicans. Four members of the committee are randomly selected to lead a U.S. delegation on SALT III negotiations with the Soviet Union. What is the probability that 2 Democrats and 2 Republicans will be selected to lead the U.S. delegation?

4.31 Among the 15 participants in an executive training seminar, 3 have an engineering degree. Five participants are selected at random. What is the probability that none of the participants selected have an engineering degree?

4.32 The United Nations Security Council consists of 21 member nations, 8 of which have a pro-Western stand. A committee of 3 member nations is randomly selected from the 21 members to supervise a national referendum in El Salvador. What is the probability that the committee will have a pro-Western majority?

4.33   Among the 19 university presidents in the California State University system, six have a D.B.A. If 3 presidents are randomly selected to represent the system on the State Commission on Higher Education, what is the probability that at least one of the presidents chosen has a D.B.A.?

THE POISSON DISTRIBUTION

The **Poisson distribution** is used as a model to describe the probability distribution of such events as the arrivals of cars at a service station, the arrivals of airplanes at an airport, and the arrivals of customers at a restaurant.

To illustrate, we can assume that the average number of cars, μ, that arrive at a particular service station is 20 per hour. If the Poisson distribution is used to describe car arrivals in this case, we must further assume the following.

1. The probability of a single car arriving at the service station during a very short interval, say 1 second, is proportional to the length of the time interval; that is, $20/(60 \cdot 60) = \frac{1}{180}$. Such a very short time interval is generally called a *subinterval.*

2. The probability that *two* or more cars will arrive during a subinterval is virtually zero.

3. The number of cars that arrive during any subinterval is *independent* of the number of cars that arrive *outside* the subinterval.

The Poisson distribution is also used to describe such experiments as the number of typing errors per page, the number of defective rivets in an airplane, and the number of bacteria in a cubic centimeter of ocean water. In these experiments, it is assumed that the average number of occurrences (generally called "successes") in a specified region is known. The specific region can be a unit of length, an area, or a volume. It is also assumed that the probability of a single success occurring within a very small region (subregion) is proportional to the size of the subregion and is independent of the number of successes occurring outside the subregion. Finally, it is assumed that the probability of two or more successes occurring in a subregion is approximately zero.

In any Poisson experiment, the probability of getting *exactly* x successes, denoted by $P(X = x)$, is

$$P(X = x) = \frac{\mu^x e^{-\mu}}{x!},$$

for $x = 0, 1, 2, \ldots$, where μ is the average number of successes during a given time interval (or in a specific region), and e is $2.71828 \ldots$ (the base of the natural logarithm system).

Example The average number of claims filed against an insurance company is 2 per day. What is the probability that on any given day

    a) exactly 1 claim is filed against the insurance company?

    b) no claim is filed against the insurance company?

    c) exactly 3 claims are filed against the insurance company?

Solution:

    a) Let

$$\mu = 2: \quad \text{average number of claims per day,}$$

$$x = 1: \quad \text{exact number of claims filed.}$$

According to the Poisson distribution,

$$P(X = x) = \frac{\mu^x e^{-\mu}}{x!}$$

$$P(X = 1) = \frac{(2)^1 (2.71828)^{-2}}{1!}$$

$$= \frac{2}{(2.71828)^2} = \frac{2}{7.38905} = .27067.$$

    b) Let

$$\mu = 2: \quad \text{average number of claims per day,}$$

$$x = 0: \quad \text{exact number of claims filed.}$$

According to the Poisson distribution,

$$P(X = x) = \frac{\mu^x e^{-\mu}}{x!}$$

$$P(X = 0) = \frac{(2)^0 (2.71828)^{-2}}{0!}$$

$$= \frac{1}{(2.71828)^2} = \frac{1}{7.38905} = .13534.$$

    c) Using a Poisson distribution with $\mu = 2$ and $x = 3$, we find

$$P(X = 3) = \frac{(2)^3(2.71828)^{-2}}{3!}$$

$$= \frac{8}{(6)(7.38905)} = .18045.$$

Example A student makes, on average, 1 typing error per page. What is the probability that the student will make exactly 2 typing errors in a 3-page term paper?

Solution: It is necessary here to define μ as the average number of typing errors per *3* pages. Hence,

$\mu = 3$:   average number of typing errors per 3 pages,

$x = 2$:   exact number of typing errors in a 3-page paper.

According to the Poisson distribution,

$$P(X = x) = \frac{\mu^x e^{-\mu}}{x!}$$

$$P(X = 2) = \frac{(3)^2(2.71828)^{-3}}{2!} = \frac{9}{2(2.71828)^3} = .22404.$$

Cumulative Poisson Tables

Cumulative Poisson probabilities have been computed and tabulated for values of μ ranging from .1 to 10. See Table H at the end of the book. The value of μ is found at the head of the column, and the values of $X(x = 0, 1, 2, \ldots)$ are located in the left column of the table. The probability in any section in the table is the probability of getting *x or fewer* successes, that is, $P(X \le x)$. The use of Table H is illustrated with the following two examples.

Example A car salesperson sells, on average 2.5 cars per day. Use Table H to determine the probability that on a given day the salesperson will sell (a) at most 4 cars, (b) exactly 4 cars.

Solution:

a) Since Table H shows the cumulative probabilities $P(X \le x)$, the probability of selling 4 or fewer cars is found directly from Table H. Thus with $\mu = 2.5$, Table H shows $P(X \le 4) = .8912$.

b) The probability of selling exactly 4 cars, $P(X = 4)$, can be found as follows:

$$P(X = 4) = P(X \le 4) - P(X \le 3).$$

Hence, with $\mu = 2.5$, according to Table H,

$$P(X = 4) = .8912 - .7576 = .1336.$$

Example The number of traffic accidents that take place on the Hollywood Freeway on a weekday between 7:00 A.M. and 8:00 A.M. is, on average, .7. Use Table H to determine the probability that more than 2 traffic accidents will occur on the Hollywood Freeway on Tuesday morning between 7:00 A.M. and 8:00 A.M.

Solution: Using a Poisson distribution with $\mu = .7$, and according to Table H, we find

$$P(X > 2) = 1 - P(X \le 2)$$
$$= 1 - .9659 = .0341.$$

The Poisson Approximation to the Binomial Distribution

Let us consider a binomial distribution with $\pi = .02$ and $n = 100$ and find the probability that $X = 3$. Using the binomial formula, we can find the *exact* probability as

$$P(X = 3) = \frac{100!}{3!97!}(.02)^3(.98)^{97} = .1823.$$

But as you may already have noticed, the use of the binomial formula in this case involves many tedious computations. Fortunately, however, when the value of π is close to zero and n is very large (as it is in the case), the binomial distribution can be approximated by a Poisson distribution with $\mu = n\pi$. Using a Poisson distribution with

$$\mu = n\pi = 100(.02) = 2,$$

we find that the probability that $X = 3$ is

$$P(X = 3) = \frac{\mu^x e^{-\mu}}{x!}$$

$$= \frac{(2)^3(2.71828)^{-2}}{3!} = \frac{8}{(6)(2.71828)^2} = .1805.$$

Thus, using the binomial formula, we find that the probability that $X = 3$ is exactly .1823. When we use the Poisson distribution as an approximation to the binomial, we find that the probability that $X = 3$ is approximately .1805.

The approximation of binomial probabilities by Poisson probabilities improves as the value of π gets closer to zero and as the value of n becomes large. As a rule of thumb, the Poisson approximation is considered appropriate when $\pi \le .05$ and $n \ge 20$.

Example A machine is producing parts that contain, on average, .02 defectives. In a random sample of 75 parts, what is the probability of obtaining exactly 3 defective parts?

Solution: This is a binomial distribution with $\pi = .02$ and $n = 75$. Since π is close to 0 and n is large, we will use a Poisson distribution as an approximation to the binomial. Hence,

$$\mu = n\pi = 75(.02) = 1.5,$$

we find, from Table H,

$$P(X = 3) = .9344 - .8088 = .1256.$$

EXERCISES

4.34 The average number of homicides per day in Los Angeles County is 2. Use the Poisson distribution to determine the probability that on a given day

a) there will be 3 or fewer homicides in Los Angeles County,

b) there will be exactly 3 homicides.

4.35 The average number of earthquakes per year in California is .5. Use the Poisson distribution to determine the probability that there will be no earthquakes in California in the next three years.

4.36 The average number of major fires per month in a certain city is 1.5. Use the Poisson distribution to determine the probability that there will be exactly 1 major fire in a period of two months.

4.37 Telephone calls come into the Watergate Hotel switchboard at a rate of 10 per minute. Use the Poisson distribution to determine the probability of the switchboard's receiving exactly 4 calls in a 30-second interval.

4.38 The average number of defects in a roll of a certain type of wallpaper is 2.5. Use the Poisson distribution to determine the probability that a roll will have 4 or more defects.

4.39 A machine is producing parts that contain, on the average, 2% defectives. Use the Poisson distribution to approximate the probability of obtaining exactly 2 defective parts in a random sample of 40 parts.

4.40 The probability that a sales contact will result in a sale is $\frac{1}{20}$. If 200 sales contacts are made on a given day, what is the probability that at least 12 sales are made? Use the Poisson approximation to the binomial.

THE NORMAL DISTRIBUTION

Consider the following variables: the number of workers in a given establishment, the number of heads in 14 tosses of a balanced coin, the number of students in a statistics class. These variables can assume only the limited values 0, 1, 2, ... Consequently, they are *discrete variables.*

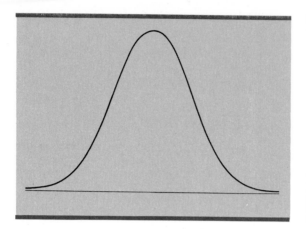

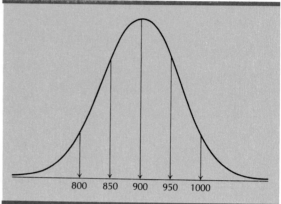

Figure 4.4   The normal distribution

Figure 4.5

By contrast, consider the following variables: the weight of a jar of instant coffee, the height of a telephone pole, the temperature at a certain time of day. Each of these variables can assume an infinite number of values on a measuring scale. The weight of a jar of instant coffee, for example, can be 4.5 ounces, 4.512 ounces, 4.512718 ounces, and so on. Similarly, the height of a telephone pole can be 103 feet, 103.178 feet, 103.178912 feet, ... Consequently, these variables are *continuous variables.*

As you may already suspect, the binomial distribution and the Poisson distribution can represent the probability distribution of only discrete variables. What about continuous variables? The probability distribution of some continuous variables can be described by a very common continuous distribution called the **normal distribution.**

Let us consider some continuous variables: the height of a soldier in an army regiment, the life of a 100-watt electric bulb in a large lot of a certain brand, and the weight of a 10-ounce jar of instant coffee in a very large shipment. The probability distribution of each of these continuous variables may very well be described by the normal distribution, illustrated in Fig. 4.4.

The normal distribution can best be explained by a concrete example. Consider the case of a manufacturer receiving a very large shipment of 100-watt electric bulbs. Assume further that the average life of these bulbs is 900 hours, with a standard deviation of 50 hours ($\mu = 900$ hours, $\sigma = 50$ hours). Now, if the lives of these bulbs are normally distributed, then we expect most of the bulbs to have a life of about 900 hours. Furthermore, there will be as many bulbs lasting longer than 950 hours as there are bulbs lasting less than 850 hours. Similarly, there will be as many bulbs lasting more than 1000 hours as there are bulbs lasting less than 800 hours (See Fig. 4.5). These remarks about the normal distribution are informal and made to give you a general idea of what the normal distribution is all about. Now we will be more specific and rigorous.

The normal distribution is completely specified by its mean and standard deviation. In other words, you will know all you want to know about the electric bulbs once you know the mean and the standard deviation of their lives. For example, you will be able to determine the percentage of bulbs that should last longer than 917 hours, from 927 to 1071 hours, or less than 892 hours.

It is a fact, for example, that 34% of the area under the normal curve is between μ and $\mu + 1.0\sigma$ (Fig. 4.6). This means that the lives of 34% of all bulbs are expected to be between μ and $\mu + 1\sigma$, or 900 and 900 + 50—that is, between 900 and 950 hours (Fig. 4.7). We can also conclude that the probability is .34 that any one bulb will last from 900 to 950 hours.

These facts concerning the area under the normal curve are obtained from Table A at the end of the book, which shows the area enclosed between the mean and any other value x (x can be above or below the mean). The letter z labeling the first column in the table indicates how many standard deviations x is away from the mean. Table A shows, for example, the following facts.

1. .4332 of the area under the normal curve is between μ and $\mu + 1.5\sigma$ (See Fig. 4.8).
2. .3869 of the area under the normal curve is enclosed between μ and $\mu - 1.21\sigma$ (See Fig. 4.9).
3. .4830 of the area under the normal curve is enclosed between either μ and $\mu + 2.12\sigma$ or between μ and $\mu - 2.12\sigma$ (See Fig. 4.10).

Let us now consider a normal distribution, the ages of workers in a large plant, with a mean of 50 years and a standard deviation of 5 years ($\mu = 50$ years, $\sigma = 5$ years). The following questions can be answered using Table A.

Figure 4.6

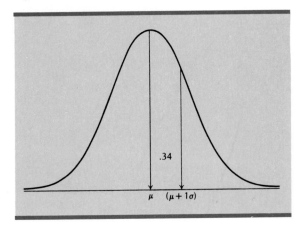

Figure 4.7

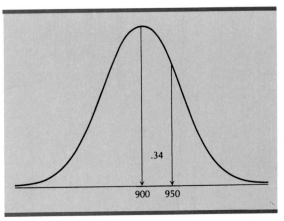

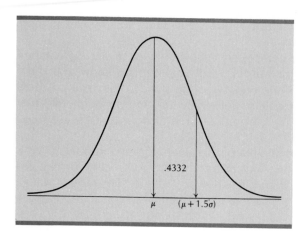

Figure 4.8

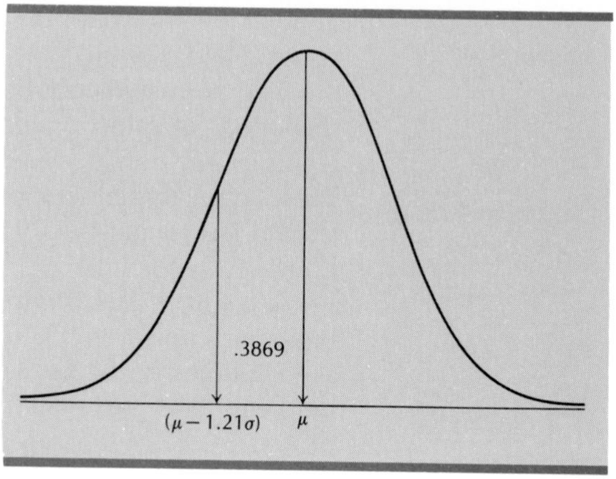

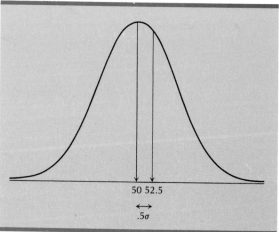

Figure 4.9

a) What is the percentage of workers whose ages are between 50 and 52.5 years?

This problem can be solved in two steps:

1. $52.5 - 50 = 2.5$ years (the difference between x and μ in years),
2. $2.5 \div 5 = .5$ (x exceeds μ by $.5\sigma$).

From Table A we find that .1915 of the area under the normal curve is enclosed between μ and $\mu + .5\sigma$. Thus 19.15% of the workers are between 50 and 52.5 years old (Fig. 4.11). The two steps above can be combined in

Figure 4.10

Figure 4.11

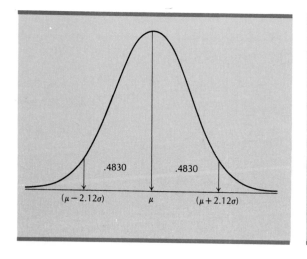

the following formula:

$$z = \frac{x - \mu}{\sigma} = \frac{52.5 - 50}{5} = .5,$$

where z is the deviation of x from the mean, measured in standard deviations. Thus 52.5 deviates from the mean by $.5\sigma$. Once again, 19.15% of the workers are between 50 and 52.5 years old.

b) What is the probability that any one worker is 45 years or younger?

Determining the probability that any one worker is 45 years or younger is the same as determining the percentage of workers who are younger than 45 years:

$$z = \frac{x - \mu}{\sigma} = \frac{45 - 50}{5} = -1.0.$$

Since .3413 of the area under the normal curve is between μ and $\mu - 1\sigma$, the area that lies to the left of $\mu - 1\sigma$ is

$$.5000 - .3413 = .1587.$$

Thus 15.87% of the workers are younger than 45 years (Fig. 4.12). Stated differently, the probability is .1587 that any one worker is younger than 45. Symbolically, we may write $P(X < 45) = .1587$.

c) What is the probability that any one worker is between 41 and 58 years?

Let us denote by A_1 the area between 58 and 50 and by A_2 the area

Figure 4.12

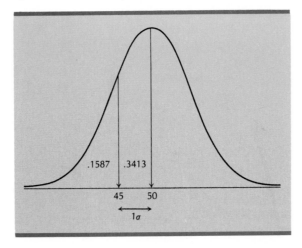

between 41 and 50. Then

$$P(41 \le X \le 58) = A_1 + A_2.$$

See (Fig. 4.13.) We proceed as follows:

$$z_2 = \frac{X - \mu}{\sigma} \qquad z_1 = \frac{X - \mu}{\sigma}$$

$$= \frac{41 - 50}{5} \qquad = \frac{58 - 50}{5}$$

$$= -1.8 \qquad = 1.6$$

$$A_2 = .4641 \qquad A_1 = .4452$$

Therefore,

$$P(41 \le X \le 58) = A_1 + A_2$$
$$= .4452 + .4641$$
$$= .9093.$$

Thus the probability that any one worker is between 41 and 58 years is .9093.

d) What is the probability that any one worker is between 55 and 60 years?

We denote by A_1 the area between 60 and 50 and by A_2 the area between 55 and 50. Then

$$P(55 \le X \le 60) = A_1 - A_2.$$

Figure 4.13

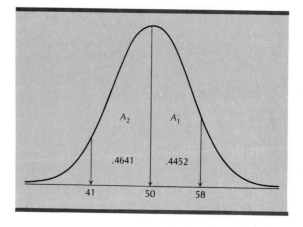

(See Fig. 4.14.) We calculate as follows:

$$z_2 = \frac{x - \mu}{\sigma} \qquad z_1 = \frac{x - \mu}{\sigma}$$

$$= \frac{55 - 50}{5} \qquad = \frac{60 - 50}{5}$$

$$= 1.0 \qquad = 2.0$$

$$A_2 = .3413 \qquad A_1 = .4772$$

Therefore,

$$P(55 \le X \le 60) = A_1 - A_2$$
$$= .4772 - .3413$$
$$= .1359.$$

Thus the probability that any one worker is between 55 and 60 years old is .1359.

e) Twenty percent of the workers are below a certain age. What is this age?

Table A shows that .2995 or .30 of the area under the normal curve is between μ and $\mu - .84\sigma$. Thus if x is located at a distance of $-.84\sigma$ from the mean, then .2005 of the workers will not have reached age x (Fig. 4.15).

Figure 4.14

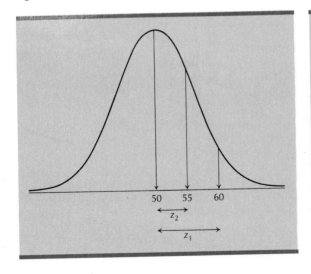

Figure 4.15

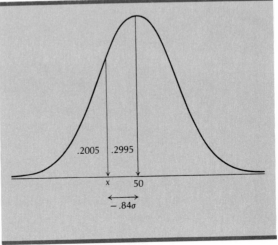

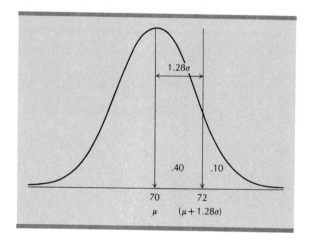

Figure 4.16

Therefore,

$$X = \mu - .84\sigma$$
$$= 50 - .84(5) = 50 - 4.20$$
$$= 45.80 \text{ years.}$$

Thus about 20% of all workers are younger than 45.8 years.

Example   The mean height of soldiers in an army regiment is 70 inches. Ten percent of the soldiers in the regiment are taller than 72 inches. Assuming that the heights of the soldiers in this regiment are normally distributed, what is the standard deviation?

Solution: Since 10% of the soldiers are taller than 72 inches, 40% of the soldiers are between 70 and 72 inches tall. But according to Table A, approximately 40% (.3997) of the area under the normal curve is between μ and $\mu + 1.28\sigma$ (Fig. 4.16). Consequently,

$$\mu + 1.28\sigma = 72, \qquad 70 + 1.28\sigma = 72, \qquad 1.28\sigma = 2,$$

$$\sigma = \frac{2}{1.28}, \qquad \sigma = 1.56 \text{ inches.}$$

Example   A food processor packages instant coffee in small jars. The weights of the jars are normally distributed with a standard deviation of .3 ounce. If 5% of the jars weigh more than 12.492 ounces, what is the mean weight of the jars?

Solution: Since approximately 45% (.4495) of the jars weigh between μ and 12.492 ounces, according to Table A the point 12.492 is at a distance of 1.64σ

from μ (Fig. 4.17). In other words,

$$12.492 = \mu + 1.64\sigma$$
$$= \mu + 1.64(.3)$$
$$= \mu + .492$$
$$\mu = 12.492 - .492 = 12 \text{ ounces}.$$

Example   The heights of soldiers are normally distributed. If 13.57% of the soldiers are taller than 72.2 inches and 8.08% are shorter than 67.2 inches, what are the mean and the standard deviation of the heights of the soldiers?

Solution: Since .3643 of all the area under the normal curve is enclosed between μ and 72.2, according to Table A the point 72.2 is at a distance of 1.1σ from μ (Fig. 4.18). In other words,

$$72.2 = \mu + 1.1\sigma.$$

Similarly, since .4192 of the area under the normal curve is between μ and 67.2, according to Table A the point 67.2 is 1.4σ to the left of μ. In other words,

$$67.2 = \mu - 1.4\sigma.$$

Now we have two simultaneous equations containing the two unknowns σ and μ. Solving the equations, we have

$$72.2 = \mu + 1.1\sigma$$
$$\underline{67.2 = \mu - 1.4\sigma}$$
$$5 \quad = 0 + 2.5\sigma$$
$$\sigma \quad = \tfrac{5}{2.5} = 2 \text{ inches,}$$

Figure 4.17

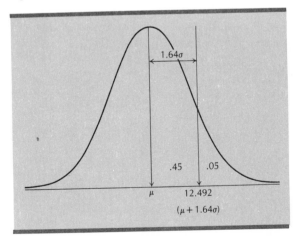

Figure 4.18

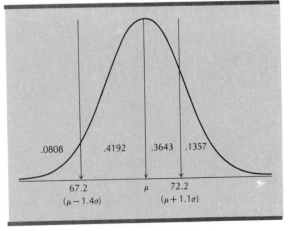

and the value of μ can be found from either of the two equations.

$$72.2 = \mu + 1.1\sigma$$
$$= \mu + 1.1(2)$$
$$= \mu + 2.2$$
$$\mu = 72.2 - 2.2 = 70 \text{ inches.}$$

Example   The diameters of a large shipment of ball bearings are normally distributed with a mean of 2.0 inches and a standard deviation of .01 inch. If three ball bearings are selected at random from the shipment, what is the probability that exactly two of the selected ball bearings will have a diameter larger than 2.02 inches?

Solution: First, let us determine the probability that the diameter of any *one* ball bearing is greater than 2.02 inches (See Fig. 4.19):

$$Z = \frac{x - \mu}{\sigma}$$

$$= \frac{2.02 - 2.00}{.01} = 2.$$

Therefore,

$$P(X > 2.02) = .5000 - .4772$$
$$= .0228.$$

Now, let

$\pi = .0228$:   probability that the diameter of any one ball bearing is larger than 2.02 inches;
$n = 3$:   sample size;
$x = 2$:   number of ball bearings with a diameter larger than 2.02 inches.

Figure 4.19

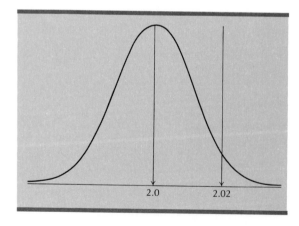

Using the binomial formula, the probability that exactly two of the selected ball bearings will have a diameter greater than 2.02 inches is

$$P(X = x) = \frac{n!}{x! \, (n - x)!} \, \pi^x (1 - \pi)^{n-x}$$

$$P(X = 2) = \frac{3!}{2! \, 1!} \, (.0228)^2 (.9772)^1$$

$$= 3(.00051984)(.9772) = .00152.$$

Example   The production manager believes that the life of machine K is normally distributed with a mean of 3000 hours. If the manager also believes there is a .50 chance that chance that machine K could last less than 2632 or more than 3368 hours, what is the standard deviation?

Solution: Since the manager believes there is a .50 chance that machine K could last less than 2632 or more than 3368 hours, the probability is .50 that the life of machine K is between 2632 and 3368 hours. And because of the symmetry of the area under the normal curve, the probability is .25 that the machine life is between 3000 and 3368 hours (See Fig. 4.20).

But according to Table A, approximately .25 (.2486) of the area under the normal curve is between μ and $\mu + .67\sigma$ (Fig. 4.20). Consequently,

$$.67\sigma = 3368 - 3000$$

$$= 368 \text{ hours}$$

$$\sigma = {}^{368}\!/_{.67} = 549.25 \text{ hours.}$$

Figure 4.20

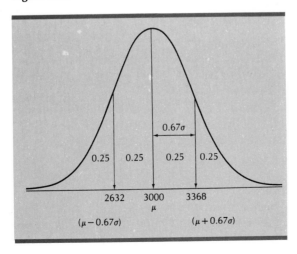

4.41 The heights of soldiers in an army regiment are normally distributed with a mean of 69 inches and a standard deviation of 2 inches.

a) What is the probability that any one soldier is taller than 72 inches?

b) What is the percentage of soldiers who are between 69 and 73 inches tall?

c) If the tallest 20% of the soldiers in the regiment are eligible to perform a certain task, what is the minimum height required to perform such a task?

4.42 A ball bearing is considered defective and therefore is rejected if its diameter is greater than 2.02 inches or less than 1.98 inches. What is the expected number of rejected ball bearings if the diameters in a lot of 10,000 ball bearings are normally distributed with a mean of 2 inches and a standard deviation of .01 inch?

4.43 The final examination scores in a psychology class are normally distributed. The mean score is 60 and the standard deviation is 10.

a) If the lowest passing grade is 48, what percentage of the class is failing?

b) If the highest 80% of the class are to pass, what is the lowest passing score?

4.44 A food processor markets flour in a NET WT. 12 OZ. package. The filling process can be adjusted so that the mean fill can be set to any level. If the fill is normally distributed with a standard deviation of .2 ounce,

a) at what level should the mean fill be set so that only .1% of the packages will have a net weight less than 12 ounces?

b) at what level should the mean fill be set so that only 5% of the packages will have a net weight exceeding 12.4 ounces?

4.45 The mean weight of pineapples in a very large shipment is 5 pounds. Ten percent of the pineapples weigh less than 4 pounds. Assuming that the weights are normally distributed, what is the standard deviation in the shipment?

4.46 The lives of a certain brand of 9-volt batteries are normally distributed. If 6.68% of the batteries last more than 56 hours and 30.85% last less than 52 hours, what are the mean and the standard deviation of the life of this brand of batteries?

4.47 Mr. Mode, a statistical analyst for the Data Kontrol Corporation, drives to work every day. The time required for the trip from his apartment to the office can be approximated by a normal distribution with a mean of 20 minutes and a standard deviation of 5 minutes. At what time should Mr. Mode leave his apartment to give himself a .95 chance that he will be at the office by 9 A.M.?

4.48 The lives of 40-watt electric bulbs of brand A are normally distributed with a mean of 850 hours and a standard deviation of 50 hours. In a random sample of 4 bulbs, what is the probability that exactly 3 bulbs will last 822 hours or more?

4.49 The lives of 40-watt electric bulbs of brand A have a mean of 850 hours with a standard deviation of 50 hours. The mean life of brand B 40-watt electric bulbs is 820 hours with a standard deviation of 40 hours. The life of each brand of bulbs is normally distributed. If one bulb is to be selected from each brand at random, what is the probability that bulb A will last longer than 825 hours and bulb B less than 840 hours?

4.50 A magazine publisher is considering publishing a special Christmas edition. The publisher believes that sales of the special edition are normally distributed with a mean of 100,000 copies. If the publisher furthermore believes that the probability is .20 that sales could exceed 120,000 copies, what is the standard deviation?

4.51 The credit manager of a department store estimates bad debt losses in the current year as follows: the loss is normally distributed with a mean of $30,000, and the probability is .50 that the loss could be greater than $35,000 or less than $25,000. What is the standard deviation?

4.52 Arithmetic test scores of 1000 eleventh graders are normally distributed with a mean of 60 and a standard deviation of 8. Scores of the same test for 800 twelfth graders are also normally distributed with a mean of 68 and a standard deviation of 10.

a) How many of the eleventh graders score above the average twelfth grader?

b) How many of the twelfth graders score below the average eleventh grader?

4.53 Variable X is normally distributed with $\mu = 100$ and $\sigma = 10$. Find a) $P(X > 112)$, b) $P(95 < X < 110)$, c) $P(85 \leq X \leq 95)$.

4.54 The lives of tires used by a trucking company are normally distributed with a mean of 80,000 miles and a standard deviation of 2000 miles. To avoid a tire blowout, the company replaces each tire after it has been used for a given number of miles. After how many miles of use should a tire be replaced if the chance of a tire blowout is to be limited to .001?

4.55 An electronic device is used in an ocean exploration apparatus. The operational life of the device is normally distributed with a mean of 500 hours and a standard deviation of 50 hours.

a) What is the probability that the device will fail before 420 hours of operation time?

b) After how many hours of operation time should the device be replaced if the probability of failure is to be approximately .05?

4.56   Weekly demand for product X is normally distributed with μ = 10 units and σ = 2 units. Assume that supply is fixed at 12 units per week. What is the probability that the quantity demanded in a given week will exceed supply?

4.57   Bank of America operates a training center for its new tellers. A study shows that the time required to successfully complete the training program is normally distributed with a mean of 120 hours and a standard deviation of 20 hours. A participant is selected at random.

a) What is the probability that the participant will need more than 130 hours to complete the program successfully?

b) What is the probability that the participant will require between 110 and 140 hours?

c) Thirty percent of the participants require less than X hours. Find X.

4.58   In California the automobile accident settlement cost is normally distributed with a mean of $800 and a standard deviation of $160.

a) What is the probability that an automobile accident settlement cost exceeds $1000?

b) What is the probability that an automobile settlement cost is between $900 and $1000?

c) The probability is .90 that an accident settlement cost exceeds X. Find X.

4.59   The hourly wage rates for automobile mechanics in Los Angeles are normally distributed with a mean of $9.20 and a standard deviation of $.80. A mechanic is selected at random.

a) What is the probability that the mechanic earns more than $10.50?

b) What is the probability that the mechanic earns between $9.00 and $10.50?

c) The probability is .80 that the mechanic earns between X_1 and X_2. Find X_1 and X_2 using symmetrical limits around the mean.

4.60   Assume that admission test scores for the 10,000 applicants to the Harvard Graduate School of Business are normally distributed with a mean of 600 and a standard deviation of 100.

a) How many of the applicants score between 560 and 670?

b) If the school accepts the highest 15% of its applicants, what is the minimum score needed to be accepted?

4.61   California Federal Savings and Loan reports that the balance in the savings accounts of its depositors is normally distributed with a mean of $5000 and a standard deviation of $800. One account is selected at random.

a) What is the probability that the account exceeds a balance of $6000?

b) What is the probability that the balance is between $4500 and $5700?

c) A bonus is to be awarded to the holders of the largest 10% of accounts. What is the minimum balance needed to qualify for a bonus?

4.62 A manufacturer of a seasonal novelty believes that demand for the coming season is normally distributed with a mean of 100,000 units and a standard deviation of 15,000 units. Because of the nature of the product, only one production run is possible.

a) If the manufacturer produces 120,000 units, what is the probability that the quantity demanded will exceed supply?

b) How many units should the manufacturer produce so that the probability of being out of stock is .05?

THE NORMAL CURVE APPROXIMATION TO THE BINOMIAL DISTRIBUTION

Let us determine the probability of getting 6 heads in 16 tosses of a balanced coin. Since this is a binomial experiment with $\pi = \frac{1}{2}$ and $n = 16$, we can use the binomial formula to determine the *exact* probability of obtaining 6 heads in this experiment.

$$P(X = 6) = \frac{16!}{6!\ 10!} \left(\frac{1}{2}\right)^6 \left(\frac{1}{2}\right)^{10}$$

$$= 8008 \left(\frac{1}{2}\right)^{16} = \frac{8008}{65,536} = .122$$

The probability of getting 6 heads in 16 tosses of a balanced coin can be approximated using the normal distribution as an approximation to the binomial distribution. The approximation is obtained as follows:

1. Determine the mean and the standard deviation of the binomial distribution. The mean is

$$\mu = n\pi = 16(\tfrac{1}{2}) = 8 \text{ heads,}$$

and the standard deviation is

$$\sigma = \sqrt{n\pi(1 - \pi)} = \sqrt{16(\tfrac{1}{2})(\tfrac{1}{2})} = 2 \text{ heads.}$$

2. Approximate the binomial distribution by a normal distribution with $\mu = 8$ and $\sigma = 2$ (See Fig. 4.21).

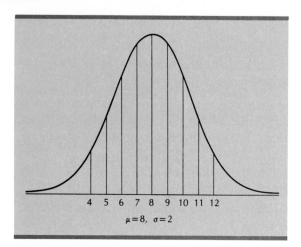

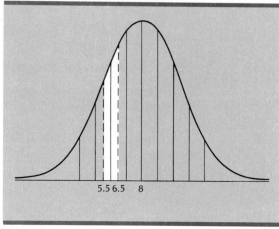

Figure 4.21   **Figure 4.22**

3. The probability of obtaining 6 heads is approximated by the area under the normal curve between $x = 5.5$ and $x = 6.5$ (shaded area in Fig. 4.22). We have

$$z_1 = \frac{5.5 - 8}{2} \qquad z_2 = \frac{6.5 - 8}{2}$$

$$= \frac{-2.5}{2} \qquad = \frac{-1.5}{2}$$

$$= -1.25; \qquad = -.75;$$

$$A_1 = .3944. \qquad A_2 = .2734.$$

Therefore,

$$P(5.5 \le X \le 6.5) = .3944 - .2734$$

$$= .121.$$

Thus, using the binomial distribution, the probability of getting 6 heads in 16 tosses of a balanced coin is exactly .122. On the other hand, when we use the normal curve as an approximation to the binomial distribution, the probability of getting 6 heads in 16 tosses of a balanced coin is approximately .121.

The probability of getting a given number of heads in 16 tosses of a balanced coin can be approximated in a similar fashion. The probability of getting 8 heads, for example, is approximated by the area under the normal curve between $x = 7.5$ and $x = 8.5$. Similarly, the probability of getting 10 heads is approximated by the area under the normal curve between $x = 9.5$ and $x = 10.5$. In general, the probability of obtaining x number of heads is approximated by the area under the normal curve enclosed between $x - \frac{1}{2}$ and $x + \frac{1}{2}$.

The usefulness of the normal-curve approximation to the binomial distribution becomes evident when we consider the following example. Let us determine the probability of getting 6 or more heads in 16 tosses of a balanced coin.

To determine the exact probability, we must use the binomial formula to determine the probability of getting 6 heads, the probability of getting 7 heads, the probability of getting 8 heads, and so on, up to the probability of getting 16 heads. The exact probability of getting 6 or more heads is the sum of the individual probabilities:

$$P(X \geq 6) = P(X = 6) + P(X = 7) + \cdots + P(X = 16)$$

$$= \frac{16!}{6! \, 10!} \left(\frac{1}{2}\right)^6 \left(\frac{1}{2}\right)^{10} + \cdots + \frac{16!}{16! \, 0!} \left(\frac{1}{2}\right)^{16} \left(\frac{1}{2}\right)^0.$$

The binomial formula requires some lengthy computations, but the probability of getting 6 or more heads in our binomial experiment can easily be approximated by the area under the normal curve lying to the right of 5.5 (shaded area in Fig. 4.23):

$$z = \frac{x - \mu}{\sigma} = \frac{5.5 - 8}{2}$$

$$= \frac{-2.5}{2} = -1.25;$$

$$A = .3944.$$

Figure 4.23

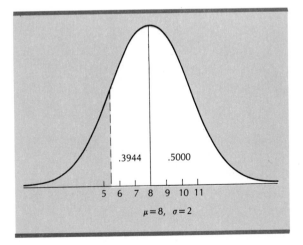

Therefore,

$$P(X \geq 5.5) = .3944 + .5000$$
$$= .8944.$$

Thus the probability of getting 6 or more heads in 16 tosses of a balanced coin is approximately .8944.

Finally, let us approximate the probability of getting from 5 to 10 heads in 16 tosses of a balanced coin. This probability is approximated by the area under the normal curve between 4.5 and 10.5 (shaded area in Fig. 4.24);

$$z_1 = \frac{4.5 - 8}{2} \qquad z_2 = \frac{10.5 - 8}{2}$$

$$= \frac{-3.5}{2} \qquad = \frac{2.5}{2}$$

$$= -1.75; \qquad = 1.25;$$

$$A_1 = .4599. \qquad A_2 = .3944.$$

Therefore,

$$P(4.5 \leq X \leq 10.5) = A_1 + A_2$$
$$= .4599 + .3944$$
$$= .8543.$$

Thus the probability of getting from 5 to 10 heads in 16 tosses of a balanced coin is approximately .8543.

You may wonder about the accuracy of the normal-curve approximation to the binomial distribution. The degree of accuracy depends on the values of n

Figure 4.24

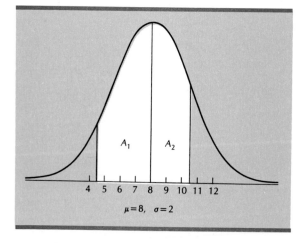

$\mu = 8, \quad \sigma = 2$

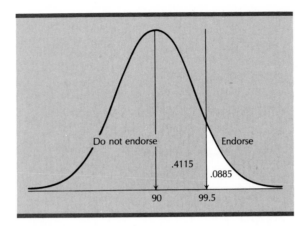

Figure 4.25

and π. Accuracy improves as n gets larger and as the value of π becomes closer to $\frac{1}{2}$. As a rule, the approximation is regarded as satisfactory if both $n\pi$ and $n(1 - \pi)$ are greater than 5.

Example Congressional candidate X will base her decision about whether to endorse the Educational Opportunity Act on the results of a poll of a random sample of 200 registered voters from her district. She will endorse the Educational Opportunity Act only if 100 or more voters are in favor of it.

a) What is the probability that candidate X will endorse the act if 45% of all registered voters in her district are in favor of it?

b) What is the probability that candidate X will not endorse the act if 52% of all voters in the district are in favor of it?

Solution:

a) The random selection of 200 voters from a district in which 45% of all voters are in favor of the Educational Opportunity Act can be regarded as a binomial experiment with $n = 200$ and $\pi = .45$. The mean μ and the standard deviation σ of this binomial experiment are as follows.

$$\mu = n\pi = 200(.45) = 90 \text{ voters}$$
$$\sigma = \sqrt{n\pi(1 - \pi)} = \sqrt{200(.45)(.55)} = \sqrt{49.5} = 7.04 \text{ voters}$$

Candidate X will endorse the act only when 100 or more (100, 101, 102, . . . , or 200) voters are in favor of it. Using the normal distribution as an approximation to the binomial distribution, the probability that the act is favored by 100 or more voters is approximated by the area under the normal curve lying to the right of $x = 99.5$ (shaded area in Fig. 4.25). We calculate

$$z = \frac{x - \mu}{\sigma} = \frac{99.5 - 90}{7.04}$$

$$= \frac{9.5}{7.04} = 1.35;$$

$$A = .4115.$$

Therefore,

$$P(X \geq 99.5) = .50 - .4115$$
$$= .0885.$$

Thus the probability that candidate X will endorse the Educational Opportunity Act is .0885.

b) The random selection of 200 voters from a district in which 52% of all voters favor the Educational Opportunity Act can be regarded as a binomial experiment with $n = 200$ and $\pi = .52$. The mean and the standard deviation of this binomial experiment are as follows.

$$\mu = n\pi = 200(.52) = 104 \text{ voters}$$
$$\sigma = \sqrt{n\pi(1 - \pi)} = \sqrt{200(.52)(.48)} = \sqrt{49.92} = 7.07 \text{ voters}$$

Candidate X will not endorse the act if fewer than 100 (99, 98, 97, . . . , or 0) voters are in favor of it. The probability that the act is favored by 99 or fewer voters is approximated by the area under the normal curve lying to the left of $x = 99.5$ (shaded area in Fig. 4.26). We calculate

$$z = \frac{x - \mu}{\sigma}$$

$$= \frac{99.5 - 104}{7.06}$$

$$= \frac{-4.5}{7.07} = -.64;$$

$$A = .2389.$$

Therefore,

$$P(X \leq 99.5) = .50 - .2389$$
$$= .2611.$$

Thus the probability that candidate X will not endorse the Educational Opportunity Act is .2611.

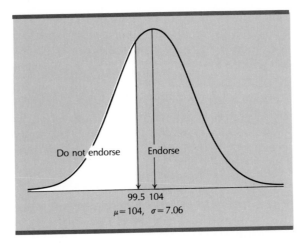

Do not endorse | Endorse

99.5 104

$\mu = 104$, $\sigma = 7.06$

Figure 4.26

4.63 A balanced coin is tossed 36 times. What is the probability

a) of getting 15 heads?

b) of getting fewer than 20 heads?

4.64 Determine the probability of getting 110 or more sixes when a fair die is rolled 720 times.

4.65 If 64% of all students attending this college are male, what is the probability that a random sample of 400 students will contain 250 or more male students?

4.66 A fair coin is to be tossed 100 times. The player receives $10 if the number of heads is 57 or more, and the player loses $5 if the number of heads is 47 or less; no gain or loss is incurred otherwise. Determine the expected value of this game to the player.

4.67 The following rule is used in controlling the operation of a machine that produces parts. Select a random sample of 400 parts every hour. If the number of defective parts is 12 or more, stop the machine. If the number of defective parts is fewer than 12, continue the operation of the machine. What is the probability

a) of stopping the machine when it produces, on the average, 2% defective parts?

b) of continuing the machine operation when it produces, on the average, 4% defective parts?

4.68   A pair of dice consists of a red die and a blue die. The pair is to be rolled 180 times. In order to win, a player must get at least 37 sixes with the red die and no more than 27 sixes with the blue die. If the player wins, he or she receives $21. Determine the expected value of this game if it costs the player $1 to play.

4.69   It is claimed that 10% of all students attending this college have an I.Q. score of 125 or more. What can you conclude about this claim if a random sample of 900 students shows that fewer than 50 students have an I.Q. score of 125 or more?

KEY TERMS

probability distribution   A listing of all the possible values and the corresponding probabilities for a random variable.

permutation   An arrangement of distinct objects. There are $n!$ permutations of n distinct objects and $n!/(n - r)!$ permutations of r objects taken from n distinct objects.

combination   A collection of objects that disregards the order of selection. Thus *ADF, DAF, AFD, FAD, DFA,* and *FDA* are the six permutations of the single combination of letters *ADF.*

binomial distribution   The probability distribution of the number of successes in n trials, where each trial has only two possible outcomes (success and failure), the probability of success (π) on any trial is the same for each trial, and the trials are independent of each other.

hypergeometric distribution   The probability distribution of the number of successes in a random sample of n taken without replacement from a finite population.

Poisson distribution   The probability distribution of the number of occurrences of some event during a fixed period of time (or in a fixed area or volume). The rate of occurrences per period (or area or volume) is μ.

normal distribution   A distribution used with many continuous random variables that have a bell-shaped distribution.

SUMMARY OF FORMULAS

permutations of n distinct objects $n!$

permutations of r objects taken $_nP_r = n!/(n - r)!$
from n distinct objects

combinations of r objects taken from n distinct objects

$$\binom{n}{r} = \frac{n!}{(n - r)!\, r!}$$

permutations of n objects of which r are of one kind and $n - r$ are of another kind

$$\binom{n}{r} = \frac{n!}{r!\, (n - r)!}$$

binomial formula

$$P(X = x) = \frac{n!}{x!\, (n - x)!}\, \pi^x\, (1 - \pi)^{n-x}$$

binomial mean

$$\mu = n\pi$$

binomial standard deviation

$$\sigma = \sqrt{n\pi(1 - \pi)}$$

hypergeometric formula

$$P(X = x) = \frac{\binom{a}{x}\binom{b}{n - x}}{\binom{a + b}{n}}$$

Poisson formula

$$P(X = x) = \frac{\mu^x\, e^{-\mu}}{x!}$$

normal formula (to use with Table A)

$$z = \frac{x - \mu}{\sigma}$$

CUMULATIVE REVIEW

1. Given the following information concerning a population of 100 accounts receivable:

$$x = \text{amount of any individual account,}$$
$$\Sigma x = \$13,000,$$
$$\Sigma(x - \mu)^2 = \$62,500.$$

   Determine the population mean and standard deviation.

2. Given the sets

$$A = \{x \mid x^2 - 2x - 24 = 0\}, \qquad B = \{x \mid x^2 + 2x = 8\}.$$

   Find $P(A \cap B)$.

3. An experiment consists of drawing three cards from an ordinary deck of playing cards and observing the color of each card.
   a) Denoting a red card by R and a black card by B, list all the elements of the sample space S of this experiment.
   b) List the elements of S contained in the event that there is exactly one red card.
   c) How do you define event A where

$$A = \{B, B, B\}?$$

4. A population consists of the following 10 accounts receivable: $26, $20, $18, $22, $20, $12, $24, $24, $20, $14.

   a) Determine the arithmetic mean and the standard deviation.

   b) One account receivable is to be selected at random. What is the probability that it will fall in the range $\mu \pm 1\sigma$?

5. A committee consists of 4 Republicans and 6 Democrats. Two persons are to be selected at random, the first to be the committee chairperson and the second to be vice-chairperson.

   a) What is the probability that the committee chairperson will be a Republican?

   b) What is the probability that the chairperson and vice-chairperson will be Republicans?

   c) What is the probability that only the vice chairperson will be a Republican?

6. The probability that Oscar will marry a blue-eyed woman is .20. The probability that he will marry an intelligent woman is .60, and the probability that he will marry a rich woman is .05. Assuming that the three characteristics are independent, what is the probability that Oscar will marry a rich, intelligent, blue-eyed woman?

7. The probability of an engine failure on an aircraft is .10. With how many engines should the aircraft be equipped to be .999 sure against an engine failure, assuming that only one engine is needed for a successful operation of the aircraft?

8. The probability that a sharpshooter hits the target with any single shot is .4.

   a) What is the probability of missing the target in 4 consecutive shots?

   b) What is the probability of hitting the target at least once in 4 consecutive shots?

   c) How many shots should the sharpshooter fire to be approximately .95 sure that the target is hit at least once?

9. A system consists of four independent components: A, B, C_1, and C_2. The probability of failure is .01 for A, .02 for B, .10 for C_1, and .10 for C_2. If component A, component B, and at least one of components C are needed for successful operation of the system, what is the probability that the system will succeed?

10. Ms. Smith leaves work promptly at 4:45 P.M. The probability is .7 that she goes directly home; the probability is .3 that she stops at a store before going home. If Ms. Smith goes directly home, the probability is .90 that she arrives home by 6:00 P.M. If she stops at the store after work, the probability is only .05 that she will arrive home by 6:00 P.M. Given that Ms. Smith

arrived at home after 6:00 P.M., what is the probability that her delay was due to a stop at the store?

11. Professor X teaches statistics and would like to give a quiz at every class meeting. Being aware that he sometimes forgets to come to class, Professor X has arranged for his graduate assistant to take over the class in his absence. If Professor X appears in class, the probability is 70% that he will give a quiz. In his absence, the probability is only 10% that his graduate assistant will give a quiz. Professor X is known to be absent 80% of the time.

    a) What is the probability that there will be a quiz in any given class meeting?

    b) Assuming that there was a quiz in a given class meeting, what is the probability that Professor X was present?

12. Urn A contains 3 white, 5 black, and 2 green marbles; urn B contains 4 white, 3 black, and 3 green marbles. One marble is to be selected at random from each urn. You will win $4.00 when the two marbles selected are white, $3.00 when both are black, and $5.00 when both are green. If it costs you $1.50 to play the game, what is the expected value of this game to you?

13. A true/false quiz consists of five questions. Assuming that you answer each question by sheer guess,

    a) what is the probability that you answer only the first two questions correctly?

    b) what is the probability that you answer exactly two questions correctly?

14. Ms. Monday is an amateur thief. The probability that she opens a jewel safe on any single trial is .2.

    a) What is the probability that it will take Ms. Monday exactly two trials to open the safe?

    b) What is the probability that Ms. Monday will open the safe by the third trial?

15. It is known that 80% of all students at Valley State College are undergraduates. Four students are selected at random.

    a) What is the probability that exactly 3 students are undergraduates?

    b) Calculate the mean number of undergraduate students in the random sample. Also calculate the standard deviation.

16. It is known that 60% of all registered voters in the 27th congressional district are Democrats. Four registered voters are selected at random from the district.

    a) What is the probability that there will be exactly two Democrats in the sample?

    b) What is the probability that the sample will contain at least one Democrat?

    c) What is the probability that only the first two voters selected are Democrats?

17. Fifty percent of all students at Bradford College are freshmen, 25% are sophomores, 15% are juniors, and 10% are seniors. Five students are selected at random.

    a) What is the probability that exactly two of the students selected are freshmen?

    b) What is the probability that none of the students selected are juniors or seniors?

18. The probability of success in a single trial is $\frac{1}{2}$.

    a) What is the probability of getting exactly two successes in three consecutive trials?

    b) What is the probability of having at least one success in three consecutive trials?

    c) How many consecutive trials should be performed to be .9375 sure of obtaining at least one success?

19. The heights of orange trees are normally distributed. 2.28% of the trees are taller than 14 feet and 84.13% are shorter than 12 feet. Find the mean height of the orange trees. Find the standard deviation.

20. Beta Airlines has introduced the Red-Eye Special, a nonstop midnight flight between Los Angeles and Atlanta. Flight time is normally distributed with a mean of 4 hours and a standard deviation of 1 hour. If an aircraft leaves Los Angeles at 12:00 A.M., what is the probability that it will arrive in Atlanta by 6:00 A.M. (Los Angeles time)?

21. The Hob-Nob Bar has installed an automatic draft beer machine. The machine can be regulated so that the average fill per glass can be set at any level. At any given level, however, the amount of beer discharged is normally distributed with a standard deviation of .2 ounce.

    a) If the filling level is set at 10.3 ounces per glass, what percentage of glasses will contain less than 10 ounces?

    b) At what filling level should the machine be set if it is desired that 2.28% of the glasses contain less than 10 ounces?

    c) At what filling level should the machine be set if it is desired that 84.13% of the glasses contain less than 10.6 ounces?

22. The life of a certain brand of batteries is normally distributed with a mean of 80 hours and a standard deviation of 10 hours. The manufacturer guarantees to replace any battery that fails prior to a specified time. How long a

guarantee should the manufacturer give so that no more than 5% of the batteries fail before the guaranteed time?

23. The ABC Tire Company produces a radial tire with a mean lifetime of 50,000 miles and a standard deviation of 5000 miles. Assume that the lifetime is normally distributed.

   a) What is the probability that any one tire will last longer than 60,000 miles?

   b) Fifty percent of the tires will last between x_1 and x_2. Find the values of x_1 and x_2 using symmetrical limits around the mean.

   c) The manufacturer guarantees to replace any tire that lasts less than x miles. Determine the value of x so that the manufacturer would have to replace only 1% of the tires.

24. The machine time required to produce a unit of product A is normally distributed with a mean of 50 minutes and a standard deviation of 5 minutes. A lot of 4000 units of product A is to be produced.

   a) How many units of the lot are expected to require more than 53 minutes of machine time?

   b) How many units of the lot are expected to require no less than 48 minutes and no more than 53 minutes of machine time?

   c) Fifty percent of the lot require machine time greater than X_1 minutes but less than X_2 minutes. Determine X_1 and X_2 using symmetrical limits around the mean.

25. In deciding on whether to undertake a public housing project in South Chicago, the Public Housing Administration adopted the following rule: Select 100 housing units from South Chicago at random. If 40% or more of the units selected are dilapidated, undertake the project. If fewer than 40% are dilapidated, do not undertake the project.

   a) What is the probability of undertaking the public housing project when only 36% of *all* housing units in South Chicago are dilapidated?

   b) What is the probability of not undertaking the public housing project when 50% of *all* housing units in South Chicago are dilapidated?

26. A firm markets its product exclusively by mail to a list of 100,000 customers. The firm is considering marketing a new gadget. In deciding whether to market the gadget, the firm adopted the following rule: Select and contact 100 persons at random from the customer list. If 30 or more of the customers contacted wish to purchase the gadget, market it. If fewer than 30 of those contacted desire to purchase the gadget, do not market it.

   a) What is the probability of marketing the gadget when 20% of *all* customers on the list would purchase the gadget?

b) What is the probability of not marketing the gadget when 36% of *all* customers would purchase the gadget?

27. An electronic device is used in the operation of an aircraft. The life of the device is normally distributed with a mean of 100 hours and a standard deviation of 10 hours.

    a) What is the probability that a given device will last longer than 112 hours?

    b) After how many hours of use should a device be replaced if the probability of a device failure is to be approximately .001?

28. Urn X contains four balls numbered 1 through 4; urn Y contains three balls numbered 6, 7, and 8. One ball is selected from each urn.

    a) What is the probability that the sum of the two numbers selected is 11?

    b) What is the probability that the sum of the two numbers selected is 10?

29. Arithmetic test scores are normally distributed with a mean of 60 and a standard deviation of 10. English test scores are normally distributed with a mean of 70 and a standard deviation of 15. Tom's test score in arithmetic is 72. How high should Tom score in English to attain an equivalent level of achievement in both subjects?

30. A manufacturer estimates the daily demand for a product as follows.

Number of Units Sold per Day	Probability
5	.2
6	.5
7	.3

    a) What is the probability that the manufacturer will sell six units in two successive days?

    b) Determine the expected number of units sold per day.

31. Joe is an insurance salesperson who makes several personal sales contacts during the day. It is known that 50% of his contacts result in signed contracts. Assume that Joe makes five sales contacts on a given day.

    a) What is the probability that Joe signs exactly one contract on that day?

    b) What is the probability that he signs at least one contract?

32. An automobile agency sells either 2, 3, or 5 cars per day, with probability of .2, .3, and .5, respectively. The selling price of an automobile is either $4000, $5000, or $8000, with probability of .6, .2, and .2, respectively.

   a) What is the expected number of automobiles sold per day?

   b) What is the expected price per automobile sold?

   c) Determine the agency's expected sales per day.

33. A certain type of electronic tube has an average life of 100 hours with a standard deviation of 10 hours.

   a) What is the probability that a single tube will fail before 95 hours of operation?

   b) What is the probability that in a random sample of five tubes three will fail before 95 hours of operation time?

34. The owner of a newspaper stand estimates daily sales for a certain newspaper as follows.

Number of Newspapers Sold	Probability
30	¼
40	½
50	¼

   a) What is the probability that the owner will sell 30 newspapers in two consecutive days?

   b) What is the probability that the owner will sell 30 papers in two days out of five?

   c) What is the expected number of newspapers sold per day?

35. An urn contains 4 white marbles and 6 black marbles. Marbles are drawn at random, one at a time and without replacement. The selection is terminated as soon as two white marbles are obtained.

   a) What is the probability that the drawing is terminated by the third selection?

   b) What is the probability that exactly four drawings are needed to terminate the selection?

36. A college graduate applies for a job at three different companies: A, B, and C. She assesses the probability of getting an offer from company A as .8,

from company B as .5, and from company C as .6. Assume the offers are independent.

a) What is the probability that the graduate is offered a job by both A and B?

b) What is the probability that she is offered a job by A and B but not by C?

c) What is the probability that she is offered exactly two jobs?

37. The amounts of money market accounts maintained by customers with Fidelity Mutual Fund are normally distributed with a mean of $5000 and a standard deviation of $1000.

a) If an account is selected at random, what is the probability that it exceeds $7500?

b) The largest 5% of all accounts are to receive an extra $\frac{1}{2}$% interest as a bonus. What is the minimum balance required to qualify for the bonus?

38. Dr. Glassman, an optometrist, estimates his monthly expenditures and gross revenues for any given month as follows.

Expenditures ($1000)	Probability	Gross Revenues ($1000)	Probability
70	.5	100	.2
80	.4	120	.3
100	.1	150	.5

a) Find Dr. Glassman's expected monthly gross revenues.

b) Find his expected monthly net income.

c) What is the probability that his expenditures are $70,000 in two consecutive months?

d) What is the probability that he will have a net income of $50,000 in any given month? Assume that expenditures and gross revenues are independent.

39. An tire manufacturer observed that 2% of its tires are defective. The company uses a certain test to detect defective tires, but this test is not entirely accurate. If a tire is really defective, the probability that the test will indicate that it is defective is .90. But if the tire is not defective, the probability that the test will indicate that it is nondefective is .95. A tire is

tested and the test indicates that it is defective. What is the probability that the tire really is defective?

40. In a game of chance, a pair of dice is tossed over and over again. The game is terminated as soon as the sum 7 appears three times.

a) What is the probability that it will take exactly four trials to terminate the game?

b) What is the probability that the game will be terminated by the fourth trial?

41. A sharpshooter fires at a target, and the firing is terminated as soon as the target is hit exactly three times. The probability of hitting the target on any given shot is .8, and each shot is independent of the others.

a) What is the probability that exactly four shots are needed to terminate the game?

b) What is the probability of terminating the game by the fourth shot?

42. Fifty percent of all registered voters in California are Democrats, 40% are Republicans, and 10% are Independents. Gubernatorial candidate X is favored by 70% of the Democrats, 40% of the Republicans, and 20% of the Independents. One registered voter is selected at random. Given that the selected voter favors candidate X, what is the probability that the voter is a Democrat?

43. The manager of the Tie and Shirt Shop estimates her daily demand of ties and shirts as follows.

Number of Ties (x)	P(x)	Number of Shirts (y)	P(y)
5	.2	10	.1
10	.3	20	.2
15	.5	30	.7

a) What is the expected daily sales for ties?

b) What is the expected daily sales for shirts?

c) What is the probability of selling 30 shirts on each of two consecutive days?

d) What is the probability of selling an equal number of shirts and ties on a given day? Assume the sales of ties and shirts are independent.

44. The training department of a multinational corporation operates an in-house management training program. Past records indicate that the time

needed by participants to complete the program is normally distributed with a mean of 600 hours and a standard deviation of 120 hours.

a) A participant is selected at random. What is the probability that the participant will require more than 750 hours to complete the program?

b) What percentage of the participants will require between 650 and 700 hours to complete the program?

c) Sixty percent of the participants will require less than X hours to complete the program. Find the value of X.

SAMPLING

5

We have defined statistics as a field of knowledge that enables us to derive and evaluate conclusions about a population from sample data. It is obvious that the validity and usefulness of these conclusions depend on how well the samples represent the population. This chapter presents the various methods used in selecting a representative sample.

In many problems it is either impossible or unnecessary to have complete population data. A part of the population data can provide the information necessary to make a decision or to test a hypothesis concerning the entire population. It is not practical, for example, to burn all electric bulbs of a certain brand to determine the bulbs' average life. The average life may be estimated by testing only 100 bulbs.

Any part of a population is called a **sample.** The objective of sampling is to select the part that is representative of the entire population. Various sampling techniques and designs have been developed in attempts to improve representation. Each design is suitable for certain types of problems.

Samples are classified into *probability samples* and *nonprobability samples.* A sample is a probability sample if each unit in the population is given *some* chance of being selected in the sample. The probability of selecting each unit must be known. Contrary to general belief, therefore, it is not necessary that all units in the population be given an *equal* chance of being selected in the sample. Each unit in the population must be given a chance of being selected, and this chance must be known to the investigator.

Since the probability of selecting each population unit is known, a statistician can utilize the various rules and laws of probability to evaluate the reliability of conclusions derived from probability samples. In other words, when a sample is a probability sample, the risk of incorrect decisions and conclusions can be measured using the theory of probability.

A sample is a nonprobability sample when some units in the population are not given any chance of being selected and when the probability of selecting any unit into the sample cannot be determined or is not known.

When a decision is made on the basis of sample information, there is always the risk of error. If 1000 items selected from the output of machines A and B contain 20% and 24% defectives, respectively, there is a risk in concluding that machine A is better than machine B. It is always possible that the two machines are of the same efficiency, and the observed difference is due to chance or to sampling fluctuations. The risk of arriving at the wrong conclusion can be measured only when the sample is a probability sample; it cannot be determined for a nonprobability sample. For this reason, only probability samples are subject to statistical treatment and analysis. The simple random sample, the most common type of probability sample, is treated in great detail in this chapter. Other sample designs are surveyed briefly.

SIMPLE RANDOM SAMPLE

To illustrate the procedure used in selecting a simple random sample, let the population of interest consist of five people: Adams, Bakers, Camel, Daniels, and Edwards. We want to select a committee (a sample) of three members from this population, using a simple random selection.

How many possible samples of three can we select from this population? Referring to the names by their initials, we have ten possible samples.

ABC	ACD	BCD
ABD	ACE	BCE
ABE	ADE	BDE
	CDE	

Our method of selection would result in a simple random sample if each of the 10 samples were given an equal chance of being selected. One way of accomplishing this is to write each combination on a slip of paper, thoroughly mix the slips in a bowl, and draw one slip from the bowl. If the combination drawn is *CDE,* our sample consists of Camel, Daniels, and Edwards. Although this method of selecting a simple random sample is straightforward, statisticians prefer an alternative procedure that is equally sound but easier to apply.

It has been found that each of the ten possible samples is given an equal chance of being selected if each of the five names is written on a slip of paper, the slips thoroughly mixed, and three slips drawn in succession from the bowl. This alternative method eliminates the task of enumerating all possible samples of a given size that can be selected from a population—an enormous task when the number of elementary units in the population is very large.

It may be interesting to prove that both methods of selecting a simple random sample give all possible samples an equal chance of being selected. Under the first method, all ten possible samples are given the same chance of being selected. The probability of selecting any one of these samples, say *ABC* (Adams, Bakers, and Camel), is $1/10$. To prove our proposition, therefore, we must show that the probability of selecting a committee consisting of Adams, Bakers, and Camel under the second method of selection is also $1/10$.

Using the second method, there are six ways in which we can obtain a sample consisting of Adams, Bakers, and Camel. The resulting sample is Adams, Bakers, and Camel if Adams is selected on the first draw, Bakers is selected on the second draw, and Camel is selected on the third draw. The resulting sample is also Adams, Bakers, and Camel if Adams is selected on the first draw, Camel on the second draw, and Bakers on the third draw. The six possible ways of selecting a committee consisting of Adams, Bakers, and Camel are listed below.

1. Adams, then Bakers, then Camel (*ABC*)
2. Adams, then Camel, then Bakers (*ACB*)
3. Bakers, then Adams, then Camel (*BAC*)
4. Bakers, then Camel, then Adams (*BCA*)
5. Camel, then Adams, then Bakers (*CAB*)
6. Camel, then Bakers, then Adams (*CBA*)

Thus each of the six events represents the selection of a committee (a simple random sample) consisting of Adams, Bakers, and Camel. Since the six events are mutually exclusive, the probability of selecting a committee consisting of Adams, Bakers, and Camel is equal to the sum of the probabilities of the six events.

$$P(A \cap B \cap C) = \frac{1}{5} \cdot \frac{1}{4} \cdot \frac{1}{3} = \frac{1}{60}$$

$$P(A \cap C \cap B) = \frac{1}{5} \cdot \frac{1}{4} \cdot \frac{1}{3} = \frac{1}{60}$$

$$P(B \cap A \cap C) = \frac{1}{5} \cdot \frac{1}{4} \cdot \frac{1}{3} = \frac{1}{60}$$

$$P(B \cap C \cap A) = \frac{1}{5} \cdot \frac{1}{4} \cdot \frac{1}{3} = \frac{1}{60}$$

$$P(C \cap A \cap B) = \frac{1}{5} \cdot \frac{1}{4} \cdot \frac{1}{3} = \frac{1}{60}$$

$$P(C \cap B \cap A) = \frac{1}{5} \cdot \frac{1}{4} \cdot \frac{1}{3} = \frac{1}{60}$$

$$P(\text{selecting sample } ABC) = \frac{6}{60} = \frac{1}{10}$$

Use of Random Digits

Using slips of paper and a bowl in the selection of a simple random sample is a rather crude approach, and it becomes even more cumbersome and unmanageable as the number of elementary units in the population gets larger. In practice, therefore, a table of random digits is used instead of the bowl.

Random digits are the digits 0, 1, 2, 3, 4, 5, 6, 7, 8, and 9 scrambled in a particular fashion. Table 5.1 is an example of a table of random digits. The various digits are arranged in such a way that all digits appear with approximately the same frequency in the table. Furthermore, any given digit has no relation to the digit above, below, to the right, or to the left of it. In other words, the various digits are scattered at random. For convenience, 40 digits, in groups of 5, are placed on each line.

A practical sampling problem will best illustrate the use of the table of random digits in selecting a simple random sample. Let us assume that we wish to select 10 accounts receivable from a ledger containing 6532 accounts.

As a first step, we must assign a serial number to each account in the ledger—in this case, a four-digit number. (If the number of accounts in the ledger was 623, we would have assigned a three-digit serial number to each account. The number of digits of which a serial number consists depends on the total number of accounts in the ledger.) We now assign 0001 to the first account, 0002 to the second account, 0123 to the 123rd account, and 6532 to the last account. Once all accounts in the ledger are serialized, we can begin to select our sample by reading the first four digits from the first line of the table of random digits. The resulting number is 7899. Since no account in the ledger corresponds to this number, we move down and read the first four digits of the second line. The number 0490 corresponds to the 490th account in the ledger, which becomes our first account in the sample. Continuing in the same fashion, we obtain the other nine accounts for our sample:

4658, 2924, 1715, 5071, 3944, 0102, 0833, 3970, 2590.

(Note that if a serial number appears twice, it must be ignored on the second appearance.)

The table of random digits could have been used in some other manner. We could have obtained the first four digits from any place in the table. In selecting the second four digits, we could have moved sideways or crosswise, as long as our movement remained systematic.

To select a simple random sample, one must obtain a list of all elementary units in the population. Such a list is called a *population frame.* Ideally, a population frame should contain each elementary unit in the population and exclude duplication of any units.

In many market research surveys, it is somewhat difficult to obtain a good population frame. Researchers have often used various "workable" frames

TABLE 5.1   AN ILLUSTRATIVE TABLE OF RANDOM DIGITS

Line	(1)	(2)	(3)	(4)	(5)	(6)	(7)	(8)
1	78994	36244	02673	25475	84953	61793	50243	63423
2	04909	58485	70686	93930	34880	73059	06823	80257
3	46582	73570	33004	51795	86477	46736	60460	70345
4	29242	89792	88634	60285	07190	07795	27011	85941
5	68104	81339	97090	20601	78940	20228	22803	96070
6	17156	02182	82504	19880	93747	80910	78260	25136
7	50711	94789	07171	02103	99057	98775	37997	18325
8	39449	52409	75095	77720	39729	03205	09313	43545
9	75629	82729	76916	72657	58992	32756	01154	84890
10	01020	55151	36132	51971	32155	60735	64867	35424
11	08337	89989	24260	08618	66798	25889	52860	57375
12	76829	47229	19706	30094	69430	92399	98749	22081
13	39708	30641	21267	56501	95182	72442	21445	17276
14	89836	55817	56747	75195	06818	83043	47403	58266
15	25903	61370	66081	54076	67442	52964	23823	02718
16	71345	03422	01015	68025	19703	77313	04555	83425
17	61454	92263	14647	08473	34124	10740	40839	05620
18	80376	08909	30470	40200	46558	61742	11643	92121
19	45144	54373	05505	90074	24783	86299	20900	15144
20	12191	88527	58852	51175	11534	87218	04876	85584
21	62936	59120	73957	35969	21598	47287	39394	08778
22	31588	96798	43668	12611	01714	77266	55079	24690
23	20787	96048	84726	17512	39450	43618	30629	24356
24	45603	00745	84635	43079	52724	14262	05750	89373
25	31606	64782	34027	56734	09365	20008	93559	78384
26	10452	33074	76718	99556	16026	00013	78411	95107
27	37016	64633	67301	50949	91298	74968	73631	57397
28	66725	97865	25409	37498	00816	99262	14471	10232

(Continued)

TABLE 5.1 *(Continued)*

Line	(1)	(2)	(3)	(4)	(5)	(6)	(7)	(8)
29	07380	74438	82120	17890	40963	55757	13492	68294
30	71621	57688	58256	47702	74724	89419	08025	68519
31	03466	13263	23917	20417	11315	52805	33073	07723
32	12692	32931	97387	34822	53775	91674	76549	37635
33	52192	30941	44998	17833	94563	23062	95725	38463
34	56691	72529	66063	73570	86860	68125	40436	31303
35	74952	43041	58869	15677	78598	43520	97521	83248
36	18752	43693	32867	53017	22661	39610	03796	02622
37	61691	04944	43111	28325	82319	65589	66048	98498
38	49197	63948	38947	60207	70667	39843	60607	15328
39	19436	87291	71684	74850	76501	93456	95714	92518
40	39143	64893	14606	13543	09621	68301	69817	52140
41	82244	67549	76491	09761	74494	91307	64222	66592
42	55847	56155	42878	23708	97999	40131	52360	90390
43	94095	95970	07826	25991	37584	56966	68623	83454
44	11751	69469	25521	44097	07511	88976	30122	67542
45	69902	08995	27821	11758	64989	61902	32121	28165
46	21850	25352	25556	92161	23592	43294	10479	37879
47	75850	46992	25165	55906	62339	58958	91717	15756
48	29648	22086	42581	85677	20251	39641	65786	80689
49	82740	28443	42734	25518	82827	35825	90288	32911
50	36842	42092	52075	83926	42875	71500	69216	01350

A portion of page 5 of *Table of 105,000 Random Decimal Digits,* constructed by H. Burke Horton and R. Tynes Smith III for the Bureau of Transport Economics and Statistics, Interstate Commerce Commission.

such as city directories, tax assessors' lists, telephone directories, voter registration records, auto registrations, or lists prepared by name-gathering agencies. Although some of these frames, such as city directories and tax assessors' lists, are better than others, all such frames are subject to considerable imperfections that limit their use and introduce some hazards.

Our discussion so far has dealt with the selection of a simple random sample from a finite population for which it is possible to prepare a list of all elementary units. But how can we select a simple random sample from an infinite population for which such a list cannot be obtained? How can we select, for example, a simple random sample of 100 electric bulbs from a production process that produces thousands day after day? The answer is simple: a production process is a random process, and any 100 bulbs are a simple random sample of the entire output. Fortunately, most infinite populations are generated by more or less random processes, and any number of elementary units is a simple random sample of all elementary units that can be produced by a process.

A Statistic

A **statistic** is a number that describes a certain aspect of a sample. The arithmetic mean, the median, the mode, the proportion, and the standard deviation are all statistics if they are computed from a sample.

A clear distinction must be made between a parameter and a statistic. While a parameter describes a certain aspect of a population, a statistic describes a certain aspect of a sample. The arithmetic mean is a parameter if it is computed from complete population data. If the arithmetic mean is computed from a sample, it is called a statistic.

Since a parameter is computed from complete population data, its value is constant. The value of a statistic, however, varies from sample to sample. Thus a statistic is a *variable*. To illustrate this point, let our population of interest consist of the ages of five houses:

$$x_1 = 2 \text{ years}, \qquad x_3 = 4 \text{ years},$$
$$x_2 = 2 \text{ years}, \qquad x_4 = 5 \text{ years},$$
$$x_5 = 2 \text{ years}.$$

The arithmetic mean of the population is constant and is equal to 3:

$$\mu = \frac{2 + 2 + 4 + 5 + 2}{5} = \frac{15}{5} = 3 \text{ years}.$$

If we select two houses as a simple random sample, and these two happen to be the first and the second houses, the arithmetic mean of this sample is 2 years. If our sample consists of the third and the fourth houses, the arithmetic mean is equal to 4.5 years. Thus the arithmetic mean differs from sample to sample.

The most popular statistics are the arithmetic mean, the proportion, and the standard deviation. The arithmetic mean of a simple random sample, denoted by $\overline{x}$, is calculated in the same manner as the arithmetic mean of a population. Symbolically,

$$\overline{x} = \frac{\sum_{i=1}^{n} x_i}{n},$$

where x_i indicates the ith member of the sample and n refers to the sample size. The proportion of a simple random sample, denoted by p, is also calculated in the same manner as the population proportion.

$$p = \frac{\text{Number of, items in sample with characteristic of interest}}{n}.$$

The standard deviation of a simple random sample, on the other hand, is calculated in a slightly different way from the standard deviation of a population. Denoted by s, the standard deviation of a sample can be written symbolically as

$$s = \sqrt{\frac{\sum_{i=1}^{n} (x_i - \bar{x})^2}{n - 1}} \;^{*}$$

STRATIFIED SAMPLE

In a **stratified sample** the population is divided into a number of groups, or strata. The objective of such stratification is to obtain a more homogeneous group with respect to the characteristic under study. A simple random sample is selected from each group or stratum, and these subsamples are combined into one grand sample.[†]

To estimate the annual family expenditure on rent in Los Angeles, for example, it might be desirable to divide Los Angeles families into three groups: those earning less than $10,000 a year, those with annual incomes ranging from $10,000 to $30,000, and those whose annual earnings exceed $30,000. After the population is divided into these three strata, a simple random sample is selected from each group and the three subsamples are combined into one sample.

Provided the stratification is successful in dividing the population into more homogeneous groups with respect to annual rent expenditures, we will obtain a more accurate estimate of average annual rent using a stratified sample than using a simple random sample selected from the population at large, assuming that the two samples are of the same size. Stratification has another, related advantage: information is obtained about the individual strata as well as about the entire population. It must be mentioned, however, that the cost of obtaining a stratified sample is higher than that of obtaining a simple random sample of the same size, since stratification entails the additional work of classifying the population into various groups.

---

[*] It is beyond the scope of this text to explain why the sum of squared deviations is divided by $n - 1$ instead of by n.

[†] The formulas used in computing the various statistics (mean, standard deviation, and so on) from a stratified sample are entirely different from those used to compute the same statistics for a simple random sample.

NONPROBABILITY SAMPLES

Nonprobability samples are characterized by the fact that the chance of including any elementary unit of the population in the sample cannot be determined. For this reason, there is no means of measuring the risk of making erroneous conclusions derived from nonprobability samples. Since the reliability of the results of nonprobability samples cannot be measured, such samples do not lend themselves to statistical treatment and analysis. Convenience and judgment samples are the most common types of nonprobability samples.

The elementary units to be included in a convenience sample are chosen because they can be reached more easily and conveniently than other units. A manufacturer of a certain brand of food can use a convenience sample to obtain information about consumer preference for a product. The manufacturer may insert a refund coupon in a number of packages of the product asking customers to provide the needed information. Returned coupons provide the manufacturer with a convenience sample. Samples of this sort are popular among manufacturers of consumer products.

The elementary units to be included in a judgment sample are chosen by an expert on the basis that the units are representative of the majority of elementary units in the population. Judgment samples are used whenever such limitations as time and cost make it necessary to choose a very small sample.

EXERCISES

5.1 The final grades of 112 students enrolled in an elementary statistics class are listed in Table 5.2. Use the table of random digits (Table 5.1) to select a random sample of 10 grades and calculate the sample mean.

5.2 A random sample of 100 accounts receivable is selected from a retail store ledger. The sample results are summarized below.

$$x = \text{amount of an account receivable in dollars}$$
$$\sum x = \$12,000$$
$$\sum (x - \bar{x})^2 = \$89,100$$

Compute the mean and the standard deviation of the sample.

5.3 The nicotine contents of five cigarettes of a certain brand, measured in milligrams, are as follows: 21, 19, 23, 19, 23. Determine the mean nicotine content in the sample. Determine the standard deviation.

5.4 Under what circumstances is a stratified sample more desirable than a simple random sample?

5.5 What is the difference between a statistic and a parameter?

TABLE 5.2

Student	Grade	Student	Grade	Student	Grade	Student	Grade
1	78	29	89	57	67	85	58
2	46	30	81	58	56	86	32
3	68	31	94	59	95	87	43
4	50	32	52	60	69	88	71
5	39	33	82	61	46	89	14
6	75	34	55	62	22	90	76
7	76	35	89	63	42	91	42
8	39	36	47	64	70	92	93
9	89	37	55	65	88	93	51
10	71	38	61	66	97	94	60
11	61	39	92	67	82	95	77
12	80	40	88	68	75	96	72
13	45	41	59	69	76	97	51
14	62	42	96	70	36	98	56
15	45	43	96	71	56	99	75
16	66	44	64	72	66	100	54
17	71	45	33	73	58	101	68
18	52	46	64	74	73	102	90
19	56	47	97	75	43	103	51
20	74	48	74	76	84	104	43
21	61	49	57	77	84	105	56
22	82	50	30	78	76	106	99
23	94	51	72	79	67	107	53
24	69	52	43	80	82	108	92
25	74	53	43	81	58	109	55
26	82	54	63	82	97	110	85
27	58	55	87	83	44	111	25
28	73	56	64	84	66	112	83

5.6 J. Paula Betty, an investor, wishes to invest a sum of $100,000 in either of two stocks: A or B. Ms. Betty is a prudent woman. Before investing this large sum of money, she decides to engage the services of an investment counselor, Harriet Goldstein. Ms. Goldstein consequently decides to gather pertinent information concerning the performance of the two stocks over the last two years, and obtains the following information.

Stock A	Stock B
$\bar{x} = \$80$	$\bar{x} = \$80$
$s = \$30$	$s = \$5$

Assuming that the current prices of the two stocks are the same, which stock should Ms. Goldstein recommend and why?

5.7. A random sample of 9 one-pound packages of Oscar Mire's hot dogs is selected to estimate the amount of meat contained in the product. The sample revealed the following amounts (in ounces): 14, 5, 6, 11, 13, 14, 14, 5, 8.

a) Find the sample mean.

b) Find the sample standard deviation.

c) Determine the proportion of packages p that contain at least 10 ounces of meat.

KEY TERMS

sample   A part of a population.

simple random sample   A sample chosen in such a way that all possible samples have an equal chance of being selected.

random digits   The digits 0, 1, 2, . . . , 8, 9 scrambled in such a way that any given digit has no fixed relation to those around it.

statistic   A number that describes a certain aspect of a sample. The sample mean and sample standard deviation are statistics.

stratified sample   A sample chosen with a predetermined number of items from each of several groups or strata. A simple random sample is used within each stratum.

SUMMARY OF FORMULAS

sample mean

$$\overline{x} = \frac{\sum_{i=1}^{n} x_i}{n}$$

proportion

$$p = \frac{\text{Number of items in sample with characteristic of interest}}{n}$$

sample standard deviation

$$s = \sqrt{\frac{\sum_{i=1}^{n} (x_i - \overline{x})^2}{n-1}}$$

ESTIMATING THE POPULATION MEAN

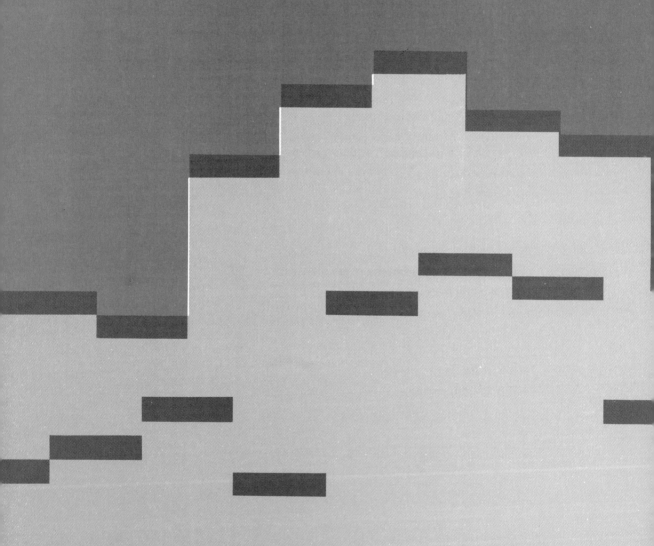

6

The population mean or average is the most widely used parameter. This chapter demonstrates how to estimate the population mean from a simple random sample. Before we embark on this task, we will study the relation between the sample mean $\bar{x}$ and the population mean μ. The central limit theorem describes an important aspect of this relation.

The principal objective in many statistics problems is to determine the value of a population parameter such as the arithmetic mean μ. To achieve this objective, statisticians rarely calculate the value of the parameter using the complete population data but instead try to estimate its value from a carefully selected sample.

Statisticians thus use the sample mean $\bar{x}$ as an estimate of the population mean μ. They also use the sample proportion p as an estimate of the population proportion π and the sample standard deviation s as an estimate of the population standard deviation σ. But how reliable is $\bar{x}$ as an estimate of μ? The value of μ is constant. The value of $\bar{x}$ varies from sample to sample. The reliability of $\bar{x}$ as an estimate of μ cannot be determined unless we can precisely describe the behavior of $\bar{x}$ or its pattern of variability from sample to sample. If μ is known, what are the possible values that $\bar{x}$ can assume in different samples? If this question is answered satisfactorily, the reliability of $\bar{x}$ as an estimate of μ can easily be assessed.

The first part of this chapter describes the behavior of $\bar{x}$ in relation to μ. The latter part deals with the problem of estimating μ from sample data.

PATTERN OF BEHAVIOR OF SAMPLE MEANS

The relation between the population mean and the means of the various samples that can be selected from the population can best be illustrated by an actual sampling operation from a known population. Let the known population consist of the heights of five different plants. The individual heights of these plants are: $x_1 = 2$ feet, $x_2 = 4$ feet, $x_3 = 6$ feet, $x_4 = 8$ feet, and $x_5 = 10$ feet. The population mean μ and the population standard deviation σ are calculated in the following table.

x_i	$(x_i - \mu)$ $(x_i - 6)$	$(x_i - \mu)^2$
2	-4	16
4	-2	4
6	0	0
8	$+2$	4
10	$+4$	16
$\sum x = 30$		$\sum(x - \mu)^2 = 40$

$$\mu = \frac{\sum x}{N} = \frac{30}{5}$$
$$= 6 \text{ feet}$$

$$\sigma = \sqrt{\frac{\sum(x - \mu)^2}{N}}$$
$$= \sqrt{\frac{40}{5}} = \sqrt{8}$$
$$= 2.83 \text{ feet}$$

Thus the mean of the population is 6 feet and the standard deviation is 2.83 feet.

Before proceeding further to our discussion, let us summarize the results of our calculations:

$N = 5$ (population size)

$$\mu = \frac{\Sigma x}{N} = \frac{30}{5} = 6 \text{ (population mean)}$$

$$\sigma = \sqrt{\frac{\Sigma(x - \mu)^2}{N}} = \sqrt{\frac{40}{5}} = 2.83 \text{ (population standard deviation)}$$

Now let us select all possible samples of size 2 from this population, and compute the mean of each sample.

Possible Samples	Sample Mean (feet)
x_1, x_2 (2, 4)	$\bar{x}_1 = 3$
x_1, x_3 (2, 6)	$\bar{x}_2 = 4$
x_1, x_4 (2, 8)	$\bar{x}_3 = 5$
x_1, x_5 (2, 10)	$\bar{x}_4 = 6$
x_2, x_3 (4, 6)	$\bar{x}_5 = 5$
x_2, x_4 (4, 8)	$\bar{x}_6 = 6$
x_2, x_5 (4, 10)	$\bar{x}_7 = 7$
x_3, x_4 (6, 8)	$\bar{x}_8 = 7$
x_3, x_5 (6, 10)	$\bar{x}_9 = 8$
x_4, x_5 (8, 10)	$\bar{x}_{10} = 9$

There are ten possible samples of size 2 that can be selected from the population of five plants. Consequently, there are ten possible sample means. How representative are these sample means of the true population mean? While the means of the first and tenth samples ($\bar{x}_1 = 3, \bar{x}_{10} = 9$) differ from the mean of the population by 3 feet, the means of the fourth and sixth samples ($\bar{x}_4 = 6, \bar{x}_6 = 6$) are exactly equal to the population ($\mu = 6$). The means of the remaining six samples are either above or below the true mean by 1 or 2 feet.

To examine these sample means in greater detail, we first calculate their arithmetic mean, or average. The average of all sample means is noted by $E(\bar{x})$:

$$E(\bar{x}) = \frac{\bar{x}_1 + \bar{x}_2 + \bar{x}_3 + \bar{x}_4 + \bar{x}_5 + \bar{x}_6 + \bar{x}_7 + \bar{x}_8 + \bar{x}_9 + \bar{x}_{10}}{10}$$

$$= \frac{3 + 4 + 5 + 6 + 5 + 6 + 7 + 7 + 8 + 9}{10}$$

$$= \frac{60}{10} = 6 = \mu.$$

We can thus say that the average of all possible sample means is equal to the population mean, or $E(\bar{x}) = \mu$. However, individual sample means may either overstate or understate the population mean, but their arithmetic mean is always equal to the population mean.

Continuing our examination of the properties of the sample means, we can calculate the standard deviation of the ten possible sample means. Their standard deviation, called the **standard error of the mean** (denoted by $\sigma_{\bar{x}}$) is computed in the following table.

$\bar{x}$	$(\bar{x} - \mu)$	$(\bar{x} - \mu)^2$
3	−3	9
4	−2	4
5	−1	1
6	0	0
5	−1	1
6	0	0
7	+1	1
7	+1	1
8	+2	4
9	+3	9

$$E(\bar{x}) = \mu = 6 \qquad \sigma_{\bar{x}} = \sqrt{\frac{\Sigma\,(\bar{x} - \mu)^2}{\text{No. of samples}}} \qquad \Sigma\,(\bar{x} - \mu)^2 = 30$$

$$= \sqrt{\frac{30}{10}} = \sqrt{3}$$

$$= 1.73 \text{ feet}$$

The standard error of the mean indicates the average difference between the various $\bar{x}$'s and μ.* The first sample mean differs from the population mean by 3 feet, the second sample mean by 2 feet, the third by 1 foot, and so on. On the average, each sample mean differs from the population mean by 1.73 feet.

A small value for $\sigma_{\bar{x}}$ indicates two facts: first, that the various values of $\bar{x}$ are close to each other; second, that the average difference between the $\bar{x}$'s and μ is small. Consequently, any one $\bar{x}$ is a good estimate of μ.

Although the standard error of the mean measures the average difference between all possible sample means and the population mean, it is not necessary to consider all the samples to determine the error. Fortunately, the standard error of the mean can be determined if the standard deviation of the

*To be specific, $\sigma_{\bar{x}}$ is the square root of the average square difference.

original population is known. It has been found that

$$\sigma_{\bar{x}} = \frac{\sigma}{\sqrt{n}} \frac{\sqrt{N-n}}{\sqrt{N-1}},$$

where σ is the standard deviation in the population, N is the population size, and n is the sample size.

In reference to the population of five plants with $\mu = 6$ feet and $\sigma = 2.83$ feet, the standard error of the mean for all possible samples of size 2 is

$$\sigma_{\bar{x}} = \frac{\sigma}{\sqrt{n}} \sqrt{\frac{N-n}{N-1}}$$

$$= \frac{2.83}{\sqrt{2}} \sqrt{\frac{5-2}{5-1}} = \frac{2.83}{\sqrt{2}} \sqrt{\frac{3}{4}}$$

$$= \frac{2.83}{1.414} \frac{1.73}{2} = \frac{(2.83)(1.73)}{2.83}$$

$$= 1.73 \text{ feet.}$$

The above value for $\sigma_{\bar{x}}$ is identical to the one we obtained in the preceding table.

Thus we can say that if all possible samples of size n are selected from a given population, then

$$E(\bar{x}) = \mu \qquad \text{and} \qquad \sigma_{\bar{x}} = \frac{\sigma}{\sqrt{n}} \sqrt{\frac{N-n}{N-1}}.$$

The term $\sqrt{(N-n)/(N-1)}$, called the **finite population correction,** is approximately equal to 1 whenever we sample from an infinite population. If the population is finite but the sample size is small in relation to the population (the sample size is 10% or less of the population size), the finite population correction will approach unity. If in a certain problem, for example, $N = 1001$ and $n = 49$, then the finite population correction is

$$\sqrt{\frac{N-n}{N-1}} = \sqrt{\frac{1001-49}{1001-1}} = \sqrt{\frac{952}{1000}}$$

$$= \sqrt{.952} = .9757.$$

In the following discussion, whenever a population is finite we assume that the sample is less than 10% of the population (a very realistic assumption indeed). Consequently, the finite population correction approaches 1, and it can, therefore, be completely ignored. Under such circumstances, the standard error of the mean is equal to the population standard deviation divided by the square root of the sample size:

$$\sigma_{\bar{x}} = \frac{\sigma}{\sqrt{n}}.$$

In the real world, the population is usually quite large and the sample represents only a small fraction of the population. Therefore, this standard error of the mean formula (without the finite population correction) is used in practice and throughout this book.

It is very interesting to observe that the standard error of the mean becomes smaller and smaller as the sample size gets larger and larger. As the sample size increases, the various sample means become more uniform in value and, consequently, any one sample mean is a good estimate of the population mean. In other words, a large sample is more reliable than a small one.

Concluding our examination of the properties of the sample mean, we add a final, important property. The sample means are approximately normally distributed whenever the sample size is 30 or more. It must be emphasized that this statement is true even when the samples are obtained from a population that is not normally distributed. For example, the first part of Fig. 6.1 represents a population that looks like a rectangle (called *rectangular distribution*). If repeated samples of size 2 are drawn from this population, the resulting sample means will have a distribution that looks like a triangle (see second part of Fig. 6.1). However, as the sample size increases, the distribution of the sample means becomes more normal. The third and fourth parts of Fig. 6.1 represent the distributions of sample means when $n = 5$ and $n = 30$, respectively. Hence, as shown in the fourth part of Fig. 6.1, when repeated samples of size 30 are drawn from the rectangular population, the resulting sample means are approximately normally distributed.

The original populations in Figs. 6.2 and 6.3 are not in fact normally distributed. However, the distributions of the sample means are approximately normally distributed when $n = 30$. When the original population is normally distributed, as in Fig. 6.4, the sample means are normally distributed no matter how small the sample size is.

In conclusion we can state: If all possible samples of size n ($n \geq 30$) are selected from a given population, the various sample means are approximately normally distributed, have an average equal to the population mean, and have a standard error equal to the population standard deviation divided by the square root of the sample size (Fig. 6.5). This fact is called the *central limit theorem*.

Example Two thousand different simple random samples of 100 students each are selected from a very large university, where the average age of the student μ is 20 years and the standard deviation σ is 2 years. There will be 2000 sample means. The mean of the first sample may be 22 years; the mean of the second sample, 19; of the third sample, 20, and so on. However, according to the central limit theorem the 2000 sample means will be approximately normally distributed and will have an average of 20 years and a standard deviation or a standard error of $2/\sqrt{100}$ or .2 year (see Fig. 6.6).

The mean of each of the 2000 samples may or may not be 20 years. According to Table A, 68% of the sample means will be in the range

$$\mu \pm 1\sigma_{\bar{x}} = 20 \pm .2,$$

or between 19.8 years and 20.2 years (Fig. 6.7).

Figure 6.1

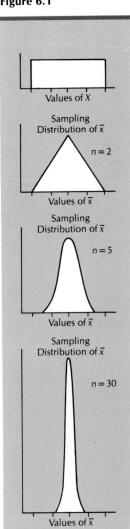

Figure 6.2

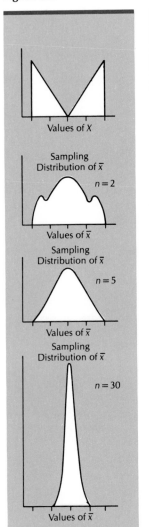

Figure 6.3

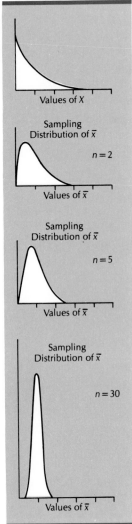

Figure 6.4

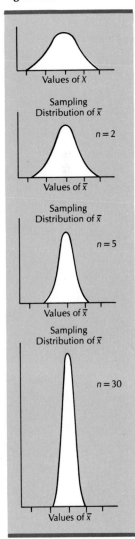

Figures 6.1, 6.2, 6.3, and 6.4 have been reproduced with permission from Kurnow, Glasser, and Ottman, *Statistics for Business Decisions* (Homewood, Ill.: Richard D. Irwin, Inc., © 1959), pp. 182–183.

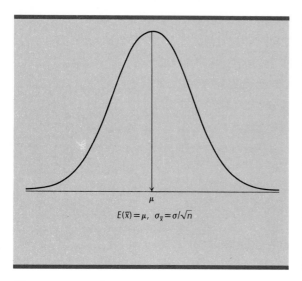

Figure 6.5

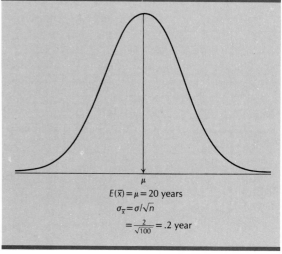

Figure 6.6

In the same manner, according to Table A, 95% of all sample means will be in the range

$$\mu \pm 1.96\sigma_{\bar{x}} = 20 \pm 1.96(.2) = 20 \pm .4,$$

or between 19.6 years and 20.4 years (Fig. 6.8).

Figure 6.7   **Figure 6.8**

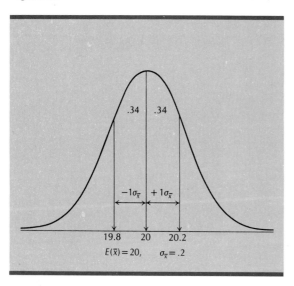

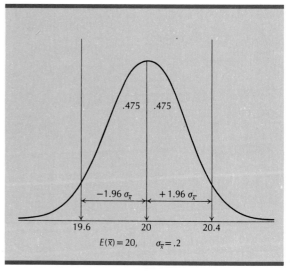

Example The average account receivable in a ledger is $125 with a standard deviation of $24 ($\mu = 125$, $\sigma = 24$). What is the probability that a simple random sample of 36 accounts selected from the ledger will show an average of $115 or less per account?

Solution: If all possible samples of size 36 are selected from this ledger, then all $\bar{x}$'s are normally distributed and have an average of $125 and a standard error of $24/\sqrt{36}$, or $4 (Fig. 6.9).

The probability that the mean of a sample of size 36 is $115 or less can be calculated as follows:

$$z = \frac{\bar{x} - \mu}{\sigma_{\bar{x}}} = \frac{115 - 125}{4} = -2.5.$$

Therefore,

$$P(\bar{x} \le 115) = .5000 - .4938 = .0062.$$

See Fig. 6.10.

Example The mean I.Q. score of all students attending a particular college is 110 with a standard deviation of 10.

a) If the I.Q. scores are normally distributed, what is the probability that the score of any one student is greater than 112?

b) What is the probabilty that the mean score in a random sample of 36 students is greater than 112?

Figure 6.9

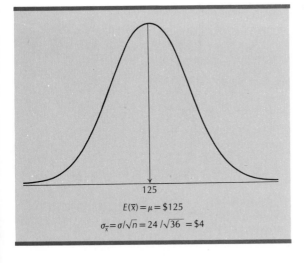

$E(\bar{x}) = \mu = \$125$

$\sigma_{\bar{x}} = \sigma/\sqrt{n} = 24/\sqrt{36} = \$4$

Figure 6.10

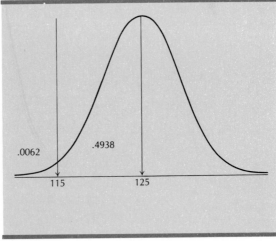

c) What is the probability that the mean score in a random sample of 100 students is greater than 112?

Solution:

a) The probability that the I.Q. score of any one student is greater than 112 is calculated as follows:

$$z = \frac{x - \mu}{\sigma} = \frac{112 - 110}{10} = .2.$$

Therefore,

$$P(x > 112) = .5000 - .0793 = .4207.$$

We must note here that the normal distribution in Fig. 6.11 describes a real population consisting of the I.Q. scores of all students attending the college. The mean of this population is 110 and its standard deviation is 10 ($\mu = 110$, $\sigma = 10$).

b) The means of the various samples of 36 students are described by the normal distribution shown in Fig. 6.12. The probability that the mean I.Q. score in a random sample of 36 students is greater than 112 can now be calculated as follows (see Fig. 6.13):

$$z = \frac{\bar{x} - \mu}{\sigma_{\bar{x}}} = \frac{112 - 110}{1.67} = 1.2.$$

Figure 6.11

Figure 6.12

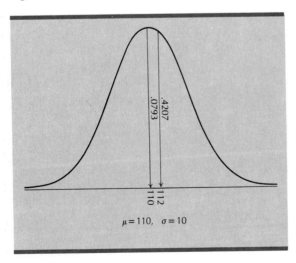

$\mu = 110$, $\sigma = 10$

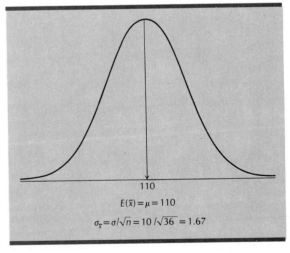

110

$E(\bar{x}) = \mu = 110$

$\sigma_{\bar{x}} = \sigma/\sqrt{n} = 10/\sqrt{36} = 1.67$

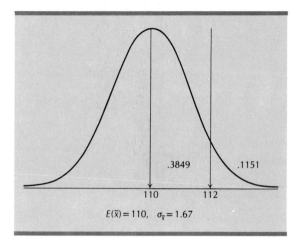

Figure 6.13

Therefore,

$$P(\bar{x} > 112) = .5000 - .3849$$
$$= .1151.$$

It may be useful to compare the two normal distributions used in parts a and b of this example. The normal distribution in a describes a real population consisting of the I.Q. scores of all students. The mean of this population is 110 and the standard deviation is 10 ($\mu = 110$, $\sigma = 10$). The normal distribution in b, on the other hand, describes a theoretical population consisting of the means of all possible random samples of 36 students that can be selected from the college. The mean of this population is also 110, but its standard deviation, called *standard error,* is only 1.67 [$E(\bar{x}) = 110$ and $\sigma_{\bar{x}} = 1.67$].

c) The means of the various samples of 100 students are described by the normal distribution shown in Fig. 6.14. The probability that the mean I.Q. score in a random sample of 100 students is greater than 112 can now be determined as follows (Fig. 6.15):

$$z = \frac{\bar{x} - \mu}{\sigma_{\bar{x}}} = \frac{112 - 110}{1} = 2.0.$$

Therefore,

$$P(\bar{x} > 112) = .5000 - .4772 = .0228.$$

We may finally note that the normal distribution in Fig. 6.15 also describes a theoretical population. This population, however, consists of the *means* of all possible random samples of 100 students that can be selected from this college. The mean of this population is 110 and its standard deviation is 1($E(\bar{x}) = 110$, $\sigma_{\bar{x}} = 1$).

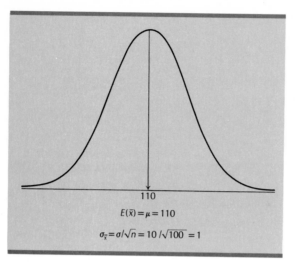

$$E(\bar{x}) = \mu = 110$$

$$\sigma_{\bar{x}} = \sigma/\sqrt{n} = 10/\sqrt{100} = 1$$

Figure 6.14

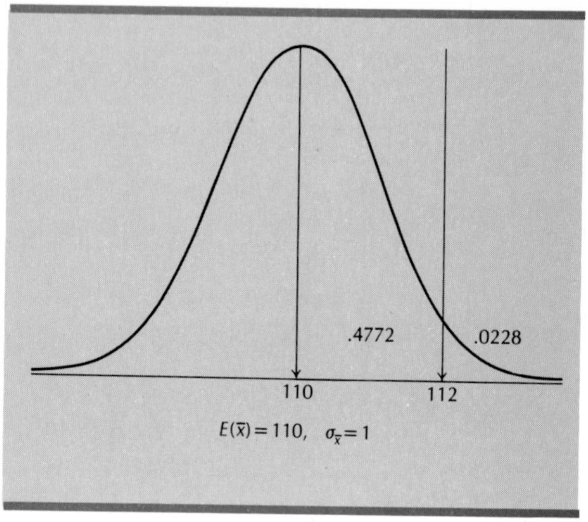

.4772   .0228

110   112

$$E(\bar{x}) = 110, \quad \sigma_{\bar{x}} = 1$$

Figure 6.15

EXERCISES

6.1 A population consists of children's ages in a family of four children, as follows:

$$X_1 = 2 \text{ years,}$$
$$X_2 = 4 \text{ years,}$$
$$X_3 = 6 \text{ years,}$$
$$X_4 = 8 \text{ years.}$$

a) Determine the mean μ and the standard deviation σ of the population.

b) List *all* possible samples of two children that can be selected from this family, and determine the arithmetic mean $\bar{x}$ for each sample.

c) Determine the mean $E(\bar{x})$ and the standard deviation $\sigma_{\bar{x}}$ of the six sample means.

d) Demonstrate that

$$\sigma_{\bar{x}} = \frac{\sigma}{\sqrt{n}} \sqrt{\frac{N-n}{N-1}}.$$

6.2 The mean height of all soldiers in the U.S. Army is 69 inches, with a standard deviation of 2 inches.

a) Assume that very many random samples of 100 soldiers are selected and the mean height is computed for each sample. Determine an interval within which 90% of all sample means are expected to fall.

b) Assume that very many random samples of 400 soldiers are selected and the mean height is computed for each sample. Determine an interval within which 90% of all sample means are expected to fall.

c) Explain why the interval in part a is larger than that in part b.

6.3 A radio manufacturer receives a shipment of 100,000 9-volt batteries each week from a supplier. The following sampling rule is used in deciding whether to accept or reject a shipment: Measure the life of 36 batteries from each shipment received. If the mean life of the sample is 50 hours or more, accept the shipment; otherwise reject the shipment.

a) What is the probability of the manufacturer's accepting a shipment that has a mean life of 49 hours with a standard deviation of 3 hours?

b) What is the probability of the manufacturer's rejecting a shipment that has a mean life of 50.5 hours with a standard deviation of 3 hours?

c) What is the probability of the manufacturer's rejecting a shipment that has a mean life of 50 hours? Of accepting such a shipment?

6.4 A certain brand of tire has a mean life of 21,000 miles, with a standard deviation of 800 miles.

a) Assuming that the lives of the tires are normally distributed, what is the probability that any one tire will last less than 20,900 miles?

b) What is the probability that the mean life of 64 tires is less than 20,900 miles?

c) What is the probability that the mean life of 256 tires is less than 20,900 miles?

6.5 A food processor packages coffee in one-pound cans, using the following sampling rule to decide whether to stop the filling process: Select a sample of 64 cans every hour. If the mean weight of the sample is less than a critical level L, stop and readjust the process. If the sample mean weight is equal to or greater than L, continue the operation. Determine the value of L so that the probability is only .05 of stopping a process that turns out, on average, 16.3-ounce cans with a standard deviation of .1 ounce ($\mu = 16.3$, $\sigma = .1$).

6.6 The life of a certain type of electronic tube is normally distributed, with $\mu = 50$ hours and $\sigma = 5$ hours.

a) What is the probability that a single tube will last longer than 55 hours?

b) What is the probability that the mean $\bar{x}$ of a simple random sample of 100 tubes will be greater than 51 hours?

c) The probability is .90 that the mean of a random sample of 100 tubes is between L_1 and L_2. Find L_1 and L_2 using symmetrical limits about μ.

6.7 Jack Shaft is considering opening a new health spa in Encino, California. Jack adopted the following decision rule in deciding about whether to open the new spa: Select a random sample of 50 families from Encino and determine the mean family income. If the sample mean is $80,000 or more, open the new spa. If the sample mean is less than $80,000, do not start the project.

a) What is the probability that Jack will open the spa, assuming that the average annual family income in Encino is $78,000 with a standard deviation of $10,000?

b) What is the probability of Jack's not opening the spa, assuming that the average annual family income in Encino is $82,500 with a standard deviation of $10,000?

6.8 The mean annual salary of all typists employed by Los Angeles County is $12,000 with a standard deviation of $1500 ($\mu = $12,000$, $\sigma = 1500).

a) Is it correct to state that 95% of all county typists earn somewhere between $9060 and $14,940? Explain fully.

b) Is it correct to state that the mean salary of a random sample of 225 county typists can be expected to fall somewhere between $11,804 and $12,196, with probability .95? Explain fully.

6.9 Savings accounts maintained at University Credit Union have a mean μ and a standard deviation of $1200. If a sample of 100 savings accounts is selected at random, what is the probability that the sample mean will be greater than the population mean by $180 or more?

6.10 A state's Department of Education is considering establishing a new grant program for college students. The following sampling rule is used in deciding whether to enact such a program: Select a random sample of 1000 college students and determine the mean annual college expense per student. If the sample mean $\overline{X}$ is $10,000 or more, establish the program. If $\overline{X}$ is less than $10,000, do not establish it.

a) What is the probability of not enacting the program, assuming that the actual average cost of attending college is $10,200 per year with a standard deviation of $3000?

b) What is the probability of enacting the program, assuming the actual average cost of college is $9,850 per year with a standard deviation of $3000?

6.11 A commercial bank uses the following sampling rule in deciding whether to open a branch in any new community: Select a random sample of 80 families from the community and determine their mean annual family income. If the sample mean is $10,000 or more, open a branch in the community. If the sample mean is less than $10,000, do not open a branch.

a) What is the probability that the bank will open a branch in a community where average annual family income in the community is $9500 with a standard deviation of $1500?

b) What is the probability that the bank will not open a branch in a community with an average family income of $10,300 and a standard deviation of $1500?

c) What is the probability that the bank will open a branch in a community with an average annual family income of $10,000?

ESTIMATING THE POPULATION MEAN FROM A SAMPLE

We have already stated that the population mean μ is rarely calculated using the complete population data; rather, it is estimated from a carefully selected sample. With a simple random sample we may use the sample mean $\bar{x}$ as an estimate of the population mean μ. For example, if the mean age of a random sample of several students selected from a college is 23.7 years ($\bar{x} = 23.7$ years), we may *estimate* the average student age in the entire college, μ, as 23.7 years. Denoting the estimated value of μ by the symbol $\hat{\mu}$, we can write

$$\hat{\mu} = \bar{x}$$
$$= 23.7 \text{ years.}$$

Thus we have estimated the population mean μ by a single number, which is $\bar{x}$. This type of estimate is called a *point estimate.*

A point estimate of μ is subject to sampling error, since the sample mean $\bar{x}$ may either overstate or understate the true value of μ. To measure the sampling error, we must consider some other relevant factors such as the sample size n and the sample standard deviation s. By incorporating this additional sample information, we will be able to estimate μ by a range or as an interval instead of just as a single point.

When the population mean μ is estimated as an interval, we can further apply some probability rules and theorems to assess the reliability of the estimate. In other words, we can now assign a certain degree of confidence to the estimation method when μ is estimated as an interval rather than as a single point.

Interval Estimate of μ from a Large Sample*

The central limit theorem states that when all possible random samples of size n are selected from a population with a mean μ and a standard deviation σ, then the sample means are approximately normally distributed. Furthermore, the

---

*A sample is regarded as large for our purposes when $n \geq 30$. Estimating the population mean from a small sample is discussed later in the chapter. Other rules of thumb are used to define "large" in other statistical situations.

various sample means have a mean equal to μ and a standard error equal to $\sigma\sqrt{n}$ (see Fig. 6.16).

Since the sample means are normally distributed, we expect 95% of the $\bar{x}$'s to fall in the range defined by

$$\mu \pm 1.96\sigma_{\bar{x}} \qquad \text{or} \qquad \mu \pm 1.96\,\frac{\sigma}{\sqrt{n}}.$$

See Fig. 6.17. We can also conclude that if only one sample of size n is selected, there is a .95 chance that its mean $\bar{x}$ falls within the interval $\mu \pm 1.96\sigma_{\bar{x}}$. The probability that it falls outside this interval is .05.

Now let us assume that a simple random sample of size n is selected and its arithmetic mean calculated. The interval $\bar{x} \pm 1.96\sigma_{\bar{x}}$ may or may not contain μ. If the mean of the sample happens to be from within any part of the shaded area under the normal curve shown in Fig. 6.18 (selected from within the interval $\bar{x} \pm 1.96\sigma_{\bar{x}}$), the interval $\bar{x} \pm 1.96\sigma_{\bar{x}}$ will certainly contain μ (see Figs. 6.18 and 6.19).

If, on the other hand, $\bar{x}$ happens to be from the unshaded area under the normal curve shown in Fig. 6.20 (selected from outside the range $\mu \pm 1.96\sigma_{\bar{x}}$), the interval $\bar{x} \pm 1.96\sigma_{\bar{x}}$ will not contain μ.

We may conclude that if all possible samples of size n are selected and the interval $\bar{x} \pm 1.96\sigma_{\bar{x}}$ is established for each sample, then .95 of all such intervals are expected to contain μ. The interval $\bar{x} \pm 1.96\sigma_{\bar{x}}$ or $\bar{x} \pm 1.96(\sigma/\sqrt{n})$ is called a .95 **confidence interval estimate of** μ.

To determine the above interval estimate of μ, we must know the standard deviation of the population, but the standard deviation of the population is not

Figure 6.16

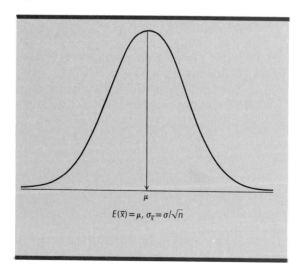

Figure 6.17

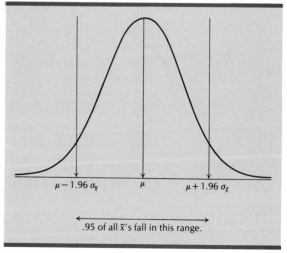

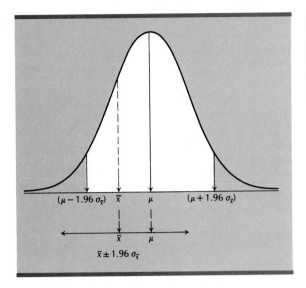

Figure 6.18

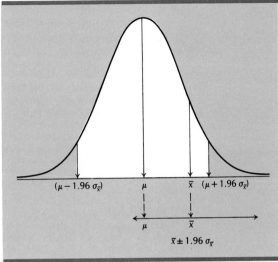

Figure 6.19

known. When the sample size is 30 or more, the standard deviation in the population, σ, may be approximated by the sample standard deviation s, and the exact confidence interval estimate $\bar{x} \pm 1.96(\sigma/\sqrt{n})$ is approximated by the interval $\bar{x} \pm 1.96(s/\sqrt{n})$. This interval is called an *approximate .95 confidence interval estimate* of μ. In the same manner, the range $\bar{x} \pm 2.58(s/\sqrt{n})$ is called

Figure 6.20

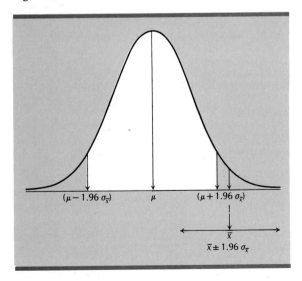

an *approximate .99 confidence interval estimate* of μ. In general, the range $\bar{x} \pm z(s/\sqrt{n})$ is an approximate confidence interval estimate of μ, where the value of z is determined by the degree of confidence required in estimating μ.

Example A random sample of 100 students from a college showed an average I.Q. score of 112 with a standard deviation of 10.

    a) Establish a .95 confidence interval estimate of the mean I.Q. score of all students attending the college.

    b) Establish a .99 confidence interval estimate of the mean I.Q. score of all students in the college.

Solution:

    a) The .95 confidence interval estimate of μ is

$$\bar{x} \pm 1.96 \frac{s}{\sqrt{n}} = 112 \pm 1.96 \frac{10}{\sqrt{100}}$$

$$= 112 \pm 1.96(1)$$

$$= 112 \pm 1.96,$$

between 110.04 and 113.96.

    b) The .99 confidence interval estimate of μ is

$$\bar{x} \pm 2.58 \frac{s}{\sqrt{n}} = 112 \pm 2.58 \frac{10}{\sqrt{100}}$$

$$= 112 \pm 2.58(1)$$

$$= 112 \pm 2.58,$$

or between 109.42 and 114.58.

Example A sample survey of 400 families in Cairo, Egypt, shows an average annual expenditure of $74 per family on shoes. The standard deviation of the sample is $40.

    a) Establish a .95 confidence interval estimate of the average annual expenditure on shoes by a family in Cairo.

    b) What can we conclude with .99 confidence about the maximum error in our estimate if the average annual expenditure on shoes by a family in Cairo is estimated as $74?

    c) With what degree of confidence can we assert that the average annual family expenditure on shoes in Cairo is between $71 and $77?

Solution:

a) The .95 confidence interval estimate of μ is

$$\bar{x} \pm 1.96 \frac{s}{\sqrt{n}} = 74 \pm 1.96 \frac{40}{\sqrt{400}}$$

$$= 74 \pm 1.96(2)$$

$$= 74 \pm 3.92,$$

Therefore, we can say with .95 confidence that the average annual family expenditure on shoes is somewhat between $70.08 and $77.92.

b) The .99 confidence interval estimate of μ is

$$\bar{x} \pm 2.58 \frac{s}{\sqrt{n}} = 74 \pm 2.58 \frac{40}{\sqrt{400}}$$

$$= 74 \pm 2.58(2)$$

$$= 74 \pm 5.16,$$

or between $68.84 and $79.16. Since we have added and subtracted the expression $2.58(40/\sqrt{400})$, or 5.16, from the sample mean, $74, to establish a .99 confidence interval estimate of μ, we can assert with a probabilty of .99 that our maximum error is $5.16 if μ is estimated as $74. In general, the maximum expected error in a point sample estimate of μ is determined by the expression $z(s/\sqrt{n})$.

c) If μ is estimated to be between $71 and $77, then we must have added and subtracted $3 from the sample mean, $74, to obtain this interval estimate of μ. In other words, our interval estimate was obtained as follows:

$$\bar{x} \pm z \frac{s}{\sqrt{n}} = 74 \pm 3.$$

Therefore,

$$z \frac{s}{\sqrt{n}} = 3$$

$$z \frac{40}{\sqrt{400}} = 3$$

$$z(2) = 3$$

$$z = 1.5.$$

Using the area under the normal curve in Table A, we conclude that the range $71 to $77 is the .8664 confidence interval estimate of μ (see Fig. 6.21).

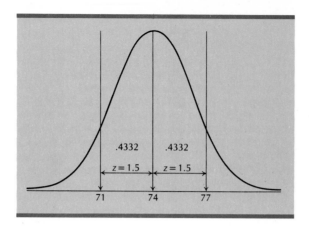

Figure 6.21

Example   A survey was conducted in 1984 to determine the average hourly earnings of sales clerks employed by a department store in metropolitan Detroit. A simple random sample of 225 clerks was selected and the following information obtained:

$$x = \text{Hourly wage rate earned by a female sales clerk,}$$
$$\Sigma x = \$450.00,$$
$$\Sigma(x - \bar{x})^2 = \$2016.00.$$

What is the .99 confidence interval estimate of the average hourly wage rate?

Solution:

Step 1.

$$\bar{x} = \frac{\Sigma x}{n}$$

$$= \frac{\$450.00}{225}$$

$$= \$2.00 \text{ (sample mean).}$$

Step 2.

$$s = \sqrt{\frac{\Sigma(x - \bar{x})^2}{n - 1}}$$

$$= \sqrt{\frac{2016.00}{224}}$$

$$= \sqrt{9.00} = 3.00 \text{ (standard deviation of the sample).}$$

Step 3.

$$\bar{x} \pm 2.58 \frac{s}{\sqrt{n}} = 2.00 \pm 2.58 \frac{3.00}{\sqrt{225}}$$

$$= 2.00 \pm 2.58 \left(\frac{3.00}{15}\right)$$

$$= 2.00 \pm 2.58(.20) = 2.00 \pm .52.$$

Thus the average hourly earnings of sales clerks is estimated to be between $1.48 and $2.52.

Example A department store has 10,000 customer charge accounts. To estimate the total amount owed by its customers, it selected a random sample of 36 charge accounts, which showed a mean amount of $150 per account and a standard deviation of $60 ($\bar{x} = 150$, $s = 60$). Establish a .95 confidence interval estimate of the *total amount* owed by customers to the department store.

Solution: This problem is solved in two steps. In the first step we will establish a .95 confidence interval estimate of the average amount owed per customer (a .95 confidence interval estimate of μ). In the second step we will multiply the range established for μ by the number of customers to obtain a range for the total amount owed by customers.

Step 1. The .95 confidence interval estimate of μ is

$$\bar{x} \pm 1.96 \left(\frac{s}{\sqrt{n}}\right) = 150 \pm 1.96 \left(\frac{60}{\sqrt{36}}\right)$$

$$= 150 \pm 1.96\,(10)$$

$$= 150 \pm 19.60,$$

or between $130.40 and $169.60. This is a 0.95 confidence-interval estimate of the average amount owed per customer.

Step 2. Since the department store has 10,000 customers, the .95 confidence interval estimate for the total amount owed by customers can be obtained as

$$10,000\,(130.40 \le \mu \le 169.60),$$

or between $1,304,000 and $1,696.000.

It may be useful now to summarize the solution to our problem. A .95 confidence interval estimate of the total amount owed by customers to the department store can be determined as

$$N\left(\bar{x} \pm z\left(\frac{s}{\sqrt{n}}\right)\right) = 10,000\left(150 \pm 1.96 \frac{60}{\sqrt{36}}\right),$$

or between $1,304,000 and $1,696,000.

Determining Sample Size

The question of sample size must be resolved before a sample is selected. How large should the sample be? Generally speaking, the sample size is determined by the desired degree of accuracy required in estimating the population mean from a sample.

There are two aspects to the degree of accuracy required: (1) the magnitude of the maximum allowable error; (2) the degree of confidence that the error in the estimate will not exceed the maximum allowable error.

If we are asked by the Austin city council to estimate the average annual family earnings in Austin to within $500, the maximum allowable error is $500. Regardless of the size of the sample selected, however, there is always a chance that the error in our estimate will exceed $500. The larger the sample size, the smaller the risk that the allowable error will be exceeded or the greater the confidence that our estimate will be within the allowable error. If the city council states that there should be .95 confidence that the error in the estimate will not exceed $500, the two aspects of accuracy become the following:

1. The maximum allowable error, denoted by e, is $500.

2. The degree of confidence that the maximum allowable error will not be *exceeded* is .95.

Having determined the two accuracy requirements of our estimate, we must determine the sample size that satisfies the requirements. Specifically, we must have a sample size n that will ensure that $1.96\sigma_{\bar{x}} = \$500$. (See Fig. 6.22.)

Figure 6.22

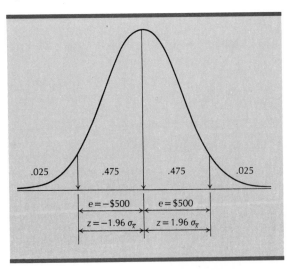

In general, the sample size is manipulated until

$$z\sigma_{\bar{x}} = e,$$

where z is determined by the degree of confidence. Since

$$\sigma_{\bar{x}} = \sigma/\sqrt{n},$$

it follows that

$$z\frac{\sigma}{\sqrt{n}} = e,$$

or

$$\sqrt{n} = \frac{z\sigma}{e}$$

$$n = \frac{z^2\sigma^2}{e^2}.$$

Thus the sample size is determined by e, z, and σ, where e is equal to the maximum allowable error, z is determined by the degree of confidence, and σ is the standard deviation in the population whose mean we are trying to estimate.

The value of z is determined by the degree of confidence. Thus if the degree of confidence is .95, z is equal to 1.96. If it is required that the degree of confidence be .99, z is equal to 2.58. The value of z is 1.64 if the degree of confidence is .90. All these values are obtained from the area under the normal curve.

In addition to e and z, the standard deviation, σ, of the population from which the sample is selected must be known. We can obtain σ from previous surveys or census records if such records exist. Otherwise, we may have to select a preliminary sample to estimate the standard deviation in the population.

It is interesting to note that as the value of σ (the variability of the population we are sampling) increases, we must increase the size of the sample. The conclusion is logical indeed: for example, if each family in Austin had the same annual income, a sample of size 1, would be sufficient; but the greater the disparity in family earnings, the larger the required sample size.

To summarize: The sample size must be increased as

1. the allowable error becomes smaller,
2. the degree of confidence increases, and
3. the variability in the population from which the sample is chosen increases.

Example What sample size is required to estimate the average family income in Austin if it is specified that there be .95 confidence that the error in the estimate will not exceed $500? The 1980 census shows an average family income of $15,000 with a standard deviation of $4000.

Solution: Let

$$e = 500,$$

$$z = 1.96$$

$$\sigma = \$4000.$$

$$n = \frac{z^2\sigma^2}{e^2} \quad \text{or} \quad n = \frac{(1.96)^2(4000)^2}{(500)^2},$$

so

$$n = 245.8, \quad \text{or} \quad 246 \text{ families.}$$

Estimating μ from a Small Sample

We have already learned that when the sample size is 30 or more, the confidence interval estimate of the population mean $\bar{x} \pm z(\sigma/\sqrt{n})$, is approximated by the interval $\bar{x} \pm z(s/\sqrt{n})$. But when the sample size is small, say 10, such an approximation is no longer appropriate. Consequently, we must develop an alternative approach for estimating the population mean from a small sample.

Let us begin this alternative approach by assuming that there is a normally distributed population with a mean of μ and that the standard deviation of this population is unknown. Let us further assume that all possible simple random samples of size n are selected from this population and the mean $\bar{x}$ and the standard deviation s of each of these samples are computed. If the variable t, where

$$t = \frac{\bar{x} - \mu}{s/\sqrt{n}},$$

is computed for each of these samples, then according to statistical theory the various values of t are distributed according to what is called the **Student *t*-distribution.** A Student *t*-distribution and a standard normal distribution are shown in Fig. 6.23 (in a standard normal distribution, $\mu = 0$ and $\sigma = 1$).

In studying the *t*-distribution, we must recognize that there are not only one but several *t*-distributions. Each is associated with the number of **degrees of freedom** (df), which in this case is equal to the sample size minus 1.

Thus the distribution of the *t*-values of samples of size 6 can be described by a *t*-distribution of 5 degrees of freedom. Similarly, a *t*-distribution of 10 degrees of freedom describes the distribution of the *t*-values of samples of size 11. Two distinct *t*-distributions (one with 5 degrees of freedom and the other with 10 degrees of freedom), together with the normal distribution, are shown in Fig. 6.24. As you can see in the figure, a t-distribution, like the normal distribution, is bell-shaped and symmetrical. Unlike the normal distribution, a t-distribution has a greater dispersion, which becomes larger as the number of degrees of freedom decreases.

Information concerning t-distributions can be obtained from Table E. Each row in Table E corresponds to one particular t-distribution. The fifth row, for example, corresponds to a t-distribution with 5 degrees of freedom. Similarly, the tenth row deals with a t-distribution having 10 degrees of freedom. We will confine our discussion to the t-distribution with 5 degrees of freedom to explain the various values recorded in that row. The value 2.571, located in the column labeled $t_{.025}$, indicates that 2.5% of the area under this particular t-curve is to the right of $+2.571$ and 2.5% of the area is to the left of -2.571 (see Fig. 6.25). Consequently, 95% of the area under this t-curve is enclosed in the interval ± 2.571; the probability is .95 that the variable t is in the interval ± 2.571.

Similarly, the value 4.032, located in the column labeled $t_{.005}$, indicates that .005 of the area under the t-curve is to the right of $+4.032$ and to the left of -4.032 (see Fig. 6.26). Consequently, .99 of the area under the t-curve is enclosed in the interval ± 4.032; the probability is .99 that the variable t is in the interval ± 4.032.

Other entries in Table E can be interpreted in a similar fashion. The value

Figure 6.23

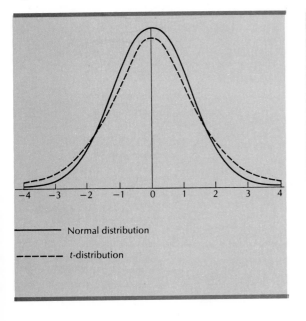

Figure 6.24

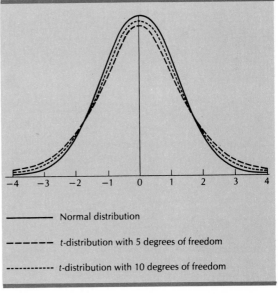

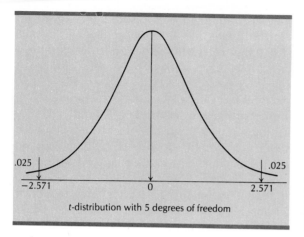

Figure 6.25   **Figure 6.26**

1.812, for example, located in the tenth row and in the column labeled $t_{.050}$, indicates that in a t-distribution with 10 degrees of freedom 5% of the area under the t-curve is to the right of $+1.812$ and to the left of -1.812. Consequently, 90% of the area under the t-curve is enclosed in the interval ± 1.812; the probability is .90 that the variable t is in the interval ± 1.812.

Again confining our discussion to a t-distribution with 5 degrees of freedom, we find from Table E that 95% of the area under this particular t-curve is in the interval ± 2.571; the probability is .95 that

$$-2.571 \le t \le +2.571.$$

Since

$$t = \frac{\bar{x} - \mu}{s/\sqrt{n}},$$

the inequality becomes

$$-2.571 \le \frac{\bar{x} - \mu}{s/\sqrt{n}} \le +2.571,$$

which, finally, can be written as

$$\bar{x} - 2.571 \frac{s}{\sqrt{n}} \le \mu \le \bar{x} + 2.571 \frac{s}{\sqrt{n}}.$$

Thus the probability is .95 that μ is in the interval $\bar{x} \pm 2.571(s/\sqrt{n})$.

We can therefore state that when the sample size is 6 (df = 5), there is .95 confidence that μ is in the interval

$$\bar{x} \pm 2.571 \frac{s}{\sqrt{n}}.$$

Similarly, we can show that when the sample size is 6, there is .99 confidence that μ is in the interval

$$\bar{x} \pm t_{.005} \frac{s}{\sqrt{n}}, \quad \text{or} \quad \bar{x} \pm 4.032 \frac{s}{\sqrt{n}}.$$

To summarize, we can construct a confidence interval estimate of the population mean based on a small sample by choosing the appropriate value of t in the formula $\bar{x} \pm t(s/\sqrt{n})$. The appropriate value of t is determined by the number of degrees of freedom ($df = n - 1$) and by the degree of confidence required in estimating the population mean. As an illustration, several confidence interval estimates of the population mean based on a random sample of size 23 ($df = 22$) are shown below.

$$\bar{x} \pm t_{.050} \frac{s}{\sqrt{n}} \text{ (.90 confidence interval estimate of } \mu); \bar{x} \pm 1.717 \frac{s}{\sqrt{n}}$$

$$\bar{x} \pm t_{.025} \frac{s}{\sqrt{n}} \text{ (.95 confidence interval estimate of } \mu); \bar{x} \pm 2.074 \frac{s}{\sqrt{n}}$$

$$\bar{x} \pm t_{.005} \frac{s}{\sqrt{n}} \text{ (.99 confidence interval estimate of } \mu); \bar{x} \pm 2.819 \frac{s}{\sqrt{n}}$$

Example   Nine cars of the same model were driven in an identical manner, using one gallon of unleaded gasoline. The mean distance traveled by the cars was 19 miles, with a standard deviation of 2.7 miles. Establish a .95 confidence interval estimate of the average mileage per gallon for this car model.

Solution:

Step 1.   Determine the number of degrees of freedom:

$$df = n - 1$$
$$= 8.$$

Step 2.   Determine the appropriate value of t: With 8 degrees of freedom and a desired .95 confidence interval estimate of μ, the appropriate value of t is located at the intersection of row 8 and the column labeled $t_{.025}$ in Table E. This t-value is 2.306.

Step 3.   Construct the interval estimate of μ:

$$\bar{x} \pm t_{.025} \frac{s}{\sqrt{n}} = 19 \pm 2.306 \frac{2.7}{\sqrt{9}}$$
$$= 19 \pm (2.306)(.9)$$
$$= 19 \pm 2.0754.$$

The interval estimate is between 16.9246 and 21.0754 miles.

Example   The nicotine contents of five cigarettes of a certain brand, measured in milligrams, are 21, 19, 23, 19, 23. Establish a .99 confidence interval estimate of the average nicotine content of this brand of cigarettes.

Solution:

Step 1.   Determine the mean of the sample.

$$\bar{x} = \frac{21 + 19 + 23 + 19 + 23}{5} = \frac{105}{5} = 21 \text{ milligrams}$$

Step 2.   Determine the standard deviation of the sample.

x	$(x - \bar{x})$	$(x - \bar{x})^2$
21	0	0
19	-2	4
23	$+2$	4
19	-2	4
23	$+2$	4
		$\sum(x - \bar{x})^2 = 16$

$$s = \sqrt{\frac{\sum(x - \bar{x})^2}{n - 1}} = \sqrt{\frac{16}{5 - 1}}$$

$$= 2 \text{ milligrams}$$

Step 3.   Determine the number of degrees of freedom.

$$df = n - 1 = 5 - 1 = 4$$

Step 4.   Construct the .99 confidence interval estimate of μ:

$$\bar{x} \pm t_{.005} \frac{s}{\sqrt{n}} = 21 \pm 4.604 \frac{2}{\sqrt{5}}$$

$$= 21 \pm 4.604(.8944)$$

$$= 21 \pm 4.1178.$$

The interval is between 16.8822 and 25.1178.

Before we conclude this chapter, it is useful to compare the two methods used in estimating the population mean for small versus large samples. In the small-sample method, the range

$$\bar{x} \pm t \frac{s}{\sqrt{n}}$$

is an *exact* confidence interval estimate of the population mean. In the large-sample method, the range

$$\bar{x} \pm z \frac{s}{\sqrt{n}}$$

is only an approximate confidence interval estimate of the population mean. If this is the case, then why not use the small-sample method all the time?

In the small-sample method, the range $\bar{x} \pm t(s/\sqrt{n})$ is an exact confidence interval estimate of the population mean only when such a population is *normally distributed.* If a population is not normally distributed, the use of the small sample cannot be justified.

In comparison, the large-sample method of estimating the population mean does not require any assumption about the nature of the population distribution. The only requirement is that the sample standard deviation s be a good approximation of the population standard deviation σ. Thus we conclude that the small-sample method of estimating the population mean should not supplant the large-sample method unless the assumption of normality of the population is justified.

EXERCISES

6.12 A random sample of 30 members was selected from the faculty of a large university to estimate the average length of teaching experience of faculty members. The records of teaching experience (measured in years) for the 30 members are

3,	4,	4,	6,	2,	3,	4,	6,	2,	4,
6,	4,	3,	4,	4,	7,	3,	4,	5,	6,
1,	6,	4,	5,	4,	3,	2,	4,	3,	4.

Using the data, establish a .99 confidence interval estimate of the average length of teaching experience of faculty members.

6.13 The management of a manufacturing concern wishes to determine the average time required to complete a certain manual operation. There should be .95 confidence that the error in the estimate will not exceed 2 minutes.

a) What sample size is required if the standard deviation of the time needed to complete the manual operation is estimated by a time and motion study expert as 10 minutes?

b) What sample size is required if the standard deviation of the time needed to complete the manual operation is estimated by a time and motion study expert as 16 minutes?

c) Explain intuitively (without referring to the formula) why the required sample size is larger in b than in a.

6.14   The nicotine content of 36 cigarettes of a certain brand is measured, and the results are summarized below.

$$x = \text{nicotine content in milligrams}$$
$$\Sigma x = 756 \text{ milligrams}$$
$$\Sigma(x - \bar{x})^2 = 315 \text{ milligrams}$$

Establish a .95 confidence interval estimate of the average nicotine content of this brand of cigarettes.

6.15   The Miser Saving and Loan Association wishes to determine the mean amount of its customers' savings accounts. The standard deviation of all savings accounts is estimated by the manager as $400.

a) What sample size is required to ensure with .95 confidence that the error in the estimate will not exceed $20?

b) What sample size is required to ensure with .95 confidence that the error in the estimate will not exceed $40?

c) Compare the sample size and the maximum allowable error in a and b. What happens to the sample size when the maximum allowable error is doubled?

6.16.   The systolic blood pressure of 100 patients taking 20 milligrams of a certain drug exhibits a mean increase of 18 with a standard deviation of 6.

a) Establish a .99 confidence interval estimate of the increase in blood pressure caused by 20 milligrams of this drug.

b) What can we assert with probability .95 about the maximum error in our estimate if the average increase in blood pressure is estimated as 18?

6.17   A construction firm wishes to estimate the average shearing strength of steel bars used in the construction of several high-rise apartment buildings. What sample size is required to ensure that there will be only a .001 risk of an error of 10 pounds or more in the estimate? The standard deviation of the sheering strength of this type of steel bar is estimated as 50 pounds.

6.18   Forty-nine pigs were fed a special feed for three months. The mean weight gain in these three months was 120 pounds, with a standard deviation of 14 pounds. With what degree of confidence can we assert that this feed will cause an average weight gain of 118.5 to 121.5 pounds in a period of three months?

6.19   Construct a .98 confidence interval estimate of the population mean based on each of the following samples.

a) $n = 9$, $\bar{x} = 40$, $s = 6$

b) $n = 16$, $\bar{x} = 20$, $s = 2$

c) $n = 25$, $\bar{x} = 70$, $s = 10$

6.20 A random sample of 64 accounts receivable was selected from a ledger containing 10,000 accounts. The sample showed a mean amount of $120 per account with a standard deviation of $40.

a) Establish a .90 confidence interval estimate of the average account receivable in the ledger.

b) What can we assert with a probability of .95 about the maximum error in our estimate if the average account receivable in the ledger is estimated as $120?

6.21 A sample of five jars of instant coffee is selected from a production process. The contents of these jars, measured in ounces, are as follows: 10.5, 10.7, 10.3, 10.6, and 10.4. Establish a .95 confidence interval estimate of the average net weight of jars turned out by this production process.

6.22 To estimate the total amount of customers' demand deposits, a commercial bank selected a random sample of 400 demand deposit accounts. The sample showed a mean amount of $500 per account and a standard deviation of $100. Assuming that the bank has 12,000 demand deposit accounts, establish a .99 confidence interval estimate of the aggregate amount of demand deposits held by the bank.

6.23 A random sample of 100 families was selected from a community of 5000 families. The sample showed an average annual family income of $15,000 with a standard deviation of $2000. Establish a .90 confidence interval estimate of aggregate annual income in that community.

6.24 A random sample of 100 families in Boston shows an average family income of $12,000, with a standard deviation of $4000.

a) Establish a .99 confidence interval estimate of the average family income in Boston.

b) With what degree of confidence can we assert that average family income in Boston is between $11,400 and $12,600?

6.25 A random sample of five batteries of a certain brand is tested to determine the average life. The lives of the batteries tested, measured in hours, are 52, 48, 50, 44, 56. Establish a .95 confidence interval estimate of the average battery life.

6.26 Quality Food employs 10,000 sales representatives who call on retail grocery outlets to merchandise the company's products. Sharon Hill, vice-president of sales, is interested in determining the average number of calls sales representatives make per retail customer during the month. Ms. Hill examined the records of 50 randomly selected sales representatives. The sample showed an average of 12 calls per customer per month, with a standard deviation of 4.

a) Establish a .95 confidence interval estimate of the average number of sales calls per customer per month for all sales representatives of Quality Food.

b) With what degree of confidence can we assert that the average is between 11 and 13 calls?

6.27 A random sample of 120 students is selected from the 22,000 students attending CSUN. The sample shows a mean expenditure of $220 per student per year on textbooks and supplies, with a standard deviation of $40. Establish a .99 confidence interval estimate of the total amount spent by CSUN students on textbooks and school supplies.

6.28 Edsel E. Lemons, a used-car dealer, wishes to estimate his average weekly sales for used cars. A random sample of five weeks shows the following number of cars sold: 50, 47, 52, 56, 45. Establish a .90 confidence interval estimate of Lemon's average weekly sales.

6.29 A random sample of 100 savings accounts maintained at American Savings and Loan Association shows a mean balance of $25,000 per account, with a standard deviation of $12,000.

a) With what degree of confidence can we assert that the mean balance of *all* savings accounts maintained at American Savings is between $21,904 and $28,096?

b) Can we assert that 95% of all savings accounts maintained at American Savings have a balance between $22,648 and $27,352?

6.30 A company ledger contains 10,000 accounts receivable. A simple random sample of 49 accounts is selected from the ledger. The sample shows a mean of $1500 per account, with a standard deviation of $580.

a) Establish a .95 confidence interval estimate of the company's *total* accounts receivable.

b) Can we assert that 99% of all accounts receivable in the ledger are between $1,286.23 and $1,713.77? Explain fully.

KEY TERMS ▬▬▬▬▬▬▬▬▬▬▬▬▬▬▬▬▬▬▬▬▬▬▬▬▬▬▬▬▬▬▬▬▬▬▬▬

standard error of the mean $(\sigma_{\bar{x}})$ The standard deviation of the distribution of $\bar{x}$. The standard error of the mean tells us how far a typical sample $\bar{x}$ will be from the population mean μ.

finite population correction The factor $\sqrt{(N-n)/(N-1)}$ used in computing the standard error of the mean in sampling without replacement from a finite population.

confidence interval estimate An interval estimate of a population parameter. The level of confidence is the probability that a sample will yield an interval containing the true value of the parameter.

Student _t_-distribution   The distribution of $(\bar{x} - \mu)/(s/\sqrt{n})$ when the data are normally distributed. The _t_-distribution is most often used for small samples when σ is unknown.

degrees of freedom   The parameter of the _t_-distribution. The number of degrees of freedom for estimating the mean from a sample of size n is $n - 1$.

SUMMARY OF FORMULAS

mean of $\bar{x}$	$E(\bar{x}) = \mu$
standard error of the mean (sampling without replacement)	$\sigma_{\bar{x}} = \dfrac{\sigma}{\sqrt{n}} \sqrt{\dfrac{N - n}{N - 1}}$
finite population correction	$\sqrt{(N - n)/(N - 1)}$
standard error of the mean (n/N is small or sampling with replacement)	$\sigma_{\bar{x}} = \dfrac{\sigma}{\sqrt{n}}$
approximate confidence interval for μ (large n, σ unknown)	$\bar{x} \pm z\hat{\sigma}_{\bar{x}} = \bar{x} \pm z\dfrac{s}{\sqrt{n}}$
sample size needed	$n = \dfrac{z^2\sigma^2}{e^2}$
confidence interval for μ (normal data, σ unknown)	$\bar{x} \pm t\dfrac{s}{\sqrt{n}}$

TESTING HYPOTHESES ABOUT THE POPULATION MEAN

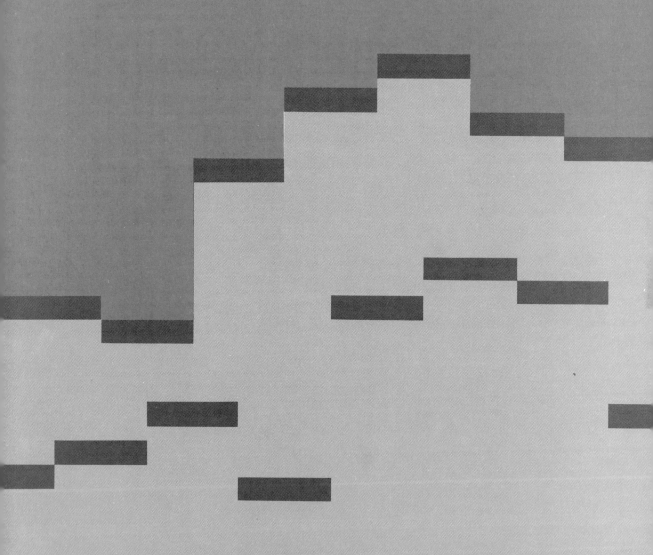

7

Statistical inference is the central theme in statistics. We make inferences about an entire population based on sample data. Inferences about a population are classified into two types: estimating the population parameter and testing hypotheses about parameters. Chapter 6 dealt with estimating the parameter μ. This chapter deals with testing hypotheses about a single population mean.

Chapter 6 dealt with the problem of estimating the population mean, μ. Specifically, μ is unknown, and a random sample is selected from the population and used to provide an estimate of μ.

In some other problems, a claim may have been made about the value of μ. A tire manufacturer may claim that the average life of its radial tires is 50,000 miles ($\mu = 50,000$). The claim, of course, can be either true or false. In the same manner, a supermarket may claim that its lean hamburger contains, on average, 10% fat ($\mu = .10$). Once again, the claim can be either true or false.

Pursuing the case of the supermarket claim, let us assume that a government consumer protection agency receives several complaints that the supermarket hamburger contains more than 10% fat. The claim is that $\mu = .10$; the counterclaim is that $\mu > .10$. To test the validity of the supermarket claim that $\mu = .10$, the agency selects several hamburger packages and measures the fat content of each package. If the sample result is inconsistent with the supermarket claim (if the sample average fat content is substantially more than 10%), the supermarket claim is rejected and the agency concludes that the supermarket has understated the fat content of its hamburger. On the other hand, if the sample result is consistent with the supermarket claim (if the sample average fat content is "reasonably close" to 10%), then the supermarket claim is not rejected and the agency concludes that the supermarket is not guilty of false labeling.

NULL HYPOTHESIS AND ALTERNATIVE HYPOTHESIS

In statistical terminology, the supermarket case can be restated as follows: The supermarket claim that its hamburger contains 10% fat ($\mu = .10$) is a hypothesis that can be either true or false. This hypothesis is called the **null hypothesis,** denoted by H_0. The consumers' counterclaim that the average fat content is greater than 10% ($\mu > .10$) is called the **alternative hypothesis,** denoted by H_1. We must now clearly note that both hypotheses are concerned with the value of the population parameter μ. Stated rigorously, our two hypotheses about the population mean are

$$H_0: \quad \mu = .10,$$

$$H_1: \quad \mu > .10.$$

To test the null hypothesis, H_0, which states that the mean of the population is .10 ($\mu = .10$), against the alternative hypothesis, which states that the mean of the population is greater than .10 ($\mu > .10$), a sample is selected from the population. Depending on the findings in the sample, the investigator either rejects the null hypothesis or does not reject it. The null hypothesis is rejected if the sample findings are inconsistent with it. The null hypothesis is not rejected if the sample findings do not contradict it.

Such a procedure is analogous to a court trial. Under the U.S. legal system, an accused individual is assumed to be innocent, and it is the duty of the prosecutor to prove otherwise. The prosecutor must present enough evidence to prove, beyond a reasonable doubt, that the accused is guilty. Similarly, in testing a claim (a null hypothesis), it is assumed that the null hypothesis is true and the sample selected must provide strong and convincing evidence to prove that the null hypothesis is false before it is rejected.

We have so far described the notion of hypothesis testing in general. Now we discuss the exact procedure using several illustrative examples.

Example   A manufacturer of a certain brand of 9-volt batteries claims that the average life of the battery is 50 hours, with a standard deviation of 5 hours. A simple random sample of 100 batteries shows an average life of 40 hours. What do you conclude about the manufacturer's claim?

Solution: If the manufacturer's claim is true, and an infinite number of samples of size 100 are selected from the population, then we expect all possible $\bar{x}$'s to be normally distributed and to have a mean of 50 hours and a standard error of $5/\sqrt{100}$ or .5 hour (see Fig. 7.1).

To evaluate the manufacturer's claim, let us calculate the probability that any one sample mean is 40 or fewer hours:

$$Z = \frac{\bar{x} - \mu}{\sigma_{\bar{x}}}$$

$$= \frac{40 - 50}{.5} = -20.$$

Therefore, $P(\bar{x} \le 40)$ is null and the manufacturer's claim is rejected.

Figure 7.1

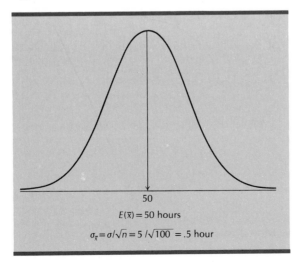

50

$E(\bar{x}) = 50$ hours

$\sigma_{\bar{x}} = \sigma/\sqrt{n} = 5/\sqrt{100} = .5$ hour

Example Suppose that the sample in the previous example has an average life of 49 hours. Do you still reject the manufacturer's claim?

To evaluate the claim, let us calculate the probability of any one sample mean being 49 or fewer hours:

$$z = \frac{\overline{x} - \mu}{\sigma_{\overline{x}}}$$

$$= \frac{49 - 50}{.5} = -2.0.$$

Therefore,

$$P(\overline{x} \le 49) = .5000 - .4772$$
$$= .0228.$$

If the manufacturer's claim is true, there is a probability of only .0228 that $\overline{x}$ will be 49 or fewer just by chance. Are we willing to reject the claim when $\overline{x} = 49$? The answer to this question depends on the consequences of rejecting the claim when it is true.

Example A manufacturer of synthetic fiber advertises that its fiber has an average tensile strength of 30 pounds. A simple random sample of 100 fibers is tested for breaking strength. It shows an average of 28 pounds and a standard deviation of 12 pounds. Test the manufacturer's claim against the hypothesis that the average tensile strength of the fiber is less than 30 pounds.

Solution: If the manufacturer's claim is true, and an infinite number of samples of 100 fibers are selected from its product, then the various sample means $\overline{x}$ are normally distributed and have an average of 30 pounds and a standard error of $\sigma/\sqrt{100}$. But since the standard deviation in the population, σ, is not known, we use the standard deviation of the sample s, as an estimate of σ. The estimated standard error of the mean, denoted by $\hat{\sigma}_{\overline{x}}$, will be $s/\sqrt{n}$. (This is in contrast to the true standard error of the mean, which is $\sigma/\sqrt{n}$.) See Fig. 7.2.

To test the manufacturer's claim, let us calculate the probability that a sample mean of 100 fibers will be 28 pounds or less.

$$z = \frac{\overline{x} - \mu}{\hat{\sigma}_{\overline{x}}}$$

$$= \frac{28 - 30}{1.2} = 1.67.$$

Therefore,

$$P(\overline{x} \le 28) = .5000 - .4525$$
$$= .0475.$$

If the manufacturer's claim is true, there is a probability of only .0475 that $\overline{x}$ will be 28 pounds or less just by chance.

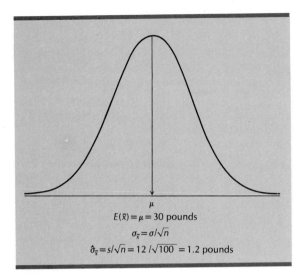

$E(\bar{x}) = \mu = 30$ pounds

$\sigma_{\bar{x}} = \sigma/\sqrt{n}$

$\hat{\sigma}_{\bar{x}} = s/\sqrt{n} = 12/\sqrt{100} = 1.2$ pounds

Figure 7.2

The preceding example is a typical problem in testing a hypothesis about a population. In our case, the hypothesis is made by the manufacturer who claims that the average tensile strength μ of all its fibers is 30 pounds. The hypothesis is tested against a hypothesis that states that μ is less than 30 pounds. In the fiber problem, we find that the two hypotheses are

H_0: $\mu = 30$ pounds (null hypothesis),

H_1: $\mu < 30$ pounds (alternative hypothesis).

If the null hypothesis is not rejected, because the sample findings do not contradict it, statisticians prefer to say they reserve judgment (rather than saying they accept the null hypothesis). They mean by "reserving judgment" that, on the basis of the sample information, they do not have enough evidence to reject the null hypothesis. For all practical purposes, however, statisticians reserving judgment in a way accept the null hypothesis without really saying so and without commitment.

If the null hypothesis is rejected, there is always a risk that a true hypothesis is being rejected. The risk of rejecting the null hypothesis when it is true is called the α-risk, and the resulting error is called a type I error. The symbol α represents the probability of the type I error. (This is discussed more fully later in the chapter.)

How great a risk should statisticians take in rejecting a true hypothesis? Generally, the greater the consequence of rejecting the null hypothesis when it is true, the smaller the risk they should take. Statisticians have set arbitrary limits of .05 or .01. Each limit is called a **level of significance.**

The .05 level of significance is used whenever it is desired that the α-risk (the risk of rejecting the null hypothesis when it is true) not exceed .05. The .01 level of significance is used when the risk must not exceed .01.

Returning to the fiber problem, we have found that the probability of obtaining a sample mean of 28 pounds or less is only .0475 if the null hypothesis ($\mu = 30$) is true. Hence if we decide to reject the null hypothesis whenever $\bar{x}$ is 28 or less, there is a .0475 risk that when the null hypothesis is true we will reject it by accident.

In this example, the decision of whether to reject the null hypothesis or to reserve judgment depends on the maximum risk we are willing to take. Using the .05 level of significance, we reject the null hypothesis since the maximum allowable risk is .05 and the actual risk is .0475. Using the .01 level of significance, we must reserve judgment (maximum allowable risk is .01 and actual risk is .0475).

Example   In justifying their demand for higher wages, the employees in the shipping department of a large mail order house report that, on average, the department completes an order in 13 minutes. As a general manager for this firm, what can you conclude if a sample of 400 orders shows an average completion time of 14 minutes, with a standard deviation of 10 minutes? Use a .05 level of significance.

Solution: Denoting the null hypothesis by H_0, and the alternative hypothesis by H_1, we can summarize the problem as follows:

$$H_0: \quad \mu = 13 \text{ minutes},$$

$$H_1: \quad \mu > 13 \text{ minutes},$$

$$\text{Level of significance} = .05.$$

Note that in this example the null hypothesis is tested against an alternative hypothesis that states that the average completion time is *greater than* 13 minutes. This is because management feels that the demand for a wage increase is unjustified if the true mean is greater than 13 minutes.

To test the null hypothesis, let us calculate the probability of obtaining a sample mean of 14 minutes or more from a population for which the true mean is 13 minutes (see Fig. 7.3).

$$
\begin{aligned}
z &= \frac{\bar{x} - \mu}{\hat{\sigma}_{\bar{x}}} \\
&= \frac{\bar{x} - \mu}{s/\sqrt{n}} \\
&= \frac{14 - 13}{10/\sqrt{400}} = \frac{1}{.5} = 2.0.
\end{aligned}
$$

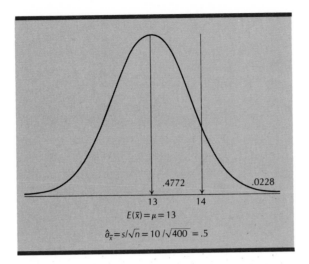

Figure 7.3

Therefore,

$$P(\bar{x} \geq 14) = .5000 - .4772$$
$$= .0228.$$

Using the .05 level of significance, we reject the null hypothesis.

You may have observed that the decision whether to reject the null hypothesis or to reserve judgment becomes obvious once the z-value is calculated. Using the .05 level of significance, we reject the null hypothesis if the *absolute value* of z exceeds 1.64. (If the z value is greater than 1.64, the risk of rejecting the null hypothesis when it is true is less than .05.) This is shown in Fig. 7.4. If the .01 level of significance is used instead, the null hypothesis is rejected only when the absolute z-value is greater than 2.33. (If the z-value is greater than 2.33 the risk is less than .01.) (See Fig. 7.5.)

Example In investigating several complaints concerning the weight of the NET WT. 12 OZ. jar of a local brand of peanut butter, the Better Business Bureau selects a sample of 36 jars. The sample shows an average net weight of 11.92 ounces and a standard deviation of .3 ounce. Using the .01 level of significance, what would the bureau conclude about the operation of the local firm?

Solution: The problem is formulated as follows:

$$H_0: \quad \mu = 12 \text{ ounces,}$$
$$H_1: \quad \mu < 12 \text{ ounces,}$$

Level of significance = .01.

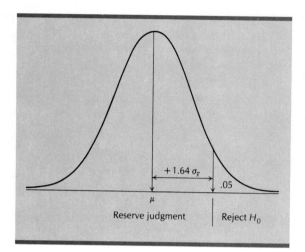

Figure 7.4   **Figure 7.5**

To test the null hypothesis, let us calculate the deviation of a sample mean of 11.92 ounces from a population mean of 12 ounces (the deviation is measured in units of z):

$$z = \frac{\bar{x} - \mu}{\hat{\sigma}_{\bar{x}}} = \frac{11.92 - 12.00}{.3/\sqrt{36}} = \frac{-.08}{.05} = -1.60.$$

Using the .01 level of significance, we must reserve judgment (z is less than 2.33). In other words, the sample evidence is not strong enough to indicate that the local firm is not maintaining the advertised weight.

Two-Sided Test

The alternative hypotheses in all the problems discussed so far are essentially of two kinds. In some, the alternative hypothesis states that the mean of the population is less than a given number. In others, that the mean of the population is greater than a given number.

When the alternative hypothesis is formulated as "less than," we obviously do not mind when the mean of the population is actually above the figure stated by the null hypothesis. In the fiber problem, for example, the null hypothesis states that the average tensile strength of the fiber is 30 pounds. The alternative hypothesis is formulated to state that the average is less than 30 pounds, simply because we are not concerned, and may even be delighted, if the average tensile strength is actually greater than 30 pounds. For exactly the same reason, the null hypothesis in the peanut butter problem, which states that the average weight of all jars is 12 ounces, is tested against the alternative hypothesis that the average weight of all jars is less than 12 ounces. Customers will be very happy indeed if the average weight is greater than 12 ounces.

At other times, the investigator is concerned only when the mean of the population is greater than the value stipulated by the null hypothesis. Under such circumstances, the alternative hypothesis is formulated in "greater than" form. The null hypothesis in the mail order house problem, for example, is tested against the alternative hypothesis that the average completion time is greater than 13 minutes. An alternative hypothesis of the "greater than" type is certainly appropriate in that case, since the shipping department would be operating more efficiently than stated in the report if the average completion time turned out to be less than 13 minutes. Management will be concerned and feel that the demand for wage increase is unjustified only if the average completion time is greater than 13 minutes.

When the null hypothesis is tested against an alternative hypothesis of a "greater than" or a "less than" type, the test is called a *one-sided test.* As we have already learned, in such problems the null hypothesis is rejected only if the absolute value of z exceeds 1.64 or 2.33, depending on whether we are using the .05 or the .01 level of significance.

In contrast to the one-sided test problems, some problems will cause the investigator to be equally concerned whether the mean of the population is understated or overstated by the null hypothesis. In such cases, the null hypothesis is rejected whenever the sample data strongly suggest that the population mean is greater than or less than the value stipulated in the null hypothesis. To clarify this point, let us assume that a manufacturing firm places an order for 10,000 ball bearings of 2-inch diameter. On receiving the shipment, the firm would be equally alarmed if the actual average diameter was smaller or greater than 2 inches. In other words, the consequences are very grave when the average diameter is not equal to 2 inches.

If the null hypothesis is rejected whenever sample evidence indicates that the population mean is overstated or understated by the null hypothesis, the test is called a *two-sided* or *two-tailed test.* In a two-sided test problem, therefore, the null hypothesis, which states that the mean of the population is equal to a given value, is tested against the alternative hypothesis that the mean is not equal to that value ("not equal" means "greater than" or "less than").

Using the .05 level of significance, the null hypothesis is rejected in a two-sided test whenever the *total* risk of rejecting the null hypothesis when it is true does not exceed .05. And since the null hypothesis is rejected whether the mean of the population is greater than or less than the value stipulated by the null hypothesis, the total .05 risk must be divided equally on both sides of the normal curve, as shown in Fig. 7.6. Hence, the null hypothesis can be rejected only when the absolute value of z exceeds 1.96.

Using the .01 level of significance, on the other hand, we must reject the null hypothesis in a two-sided test whenever the absolute value of z exceeds 2.58 (see Fig. 7.7).

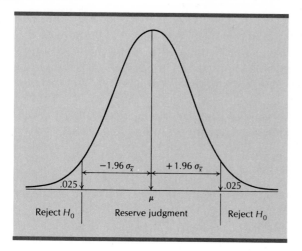

Figure 7.6

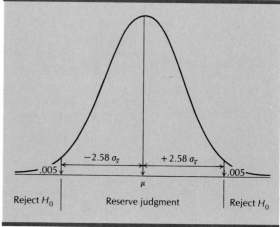

Figure 7.7

Example   A circuit fuse is designed to burn out as the electric current reaches 20 amperes. From a lot of 10,000 fuses, 36 are selected and tested for their breaking point. What do you conclude about the amperage specification of the lot if the sample reveals a mean of 20.9 amperes and a standard deviation of 1.5 amperes? Use a level of significance of .01.

Solution: It is apparent that the fuse should withstand a current of up to 20 amperes and should break the circuit once the amperage exceeds 20 amperes. The null hypothesis stating that the average breaking point $\mu = 20$ amperes should, therefore, be tested against the alternative hypothesis that $\mu \neq 20$ amperes. The problem can be summarized as follows:

$$H_0: \quad \mu = 20 \text{ amperes},$$

$$H_1: \quad \mu \neq 20 \text{ amperes},$$

Level of significance $= .01$.

To test the validity of the null hypothesis, let us calculate the deviation, measured in z-units, of a sample mean of 20.9 amperes from a population mean of 20 amperes.

$$z = \frac{\bar{x} - \mu}{\hat{\sigma}_{\bar{x}}}$$

$$= \frac{20.9 - 20}{1.5/\sqrt{36}} = \frac{.9}{.25} = 3.60.$$

Since the actual z-value, 3.60, exceeds 2.58, the null hypothesis is rejected, using the .01 level of significance.

Example   In a report prepared by the economic research department of a major bank, the department manager maintains that the average annual family income in Boulder is $13,432. What do you conclude about the validity of the report if a simple random sample of 400 families shows an average income of $13,574 with a standard deviation of $2000? Use a .05 level of significance.

Solution: The problem is formulated as follows:

$$H_0: \quad \mu = \$13,432,$$

$$H_1: \quad \mu \neq \$13,432,$$

Level of significance = .05.

$$z = \frac{\bar{x} - \mu}{\hat{\sigma}_{\bar{x}}}$$

$$= \frac{13,574 - 13,432}{2000/\sqrt{400}} = \frac{142}{100} = 1.42.$$

Since the actual *z*-value, 1.42, is less than 1.96, we must reserve judgment, using the .05 level of significance.

Before concluding this chapter, we must recognize that our discussion so far has dealt with large samples. The means of large samples are approximately normally distributed. Consequently, the normal distribution is used in all the preceding testing problems. Using the normal distribution, we reject the null hypothesis whenever the *absolute value* of z exceeds some critical level. The various critical levels are summarized below.

	One-sided test	Two-sided test
.05 level of significance	1.64	1.96
.01 level of significance	2.33	2.58

What happens when the sample size is small? A hypothesis about a population mean can be tested using a small sample only if it can be assumed that the sample is selected from a *normally distributed population* with unknown standard deviation (see the section on estimating the population mean from a small sample in Chapter 6). If the assumption regarding the normality of the population can be justified, a hypothesis concerning the mean of that population can be tested by means of a small sample utilizing a *t*-distribution with $n - 1$ degrees of freedom. To test the null hypothesis in this case, a *t*-value is computed as

$$t = \frac{\bar{x} - \mu}{s/\sqrt{n}}$$

The null hypothesis is then rejected only when the absolute value of t exceeds some critical level. The critical level is determined by the nature of the test (whether it is one-sided or two-sided), by the level of signficance, and by the degrees of freedom.

The various critical levels of t are shown below.

	One-sided test	Two-sided test
.05 level of significance	$t_{.050}$	$t_{.025}$
.01 level of significance	$t_{.010}$	$t_{.005}$

The following problem illustrates the use of the t-distribution in testing a hypothesis concerning the mean of a population.

Example   The manufacturer of a certain car model claimed that the car averaged 31 miles per gallon of unleaded gasoline. A random sample of 9 cars was selected, and each car was driven with one gallon of unleaded gasoline. The sample showed a mean of 29.43 miles, with a standard deviation of 3 miles. Using the .05 level of significance, what do you conclude about the auto manufacturer's claim?

Solution:

$$H_0: \quad \mu = 31,$$
$$H_1: \quad \mu < 31,$$
$$\text{Level of significance} = .05.$$

To test the null hypothesis, we compute the *actual* value of t as

$$t = \frac{\bar{x} - \mu}{s/\sqrt{n}}$$
$$= \frac{29.43 - 31}{3/\sqrt{9}} = -1.57.$$

From Table E, we find that the critical t-value is 1.860 (row 8, column $t_{.050}$). Since the actual t-value is -1.57 and the critical level is 1.860, we reserve judgment about the manufacturer's claim.

EXERCISES

7.1   The Retail Clerks Union claims that the average hourly earnings of its members amount to $4.10. The Retail Trade Owners' Association suspects that the union understates the average hourly wage. In a random sample of 100 salesclerks, the Retail Trade Owners' Association finds that the mean hourly earnings are $4.17, with a standard deviation of $1.20. If the association is willing to reject a true claim no more than 5 times in 100, will the association reject the union's claim?

7.2   The Retail Trade Owners' Association claims that the average hourly wage of its salesclerks is $4.20. The Retail Clerks Union suspects that the association overstates the average hourly wage. In a random sample of 400 salesclerks, the Retail Clerks Union finds that the mean hourly wage is $4.11, with a standard deviation of $.80. If the Union is willing to reject a true claim no more than once in 100, will the union reject the association's claim?

7.3   A government testing agency tests a sample of 36 packages of ground beef sold by the Shop & Save Supermarket. The label on each package reads: "contains no more than 25% fat." Can the testing agency conclude that the ground beef sold by the supermarket contains more than 25% fat if the sample shows a mean fat content of .265 and a standard deviation of .030? Use a .05 level of significance.

7.4   An ice cream producer desires the fat content of the ice cream to be 10% to maintain a uniform quality. An analysis of a sample of 49 cartons of ice cream shows a mean fat content of .103 with a standard deviation of .014. Using a .05 level of significance, will the producer reject the hypothesis that the fat content of the ice cream is properly maintained?

7.5   The mean weight of a tablet of a certain drug is to be 50 milligrams. A sample of 64 tablets shows a mean weight of 50.15 milligrams, with a standard deviation of .4 milligrams. Using a .01 level of significance can we conclude that the desired weight of the tablet is not properly maintained?

7.6   A manufacturer of a certain brand of cigarettes claims that each cigarette contains, on average, 18 milligrams of nicotine. An independent testing agency examines a sample of 100 cigarettes. Using a level of significance of .01, can the agency conclude that the manufacturer understates the average nicotine content of that brand of cigarettes if the mean nicotine content in the sample is 19.2 milligrams with a standard deviation of 2 milligrams?

7.7   A manufacturer of electric ovens purchases glass components with a specified mean heat resistance of 800°. A sample of 25 components selected from a very large shipment shows an average heat resistance of 792°, with a standard deviation of 20°. Using the .01 level of significance, can the oven manufacturer conclude that the heat resistance of the glass components in the shipment is less than 800°?

7.8   It has been theorized that the melting point of a certain metal is 1657°. A metallurgist repeats the same experiment four times and observes a mean melting point of 1655°, with a standard deviation of 2°. Using a level of significance of .01, what can the metallurgist conclude about the validity of the hypothesis that the melting point of the metal is 1657°?

7.9   A manufacturer of multiple vitamin tablets asserts that each tablet contains, on average, 2.50 milligrams of riboflavin. A representative of an independent agency tests 64 tablets and finds a mean riboflavin content of 2.48 milligrams, with a standard deviation of .16 milligrams. If the representative is willing to reject a true assertion no more than 5 times in 100, will she reject the manufacturers' assertion?

7.10   A manufacturer of a certain car model claims that the average mileage of the model is 30 miles per gallon of unleaded gasoline. A consumer protection agency believes that the average mileage of the car is exaggerated by the manufacturer. Nine cars of this particular model are driven in the same manner with one gallon of unleaded gasoline. The distances traveled by the different cars are 30, 28, 26, 27, 29, 28, 31, 26, 27 miles. If the agency is willing to reject a true claim no more than once in 100, would the agency reject the manufacturer's claim?

7.11   A state department of Health and Education reports the average annual family expenditure on health care is $980. If a random sample of 100 families shows an average annual expenditure of $920, with a standard deviation of $200, would you conclude that the annual average family expenditure on health reported by the department is exaggerated?

7.12   A manufacturer of a certain brand of cigarettes claims that the nicotine content is 18 milligrams per cigarette. A government testing agency measures the nicotine content of 16 cigarettes and obtains the following information:

$$x = \text{nicotine content of a cigarette, in milligrams}$$

$$\sum x = 336 \text{ milligrams}$$

$$\sum (x - \bar{x})^2 = 240 \text{ milligrams}$$

a) Using a .05 level of significance, can the agency conclude that the nicotine content of this brand of cigarettes is underestimated by its manufacturer?

b) With what degree of confidence can we assert that the average nicotine content of this brand of cigarettes is between 18.869 and 23.131 milligrams?

7.13   The Accidental Automobile Insurance Company paid an average settlement of $512 per claim last year ($\mu = 512$). A random sample of 100 claims selected from settlements paid this year shows an average settlement cost of $556 per claim, with a standard deviation of $200. Using a level of significance of .05, can the company conclude that the average settlement cost per claim has risen since last year?

7.14   A pharmaceutical laboratory advertises that the mean time required for its brand of aspirin to dissolve is 10 minutes. A drug-testing agency tests five tablets. The times, in minutes, required to dissolve the tablets are 9, 12, 13, 11, 10. Using a level of significance of .05, can the agency conclude that the drug manufacturer exaggerates the speed with which the aspirin dissolves?

7.15 The ABC Company's balance sheet shows an aggregate accounts receivable of $1.2 million. Suspecting that this amount is overstated, an auditor selects a random sample of 150 accounts from all accounts receivable (10,000 accounts). The sample shows a mean amount of $113 per account, with a standard deviation of $40. Using a .05 level of significance, can the auditor conclude that the ABC Company has overstated its aggregate accounts receivable?

7.16 Last year the records of a sporting goods store showed that the mean amount purchased per customer was $35.17 ($\mu = 35.17$). This year a random sample of 200 sales transactions indicates that the mean amount purchased per customer is $32.87, with a standard deviation of $10.12. Using a .01 level of significance, can we conclude that the mean amount purchased per customer has declined since last year?

7.17 Senate proponents of a comprehensive national health insurance plan claim that the mean annual medical expense in the United States is $800 per family. A random sample of 500 families is selected by a Washington lobbyist for the American Medical Association. The sample shows a mean annual medical expense of $782 per family, with a standard deviation of $150. Using a .05 level of significance, can we conclude that the proponents of the national health insurance bill have exaggerated medical expenses of the average American family?

7.18 The marketing manager of a large fast-food restaurant chain is considering introducing a new product, The Big Max. The manager believes that the new product will not be profitable unless the average weekly sales are greater than 500 units per store. The Big Max is introduced at 50 randomly selected restaurants. The sample shows average weekly sales of 530 units, with a standard deviation of 40 units. Using the .01 level of significance, should the Big Max be sold at all of the chain's restaurants?

7.19 It is claimed that the average monthly food expenditure of a family of two in Chicago is $170. A random sample of 240 families of two from the city shows a mean monthly expenditure of $167, with a standard deviation of $24. Using a .05 level of significance, can we conclude that the claim is exaggerated?

TYPE I AND TYPE II ERROR

The concepts of type I and type II error can best be explained with a concrete example. Let us consider the case of a radio manufacturer who receives a very large lot of batteries from a supplier each week. Since the manufacturer cannot test all batteries in a lot, he has adopted the following rule in deciding on whether to accept or reject the weekly lot: Select a random sample of 36 batteries from each lot received. If the average life of the batteries selected is 48 hours or more, accept the entire lot. If the average battery life in the sample is less than 48 hours, reject the lot. Briefly stated, the decision is

1. if $\bar{x} \geq 48$ hours, accept the lot;
2. if $\bar{x} < 48$ hours, reject the lot.

How much protection does the use of this decision rule provide against accepting a bad lot and rejecting a good lot? Before we can answer this question, we must first describe what the manufacturer considers a good and a bad lot.

   The manufacturer considers a lot to be good when the average battery life of the entire lot, μ, is at least 50 hours. And a lot is considered to be bad when its average battery life is 47 or fewer hours.

$$\text{Good lot:} \quad \mu \geq 50 \text{ hours}$$

$$\text{Bad lot:} \quad \mu \leq 47 \text{ hours}$$

You are quite justified to ask: How does the manufacturer classify a lot whose average battery life is greater than 47 hours but less than 50 hours? For example, does he consider a lot with $\mu = 49$ hours to be a good lot or a bad lot?

   First, a lot is certainty considered to be good when $\mu \geq 50$ hours. And in this case, the manufacturer wishes to take a very small risk of rejecting such a lot. Second, a lot is certainly considered to be bad when $\mu \leq 47$ hours. And similarly, the manufacturer wishes to take a very small risk of accepting such a lot. Finally, the manufacturer is indifferent about a lot when its average battery life is between 47 and 50 hours. In other words, the manufacturer is not much alarmed whether such a lot is accepted or rejected. Having defined a good lot and a bad lot, we are ready to deal now with measuring the risks of rejecting a good lot and accepting a bad lot.

   Since the decision whether to accept or reject a lot depends on the sample outcome, and because of the nature of sample fluctuations, the use of the sample decision rule could result in any of four situations.

1. The lot received is a good lot ($\mu \geq 50$ hours), and the sample outcome indicates that the lot should be accepted ($\bar{x} \geq 48$ hours). Hence, the shipment is accepted, and the decision is correct.
2. The lot received is a good lot ($\mu \geq 50$ hours), but the sample outcome indicates that this lot should be rejected ($\bar{x} < 48$ hours). This lot is erroneously rejected, and the error committed is called type I error.
3. The lot received is a bad lot ($\mu \leq 47$ hours), and the sample outcome indicates that the lot should be rejected ($\bar{x} < 48$ hours). The lot is correctly rejected.
4. The lot received is a bad lot ($\mu \leq 47$ hours), but the sample outcome

TABLE 7.1 **SUMMARY OF DECISIONS**

Decision Dictated by Sample Outcome	Quality of Lot	
	Good ($\mu \geq 50$)	Bad ($\mu \leq 47$)
Reject lot ($\bar{x} < 48$)	Type I error	Correct decision
Accept lot ($\bar{x} \geq 48$)	Correct decision	Type II error

suggests that the lot should be accepted ($\bar{x} \geq 48$ hours). The lot is erroneously accepted, and the error committed is called type II error. Table 7.1 is a summary of these four situations.

To determine the probability of committing a type I error (rejecting a good lot), let us assume that the manufacturer receives a lot of batteries with an actual mean battery life of 50 hours and a standard deviation of 6 hours ($\mu = 50$ hours, $\sigma = 6$ hours). Although this lot is a good lot, the manufacturer would *reject* such a lot whenever the selected sample shows an average of less than 48 hours. The means of the various samples of 36 batteries that can be selected from this lot are described by the normal distribution shown in Fig. 7.8.

The probability that the mean battery life in a random sample of 36 batteries is less than 48 hours can be calculated as follows:

$$Z = \frac{\bar{x} - \mu}{\sigma_{\bar{x}}} = \frac{48 - 50}{1} = -2.$$

Figure 7.8

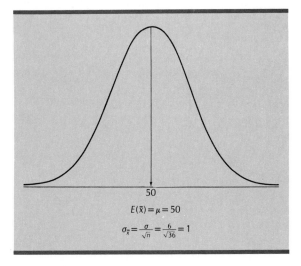

$$50$$

$$E(\bar{x}) = \mu = 50$$

$$\sigma_{\bar{x}} = \frac{\sigma}{\sqrt{n}} = \frac{6}{\sqrt{36}} = 1$$

Therefore,

$$P(\bar{x} < 48) = .5000 - .4772 = .0228.$$

See Fig. 7.9. Using the sampling decision rule, we find that the probability of rejecting a lot with $\mu = 50$ hours and $\sigma = 6$ hours is .0228. This is the probability of a type I error, denoted by the symbol α.

Similarly, to determine the probability of committing a type II error (accepting a bad lot), let us assume that the manufacturer receives a lot with an actual mean battery life of 47 hours and a standard deviation of 6 hours ($\mu = 47$ hours, $\sigma = 6$ hours). Although this lot is bad, the manufacturer would *accept* such a lot whenever the selected sample shows an average life of 48 hours or more. The means of the various samples of 36 batteries that can be selected from this lot are described by the normal distribution shown in Fig. 7.10. The probability that the mean battery life in random samples of 36 batteries is 48 hours or more can be calculated as follows (Fig. 7.11):

$$z = \frac{\bar{x} - \mu}{\sigma_{\bar{x}}} = \frac{48 - 47}{1} = 1.$$

Therefore,

$$P(\bar{x} \geq 48) = .5000 - .3413$$
$$= .1587.$$

Using the sampling decision rule, we find that the probability of accepting a lot with $\mu = 47$ hours and $\sigma = 6$ hours is .1587. This is the probability of type II error, denoted by the symbol β.

Figure 7.9

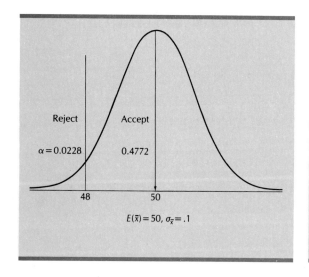

Figure 7.10

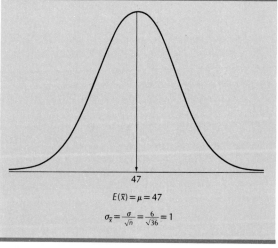

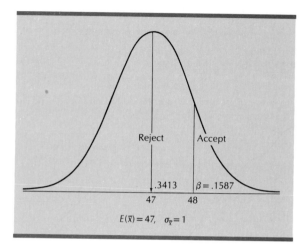

Figure 7.11

The probabilities of making type I and type II errors are displayed in Table 7.2.

To generalize our discussion concerning type I and type II errors, let the null hypothesis H_0 stand for the assumption that the lot received is a good lot and the alternative hypothesis H_1 for the assumption that the lot received is a bad lot.

$$\text{Null hypothesis } (H_0): \qquad \mu \geq 50 \text{ hours}$$

$$\text{Alternative hypothesis } (H_1): \quad \mu \leq 47 \text{ hours}$$

If the manufacturer accepts a lot, the null hypothesis is accepted and the alternative hypothesis is rejected. On the other hand, if the manufacturer rejects a lot, the null hypothesis is rejected and the alternative hypothesis is accepted. Hence, we can now define **type I error** as the error committed by rejecting H_0 when it is true (error incurred by rejecting a good lot). And we define **type II error** as the error incurred by accepting H_0 when H_0 is false (error

TABLE 7.2   SUMMARY OF DECISIONS

Decision Dictated by Sample Outcome	Quality of Lot	
	Good ($\mu = 50$)	*Bad* ($\mu = 47$)
Reject lot ($\bar{x} < 48$)	Type I error ($\alpha = .0228$)	Correct decision (Probability = .8413)
Accept lot ($\bar{x} \geq 48$)	Correct decision (Probability = .9772)	Type II error ($\beta = .1587$)

TABLE 7.3   TYPE I AND II ERRORS

Decision Dictated by Sample Outcome	H_0 True	H_1 True
Reject H_0	Type I error	Correct decision
Accept H_0	Correct decision	Type II error

incurred by accepting a bad lot).* The probability of making a type I error is denoted by the symbol α and the probability of making a type II error by the symbol β. These generalizations are summarized in Table 7.3.

Effect of Changing Sample Size on Type I and Type II Errors

We repeat the decision rule adopted by the radio manufacturer: Select a random sample of 36 batteries from each lot received. If the average life of the batteries selected is 48 hours or more, accept the entire lot; if the observed sample mean is less than 48 hours, reject the lot. Briefly stated,

1. if $\bar{x} \geq 48$ hours, accept the lot,
2. if $\bar{x} < 48$ hours, reject the lot.

This decision rule can be generalized as follows: Select a random sample of size n from each lot received. If the observed sample mean $\bar{x}$ is equal to or greater than some critical value (denoted by c^*), accept the lot; if $\bar{x}$ is less than this critical value, reject the lot. Briefly stated, the general decision rule is

1. if $\bar{x} \geq c^*$, accept the lot.
2. if $\bar{x} < c^*$, reject the lot.

In formulating the decision rule, the manufacturer has adopted a sample size of 36 and a critical value of 48 hours ($n = 36, c^* = 48$).

We must emphasize that in formulating a decision rule of this kind, two elements are of utmost importance: the sample size (n) and the critical value (c^*). In fact, the probabilities of type I and type II errors depend entirely on the values assigned to n and c^*.

Although we are mainly interested in examining the effect of changing the sample size on type I and type II errors, it is useful to examine the effect of modifying the value of c^* first.

Let us assume that the manufacturer modifies the original decision rule. The modified rule is the following: Select a random sample of 36 batteries from each shipment received. If the observed sample mean $\bar{x}$ is equal to or greater

---

*It is useful to point out that type II error is not committed when the decision maker *reserves judgment* instead of accepting H_0.

than 48.4 hours, accept the lot; if the sample mean is less than 48.4 hours, reject the lot. The critical value c^* is changed from 48 to 48.4 and the sample size is kept the same. We will examine the effect of modifying the value of c^* on type I error and type II error in turn.

To determine the effect of modifying the value of c^* on type I error, let us once again assume that the manufacturer receives a lot with $\mu = 50$ hours and $\sigma = 6$ hours. Although this lot is a good lot, the manufacturer would reject such a lot (commit type I error) whenever the selected sample shows an average of less than 48.4 hours. The means of the various samples of 36 batteries that can be selected from this lot are described by the normal distribution shown in Fig. 7.12. The probability that the mean battery life in a random sample of 36 is less than 48.4 hours can be calculated as follows:

$$Z = \frac{\bar{x} - \mu}{\sigma_{\bar{x}}} = \frac{48.4 - 50}{1} = -1.6.$$

Therefore,

$$P(\bar{x} < 48.4) = .5000 - .4452 = .0548.$$

See Fig. 7.13. Thus, using the modified decision rule ($n = 36$, $c^* = 48.4$), we see that the probability of making type I error is .0548. You may recall, however, that in using the original decision rule ($n = 36$, $c^* = 48$), the probability of making type I error is .0228. Hence by changing the critical value, c^*, from 48 hours to 48.4 hours, the probability of making type I error has increased from .0228 to .0548.

Similarly, to determine the effect of modifying the value of c^* on type II

Figure 7.12
Figure 7.13

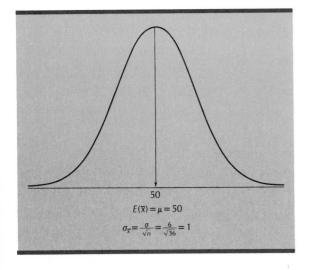

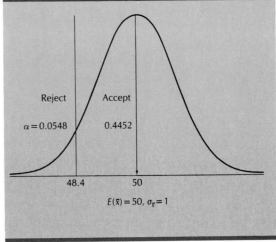

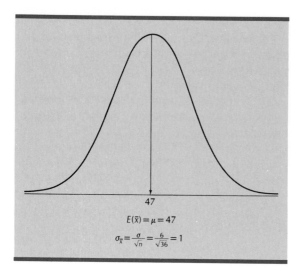

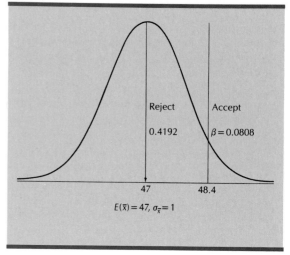

Figure 7.14   **Figure 7.15**

error, let us assume that the manufacturer receives a lot with $\mu = 47$ hours and $\sigma = 6$ hours. Although this lot is a bad lot, the manufacturer would accept such a lot (commit type II error) whenever the observed sample mean is equal to or greater than 48.4 hours. The means of various battery samples of size 36 that can be selected from this lot are described by the normal distribution shown in Fig. 7.14. The probability that the mean battery life in a random sample of 36 batteries is 48.4 hours or more can be calculated as follows (Fig. 7.15):

$$z = \frac{\overline{x} - \mu}{\sigma_{\overline{x}}} = \frac{48.4 - 47}{1} = 1.4.$$

Therefore,

$$P(\overline{x} \geq 48.4) = .5000 - .4192 = .0808.$$

Thus, using the modified decision rule ($n = 36$, $c^* = 48.4$), the probability of making type II error is .0808. Using the original decision rule ($n = 36$, $c^* = 48$), the probability of making type II error is .1587. Hence, the probability of type II error is reduced from .1587 to .0808 as a result of changing the critical value, c^*, from 48 to 48.4.

The effect of modifying the critical value of a decision rule on the probability of making type I and type II errors can be summarized as follows: as a result of changing the critical value c^* from 48 to 48.4, the probability of making type I error is increased from .0228 to .0548, but the probability of making type II error is decreased from .1587 to .0808. We can now generalize these results: As the critical value c^* is modified, the probabilities of making type I error and type II error change in opposite directions. While the probability of making one type of error decreases, the probability of making the other type of error increases.

We will now demonstrate that the probabilities of making both type of errors can simultaneously be reduced by increasing the sample size in the decision rule.

To show that enlarging the sample size n reduces the probability of making both types of errors, let us modify the original decision rule: Select a random batch of 64 batteries from each lot received. If average battery life in the observed sample is equal to or greater than 48 hours, accept the lot; if the sample mean is less than 48 hours, reject the lot. Compared to the original decision rule, n is increased from 36 to 64 and c^* is kept the same, at 48. To measure the probability of type I error under this modified rule, let us once again assume that the manufacturer receives a lot with $\mu = 50$ hours and $\sigma = 6$ hours. Although the received lot is a good lot, the manufacturer would reject such a lot (commit type I error) whenever the selected sample reveals an average of less than 48 hours. The means of the various samples of 64 batteries that can be selected from this lot are described by the normal distribution shown in Fig. 7.16. The probability that the mean battery life in a random sample of 64 is less than 48 hours can be calculated as follows (Fig. 7.17):

$$z = \frac{\bar{x} - \mu}{\sigma_{\bar{x}}} = \frac{48 - 50}{.75} = -2.67$$

Therefore,

$$P(\bar{x} < 48) = .5000 - .4962 = .0038.$$

Figure 7.16

Figure 7.17

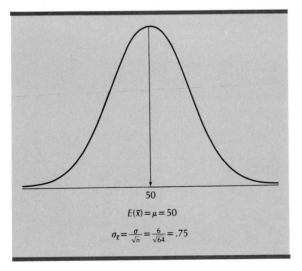

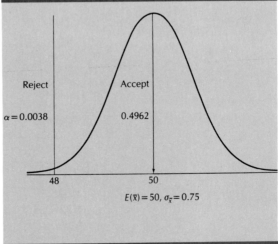

Thus, using the modified decision rule ($n = 64$, $c^* = 48$), the probability of making type I error is .0038. With the original decision rule ($n = 36$, $c^* = 48$), on the other hand, the probability of making type I error is .0228. Hence, the probability of making type I error is reduced from .0228 to .0038 as a result of changing the sample size from 36 to 64 batteries.

Similarly, to measure the probability of making type II error using the modified rule ($n = 64$, $c^* = 48$) let us assume again that the manufacturer receives a lot with $\mu = 47$ hours and $\sigma = 6$ hours. Although the lot received is a bad lot, the manufacturer would accept such a lot (commit type II error), whenever the sample selected from the lot shows an average equal to or greater than 48 hours. The means of the various samples of 64 batteries that can be selected from this lot are described by the normal distribution shown in Fig. 7.18. The probability that the mean battery life in a random sample of 64 is greater than or equal to 48 hours can be calculated as follows (Fig. 7.19):

$$z = \frac{\overline{x} - \mu}{\sigma_{\overline{x}}} = \frac{48 - 47}{.75} = 1.33.$$

Therefore,

$$P(\overline{x} \geq 48) = .5000 - .4082 = .0918.$$

Thus, using the modified decision rule ($n = 64$, $c^* = 48$), we find that the probability of making type II error is .0918. With the original decision rule ($n = 36$, $c^* = 48$), on the other hand, the probability of making type II error is .1587. Hence the probability of type II error is reduced from .1587 to .0918 as a result of enlarging the sample size from 36 to 64 batteries. In conclusion, we can now

Figure 7.18

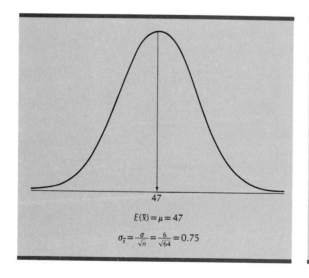

$$E(\overline{x}) = \mu = 47$$

$$\sigma_{\overline{x}} = \frac{\sigma}{\sqrt{n}} = \frac{6}{\sqrt{64}} = 0.75$$

Figure 7.19

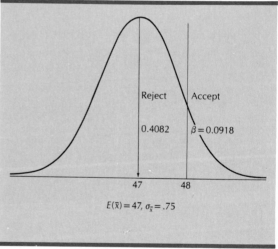

$$E(\overline{x}) = 47, \ \sigma_{\overline{x}} = .75$$

generalize: As the sample size n is increased, the probabilities of making both type I and type II errors are reduced.

Example   A soft-drink bottling process is considered to be operating satisfactorily when the mean fill per bottle is 355 ml ($\mu = 355$). The following decision rule is adopted to ascertain whether the process continues to operate in a satisfactory manner: Select a random sample of 40 bottles each hour and determine their average fill. If this average, $\bar{x}$, is between 350 ml and 360 ml, let the process continue; otherwise stop and readjust the process. (Assume that the standard deviation of the process always remains 15 ml.)

a) Formulate the null hypothesis and the alternative hypothesis.

b) What is the risk of type I error?

c) What is the risk of type II error when $\mu = 365$ (excessive overfilling)?

Solution:

a) The null hypothesis is that the process is operating satisfactorily, or $\mu = 355$ ml. The alternative hypothesis is that the value of μ is no longer 355 ml and the process is either overfilling or underfilling. Stated briefly, the two hypotheses are

$$H_0: \quad \mu = 355,$$
$$H_1: \quad \mu \neq 355.$$

b) Type I error is committed when the process is operating satisfactorily ($\mu = 355$) but the process is erroneously stopped because the mean of the sample selected does not fall between 350 and 360. Referring to the normal curve in Fig. 7.20, we can determine the probability of type I error (stopping the process erroneously) as follows: We denote the area under the normal curve between 350 and 355 by A_1 and the area between 355 and 360 by A_2. Then

$$P(\text{stop}) = P(\bar{x} \leq 350) + P(\bar{x} \geq 360),$$
$$= (.5 - A_1) + (.5 - A_2),$$

which is the shaded area in Fig. 7.20. We now proceed to find A_1 and A_2:

$$z_1 = \frac{\bar{x} - \mu}{\sigma_{\bar{x}}} \qquad\qquad z_2 = \frac{\bar{x} - \mu}{\sigma_{\bar{x}}}$$

$$= \frac{350 - 355}{2.37} \qquad\qquad = \frac{360 - 355}{2.37}$$

$$= -2.11; \qquad\qquad\qquad = 2.11;$$

$$A_1 = .4826. \qquad\qquad\qquad A_2 = .4826.$$

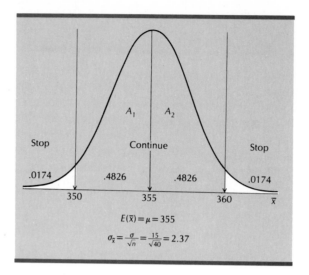

Figure 7.20

Therefore,

$$P(\text{stop}) = (.5 - .4826) + (.5 - .4826)$$
$$= .0174 + .0174$$
$$= .0348.$$

Thus, using the sampling decision rule, we find that the probability of stopping a satisfactory process is .0348. This is the probability of type I error.

c) When $\mu = 365$ the process is overfilling and hence should be stopped. However, the process is allowed to continue (type II error is committed) whenever the mean of the sample selected falls between 350 and 360. We refer to Fig. 7.21 to calculate the probability of committing this error as follows: We denote the area under the normal curve between 350 and 365 by A_1 and the area between 360 and 365 by A_2; then

$$P(\text{continue}) = A_1 - A_2.$$

We proceed to find A_1 and A_2:

$$Z_1 = \frac{\bar{x} - \mu}{\sigma_{\bar{x}}} \qquad\qquad Z_2 = \frac{\bar{x} - \mu}{\sigma_{\bar{x}}}$$

$$= \frac{350 - 365}{2.37} \qquad\qquad = \frac{360 - 365}{2.37}$$

$$= -6.33; \qquad\qquad = -2.11;$$

$$A_1 = .5000. \qquad\qquad A_2 = .4826.$$

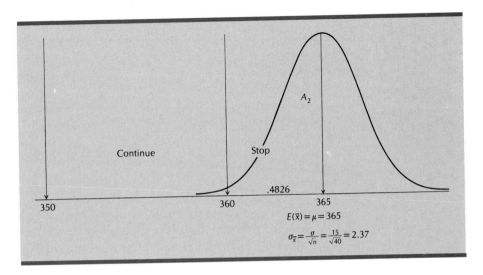

Figure 7.21

Therefore,

$$P(\text{continue}) = A_1 - A_2$$
$$= .5000 - .4826$$
$$= .0174.$$

Thus, although the process is overfilling ($\mu + 365$), this process is allowed to continue with a probability of .0174.

Example   A government housing agency undertakes public housing projects in various communities. The housing agency considers a project essential to a community when the average family income, μ, in that community is $5000 or less. The project is deemed unjustified when average income is $6000 or more. The agency develops the following sampling decision rule to be used in deciding whether to undertake a given project. Select a number of families n from a given community and determine the average income. If this average, $\bar{x}$, is equal to c^* or less, undertake the project. If it is greater than c^*, do not undertake the project. Determine the values of n and c^* so that the probability of not undertaking the project when it is justified (the probability of type I error) is $\alpha = .05$ and the probability of undertaking the project when it is not justified (probability of type II error) is $\beta = .10$. Assume that for every community considered by the agency the standard deviation is $2000 ($\sigma = \$2000$).

Solution: We need to develop a sampling rule (determine n and c^*) that will satisfy the conditions stipulated by the agency. We summarize these conditions in Table 7.4. According to Table 7.4, when $\mu = \$5000$, then application of the sampling rule should result in undertaking a project with a probability of .95

TABLE 7.4   **SUMMARY OF DECISIONS**

Decision Dictated by Sample Outcome	Average Family Income	
	H_0 ($\mu = \$5000$)	H_1 ($\mu = \$6000$)
Undertake project ($\bar{x} \le c^*$)	Correct decision (probability = .95)	Type II error ($\beta = .10$)
Do not undertake project ($\bar{x} > c^*$)	Type I error ($\alpha = .05$)	Correct decision (probability = .90)

and not undertaking it with probability of .05. When $\mu = \$6000$, on the other hand, application of the sampling rule should result in undertaking a project with a probability of .10 and not undertaking it with a probability of .90. In summary, we must find the values for n and c^* that will render the risk of type I error .05 and the risk of type II error .10. We consider the implications of these two conditions in turn.

Type I error is committed when a project is justified ($\mu = \$5000$) but is erroneously not undertaken because the mean of the sample selected is greater than c^*. The probability of committing this error is set as .05.

The means of the various samples of size n that can be selected from a population with $\mu = 5000$ and $\sigma = 2000$ are described by the normal distribution shown in Fig. 7.22. Since the probability of committing type I error is set as .05, we specify the value of c^* so that .05 of the area under the normal curve is to the right of c^*, as in Fig. 7.23.

Figure 7.22

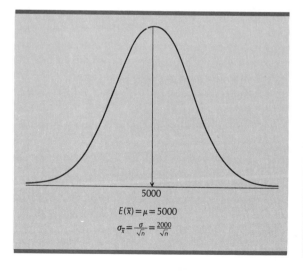

Figure 7.23

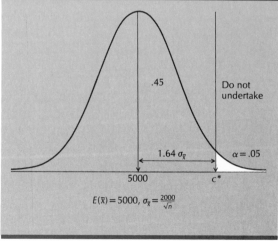

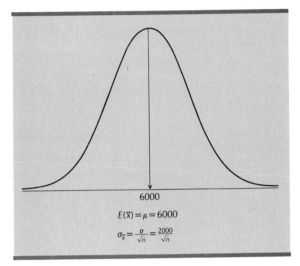

Figure 7.24

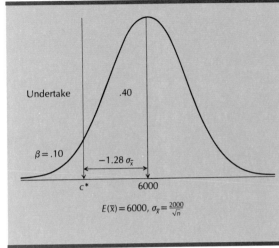

Figure 7.25

With .45 of the area under the normal curve between 5000 and c^*, Table A indicates that

$$c^* = 5000 + 1.64\sigma_{\bar{x}}$$

$$= 5000 + 1.64\,\frac{2000}{\sqrt{n}},$$

or

$$c^* = 5000 + \frac{3280}{\sqrt{n}}. \tag{I}$$

Equation (I) contains the unknowns n and c^*. By considering type II error next, we will obtain another equation containing the same unknowns. We will then simultaneously solve the two equations to find c^* and n.

Type II error is committed when a project is not justified ($\mu = \$6000$) but is undertaken because the mean of the sample selected is below c^*. The probability of committing this error is set as .10.

The means of the various samples of size n that can be selected from a population with $\mu = 6000$ and $\sigma = 2000$ are described by the normal curve shown in Fig. 7.24. Since the probability of type II error is set as .10, we specify the value of c^* so that .10 of the area under the normal curve is to the left of c^*, as in Fig. 7.25. With .40 of the area under the normal curve between c^* and 6000, Table A indicates that

$$c^* = 6000 - 1.28\sigma_{\bar{x}}$$

$$= 6000 - 1.28\,\frac{2000}{\sqrt{n}},$$

or

$$c^* = 6000 - \frac{2560}{\sqrt{n}}. \tag{II}$$

Equation (II) can be combined with Eq. (I) to solve for c^* and n. We proceed by subtracting Eq. (II) from Eq. (I) to obtain Eq. (III).

$$c^* = \quad 5000 + \frac{3280}{\sqrt{n}} \tag{I}$$

$$c^* = \quad 6000 - \frac{2560}{\sqrt{n}} \tag{II}$$

$$0 = -1000 + \frac{5840}{\sqrt{n}} \tag{III}$$

We solve for n in Eq. (III) as follows:

$$\frac{5840}{\sqrt{n}} = 1000$$

$$\sqrt{n} = \frac{5840}{1000} = 5.84.$$

Hence,

$$n = (5.84)^2 = 34.11.$$

Substituting $\sqrt{n} = 5.84$ in Eq. (I) gives

$$c^* = 5000 + \frac{3280}{5.84} = 5561.64.$$

With $n = 34.11$ (say 35 for convenience) and with $c^* = 5561.64$, the sampling decision rule becomes the following: Select a random sample of 35 families from any given community and determine their average annual income. If this average is equal to or less than \$5561.64, undertake the project. If it is greater than \$5561.64, do not undertake the project.

Example Given the two hypotheses

$$H_0: \quad \mu = 80,$$

$$H_1: \quad \mu \neq 80,$$

use a sample of 40 observations ($n = 40$) to develop a sampling decision rule so that the probability of committing type I error is .05. Assume that the population standard deviation, σ, is 12.

Solution: This is a two-sided test. The null hypothesis is rejected when $\mu < 80$ as well as when $\mu > 80$. Consequently, the appropriate decision rule is the following: Select a random sample of 40 observations and determine the mean of the sample, $\bar{x}$. If $\bar{x}$ does not fall between c_1^* and c_2^*, reject H_0. We must now find the values of c_1^* and c_2^* so that the probability of committing type I error is .05.

Type I error is committed when H_0 is true ($\mu = 80$), but the hypothesis is erroneously rejected because the mean of the sample selected does not fall between c_1^* and c_2^*. The probability of committing such error is set as .05.

The means of the various samples of size 40 that can be selected from a population with $\mu = 80$ and $\sigma = 12$ are described by the normal curve shown in Fig. 7.26. Since the probability of committing type I error is set as .05, we specify the values of c_1^* and c_2^* so that .025 of the area under the normal curve is to the left of c_1^* and .025 of the area is to the right of c_2^*, as shown in Fig. 7.27.

With .475 of the area under the normal curve between c_1^* and 80, Table A indicates that

$$c_1^* = 80 - 1.96\sigma_{\bar{x}}$$
$$= 80 - 1.96(1.90)$$
$$= 76.276.$$

In a similar fashion we find

$$c_2^* = 80 + 1.96\sigma_{\bar{x}}$$
$$= 80 + 1.96(1.90)$$
$$= 83.724.$$

Hence, our sampling decision rule is as follows: Select a random sample of 40

Figure 7.26

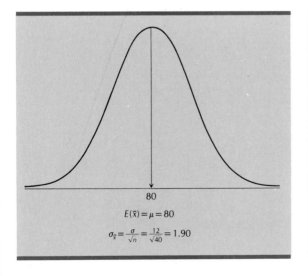

Figure 7.27

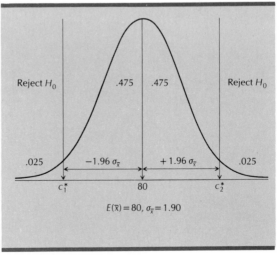

observations and determine the mean of the sample. If this mean does not fall between 76.276 and 83.724, reject H_0. With this decision rule, the probability of committing type I error is .05.

Example   Given the two hypotheses

$$H_0: \quad \mu = 80,$$

$$H_1: \quad \mu < 80,$$

use a sample of 40 observations to develop a sampling decision rule so that the probability of type I error is .05. Assume that the population standard deviation is 12.

Solution: In contrast to the previous example, this is a one-sided test. The null hypothesis is rejected only when $\mu < 80$. Consequently, the appropriate decision rule is as follows: Select a random sample of 40 observations and determine the mean of the sample, $\bar{x}$. If $\bar{x}$ is less than c^*, reject H_0. We must now find the value of c^* so that the probability of committing type I error is .05.

Type I error is committed when H_0 is true ($\mu = 80$), but the hypothesis is erroneously rejected because the mean of the sample selected is less than c^*. Since the probability of committing such error is set as .05, we must specify the value of c^* so that .95 of the area under the normal curve is to the left of c^*, as indicated in Fig. 7.28.

With .45 of the area under the normal curve between c^* and 80, Table A indicates that

$$c^* = 80 - 1.64\sigma_{\bar{x}}$$

$$= 80 - 1.64(1.90)$$

$$= 76.865.$$

Figure 7.28

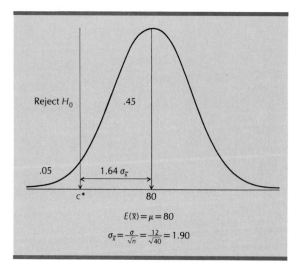

Hence, our sampling decision rule is the following: Select a random sample of 40 observations and determine the mean of the sample. If this mean is less than 76.865, reject H_0. With this decision rule, the probability of committing type I error is .05.

7.20 A foundry desires to produce iron castings with an average weight of 20 pounds and a standard deviation of 2 pounds ($\mu = 20$, $\sigma = 2$). To decide whether the manufacturing process is operating satisfactorily a sample of 40 castings is selected each hour from the output of the process and their average weight is determined. If this average is between 19.5 and 20.5 pounds, no action is taken; otherwise, the process is stopped and corrected. Assume that the standard deviation of the process is always 2 pounds.

a) What is the probability of type I error?

b) What is the probability of type II error when $\mu = 19.0$ pounds?

c) What is the probability of type II error when $\mu = 21.1$ pounds?

7.21 The Standard Shoe Company operates a growing chain of retail shoe stores in various communities throughout Arizona. The company wishes to have a branch in any community with an average annual family expenditure on shoes of $150 or more. The company considers it unprofitable to operate a store in a community where an average expenditure on shoes is $125 or less. The company develops a decision rule to be used in deciding whether to open a new branch: Select a number of families n from a given community and determine their average annual expenditure on shoes. If this average is equal to or more than c^*, establish a store in that community. If it is less than c^*, do not open a store. Determine the values of n and c^* so that the probability of not establishing a store when $\mu = $150 is .01 and the probability of establishing a store when $\mu = $125 is .05. Assume that the standard deviation of annual family expenditure on shoes, σ, is $50.

7.22 A manufacturer of oleomargarine uses national television advertising to promote its product. In addition, the company undertakes local advertising campaigns to supplement national advertising in some areas. The manufacturer believes that local advertising is not necessary in areas where the average weekly amount of oleomargarine used by a family is 2 pounds or more. Local advertising is needed when average weekly consumption is 1.5 pounds or less. To decide whether to undertake a local advertising campaign in any given area, the market research department has adopted the following decision rule: Select a random sample of 36 families from the area and determine their average weekly consumption of oleomargarine. If this average is 1.8 pounds or more, do not advertise locally. If it is less than 1.8 pounds, advertise. Assume that the standard deviation of the amount of oleomargarine consumed per family per week is .6 pound.

a) Formulate the null hypothesis and the alternative hypothesis.

b) What is the risk of type I error?

c) What is the risk of type II error when $\mu = 1.5$ pounds?

7.23 Automobile insurance companies have petitioned a state insurance commission for an increase in automobile insurance rates, claiming rising accident settlement costs. Last year the average settlement cost was $502 per claim with a standard deviation of $182 ($\mu = 502$, $\sigma = 182$). To decide whether to approve the increase in premium rate, the state commission adopted the following decision rule: Select a random sample of 50 claims from settlements paid this year and determine the average amount paid per claim. If it is less than $550, do not approve the increase. Assume that the population standard deviation, σ, remains $182.

a) Formulate the null hypothesis and the alternative hypothesis.

b) What is the probability of type I error?

c) What is the probability of type II error when $\mu = \$600$?

7.24 The Department of Health and Human Services has adopted the following decision rule in deciding on whether to introduce a comprehensive national health insurance plan: Select a random sample of n families and determine their average annual medical expenses. If this average is equal to or more than c^*, introduce the insurance plan. If it is less than c^*, do not introduce the plan. Determine the value of n and c^* so that the probability of introducing the plan is .05 when average family medical expenses are $800 per year ($\mu = \$800$) and the probability of not introducing the plan is .01 when $\mu = \$1000$. Assume that the population standard deviation for medical expenses, σ, is $300.

7.25 Given the two hypotheses

$$H_0: \quad \mu = 150,$$

$$H_1: \quad \mu > 150,$$

use a sample of 64 observations to develop a sampling decision rule so that the probability of type I error is .05. Assume that the population standard deviation is 16.

7.26 Given the two hypotheses

$$H_0: \quad \mu = 65,$$

$$H_1: \quad \mu \neq 65,$$

use a sample of 49 observations to develop a sampling decision rule so that the probability of type I error is .01. Assume that the population standard deviation is 14.

7.27 Given the two hypotheses

$$H_0: \quad \mu = 90,$$

$$H_1: \quad \mu < 90,$$

use a sample of 40 observations to develop a sampling decision rule so that the probability of type II error is .10 when $\mu = 83$. Assume that the population standard deviation is 15.

7.28 A large real estate investment company has adopted the following decision rule in deciding whether to build custom single-family homes in St. Louis: Select a random sample of n families from St. Louis and determine the mean annual family income ($\bar{x}$). If this mean is equal to or more than c^*, build the new homes. If it is less than c^*, do not start the project. Determine the value of n and c^* so that the probability of undertaking the project is .01 when the average annual family income is $50,000 ($\mu = \$50,000$) and the probability of not undertaking the project is .10 when $\mu = \$55,000$. Assume that the standard deviation for income is $12,000.

KEY TERMS

null hypothesis (H_0)   A claim about a population parameter that can be either accepted or rejected after data are collected.

alternative hypothesis (H_1)   A claim about a population parameter that is in opposition to the null hypothesis.

type I error (α)   The error committed if H_0 is rejected when it is actually true.

α The probability of type I error.

level of significance   The maximum value of the probability of a type I error.

type II error (β)   The error committed if H_0 is accepted when it is actually false.

β The probability of type II error.

SUMMARY OF FORMULAS

z-value $z = \dfrac{\bar{x} - \mu}{\sigma_{\bar{x}}} = \dfrac{\bar{x} - \mu}{\sigma/\sqrt{n}} = \dfrac{\bar{x} - \mu}{s/\sqrt{n}}$

t-value $t = \dfrac{\bar{x} - \mu}{s/\sqrt{n}}$

TESTING HYPOTHESES ABOUT SEVERAL POPULATION MEANS

8

This chapter deals with testing hypotheses about the means of several populations. We can now test the hypothesis that average annual family income in Chicago is the same as that in Boston, for example. Similarly, we can test the hypothesis that the average lives of four brands of batteries are the same.

When a random sample of students from Delmore State College shows a mean age of 23 years and a random sample from Eastern University shows a mean age of 24 years, can we safely conclude that the average ages in the two schools are really different? In other words, can we use the difference between the means of the two samples as conclusive evidence that the means of the two populations are not the same? Similarly, when three samples from three different brands of 9-volt batteries show average lives of 40, 50, and 60 hours, respectively, are we justified in concluding that these brands are different in regard to their average lives? The theoretical foundations and techniques needed to provide a satisfactory answer to these questions are the subject of this chapter. Specifically, the first two sections deal with the theory and procedure used in comparing the means of two populations. The technique of comparing more than two population means is dealt with in the third section.

SAMPLING DISTRIBUTION OF THE DIFFERENCE BETWEEN TWO SAMPLE MEANS

Let us assume that we have two distinct populations: the first consists of the ages of all students attending Harman University, and the second consists of the ages of all students attending Columbo University. The mean ages and the standard deviation for the two populations are as follows:

	Harman	*Columbo*
Population mean	$\mu_1 = 24$ years	$\mu_2 = 22$ years
Population standard deviation	$\sigma_1 = 7$ years	$\sigma_2 = 6$ years

If we select *many* random samples of 100 students from the Harman population and record the mean age of each sample, the various sample means might be shown as follows.

Harman Sample Means *(years)*
24
23
25
23
22
.
.
.
25

Thus the mean of the first sample of 100 students is 24 years, the mean of the second sample is 23 years, and the mean of the last sample is 25 years.

Similarly, let us assume that we have selected an equal number of random samples of 50 students from Columbo University. The means of these samples might be as follows.

Columbo Sample Means (years)
23
21
22
20
21
.
.
.
22

In comparing the results of the two sets of sample means, let us randomly pair the samples and compute the difference between the means of each pair. The difference is denoted by d. See Table 8.1.

Remembering that the $\bar{x}_1$'s are sample means drawn from a population with $\mu_1 = 24$ and that the $\bar{x}_2$'s are sample means drawn from a population with $\mu_2 = 22$, let us examine some of the properties of the differences recorded in the last column of Table 8.1.

TABLE 8.1

$\bar{x}_1$ (Harman)	$\bar{x}_2$ (Columbo)	$d = \bar{x}_1 - \bar{x}_2$
24	23	1
23	21	2
25	22	3
23	20	3
22	21	1
.	.	.
.	.	.
.	.	.
25	22	3

First, although the difference between the means of the first pair of samples is 1 year, that between the second pair is 2 years, and that between the last pair is 3 years, we would expect the average of these differences to be 2 years (that is, $24 - 22$). The first property of the differences between two sample means is therefore

$$E(d) = \mu_1 - \mu_2,$$

where $E(d)$ is the average of *all* differences, μ_1 is the mean of the population from which the first set of samples is selected (Harman), and μ_2 is the mean of the population from which the second set of samples is selected (Columbo).

Statisticians have studied these differences in great detail. They have discovered that the differences are approximately normally distributed and have a standard deviation or standard error equal to

$$\sqrt{\frac{\sigma_1^2}{n_1} + \frac{\sigma_2^2}{n_2}},$$

where σ_1 is the standard deviation of the population from which the first set of samples is drawn (Harman), n_1 is the size of each sample of the first set of samples (100 students), σ_2 is the standard deviation of the population from which the second set of samples is drawn (Columbo), and n_2 is the size of each sample of the second set (50 students).

Denoting the standard deviation or standard error of the differences by σ_d, we summarize the properties of these differences in Fig. 8.1. For our samples from Harman and Columbo, the properties given in Fig. 8.1 imply that the average of all differences between the means of paired samples is 2 years and their standard error is 1.1 years (see the computations in Fig. 8.2).

Having determined the mean and the standard error of the differences between the means of the paired samples, we can draw some useful conclusions. Since the differences are approximately normally distributed, we expect 68% of the differences to fall within the range

$$E(d) \pm 1\sigma_d = 2 \pm 1.1,$$

or between .9 and 3.1 years (Fig. 8.3). In the same manner, we expect 95% of all the differences to fall within the range

$$E(d) \pm 1.96\sigma_d = 2 \pm 1.96(1.1)$$
$$= 2 \pm 2.16,$$

or between $-.16$ and 4.16 years (Fig. 8.4).

We can summarize the implications of the preceding discussion. Let us assume that the mean ages at Harman and Columbo are 24 and 22 years, respectively, and that the respective standard deviations are 7 and 6 years. Then, if a random sample of 100 students is selected from Harman and another

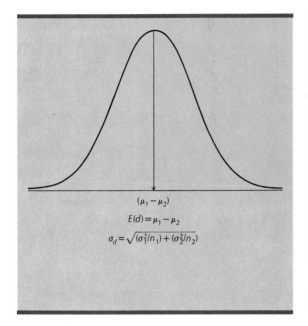

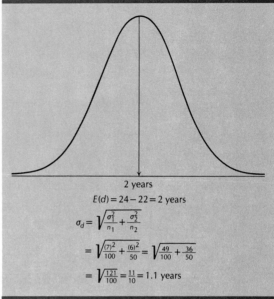

Figure 8.1

Figure 8.2

sample of 50 students from Columbo, we expect the mean of the Harman sample to be, *on the average,* higher than the mean of the Columbo sample by 2 years. However, the difference between the means of the two samples may very well be smaller or greater than 2 years. For example, the Harman sample mean could exceed the Columbo mean by 4.16 years or more or it could be

Figure 8.3

Figure 8.4

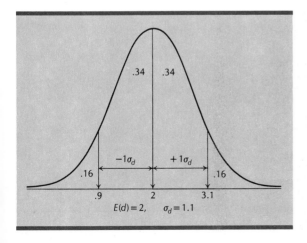

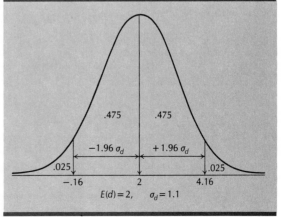

lower than the Columbo mean by .16 year or more. But the probability of obtaining either of these extreme results is only .025 (see Fig. 8.4).

Finally, let us assume that we have selected a sample of 64 students from Harman and a sample of 32 students from Columbo. What is the probability that the Harman sample mean exceeds that of Columbo by 3 years or more? We have already learned that if *many* samples of 64 students are selected from Harman and many samples of 32 students from Columbo, then the differences between the means of paired samples are normally distributed with an average equal to $(\mu_1 - \mu_2)$ and a standard deviation or standard error equal to

$$\sqrt{\frac{\sigma_1^2}{n_1} + \frac{\sigma_2^2}{n_2}}.$$

See Fig. 8.5. Having determined the mean and the standard error of the differences between the sample means, we can now calculate the probability that the difference between any two sample means is 3 years or more (see Fig. 8.6):

$$z = \frac{d - E(d)}{\sigma_d}$$

$$= \frac{3 - 2}{1.375} = \frac{1}{1.375} = .73.$$

Figure 8.5

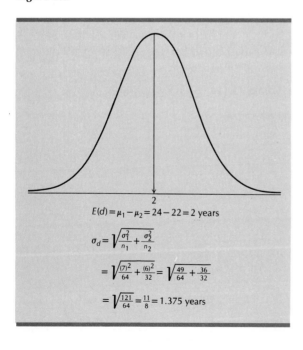

$$E(d) = \mu_1 - \mu_2 = 24 - 22 = 2 \text{ years}$$

$$\sigma_d = \sqrt{\frac{\sigma_1^2}{n_1} + \frac{\sigma_2^2}{n_2}}$$

$$= \sqrt{\frac{(7)^2}{64} + \frac{(6)^2}{32}} = \sqrt{\frac{49}{64} + \frac{36}{32}}$$

$$= \sqrt{\frac{121}{64}} = \frac{11}{8} = 1.375 \text{ years}$$

Figure 8.6

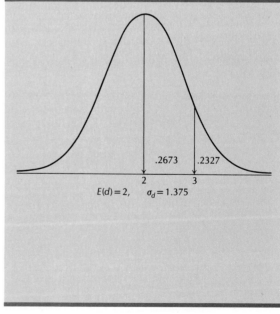

.2673   .2327

$$E(d) = 2, \quad \sigma_d = 1.375$$

Therefore,

$$P(d \geq 3) = .5000 - .2673 = .2327.$$

TEST OF HYPOTHESIS ABOUT THE DIFFERENCE BETWEEN TWO POPULATION MEANS

A simple random sample of 100 students attending Delmore College showed an average of 23 years and a standard deviation of 4 years, while a simple random sample of 50 Eastern University students revealed an average age of 21 years and a standard deviation of 5 years. From the results of these two samples, can we safely conclude that the average age in the two colleges is not the same?

The mere fact that the mean of a sample of Delmore College is higher than the mean of a sample from Eastern University is not conclusive evidence that the average age in the two schools is not the same. Remembering that two samples drawn from the *same* population rarely show the same arithmetic mean, we must be very careful in interpreting the difference between the means of two samples.

Generally speaking, when given two populations, we have two hypotheses to explore. First is the null hypothesis that the two populations from which the two samples originate have the same mean ($H_0 : \mu_1 = \mu_2$). If this is the case, the two sample means should be close together and the observed difference between the two sample means should be small. If the observed difference between the two sample means is in fact small, the difference is deemed *not significant* and is attributed to chance or random sampling fluctuations. The second hypothesis to be explored is that the two samples are drawn from populations that have different means ($H_1 : \mu_1 \neq \mu_2$). If this alternative hypothesis is true, the two sample means should be far apart and the observed difference between the two sample means should be large. If the observed difference between the two sample means is in fact large, the difference is deemed a **significant difference.**

When two sample means are different, how can we decide whether the difference between the two means is significant? The standard procedure is to test the validity of the null hypothesis, which states that $\mu_1 = \mu_2$, utilizing the information from the two samples. On the basis of the evidence produced by the two samples, we will either reject the null hypothesis or reserve judgment. If the null hypothesis is rejected, the observed difference between the two sample means is deemed significant. However, the observed difference is deemed not significant whenever judgment is reserved.

Having outlined the general nature of our test, we can now proceed with the solution to our problem. For clarity, the problem is divided into four sections.

1. Data:

Delmore College	Eastern University
$\bar{x}_1 = 23$ years	$\bar{x}_2 = 21$ years
$s_1 = 4$ years	$s_2 = 5$ years
$n_1 = 100$ students	$n_2 = 50$ students

2. Question: Is the observed difference between the two sample means significant or not?

3. Hypothesis:

$$H_0: \quad \mu_1 = \mu_2,$$
$$H_1: \quad \mu_1 \neq \mu_2.$$

4. Solution: Let us assume that we have selected many samples of size 100 from Delmore College and an equal number of samples of size 50 from Eastern University. When these two sets of samples are paired and the difference between the means of each pair is recorded, then according to what we have already learned, the average of all these differences is equal to $(\mu_1 - \mu_2)$ and the standard error σ_d is equal to

$$\sqrt{\frac{\sigma_1^2}{n_1} + \frac{\sigma_2^2}{n_2}}.$$

But since the standard deviations in the two populations are not known, we may use the standard deviation of the sample as an approximation for the standard deviation of the population. Using this approximation, we find that the estimated standard error of the difference between sample means, denoted by $\hat{\sigma}_d$, is

$$\sqrt{\frac{s_1^2}{n_1} + \frac{s_2^2}{n_2}},$$

whereas the true standard error of the difference between two means is

$$\sqrt{\frac{\sigma_1^2}{n_1} + \frac{\sigma_2^2}{n_2}}.$$

If the null hypothesis is true, that is, $\mu_1 = \mu_2$, then the distribution of the difference between the sample means is described by Fig. 8.7. Figure 8.7 essentially indicates that if the null hypothesis is true, although the difference between the means of any paired samples may not be zero, the average of all such differences is equal to zero. Furthermore, these differences are approximately normally distributed and their estimated standard error is .812 year.

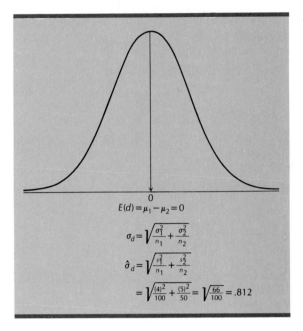

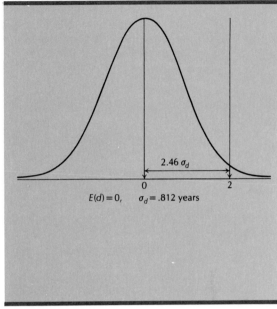

Figure 8.7   **Figure 8.8**

To evaluate the validity of the null hypothesis in light of the two samples actually selected ($\bar{x}_1 = 23$, $\bar{x}_2 = 21$, and $d = 2$), let us calculate the z-value for an observed difference of 2 years or more, assuming that the null hypothesis is true (see Fig. 8.8):

$$z = \frac{d - E(d)}{\hat{\sigma}_d}$$

$$= \frac{2 - 0}{.812} = 2.46.$$

Since the value of z is 2.46, which is greater than 1.96, the null hypothesis is rejected and the difference between the two sample means is deemed significant at the .05 level. It is not significant at the .01 level, since the actual z-value is less than 2.58. (In testing the significance of the difference between two sample means, we always formulate the alternative hypothesis as $\mu_1 \neq \mu_2$. Consequently, the test is two-tailed.)

Example   To compare the average lives of two brands of 9-volt batteries, a sample of 100 batteries from each brand is tested. The sample selected from the first brand shows an average life of 47 hours and a standard deviation of 4 hours. A mean life of 48 hours and a standard deviation of 3 hours are recorded for the sample from the second brand. Is the observed difference between the means of the two samples significant at the .05 level?

Solution: There are two hypotheses,

$$H_0:\quad \mu_1 = \mu_2,$$

$$H_1:\quad \mu_1 \neq \mu_2,$$

and if the null hypothesis is true, then $E(d) = 0$, and $\hat{\sigma}_d = .5$ hour, as shown in our calculations in Fig. 8.9.

The null hypothesis can be evaluated by computing the z-value for the observed difference between the means of the two samples ($\bar{x}_1 = 47$, $\bar{x}_2 = 48$, $d = -1$) (see Fig. 8.10):

$$z = \frac{d - E(d)}{\hat{\sigma}_d}$$

$$= \frac{-1 - 0}{.5} = -2.0.$$

Since the absolute z-value is greater than 1.96, the null hypothesis is rejected, and the difference between the means of the two samples is regarded as significant at the .05 level.

In testing the significance of the difference between two sample means, we have tacitly assumed that both samples are large-size samples. We have

Figure 8.9

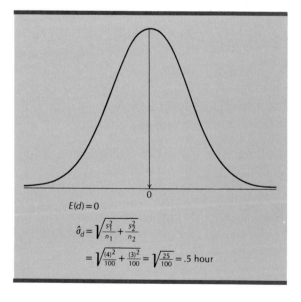

$$E(d) = 0$$

$$\hat{\sigma}_d = \sqrt{\frac{s_1^2}{n_1} + \frac{s_2^2}{n_2}}$$

$$= \sqrt{\frac{(4)^2}{100} + \frac{(3)^2}{100}} = \sqrt{\frac{25}{100}} = .5 \text{ hour}$$

Figure 8.10

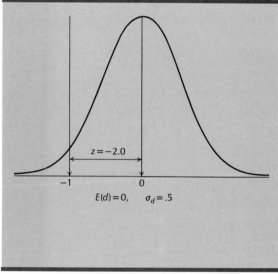

$z = -2.0$

$$E(d) = 0, \qquad \sigma_d = .5$$

furthermore utilized a technique that essentially consists of computing a value of z, where

$$z = \frac{d}{\hat{\sigma}_d} = \frac{\bar{x}_1 - \bar{x}_2}{\sqrt{(s_1^2/n_1) + (s_2^2/n_2)}}.$$

When the above absolute value of z exceeds 1.96, the difference between the two sample means is regarded as significant at the .05 level. Similarly, the difference between the two sample means is regarded as significant at the .01 level when the absolute value of z exceeds 2.58.

The preceding technique is slightly modified when the means to be compared belong to small-size samples. Instead of the normal distribution, a t-distribution with $(n_1 + n_2 - 2)$ degrees of freedom is used.* Consequently, we must compute a t-value, where

$$t = \frac{d}{\hat{\sigma}_d} = \frac{\bar{x}_1 - \bar{x}_2}{\sqrt{\frac{(n_1 - 1)s_1^2 + (n_2 - 1)s_2^2}{n_1 + n_2 - 2}} \sqrt{\frac{1}{n_1} + \frac{1}{n_2}}}.$$

Using $(n_1 + n_2 - 2)$ degrees of freedom, we compare the above value of t with a critical value of $t_{.025}$ or $t_{.005}$, depending on whether the .05 or .01 level of significance is used. The difference between the means of the two samples is regarded as significant when the observed absolute value of t exceeds $t_{.025}$. Similarly, when the observed absolute value of t exceeds $t_{.005}$, the difference between the two sample means is regarded as significant at the .01 level. We now clarify this procedure with an example.

Example A reading test is given to an elementary school class that consists of 12 Anglo-American children and 10 Mexican-American children. The results of the test are as follows.

Anglo-American	Mexican-American
$\bar{x}_1 = 74$	$\bar{x}_2 = 70$
$s_1 = 8$	$s_2 = 10$

Is the difference between the means of the two samples significant at the .05 level?

---

*The use of the t-distribution requires two assumptions: (1) the two samples selected are independent random samples; (2) the parent populations are normally distributed with equal variances.

Solution:

$$H_0: \quad \mu_1 = \mu_2,$$

$$H_1: \quad \mu_1 \neq \mu_2,$$

Level of significance = .05.

To test the null hypothesis, we compute the observed value of t as

$$t = \frac{\bar{x}_1 - \bar{x}_2}{\sqrt{\dfrac{(n_1 - 1)s_1^2 + (n_2 - 1)s_2^2}{n_1 + n_2 - 2}} \sqrt{\dfrac{1}{n_1} + \dfrac{1}{n_2}}}.$$

$$= \frac{74 - 70}{\sqrt{\dfrac{(12 - 1)(8)^2 + (10 - 1)(10)^2}{12 + 10 - 2}} \sqrt{\dfrac{1}{12} + \dfrac{1}{10}}}$$

$$= \frac{4}{\sqrt{\dfrac{1604}{20}} \sqrt{\dfrac{22}{120}}}$$

$$= \frac{4}{\sqrt{14.703}}$$

$$= 1.043.$$

With 20 degrees of freedom (df = 12 + 10 − 2), the critical value of $t_{.025}$ is 2.086. Since the actual value of t is 1.043 and the critical value is 2.086, the difference between the means of the two groups of children is not regarded as significant at the .05 level.

EXERCISES

8.1   The mean height of soldiers in the U.S. army is 69 inches, with a standard deviation of 2 inches. The mean height of soldiers in the French army is 67 inches, with a standard deviation of 1 inch. If a random sample of 80 soldiers is selected from each army, what is the probability that the mean height

a) in the U.S. sample is greater than that of the French sample by 2.4 inches or more?

b) in the French sample is smaller than that of the U.S. sample by 1.8 inches or less?

8.2   The following data are given on the lives of two different brands of 9-volt batteries.

Brand A (hours)	Brand B (hours)
$\mu_1 = 51$	$\mu_2 = 50$
$\sigma_1 = 8$	$\sigma_2 = 6$

If a random sample of 100 batteries is selected from each brand, what is the probability that the mean life of sample B is

a) greater than that of A by .6 hour or more?

b) smaller than that of A by .6 or more?

8.3   To assess the impact of windowless schools on the psychological development of schoolchildren, an anxiety test was given to a class of 40 children in a windowless school. The same test was also given to a similar class of 30 students in a school with windows. The results of the test are shown below.

Windowless Schools	Schools with Windows
$\bar{x}_1 = 117$	$\bar{x}_2 = 112$
$s_1 = 10$	$s_2 = 12$
$n_1 = 40$	$n_2 = 30$

If you are willing to reject a true hypothesis no more than 5 times in 100, can you conclude that the impact of the two types of school on the anxiety of the children is not the same?

8.4   The systolic blood pressure of a group of 64 persons from a South Pacific island was compared with that of a similar group of 64 persons living in New York City. The data below summarize the findings.

	South Pacific Island	New York City
$\sum x$	9088	9472
$\sum (x - \bar{x})^2$	9072	16128
n	64	64

Is the difference between the means of the two sample groups significant at the .05 level?

8.5   To compare the vitamin A content of two different brands of vitamin capsules, a sample of 6 capsules was selected from each brand. The results are given below.

	First Brand (USP units)	Second Brand (USP units)
Mean	5000	4800
Standard deviation	400	300

If you are willing to reject a true hypothesis no more than once in 100, can you conclude that the vitamin A contents of the two brands of capsules are not the same?

8.6   Given: the following nicotine content of several cigarettes taken from two different brands.

Brand X: 17, 20, 20, 23
Brand Y: 18, 20, 21, 22, 24

Using the .05 level of significance, can you conclude that the nicotine content of the two brands of cigarettes is not the same?

8.7   In a study concerning the effect of film rating on box office gross, a random sample of 50 films is selected from each of the G-rated and R-rated categories. The two samples show the following information.

	G-Rated	R-Rated
Mean gross (millions of dollars)	16.2	17.7
Standard deviation (millions of dollars)	4.1	3.3

Using the .01 level of significance, can we conclude that the two categories gross equal amounts at the box office?

8.8   In a study concerning the characteristics of an effective salesperson, sales vice-president Willy Loman randomly selected several individuals from among the best and worst salespeople. The study revealed the following information.

	Successful Salespeople	Unsuccessful Salespeople
Sample size	50	40
Aggressiveness mean score	17	21
Standard deviation	3	4

Using the .05 level of significance, can Mr. Loman conclude that the degree of aggressiveness for successful and unsuccessful salespeople is the same?

8.9 A sample survey is conducted to compare the mean annual family income for Mexican-Americans and blacks in metropolitan Los Angeles. A random sample of 200 families is selected from each group. The samples show the following results.

Mexican-Americans	Blacks
$n_1 = 200$	$n_2 = 200$
$\bar{x}_1 = \$14,225$	$\bar{x}_2 = \$15,212$
$s_1 = \$1,800$	$s_2 = \$2,400$

Using the .05 level of significance, can we conclude that annual family income for the two groups is not the same?

COMPARING SEVERAL POPULATION MEANS: ANALYSIS OF VARIANCE

A sample of five batteries was selected from each of three different brands. The lifetime in hours was recorded for each individual battery. The results are shown below.

Brand A (hours)	Brand B (hours)	Brand C (hours)
40	50	60
30	50	60
40	50	60
60	60	70
30	40	50
$\bar{x}_1 = 40$	$\bar{x}_2 = 50$	$\bar{x}_3 = 60$

Are these brands different with respect to their average lives?

When several samples reveal different means, an investigator has two hypotheses to explore. First, there is the null hypothesis that these samples are from populations with equal means, that is, $\mu_1 = \mu_2 = \mu_3$. If this is the case, then the observed differences among sample means are due to sampling fluctuations and hence are not significant.

The alternative hypothesis to be explored is that each of the three samples is obtained from a given population and that means of the three populations are not all equal. According to this hypothesis, the differences between some or all sample means are significant.

In comparing the several sample means, the investigator tests the validity of the null hypothesis, utilizing the information contained in the samples. On the basis of such information, the investigator either rejects the null hypothesis or reserves judgment. If the null hypothesis is rejected, the differences between some or all sample means are regarded as significant. On the other hand, if the investigator reserves judgment, the differences are not regarded as significant.

We must know clearly two basic assumptions underlying our method of analysis before we can proceed. First, our method of analysis assumes that each of our three samples is obtained from a normally distributed population. Second, it is assumed that the three populations have the same standard deviation, that is, $\sigma_1 = \sigma_2 = \sigma_3$. If these two assumptions can be justified, then the null hypothesis, which states that $\mu_1 = \mu_2 = \mu_3$, can be extended to mean that the three samples are from one and the same population.

The general procedure used in our test is to assume first that the null hypothesis is true, that is, that all the samples belong to the same population. We then make two estimates of the population variance, σ^2. These two estimates are called the **variance within samples** and the **variance between samples.** If the disparity between the two estimates is "considerable," the null hypothesis is rejected and the differences between the various sample means are regarded as significant.

Assuming that our three samples do belong to the same population, how can we estimate the variance of this population, σ^2? A logical and reasonable approach is to compute the variance of each sample and to use the average of the variances of the three samples as an estimate of σ^2. This estimate, called the *variance within samples,* is then contrasted with a second estimate of σ^2 obtained by means of an alternative procedure (to be discussed later in this section). The computations used in determining the variance within samples are carried out in the following section.

Estimating the Population Variance: Variance Within Samples

Recalling that the variance is the square of the standard deviation, we compute the variance of each of the three samples, using the following formula (see Table 8.2):

$$s^2 = \frac{\sum (x - \bar{x})^2}{n - 1}.$$

TABLE 8.2

Sample 1		Sample 2		Sample 3	
x	$(x - \bar{x})^2$	x	$(x - \bar{x})^2$	x	$(x - \bar{x})^2$
40	0	50	0	60	0
30	100	50	0	60	0
40	0	50	0	60	0
60	400	60	100	70	100
30	100	40	100	50	100
$\bar{x}_1 = 40$	600	$\bar{x}_2 = 50$	200	$\bar{x}_3 = 60$	200

$$n = 5 \qquad\qquad n = 5 \qquad\qquad n = 5$$

$$s_1^2 = \frac{\sum (x - \bar{x}_1)^2}{n - 1} \qquad s_2^2 = \frac{\sum (x - \bar{x}_2)^2}{n - 1} \qquad s_3^2 = \frac{\sum (x - \bar{x}_3)^2}{n - 1}$$

$$s_1^2 = \frac{600}{4} \qquad\qquad s_2^2 = \frac{200}{4} \qquad\qquad s_3^2 = \frac{200}{4}$$

$$s_1^2 = 150 \qquad\qquad s_2^2 = 50 \qquad\qquad s_3^2 = 50$$

The population variance can be estimated as the average of the three sample variances:

$$\hat{\sigma}^2 = \frac{s_1^2 + s_2^2 + s_3^2}{3}$$

$$= \frac{150 + 50 + 50}{3}$$

$$= \frac{250}{3} = 83.33.$$

We obtain this estimate of the population variance utilizing the three sample *variances.* Alternatively, we can estimate the population variance, utilizing the *means* of the three samples. The estimate obtained in this way is called *variance between samples.* As mentioned earlier, the two estimates for the population variance obtained by these two methods are compared, and the decision of whether to reject the null hypothesis depends on the magnitude of the disparity between the two estimates.

Estimating the Population Variance: Variance Between Samples

Three samples have been selected. Their arithmetic means are 40, 50, and 60 hours. If these samples belong to the same population, what is our best estimate of the mean of that population? The mean of the population can best be estimated by averaging the three sample means. Denoted by $\hat{\mu}$, the estimated population mean is therefore

$$\hat{\mu} = \frac{\bar{x}_1 + \bar{x}_2 + \bar{x}_3}{3}$$

$$= \frac{40 + 50 + 60}{3}$$

$$= \frac{150}{3} = 50 \text{ hours.}$$

In general, the estimated population mean is

$$\hat{\mu} = \frac{\bar{x}_1 + \bar{x}_2 + \cdots + \bar{x}_k}{k},$$

where there are k sample means to be compared.

Now we have three sample means: $\bar{x}_1 = 40$, $\bar{x}_2 = 50$, $\bar{x}_3 = 60$, which, according to the null hypothesis, belong to a population whose mean has been estimated as $\hat{\mu} = 50$. Using these three sample means, let us calculate the square of their standard deviation or the square of their standard error.

$$\hat{\sigma}_{\bar{x}}^2 = \frac{(\bar{x}_1 - \hat{\mu})^2 + (\bar{x}_2 - \hat{\mu})^2 + (\bar{x}_3 - \hat{\mu})^2}{\text{Number of samples} - 1}$$

$$= \frac{(40 - 50)^2 + (50 - 50)^2 + (60 - 50)^2}{3 - 1}$$

$$= \frac{100 + 0 + 100}{2} = 100.$$

In general,

$$\hat{\sigma}_{\bar{x}}^2 = \frac{(\bar{x}_1 - \hat{\mu})^2 + (\bar{x}_2 - \hat{\mu})^2 + \cdots + (\bar{x}_k - \hat{\mu})^2}{k - 1},$$

where k is the number of sample means to be compared and $\hat{\sigma}_{\bar{x}}^2$ is the square of their standard error.

But we have already learned from the theory dealing with the distribution of the sample means (Chapter 6) that when all possible random samples are selected from a given population, the standard deviation or the standard error of these sample means is equal to the standard deviation in the *population* divided by the square root of the sample size. Symbolically,

$$\sigma_{\bar{x}} = \frac{\sigma}{\sqrt{n}}.$$

Squaring both sides, we obtain

$$\sigma_{\bar{x}}^2 = \sigma^2/n,$$

and solving for σ^2, we have

$$\sigma^2 = n\sigma_{\bar{x}}^2.$$

Thus we conclude that the variance in the population from which the three samples originate can be estimated as the product of the sample size times the square of the standard error the mean.

We have already determined that $\hat{\sigma}_{\bar{x}}^2$ is 100. With a sample size of 5, the variance in the population is estimated as follows:

$$\hat{\sigma}^2 = n\hat{\sigma}_{\bar{x}}^2$$
$$= 5 \cdot 100 = 500.$$

Thus, utilizing the sample means we estimate the variance in the population as 500.

Now we are ready to compare the two estimates obtained for the variance in the population. Utilizing the *variances* in the sample, we have obtained an estimate of 83.33 hours (variance within samples). An estimate of 500, on the other hand, is obtained when the sample *means* are utilized (variance between samples). The disparity between the two estimates can be measured by what is called the *F*-ratio, where

$$F = \frac{\text{Variance between samples}}{\text{Variance within samples}}$$

$$= \frac{500}{83.33} = 6.0.$$

If the null hypothesis is true, that is, if there is no significant difference between the three brands, then the two estimates for the population variance must be reasonably close and the *F*-ratio is expected to be unity.

If the three brands are different, however, the variance *between* samples would be larger than the variance *within* samples. This is due to the fact that while the variance within samples is a good estimate of the population variance, the variance between samples consists of the population variance plus an additional variance reflecting the differences between the three brands of batteries. Thus, when the three brands differ with respect to their average life, the F-ratio is expected to be greater than unity. Furthermore, the greater the difference between the various brands, the greater the F-ratio.

To determine whether the differences between brands are significant at the .05 level, the *actual F-ratio* is compared against what is called a *critical* $F_{.05}$-*ratio* (see Table B at the end of the book). From Table B we see that each critical $F_{.05}$-ratio is determined by a combination of numerator and denominator degrees of freedom. The numerator degrees of freedom are equal to $k - 1$, where k is the number of samples to be compared. The denominator degrees of freedom are equal to $k(n - 1)$, where n is the size of each sample.

To determine the critical $F_{.05}$-ratio in our problem, the numerator and denominator degrees of freedom must be determined first.

$$\text{Numerator degrees of freedom} = k - 1$$
$$= 3 - 1$$
$$= 2$$

$$\text{Denominator degrees of freedom} = k(n - 1)$$
$$= 3(5 - 1)$$
$$= 12$$

For a combination of 2 numerator and 12 denominator degrees of freedom, Table B lists a critical $F_{.05}$-ratio of 3.89, which means that with this particular combination of degrees of freedom, there is only a .05 probability of obtaining an F-ratio of 3.89 or more as a result of random sampling fluctuations. Furthermore, the probability of obtaining an F-ratio greater than 3.89 is less than .05 (see Fig. 8.11).

Thus, whenever our actual F-ratio exceeds the critical $F_{.05}$-ratio, the null hypothesis is rejected and the differences between the several sample means are regarded as significant at the .05 level. However, the differences between the various sample means are not significant when the actual F-ratio is less than the critical $F_{.05}$-ratio.

Figure 8.11

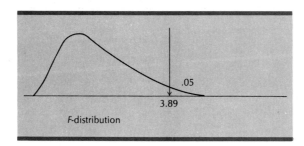

Similarly, the differences between several sample means are regarded as significant at the .01 level when the actual F-ratio is greater than the $F_{.01}$-ratio in Table C at the end of the book.

The actual F-ratio in our problem is 6.0, while the critical $F_{.05}$- and $F_{.01}$-ratios are 3.89 and 6.93, respectively. Since our actual F-ratio is greater than $F_{.05}$ but less than $F_{.01}$, the differences between the means of the three samples are significant at the .05 level but not at the .01 level. In other words, if the three brands of batteries do have the same average life, there is less than a .05, but more than a .01, chance that the F-ratio will be 6.0 or more. If we reject the null hypothesis of equal means whenever the F-ratio is 6.0 or more, there is a probability of between .01 and .05 that, when the brands are actually equal, we will mistakenly conclude that the brands of batteries are different.

Before concluding this chapter, we will summarize the various steps used in comparing several means, as well as the solution to our problem.

Step 1. Compute the variance within samples.

$$\text{Variance within samples} = \frac{S_1^2 + S_2^2 + \cdots + S_k^2}{k},$$

where

$$S^2 = \frac{\sum (x - \bar{x})^2}{n - 1},$$

$k =$ number of samples to be compared,

$n =$ size of each sample.

Step 2. Compute the variance between samples.

$$\text{Variance within samples} = n\hat{\sigma}_{\bar{x}}^2$$

$$= n \left[\frac{(\bar{x}_1 - \hat{\mu})^2 + (\bar{x}_2 - \hat{\mu})^2 + \cdots + (\bar{x}_k - \hat{\mu})^2}{k - 1} \right],$$

where

$$\hat{\mu} = \frac{\bar{x}_1 + \bar{x}_2 + \cdots + \bar{x}_k}{k}.$$

Step 3. Determine the actual F-ratio.

$$F = \frac{\text{Variance between samples}}{\text{Variance within samples}}$$

Step 4. Determine the degrees of freedom.

$$\text{Numerator degrees of freedom} = k - 1$$
$$\text{Denominator degrees of freedom} = k(n - 1)$$

Step 5.   Compare the actual *F*-ratio with the critical *F*-ratio.

If $F > F_{.05}$, the difference is significant at the .05 level. If $F > F_{.01}$, the difference is significant at the .01 level.

Solution:

Data and Preliminary Computations

Brand A		Brand B		Brand C	
x	$(x - \bar{x}_1)^2$	x	$(x - \bar{x}_2)^2$	x	$(x - \bar{x}_3)^2$
40	0	50	0	60	0
30	100	50	0	60	0
40	0	50	0	60	0
60	400	60	100	70	100
30	100	40	100	50	100
$\bar{x}_1 = 40$	600	$\bar{x}_2 = 50$	200	$\bar{x}_2 = 60$	200

$$n = 5$$
$$s_1^2 = \frac{\Sigma (x - \bar{x}_1)^2}{n - 1}$$
$$= \frac{600}{4} = 150$$

$$n = 5$$
$$s_2^2 = \frac{\Sigma (x - \bar{x}_2)^2}{n - 1}$$
$$= \frac{200}{4} = 50$$

$$n = 5$$
$$s_3^2 = \frac{\Sigma (x - \bar{x}_3)^2}{n - 1}$$
$$= \frac{200}{4} = 50$$

$$\hat{\mu} = \frac{\bar{x}_1 + \bar{x}_2 + \bar{x}_3}{3}$$
$$= \frac{40 + 50 + 60}{3} = 50$$

Step 1.

$$\text{Variance within samples} = \frac{s_1^2 + s_2^2 + s_3^2}{3}$$
$$= \frac{150 + 50 + 50}{3}$$
$$= \frac{250}{3} = 83.33$$

Step 2.

$$\text{Variance between samples} = n \left[\frac{(\bar{x}_1 - \hat{\mu})^2 + (\bar{x}_2 - \hat{\mu})^2 + (\bar{x}_3 - \hat{\mu})^2}{3 - 1} \right]$$

$$= 5 \left[\frac{(40 - 50)^2 + (50 - 50)^2 + (60 - 50)^2}{2} \right]$$

$$= 5 \left[\frac{100 + 0 + 100}{2} \right] = 500$$

Step 3.

$$F = \frac{\text{Variance between samples}}{\text{Variance within samples}}$$

$$= \frac{500}{83.33} = 6.0$$

Step 4.

$$\text{Numerator degrees of freedom} = (k - 1)$$
$$= (3 - 1)$$
$$= 2$$
$$\text{Denominator degrees of freedom} = k(n - 1)$$
$$= 3(5 - 1)$$
$$= 12$$

Step 5.

$$F_{.05} = 3.89 \quad \text{(Table B)}$$
$$F_{.01} = 6.93 \quad \text{(Table C)}$$

Conclusion: Since the actual F-ratio is 6.0, which is greater than $F_{.05}$ but less than $F_{.01}$, the differences between the three sample means are significant at the .05 level but not significant at the .01 level.

EXERCISES

8.10 To compare the effectiveness of three distinct methods of teaching arithmetic, 15 homogeneous fourth-grade students were divided into three equal subgroups, and each subgroup was taught arithmetic using one of the three methods. After one year, the pupils were given the same examination. The examination scores were as follows.

First Method	Second Method	Third Method
77	73	76
78	76	77
80	76	82
82	77	83
83	78	87

If the subgroups were taught by teachers who were very much alike in all pertinent attributes, is there evidence that the effectiveness of the three teaching methods is not the same? Use a .05 level of significance.

8.11   Three cars from each of the four different brands F, C, D, and R were driven in the same manner with one gallon of regular gasoline. The distance traveled by each car, in miles, is shown below.

F	C	D	R
18	21	23	20
20	22	26	19
22	26	26	21

If you are willing to reject a true hypothesis no more than 5 times in 100, do you conclude that the average mileage of the four brands of cars is not the same?

8.12   Each of three fertilizer mixtures, X, Y, and Z, was applied to 6 test plots planted with a certain variety of wheat. The wheat yields, in bushels per acre, for the 18 test plots are given below.

Mixture X	Mixture Y	Mixture Z
50	55	70
55	57	68
57	59	66
56	60	71
59	57	67
53	54	66

What is your conclusion regarding the effectiveness of the three fertilizer mixtures? Use a .01 level of significance.

8.13   The means and the standard deviations of social maturity scores received by individuals belonging to four occupational groups are as follows.

	Dentists	Bankers	Machinists	Research Scientists
n	6	6	6	6
$\bar{x}$	57	59	43	61
s	10	10	10	10

Test the hypothesis that the social maturity of the four occupational groups is the same against the alternative hypothesis that their social maturity is not the same. Use a level of significance of .05.

KEY TERMS

significant difference   When the sample means are so far apart that the null hypothesis $\mu_1 = \mu_2$ is rejected, the difference in the sample means is significant.

variance between samples   An estimate of the variance made by comparing the sample means.

variance within samples   An estimate of the variance made by averaging the sample variances for all the samples.

F-ratio   The ratio of the variance between samples to the variance within samples. The F-ratio is used to test the hypothesis that the means of several populations are equal.

SUMMARY OF FORMULAS

expected difference between sample means

$$E(d) = E(\bar{x}_1 - \bar{x}_2) = \mu_1 - \mu_2$$

standard deviation of difference between sample means

$$\sigma_d = \sigma_{\bar{x}_1 - \bar{x}_2} = \sqrt{\frac{\sigma_1^2}{n_1} + \frac{\sigma_2^2}{n_2}}$$

z-value for the difference between two means

$$z = \frac{d}{\hat{\sigma}_d} = \frac{\bar{x}_1 - \bar{x}_2}{\sqrt{(s_1^2/n_1) + (s_2^2/n_2)}}$$

t-value for the difference of two means

$$t = \frac{d}{\hat{\sigma}_d} = \frac{\bar{x}_1 - \bar{x}_2}{\sqrt{\frac{(n_1 - 1)s_1^2 + (n_2 - 1)s_2^2}{n_1 + n_2 - 2}} \sqrt{\frac{1}{n_1} + \frac{1}{n_2}}}$$

σ^2 variance within samples

$$\hat{\sigma}^2 = \frac{s_1^2 + s_2^2 + \cdots + s_k^2}{k}$$

variance within samples

$$\hat{\sigma}^2 = n\hat{\sigma}_{\bar{x}}^2 = n\frac{\sum\limits_{i=1}^{k}(\bar{x}_1 - \hat{\mu})^2}{k - 1},$$

$$\text{where } \hat{\mu} = \frac{1}{k}\sum_{i=1}^{k}\bar{x}_1$$

F-ratio

$$F = \frac{\text{Variance between samples}}{\text{Variance within samples}}$$

CUMULATIVE REVIEW

1. A large shipment of ball bearings has a mean diameter of 2.00 inches, with a standard deviation of .02 inches ($\mu = 2.00$, $\sigma = .02$).

   a) Assuming that the diameters are normally distributed, establish a range where the probability is .95 that the diameter of a single ball bearing is expected to fall.

   b) Establish a range where the probability is .95 that the mean diameter of a sample of 400 ball bearings is expected to fall.

   c) What is the probability that the mean diameter of a random sample of 100 ball bearings will be greater than 2.003 inches?

2. The lives of 100-watt electric bulbs are normally distributed. The mean is 800 hours and the standard deviation is 50 hours ($\mu = 800$, $\sigma = 50$).

   a) Establish an interval such that the probability is .95 that the life of a single bulb is within such an interval.

   b) Establish an interval such that the probability is .99 that the average life of a random sample of 100 bulbs is within such an interval.

   c) What is the probability that any single bulb will last more than 820 hours?

   d) What is the probability that the mean life of a simple random sample of 100 bulbs will be longer than 820 hours?

3. A manufacturer of instant coffee packages the product in 12-ounce jars. To control the filling process a sample of 36 jars is selected every hour. The following decision rule is imposed: If the average weight in the sample, $\bar{x}$, is

between 12.04 ounces and 12.08 ounces, the process is continued; otherwise the process is stopped and readjusted.

a) What is the probability of stopping a process operating with a mean of 12.06 ounces per jar and a standard deviation of .3 ounce ($\mu = 12.06$, $\sigma = .3$)?

b) What is the probability of continuing a process operating with a mean of 12.08 ounces per jar and a standard deviation of .3 ounce ($\mu = 12.08$, $\sigma = .3$)?

4. The average age of all students attending Riverside College is 22 years, with a standard deviation of 4 years ($\mu = 22$, $\sigma = 4$).

a) What is the probability that the mean age in a random sample of 64 students will be between 21.5 and 23.0 years?

b) What sample size is required to estimate the average age of a Riverside student if it is desired that there be a .99 confidence that the error in the estimate does not exceed 1 year?

5. In a very large shipment of batteries, the useful life of a battery is normally distributed, with a mean of 400 hours. It is also known that 90% of the batteries have a useful life, which ranges between 318 and 482 hours. If a random sample of 100 batteries is selected from this shipment, what is the probability that the sample mean is greater than 420 hours?

6. A random sample of 64 farm workers employed in Tucson revealed the following information.

$$x = \text{hourly wage rate of a farm worker}$$
$$\sum x = \$192$$
$$\sum (x - \bar{x})^2 = \$63$$

Establish a .99 confidence interval estimate of the average hourly earnings of all farm workers employed in Tucson.

7. A random sample of a new variety of apples showed a mean weight of 10 ounces and a standard deviation of 2 ounces. Establish a .95 confidence interval estimate of the average weight of the variety of apples

a) assuming that the sample consisted of 64 apples,

b) assuming that the sample consisted of 16 apples.

8. A random sample of 5 fuses of a certain brand is tested to determine the average breaking point. The breaking points measured in amperes are as follows:

$$18, \quad 22, \quad 20, \quad 14, \quad 26.$$

With what degree of confidence can we assert that the average breaking point of this brand of fuse is between 15.736 and 24.264?

9. Mr. Smith, a farmer, desires to determine the total weight of a lot of 10,000

oranges. Since Mr. Smith has only a small scale, he selects a random sample of 16 oranges. The sample shows a mean of 7 ounces and a standard deviation of 1 ounce. Establish a .95 confidence interval estimate of the *total* weight of the entire lot.

10. The ABC Shoe Company operates a chain of retail shoe stores in Illinois. It is the policy of the company that no branch is established in any community unless the company is .99 sure that aggregate expenditures on shoes in that community are at least $1 million. The company is now considering the establishment of a branch in Springdale, a community of 20,000 families. To estimate aggregate expenditures on shoes in Springdale, a random sample of 49 families was selected. The sample revealed an average annual expenditure of $60 per family, with a standard deviation of $21. Based on this sample information, should the ABC Company establish a branch in Springdale?

11. A drug-testing agency suspects that a newly developed birth control drug has the undesirable effect of raising body temperature. The drug is administered to 64 healthy females and the following information is obtained.

$$x = \text{body temperature measured in } °F$$

$$\sum x = 6323.2$$

$$\sum (x - \bar{x})^2 = 10.08$$

Using the .05 level of significance, determine whether the agency is correct in its belief about the side effect of the new drug. The average body temperature of a healthy female is 98.6°F.

12. The Ka-Chu Nut Company markets its mixed nuts in 16-ounce jars. The jars are claimed to contain, on the average, 50% cashews and 50% peanuts. Suspecting that the mixture contains more peanuts than cashews, Ms. Nadir examined the contents of 5 jars. The proportion of cashews in these jars are

.51,   .47,   .45,   .43,   .39.

If Ms. Nadir is willing to reject a true claim no more than once in 100, would she reject the Ka-Chu Nut Company claim?

13. A random sample of 100 college professors in the United States shows the following data.

$$x = \text{age of a college professor}$$

$$\sum x = 4000 \text{ years}$$

$$\sum (x - \bar{x})^2 = 9900 \text{ years}$$

a) Establish a .95 confidence interval estimate of the average age of an American college professor.

b) With what degree of confidence can we assert that the average age of an American college professor is somewhere between 38.36 and 41.64 years?

c) An official of the American Association of University Professors claims that the average age of a college professor is 43 years. What would you conclude about the validity of this claim, using a level of significance of .01?

14. The 1980 census shows that average annual family income in Des Moines is $14,200. A random sample of 100 families from the city shows an average annual income of $14,050, with a standard deviation of $2000, in 1981. Using a level of significance of .05, test the hypothesis that mean family income has declined in 1981.

15. An arithmetic test is administered to a random sample of 100 eighth graders in the Los Angeles school district. The sample shows an average of 72 with a standard deviation of 8. When the same test is administered to a random sample of 100 eighth graders in the Pasadena school district, the sample shows an average of 75 with a standard deviation of 6. Using a level of significance of .01, can you conclude that the arithmetic performance of eighth graders in the two school districts is *not* the same?

16. The Cosmopolitan Life Insurance Company conducts an in-house training seminar for its salespersons. To measure the effectiveness of the seminar, management investigated the sales records of 100 salespersons who attended the seminar and 100 salespersons who did not attend the seminar. The investigation revealed the following information:

Salespersons Who Attended the Seminar	Salespersons Who Did Not Attend the Seminar
x = number of policies sold per month	$\bar{x}$ = number of policies sold per month
$\bar{x}$ = 7.5 policies	$\bar{x}$ = 6 policies
s = 4 policies	s = 3 policies

Using a level of significance of .01, can management conclude that the seminar is effective?

17. To compare the average nicotine content of four brands of cigarettes, 6 cigarettes of each brand were tested and the following information obtained.

	Brand			
	A	B	C	D
Mean (in milligrams)	28	27	31	30
Standard deviation (in milligrams)	2	2	2	2

Are the four brands of cigarettes significantly different with respect to their average nicotine content? Use a level of significance of .05.

18. A random sample of 400 families in Tallahassee shows an average weekly expenditure of $80 on food, with a standard deviation of $20.

   a) Establish a .95 confidence interval estimate of average weekly family expenditures on food in Tallahassee.

   b) What can we assert with .98 confidence about the possible size of our error if we estimate the mean expenditure to be $80?

   c) It is claimed that average family expenditure on food in Tallahassee is $85 per week. Use the sample information to test the hypothesis that it is less than $85.

19. A random sample of 400 families is selected from a community of 50,000 families. The sample shows an average annual expenditure of $94 per family on books and magazines, with a standard deviation of $20. Establish a .95 confidence interval estimate of *aggregate* annual expenditure on books and magazines for the entire community.

20. The U.S. Civil Aeronautics Board selected a random sample of 80 commercial pilots to determine the average length of experience of U.S. commercial pilots. The sample shows an average length of experience of 19.75 years, with a standard deviation of 4.15 years. Establish a .95 confidence interval estimate of the average experience, in years, of U.S. commercial pilots.

21. The production of machine A is monitored at 50 randomly selected hours. The production engineer observes a mean production of 120 units per hour, with a standard deviation of 20 units. Establish a .95 confidence interval estimate of machine A's output during a production period of 10,000 machine hours.

22. The personnel manager of a large automobile assembly plant wishes to determine the average number of days workers are absent during the month. A random sample of 10 employees is selected. Their files show the following number of days missed from work in a given month:

$$4, \quad 1, \quad 3, \quad 1, \quad 2, \quad 2, \quad 3, \quad 2, \quad 1, \quad 1.$$

Establish a .90 confidence interval estimate of the average number of days per month workers are absent from work in the automobile assembly plant.

23. In 1985, the average price of a single-family home sold in Northridge, California, is $89,570, with a standard deviation of $11,500 ($\mu = 89{,}570$, $\sigma = 11{,}500$).

   a) If a simple random sample of 60 homes sold in 1986 shows an average of $91,750, can we conclude that the average price of a single-family home in Northridge has increased between 1985 and 1986?

   b) Is it correct to assert that the price of 95% of all homes sold in Northridge during 1985 is between $67,030 and $112,110?

24. In a study concerning advertising practices of the top 100 U.S. national advertisers, a random sample of 5 firms is selected from the group of 100 advertisers. The sample shows the following data.

Company	Advertising as a Percent of Sales	TV Advertising as a Percent of Advertising Budget
Procter & Gamble Co.	5.7	93
General Foods Corp.	5.6	85
American Home Products	8.7	92
Bristol-Myers	8.3	92
Warner-Lambert Co.	6.7	78

   a) Establish a .90 confidence interval estimate of the mean advertising-to-sales ratio for the 100 top U.S. advertisers.

   b) With what degree of confidence can we assert that the mean ratio is somewhere between 5.210 and 8.790?

25. Use the data in the preceding problem to test the hypothesis that the top 100 U.S. national advertisers allocate, on average, at least 90% of their advertising budget to television. Use a level of significance of .01.

26. A random sample of 6 oranges is selected from a large shipment to determine the mean weight per orange for the entire shipment. The sample shows the following weights in ounces:

$$8.5, \quad 8.3, \quad 9.0, \quad 9.2, \quad 8.5, \quad 7.5.$$

   a) Establish a .90 confidence interval estimate of the mean weight per orange in the shipment.

   b) Assuming that there are 10,000 oranges in the shipment, establish a .95 confidence interval estimate of the shipment's total weight.

27. A ledger contains 100,000 accounts receivable. The mean of all accounts is $250, with a standard deviation of $50 ($\mu = 250, \sigma = 50$).

a) Can we assert that 95% of all accounts are between $152 and $348? Explain fully.

b) If a random sample of 100 accounts is selected from this ledger and the sample mean will be determined, can we assert that the probability is .95 that the sample mean will be between $240.20 and $259.80? Explain fully.

28. A simple random sample of 64 U.S. university professors shows an average annual salary of $20,000, with a standard deviation of $4000.

a) Establish a .95 confidence interval estimate of the average annual salary of a university professor in the United States.

b) Can we assert that the annual salaries of 90% of all college professors in the United States are between $19,180 and $20,820? Explain fully.

29. The average annual family income in Hinsdale, Illinois, is $25,000, with a standard deviation of $6000 ($\mu = 25,000, \sigma = 6000$).

a) Is it correct to state that 95% of all families in Hinsdale earn between $13,240 and $36,760 annually? Explain fully.

b) Is it possible to state that 95% of the families in a random sample of 64 Hinsdale families earn between $23,530 and $26,470 per year? Explain fully.

c) Is it possible to state that the probability is .99 that the mean annual income of a random sample of 100 Hinsdale families is expected to fall between $23,452 and $26,548? Explain fully.

ESTIMATING THE POPULATION PROPORTION FROM A SAMPLE

9

In the preceding three chapters we treated exclusively problems concerning the mean of a population. In this chapter and Chapter 10 we will examine problems dealing with the population proportion.

The relation between the sample proportion, p, and the population proportion, π, is described in the first part of this chapter. In the remaining sections, we are concerned with the problem of estimating the population proportion from a simple random sample.

SAMPLING DISTRIBUTION OF THE PROPORTION

The relation between the population proportion and the proportions of the various samples that can be selected from a population can best be illustrated by describing a sampling operation from a known population. Let the known population consist of 5 marbles: 1 white and 4 black. Denoting a white marble by W and a black marble by B, we display our known population below.

Marble	Color
1	W
2	B
3	B
4	B
5	B

The proportion of white marbles, denoted by π, in the above population is .20.

Now let us select all possible samples of four marbles from this population and compute the proportion p of white marbles for each sample.

Possible Samples ($n = 4$)	Sample Proportions (p)
1, 2, 3, 4 (W, B, B, B)	.25
1, 2, 3, 5 (W, B, B, B)	.25
1, 2, 4, 5 (W, B, B, B)	.25
1, 3, 4, 5 (W, B, B, B)	.25
2, 3, 4, 5 (B, B, B, B)	.00

Thus, while the true population proportion π of white marbles is .20, the sample proportion p is .25 in four of the above samples, and it is zero in the last sample.

To examine these five possible sample proportions in greater detail, let us first calculate their arithmetic mean, or average. The average of all sample proportions, denoted by $E(p)$, is

$$E(p) = \frac{p_1 + p_2 + p_3 + p_4 + p_5}{5}$$

$$= \frac{.25 + .25 + .25 + .25 + .00}{5}$$

$$= .20 = \pi.$$

We can thus say that although individual sample proportions may either overstate or understate the true population proportion, their average is always equal to the population proportion.

Let us now calculate the standard deviation of these five possible sample proportions. Their standard deviation, called the **standard error of the proportion** (denoted by σ_p) is computed in the following table.

p	$(p - \pi)$	$(p - \pi)^2$
.25	.05	.0025
.25	.05	.0025
.25	.05	.0025
.25	.05	.0025
.00	−.20	.0400

$$\Sigma (p - \pi)^2 = .0500$$

$$\sigma_p = \sqrt{\frac{\Sigma (p - \pi)^2}{\text{No. of samples}}}$$

$$= \sqrt{\frac{.0500}{5}} = \sqrt{.01} = .10$$

The standard error of the proportion indicates the "average" disparity between the various p's and π. The first four sample proportions are different from the population mean by .05 and the fifth sample proportion is different by .20. However, on the average, each sample proportion is different from the population proportion by .10.

A small value of σ_p indicates two facts: (1) the various values of p are close to each other; (2) the average difference between these p's and π is small. Consequently any one p is a good estimate of π.

Although the standard error of the proportion measures the average difference of all possible sample proportions from the population proportion, it is not necessary to actually select all such samples to determine its value. Fortunately, there is an alternative way of determining the standard error of the proportion. It has been found that

$$\sigma_p = \sqrt{\frac{\pi(1 - \pi)}{n}} \sqrt{\frac{N - n}{N - 1}},$$

where π is the population proportion, N is the population size, and n is the sample size.

For our population of 5 marbles, where $\pi = .20$, the standard error of the proportion for all possible samples of size 4 is

$$\sigma_p = \sqrt{\frac{\pi(1 - \pi)}{n}} \sqrt{\frac{N - n}{N - 1}}$$

$$= \sqrt{\frac{.20 \cdot .80}{4}} \sqrt{\frac{5 - 4}{5 - 1}}$$

$$= \sqrt{\frac{.16}{4}} \sqrt{\frac{1}{4}} = \sqrt{.01} = .10.$$

The above value is exactly identical to the one previously obtained.

Thus we can say that if all possible samples of size n are selected from a given population, then

$$E(p) = \pi \qquad \text{and} \qquad \sigma_p = \sqrt{\frac{\pi(1 - \pi)}{n}} \sqrt{\frac{N - n}{N - 1}}.$$

Furthermore, the finite population correction, $\sqrt{(N - n)/(N - 1)}$, will approach unity whenever we sample from an infinite population or whenever the sample size is less than 10% of the population. Under either condition, therefore, the standard error of the proportion becomes

$$\sigma_p = \sqrt{\frac{\pi(1 - \pi)}{n}}.$$

Concluding our examination of the properties of the various sample proportions, we add one final but important property: The sample proportions are approximately normally distributed whenever the sample size is fairly large.

In summary, we may therefore state this general theorem (see Fig. 9.1):

If all possible simple random samples of size n are selected from a population having a proportion of π, then the resulting sample proportions are approximately normally distributed, have an average equal to π and a standard deviation or a standard error equal to $\sqrt{\pi(1 - \pi)/n}$.

To clarify the implications of the theorem, let us assume that all possible random samples of 100 students are selected from a college where the actual proportion of senior students is 20%. According to the theorem, the various sample proportions would be approximately normally distributed and have an average of 20% and a standard error of 4%. (See computations in Fig. 9.2.)

Since the various sample proportions are approximately normally distributed, 68% of all such proportions will be in the range

$$\pi \pm 1.0\sigma_p = .20 \pm 1.0 \cdot .04 = .20 \pm .04,$$

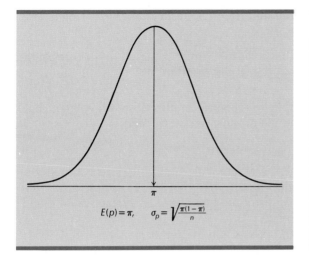

Figure 9.1

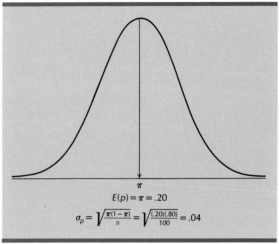

Figure 9.2

or between 16% and 24% (Fig. 9.3). In the same manner, 95% of all such sample proportions will be in the range

$$\pi + 1.96\sigma_p = .20 \pm 1.96 \cdot .04 = .20 \pm .08,$$

or approximately between 12% and 28% (Fig. 9.4).

We now present a few examples illustrating the distribution of sample proportions.

Figure 9.3

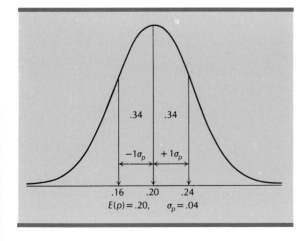

Figure 9.4

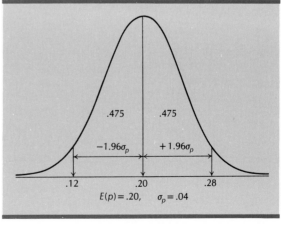

Example   It is known that 64% of all registered voters in a certain U.S. congressional district are Democrats.

a) What is the probability that a simple random sample of 100 registered voters from this district will reveal a proportion of Democrats of 60% or less?

b) If the simple random sample is increased to 400 registered voters, what is the probability that the sample proportion is 60% or less?

Solution:

a) As we have already learned, if all possible samples of size 100 registered voters are selected from this district, then the various sample proportions are approximately normally distributed and have an average of 64% and a standard error of 4.8% (Fig. 9.5).

   The probability that the proportion of Democrats in a sample of 100 registered voters will be 60% or less is calculated below (see also Fig. 9.6).

$$z = \frac{p - \pi}{\sigma_p}$$

$$= \frac{.60 - .64}{.048} = \frac{-.04}{.048} = -.83$$

Therefore,

$$P(p \le .60) = .50 - .2967 = .2033.$$

b) If many samples of size 400 registered voters are selected, then the various

Figure 9.5

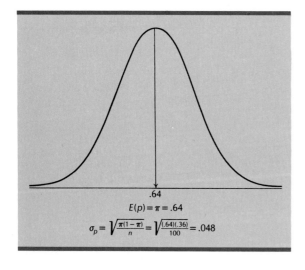

$E(p) = \pi = .64$

$\sigma_p = \sqrt{\frac{\pi(1 - \pi)}{n}} = \sqrt{\frac{(.64)(.36)}{100}} = .048$

Figure 9.6

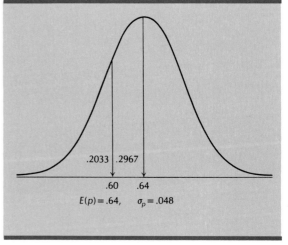

.2033 .2967

.60   .64

$E(p) = .64,$ $\sigma_p = .048$

sample proportions are approximately normally distributed and have an average of 64% and a standard error of 2.4% (see Fig. 9.7).

The probability that the proportion of Democrats in a sample of 400 registered voters is 60% or less is calculated below (see also Fig. 9.8).

$$z = \frac{p - \pi}{\sigma_p}$$

$$= \frac{.60 - .64}{.024} = \frac{-.04}{.024} = -1.67$$

Therefore,

$$P(p \le .60) = .50 - .4525 = .0475.$$

Thus, the probability that a sample of 100 voters will show a proportion of Democrats of 60% or less is .2033, but this probability is reduced to .0475 when the sample size is increased to 400 voters.

Example   Forty percent of all graduate students on a particular campus are married. If 100 graduate students are selected at random, what is the probability that the proportion of married students in this sample will be between 32% and 47%?

Solution: When several samples of 100 graduate students are selected, the distribution of the various sample proportions can be described by Fig. 9.9.

Figure 9.7

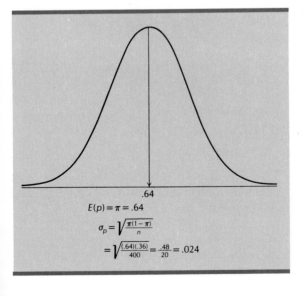

$$E(p) = \pi = .64$$

$$\sigma_p = \sqrt{\frac{\pi(1 - \pi)}{n}}$$

$$= \sqrt{\frac{(.64)(.36)}{400}} = \frac{.48}{20} = .024$$

Figure 9.8

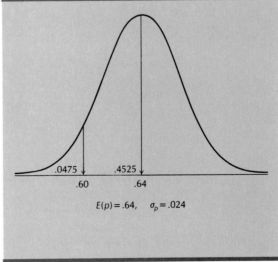

.0475   .4525

.60   .64

$$E(p) = .64, \quad \sigma_p = .024$$

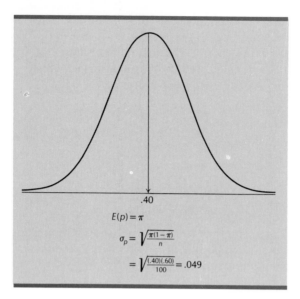

Figure 9.9

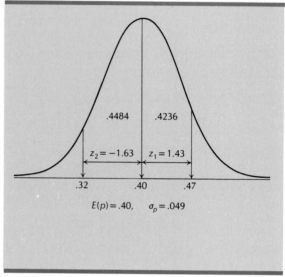

Figure 9.10

The probability that the proportion of married students in a sample of size 100 will be between 32% and 47% is determined as follows (see Fig. 9.10):

Left Side	Right Side

$$Z_2 = \frac{p - \pi}{\sigma_p}$$

$$Z_1 = \frac{p - \pi}{\sigma_p}$$

$$= \frac{.32 - .40}{.049} = \frac{-.08}{.049} = -1.63$$

$$= \frac{.47 - .40}{.049} = \frac{.07}{.049} = -1.43$$

Area under the normal curve = .4484

Area under the normal curve = .4236

Hence the probability that the sample proportion will be between 32% and 47% is the sum of these two areas, that is,

$$P(.32 \le p \le .47) = .4484 + .4236 = .8720.$$

Example   The receiving department of a large television manufacturer uses the following rule in deciding whether to accept or reject a shipment of 100,000 small parts shipped every week by a supplier: Select a sample of 400 parts from each lot received. If 3% or more of the selected parts are defectives, reject the entire lot; if the proportion of defectives is less than 3%, accept the lot. What is the probability of rejecting a lot that actually contains 2% defectives?

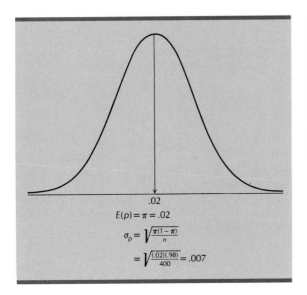

Figure 9.11

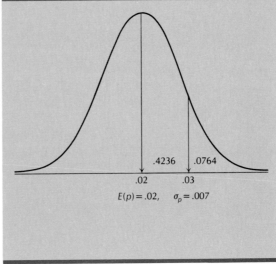

Figure 9.12

Solution: Although it is known that this lot contains 2% defectives, $\pi = .02$, it is possible that a sample of 400 parts will reveal a proportion of 3% or more defectives, and consequently the entire lot is rejected. To determine the probability of rejecting this lot, let us first describe the distribution of the various sample proportions that could be selected from such a lot (Fig. 9.11).

The probability of obtaining a sample proportion of 3% or more and consequently rejecting the lot is calculated below (see also Fig. 9.12).

$$z = \frac{p - \pi}{\sigma_p}$$

$$= \frac{.03 - .02}{.007} = 1.43$$

Hence,

$$P(p \geq .03) = .50 - .4236 = .0764.$$

EXERCISES

9.1 A population consists of the five faculty members in the psychology department at Bradford College. The marital status of each member is given below.

Faculty Member	Marital Status
A	Married
B	Single
C	Married
D	Single
E	Single

a) Determine the proportion of married members in the population.

b) Select all possible samples of two members from the population and compute the proportion of married members in each sample.

c) Compute the mean $E(p)$ and the standard deviation σ_p of the 10 sample proportions computed in part b.

d) Show that

$$\sigma_p = \sqrt{\frac{\pi(1 - \pi)}{n}} \sqrt{\frac{N - n}{N - 1}}.$$

9.2   The following information concerns a population of six persons.

Person	Education
A	College graduate
B	High school graduate
C	College graduate
D	High school graduate
E	College graduate
F	High school graduate

a) Determine the proportion of college graduates in the population.

b) Select all possible samples of three persons from the population and compute the proportion of college graduates in each sample.

c) What is the probability that the sample proportion ($n = 3$) will be over 40%? [*Hint:* How many of the 20 sample proportions are over .40?]

d) What is the probability that the sample proportion ($n = 3$) will differ from the population proportion by 20% or less?

9.3   Ten percent of all the people in a certain community have type B blood. If a random sample of 900 persons from this community is selected, what is the probability that in the sample the proportion of people with type B blood is (a) more than 12%, (b) less than 10.5%, (c) between 11% and 13%?

9.4   To decide whether to endorse gubernatorial candidate X, the Society of Independent Voters adopts the following procedure: A random sample of 400 registered voters is to be selected. The society will endorse candidate X only when 50% or more of the sample voters are in her favor. What is the probability that the society

a) will come out for candidate X when she is actually endorsed by only 45% of all voters?

b) will fail to come out for candidate X when she is actually endorsed by 55% of all voters?

9.5   The following rule is used in controlling the operation of a process that produces certain parts: Select a sample of 36 parts from the process. If the percentage of defective parts in the sample is p^*% or more, stop the process; otherwise continue the operation. Determine the value of p^* such that there is a .95 chance that a process producing, on the average, 10% defective parts will be stopped.

9.6   To decide whether to endorse gubernatorial candidate Y, the Society of Independent Voters adopts the following procedure: A random sample of n registered voters is to be selected. The society will endorse the candidate only if p^*% of the sample voters are in his favor. Determine the values of n and p^* such that there is only a .05 risk of *endorsing* the candidate when 45% of all voters are in his favor and only a .01 risk of *not endorsing* the candidate when 50% of all voters come out for him.

9.7   Fifty percent of all families in Indianapolis own at least two cars. A random sample of 400 families is selected from Indianapolis.

a) What is the probability that the sample proportion of families owning at least two cars is less than 45%?

b) The probability is .9544 that the sample proportion of the families owning at least two cars is between p_1 and p_2. Find p_1 and p_2 using symmetrical limits around π.

9.8   A manufacturer receives a shipment of 100,000 small parts each week. The following rule is adopted in deciding on whether to accept or reject each shipment: Select a random sample of 100 parts from the shipment. If the proportion of defective parts in the sample is .06 or more, reject the entire shipment; if the proportion of defective parts is léss than .06, accept the shipment.

a) What is the probability of accepting a lot that actually contains 10% defective parts?

b) What is the probability of rejecting a lot that actually contains 2% defective parts?

c) What is the probability of accepting a lot that actually contains 6% defective parts?

9.9   Assume that 60% of all California voters favor a certain property tax relief initiative on the June primary ballot. If a random sample of 150 voters is selected, what is the probability that the proportion of those favoring the initiative is between 65% and 68%?

9.10   In deciding on whether to introduce a new welfare legislation program to Congress, the administration adopted the following sampling rule: Select a random sample of 150 families. If 10% or more of the families selected earn below poverty level, introduce the new welfare legislation program to Congress; otherwise, do not introduce the program.

a) What is the probability of not introducing the new legislation to Congress assuming that 15% of all families in the United States earn below poverty level?

b) What is the probability of introducing the program assuming only 8% of all families earn below poverty level?

9.11   Susan Goldstein, a political pollster, is engaged by a newspaper to predict the outcome of the Democratic presidential primary election in Iowa. The candidates are Tom Bradshaw and Josephine Brown. Goldstein adopts the following sampling rule in predicting the winning candidates: Select a random sample of 150 registered voters. If 55% or more of the selected voters favor candidate X, then candidate X is predicted as the winner. What is the probability that Goldstein will forecast Josephine Brown as a winner

a) assuming that Brown is favored by 48% of all Iowa voters?

b) assuming that Brown is favored by 60% of all Iowa voters?

c) assuming that Brown is favored by 55% of all Iowa voters?

9.12   An accountant uses the following decision rule in deciding whether to approve an accounts receivable ledger: Select a random sample of 60 accounts from the ledger and verify the accuracy of each account. If 5% or more of the accounts examined are in error, do not approve the ledger.

a) What is the probability of approving the ledger assuming that 10% of all accounts are in error?

b) What is the probability of not approving the ledger assuming that only 3% of all accounts are in error?

9.13   An accountant uses the following decision rule in deciding whether to approve an accounts receivable ledger: Select a random sample of n accounts from the ledger and verify the accuracy of each account. If p^*% or more of the accounts examined are in error, do not approve the ledger; but if the proportion of accounts in error is less than p^*, approve the ledger. Determine the values of n and p^* such that there is only .01 risk of not approving a ledger when 3% of all accounts in the ledger are in error and such that there will be .05 risk of approving a ledger that contains 10% erroneous accounts.

ESTIMATING THE POPULATION PROPORTION

We have already stated that when repeated samples of size *n* are selected from a population having a proportion of π, then the various sample proportions, or *p*'s, are approximately normally distributed. Furthermore, these sample proportions have an average equal to π and a standard error equal to $\sqrt{\pi(1 - \pi)/n}$ (Fig. 9.13).

Since these sample proportions are approximately normally distributed, we expect .95 of all such proportions to fall within the range defined by

$$\pi \pm 1.96\sigma_p = \pi \pm 1.96 \sqrt{\pi(1 - \pi)/n}.$$

See Fig. 9.14. We can also conclude that if one sample of size *n* is to be selected, there is a .95 chance that the proportion in this sample will fall within the interval $\pi \pm 1.96\sigma_p$. The probability that it will fall outside this range is .05.

Let us assume that we *actually* select a simple random sample of size *n* and calculate the proportion *p*. The interval $p \pm 1.96\sigma_p$ may or may not contain π.

If the proportion of the sample selected happens to fall within any part of the shaded area of the normal curve (selected from *within* the interval $\pi \pm 1.96\sigma_p$) in Fig. 9.15, the interval $p \pm 1.96\sigma_p$ will certainly contain π.

If, on the other hand *p* happens to fall within the unshaded area of the normal curve (selected from *outside* the interval $\pi \pm 1.96\sigma_p$) in Fig. 9.16, the interval $p \pm 1.96\sigma_p$ will not contain π.

We may therefore conclude that if all possible samples of size *n* are

Figure 9.13

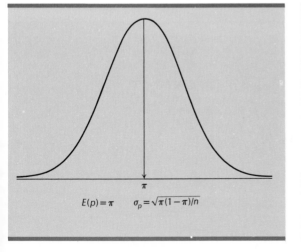

$E(p) = \pi$ $\sigma_p = \sqrt{\pi(1 - \pi)/n}$

Figure 9.14

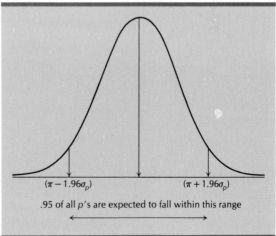

$(\pi - 1.96\sigma_p)$ $(\pi + 1.96\sigma_p)$

.95 of all *p*'s are expected to fall within this range

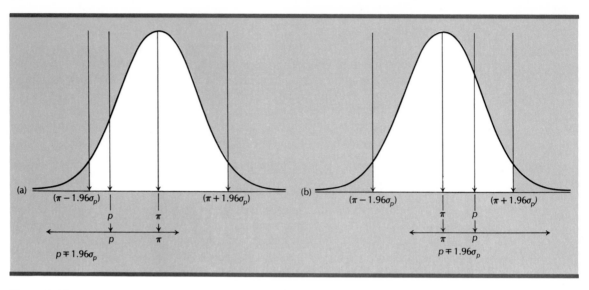

Figure 9.15

selected and the interval $p \pm 1.96\sigma_p$ is established for each sample, then .95 of all such intervals are expected to contain π. The interval $p \pm 1.96\sigma_p$ or $p \pm 1.96 \sqrt{\pi(1 - \pi)/n}$ is called a 95% confidence interval estimate of π.

To come up with the above interval estimate of π, we must know the value of π. This, however, is not known. Hence we are forced to use the sample

Figure 9.16

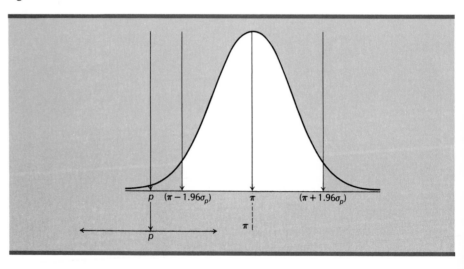

proportion p as an approximation of π. The approximate .95 confidence interval estimate of π thus becomes $p \pm 1.96\sqrt{p(1-p)/n}$. In the same manner, the range $p \pm 2.58\sqrt{p(1-p)/n}$ is called an approximate 99% confidence interval estimate of π.

Example   In assessing the desirability of windowless schools, officials asked 144 elementary schoolchildren whether or not they like windows in their classrooms. Thirty percent of the children preferred windows. Establish a .95 confidence interval estimate of the proportion of elementary school children who like windows in their classrooms.

Solution: The .95 confidence interval estimate of π is

$$p \pm 1.96\sqrt{\frac{p(1-p)}{n}} = .30 \pm 1.96\sqrt{\frac{.30 \cdot .70}{144}}$$

$$= .30 \pm 1.96\,\frac{.458}{12}$$

$$= .30 \pm 1.96 \cdot .038 = .30 \pm .074,$$

or between 22.6% and 37.4%.

Example   In a public opinion poll, 320 out of 400 persons interviewed supported the administration's policy on disarmament.

a) Establish a 95% confidence interval estimate of the proportion of persons supporting the government's stand on disarmament.

b) What can we conclude with .99 confidence about the maximum error in our estimate if the proportion of those supporting the administration policy is estimated as 80%?

c) With what degree of confidence can we assert that the proportion of persons supporting the administration policy is somewhere between 77% and 83%?

Solution:

a) The sample proportion is determined as

$$p = \frac{320}{400} = .80.$$

The .95 confidence interval estimate of π is therefore

$$p \pm 1.96\sqrt{\frac{p(1-p)}{n}} = .80 \pm 1.96\sqrt{\frac{.80 \cdot .20}{400}}$$

$$= .80 \pm 1.96 \cdot .02 = .80 \pm .0392,$$

or between 76.08% and 83.92%.

b) A .99 confidence interval estimate of π is

$$p \pm 2.58 \sqrt{\frac{p(1-p)}{n}} = .80 \pm 2.58 \sqrt{\frac{.80 \cdot .20}{400}}$$

$$= .80 \pm 2.58 \cdot .02 = .80 \pm .0516.$$

Since $2.58 \sqrt{.80 \cdot .20/400}$, or .0516, has been added to or subtracted from the sample proportion .80 to establish a .99 confidence interval estimate of π, we can assert with a probability of .99 that our maximum error is .0516 if π is estimated as 80%. In general, the maximum expected error in a point estimate of π is determined by the expression $z\sqrt{p(1-p)/n}$.

c) If π is estimated as being between .77 and .83, then .03 must have been added to or subtracted from the sample proportion .80 to establish this interval estimate of π. In other words, our interval estimate was obtained as follows:

$$p \pm z \sqrt{\frac{p(1-p)}{n}} = .80 \pm .03.$$

Therefore,

$$z \sqrt{\frac{p(1-p)}{n}} = .03$$

$$z \sqrt{\frac{.80 \cdot .20}{400}} = .03$$

$$z(.02) = .03$$

$$z = \frac{.03}{.02} = 1.5.$$

Using the area under the normal curve in Table A at the back of the book, we conclude that the range .77 to .83 is the .8664 confidence interval estimate of π (see Fig. 9.17).

Example In a community of 10,000 families, a random sample of 400 families showed that 20% of the families have an annual family income exceeding $30,000. Establish a .95 confidence interval estimate of the number of families earning over $30,000 in that community.

Solution: This problem is solved in two steps. In the first step we will establish a .95 confidence interval estimate of the *proportion* of families in the community with income exceeding $30,000 (a .95 confidence interval esti-

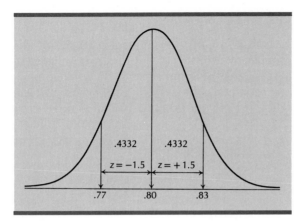

Figure 9.17

mate of π). In the second step, we will multiply the range established for π by the number of families in the community, to obtain a range for the number of families with income exceeding $30,000 in the entire community.

Step 1.   The .95 confidence interval estimate of π is

$$p \pm 1.96 \left(\sqrt{\frac{p(1-p)}{n}} \right) = .20 \pm 1.96 \left(\sqrt{\frac{.20 \cdot .80}{400}} \right)$$

$$= .20 \pm 1.96 \cdot .02 = .20 \pm .0392,$$

or between 16.08% and 23.92%.

Step 2.   Since the community consists of 10,000 families, the .95 confidence interval estimate of the number of families with income exceeding $30,000 is obtained as

$$10,000(0.1608 \le \pi \le 0.2392).$$

or between 1608 and 2392 families.

It may be useful now to summarize the solution to our problem. A 0.95 confidence-interval estimate of the number of families earning over $30,000 in the entire community can be determined as

$$N \left[p \pm z \left(\sqrt{\frac{p(1-p)}{n}} \right) \right] = 10,000 \left[0.20 \pm 1.96 \sqrt{\frac{(0.20)(0.80)}{400}} \right]$$

or between 1608 and 2392 families.

Determining the Sample Size

Whenever we are asked to estimate a population proportion from a simple random sample, we must first decide on how large our sample should be. Generally speaking, the sample size is determined by the degree of accuracy required in estimating the population proportion. The higher the required degree of accuracy in our estimate, the larger the size of the sample we must select.

There are two aspects to the degree of accuracy required in estimating the population proportion from a sample:

1. the magnitude of the maximum allowable error and
2. the degree of confidence that the error in the estimate does not exceed the maximum allowable error.

If, for example, we are asked to estimate, within 2%, the proportion of the television viewers tuned in to "Dallas" on Friday night, the maximum allowable error is .02. However, regardless of the sample size, there is always a chance that the error in our estimate will exceed .02. But the larger the sample size, the smaller the risk that the allowable error will be exceeded, or the greater the confidence that our estimate will be within the allowable error. If it is also specified that we must have .95 confidence that the error in our estimate will not exceed .02, the two aspects of accuracy in this case are as follows.

1. The maximum allowable error, denoted by e, is .02.
2. The degree of confidence that the maximum allowable error is not exceeded is .95.

Having specified the accuracy requirements of our estimate, we must determine the sample size that satisfies these two requirements. Specifically, the sample size n is manipulated until $1.96\sigma_p = .02$ (see Fig. 9.18).

In general, the size of the sample is manipulated until

$$z\sigma_p = e,$$

where z is determined by the degree of confidence. Since

$$\sigma_p = \sqrt{\pi(1 - \pi)/n},$$

it follows that

$$z\sqrt{\pi(1 - \pi)/n} = e.$$

Solving for n, we have

$$n = z^2\pi(1 - \pi)/e^2.$$

Thus the sample size is determined by z, e, and π, where e is the maximum allowable error, z is determined by the degree of confidence, and π is the population proportion we want to estimate.

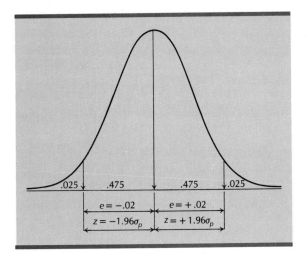

Figure 9.18

At this point you may think that we have reached an impasse: to determine the size of the sample needed to estimate the population proportion π, the value of π itself must be known. This is a problem! However, it may be overcome if the value of π can be estimated from surveys taken previously. If a previous estimate of π exists, we can use it to obtain the sample size from the formula

$$n = \frac{z^2\pi(1 - \pi)}{e^2}.$$

But what if no previous surveys were taken and the value of π is unknown? Examining the expression $\pi(1 - \pi)$ in our formula, we can show that such an expression attains its maximum value when π is equal to 50%.

π	$\pi(1 - \pi)$
.10	.10 · .90 = .09
.20	.20 · .80 = .16
.30	.30 · .70 = .21
.40	.40 · .60 = .24
.50	.50 · .50 = .25 (maximum)
.60	.60 · .40 = .24
.70	.70 · .30 = .21
.80	.80 · .20 = .16
.90	.90 · .10 = .09

Therefore we may conclude that, other things being equal, a larger sample size is required when π equals 50% than when π assumes any other value. Hence, in the absence of any previous knowledge about the value of π, we can safely set π equal to 50%, and the sample size thus obtained will be as large as or larger than required, regardless of the actual value of π.

Example An advertising agency desires to estimate the proportion of the Richmond television audience viewing "Palace," a weekly television program.

   a) Determine the sample size needed to ensure .95 confidence that the error in our estimate will not exceed .02. A survey made last season showed that 20% of the families in Richmond viewed "Palace."

   b) What would the sample size be if no previous survey had been taken?

Solution:

   a) $n = \dfrac{z^2 \pi(1 - \pi)}{e^2}$

$$= \frac{1.96^2 \cdot .20 \cdot .80}{.02^2} = \frac{3.8416 \cdot .16}{.0004}$$

$$= 1536.64 = 1537 \text{ families}$$

   b) In the absence of any previous knowledge about the value of π, we assume that $\pi = 50\%$ and obtain the following sample size:

$$n = \frac{z^2 \pi(1 - \pi)}{e^2}$$

$$= \frac{1.96^2 \cdot .50 \cdot .50}{.02^2} = \frac{3.8416 \cdot .25}{.0004} = 2401 \text{ families.}$$

DISTRIBUTION OF SAMPLE PROPORTIONS AND THE BINOMIAL DISTRIBUTION

Note that the distribution of sample proportions is merely a modified version of the binomial distribution. To examine the relation between these two distributions, let us first summarize what we know about them.

	Binomial Distribution	Distribution of Sample Proportions
Mean	$n\pi$	π
Standard deviation	$\sqrt{n\pi(1 - \pi)}$	$\sqrt{\dfrac{\pi(1 - \pi)}{n}}$

The mean and the standard deviation of the distribution of sample proportions are obtained by dividing the mean and the standard deviation of the binomial distribution by n.

$$\text{Mean} = \frac{n\pi}{n} = \pi$$

$$\text{Standard deviation} = \frac{\sqrt{n\pi(1 - \pi)}}{n} = \sqrt{\frac{\pi(1 - \pi)}{n}}$$

Thus the distribution of sample proportions is the binomial distribution expressed in percentage form.

The relation between the two distributions can perhaps be more easily understood if we consider the following problem.

Example   A machine produces, on average, 20% defective parts. If a random sample of 64 parts is selected, what is the probability that the proportion of defective parts in the sample is 25% (16 parts) or more?

We will solve this problem using two alternative methods: (a) the binomial distribution and (b) the distribution of sample proportions. We can then compare the results of the two methods.

Solution:

a) *The binomial distribution.* First, we must determine the mean and the standard deviation of the binomial distribution, with $\pi = .20$ and $n = 64$. The mean of the distribution is

$$\mu = n\pi$$
$$= 64 \cdot .20 = 12.8,$$

and the standard deviation is

$$\sigma = \sqrt{n\pi(1 - \pi)}$$
$$= \sqrt{64 \cdot .20 \cdot .80} = 3.2.$$

Using the normal-curve approximation to the binomial distribution, we can now determine the probability of obtaining 16 defective parts or more as follows (see Fig. 9.19):

$$z = \frac{x - \mu}{\sigma}$$
$$= \frac{16 - 12.8}{3.2} = \frac{3.2}{3.2} = 1.0.$$

Therefore,

$$P(x \geq 16) = .5000 - .3413 = .1587.$$

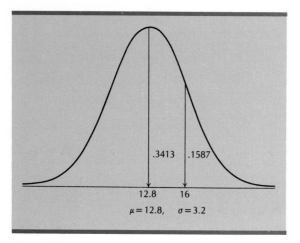

Figure 9.19   **Figure 9.20**

b) *Distribution of sample proportions.* First, we must determine the mean and the standard deviation of the distribution of sample proportions. The mean of the distribution is

$$E(p) = \pi$$
$$= .20,$$

and the standard deviation of the distribution is

$$\sigma_p = \sqrt{\frac{\pi(1 - \pi)}{n}}$$

$$= \sqrt{\frac{.20 \cdot .80}{64}} = .05.$$

The probability that the sample proportion is 25% or more can now be determined as follows (see Fig. 9.20):

$$z = \frac{p - \pi}{\sigma_p}$$

$$= \frac{.25 - .20}{.05} = 1.0.$$

Therefore,

$$P(p \geq .25) = .5000 - .3413 = .1587.$$

In comparing the results of the two solutions to our problem, we can only conclude that the two distributions are essentially the same.

EXERCISES ══

9.14   In a random sample of 400 families living in Oak Ridge, Tennessee, 80 families have more than one television set. Establish a .98 confidence interval estimate of the proportion of Oak Ridge families with more than one television set.

9.15   A random sample of 100 male students from the University of Illinois shows that 10 students belong to a social fraternity.

a) Establish a .90 confidence interval estimate of male students who belong to a social fraternity at the University of Illinois.

b) What can we assert with probability .95 about the maximum possible error if the proportion of male students who belong to a social fraternity at the University of Illinois is estimated at 10%?

9.16   Two hundred and fifty-six patients suffering from a certain disease were treated with a new drug. The drug was effective in curing 128 of the cases. With what degree of confidence can we assert that the effectiveness of this drug is between 45% and 55%?

9.17   A government agency wishes to determine the proportion of families earning less than $5000 a year in a given community. Previous studies have shown that this proportion is 20%.

a) What sample size is required to ensure .95 confidence that the error in estimating such a proportion will not exceed .05?

b) How will the required sample size change if the maximum allowable error is reduced to .01?

9.18   The dean of students is considering a new policy for student housing. Before making a final decision, she wants to select a random sample of students to estimate the proportion of students in favor of the new policy. What is the sample size needed to ensure that the risk of exceeding an error of .10 or more is only .05?

9.19   A random sample of 200 voters in a community of 5000 registered voters shows 110 voters in favor of candidate X. Establish a .99 confidence interval estimate of the number of voters favoring candidate X in the entire community.

9.20   In a university with a total enrollment of 20,000 students, a random sample of 100 students produced 64 students in favor of a new policy for student housing. Establish a .95 confidence interval estimate of the number of students in the entire university favoring the new housing policy.

9.21   A random sample of 400 students attending a particular college shows 80 married students.

a) Establish a .95 confidence interval estimate of the proportion of married students attending the college.

b) With what degree of confidence can we assert that the proportion of married students attending the college is between .16 and .24?

9.22   A bank maintains 20,000 customers' saving accounts. A random sample of 400 accounts shows that 144 accounts are in excess of $10,000. Establish a .99 confidence interval estimate of the *number* of saving accounts held by the bank that exceed $10,000.

9.23   A sample survey showed that 36% of 500 new automobiles purchased in the United States last year were Japanese imports. Assume that 15 million new automobiles were purchased in the U.S. last year. Establish a .99 confidence interval estimate of the total number of Japanese imported automobiles sold in the United States.

9.24   The marketing research department of an oven manufacturer wishes to determine the company's share of the Chicago microwave oven market. The department manager selects a random sample of 400 purchasers of microwave ovens in Chicago. The sample shows that 80 of the purchasers had bought the manufacturer's microwave ovens. With what degree of confidence can we assert that the company's share of the Chicago microwave oven market is between 16% and 24%?

9.25   In a community of 5000 families, a random sample of 200 families shows that 40% of the families own their own home.

a) Establish a .95 confidence interval estimate of the *total* number of families that own their own homes in that community.

b) With what degree of confidence can we assert that the proportion of families owning their own homes in the entire community is between 35% and 45%?

9.26   A random sample of 180 accounts is selected from a ledger that contains 15,000 accounts receivable. The sample shows 9 past-due accounts.

a) Establish a .90 confidence interval estimate of the total number of past-due accounts in the ledger.

b) With what degree of confidence can we assert the proportion of past-due accounts is between 3% and 7%?

9.27   A random sample of 400 stockholders is selected from General Motors' 2 million stockholders. Eighty percent of the selected stockholders favor the decision to manufacture the E Car, an electric car. Establish a .95 confidence interval estimate of the *total number* of GM stockholders who favor manufacturing the E Car.

KEY TERMS

standard error of the proportion (σ_p) The standard deviation of the proportion p. The standard error of the proportion tells us how far a typical sample p will be from the population proportion π.

SUMMARY
OF FORMULAS

mean of the sample proportion $\quad E(p) = \pi$

standard error of the proportion
(sampling without replacement) $\quad \sigma_p = \sqrt{\dfrac{\pi(1 - \pi)}{n}} \sqrt{\dfrac{N - n}{N - 1}}$

standard error of the proportion
(sampling with replacement or $\quad \sigma_p = \sqrt{\dfrac{\pi(1 - \pi)}{n}}$
when n/N is small)

z = value for a proportion $\qquad z = \dfrac{p - \pi}{\sigma_p}$

confidence interval for π $\qquad p \pm z\sigma_p = p \pm z \sqrt{p(1 - p)/n}$

sample size $\qquad n = \dfrac{z^2\pi(1 - \pi)}{e^2} \quad$ or $\quad n = \dfrac{z^2 .5 \cdot .5}{e^2}$

TESTING HYPOTHESES
ABOUT PROPORTIONS

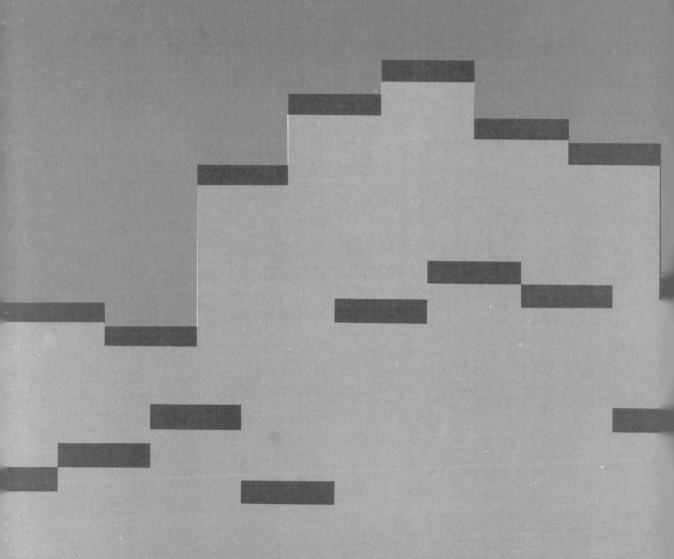

10

This chapter deals with the general question of testing hypotheses about proportions. In the first section, we test hypotheses about a single population proportion. The theoretical tools needed for testing the significance of the difference between two sample proportions are treated in the second part of the chapter, and their application is the subject matter of the third part. The chi-square test, which is used to compare several proportions, is discussed in the last section.

TESTING HYPOTHESES ABOUT A SINGLE PROPORTION

The principal objective of some statistical investigations is to test a hypothesis concerning a population proportion. We may want to evaluate, for example, a politician's claim that he or she commands 55% of all votes in a certain U.S. congressional district. Or we may want to test the hypothesis that a given drug is 90% effective in the cure of a certain disease.

How can we test a politician's claim that he or she commands 55% of all votes in a given district? A random sample of registered voters can be selected and interviewed, and, based on the result of this sample, the politician's claim can be rejected or not rejected.

Stated briefly and rigorously, the general procedure used in testing a hypothesis about a population proportion consists of the following steps: First formulate the null hypothesis and an appropriate alternative hypothesis. Then, on the basis of the sample information, either reject the null hypothesis or reserve judgment. As in any other testing problem, either a .05 or a .01 level of significance is used as the decision criterion.

To be specific, we will illustrate the procedure with three examples: a one-sided test is appropriate in the first two examples, and a two-sided test is used in the third one.

Example Mr. Dixon, a Republican, claims that he has the support of 55% of all voters in the 23rd congressional district. What will the party central committee conclude if, out of a random sample of 500 registered voters, only 245 expressed their preference for Dixon? Use a level of significance of .01.

Solution: The null hypothesis (Dixon's claim), which states that $\pi = .55$, is tested against the appropriate alternative hypothesis that $\pi < .55$.

If the null hypothesis is true, that is, $\pi = .55$, and if many samples of 500 voters are selected from this district, then the various sample proportions are distributed as shown in Fig. 10.1.

The sample shows that $245/500$, or 49%, of the voters favor Dixon. The probability of obtaining a sample proportion p of 49% or less when the null hypothesis is true is only .0032 (see Fig. 10.2 and the following computations).

$$z = \frac{p - \pi}{\sigma_p} = \frac{.49 - .55}{.022} = \frac{-.06}{.022} = -2.73$$

Therefore,

$$P(p \le .49) = .50 - .4968 = .0032.$$

Since the probability of obtaining a sample proportion of 49% or less is .0032, which is less than .01, the null hypothesis is rejected when we use a .01 level of significance.

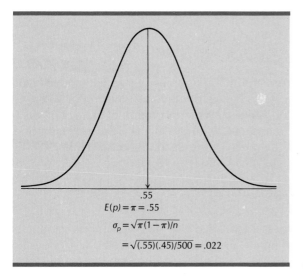

$E(p) = \pi = .55$

$\sigma_p = \sqrt{\pi(1-\pi)/n}$

$= \sqrt{(.55)(.45)/500} = .022$

Figure 10.1

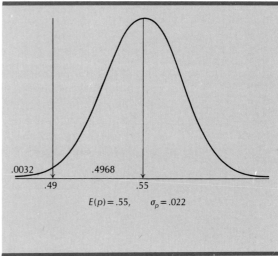

$E(p) = .55, \quad \sigma_p = .022$

Figure 10.2

It may be useful to point out again that the decision whether to reject the null hypothesis becomes obvious once the z-value is determined. The null hypotheses is rejected whenever the *absolute value* of z exceeds a critical level. These critical levels are as follows.

Level of Significance	One-Sided Test	Two-Sided Test
.05	1.64	1.96
.01	2.33	2.58

Once again, using a .01 level of significance, we reject the null hypothesis in our problem, since the absolute value of z is 2.73, which is greater than 2.33.

Example The Department of Health and Human Services reports that only 10% of all persons over 65 years of age are covered by adequate private health insurance. What would the American Medical Association (AMA) conclude about the department's claim if, out of a random sample of 900 elderly persons, 99 possessed adequate private health insurance? Use a level of significance of .05.

Solution: The two hypotheses can be formulated as

$$H_0: \quad \pi = .10,$$
$$H_1: \quad \pi > .10.$$

If the null hypothesis is true and many samples of size 900 are selected, then the various sample proportions are distributed as shown in Fig. 10.3.

The sample selected by the AMA shows a proportion of $^{99}\!/_{900}$, or 11%. To test the validity of the department's claim, let us calculate the deviation of an 11% sample proportion from the mean of the distribution, which is 10% (the deviation is measured in z-units). We obtain (Fig. 10.4)

$$z = \frac{p - \pi}{\sigma_p} = \frac{.11 - .10}{.01} = 1.0.$$

Since z is 1.0, which is less than 1.64, the null hypothesis cannot be rejected using the .05 level of significance. In other words, the AMA does not have enough evidence to reject the claim made by the Department of Health and Human Services.

Example   The sponsor of a weekly television show would like the studio audience to consist of an equal number of men and women. Out of 400 persons attending the show on a given night, 220 are men. Using a level of significance of .01, can the sponsor conclude that the desired gender composition of the audience is not properly maintained?

Figure 10.3

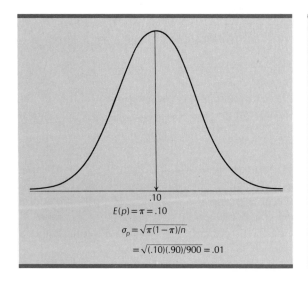

Figure 10.4

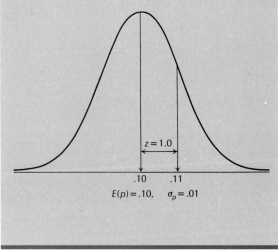

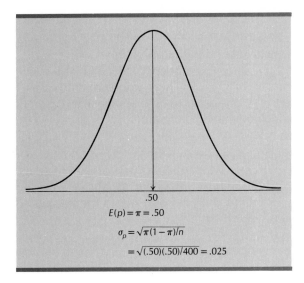

Figure 10.5

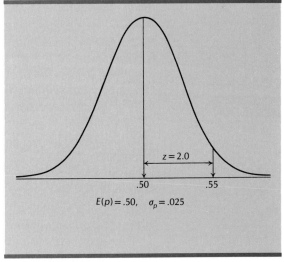

Figure 10.6

Solution: Let $\pi = 50\%$ stand for the desired proportion of males in the audience. The null hypothesis, which states that $\pi = .50$, is then tested against the alternative hypothesis that $\pi \neq .50$. The test is two-sided, since the null hypothesis is rejected whenever the sample proportion is significantly above or below 50%.

If the null hypothesis is true, then the distribution of the various sample proportions is as shown in Fig. 10.5.

The sponsor found that the proportion of men in a sample of 400 persons was $^{220}/_{400}$, or 55%. To test the validity of the null hypothesis, let us calculate the deviation of a sample proportion of 55% from the mean of the distribution, which is 50% (the deviation is measured in z-units). We have (Fig. 10.6)

$$z = \frac{p - \pi}{\sigma_p} = \frac{.55 - .50}{.025} = 2.0.$$

Since z is 2.0, which is less than 2.58, the null hypothesis cannot be rejected using the .01 level of significance. (The test is two-tailed.)

EXERCISES

10.1 A television manufacturer claims that, on average, 90% of the color television sets produced do not require any repair during the first two years of operation. A consumer protection board selects a random sample of 100 sets and finds that 15 sets require some repair in the first two years of operation. If the consumer protection board is willing to reject a true claim no more than 5 times in 100, will the board reject the manufacturer's claim?

10.2   The Johnson Pharmaceutical Laboratory has developed a certain drug for the treatment of high blood pressure. The laboratory asserts that the drug effectively lowers the blood pressure in 80% of all high blood pressure cases. If 175 out of 225 patients treated with this drug report a substantial decline in their blood pressure, do you conclude that the laboratory has exaggerated the effectiveness of the drug? Use a level of significance of .01.

10.3   The Institute of Family Relations reports that 50% of all couples living in a particular county reach a divorce court within the first year of their marriage. What do you conclude about the validity of this report if, out of a random sample of 400 marriages, only 193 reach divorce court within the first year of marriage? Use a level of significance of .01.

10.4   At a press conference, the president's press secretary states that 90% of all American voters support the president's High Society Program. An independent poll of 625 American voters shows that 550 voters are in favor of the president's program. If you are willing to reject a true hypothesis no more than once in 100, do you conclude that the popularity of the High Society Program is exaggerated by the press secretary?

10.5   When a special coin was tossed 64 times, heads came up 28 times. Using a level of significance of .05, do you conclude that the coin is biased?

10.6   A discount house is considering the purchase of a large stock of records from a supplier who claims that, on average, only 2% of the records are imperfect. In examining 400 of these records, the discount house finds that 15 are imperfect. Will the discount house reject the supplier's claim if it is willing to reject a true claim no more than once in 10?

10.7   It is claimed that 20% of all families in Los Angeles are Mexican-Americans.

a)   What do you conclude about the validity of this claim if a random sample of 400 families shows 90 Mexican-American families?

b)   What do you conclude about the validity of this claim if a random sample of 400 families shows 120 Mexican-American families?

10.8   Twenty percent of all color televisions sold in Alabama in 1984 are of brand X. A random sample of 100 color television sets sold in Alabama in 1985 shows that only 17 sets are of brand X. Using a level of significance of .01, can you conclude that the brand X color television share of the Alabama market has declined between 1984 and 1985?

10.9   The student newspaper at the state college just published the results of a recent student poll concerning a proposal that all student dorms become coed. In this poll, 100 students were sampled and 80 students stated that they were in favor of the proposal. The college president quickly ruled against the proposal, claiming that the sample result did not prove beyond a reasonable doubt that the majority of the students favor it.

a) Construct a .80 confidence interval estimate for the proportion of the student population in favor of the proposal.

b) If a .05 level of significance is used, is the president's conclusion valid?

10.10   Kelly Log owns a large breakfast food company. One of the cereals, Trixx, is quite popular. Trixx comes in a 16-ounce package. Suppose government regulations require that at least 80% of the boxes must contain 16 ounces or more of cereal if the packages are to use the 16-ounce label. A recent analysis, conducted by government inspectors, revealed that of 400 boxes of Trixx, 300 boxes contained 16 ounces or more of cereal. Using a .05 level of significance, can the government prove a violation?

10.11   It is claimed that 50% of all elementary school students in the Atlanta school district are black. What do you conclude about the validity of the claim if a random sample of 500 students shows 225 black students? Use a level of significance of .01.

10.12   A mail order house is considering marketing a new home food processor, La Cuisine. A random sample of 200 customers is selected from the company's list of 8000 active customers. The sample shows that 43 customers wish to purchase the new product.

a) Establish a .95 confidence interval estimate of the proportion of the company's active customers who desire to purchase the new product.

b) The marketing manager claims that 30% of the company's active customers would purchase La Cuisine. Using the .01 level of significance, can we conclude that the marketing manager exaggerated the sales potential of La Cuisine?

10.13   It is claimed that 80% of all American families change houses within five years. What can you conclude about the validity of this claim if in a random sample of 1200 American families 900 families changed their houses within five years? Use a level of significance of .01.

SAMPLING DISTRIBUTION OF THE DIFFERENCE BETWEEN TWO SAMPLE PROPORTIONS

Let π_1 stand for the proportion of senior students in Delmore College, and let π_2 stand for the proportion of senior students at Eastern University. Let us further assume that these two proportions are 24% and 20% respectively.

If we select many random samples of 200 students from Delmore College and record the proportion of senior students in each sample, the various sample proportions may show the results in Example A. Similarly, if an equal number of samples of 400 students are selected from Eastern University, the proportions of senior students in the various samples might be as shown in Example B.

Example A	*Example B*
Delmore College *Sample Proportions* (p_1)	*Eastern University* *Sample Proportions* (p_2)
.24	.20
.22	.19
.26	.22
.21	.23
.25	.19
.23	.17
. . .	. . .
.25	.22

In comparing the results of these two sets of proportions, let us randomly pair the samples and compute the difference d between the proportions of each pair, as shown in the following table.

p_1	p_2	$(p_1 - p_2) = d$
.24	.20	.04
.22	.19	.03
.26	.22	.04
.21	.23	−.02
.25	.19	.06
.23	.17	.06
. . .	. . .	. . .
.25	.22	.03

Remembering that the p_1's are the proportions of samples drawn from a population with $\pi_1 = .24$ and that the p_2's are the proportions of samples drawn from a population with $\pi_2 = .20$, let us examine the properties of the differences recorded in the last column of the table.

First, although the difference between the proportions of the first pair of samples is .04, of the second pair .03, and of the last pair .03, we expect these differences to have an average of .04 (that is, .24 − .20). Hence the first property of the differences between two sample proportions is

$$E(d) = \pi_1 - \pi_2,$$

where $E(d)$ is the average of all differences, π_1 is the proportion in the population from which the first set of samples is selected (in this case Delmore College), and π_2 is the proportion in the population from which the second set of samples is selected (Eastern University).

Statisticians have studied these differences in great detail and have found that they are approximately normally distributed and have a standard deviation or a standard error equal to

$$\sqrt{\frac{\pi_1(1 - \pi_1)}{n_1} + \frac{\pi_2(1 - \pi_2)}{n_2}}.$$

Denoting the standing error of these differences by σ_d, we summarize their properties in Fig. 10.7.

For our samples from Delmore College and Eastern University, these properties imply that the average of all differences between the proportions of paired samples is .04 and their standard error is .036 (Fig. 10.8).

Figure 10.7

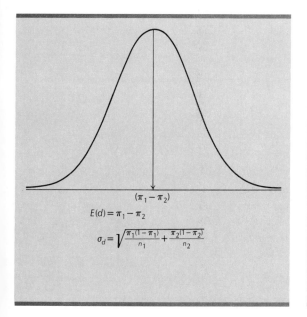

Figure 10.8

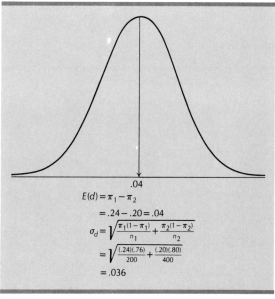

Having determined the mean and the standard error of the differences between the proportions of the paired samples, we can draw some interesting conclusions. Since these differences are approximately normally distributed, we expect 68% of the differences to fall within the range

$$E(d) \pm 1.0\sigma_d = .04 \pm .036,$$

or between .004 and .076 (Fig. 10.9).

In the same manner, we expect 95% of all these differences to fall within the range

$$E(d) \pm 1.96\sigma_d = .04 \pm 1.96 \cdot .036$$
$$= .04 \pm .07,$$

or between $-.03$ and .11 (Fig. 10.10).

Let us now summarize the implications of the preceding discussion. We assume that the proportions of senior students in Delmore College and Eastern University are 24% and 20% respectively. Then, if a random sample of 200 students is selected from Delmore and a sample of 400 students from Eastern, we expect the proportion of seniors in the Delmore sample to be, on average, .04 higher than the proportion of seniors in the Eastern sample. However, the difference between the two sample proportions may very well be smaller or greater than .04. It is even possible, for example, that the proportion of seniors in the Delmore sample will be .11 (or more) *higher* than that in the Eastern sample, and it is also possible that the Delmore sample proportion will be .03 (or more) *lower* than that of Eastern. But the probability of either of these extreme results is only .025 (see Fig. 10.10).

Figure 10.9

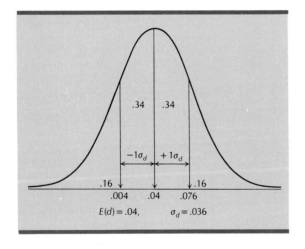

Figure 10.10

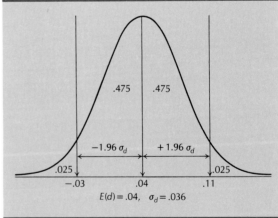

TESTING HYPOTHESES ABOUT THE DIFFERENCE BETWEEN TWO POPULATION PROPORTIONS

If the proportion of senior students in a random sample of 200 students from UCLA is 18% and the same proportion in a random sample of 400 students from USC is 15%, can we safely conclude that the proportions of senior students in the two schools are not the same?

When there are two populations, we have two hypotheses to explore, as we did when we were dealing with population means. First is the null hypothesis, which states that the two populations from which the two samples originate have the same proportion (H_0: $\pi_1 = \pi_2$). If this is the case, the two sample proportions should be close together and the observed difference between the two sample proportions should be small. If the observed difference is in fact small, the difference is deemed not significant and is attributed to chance or random sampling fluctuations. The alternative hypothesis to be explored is that the two samples are drawn from two different populations, each having a distinct proportion (H_1: $\pi_1 \neq \pi_2$). If this alternative is true, the observed difference between the two sample proportions should be large. If the observed difference is in fact large, the difference is deemed significant.

Stated briefly, the two hypotheses in our example are as follows:

$$\text{Null hypothesis:} \quad \pi_1 = \pi_2,$$
$$\text{Alternative hypothesis:} \quad \pi_1 \neq \pi_2,$$

where π_1 is the proportion of seniors in the first population (UCLA) and π_2 is the proportion of seniors in the second population (USC).

Now let us assume that the null hypothesis is true, that is, π_1 and π_2 are the same, each equal to π. If this is the case, then the sampling distribution of the differences between two sample proportions can be described as in Fig. 10.11.

The above result can be interpreted in the following manner: Let us assume that the proportions of seniors at UCLA and USC are the same and that many samples of 200 students are selected from the first school and equally many samples of 400 students are selected from the second school. When these two sets of samples are paired and the difference between the proportions of seniors in each pair is recorded, then the average of all these differences is equal to zero and their standard error, or standard deviation, is

$$\sqrt{\pi(1 - \pi)\left(\frac{1}{n_1} + \frac{1}{n_2}\right)}.$$

If the null hypothesis is true, the proportion of seniors in both schools is the same. This proportion, denoted by π, is certainly unknown. But it can be

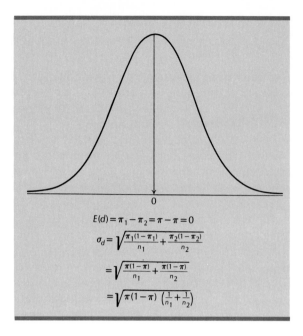

$$E(d) = \pi_1 - \pi_2 = \pi - \pi = 0$$

$$\sigma_d = \sqrt{\frac{\pi_1(1-\pi_1)}{n_1} + \frac{\pi_2(1-\pi_2)}{n_2}}$$

$$= \sqrt{\frac{\pi(1-\pi)}{n_1} + \frac{\pi(1-\pi)}{n_2}}$$

$$= \sqrt{\pi(1-\pi)\left(\frac{1}{n_1} + \frac{1}{n_2}\right)}$$

Figure 10.11

approximated by

$$\hat{\pi} = \frac{n_1 p_1 + n_2 p_2}{n_1 + n_2}$$

$$= \frac{200(.18) + 400(.15)}{200 + 400}$$

$$= \frac{96}{600} = 16\%,$$

and the sampling distribution of the difference between the two sample proportions is as described by Fig. 10.12.

The validity of the null hypothesis is evaluated in terms of the results of the two samples actually selected. The difference between these two sample proportions is .03(.18 − .15), which deviates from the mean of the distribution by .94 unit of z (see Fig. 10.13 and following computations).

$$z = \frac{d - E(d)}{\hat{\sigma}_d}$$

$$= \frac{.03 - 0}{.032} = .94$$

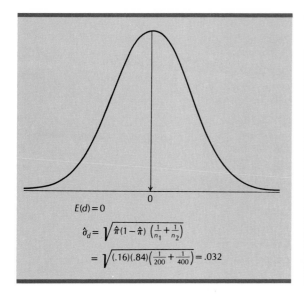

Figure 10.12

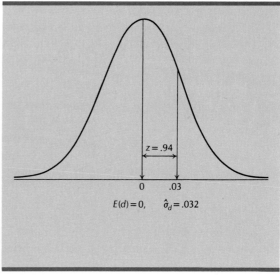

Figure 10.13

Since the test is two-sided, and $z < 1.96$, the difference between the two sample proportions is not significant at the .05 level. In other words, on the basis of the evidence provided by the two samples, one cannot reject the hypothesis that the proportion of seniors in the two schools is the same.

Summarizing the procedure used in testing the significance of the difference between two sample proportions, one must first calculate the value of z:

$$z = \frac{d}{\hat{\sigma}_d} = \frac{p_1 - p_2}{\sqrt{\hat{\pi}(1 - \hat{\pi})\left(\dfrac{1}{n_1} + \dfrac{1}{n_2}\right)}},$$

where

$$\hat{\pi} = \frac{n_1 p_1 + n_2 p_2}{n_1 + n_2}.$$

If $z > 1.96$, the difference is significant at the .05 level. If $z > 2.58$, the difference is significant at the .01 level.

Example   In a public opinion poll of 400 men and 600 women, 70% of the men and 75% of the women expressed approval of the nuclear freeze. Using a level of significance of .05, can we conclude that the observed difference between these two proportions is significant?

Solution:

Given

$$p_1 = .70, \quad p_2 = .75, \quad n_1 = 400, \quad n_2 = 600.$$

Therefore,

$$\hat{\pi} = \frac{n_1 p_1 + n_2 p_2}{n_1 + n_2}$$

$$= \frac{400(.70) + 600(.75)}{400 + 600} = .73,$$

and

$$z = \frac{p_1 - p_2}{\sqrt{\hat{\pi}(1 - \hat{\pi})\left(\dfrac{1}{n_1} + \dfrac{1}{n_2}\right)}}$$

$$= \frac{.70 - .75}{\sqrt{(.73)(.27)\left(\dfrac{1}{400} + \dfrac{1}{600}\right)}}$$

$$= \frac{-.05}{.028} = -1.72.$$

Since the absolute value of z is less than 1.96, the difference between the two sample proportions is not significant at the .05 level.

EXERCISES

10.14   It is known that the percentages of families with an annual income of $20,000 or more in Los Angeles and San Francisco are 25% and 20%, respectively. If a random sample of 100 families is selected from each of these two cities and the proportions of families earning $20,000 or more in the two samples are compared, what is the probability that the Los Angeles sample proportion will be

a) greater than that of San Francisco's by 3% or more?

b) smaller than that of San Francisco's by 3% or more?

10.15   A researcher selected random samples of 120 psychologists and 80 psychiatrists to investigate their views on whether schizophrenia is a biochemical abnormality or a maladjustment to others dating from childhood. The data below are the result of this investigation.

	Psychologists	*Psychiatrists*
Biochemical abnormality	60	50
Childhood maladjustment	60	30
Total	120	80

If you are willing to reject a true hypothesis no more than once in 100, will you reject the hypothesis that the views of the psychologists and psychiatrists on the cause of schizophrenia are the same?

10.16   On August 20 a poll of 200 registered voters showed 120 voters in favor of candidate X. A month later, a poll of 300 registered voters showed only 150 voters in her favor. Does this indicate that the popularity of candidate X has changed during the time between the two polls? Use a level of significance of .05.

10.17   A random sample of 400 consumers selected by a market research organization showed that 20% preferred brand X coffee to all other competing brands. After completion of an intensive radio and television advertising campaign, a second sample of 600 consumers was selected to assess the effectiveness of the campaign. The post-advertising sample showed 22% of the consumers in favor of brand X. If you are willing to reject a true hypothesis no more than once in 10, will you reject the hypothesis that the advertising program was ineffective?

10.18   A random sample of 1000 state employees consists of 400 men and 600 women. The sample shows that 70% of the men prefer a new retirement plan. Of the women, 80% prefer the new retirement plan. Using the .05 level of significance, test the hypothesis that the new retirement plan is equally preferred by men and women.

10.19   To compare the family savings habits in New York and Los Angeles, a random sample of 500 families is selected from each city. In New York, 60% of the families interviewed maintain a savings account; in Los Angeles 56% of the families interviewed have savings accounts. Using a significance level of .01, test the hypothesis that there is no difference in the proportion of families with savings accounts between New York and Los Angeles.

10.20   In Kansas City a random sample of 200 dwelling units shows a vacancy rate of 8%. In comparison, the proportion of vacant units in a random sample of 300 dwelling units in Atlanta is 10%. Using the .01 level of significance, can we conclude that the vacancy rate in the two cities is not the same?

10.21   In Arizona a sample survey of 500 adults showed that 80% of those interviewed support the new administration's economic policy. By contrast, a random sample of 700 adults in Idaho showed that 75% are in favor of the new administration's policy. Use the .01 level of significance to test the hypothesis that the administration's economic policy is equally preferred in Arizona and Idaho.

COMPARISON OF SEVERAL PROPORTIONS: CHI-SQUARE ANALYSIS

Random samples of 160, 240, and 200 persons were selected from Los Angeles, Chicago, and New York, respectively. The persons selected were asked, "What type of television program do you like best: drama, western, documentary, or comedy?" The responses are summarized in the following table.

Type of Program	Los Angeles		Chicago		New York	
	No. of persons	%	No. of persons	%	No. of persons	%
Drama	60	37.50	100	41.67	80	40.00
Western	30	18.75	30	12.50	30	15.00
Documentary	30	18.75	40	16.67	50	25.00
Comedy	40	25.00	70	29.16	40	20.00
Total	160	100.00	240	100.00	200	100.00

Examining the results in the table, we note that drama was preferred by 37.50% of persons interviewed in Los Angeles, 41.67% of those interviewed in Chicago, and 40.00% of those interviewed in New York. The question therefore arises whether the observed difference between these three proportions is due to a real difference in television preferences among the residents of the three cities or to random sampling fluctuations. Similarly, one wonders whether the observed difference between the sample proportions of those who preferred westerns (Los Angeles, 18.75%; Chicago, 12.50%; and New York, 15.00%) is significant.

Although there are many proportions to be compared, the central issue in this problem can be stated as follows: From the sample information, can we safely conclude that the residents of these three metropolitan areas differ in their preference for type of television program? Specifically, the investigator has two hypotheses to explore. First is the null hypothesis that preference for the various types of television programs in the three cities is essentially the same and that any observed sampling differences are due to random sampling fluctuations and hence are not significant. The alternative hypothesis is that there exists a real difference in preferences. On the basis of the results of the three samples selected, the investigator may either reject the null hypothesis or not reject it.

Before testing the validity of the null hypothesis, let us organize our sample data in a manner that will facilitate analysis.

Type of program	Number of persons		
	Los Angeles	Chicago	New York
Drama	60	100	80
Western	30	30	30
Documentary	30	40	50
Comedy	40	70	40
Total	160	240	200

We see that the data are organized in a table that has four rows (drama, western, documentary, and comedy) and three columns (Los Angeles, Chicago, and New York). This table is said to be a 4-by-3 array, since it contains four rows and three columns. Furthermore, it contains 12 cells. Note that the number in each cell indicates the *number* of people (not the percent of people) residing in a certain city and preferring a certain television program. The number 60, for example, which is located in the first cell, indicates that 60 persons out of the 160 interviewed in Los Angeles prefer drama.

Let us proceed as in any other testing problem; that is, let us assume that the null hypothesis is true, that there is no difference in preferences among the three cities. If this is the case, then one expects the proportion of those who prefer drama to be the same in all three cities. We estimate this proportion as follows:

$$\frac{60 + 100 + 80}{160 + 240 + 200} = \frac{240}{600} = 40\%.$$

That is, out of all persons interviewed, the proportion of those who prefer drama is 40%. We next estimate the proportions of those who prefer westerns, documentaries, and comedies, as follows.

$$\frac{30 + 30 + 30}{160 + 240 + 200} = \frac{90}{600} = 15\%:$$

that is, out of all persons interviewed, the proportion of those who prefer westerns is 15%.

$$\frac{30 + 40 + 50}{160 + 240 + 200} = \frac{120}{600} = 20\%:$$

that is, out of all persons interviewed, the proportion of those who prefer documentaries is 20%.

$$\frac{40 + 70 + 40}{160 + 240 + 200} = \frac{150}{600} = 25\%:$$

that is, out of all persons interviewed, the proportion of those who prefer comedy is 25%.

These calculations are summarized in the following table.

ACTUAL NUMBER OF RESPONSES

	Los Angeles	Chicago	New York	Total	Percent
Drama	60	100	80	240	$^{240}/_{600} = 40\%$
Western	30	30	30	90	$^{90}/_{600} = 15\%$
Documentary	30	40	50	120	$^{120}/_{600} = 20\%$
Comedy	40	70	40	150	$^{150}/_{600} = 25\%$
Total	160	240	200	600	

If the null hypothesis is true, then in any sample (whether from Chicago, Los Angeles, or New York), we expect 40% to prefer dramas; 15%, westerns; 20%, documentaries; and 25%, comedies. Applying these percentages to the three samples actually selected, we expect the following responses in each cell.

EXPECTED NUMBER OF RESPONSES

	Los Angeles	Chicago	New York
Drama	$160 \cdot .40 = 64$	$240 \cdot .40 = 96$	$200 \cdot .40 = 80$
Western	$160 \cdot .15 = 24$	$240 \cdot .15 = 36$	$200 \cdot .15 = 30$
Documentary	$160 \cdot .20 = 32$	$240 \cdot .20 = 48$	$200 \cdot .20 = 40$
Comedy	$160 \cdot .25 = 40$	$240 \cdot .25 = 60$	$200 \cdot .25 = 50$
Total	160	240	200

To find the expected number of responses in the first cell, that is, the drama fans in Los Angeles, we multiply the number of persons interviewed in Los Angeles by the expected proportion of those who prefer drama. Thus the expected number of responses in the first cell is

$$160 \cdot .40 = 64 \text{ persons.}$$

This result differs from the actual number of responses in that cell, which is only 60.

If the null hypothesis is true, then the actual and expected numbers of responses in each cell should be reasonably close. The greater the disparity between these two sets of responses, the more doubtful the null hypothesis.

To facilitate the analysis of the data, let us list both the actual and the expected response distributions in one table. The expected responses are enclosed in parentheses.

ACTUAL AND EXPECTED NUMBER OF RESPONSES

	Los Angeles	Chicago	New York
Drama	60 (64)	100 (96)	80 (80)
Western	30 (24)	30 (36)	30 (30)
Documentary	30 (32)	40 (48)	50 (40)
Comedy	40 (40)	70 (60)	40 (50)

We can measure the disparity between the actual and expected distributions of responses by computing the term

$$\frac{(\text{Actual} - \text{Expected})^2}{\text{Expected}}$$

for each cell and adding the 12 terms. The sum, called **chi-square** and denoted by x^2, is computed as follows:

$$x^2 = \frac{(60 - 64)^2}{64} + \frac{(100 - 96)^2}{96} + \frac{(80 - 80)^2}{80} + \frac{(30 - 24)^2}{24}$$

$$+ \frac{(30 - 36)^2}{36} + \frac{(30 - 30)^2}{30} + \frac{(30 - 32)^2}{32} + \frac{(40 - 48)^2}{48}$$

$$+ \frac{(50 - 40)^2}{40} + \frac{(40 - 40)^2}{40} + \frac{(70 - 60)^2}{60} + \frac{(40 - 50)^2}{50}$$

$$= .25 + .16 + 0 + 1.38 + 1.00 + 0 + .12 + 1.33$$

$$+ 2.50 + 0 + 1.66 + 2.00$$

$$= 10.40.$$

If the preferences for television programs are the same in all three cities, the actual and expected responses must be reasonably close and the value of x^2 must be very small. Furthermore, the greater the disparity between the two sets of responses, the larger the value of x^2 and the more doubtful the hypothesis that the preferences are the same. But how large a value should x^2 reach before we can safely conclude that the preferences are not the same?

This question can be answered after we have examined the theoretical sampling distribution of χ^2 in Table D at the end of the book.

Table D shows the various values of χ^2 that can be obtained as a result of pure sampling fluctuations. The probability given at the top of each column indicates the chance of obtaining a larger value than the one specified in the table. In addition, each row in the table is associated with the number of degrees of freedom (to be explained later).

Thus, with 6 degrees of freedom, for example, there is a .05 chance that a $\chi^2 > 12.592$ could occur as a result of pure random sampling fluctuations (see Fig. 10.14). With the same number of degrees of freedom, the probability is only .01 that $\chi^2 > 16.812$ as a result of sampling fluctuations (Fig. 10.15).

We have already mentioned that each row in Table D is associated with a certain number of degrees of freedom. What are these degrees of freedom? The number of degrees of freedom in any given problem is determined as follows:

$$\text{Degrees of freedom} = (r - 1)(c - 1),$$

where r is the number of rows in the problem and c is the number of columns in the problem.

In our problem, there are four rows (drama, western, documentary, and comedy) and three columns (Los Angeles, Chicago, and New York). Therefore, the number of degrees of freedom is

$$df = (r - 1)(c - 1)$$
$$= (4 - 1)(3 - 1) = 6.$$

You may recall that we have obtained an *actual* χ^2-value of 10.40. With 6 degrees of freedom, Table D shows that there is a .10 chance that $\chi^2 > 10.645$ could occur as a result of sampling fluctuations. The probability is greater than .10, therefore, that we will obtain $\chi^2 > 10.40$, although the preference for the various television programs is the same in the three cities.

Generally speaking, the null hypothesis is rejected only when the chance

Figure 10.14 Chi-square distribution (6 df)

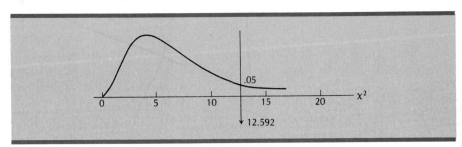

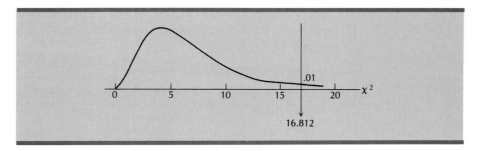

Figure 10.15 Only .01 chance that x^2 is larger than 16.812

of obtaining an observed value of x^2 is less than .05 or .01. These are the two levels of significance most frequently used.

Thus, using either the .01 or .05 level of significance, we cannot reject the null hypothesis that preferences are the same.

Example In a public opinion poll, 1000 Americans were asked, "How do you rate the job Mr. X is doing as secretary of state: good, fair, or poor?" The responses, classified according to the educational level of the respondents, are shown in the following table.

ACTUAL DISTRIBUTION OF RESPONSES BY EDUCATIONAL LEVEL

	Eighth grade or Less	High School	College	Total
Good	82	427	191	700
Fair	10	110	60	180
Poor	8	63	49	120
Total	100	600	300	1000

Using a level of significance of .05, can we conclude that the ratings are the same for all educational levels of the respondents?

If the secretary of state's rating is the same regardless of the educational level of the respondent (the null hypothesis), then we expect

$$\frac{700}{1000} = 70\% \text{ to respond "good,"}$$

$$\frac{180}{1000} = 18\% \text{ to respond "fair,"}$$

$$\frac{120}{1000} = 12\% \text{ to respond "poor."}$$

Applying these three ratios to the number of people selected from each of the three educational levels, we obtain the following expected or theoretical distribution of responses.

EXPECTED DISTRIBUTION OF RESPONSES

	Eighth Grade or Less	High School	College
Good	$100 \cdot .70 = 70$	$600 \cdot .70 = 420$	$300 \cdot .70 = 210$
Fair	$100 \cdot .18 = 18$	$600 \cdot .18 = 108$	$300 \cdot .18 = 54$
Poor	$100 \cdot .12 = 12$	$600 \cdot .12 = 72$	$300 \cdot .12 = 36$
Total	100	600	300

Before computing the observed value of x^2, let us combine the actual and the expected response distributions in one table. The expected number of responses is placed in parentheses.

	Eighth Grade or Less	High School	College
Good	82 (70)	427 (420)	191 (210)
Fair	10 (18)	110 (108)	60 (54)
Poor	8 (12)	63 (72)	49 (36)

The following are the computations for the observed value of x^2.

$$x^2 = \frac{(82 - 70)^2}{70} + \frac{(427 - 420)^2}{420} + \frac{(191 - 210)^2}{210} + \frac{(10 - 18)^2}{18}$$

$$+ \frac{(110 - 108)^2}{108} + \frac{(60 - 54)^2}{54} + \frac{(8 - 12)^2}{12} + \frac{(63 - 72)^2}{72}$$

$$+ \frac{(49 - 36)^2}{36}$$

$$= 2.507 + .116 + 1.719 + 3.555 + .037 + .666 + 1.333$$

$$+ 1.125 + 4.694$$

$$= 15.752.$$

Before we can determine the probability of obtaining $x^2 > 15.752$ as a result of sampling fluctuations, we must determine the number of degrees of freedom in our problem:

$$\text{Degrees of freedom} = (r - 1)(c - 1)$$
$$= (3 - 1)(3 - 1) = 4.$$

With 4 degrees of freedom, Table D shows that there is only a .01 chance that $x^2 > 13.277$ could occur as a result of sampling fluctuations. Thus the probability is less than .01 that $\chi^2 > 15.752$ will occur if ratings for all educational levels are the same. Using the .05 level of significance (or even the .01 level), we must therefore conclude that the secretary of state's rating is not the same for all educational levels of the respondents.

EXERCISES

10.22   In a public opinion poll, 500 American adults were asked, "Do you approve of the escalation of the war in Chad? Yes, no, or no opinion." The responses, cross-classified by party affiliation, are shown in the following table.

	Yes	No	No Opinion
Democrats	95	110	45
Republicans	80	75	45
Independents	25	15	10

Test the hypothesis that the attitude of American adults toward the escalation of the war in Chad is the same for all political parties. Use a level of significance of .05.

10.23   Three drugs—Cloroquine, Pyrimethamine, and Sulformethoxine— were used in the treatment of 240 cases of falciparum malaria. The number of patients cured with each drug, as well as the relapse rates, are shown in the following table.

	Cloroquine	Pyrimethamine	Sulformethoxine
Number of cured cases	60	80	100
Relapse rate	40%	30%	12%

Using a level of significance of .01, do the data present evidence that the relapse rates of the three drugs are not the same?

10.24   The following is a percentage distribution, by home ownership and income level, of a random sample of 400 families in Tulsa, Oklahoma.

	Annual Income		
	Less than $10,000	$10,000–$20,000	More than $20,000
Home owners	5%	35%	10%
Renters	15%	25%	10%

Test the hypothesis that in Tulsa home ownership is the same for all levels of family income. Use a level of significance of .01.

10.25 The governor's reelection committee mailed letters soliciting political contributions to a random sample of 1000 Republicans. Of these 1000 letters, 400 were originally typed personal letters, and 600 were mimeographed form letters. The committee received the following responses from the two kinds of letters:

	Typed Letters	Mimeographed Forms
Contribution under $100	200	200
Contribution of $100 or more	100	200
No response	100	200
	400	600

Test the hypothesis that political contributions are the same for all types of letters used in soliciting. Use a level of significance of .01.

10.26 In a public opinion poll, 300 adults are asked, "Do you attend a weekly religious service? Never, occasionally, or regularly." The responses, classified by gender of respondents, are shown below:

	Male	Female
Never	80	70
Occasionally	50	70
Regularly	10	20

Test the hypothesis that attendance at religious service is independent of gender. Use a level of significance of .01.

10.27 A random sample of 200 American, middle-class, married men and 200 such women were asked what they enjoyed doing most in their leisure time. The survey showed the following percentage distribution of their first-choice leisure activity:

	Reading	Watching TV	Other Activities	Total
Men	23%	40%	37%	100%
Women	47%	43%	10%	100%

Using the .05 level of significance, can we conclude that American, middle-class, married men and women prefer the same activities in their leisure time?

10.28 KPFK is a Los Angeles radio station that is supported by its subscribers. Its management wishes to determine whether various age groups prefer different kinds of music. The station's manager randomly selected 400 of its subscribers and asked them which music they preferred: classical, popular, or country. The following results were obtained.

	Number of Respondents (by age)		
	Under 30	30–50	Over 50
Classical	10	20	10
Popular	90	140	50
Country	20	40	20

Test the hypothesis that music preference is the same for all the subscriber age groups. Use a level of significance of .05.

10.29 A study is conducted by the Boston school district to determine the effect of television viewing time on children's school performance. An academic aptitude test is administered to a random sample of 400 sixth-grade children whose television viewing habits have been analyzed. The study's results are as follows.

Test Result	Average Television Viewing Time per Day		
	1 hour or less	1–2 hours	Over 2 hours
Passing	150	100	50
Failing	10	40	50
Total	160	140	100

Using the .05 level of significance, can you conclude that the length of television viewing time does not influence children's academic performance?

KEY TERMS

chi-square analysis A method of analyzing several discrete distributions to test whether the proportions are the same for all the distributions.

chi-square statistic   The statistic computed by summing (Actual − Expected)^2/Expected over all the cells in the table of actual and expected responses.

chi-square distribution   The theoretical distribution of the chi-square statistic when the proportions are the same for all the populations, and only sampling fluctuations are present.

SUMMARY OF FORMULAS

z-value for testing a proportion

$$z = \frac{p - \pi}{\sigma_p}$$

expected difference between two sample proportions

$$E(d) = E(p_1 - p_2) = \pi_1 - \pi_2$$

standard deviation of the difference between two proportions

$$\sigma_d = \sigma_{p_1 - p_2} = \sqrt{\frac{\pi_1(1 - \pi_1)}{n_1} + \frac{\pi_2(1 - \pi_2)}{n_2}}$$

standard deviation of the difference between two proportions when $\pi_1 = \pi_2 = \pi$

$$\sigma_d = \sigma_{p_1 - p_2} = \sqrt{\pi(1 - \pi)\left(\frac{1}{n_1} + \frac{1}{n_2}\right)}$$

pooled estimate of π from two samples assuming $\pi_1 = \pi_2 = \pi$

$$\hat{\pi} = \frac{n_1 p_1 + n_2 p_2}{n_1 + n_2}$$

z-value for testing the equality of two proportions

$$z = \frac{d}{\hat{\sigma}_d} = \frac{p_1 - p_2}{\sqrt{\hat{\pi}(1 - \hat{\pi})\left(\frac{1}{n_1} + \frac{1}{n_2}\right)}}$$

chi-square

$$\chi^2 = \sum \frac{(\text{Actual} - \text{Expected})^2}{\text{Expected}}$$

degrees of freedom for chi-square

$$\begin{aligned} df &= (\text{rows} - 1)(\text{columns} - 1) \\ &= (r - 1)(c - 1) \end{aligned}$$

CUMULATIVE REVIEW

1. It is known that 64% of all registered voters in the 27th congressional district are Democrats. What is the probability that in a random sample of 400 voters from this district there will be 240 or more Democrats?

2. It is known that 10% of all families in a certain city are Irish-American. If 100 families are selected at random from this city, what is the probability that the percentage of Irish-Americans will be

   a) greater than 13 percent?

   b) between 13 and 16 percent?

3. Assume that 50 percent of all adults in Utah favor admitting the newly formed Republic of Bangal to the United Nations.

   a) What is the probability that in a random sample of 300 adult Utah residents, 55% or more of those interviewed will favor admitting the Republic of Bangal to the United Nations?

   b) The probability is 90% that the proportion of adult Utah residents who favor admitting the new country to the United Nations in a random sample of 100 is between p_1 and p_2. Find p_1 and p_2 using symmetrical limits around the mean.

4. Twenty percent of all students attending a given college are nonresident students.

   a) What is the probability that a random sample of 500 students will reveal 22% or more nonresident students?

b) The probability is .50 that the percentage of nonresident students in a random sample of 1600 is between p_1 and p_2. Find p_1 and p_2 using symmetrical limits around the mean of the sampling distribution of the proportion.

c) Construct an interval where there is .80 chance that the proportion of nonresidents in a random sample of 100 students will fall.

5. A very large shipment of small parts contains 10% defective parts. A random sample of 225 parts is selected from this shipment.

a) What is the probability that the sample proportion will be between .07 and .13?

b) Establish an interval where there is .95 confidence that the sample proportion will fall within that interval.

6. A random sample of 200 consumers showed that 72 preferred brand X coffee to all other competing brands. Establish a .95 confidence interval estimate of the proportion of consumers favoring brand X coffee.

7. A random sample of 400 families in Wilmington, Delaware, revealed that 200 families have two cars or more.

a) Establish a .90 confidence interval estimate of the proportion of families owning two cars or more in Wilmington.

b) With what degree of confidence can we assert that the proportion of families with two cars or more in Wilmington is between 45% and 55%?

8. A random sample of 400 files of students who visited the student health center at a given college last year shows that 80 students had an illness of a psychosomatic nature.

a) With what degree of confidence can we assert that 16% to 24% of *all* students who visited the health center last year had a psychosomatic illness?

b) Assume that 2000 students visited the health center last year. How many of these students had a psychosomatic illness? What degree of confidence can you attach to your estimate?

9. It is claimed that chloroquine is 80% effective in the cure of malaria. Eight hundred malaria cases were treated with chloroquine and only 600 were cured. Would you conclude that the effectiveness of chloroquine in the cure of malaria is exaggerated?

10. Elisa Smith, a life insurance salesperson, reports to the regional sales manager that 20% of the prospects assigned to her would purchase a life insurance policy.

a) What would the manager conclude about Smith's claim if a random sample of 100 prospects assigned to her shows that 18% of the prospects purchased a life insurance policy?

b) Would the manager's conclusion be different if only 7% of the sampled prospects purchased a life insurance policy? Justify your answer.

11. Machine 36 produces product X. Several years of experience have shown that machine 36 produces, on average, 10% defective units. Recently, the quality-control engineer suspected that the quality of product X has deteriorated. He selected a random sample of 100 units. The sample revealed 14 defective units. Using a level of significance of .05, can the quality-control engineer conclude that the quality of product X has deteriorated?

12. A random sample of 1000 college professors in the United States shows 200 females.

a) Establish a .95 confidence interval estimate of female college professors in the United States.

b) An official of the AAUP claims that 24% of all college professors in the United States are females. Test the validity of this claim, using a level of significance of .01.

13. A random sample of 500 students from a college shows 100 freshmen students.

a) Establish a .95 confidence interval estimate of the proportion of freshmen students in the college.

b) The dean of students claims that the proportion of freshmen is 15%. Test the validity of this claim using a .01 level of significance.

c) Estimate the number of freshmen, assuming that the college has a total enrollment of 20,000 students. Justify your answer.

14. A sample survey is conducted in a Midwestern city of 10,000 families to determine the proportion of families who own a color television set. A random sample of 200 families shows 160 families own color television sets.

a) Establish a .95 confidence interval estimate of the proportion of families who own color television sets in the city.

b) The president of the local chamber of commerce claims that at least 8500 families in the city own color television sets. Test this claim using a .01 level of significance.

15. A random sample of 400 new automobiles sold in the United States in 1985 showed 96 foreign-made cars.

a) Establish a .95 confidence interval estimate of the proportion of new foreign-made automobiles sold in the United States in 1985.

b) Assuming that 20% of *all* new automobiles sold in the United States in 1984 were foreign-made, test the hypothesis that the proportion of foreign-made cars increased between 1984 and 1985. Use a level of significance of .05.

16. A random sample of 500 college professors in the United States reveals 400 men and 100 women. The sample furthermore shows that of the men, 240 hold doctorates. Of the women, 80 have doctorates. Using the .05 level of significance, can you conclude that the percentage of those holding doctorates is different between men and women?

17. A sample survey of 100 female and 100 male students from a college showed 55 females and 45 males in favor of coed housing. If you are willing to reject a true hypothesis no more than once in 100, would you reject the hypothesis that there is no real difference of opinion between male and female students at the college in regard to coed housing?

18. Random samples of 40, 40, and 120 parts are taken from the weekly production of machines A, B, and C, respectively. The number of defective parts found in the samples are 15, 5, and 30 for machines A, B, and C, respectively. Using a .05 level of significance, can you conclude that the percentage of defective parts turned out by the three machines is essentially the same?

19. To decide whether to endorse proposition 10, Governor Black adopts the following decision rule: A random sample of 200 Alabama registered voters is selected. The governor will endorse proposition 10 only when 55% or more of the sample voters are in favor of proposition 10. What is the probability that Governor Black

   a) will endorse proposition 10 when the proposition is favored by 48% of *all* Alabama voters?

   b) will fail to endorse proposition 10 when the proposition is favored by 60% of all Alabama voters?

20. In a university with a total enrollment of 30,000 students, a random sample of 150 students shows that 57 have transferred from other colleges and universities.

   a) Establish a .90 confidence interval estimate of the total number of transfer students at the university.

   b) With what degree of confidence can we assert that the proportion of transfer students in the entire university is between 31% and 45%?

21. Procter & Gamble uses the following sampling rule in deciding whether to introduce a new product line: Select a random sample of 100 retail merchants and determine the proportion of merchants who favor the decision to add the new line. If the sample proportion is 50% or more, the

company will adopt the new product line; otherwise the new product line will not be added.

   a) What is the probability of adopting the new product line, assuming that 45% of *all* retail merchants prefer the new line?

   b) What is the probability of not adding the new product line when 60% of all retailers are in favor of introducing it?

22. In a marketing survey conducted in several major U.S. cities, the Chrysler Corporation reported that 600 of 1000 persons preferred its K Car over similar Japanese models. Establish a .99 confidence interval estimate of the proportion of people who favor Chrysler's K Car over the competing Japanese models.

SIMPLE LINEAR REGRESSION AND CORRELATION

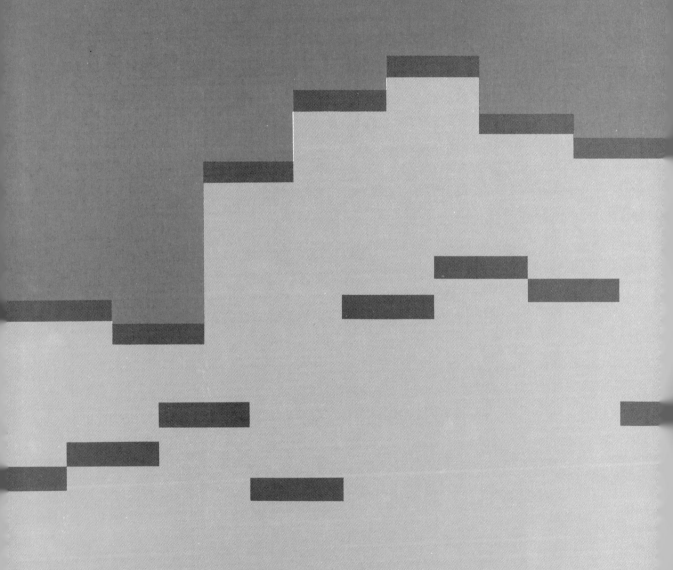

11

This and the next two chapters deal with two closely related topics: regression and correlation. The main purpose of regression is to predict a particular variable, such as sales, from closely related variables such as income, population growth, advertising outlay, and the like. Correlation is mainly concerned with measuring the strength of the relationship among such variables. In this chapter we develop a method to describe a relationship between only two variables, Y and X. We also learn how to calculate measures that describe various aspects of this relationship.

The success of every organization, private or public, depends to a large extent on the proper formulation of its current and future plans of operation, and prediction or forecasting plays a crucial role in the formulation of these plans. Public organizations strive to obtain an accurate prediction of revenues and expenditures; and business firms seek to forecast as accurately as possible various economic variables such as sales, cost of production, capital requirements, inventories, cash flow, and so on.

The term **regression** refers to the process of predicting the value of one variable from a known and related variable (or variables). The variable to be predicted is called a dependent variable and is denoted by Y; the known variable is called the independent variable and is denoted by X. To predict the dependent variable Y from the known and independent variable X, we must first establish a relationship between them. A mathematical equation is often used to express such a relationship. For example, we can let the regression equation

$$Y = 5000 + 200X$$

express the relationship between total cost (Y) and the number of units produced (X) by a certain manufacturing firm. If the manufacturing firm plans to produce 50 units in the coming month, the predicted total cost can be determined as follows:

$$\begin{aligned} Y &= 5000 + 200X \\ &= 5000 + 200(50) \\ &= \$15{,}000 \end{aligned}$$

In this chapter we will not only learn how to determine the regression equation but we will also discuss some issues that relate to the accuracy of the prediction and to the strength of the relationship between the variables Y and X. The term *correlation* refers to the strength of the relationship between pairs of variables.

Before we embark on the topics of regression and correlation we begin by briefly discussing the concept of a simple linear equation.

SIMPLE LINEAR EQUATIONS

Let us assume that two variables, X and Y, are related in the following fashion: $Y = 3 + 1.5X$. This relationship enables us to compute the value of Y for any given value of X. If X is known to be 2, for example, $Y = 6$. Similarly, $Y = 9$ when X is known to be 4. The data below show various values of Y, each of which is associated with a given value of X.

Predicted Value of Y	Known Value of X	Change in Y
4.5	1	–
6.0	2	1.5
7.5	3	1.5
9.0	4	1.5
10.5	5	1.5

The last column of the table indicates that the value of Y increases by 1.5 units as the value of X is increased by 1 unit.

An equation like $Y = 3 + 1.5X$ not only enables us to determine the value of Y associated with any given value of X, but it also describes the effect of a change in variable X on the values assumed by variable Y. Specifically, the coefficient of the variable X indicates the change in the value of Y caused by one unit change in X. Thus, in the equation $Y = 3 + 1.5X$ the value of Y increases by 1.5 units as the value of X is increased by 1 unit. Similarly, the value of Y in the equation $Y = 6 + .2X$ increases by .2 unit as the value of X is increased by 1 unit. In both equations, variable Y increases as variable X increases, and the two variables are said to be *directly related*. On the other hand, in the equation $Y = 100 - 2X$, the value of Y decreases by 2 units as X is increased by 1 unit, and X and Y are said to be *inversely related*. The sign of the coefficient of X in the equation indicates whether the two variables are directly or inversely related. A positive coefficient indicates a direct relationship, and a negative coefficient indicates an inverse one.

The equation $Y = 3 + 1.5X$ is a *first-degree equation*, and the equations $Y = 3 + 2X + 4X^2$ and $Y = 3 + 7X + 5X^3$ are called *second-degree* and *third-degree equations*, respectively. The degree of an equation refers to the highest power of X in the equation. All three equations, however, are called *simple equations* because they express a relationship between only two variables, Y and X. An equation such as $Y = 3X + 8Z$, which expresses a relationship between more than two variables, is called a *multiple equation*. In this chapter our discussion is limited to simple first-degree relationships.

Let us see how a simple first-degree equation such as $Y = 3 + 1.5X$ can be represented graphically. To represent any equation by a graph, we must first prepare a table that shows several values for variable X and the corresponding values for Y.

X	1	2	3	4	5
Y	4.5	6.0	7.5	9.0	10.5

We measure off the value of X on the horizontal axis and the value of Y on the vertical axis on a graph such as that in Fig. 11.1. Then each pair of values of X

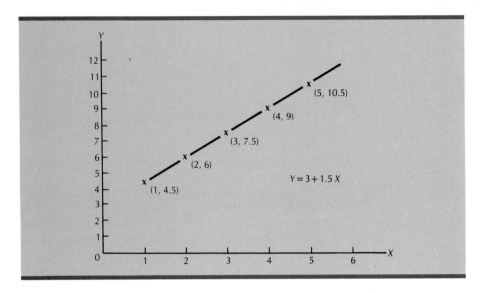

Figure 11.1

and Y, such as (1, 4.5), (2, 6), and (3, 7.5), represent a point in the graph. The five paired values in the preceding table are plotted in Fig. 11.1. Examining the figure, we can also readily observe that the five points lie on a straight line. This line is the graphic representation of the equation $Y = 3 + 1.5X$.

The equation $Y = a + bX$ is the general form of a simple first-degree equation (in the equation $Y = 3 + 1.5X$, we have $a = 3$ and $b = 1.5$). Since the graphic representation of such an equation is a straight line, a simple first-degree equation is also called a *simple linear equation.*

SIMPLE LINEAR REGRESSION

The principal objective in simple regression analysis is to establish a quantitative relationship (in the form of an equation) between two related variables. Once this relationship is established, we can predict the value of one of the variables, Y, if the value of the other variable, X, is known.

To establish the quantitative relationship between Y and X, we must obtain certain sample data. These data consist of a number of paired observations on Y and X, where each pair belongs to one particular elementary unit in the sample.

To be specific, let us assume that we wish to determine the simple linear relationship between the height and the age of a papaya tree, based on a sample of five trees. If the height and the age of each tree are recorded, our data will then consist of five paired observations, with each pair referring to the height and the age of one tree. These five paired observations are shown in the following table.

Y (feet)	9	5	7	14	10
X (years)	3	1	2	5	4

The first pair of observations ($Y = 9$, $X = 3$) indicates that the first tree is 9 feet high and 3 years old. In the same manner, the second pair ($Y = 5$, $X = 1$) refers to the second tree, whose height is 5 feet and whose age is 1 year. The pair ($Y = 10$, $X = 4$) refers to the height and the age of the fifth tree.

Once the necessary data are obtained, the relationship between the two variables can be determined either graphically or mathematically, by the least-squares method.

The Graphic Method

In the graphic method, each pair of observations is represented by a point on a chart. A point is obtained by plotting the independent variable, X, along the horizontal axis and the dependent variable, Y, along the vertical axis. The pair ($Y = 9$, $X = 3$), for example, is represented by point (1) in Fig. 11.2; point (1) is located at the intersection of 3 on the horizontal axis and 9 on the vertical axis. The remaining four pairs of observations are plotted in a similar fashion. A plot of all observations is called a *scatter diagram*.

Once all observations are plotted, we draw a straight line that best represents the relationship between the two variables. Such a line (as in Fig. 11.2) is called the *estimated regression line*. It enables us to predict the value of Y for any given value of X. If X is known to be 7, for example, the value of Y is expected to be approximately 17, as shown by the dashed lines.

The graphic method for determining the relationship between two variables is certainly simple and straightforward. Its main drawback, however, is its subjective nature. Different people will most likely draw different regression lines. The mathematical or least-squares method, on the other hand, will always yield the same equation, an equation that best describes the linear relationship between two variables.

The Least-Squares Method

We have already learned that a linear relationship between two variables is represented by a straight line whose general equation is $Y = a + bX$. The **least-squares method** is the mathematical procedure used to determine the numerical value of the constants a and b in this equation. The general equation $Y = a + bX$ is called the *regression equation* and the constants a and b are called the *regression coefficients*.

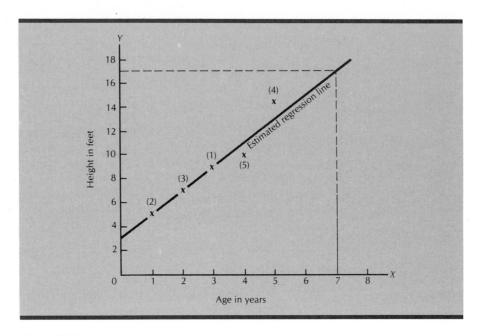

Figure 11.2

Like the graphic method, the least-squares method utilizes a set of paired observations on Y and X. Returning to our example of determining the simple linear relationship between the height and the age of a papaya tree, we repeat the set of five paired observations.

Y (feet)	9	5	7	14	10
X (years)	3	1	2	5	4

A few preliminary computations facilitate the procedure used to determine the numerical values of the constants a and b. These calculations are carried out, explained, and summarized in the following table and discussion.

Preliminary Computations:

Y	X	Y^2	X^2	XY
9	3	81	9	27
5	1	25	1	5
7	2	49	4	14
14	5	196	25	70
10	4	100	16	40
$\sum Y = 45$	$\sum X = 15$	$\sum Y^2 = 451$	$\sum X^2 = 55$	$\sum XY = 156$

Explanation of Table: The first column contains the various values of Y, together with their sum. The second column contains the various values of X, together with their sum. The third column lists the squares of the individual values of Y in column 1, together with their sum. Thus, for example, the 81 in column 3 is obtained by squaring the 9 in column 1. The fourth column lists the squares of the individual values of X in column 2, together with their sum. Thus, for example, the 9 in column 4 is obtained by squaring the 3 in column 2. The fifth column lists the cross-products of the corresponding Y- and X-values in columns 1 and 2, together with their sums. Thus, for example, the 27 in column 5 is the cross-product of the 9 and 3 from columns 1 and 2.

Summary of Computations:

$$\sum Y = 45, \qquad \sum Y^2 = 451,$$
$$\sum X = 15, \qquad \sum X^2 = 55,$$
$$\sum XY = 156.$$

Once the sum of each variable, the sum of each of their squares, and the sum of their cross-products are computed, the next step is to substitute these values in what is called the two **normal equations.**
The two normal equations are

$$\sum Y = na + b \sum X,$$
$$\sum XY = a \sum X + b \sum X^2,$$

where n refers to the number of paired observations used in the regression (we have 5 paired observations here, that is, $n = 5$) and a and b are the regression coefficients we want to determine.
Substituting the values $\sum Y = 45$, $n = 5$, $\sum X = 15$, $\sum XY = 156$, and $\sum X^2 = 55$ in the two normal equations, we obtain the following two simultaneous equations:

$$45 = 5a + 15b,$$
$$156 = 15a + 55b.$$

Solving these two equations, we find that the regression coefficients b and a are 2.1 and 2.7, respectively, and hence the regression equation is

$$Y = 2.7 + 2.1X.$$

This equation enables us to estimate the value of Y for any given value of X. If X is known to be 10 years, for example, the estimated value of Y is 23.7 feet. The regression equation, furthermore, indicates that the value of Y increases by 2.1 feet as the value of X increases by 1 year. In other words, each additional year will add 2.1 feet to the height of a papaya tree.
Before concluding this discussion, we must make a clear distinction between the *observed* value of Y and the *estimated* value of Y. The observed

value of Y refers to the *actual* height of a given tree, and the estimated value of Y is the *estimated* height of a tree, using the regression equation as a means of estimation. The observed and the estimated height of a tree may or may not be the same. This point becomes clear if one refers to any of the trees in the sample. For example, the second tree, which is 1 year old, has an observed, or actual, height of 5 feet. However, using the regression equation $Y = 2.7 + 2.1X$, we obtain its estimated height as 4.8 feet (the estimated height is obtained by substituting $X = 1$ in the regression equation). Thus, while the observed value of Y is 5 feet, the estimated value is 4.8 feet; the two values are not the same. To distinguish between the observed and the estimated height of a given tree, we use Y to denote the observed height and Y' to denote the estimated height. Thus the regression equation, which always refers to the *estimated* value of the dependent variable, must be written $Y' = 2.7 + 2.1X$ (see Fig. 11.3).

STANDARD ERROR OF THE ESTIMATE

The **standard error of the estimate,** denoted by S_{YX}, measures the "average" disparity between the actual and estimated values of the variable Y. To determine the standard error of the estimate, we must begin by computing the estimated height of each tree in that sample; that is, we must substitute the age of each tree in the regression equation $Y' = 2.7 + 2.1X$. The observed height, Y, the age, X, and the estimated height, Y', of the five trees are shown in the first, second, and third columns in the following table.

Y	X	Y'	$(Y - Y')$	$(Y - Y')^2$
9	3	9.0	.0	.0
5	1	4.8	+.2	.04
7	2	6.9	+.1	.01
14	5	13.2	+.8	.64
10	4	11.1	−1.1	1.21
				$\sum(Y - Y')^2 = 1.90$

Column 4 shows the difference between the observed and estimated height of each tree. These differences are squared and entered in column 5. The total of column 5 is $\sum(Y - Y')^2$. The standard error of the estimate can now be computed as

$$S_{YX} = \sqrt{\frac{\sum(Y - Y')^2}{n - 2}}$$

$$= \sqrt{\frac{1.90}{5 - 2}} = \sqrt{\frac{1.90}{3}} = \sqrt{.633} = .80 \text{ foot.}$$

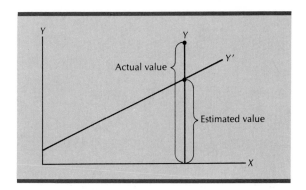

Figure 11.3

Since the standard error of the estimate measures the "average" disparity between the actual and estimated heights of a tree in the sample, it can be regarded as an indication of how well the regression equation predicts the dependent variable. If S_{yx} is small, the actual and estimated values of Y must be reasonably close, and the regression equation is a good means of prediction. When $S_{yx} = 0$, for example, the actual and estimated values of Y must be identical. A large standard error of the estimate, on the other hand, means a large disparity between the actual and estimated values of Y; in this case, the regression equation is regarded as a poor means of prediction.

The standard error of the estimate is measured in the same units as Y; in the case of the papaya trees, both are measured in feet. If we had measured the height of each tree in inches, the standard error of the estimate would also be in inches. Furthermore, its numerical value would be 12 times as large. In other words, the standard error is affected by changes in the units of Y.

While S_{yx} measures the accuracy of predicting the value of Y (in some rough fashion),* another measure, called the **correlation coefficient,** measures the strength of the relationship between the two variables Y and X. The correlation coefficient is a unitless measure whose value ranges between -1 and 1. When the correlation coefficient is equal to 1 or -1, there is perfect correlation between the two variables. On the other hand, a correlation coefficient of zero indicates no correlation at all.

THE CORRELATION COEFFICIENT

The regression equation $Y' = 2.7 + 2.1X$ was derived from a sample of five trees whose actual or observed heights are $Y_1 = 9$ feet, $Y_2 = 5$ feet, $Y_3 = 7$ feet, $Y_4 = 14$ feet, and $Y_5 = 10$ feet. The average height of a tree in this sample can

---

*A detailed discussion concerning the accuracy of predicting the value of Y is found in the next chapter.

be computed as

$$\overline{Y} = \frac{Y_1 + Y_2 + Y_3 + Y_4 + Y_5}{5}$$

$$= \frac{9 + 5 + 7 + 14 + 10}{5} = \frac{45}{5} = 9 \text{ feet.}$$

We measure the variation in the heights of the five trees by computing the sum of the squared deviations, that is, differences between the actual height of the individual tree and the mean height, $\sum(Y - \overline{Y})^2$, as shown in the following table.

Y	$\overline{Y}$	$(Y - \overline{Y})$	$(Y - \overline{Y})^2$
9	9	0	0
5	9	-4	16
7	9	-2	4
14	9	$+5$	25
10	9	$+1$	1
			$\sum(Y - \overline{Y})^2 = 46$

The sum $\sum(Y - \overline{Y})^2$, which measures variations in the heights of the five trees, is called **total variation** (depicted in Fig. 11.4).

We can now ask an interesting question: Can we account for or explain this variation in the heights of the trees? There are certainly many factors responsible for it: the variation in the soil in which these trees are planted, the variation in climate, and, above all, the variation in the ages of the individual trees. The next question to be asked is: Since we are interested in the relationship

Figure 11.4

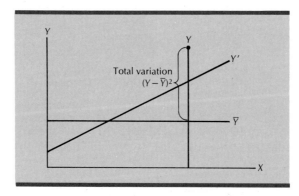

between height and age, why not separate the effect of variation in age from the effect of all other factors? This is precisely what we will attempt to do. The total variation in height will be subdivided into two components. The first component is the variation in height that is associated with, or could be explained by, variation in age. This component is called **explained variation.** The remaining component of total variation is attributed to all other factors that influence height, such as soil and climate. That component is called the **unexplained variation,** since it is not explained by variation in age but by variations in all other factors.

We measure the explained variation by computing the sum of the squared deviations as the difference between the estimated height of each tree and the mean height in the sample, that is, $\sum(Y' - \bar{Y})^2$. The results of the computations are shown in the following table. Explained variation is shown in Fig. 11.5.

Y'	$\bar{Y}$	$(Y' - \bar{Y})$	$(Y' - \bar{Y})^2$
9.0	9	0	.00
4.8	9	-4.2	17.64
6.9	9	-2.1	4.41
13.2	9	$+4.2$	17.64
11.1	9	$+2.1$	4.41
			$\sum(Y' - \bar{Y})^2 = 44.10$

To measure the unexplained variation, we compute the sum of the squared deviations, as differences between the actual and estimated heights of each tree, that is, $\sum(Y - Y')^2$, shown in the following table. Unexplained variation is shown in Fig. 11.6.

Figure 11.5

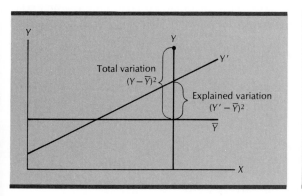

Figure 11.6

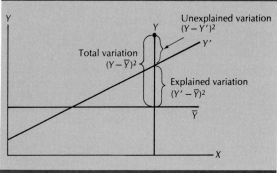

Y	Y′	(Y − Y′)	(Y − Y′)²
9	9.0	.0	.00
5	4.8	+.2	.04
7	6.9	+.1	.01
14	13.2	+.8	.64
10	11.1	−1.1	1.21
			$\sum(Y - Y')^2 = 1.90$

We can now summarize the computations required to obtain the total variation, explained variation, and unexplained variation.

Y	$\bar{Y}$	Y′	(Y − $\bar{Y}$)	(Y − $\bar{Y}$)²	(Y′ − $\bar{Y}$)	(Y′ − $\bar{Y}$)²	(Y − Y′)	(Y − Y′)²
9	9	9.0	0	0	0	.00	.0	.00
5	9	4.8	−4	16	−4.2	17.64	+.2	.04
7	9	6.9	−2	4	−2.1	4.41	+.1	.01
14	9	13.2	+5	25	+4.2	17.64	+.8	.64
10	9	11.1	+1	1	+2.1	4.41	−1.1	1.21
			$\sum(Y - \bar{Y})^2 = 46$ Total variation		$\sum(Y' - \bar{Y})^2 = 44.10$ Explained variation		$\sum(Y - Y')^2 = 1.90$ Unexplained variation	

You may already have observed that

Total variation = Explained variation + Unexplained variation.
46   =   44.10   +   1.90.

This is by no means a coincidence. The total variation in height has indeed been subdivided into two components: the explained variation, which is associated with age, and the unexplained variation, which is associated with other factors.

The ratio of explained variation to total variation is called the **coefficient of determination.** Denoted by r^2, the coefficient of determination is

$$r^2 = \frac{\text{Explained variation}}{\text{Total variation}}$$

$$= \frac{\sum(Y' - \bar{Y})^2}{\sum(Y - \bar{Y})^2}$$

$$= \frac{44.10}{46} = .96.$$

It expresses the proportion of the variation in Y that is associated with, or related to, the variation in X. In our example, we may therefore conclude that

96% of the variation in the heights of the five papaya trees is related to, or explained by, the variation in the ages of the trees.

Now let us consider the possible numerical values that can be assumed by the coefficient of determination. If there is an exact relationship between X and Y, then, as we have already learned, the actual and estimated values of Y will be identical for every observation in the sample. In this case, the unexplained variation, $\sum(Y - Y')^2 = 0$, and the explained variation will be equal to the total variation. Consequently, $r^2 = 1$, which is the highest value the coefficient of determination can have. It indicates a perfect correlation between the two variables, since all the variation in Y is associated with, or explained by, the variation in X. On the other hand, if X and Y are unrelated, the explained variation is zero, and hence $r^2 = 0$. The stronger the relationship between X and Y, the higher the value of r^2.

The coefficient of correlation r is the square root of the coefficient of determination r^2. Its numerical value, therefore, is also between 0 and 1. But whereas r^2 is always positive, r can be either positive or negative. We find that r is positive when X and Y are directly related, and r is negative when X and Y are inversely related. Stated differently, r always assumes the same sign as the regression coefficient b in the regression equation $Y' = a + bX$. (See Fig. 11.7.)

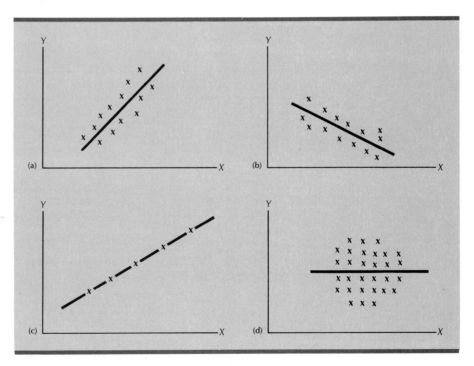

Figure 11.7 (a) Direct relationship (r is positive); (b) inverse relationship (r is negative); (c) perfect correlation ($r = 1$); (d) no apparent relationship ($r = 0$)

For our problem of the papaya trees, $r^2 = .96$. Hence $r = \sqrt{.96}$, or .98. Furthermore, r is positive because X and Y are directly related, as indicated by the positive sign of the regression coefficient b in the regression equation $Y' = 2.7 + 2.1X$.

Before we conclude this discussion, a few words of caution are in order. Both r^2 and r measure the strength of a linear relationship between two variables. Both measures assume the value 1 when the correlation is perfect and the value 0 when there is absolutely no correlation. Except in these two extreme cases, however, r^2 is the more meaningful of the two measures, because it is r^2 and not r that measures the percentage of the variation in Y explained by the variations in X.

CORRELATION AND REGRESSION: SHORTCUT METHOD

We can calculate the three measures—the regression coefficients, the standard error of the estimate, and the correlation coefficient—using an alternative method, called the *shortcut method.* It consists of the following seven steps:

Step 1. Construct five columns to record the actual values of X and Y, their squares, and their cross-products. (Use uppercase letters for X and Y.) Then total each column.

Y	X	Y^2	X^2	XY
9	3	81	9	27
5	1	25	1	5
7	2	49	4	14
14	5	196	25	70
10	4	100	16	40
$\sum Y = 45$	$\sum X = 15$	$\sum Y^2 = 451$	$\sum X^2 = 55$	$\sum XY = 156$

Step 2. Compute the mean of Y and the mean of X. The mean of the dependent variable Y is computed as

$$\bar{Y} = \frac{\sum Y}{n} = \frac{45}{5} = 9 \text{ feet}$$

The mean of the independent variable X is computed as

$$\bar{X} = \frac{\sum X}{n} = \frac{15}{5} = 3 \text{ years}$$

Step 3. Compute $\sum y^2$, $\sum x^2$, and $\sum xy$. (Note that we use lowercase letters for these terms, which are completely different from the terms denoted by uppercase letters that we computed previously.) Use the following three equations:*

$$\sum y^2 = \sum Y^2 - n(\bar{Y})^2$$
$$= 451 - 5(9)^2 = 46$$

$$\sum x^2 = \sum X^2 - n(\bar{X})^2$$
$$= 55 - 5(3)^2 = 10$$

$$\sum xy = \sum XY - n\bar{X}\bar{Y}$$
$$= 156 - 5(9)(3) = 21$$

Step 4. Compute the regression coefficient b:

$$b = \frac{\sum xy}{\sum x^2} = \frac{21}{10} = 2.1.$$

Step 5. Compute the regression coefficient a.

$$a = \bar{Y} - b\bar{X}$$
$$= 9 - (2.1)(3)$$
$$= 9 - 6.3$$
$$= 2.7.$$

Hence the regression equation is

$$Y' = 2.7 + 2.1X.$$

Step 6. Compute the standard error of the estimate:

$$S_{YX} = \sqrt{\frac{\sum y^2 - b \sum xy}{n - 2}}$$

$$= \sqrt{\frac{46 - (2.1)(21)}{5 - 2}}$$

$$= \sqrt{\frac{46 - 44.1}{3}}$$

$$= \sqrt{\frac{1.90}{3}} = .80.$$

---

*The terms $\sum x^2$, $\sum y^2$, and $\sum xy$ are obtained as follows:
$$\sum x^2 = \sum(X - \bar{X})^2, \sum y^2 = \sum(Y - \bar{Y})^2, \sum xy = \sum(X - \bar{X})(Y - \bar{Y}).$$
However, we can readily compute them, using the three equations given in step 3.

Step 7.   Compute the correlation coefficient.

$$r = \frac{\sum xy}{\sqrt{\sum x^2 \sum y^2}}$$

$$= \frac{21}{\sqrt{(10)(46)}} = \frac{21}{\sqrt{460}} = \frac{21}{21.16} = .98.$$

THE SIGNIFICANCE OF CORRELATION

Since the correlation coefficient *r* is computed from sample data, an interesting question always arises: How is the sample correlation coefficient related to the true population correlation coefficient? If the sample correlation coefficient is .60, for example, what can we say about the magnitude of the population correlation coefficient?

The relationship between the sample correlation coefficient and the population correlation coefficient is very complex, and its examination in depth is beyond the scope of this book. However, we will discuss some of its aspects in a somewhat simplified form.

Let us assume that the population correlation coefficient is equal to zero; that is, there is no correlation between two variables in the population. If a random sample of *n* paired observations is drawn from this population, will the sample correlation coefficient be equal to zero? Of course not. Stated differently, the mere fact that the absolute value of a sample correlation coefficient is greater than zero is by no means conclusive evidence that a correlation exists in the population.

When the absolute value of the sample correlation coefficient is greater than zero, we have two hypotheses to explore. First is the null hypothesis that there is no correlation between the two variables in the population. In this case the sample correlation coefficient should be close to zero. If in fact the absolute value of the sample correlation coefficient is small, the sample correlation coefficient is deemed not significant and we cannot reject the null hypothesis. The second hypothesis to be explored is that a correlation does exist in the population. If this is the case, the sample correlation coefficient should not be close to zero. If in fact the absolute value of the sample correlation coefficient is large, the sample correlation coefficient is deemed significant and we reject the null hypothesis. Table F is used to infer, with specified risk, whether a particular sample correlation coefficient is significant.

The first column in Table F lists numbers of degrees of freedom. In a simple correlation problem, the number of degrees of freedom is equal to the sample size minus 2, that is $(n - 2)$. Thus in a correlation problem with 19 paired observations, the number of degrees of freedom is 17.

The entries in the column labeled $r^*_{.05}$ are critical levels of *r*, each associated with a given number of degrees of freedom. Each of these critical levels can be interpreted as follows: If the null hypothesis is true, that is, there is no correlation in the population, then the probability is only .05 that a sample correlation coefficient will be as large as or larger than this critical level. Therefore, when the sample correlation coefficient exceeds this critical level, the null hypothesis is rejected and the sample correlation coefficient is regarded to be significant at the .05 level. Thus, in a simple correlation problem of 19 paired observations (df $=$ 17), the sample correlation coefficient is regarded as significant at the .05 level whenever its absolute value exceeds .456. Likewise, in a correlation problem of 30 paired observations (df $=$ 28), the correlation coefficient is regarded as significant at the .05 level whenever its absolute value exceeds the critical level of .361.

The entries in the last column, labeled $r_{.01}^*$, can be interpreted in a similar fashion. These entries, however, are the critical 1% levels of r. Consequently, a sample correlation coefficient is regarded as significant at the .01 level only when its absolute value exceeds the corresponding critical level in this column.

Before concluding this discussion, let us reexamine the degree of the relationship between the height and the age of the papaya trees. Based on a sample of five trees, the correlation coefficient was .98. With three degrees of freedom this correlation coefficient is significant at the .01 level (r is greater than the critical 1% level of .959).

We conclude the chapter with two comprehensive examples.

Example General Food employs 10,000 sales representatives whose duty is to call on retail grocery outlets for the purpose of merchandising the company's food products. Sales vice-president Mary Saunders wishes to determine the relationship between the number of monthly calls a sales representative makes on a given retail outlet and the amount of the company's food products purchased by the outlet. Ms. Saunders selected 5 retail stores at random and obtained information in the following table.

Retail Grocery Outlet	Number of Sales Calls During One Month	Monthly Sales to Outlet (thousands of dollars)
A	7	73
B	6	68
C	5	60
D	3	45
E	4	54

a) Determine the linear regression equation using the shortcut method of least squares with the number of sales calls as the independent variable.

b) What is the meaning of the regression coefficient *b* in this case?

c) Harold Hill, a sales representative, makes 6 sales calls on Cohen's Delicatessen and Food Market during the month. Estimate monthly sales to Cohen's.

d) Determine the standard error of the estimate.

e) Is there a significant correlation between sales volume and the number of sales calls? Use the .05 level of significance.

Solution:

a) As a first step in determining the regression equation $Y' = a + bX$, we will construct a table showing the values of Y and X together with their squares Y^2 and X^2 and the product XY. These preliminary calculations are carried out in the following table.

Y	X	Y^2	X^2	XY
73	7	5329	49	511
68	6	4624	36	408
60	5	3600	25	300
45	3	2025	9	135
54	4	2916	16	216
$\sum Y = 300$	$\sum X = 25$	$\sum Y^2 = 18{,}494$	$\sum X^2 = 135$	$\sum XY = 1570$

Next we compute $\overline{Y}$ and $\overline{X}$:

$$\overline{Y} = \frac{300}{5} = 60, \qquad \overline{X} = \frac{25}{5} = 5.$$

Using the shortcut method of least squares we compute $\sum y^2$, $\sum x^2$, and $\sum xy$ as follows:

$$\sum y^2 = \sum Y^2 - n(\overline{Y})^2$$
$$= 18{,}494 - 5(60)^2 = 494;$$

$$\sum x^2 = \sum X^2 - n(\overline{X})^2$$
$$= 135 - 5(5)^2 = 10;$$

$$\sum xy = \sum XY - n\overline{X}\,\overline{Y}$$
$$= 1570 - 5(5)(60)$$
$$= 70.$$

We can now proceed to determine b:

$$b = \frac{\sum xy}{\sum x^2} = \frac{70}{10} = 7.$$

Then we determine the value of a:

$$a = \overline{Y} - b\overline{X}$$
$$= 60 - 7(5) = 25.$$

And the estimated regression equation becomes

$$Y' = 25 + 7X.$$

b) The regression coefficient, $b = 7$, indicated that each additional sales call would increase monthly sales by $7000.

c) The estimated sales to Cohen's Deli is found by substituting $X = 6$ in the regression equation.

$$Y' = 25 + 7X$$
$$= 25 + 7(6) = 67.$$

Since sales are measured in thousands of dollars, the estimated sales to Cohen's Deli are $67,000.

d) The standard error of the estimate is

$$S_{YX} = \sqrt{\frac{\sum y^2 - b \sum xy}{n - 2}}$$

$$= \sqrt{\frac{494 - (7)(70)}{5 - 2}} = \sqrt{\frac{494 - 490}{3}}$$

$$= \sqrt{\frac{4}{3}} = 1.155, \text{ or } \$1155.$$

e) The correlation coefficient r is

$$r = \frac{\sum xy}{\sqrt{\sum x^2 \sum y^2}} = \frac{70}{\sqrt{10 \cdot 494}} = .996.$$

Using the .05 level of significance and 3 degrees of freedom $(5 - 2)$, Table F shows a critical value of $r_{.05} = .878$. Since $r = .996$ is greater than $r_{.05} = .878$, we conclude that there is a significant correlation between sales volume and the number of sales calls.

Example A large real estate company administers an aptitude test for its newly hired salespeople. The company selected a random sample of 30 sales personnel files to study the relationship between sales performance and aptitude test score. The study shows the following results:

$$Y' = -200 + 10X,$$

$$S_{YX} = 50 \text{ (thousands of dollars)},$$

$$r = .4,$$

where

$X =$ Aptitude test score (range 50–95),
$Y =$ sales representative's annual first-year sales (in thousands of dollars).

a) Gladys Mahoney's test score is 80 and her first-year annual sales are $850,000. How would you rate Ms. Mahoney's sales performance compared with others who score 80 on the aptitude test?

b) Would you object to the result of the regression equation because the value of a is negative ($a = -200$)?

c) Would you conclude that there is significant correlation between sales performance and aptitude test score? Use the .05 level of significance.

Solution:

a) The expected sales for Gladys Mahoney, who scores 80 on the aptitude test, are found by substituting 80 for X in the regression equation as follows:

$$Y' = -200 + 10X$$
$$= -200 + 10(80)$$
$$= 600 \text{ (thousand dollars)}.$$

Since Ms. Mahoney's sales are $850,000 and her expected sales are only $600,000, her sales performance is $250,000 above what is expected of her. Measured in terms of standard error of the estimate ($S_{YX} = 50,000$), this excess of $250,000 represents 5 standard errors:

$$250,000 \div 50,000 = 5 \text{ units of } S_{YX}.$$

Thus, Ms. Mahoney's sales performance is excellent. Her actual sales are 5 standard errors above her expected sales of $600,000. She is a superior salesperson indeed.

b) One should not object to the fact that the intercept of the regression equation is negative in this case ($a = -200$). For the relevant values of $X(50 < X < 95)$, the estimated value of Y is positive. Hence it does not matter here whether the coefficient a is positive or negative as long as the predicted value of Y is positive for the relevant range of X.

c) According to Table F, with 28 degrees of freedom (30 − 2), the critical value of $r^*_{.05}$ = .361. Since the actual value of r is .4, which is greater than the critical value, we can conclude that there is a significant correlation between sales performances and aptitude test scores at the .05 level.

EXERCISES

11.1 A medical experiment was conducted to determine the effect of the drug ephedrine on the heart rate. A patient was given various daily dosages of the drug for six days. The data below summarize the results of the experiment.

Total Daily Dosage of Ephedrine (grains, X)	Number of Heart-beats per Minute (Y)
3	70
2	60
1	50
3	80
5	100
4	90

a) Plot a scatter diagram for the data and draw the regression line (freehand). Use the regression line to estimate the patient's heart rate for a total daily dosage of 3.5 grains of ephedrine.

b) Determine the estimated regression equation by means of the two normal equations. Use the regression equation to estimate the patient's heart rate for a total daily dosage of 3.5 grains of ephedrine.

11.2 Based on data in Exercise 11.1, the estimated regression equation is

$$Y' = 36 + 13X.$$

a) What is the average increase in the number of heartbeats associated with an *additional* dosage of 1 grain of ephedrine?

b) Estimate the heart rate of the patient when the total daily dosage is 50 grains.

c) A physician asserts that a total daily dosage of 50 grains of ephedrine reduces the heart rate to zero. In the light of this statement, discuss the validity of the estimate made in part b of this question.

11.3 Assume the data and the results of Exercise 11.1, and do not use the shortcut method.

a) Compute the total variation, explained variation, and unexplained variation. How are the three variations related?

b) Compute the standard error of the estimate.

c) Compute the coefficient of determination and correlation coefficient. Which one of the two coefficients is a more meaningful measure of the degree of relationship, and why?

11.4 A random sample of 5 families shows the following information concerning annual family income and annual expenditure on durable goods (refrigerators, washing machines, stereos, and so on):

Family	Annual Income (thousands of dollars)	Expenditures on Durable Goods (hundreds of dollars)
Addison	5	1
Baum	8	2
Cleary	7	1
Dunn	10	2
Evans	15	4

a) Determine the estimated regression equation $Y' = a + bX$.

b) Estimate the annual expenditure on durable goods of a family earning $12,000 per year.

11.5 An economist selected a random sample of five firms from a very large industry to study the relationship between total cost and volume of production. The following information was obtained:

Firm	Number of Units Produced	Total Cost (thousands of dollars)
A	2	9
B	4	12
C	6	15
D	5	14
E	3	10

a) Determine the estimated linear regression equation

$$Y' = a + bX,$$

where

Y = total cost of production, in thousands of dollars,
X = number of units produced.

b) What is the estimated total cost of producing 10 units?

c) Determine the fixed and variable costs.

11.6 A random sample of 82 supermarkets was selected to measure the relationship between annual sales (Y) and annual advertising expenditure (X). The sample revealed the following information:

$$\text{Explained variation} = \sum (Y' - \bar{Y})^2 = \$49 \text{ (million)},$$
$$\text{Unexplained variation} = \sum (Y - Y')^2 = \$51 \text{ (million)}.$$

a) Compute the correlation coefficient.

b) Test the significance of r using the .01 level of significance.

11.7 A random sample of 37 male students from the university is selected to study the relationship between the weight and the height of male college students. The heights of the students selected in the sample range from 66 to 72 inches. The results of the regression and correlation in the study are

$$Y' = -110 + 3.8X,$$
$$r = .51, \ S_{YX} = 4.2,$$

where Y = weight in pounds, X = height in inches.

a) What is the meaning of the regression coefficient b in terms of the data of this problem?

b) Mr. Smith's height is 70 inches, his weight is 140 pounds. Is Mr. Smith's weight normal? Explain.

c) How do you justify that the value of regression coefficient a is negative (that is, $a = -110$)?

d) Test the significance of the correlation coefficient using the .01 level of significance.

11.8 Data for United States disposable personal income and personal consumption expenditures from 1950 through 1977 are given below.

Year	Personal Consumption Expenditures (billions of dollars, Y)	Disposable Income (billions of dollars, X)
1950	191	207
1951	206	227
1952	217	238
1953	230	253
1954	237	257
1955	254	275
1956	267	293
1957	281	309
1958	290	319
1959	311	337
1960	325	350
1961	335	364

(Continued)

Year	Personal Consumption Expenditures (billions of dollars, Y)	Disposable Income (billions of dollars, X)
1962	355	385
1963	375	405
1964	401	438
1965	433	473
1966	466	512
1967	492	546
1968	536	591
1969	580	634
1970	618	692
1971	667	746
1972	729	803
1973	805	903
1974	877	979
1975	980	1084
1976	1094	1186
1977	1217	1322

a) Determine the linear regression equation, with personal consumption expenditures as the dependent variable. Use the shortcut method.

b) If the U.S. disposable personal income is estimated as $1550 billion in 1980, what is the amount of personal consumption expenditures in 1980?

c) Determine the degree of the relationship in part b and test its significance.

11.9 A random sample of five discount stores is selected to study the relationship between a store's sales volume and its floor space. The sample shows the following information.

Store	Annual Sales (millions of dollars)	Floor Space (thousands of square feet)
A	7	18
B	8	20
C	9	23
D	10	24
E	6	15

a) Use the least-squares method to determine the linear regression equation, with floor space as the independent variable.

b) Estimate the annual sales for a store with floor space of 22,000 square feet.

c) Store X intends to add 1000 square feet to its existing floor space. What is the expected increase in the store's annual sales?

11.10 Edsel E. Lemon, president of a national used-car dealership, appointed Harvard M.B.A. graduate Frances Fink as vice-president for strategic planning and development. The company's sales structure is organized on a territorial basis: each dealer is given an exclusive territory, and several territories are supervised by a district sales manager. To evaluate a district sales manager's performance, Ms. Fink conducted a linear regression and correlation analysis based on data collected from 32 randomly selected sales districts. The analysis shows the following results:

$$Y' = 10 + 20X,$$
$$n = 32, r = .45, S_{YX} = 120 \text{ cars},$$

where Y = average monthly number of cars sold in a sales district, X = number of salespersons employed in a sales district (range 50–80 salespersons).

a) What is the average increase in monthly sales associated with 1 additional salesperson?

b) Would you conclude that there is a significant relationship between sales volume and the number of salespersons? Use the .01 level of significance.

c) District sales manager Oscar Grouch reports average monthly sales of 730 cars. His district employs 50 salespersons. Evaluate Oscar's performance.

11.11 The following information describes the number of business failures and their current liabilities for the period 1970–1980.

Year	Number of Failures	Current Liabilities (millions of dollars)
1970	10,748	1888
1971	10,326	1917
1972	9566	2000
1973	9345	2299
1974	9915	3053
1975	11,432	4380
1976	9628	3012
1977	7919	3095
1978	6619	2656
1979	7564	2667
1980	1174	4635

Using the .05 level of significance, can we conclude that there is correlation between the number of business failures and their current liabilities?

11.12 The following data show household incomes and prices for homes that were conventionally financed in several major cities in 1983. All figures are averages.

City	Household Income (thousands of dollars)	Price of Home (thousands of dollars)
Atlanta	34.2	88.7
Boston	31.0	74.3
Chicago	33.8	85.8
Cleveland	32.1	77.4
Denver	34.4	89.2
Detroit	34.1	86.3
Miami	30.1	71.4
Minneapolis	35.3	90.2
San Francisco	40.5	128.5
Washington, D.C.	40.3	127.8

Using the .01 level of significance, can we conclude that there is correlation between family income and the purchase price of a home?

11.13 To study the relationship between bond and stock prices, the following data were collected for the period 1973–1980.

Year	Corporate Bonds, AAA (dollars per $100 bond)	Standard and Poor's Common Index (500 stocks)
1973	120.4	63.7
1974	92.9	58.8
1975	96.6	56.2
1976	114.4	58.0
1977	108.4	59.6
1978	106.3	55.8
1979	114.8	51.1
1980	134.5	41.4

a) Using the .05 level of significance, can we conclude that there is correlation between bond prices and common stock prices?

b) Explain why the correlation coefficient is negative.

KEY TERMS

linear regression   The process of finding a straight line to predict the value of a dependent variable Y on the basis of the known value of an independent variable X.

least-squares method   A mathematical procedure used to determine the numerical values of a and b of the regression equation: $Y' = a + bX$.

normal equations   Two linear equations that can be solved to find the coefficients of the least-squares regression line.

standard error of the estimate (S_{YX})   A measure of the average distance of the actual values Y from the estimated values Y'.

correlation coefficient (r)   A measure of the strength of the linear relationship between two variables.

total variation   The variation of the actual values Y about the mean $\overline{Y}$, or $\sum (Y - \overline{Y})^2$.

explained variation   The variation of the predicted values Y' about the mean $\overline{Y}$, or $\sum (Y' - \overline{Y})^2$. This variation is explained by changes in the independent variable X.

unexplained variation   The variation of the actual values Y about the predicted values Y', or $\sum (Y - Y')^2$. This variation cannot be explained by changes in the independent variable X.

coefficient of determination (r^2)   The square of the correlation coefficient r. The proportion of the total variation in Y that is explained by changes in the independent variable X.

SUMMARY OF FORMULAS

normal equations

$$\sum Y = na + b \sum X$$
$$\sum XY = a \sum X + b \sum X^2$$

standard error of the estimate

$$S_{YX} = \sqrt{\frac{\sum (Y - Y')^2}{n - 2}} = \sqrt{\frac{\sum y^2 - b \sum xy}{n - 2}}$$

correlation coefficient

$$r = \frac{\sum xy}{\sqrt{\sum x^2 \sum y^2}}$$

coefficient of determination

$$r^2 = \frac{\sum (Y' - \overline{Y})^2}{\sum (Y - \overline{Y})^2}$$

regression coefficients

$$b = \frac{\sum xy}{\sum x^2} = \frac{\sum XY - n\overline{X}\overline{Y}}{\sum X^2 - n(\overline{X})^2}$$

$$a = \overline{Y} - b\overline{X}$$

INFERENCES IN REGRESSION

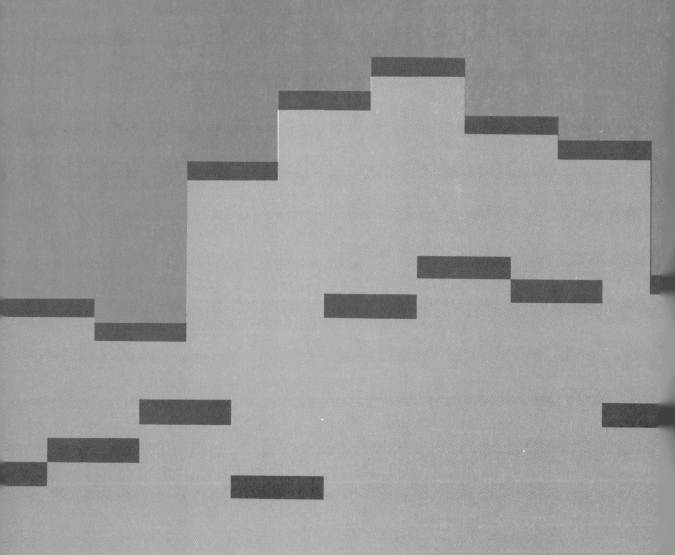

12

The subject of regression and correlation was introduced in the previous chapter. Specifically, we have learned how to determine the linear regression equation $Y' = a + bX$ from sample data. This equation is used to estimate the average value of Y for any given value of X. In addition, we have learned how to compute the standard error of the estimate S_{yx} and the correlation coefficient r. In this chapter, we will extend our treatment of regression. First we will discuss the reliability of the regression coefficient b, then we will investigate the reliability of estimating the average value of Y for any given value of X.

With a sample of n paired observations on the variables X and Y, we have used the least-squares method to obtain the coefficients a and b in the linear regression equation $Y' = a + bX$. Since the values of these regression coefficients are computed from sample data, we expect these values to vary from sample to sample. In other words, the values of regression coefficients a and b depend on the sample chosen; and an alternative sample may result in different values for these coefficients.

Throughout this text, an attempt has been made to distinguish between the population and the sample. This distinction must be brought into focus once more.

To begin, let us assume that in the *population,* the average relationship between Y and X is of the form

$$Y = A + BX.$$

This relationship is a population relationship, and both A and B are population parameters. The **population linear relationship** $Y = A + BX$ is estimated from a sample of n paired observations by means of the least-squares method. The **estimated linear relationship** is

$$Y' = a + bX,$$

where the regression coefficients a and b are sample estimates of the parameters A and B, respectively. In fact, a is called a point estimate of A and b is the point estimate of B.

In the linear relationship $Y = A + BX$, the regression coefficient B is of prime importance. The coefficient B describes the effect of a change in variable X on the values to be taken by the variable Y. Specifically, the coefficient B measures the average change in the value of Y caused by 1 unit change in the value of X. For example, in the relationship $Y = 3 + 7X$, the value of Y increases by 7 units as the value of X is increased by 1 additional unit. For this reason, the next part of our discussion will be devoted to the problem of estimating the value of B and to tests of hypotheses concerning the value of B.

ESTIMATING THE REGRESSION COEFFICIENT *B*

Once again, the population relationship $Y = A + BX$ is estimated from a sample of n paired observations on the variables X and Y. Using the least-squares method, the estimated relationship is $Y' = a + bX$. The value of b varies from sample to sample; and to establish a confidence interval estimate of B, we must take this variability into account.

As an initial step in establishing a confidence interval estimate of B, we must first define the statistic t as

$$t = \frac{b - B}{\hat{\sigma}_b}, \qquad \qquad \text{(A)}$$

where $\hat{\sigma}_b$ is an estimate of the standard error of b, a measure of the variations in the value of b from sample to sample; and the statistic t has a t-distribution with $n - 2$ degrees of freedom. For illustrative purposes, let $n = 7$, and consider the problem of finding a 95% confidence interval estimate of B. From Table E at the end of the book, with df $= 7 - 2 = 5$, we obtain $t_{.025} = 2.571$. Since

$$t = \frac{b - B}{\hat{\sigma}_b}$$

has a t-distribution with 5 degrees of freedom, the probability is .95 that t will satisfy the inequalities

$$-2.571 < t < 2.571.$$

From Eq. (A), this is equivalent to

$$-2.571 < \frac{b - B}{\hat{\sigma}_b} < 2.571.$$

Solving these inequalities for B, we arrive at

$$b - 2.571\hat{\sigma}_b < B < b + 2.571\hat{\sigma}_b.$$

Thus, $b \pm 2.571\hat{\sigma}_b$ is a 95% confidence interval estimate of B. In general, the confidence interval estimate of B is

$$b \pm t\hat{\sigma}_b.$$

As a final step, the estimated standard error, $\hat{\sigma}_b$, is given by

$$\hat{\sigma}_b = \frac{S_{YX}}{\sqrt{\sum x^2}},$$

where $S_{YX} = $ standard error of the estimate and $\sum x^2 = $ sum of squared derivations $\sum (X - \bar{X})^2$ (a term computed by the shortcut method as $\sum X^2 - n(\bar{X})^2$). Hence, the confidence interval estimate of B becomes

$$b \pm t\frac{S_{YX}}{\sqrt{\sum x^2}}.$$

We will illustrate the use of this formula with an example from Chapter 11.

Example The following data represent the heights and ages of a random sample of five papaya trees.

Y (feet)	9	5	7	14	10
X (years)	3	1	2	5	4

a) Find the regression coefficient b and the standard error of the estimate S_{YX}.

b) Establish a 95% confidence interval estimate of B.

Solution:

a) We will use the shortcut method to find the regression coefficient b and the standard error of the estimate S_{YX}. Hence, our first step is to compute the terms $\sum X^2, \sum Y^2, \sum XY, \overline{X}$, and $\overline{Y}$. These computations are carried out as follows:

Y	X	Y^2	X^2	XY
9	3	81	9	27
5	1	25	1	5
7	2	49	4	14
14	5	196	25	70
10	4	100	16	40
$\sum Y = 45$	$\sum X = 15$	$\sum Y^2 = 451$	$\sum X^2 = 55$	$\sum XY = 156$

$$\overline{Y} = \frac{\sum Y}{n} \qquad\qquad \overline{X} = \frac{\sum X}{n}$$

$$= \frac{45}{5} = 9 \text{ feet} \qquad = \frac{15}{5} = 3 \text{ years}$$

Our next step is to compute the terms $\sum x^2, \sum y^2$, and $\sum xy$ (use lowercase letters for these terms) as follows:

$$\sum y^2 = \sum Y^2 - n(\overline{Y})^2$$
$$= 451 - 5(9)^2 = 46,$$
$$\sum x^2 = \sum X^2 - n(\overline{X})^2$$
$$= 55 - 5(3)^2 = 10,$$
$$\sum xy = \sum XY - n\overline{X}\,\overline{Y}$$
$$= 156 - 5(9)(3) = 21.$$

We now compute the regression coefficient b:

$$b = \frac{\sum xy}{\sum x^2} = \frac{21}{10} = 2.1.$$

Next we compute the standard error of the estimate:

$$S_{YX} = \sqrt{\frac{\sum y^2 - b \sum xy}{n - 2}}$$

$$= \sqrt{\frac{46 - (2.1)(21)}{5 - 2}} = \sqrt{\frac{46 - 44.1}{3}}$$

$$= \sqrt{\frac{1.90}{3}} = .80.$$

b) In part a we obtained

$$b = 2.1, \qquad S_{YX} = .8, \qquad \sum x^2 = 10.$$

We will now establish a 95% confidence interval estimate of B as

$$b \pm t_{.025} \frac{S_{YX}}{\sqrt{\sum x^2}}.$$

With $n - 2 = 5 - 2 = 3$ degrees of freedom, the value of $t_{.025}$ from Table E is 3.182. Hence, the 95% confidence interval estimate of B becomes

$$b \pm 3.182 \frac{S_{YX}}{\sqrt{\sum x^2}} = 2.1 \pm 3.182 \frac{.8}{\sqrt{10}}$$

$$= 2.1 \pm .805,$$

or $1.295 \le B \le 2.905$. Hence, we may conclude that we are .95 confident that trees grow between 1.295 and 2.905 feet each year, on average.

Example In the analysis of gross national product, a great deal of attention is paid to the relationship between personal consumption expenditures and disposable personal income (disposable personal income refers to the income that consumers may either spend or save; personal consumption expenditures are the amount consumers spend on goods and services of all sorts). Various economic studies have suggested that these two variables are related in the following fashion:

$$Y = A + BX,$$

where

$$X = \text{Disposable personal income,}$$
$$Y = \text{Personal consumption expenditures.}$$

In this relationship the regression coefficient B is of great importance to the economist. Called the *marginal propensity to consume,* the regression coefficient B represents the amount that individuals spend out of each additional

TABLE 12.1   U.S. DISPOSABLE PERSONAL INCOME AND PERSONAL CONSUMPTION EXPENDITURES, 1950–1974

Year	Personal Consumption Expenditures (billions of dollars, Y)	Disposable Income (billions of dollars, X)
1950	191	207
1951	206	227
1952	217	238
1953	230	253
1954	237	257
1955	254	275
1956	267	293
1957	281	309
1958	290	319
1959	311	337
1960	325	350
1961	335	364
1962	355	385
1963	375	405
1964	401	438
1965	433	473
1966	466	512
1967	492	546
1968	536	591
1969	580	634
1970	618	692
1971	667	746
1972	729	803
1973	805	903
1974	877	979

dollar of income. Economists believe that the magnitude of the marginal propensity to consume, B, is a crucial factor in determining the effectiveness of governmental fiscal policies.*

In this example, we will establish a 95% confidence interval estimate of the regression coefficient B (marginal propensity to consume), based on a random sample of 25 paired observations on X and Y. These observations are obtained from the U.S. national income accounts for the years 1950–1974 and are presented in Table 12.1.

Since a 95% confidence interval for B is

$$b \pm t_{.025} \frac{S_{YX}}{\sqrt{\sum x^2}},$$

we must first calculate the regression coefficient, b, and the standard error of the estimate, S_{YX}. We will use the shortcut method to calculate these two

---

*Changes in government spending and changes in tax rates are the main instruments of governmental fiscal policies.

measures. Hence, the initial step in our solution is to compute the following quantities (notice the use of uppercase letters for X and Y):

$$\sum X = 11{,}536, \qquad \sum X^2 = 6{,}501{,}720, \qquad \overline{X} = \frac{11{,}536}{25} = 461.44,$$

$$\sum Y = 10{,}478, \qquad \sum Y^2 = 5{,}321{,}776, \qquad \overline{Y} = \frac{10{,}478}{25} = 419.12.$$

$$\sum XY = 5{,}881{,}794$$

Our next step is to compute the terms $\sum x^2$, $\sum y^2$, and $\sum xy$ (lowercase letters) as follows:

$$\begin{aligned}
\sum x^2 &= \sum X^2 - n(\overline{X})^2 \\
&= 6{,}501{,}720 - 25(461.44)^2 \\
&= 1{,}178{,}548,
\end{aligned}$$

$$\begin{aligned}
\sum y^2 &= \sum Y^2 - n(\overline{Y})^2 \\
&= 5{,}321{,}776 - 25(419.12)^2 \\
&= 930{,}237,
\end{aligned}$$

$$\begin{aligned}
\sum xy &= \sum XY - n(\overline{X})(\overline{Y}) \\
&= 5{,}881{,}794 - 25(461.44)(419.12) \\
&= 1{,}046{,}826.
\end{aligned}$$

We are ready now to compute the regression coefficient b:

$$b = \frac{\sum xy}{\sum x^2} = \frac{1{,}046{,}826}{1{,}178{,}548} = .888.$$

We also compute the standard error of the estimate S_{YX}:

$$S_{YX} = \sqrt{\frac{\sum y^2 - b \sum xy}{n - 2}}$$

$$= \sqrt{\frac{930{,}237 - (.888)(1{,}046{,}826)}{25 - 2}} = 5.339.$$

So far, we have computed the following measures:

$$b = .888, \qquad S_{YX} = 5.339, \qquad \sum x^2 = 1{,}178{,}548.$$

Using these results, we will now establish a .95 confidence interval estimate of B as

$$b \pm t_{.025} \frac{S_{YX}}{\sqrt{\sum x^2}}.$$

With $n - 2$, or $25 - 2 = 23$ degrees of freedom, the value of $t_{.025}$ from Table E is 2.069. Hence, the .95 confidence interval estimate of B becomes

$$b \pm 2.069 \frac{S_{YX}}{\sqrt{\sum x^2}} = .888 \pm 2.069 \frac{5.339}{\sqrt{1,178,548}}$$

$$= .888 \pm .010,$$

or $.878 < B < .898$.

TEST OF HYPOTHESIS ABOUT THE VALUE OF B

In the population regression relationship

$$Y = A + BX,$$

the regression coefficient, B, indicates the average change in the value of Y for a unit change in X. The preceding section dealt with the problem of estimating the value of the parameter B from a random sample of n paired observations on X and Y. In this section we will learn how to use this sample information to test a hypothesis about the value of B. For example, we may test the hypothesis that $B = 0$, that is, that there is no relationship between X and Y. We will also test the hypothesis that B is equal to some specific value, say B_0.

In general, to test a null hypothesis about the value of the population regression coefficient B, we must select a random sample from such a population. Depending on the finding in the sample, we will either reject the null hypothesis or reserve judgment. We reject the null hypothesis if the sample findings are inconsistent with it. On the other hand, we reserve judgment if the sample findings do not contradict the null hypothesis.

The exact procedure to test the validity of the null hypothesis $H_0 : B = B_0$ is to compute the measure

$$t = \frac{b - B_0}{S_{YX}/\sqrt{\sum x^2}},$$

where

$t = $ a t-distribution with $n - 2$ degrees of freedom,

$B_0 = $ the value of the regression coefficient B specified by the null hypothesis,

$b = $ the sample regression coefficient,

$S_{YX} = $ the standard error of the estimate,

$\sum x^2 = $ the term $\sum (X - \overline{X})^2$, which can be computed by the shortcut method as $\sum X^2 - n(\overline{X})^2$.

The above value of t (observed value) is then compared with a critical t-value obtained from Table E. The critical t-value is determined by the level of significance (.01 or .05), by the degrees of freedom $(n - 2)$, and by the nature of the alternative hypothesis (one-sided vs. two-sided test). We reject the null hypothesis when the observed absolute value of t exceeds the critical t-value; otherwise we reserve judgment. We will clarify this procedure with two examples.

Example The following information is related to the height in feet, Y, and the age in years, X, of a random sample of five papaya trees:

$$Y' = 2.7 + 2.1\,X \quad \text{(sample regression equation)},$$

$$S_{YX} = .8 \text{ foot}, \qquad \sum x^2 = 10.$$

Use this information to test the null hypothesis $H_0 : B = 0$ against the alternative hypothesis $H_1 : B \neq 0$. Use a level of significance of .01.

Solution:

$$H_0 : \quad B = 0,$$

$$H_1 : \quad B \neq 0,$$

Level of significance: $\quad \alpha = .01$.

To test the null hypothesis that $B = 0$, we compute the observed value of t as

$$t = \frac{b - B}{S_{YX}/\sqrt{\sum x^2}}$$

$$= \frac{2.1 - 0}{.8 \div \sqrt{10}} = 8.30.$$

Since the alternative hypothesis is two-sided and the level of significance is .01, the critical value of t is found under the column labeled $t_{.005}$ in Table E. With $n - 2 = 5 - 2 = 3$ degrees of freedom, this critical value of $t_{.005}$ is 5.841. Since the observed value of t is 8.30, which is greater than the critical value, 5.841, the null hypothesis is rejected. In other words, we conclude that $B \neq 0$ and that the height of a papaya tree is related to its age.

Example Use the information provided in the preceding example to test the null hypothesis that a papaya tree grows, on average, 2 feet per year against the alternative hypothesis that the average growth is greater than 2 feet per year. Use a level of significance of .05.

Solution:

$$H_0: \quad B = 2 \text{ feet per year,}$$

$$H_1: \quad B > 2 \text{ feet per year,}$$

Level of significance: $\quad \alpha = .05.$

To test the null hypothesis that $B = 2$, we compute the observed value of t as

$$t = \frac{b - B_0}{S_{YX}/\sqrt{\sum x^2}}$$

$$= \frac{2.1 - 2.0}{.8/\sqrt{10}} = .40.$$

From Table E, we find that the critical value of t is 2.353 ($t_{.050}$ with 3 degrees of freedom in a one-sided test). Since the observed value of t is .40, which is less than the critical value, 2.353, we must reserve judgment. In other words, the information provided by the sample does not give us enough evidence to reject the null hypothesis that the average growth in height is 2 feet per year.

ESTIMATING THE MEAN VALUE OF Y

The regression equation $Y' = a + bX$ enables us to estimate the *average* value of Y for any given value of X. For example, the regression equation

$$Y' = 2.7 + 2.1X,$$

where

$$X = \text{the age of a papaya tree in years,}$$

$$Y = \text{the height of a tree in feet,}$$

enables us to estimate the average height of a papaya tree for any given age. According to this equation, for instance, the average height of a 7-year-old tree is 17.4 feet.

Once more, the regression equation enables us to estimate the *average* value of Y for a given value of X. This estimate, furthermore, is a **point estimate.** A confidence interval estimate of the average value of Y for any given value of X, on the other hand, is established as follows:

$$Y' \pm tS_{YX} \sqrt{\frac{1}{n} + \frac{(X_g - \bar{X})^2}{\sum x^2}},$$

where

$$Y' = \text{a point estimate of the average value of } Y,$$

$$t = \text{a } t\text{-distribution with } n - 2 \text{ degrees of freedom.}$$

$$S_{YX} = \text{standard error of the estimate,}$$

$$X_g = \text{the given value of } X \text{ for which}$$
the average value of Y is to be predicted,

$$\sum x^2 = \text{the sum of the squared derivations, } \sum (X - \bar{X})^2.$$

We will illustrate the use of this formula with a familiar example.

Example The following information relates to the height in feet, Y, and the age in years, X, of a random sample of five papaya trees:

$$Y' = 2.7 + 2.1X \quad \text{(regression equation)},$$

$$S_{YX} = .8 \text{ foot}, \qquad \bar{X} = 3 \text{ years}, \qquad \sum x^2 = 10.$$

Use this information to find

a) a point estimate of the average height of a 7-year-old papaya tree;

b) a 95% confidence interval estimate of the average height of a 7-year-old papaya tree;

c) a 95% confidence interval estimate of the average height of a 10-year-old papaya tree.

Solution:

a) A point estimate of the average height of a 7-year-old papaya tree is obtained by substituting $X = 7$ in the regression equation

$$Y' = 2.7 + 2.1X.$$

Hence, this point estimate is

$$Y' = 2.7 + 2.1(7)$$

$$= 17.4 \text{ feet.}$$

b) A 95% confidence interval estimate of the average height of a 7-year-old papaya tree is established according to the formula

$$Y' \pm t_{.025}S_{YX} \sqrt{\frac{1}{n} + \frac{(X_g - \bar{X})^2}{\sum x^2}}.$$

We substitute the following values in this formula:

$Y' = 17.4$ (the point estimate of the average
    height of a 7-year-old tree),

$t_{.025} = 3.182$ (the value of $t_{.025}$ with $5 - 2 = 3$ degrees of freedom),

$S_{YX} = .8$ (standard error of the estimate),

$n = 5$ (sample size),

$X_g = 7$ (the given value of X for which the average
    value of Y is to be predicted),

$\overline{X} = 3$ (mean of X),

$\sum x^2 = 10$ (sum of squared deviations).

The substitutions result in the range

$$Y' \pm t_{.025}\, S_{YX} \sqrt{\frac{1}{n} + \frac{(X_g - \overline{X})^2}{\sum x^2}} = 17.4 \pm (3.182)(.8) \sqrt{\frac{1}{5} + \frac{(7 - 3)^2}{10}}$$

$$= 17.4 \pm 3.4,$$

or between 14.0 feet and 20.8 feet. Hence, a 95% confidence interval of the average height of a 7-year-old tree is between 14.0 feet and 20.8 feet.

c) To establish a 95% confidence interval estimate of the average height of a 10-year-old tree, we must first determine the point estimate, Y', for a tree at that age. The point estimate is obtained by substituting $X = 10$ in the regression equation, as follows:

$$Y' = 2.7 + 2.1X$$

$$= 2.7 + 2.1(10)$$

$$= 23.7 \text{ feet.}$$

A .95 confidence interval estimate of the average height of a 10-year-old papaya tree can be established using the formula

$$Y' \pm t_{.025}\, S_{YX} \sqrt{\frac{1}{n} + \frac{(X_g - \overline{X})^2}{\sum x^2}}.$$

With $Y' = 23.7$ feet and $X_g = 10$ years, and with all other values the same as in part b of this example, our formula would result in the following range:

$$23.7 \pm (3.182)(.8) \sqrt{\frac{1}{5} + \frac{(10 - 3)^2}{10}} = 23.7 \pm 5.7,$$

or between 18.0 feet and 29.4 feet. Hence, a .95 confidence interval estimate of the average height of a 10-year-old papaya tree is between 18.0 feet and 29.4 feet.

EXERCISES

12.1   The following data give the gross national product (GNP) and the values of exports for a random sample of nine Western European countries in a given year.

Country	GNP (billions of dollars)	Exports (billions of dollars)
Belgium	26	16
Ireland	5	2
Finland	13	3
Switzerland	30	7
Norway	15	3
United Kingdom	134	24
Germany	260	46
France	238	26
Spain	46	4

a) Determine the linear regression equations with GNP as the independent variable.

b) Establish a .95 confidence interval estimate of the population regression coefficient.

c) Test the null hypothesis that $B = .10$ against the alternative hypothesis that $B > .10$. Use a level of significance of .01.

12.2   A random sample of ten Western countries shows the following information concerning their per capita gross national product and per capita consumption in a given year.

Country	GNP per Capita (thousands of dollars)	Consumption per Capita (thousands of dollars)
United States	5.2	3.3
Canada	4.3	2.4
Switzerland	4.2	2.5
Norway	3.5	1.9
West Germany	3.8	2.0
Belgium	3.3	2.0
United Kingdom	2.7	1.7
Italy	2.0	1.3
Greece	1.2	.8
France	3.5	2.0

a) Determine the linear regression equation with GNP as the independent variable.

b) Establish a .99 confidence interval estimate of the population regression coefficient.

c) Test the null hypothesis that $B = .60$ against the alternative hypothesis that $B < .60$. Use a level of significance of .05.

12.3   A random sample of 12 clothing shops in Atlanta, Georgia, shows the following information about annual sales and annual expenditures on advertising.

Annual Sales (thousands of dollars)	Advertising Expenditures (thousands of dollars)
170	10
135	7
148	8
205	13
120	6
180	11
155	9
142	8
125	6
110	10
144	8
190	12

a) Use the least-squares method to determine the linear regression equation with advertising expenditures as the independent variable.

b) What is the average increase in annual sales associated with an additional advertising expenditure of $1000?

c) Use a level of significance of .05 to test the hypothesis that $B = 10$ against the alternative hypothesis that $B > 10$.

d) Establish a 90% confidence interval estimate of average annual sales when annual advertising expenditures are $15,000.

12.4   The general manager of a gambling casino in Las Vegas wishes to find an accurate method of forecasting the number of customers visiting the casino each week. The manager noted that the number of customers in any given week seems to be linearly related to the number of conventions being held in Las Vegas at that time. Ten weeks, selected at random, reveal the following information.

Number of Customers (in hundreds)	Number of Conventions
27	3
46	7
27	4
31	4
26	3
48	8
52	9
42	6
41	6
60	10

a) Use the least-squares method to determine the linear relationship with the number of conventions as the independent variable.

b) Interpret the meaning of the regression coefficient b in this problem.

c) Establish a .90 confidence interval estimate of the population regression coefficient.

d) Establish a 99% confidence interval estimate of the average number of customers visiting the gambling casino during a week for which 8 conventions are scheduled.

12.5 A post office district maintains a fleet of small mail delivery trucks. The following data are from a random sample of 15 mail delivery truck records.

Truck	Age (years)	Annual Repair Costs (dollars)
1	5	525
2	1	80
3	4	421
4	4	356
5	6	684
6	3	222
7	4	490
8	2	144
9	4	473
10	3	384
11	5	507
12	2	203
13	3	332
14	2	206
15	2	219

a) Use the least-squares method to determine the linear regression equation with the age of the truck as the independent variable.

b) How do you justify that the value of a is negative?

c) What is the average increase in repair costs as a truck becomes 1 year older?

d) Test the null hypothesis that $B = \$100$ against the alternative hypothesis that $B > \$100$. Use a level of significance of .01.

e) What is the average repair cost of a 4-year-old truck? Establish a 95% confidence interval estimate of this cost.

12.6 Sixteen families are randomly selected in a given community. The sample shows the following information concerning annual family income and monthly housing expenditures.

Family	Annual Income (thousands of dollars)	Housing Expenditures
A	22	306
B	30	332
C	15	350
D	40	740
E	7	143
F	24	320
G	15	451
H	14	250
I	21	314
J	17	265
K	19	503
L	50	350
M	25	400
N	19	362
O	7	245
P	13	400

What is the average monthly housing expenditures of a family earning $15,000 a year? Establish a .99 confidence interval estimate of this average.

KEY TERMS

population linear relationship   The true average relationship in the population, $Y = A + BX$.

estimated linear relationship   The least-squares line computed from the data, $Y' = a + bX$.

regression coefficients   The estimated intercept and slope, a and b.

point estimate of the mean value of Y   The estimate of the population mean of Y for a fixed value of X. The point estimate of the mean is $Y' = a + bX$.

SUMMARY
OF FORMULAS

estimated standard error of b	$\hat{\sigma}_b = \dfrac{S_{YX}}{\sqrt{\sum x^2}}$
confidence interval estimate of B	$b \pm t\hat{\sigma}_b = b \pm t\dfrac{S_{YX}}{\sqrt{\sum x^2}}$
t-value for test of H_0: $B = B_0$	$t = \dfrac{b - B_0}{S_{YX}/\sqrt{\sum x^2}}$
confidence interval for the mean value of Y	$Y' \pm tS_{YX}\sqrt{\dfrac{1}{n} + \dfrac{(X_g - \bar{X})^2}{\sum x^2}}$

MULTIPLE REGRESSION AND CORRELATION

13

In this chapter we extend our analysis of regression and correlation to cover the case of *multiple* regression and correlation. Specifically, we will develop a method to predict the dependent variable Y using several independent variables (X_1, X_2, X_3, . . .). We will also deal with certain measures associated with multiple regression and correlation, and we conclude with an introduction to computer programs that are designed to carry out the lengthy and time-consuming computations.

In the previous two chapters we learned how to use the least-squares method to determine the coefficients of the linear regression equation

$$Y' = a + bX.$$

This equation is used to estimate the value of the dependent variables Y for any given value of the independent variable X. In addition, we also learned how to compute the standard error S_{yx} and the coefficient of determination r^2. The standard error S_{yx} is the standard deviation of the actual value of Y around its estimated value Y'; and the coefficient of determination r^2 is the percentage variation in Y that is related to the variation in X.

When the value of the dependent variable Y is estimated using *one* independent variable, the regression is called *simple regression*. We can estimate the dependent variable Y using two or more independent variables, and the regression is called **multiple regression.** In this chapter, we will confine our discussion first to the case where only two independent variables are used. The two variables are denoted by X_1 and X_2. Furthermore, we assume that the relationship between the dependent variable Y and the two independent variables X_1 and X_2 is linear. Consequently, we will use the least-squares method to determine the regression coefficients of the multiple linear regression equation

$$Y' = a + b_1 X_1 + b_2 X_2.$$

MULTIPLE LINEAR REGRESSION

Let us consider the case of a real estate agency that operates several branch offices throughout Los Angeles. The agency wishes to develop a method to forecast the number of residential units sold per month by any of its branch offices. Management believes that the number of units sold by a branch is influenced by two factors:

1. The number of salespeople working in a branch and
2. The amount of advertising expenditure incurred by a branch in a month.

We will use the method of multiple regression to forecast the number of units sold; the number of salespeople and advertising expenditures are independent variables. We select ten branches at random. Pertinent information concerning the operation of the ten branches is shown in Table 13.1.

With the information in Table 13.1 we will use the least-squares method to determine the coefficients of the linear multiple regression equation

$$Y' = a + b_1 X_1 + b_2 X_2,$$

TABLE 13.1 MULTIPLE REGRESSION DATA

Branch	Number of Units Sold Y	Number of Salespeople X_1	Advertising Expenditures (thousands of dollars) X_2
A	25	5	10
B	20	2	11
C	30	6	12
D	25	4	13
E	25	3	14
F	32	6	15
G	25	4	12
H	21	3	11
I	20	2	10
J	27	5	12

where

$$Y = \text{Number of units sold by a branch in a month,}$$
$$X_1 = \text{Number of salespeople employed by a branch,}$$
$$X_2 = \text{Branch monthly advertising expenditures}$$
$$\text{(thousands of dollars).}$$

As a first step in determining the regression coefficients a_1, b_1, and b_2, we will construct a table showing the values of the variables Y, X_1, and X_2 together with their squares Y^2, X_1^2, X_2^2 and their cross-products YX_1, YX_2, and X_1X_2 (note the use of uppercase letters for all variables). These preliminary computations are displayed in Table 13.2.

TABLE 13.2 PRELIMINARY COMPUTATIONS

	Y	X_1	X_2	Y^2	X_1^2	X_2^2	YX_1	YX_2	X_1X_2
	25	5	10	625	25	100	125	250	50
	20	2	11	400	4	121	40	220	22
	30	6	12	900	36	144	180	360	72
	25	4	13	625	16	169	100	325	52
	25	3	14	625	9	196	75	350	42
	32	6	15	1024	36	225	192	480	90
	25	4	12	625	16	144	100	300	48
	21	3	11	441	9	121	63	231	33
	20	2	10	400	4	100	40	200	20
	27	5	12	729	25	144	135	324	60
TOTAL	250	40	120	6394	180	1464	1050	3040	489

TABLE 13.3   CONVERSION INTO DEVIATIONS FROM MEANS

$y = Y - \overline{Y}$	$x_1 = X_1 - \overline{X}_1$	$x_2 = X_2 - \overline{X}_2$

$$\sum y^2 = \sum Y^2 - n(\overline{Y})^2 = 6394 - 10(25)^2 = 144$$

$$\sum x_1^2 = \sum X_1^2 - n(\overline{X}_1)^2 = 180 - 10(4)^2 = 20$$

$$\sum x_2^2 = \sum X_2^2 - n(\overline{X}_2)^2 = 1464 - 10(12)^2 = 24$$

$$\sum yx_1 = \sum YX_1 - n(\overline{Y})(\overline{X}_1) = 1050 - (10)(25)(4) = 50$$

$$\sum yx_2 = \sum YX_2 - n(\overline{Y})(\overline{X}_2) = 3040 - (10)(25)(12) = 40$$

$$\sum x_1 x_2 = \sum X_1 X_2 - n(\overline{X}_1)(\overline{X}_2) = 489 - (10)(4)(12) = 9$$

The following summarizes the preliminary computations.

$$\sum Y = 250 \qquad \sum Y^2 = 6394 \qquad \sum YX_1 = 1050$$
$$\sum X_1 = 40 \qquad \sum X_1^2 = 180 \qquad \sum YX_2 = 3040$$
$$\sum X_2 = 120 \qquad \sum X_2^2 = 1464 \qquad \sum X_1 X_2 = 489$$
$$\overline{Y} = \frac{250}{10} \qquad \overline{X}_1 = \frac{40}{10} \qquad \overline{X}_2 = \frac{120}{10}$$
$$= 25 \qquad = 4 \qquad = 12$$

The least-squares method is greatly simplified when the original variables Y, X_1, and X_2 are converted into deviations from their mean. Denoting $(Y - \overline{Y})$, $(X_1 - \overline{X}_1)$, and $(X_2 - \overline{X}_2)$ by the lowercase letters y, x_1, and x_2, respectively, we carry out the conversion using the equations in Table 13.3.

We obtain the following data from Table 13.3.

$$\sum yx_1 = 50 \qquad \sum x_1^2 = 20$$
$$\sum yx_2 = 40 \qquad \sum x_2^2 = 24$$
$$x_1 x_2 = 9 \qquad \sum y^2 = 144$$

We are ready now to find the regression coefficients b_1 and b_2 using the two normal equations*

$$\sum yx_1 = b_1 \sum x_1^2 + b_2 \sum x_1 x_2,$$
$$\sum yx_2 = b_1 \sum x_1 x_2 + b_2 \sum x_2^2.$$

*The normal equations in Chapter 11 used the raw values X and Y. The normal equations here use the deviations x and y and are, in a sense, shortcut normal equations.

Substituting the appropriate sums into those two equations, we obtain

$$50 = 20b_1 + 9b_2,$$
$$40 = 9b_1 + 24b_2,$$

and we solve these two equations for b_1 and b_2; $b_1 = 2.105$, $b_2 = 0.877$.

The final step in determining the coefficients of the regression equation

$$Y' = a + b_1X_1 + b_2X_2$$

is to find the value of the constant a using the following formula:

$$a = \overline{Y} - b_1\overline{X}_1 - b_2\overline{X}_2.$$

With $\overline{Y} = 25$, $\overline{X}_1 = 4$, $\overline{X}_2 = 12$ (see Table 13.2), we solve for the value of a as follows:

$$a = \overline{Y} - b_1\overline{X}_1 - b_2\overline{X}_2$$
$$= 25 - 2.105(4) - .877(12)$$
$$= 6.056.$$

Now, with

$$a = 6.056,$$
$$b_1 = 2.105,$$
$$b_2 = .877,$$

the multiple regression equation becomes

$$Y' = 6.056 + 2.105X_1 + .877X_2.$$

The primary purpose of this equation is to predict the value of the dependent variables Y (the number of housing units sold) for given values of the independent variables X_1 and X_2 (number of salespeople and volume of advertising outlay). Let us assume that the manager of a given branch intends to employ 12 salespeople and plans an advertising expenditure of $15,000 for the coming month; the branch's expected sales for that month are predicted as

$$Y' = 6.056 + 2.105X_1 + .877X_2$$
$$= 6.056 + 2.105(12) + .877(15)$$
$$= 44.471 \text{ units.}$$

The regression equation enables us to predict the dependent variable Y. In addition, the regression coefficients b_1 and b_2 show the effect of changes in the independent variables X_1 and X_2 on the dependent variable Y. For example, the coefficient b_1 indicates the change in Y associated with one unit change in X_1 assuming that X_2 is held constant. Similarly, the regression coefficient b_2 shows the change in Y associated with one unit change in X_2 assuming that X_1 remains constant. In multiple regression, the regression coefficients b_1 and b_2 are called **net regression coefficients.** In the regression equation

$$Y' = 6.056 + 2.105X_1 + .877X_2,$$

the net regression coefficient b_1 (2.105) indicates that the addition of one more salesperson would increase sales by 2.105 housing units, assuming no change in advertising expenditures. Similarly, the net regression coefficient b_2 (.877) indicates that sales would increase by .877 housing units as advertising expenditures are increased by $1000 while the number of salespeople is kept the same.

We have developed the equation

$$Y' = 6.056 + 2.105X_1 + .877X_2$$

to predict housing unit sales (Y) using the number of salespersons (X_1) and advertising expenditures (X_2) as independent variables. You are now justified in asking, "How accurate is this prediction?" The accuracy of predicting sales is measured by the standard error of the estimate. As in simple regression analysis, the standard error of the estimate measures the closeness of the predicted value Y' to the actual value of Y. Specifically, the standard error of the estimate measures the disparity between estimated sales (as derived from the regression equation) and actual sales.

As a first step in computing the standard error of the estimate (and some other related measures, for that matter), it is necessary now to subdivide the total variation in Y into its two components: **explained variation** and **unexplained variation.** The procedure we use in subdividing total variation is analogous to that used in the simple regression case.

TOTAL, EXPLAINED, AND UNEXPLAINED VARIATION

The general formulas used in subdividing total variation in multiple regression are exactly the same as in the simple regression case. The formulas are as follows.

$$\text{Explained variation} = \sum (Y' - \overline{Y})^2$$
$$\text{Unexplained variation} = \sum (Y - Y')^2$$
$$\text{Total variation} = \sum (Y - \overline{Y})^2$$

where

$$Y = \text{Actual value of } Y,$$

$$Y' = \text{Estimated value of } Y \text{ (as derived from the regression equation),}$$

$$\overline{Y} = \text{Average or mean value of } Y.$$

The initial task in carrying out the subdivision of the total variation in Y is to compute the estimated values of Y for each of the ten sample observations. Referring to our illustrative problem specifically, we must now compute the estimated sales for each of the ten branch offices using the previously obtained multiple regression equation

$$Y' = 6.056 + 2.105X_1 + .877X_2.$$

These calculations are carried out in Table 13.4. The computations are self-explanatory; for example, the estimated sales of branch A are obtained by substituting the appropriate values of X_1 and X_2 in the regression equation (X_1 is the number of salespersons employed by branch A, and X_2 is its monthly advertising expenditures). With $X_1 = 5$ and $X_2 = 10$, the estimated sales for branch A are obtained as follows.

$$\begin{aligned} Y' &= 6.056 + 2.105X_1 + .877X_2 \\ &= 6.056 + 2.105(5) + .877(10) \\ &= 6.056 + 10.525 + 8.770 \\ &= 25.351 \text{ housing units.} \end{aligned}$$

Predicted sales for the other nine branches are computed in a similar fashion.

Using the estimated values of Y shown in the last column of Table 13.4 and a mean value of $\overline{Y} = 25$, we can calculate the total variation, explained variation, and unexplained variation (see Table 13.5). Once these calculations have been made, we are now ready to calculate the standard error of the estimate, which is a measure of the accuracy of predicting the dependent variable Y (sales, in this case).

TABLE 13.4   ESTIMATING THE VALUES OF Y USING THE MULTIPLE REGRESSION EQUATION $Y' = 6.056 + 2.105X_1 + .877X_2$

Branch	X_1	X_2	a	b_1X_1	b_2X_2	Estimated Value $a + b_1X_1 + b_2X_2 = Y'$
A	5	10	6.056	10.525	8.770	$6.056 + 10.525 + 8.770 = 25.351$
B	2	11	6.056	4.210	9.647	$6.056 + 4.210 + 9.647 = 19.913$
C	6	12	6.056	12.630	10.524	$6.056 + 12.630 + 10.524 = 29.210$
D	4	13	6.056	8.420	11.401	$6.056 + 8.420 + 11.401 = 25.877$
E	3	14	6.056	6.315	12.278	$6.056 + 6.315 + 12.278 = 24.649$
F	6	15	6.056	12.630	13.155	$6.056 + 12.630 + 13.155 = 31.841$
G	4	12	6.056	8.420	10.524	$6.056 + 8.420 + 10.524 = 25.000$
H	3	11	6.056	6.315	9.647	$6.056 + 6.315 + 9.647 = 22.018$
I	2	10	6.056	4.210	8.770	$6.056 + 4.210 + 8.770 = 19.036$
J	5	12	6.056	10.525	10.524	$6.056 + 10.525 + 10.524 + 27.105$

TABLE 13.5 COMPUTATIONS OF TOTAL, EXPLAINED, AND UNEXPLAINED VARIATIONS

Y	$\bar{Y}$	Y'	$(Y - \bar{Y})^2$	$(Y' - \bar{Y})^2$	$(Y - Y')^2$
25	25	25.351	0	.123	.123
20	25	19.913	25	25.878	.008
30	25	29.210	25	17.724	.624
25	25	25.877	0	.769	.769
25	25	24.649	0	.123	.123
32	25	31.841	49	46.799	.025
25	25	25.000	0	0	0
21	25	22.018	16	8.892	1.036
20	25	19.036	25	35.569	.929
27	25	27.105	4	4.431	.011
			$\sum (Y - \bar{Y})^2 = 144$	$\sum (Y' - \bar{Y})^2 = 140.308$	$\sum (Y - Y')^2 = 3.648$
			Total Variation	*Explained Variation*	*Unexplained Variation*

You may have already observed that

Total variation = Explained variation + Unexplained variation

$$144 \quad = \quad 140.308 \quad + \quad 3.648.^*$$

STANDARD ERROR OF THE ESTIMATE

The standard error of the estimate measures the "average" disparity between the actual and estimated values of Y. In other words, the standard error of the estimate indicates how accurately we can predict the value of Y using the multiple regression equation as a means of prediction.

The standard error of the estimate in a multiple regression with two independent variables, X_1 and X_2, is denoted by the symbol $S_{y.12}$. The subscript notation $y.12$ lists the variable to be predicted, y, to the left of the dot and the independent variables, X_1 and X_2, to the right of the dot. In a multiple regression case with three independent variables (X_1, X_2, X_3), the standard error of the estimate is denoted by the symbol $S_{y.123}$.

The general formula for computing the standard error in a multiple regression is

$$S_{y.123...} = \sqrt{\frac{\text{Unexplained variation}}{\text{Number of degrees of freedom}}}$$

*The two sides are not exactly equal due to rounding errors.

In a multiple correlation problem with two independent variables, the standard error of the estimate is computed using the formula

$$S_{y.12} = \sqrt{\frac{\sum (Y - Y')^2}{n - 3}},$$

where the numerator $\sum (Y - Y')^2$ is the unexplained variation and n is the sample size. The divisor $n - 3$ represents the number of degrees of freedom in this case. The number 3 in the divisor refers to the number of constants in the regression equation. The three constants in the case of our two independent variables are the constants a, b_1, and b_2 of the regression equation

$$Y' = a + b_1 X_1 + b_2 X_2.$$

Enough has been said about unpleasant and terrifying terms such as subscript, numerator, divisor, number of degrees of freedom, and so on. Let us now return to the problem at hand and compute the standard error of the estimate for predictions of real estate sales.

The formula we use to compute the standard error of the estimate in our illustrative problem is

$$S_{y.12} = \sqrt{\frac{\sum (Y - Y')^2}{n - 3}}$$

Substituting the previously obtained value of $\sum (Y - Y') = 3.648$ (see Table 13.5) into the formula, we find

$$S_{y.12} = \sqrt{\frac{\sum (Y - Y')^2}{n - 3}}$$

$$= \sqrt{\frac{3.648}{10 - 3}} = .72 \text{ housing units.}$$

This means that we can predict a branch sales with an "average" error of .72 housing units by using the number of salespersons and monthly advertising expenditures as independent variables.

It may be useful now to present the general formula for computing the standard error of the estimate in multiple regression:

$$S_{y.123...} = \sqrt{\frac{\sum (Y - Y')^2}{n - k}},$$

where

$$n = \text{Sample size,}$$
$$k = \text{Number of constants in the regression equation,}$$
$$n - k = \text{Number of degrees of freedom,}$$
$$\sum (Y - Y')^2 = \text{Unexplained variation.}$$

It is possible to establish confidence interval estimates for the mean and the individual values of Y, but such discussion is beyond the scope of this text.

As a final remark, we must mention now that there is a shortcut formula for computing the standard error of the estimate. This formula and other shortcut formulas to compute some other regression and correlation measures are presented in separate sections of this chapter.

CORRELATION ANALYSIS

The central task in correlation analysis is to measure the strength of the relationship between the dependent variable Y and all independent variables taken collectively $(X_1, X_2, X_3, \ldots)$. The strength of this relationship is measured by the **coefficient of determination.** The coefficient of determination, denoted by R^2 (with appropriate subscripts), is defined as

$$R^2 = \frac{\text{Explained variation}}{\text{Total variation}}.$$

In words, the coefficient of determination, R^2, is the proportion of the total variation in the dependent variable Y that is "explained" by the independent variables collectively.

Referring to our illustrative problem, we define and calculate the coefficient of determination as follows:

$$R^2_{y\cdot 12} = \frac{\text{Explained variation}}{\text{Total variation}}$$

$$= \frac{\sum (Y' - \bar{Y})^2}{\sum (Y - \bar{Y})^2}.$$

Substituting the values of $\sum (Y' - \bar{Y})^2 = 140.308$ and $\sum (Y - \bar{Y})^2 = 144$ (see Table 13.5) into the formula, we obtain

$$R^2_{y\cdot 12} = \frac{\sum (Y' - \bar{Y})^2}{\sum (Y - \bar{Y})^2}$$

$$= \frac{140.308}{144}$$

$$= .974.$$

Thus we can conclude that 97.4% of the variation in sales can be accounted for, or "explained," by the variation in the number of salespeople and the variation in advertising expenditures collectively. You may already have observed that the subscript notation in $R^2_{y\cdot 12}$ is the same as in $S_{y\cdot 12}$. The dependent variable Y is listed to the left of the dot and the independent variables X_1 and X_2 to the right.

The coefficient of correlation, R, is the square root of the coefficient of determination R^2. Hence, with $R^2_{y\cdot12} = .974$, the coefficient of correlation becomes

$$R_{y\cdot12} = \sqrt{.974} = .987.$$

As in the simple regression case, a correlation coefficient of 1 ($R = 1$) indicates the highest degree of correlation. In other words, when $R = 1$, there is a perfect correlation between the dependent variable Y and all independent variables combined. While $R = 1$ indicates a perfect correlation, $R = 0$ indicates no correlation at all.

Significance of Correlation

As a teacher of statistics for about 20 years, I have taught more than 1000 classes in elementary statistics with approximately 30 students in each class. When the subject of regression and correlation is discussed, I often ask each student in the classroom to state his or her age and the amount of money change he or she carries. I perform a simple linear regression and correlation analysis on the data collected and I calculate the correlation coefficient, r. In most classes where I perform this experiment, the resulting value of r is low. The sign of r, furthermore, is positive in some cases and negative in others. The value of r is low because it is only logical to assume that there is no correlation between the student's age and the amount of money change he or she carries. But once in a while when I conduct this experiment, I obtain, strictly by chance, a high value for r. The moral of the story:

When the value of the sample correlation coefficient (r or R) is not equal to zero, say $R = .62$, does this indicate a true correlation, or did we obtain such a high value of R because of pure and simple chance?

The multiple correlation coefficient R (or the regression as a whole) is tested for significance by means of the analysis of variance (explained and unexplained) utilizing the F-distribution in such a test.

In testing the significance of the regression as a whole, we begin our analysis by formulating the following two hypotheses:

H_0: The regression is *not* significant,
H_1: The regression is significant.

The null hypothesis, which states that the regression is *not* significant, is tested by computing the F-ratio where

$$F = \frac{\text{Explained variance}}{\text{Unexplained variance}}$$

$$= \frac{\text{Explained variation} \div \text{Its degrees of freedom}}{\text{Unexplained variation} \div \text{Its degrees of freedom}}.$$

Symbolically, we define the F-ratio as

$$F = \frac{\sum(Y' - \bar{Y})^2 \div (k - 1)}{\sum(Y - Y')^2 \div (n - k)},$$

where

$n = $ Sample size ($n = 10$ in our example),

$k = $ Number of constants in the regression equation ($k = 3$: a, b_1, b_2 in our example)

$\sum(Y' - \bar{Y})^2 = $ Explained variation $= 140.308$ (Table 13.5)

$k - 1 = $ Number of degrees of freedom for unexplained variation; generally called the number of degrees of freedom for the numerator of the F-ratio $= 3 - 1 = 2$

$\sum(Y - Y')^2 = $ Unexplained variation $= 3.648$ (Table 13.5)

$n - k = $ Number of degrees of freedom for unexplained variation, generally called the number of degrees of freedom for the denominator of the F-ratio $= 10 - 3 = 7$.

Substituting the values belonging to our illustrative problem into the F-ratio formula, we obtain

$$F = \frac{\sum(Y' - \bar{Y})^2 \div (k - 1)}{\sum(Y - Y')^2 \div (n - k)}$$

$$= \frac{140.308 \div (3 - 1)}{3.648 \div (10 - 3)}$$

$$= \frac{140.308 \div 2}{3.648 \div 7} = \frac{70.154}{.521} = 134.652.$$

Hence, our illustrative problems show an F-ratio of 134.652, with 2 degrees of freedom for the numerator and 7 degrees of freedom for the denominator. Once again, the decision of whether to reject or accept the null hypothesis depends entirely on the *computed* F-ratio of 134.652. The computed F-ratio is also called the *actual* F-ratio.

To determine whether the regression is significant at the .05 level, the computed or actual F-ratio ($F = 134.652$) is compared against what is called a *critical $F_{.05}$-ratio* (see Table B at the end of the book). For a combination of 2 degrees of freedom for the numerator and 7 degrees of freedom for the denominator, Table B lists a critical $F_{.05}$-ratio of 4.74, which means that with this particular combination of degrees of freedom there is only .05 probability of obtaining an F-ratio of 4.74 or more as a result of pure chance. Furthermore, the probability of obtaining an F-ratio that is greater than 4.74 is less than .05 (see Fig. 13.1).

Thus whenever our actual F-ratio exceeds the critical $F_{.05}$-ratio, the null hypothesis is rejected and the regression is regarded as significant at the .05

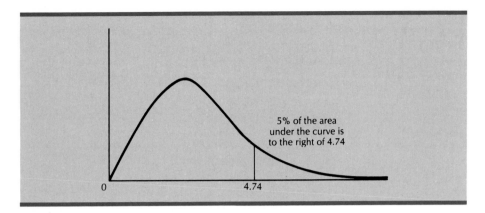

5% of the area
under the curve is
to the right of 4.74

0   4.74

Figure 13.1

level. However, the regression is regarded as *not significant* when the actual
F-ratio is less than the critical $F_{.05}$-ratio.

Similarly, the regression is significant at the .01 level when the actual
F-ratio is greater than the critical $F_{.01}$-ratio in Table C at the end of the book.

The actual F-ratio in our illustrative problem is 134.652, while the critical
$F_{.05}$ and $F_{.01}$-ratios are 4.74 and 9.55, respectively. Since our actual F-ratio is
greater than both these critical F-ratios, the regression is regarded as significant
not only at the .05 level but also at the .01 level. A summary of the analysis of
variance for our multiple regression example is displayed in Table 13.6.

The type of variation, also called source of variation, is shown in column 1
of Table 13.6. The amounts of variation, explained and unexplained, are found
in column 2. Column 3 shows the degrees of freedom for both sources of
variations. When the amount of each variation is divided by its own number of
degrees of freedom the resulting value is called *variance,* shown in column 4.
Finally, the F-ratio shown in column 5 is the ratio obtained by dividing the
explained variance by the unexplained variance. This F-ratio is the actual or
computed F-ratio.

TABLE 13.6   ANALYSIS OF VARIANCE FOR THE REGRESSION

(1) Source of Variation	(2) Amount of Variation	(3) Degrees of Freedom	(4) Variance	(5) F-ratio
Explained	$\sum(Y' - \bar{Y})^2 = 140.308$	$k - 1 = 3 - 1 = 2$	$140.308 \div 2 = 70.154$	$\dfrac{70.154}{.521} = 134.652$
Unexplained	$\sum(Y - Y')^2 = 3.648$	$n - k = 10 - 3 = 7$	$3.648 \div 7 = .521$	

TABLE 13.7   ANALYSIS OF VARIANCE FOR THE REGRESSION

(1) Source of Variation	(2) Amount of Variation (Sum of Squares = SS)	(3) Degrees of Freedom (DF)	(4) Variance (Mean Squares = MS)	(5) F ratio
Explained	$\sum(Y' - \bar{Y})^2 = 140.308$	$k - 1 = 3 - 1 = 2$	$140.308 \div 2 = 70.154$	$\dfrac{70.154}{.521} = 134.652$
Unexplained	$\sum(Y - Y')^2 = 3.648$	$n - k = 10 - 3 = 7$	$3.648 \div 7 = .521$	

Before concluding our discussion about the significance of regression, an important remark is in order. Most practical problems in regression and correlation analysis require very many lengthy and time-consuming computations. Consequently, most problems in multiple regression are solved using high-speed electronic computers, and a variety of computer programs are available to accomplish this task. Frequently used programs are STATPACK, MINITAB, and COSAP. We discuss the use of electronic computers for multiple regression analysis in the last part of this chapter, but we introduce some computer printout terminology here by displaying the analysis of variance data from Table 13.6 once more, in Table 13.7.

Tables 13.6 and 13.7 contain exactly the same data, but Table 13.7 shows some computer printout terminology in addition to the generally accepted statistical terms. In column 2, for example, the amount of variation is called the *sum of squares* (SS) in the computer printout terminology. The degrees of freedom in column 3 is abbreviated as DF. The variance in column 4 is called *mean squares,* denoted by MS in a computer printout. Additional computer printout terminology, not shown in Table 13.7, includes the terms used for the explained and unexplained variation. Explained variation is referred to as variation attributable to regression and is often called simply *regression.* The unexplained variation is referred to as deviation from regression and is often called *residuals.* Table 13.8 presents a portion of a computer printout for a

TABLE 13.8   ANALYSIS OF VARIANCE FOR THE REGRESSION,
COMPUTER STATPACK PRINTOUT

Analysis of variance for regression

Source of Variation	Sum of Squares	Degrees of Freedom	Mean Square	F Ratio
Regression	140.351	2	70.1754	134.615
Residual	3.64912	7	.521303	

**TABLE 13.9 DATA NEEDED FOR
THE SHORTCUT METHOD**

$\sum y^2 = 144$	$\sum yx_1 = 50$	$b_1 = 2.105$
$\sum x_1^2 = 20$	$\sum yx_2 = 40$	$b_2 = .877$
$\sum x_2^2 = 24$	$\sum x_1 x_2 = 9$	$k = 3$

multiple regression program called STATPACK showing the analysis of variance for our problem.*

SHORTCUT METHOD FOR COMPUTING REGRESSION MEASURES

The formula we have used so far to calculate the various measures of regression and correlation (such as $S_{y.12}$ and $R_{y.12}$) are most suitable for explaining and clarifying the various concepts in regression and correlation analysis, but they are cumbersome for computational purposes.

Most regression and correlation measures can be computed using equivalent alternative formulas, called shortcut formulas. The principal feature of the shortcut method is its extensive use of the deviations from means such as $\sum y^2$, $\sum x_1^2, \sum x_2^2, \sum yx_1, \sum yx_2, \sum x_1 x_2$, and so on.

For our illustrative example, the deviations from means have been calculated and shown in Table 13.3. We have also determined the regression equation

$$Y' = 6.056 + 2.105X_1 + .877X_2,$$

where $b_1 = 2.105$ and $b_2 = .877$. The previously obtained data that are needed for the shortcut method are shown in Table 13.9.

With the data shown in Table 13.9, we are now ready to use the shortcut method to calculate the following regression and correlation measures.[†]

1. Explained variation:

$$\begin{aligned} \sum (Y' - \overline{Y})^2 &= b_1 \sum yx_1 + b_2 \sum yx_2 \\ &= 2.105(50) + .877(40) \\ &= 140.33 \end{aligned}$$

---

*The data shown in Tables 13.6, 13.7, and 13.8 are identical. Small differences are due to rounding errors.
[†]The values for measures computed using the shortcut method may be slightly different from the previously obtained values because of rounding errors.

2. Unexplained variation:

$$\sum(Y - Y')^2 = \sum y^2 - b_1\sum yx_1 - b_2\sum yx_2$$
$$= 144 - 2.105(50) - .877(40)$$
$$= 3.67$$

3. Standard error of the estimate:

$$S_{y.12} = \sqrt{\frac{\sum y^2 - b_1\sum yx_1 - b_2\sum yx_2}{n - 3}}$$

$$= \sqrt{\frac{144 - 2.015(50) - .877(40)}{10 - 3}}$$

$$= \sqrt{\frac{3.67}{7}} = .724$$

4. Coefficient of determination:

$$R^2_{y.12} = \frac{b_1\sum yx_1 + b_2\sum yx_2}{\sum y^2}$$

$$= \frac{2.015(50) - .877(40)}{144}$$

$$= \frac{140.33}{144} = .974$$

TESTS OF HYPOTHESIS ABOUT THE POPULATION REGRESSION COEFFICIENTS

With a sample of n paired observations, also called *data points,* we have used the least-squares method to obtain the coefficients a, b_1, and b_2 in the linear regression equation

$$Y' = a + b_1X_1 + b_2X_2.$$

Since the values of these regressions are computed from sample data, we expect the values to vary from sample to sample. In other words, the values of the regression coefficients a, b_1, and b_2 depend on the sample chosen; different samples may result in different values for these coefficients.

Throughout this text, we have distinguished between the population and the sample. This distinction must be brought to focus once more. Let us assume that in the *population,* the relationship between the dependent variable Y and the two independent variables X_1 and X_2 is of the form

$$Y = A + B_1X_1 + B_2X_2$$

This relationship is a population relationship and the coefficients A, B_1, and B_2 are population parameters. The population relationship

$$Y = A + B_1X_1 + B_2X_2$$

is estimated from a sample of n observations by means of the least-squares method. The estimated relationship is

$$Y' = a + b_1X_1 + b_2X_2,$$

where the regression coefficients a, b_1, and b_2 are sample estimates of the parameters A, B_1, and B_2, respectively.

In the linear relationship $Y = A + B_1X_1 + B_2X_2$, the net regression coefficients are of prime importance. As explained earlier, the net regression coefficient B_1, for example, describes the effect of a change in variable X_1 on the values to be taken by the variable Y when the value of variable X_2 is held constant. In our illustrative problem, the net regression coefficient B_1 measures the change in sales caused by hiring one more salesperson while holding the amount of advertising expenditure at the same level. For this reason a great deal of interest is centered on assessing the reliability of the net regression coefficients b_1 and b_2 as estimators of the corresponding population parameters B_1 and B_2.

In addition to the variation due to sampling, the reliability of the net regression b_1 and b_2 is greatly affected by the degree of correlation between the independent variables X_1 and X_2.

In multiple regression, the correlation among the independent variables X_1, X_2, X_3, ... is called *multicollinearity,* or simply *intercorrelation.* A complete treatment of the subject of multicollinearity is unnecessary and beyond the scope of this text. But it is important to point out that the net regression coefficients b_1 and b_2 tend to be unreliable whenever the independent variables X_1 and X_2 are highly correlated.

The intercorrelation between the two independent variables X_1 and X_2 is measured by the simple correlation coefficient r. In this chapter, however, we denote this correlation coefficient by r_{12}. The subscript notation 12 designates the two independent variables whose degree of intercorrelation is measured. The degree of correlation between X_1 and X_2 can also be measured by the coefficient of determination r_{12}^2.

Referring to our illustrative problem, we compute the correlation coefficient between the two independent variables X_1 and X_2 by means of the formula

$$r_{12} = \frac{\sum x_1 x_2}{\sqrt{\sum x_1^2 \sum x_2^2}}.$$

Substituting the values $\sum x_1 x_2 = 9$, $\sum x_1^2 = 20$, $\sum x_2^2 = 24$ (from Table 13.3) into the formula, we obtain

$$r_{12} = \frac{\sum x_1 x_2}{\sqrt{\sum x_1^2 \sum x_2^2}}$$

$$= \frac{9}{\sqrt{20 \cdot 24}} = .410792.^*$$

When the coefficient of correlation $r_{12} = .410792$, the coefficient of determination r_{12}^2 is simply

$$r_{12}^2 = (.410792)^2 = .168750.$$

The coefficient of correlation r_{12} is incorporated into the formulas used in computing the standard errors for the net regression coefficients b_1 and b_2.

To test the significance of the net regression coefficients b_1 and b_2 we begin by computing the standard error for each of the two coefficients. The standard error of the net regression coefficient b_1, denoted by $\hat{\sigma}_{b_1}$, is calculated using the formula

$$\hat{\sigma}_{b_1} = \frac{S_{y \cdot 12}}{\sqrt{\sum x_1^2 (1 - r_{12}^2)}},$$

where

$S_{y \cdot 12} =$ Standard error of the estimate,
$r_{12}^2 =$ Coefficient of determination between the two independent variables X_1 and X_2.

Substituting the values $S_{y \cdot 12} = .724$, $\sum x_1^2 = 20$, and $r_{12}^2 = .168750$ into the formula, we obtain

$$\hat{\sigma}_{b_1} = \frac{S_{y \cdot 12}}{\sqrt{\sum x_1^2 (1 - r_{12}^2)}}$$

$$= \frac{.724}{\sqrt{20(1 - .168750)}} = \frac{.724}{\sqrt{20 \cdot .831250}}$$

$$= \frac{.724}{\sqrt{16.625}} = .177.$$

The standard error of the net regression coefficient b_2, denoted by $\hat{\sigma}_{b_2}$, is calculated using the formula

$$\hat{\sigma}_{b_2} = \frac{S_{y \cdot 12}}{\sqrt{\sum x_2^2 (1 - r_{12}^2)}}.$$

---

*The value of $r_{12} = .410792$ is carried out to six decimal places to minimize the rounding error in computing subsequent measures that utilize r_{12} in their formula.

Once again, substituting the values of $S_{y \cdot 12} = .724$, $r_{12}^2 = .168750$, and $\sum x_2^2 = 24$ into the formula, we obtain

$$\hat{\sigma}_{b_2} = \frac{S_{y \cdot 12}}{\sqrt{\sum x_2^2 (1 - r_{12}^2)}}$$

$$= \frac{.724}{\sqrt{24(1 - .168750)}} = .162.$$

Once we have determined the standard errors of the net regression coefficients b_1 and b_2, we can proceed to test the significance of both coefficients.

Beginning with the regression coefficient b_1, the null hypothesis states that the number of salespeople has no effect on sales. Formally stated, the null and the alternative hypotheses are

H_0: $B_1 = 0$ (sales are not affected by the number of salespeople),
H_1: $B_1 \neq 0$ (sales are affected by the number of salespeople).

The exact procedure to test the validity of the null hypothesis is to compute the statistic t as

$$t = \frac{b_1 - 0}{\hat{\sigma}_{b_1}} = \frac{b_1}{\hat{\sigma}_{b_1}},$$

with degrees of freedom of $n - k = 10 - 3 = 7$ in our case. Substituting the value of $b_1 = 2.105$ and $\sigma_{b_1} = .177$ into the formula, we obtain

$$t = \frac{b_1}{\hat{\sigma}_{b_1}} = \frac{2.105}{.177} = 11.893.$$

The value $t = 11.893$ (observed value) is then compared with a critical t-value obtained from Table E at the end of the book. The critical t-value is determined by the level of significance (such as .01 or .05), by the degrees of freedom ($n - k$), and by the nature of the alternative hypothesis (one-sided versus two-sided test). The null hypothesis is rejected when the observed value of t exceeds the critical t-value; otherwise we accept H_0 (a statistician would reserve judgment). Using the .01 level of significance with number of degrees of freedom $n - k = 10 - 3 = 7$, Table E lists a critical t-value of 3.499 (since the test is two-sided and the critical value of t is found under the column headed $t_{.005}$ of Table E). With the actual or observed t-value of 11.893 far exceeding the critical t-value of 3.499, the null hypothesis is rejected using the .01 level of significance. Hence we can conclude that sales are affected by the number of salespeople.

A similar procedure is used to test the significance of b_2. The null and the alternative hypotheses in this case are

H_0: $B_2 = 0$ (sales are not affected by advertising expenditures),
H_1: $B_2 \neq 0$ (sales are affected by advertising expenditures).

The observed t-value is computed as

$$t = \frac{b_2 - 0}{\hat{\sigma}_{b_2}} = \frac{.877}{.162} = 5.314.$$

Once again using the .01 level of significance, Table E lists a critical t-value of 3.499. Since the observed t-value is greater than the critical t-value (5.314 > 3.499), the null hypothesis is rejected; we can therefore conclude that sales are indeed affected by the amount of advertising expenditure.

To summarize, we can now state: Since both b_1 and b_2 are statistically significant, we can indeed conclude that sales are affected by the number of salespeople as well as by the amount of advertising expenditure.

THE COMPUTER AND MULTIPLE REGRESSION

We have already noted that most practical problems in regression analysis are complex problems with a large number of observations. Because the required amount of computation is quite lengthy and time-consuming, most practical problems in regression and correlation are solved using high-speed electronic computers. Many computer programs are available to accomplish this task (STATPACK, MINITAB, COSAP, and SPSS, among others). The computer multiple regression program called STATPACK is one of the easiest and most

TABLE 13.10   COMPUTER PROGRAM OUTPUT, STATPACK-2B

Regression of Y		NUMBER OF UNITS SOLD		
on X1		NUMBER OF SALESPEOPLE		
X2		ADVERTISING EXPENDITURES $1,000's		
Variable Name	Estimated Regression Coefficient	Estimated Standard Error of Coefficient	Value of Student's t	Degrees of freedom
Constant	6.05263			
X1	2.10526	.17708	11.88891	7
X2	.87719	.16165	5.42652	7

Multiple correlation coefficient (R) = .987248
Multiple correlation coefficient, squared (R^2) = .974659
Estimated standard error of estimate = .722013

Analysis of variance for regression

Source of Variation	Sum of Squares	Degrees of Freedom	Mean Square	F Ratio
Regression	140.351	2	70.1754	134.615
Residual	3.64912	7	.521303	

efficient for solving practical problems. The use of this program requires only one-finger typing ability to enter the data, but it requires all the knowledge we have learned in this chapter to interpret the solution provided by the computer output.

We will use STATPACK-2B to solve our illustrative problem. The solution to the problem is provided by the computer printout displayed in Table 13.10. We will now interpret the computer printout of Table 13.10 in terms of the regression equation and the various regression and correlation measures that we have previously hand-calculated. A summary of the important concepts in multiple regression and correlation is also provided. We begin our interpretation of the STATPACK-2B output with the data needed to construct the regression equation first.

The Regression Equation

The regression equation is constructed from the following section of the printout.

```
Regression of  Y            NUMBER OF UNITS SOLD
            on  X1           NUMBER OF SALESPEOPLE
            on  X2           ADVERTISING EXPENDITURES
                             $1,000's

                  Estimated
Variable          regression
name              coefficient

Constant          6.05263→a
X1                2.10526→b1
X2                 .87719→b2
```

The three arrows and the symbols a, b_1, and b_2 have been added to the computer printout to identify the regression coefficients a, b_1, and b_2 that are needed to construct the linear regression equation

$$Y' = a + b_1X_1 + b_2X_2.$$

This portion of the computer output indicates that the dependent variable Y is the number of units sold and the independent variables X_1 and X_2 are the number of salespeople and advertising expenditures, respectively. The coefficient a of the regression equation is called *constant* in a computer printout, and the values of the coefficients a, b_1, and b_2 are listed under the column headed "Estimated regression coefficient." With $a = 6.05263$, $b_1 = 2.10526$, and $b_2 = .87719$, the multiple regression equation is read as

$$Y' = 6.05263 + 2.10526X_1 + .87719X_2$$

This regression equation enables us to predict the dependent variable Y (number of units sold) for any continuation of the independent variables X_1 and

X_2 (number of salespeople and amount of advertising). In addition, the net regression coefficients b_1 and b_2 show the effect of changes in the independent variables X_1 and X_2 on the dependent variable Y. For instance, the net regression coefficient b_1 (2.10526) indicates that the addition of one more salesperson would increase sales by 2.10526 housing units, assuming no changes in advertising expenditures. The net regression coefficient b_2 (.87719) is interpreted in a similar manner.

Reliability of Net Regression Coefficient

The data needed to test the significance of the net regression coefficients b_1 and b_2 are shown in the following portion of STATPACK-2B output.

Variable name	Estimated regression coefficient	Estimated standard error of coefficient	Value of Student's t	Degrees of freedom
Constant	6.05263			
X1	b1←2.10526	σ̂b1←.17708	11.88891	7
X2	b2←.87719	σ̂b2←.16165	5.42652	7

Once again, the symbols to the left of the arrows have been added to the computer printout to facilitate the understanding of the computer output.

The values of the net regression coefficients b_1 and b_2 are listed under the column labeled "Estimated regression coefficient." The standard errors of these regression coefficients are listed under the column labeled "Estimated standard error of coefficient." This column shows the standard errors $\hat{\sigma}_{b_1} = .17708$ and $\hat{\sigma}_{b_2} = .16165$ for the net regression coefficients b_1 and b_2 respectively. The significance of both b_1 and b_2 is tested utilizing the t-distribution, where

$$t = \frac{b - 0}{\hat{\sigma}_b} = \frac{b}{\hat{\sigma}_b}.$$

These t-values are listed under the column labeled "Value of Student's t" in STATPACK-2B output.

To test the significance of any net regression coefficient, say b_1, the actual or computed t-value must first be determined as follows:

$$t = \frac{b_1}{\hat{\sigma}_{b_1}} = \frac{2.01526}{.17708} = 11.88891.$$

The column labeled "Value of Student's t" lists the actual or computed t-values for both net regression coefficients b_1 and b_2. The actual t-value must now be compared with a critical t-value obtained from Table E at the end of the book. (The critical t-value is not shown in the computer printout but must be found from Table E.) With 7 degrees of freedom (see last column in printout) Table E shows a critical $t_{.005}$ value of 3.499. Since the actual t-values for both b_1 and b_2 exceed the critical $t_{.005}$, that is, 11.88891 > 3.499 and 5.42652 > 3.499, we conclude that both b_1 and b_2 are significant at the .01 level. This means that sales are indeed affected by the number of salespeople as well as by the amount of advertising expenditures.

Standard Error of the Estimate ($S_{y.12}$)

The STATPACK-2B output in Table 13.10 shows an estimate of the standard error of the estimate of .722013. This standard error of the estimate, denoted by $S_{y.12}$, measures the average disparity between the actual values of Y and the estimated values of Y. In other words, the standard error of the estimate indicates how accurately we can predict the value of Y (sales) using the multiple regression equation as a means of prediction.

Correlation

The coefficient of correlation, R, or the coefficient of determination, R^2, measures the strength of the relationship between the dependent variable Y and all independent variables taken collectively (X_1, X_2, X_3, . . .). STATPACK output for our illustrative problem lists a multiple correlation coefficient of $R =$ .987248 and $R^2 =$ .974659, shown in the following section of the print-out:

```
Multiple correlation coefficient (R) = .987248
Multiple correlation coefficient, squared (R^2) = .974659
Estimated standard error of estimate = .722013
```

The next step is to test the multiple correlation coefficient R (or the regression as a whole) for significance by means of the analysis of variance using the F-distribution in the test. The last part of STATPACK-2B output shows the analysis of variance for our regression problem, as shown in the following section of the printout.

```
Analysis of variance for regression
```

Source of variation	Sum of squares	Degrees of freedom	Mean Square	F ratio
Regression	140.351	2	70.1754	134.615
Residual	3.64912	7	.521303	

The last column in the printout shows an actual or computed F-ratio of 134.615. To determine whether the regression is significant at, say, the .01

level, this actual F-ratio is compared against a critical $F_{.01}$-ratio from Table C at the end of the book. For a combination of 2 degrees of freedom for the numerator and 7 degrees of freedom for the denominator, Table B at the end of the book lists a critical $F_{.01}$-ratio of 9.55. Since the actual F-ratio is greater than the critical F-ratio (134.615 > 9.55), the regression is regarded as significant at the .01 level.

Next we illustrate the use of computers in regression analysis by solving another problem. In contrast to the real estate problem, which has two independent variables, the new problem has three independent variables: X_1, X_2, and X_3. Furthermore, we will use the MINITAB program instead of STATPACK to solve the problem. The computer outputs of MINITAB and STATPACK in regression analysis are essentially the same.

Example   Mr. Adams is the general sales manager for an auto parts distributing company that operates throughout New Jersey. The state is divided into 10 sales districts, each headed by a district sales manager. To forecast district sales, Adams requested each district manager to provide the following information: the district's annual sales; the number of outlets in the district carrying the company's products; the number of registered motor vehicles in the district; and the average age of the vehicles. District managers reported the following information.

District	Annual Sales (millions of dollars) Y	Number of Outlets X_1	Number of Vehicles (millions) X_2	Average Age of Vehicles (years) X_3
1	38.8	13	2.1	4.4
2	43.6	17	3.3	3.8
3	45.5	18	3.9	3.5
4	43.6	12	2.0	4.8
5	52.5	19	3.4	4.0
6	62.6	20	5.2	5.1
7	37.6	10	1.2	4.8
8	32.7	11	1.8	3.6
9	52.8	14	4.0	4.9
10	48.7	16	3.1	5.1

A multiple linear regression was carried out using MINITAB, and the computer output yielded the following data.

```
THE REGRESSION EQUATION IS
Y = - 5.96 + 0.992 X1 + 3.43 X2
    + 6.05 X3
                                    ST. DEV.      T-RATIO =
          COLUMN      COEFFICIENT   OF COEF.      COEF/SD
            -          -5.9628       8.5368        -.70
X1        C2             .9916        .5158        1.92
X2        C3            3.4287       1.4819        2.31
X3        C4            6.0460       1.4047        4.30
THE ST. DEV. OF Y ABOUT REGRESSION LINE IS
S = 2.396
WITH (10 - 4) = 6 DEGREES OF FREEDOM
R-SQUARED = 94.8 PERCENT
ANALYSIS OF VARIANCE
DUE TO              DF         SS          MS=SS/DF
REGRESSION          3        634.429       211.476
RESIDUAL            6         34.450         5.742
```

a) Ms. Smith, a district sales manager, expects her district to have in the next year 20 retail outlets and 5 million registered vehicles, with an average life of 4.5 years. Use the regression equation to predict Smith's district's total sales for the coming year.

b) Explain the meaning of each net regression coefficient. At a .05 level of significance, which regression coefficient is significant?

c) At a .05 level of significance, is the regression, as a whole, significant?

Solution

a) The MINITAB computer program output shows the regression equation as

$$Y' = -5.96 + .992X_1 + 3.43X_2 + 6.05X_3.$$

Substituting $X_1 = 20$, $X_2 = 5$, and $X_3 = 4.5$ into the regression equation, we obtain

$$Y' = -5.96 + .992(20) + 3.43(5) + 6.05(4.5)$$
$$= -5.96 + 19.84 + 17.15 + 27.225$$
$$= 58.255$$

Hence Ms. Smith's district's total sales for the coming year are predicted as $58,255,000.

b) The meaning of the three net regression coefficients is explained as follows.

1. The net regression coefficient $b_1 = .992$ indicates that the district's total sales increase by $.992 million when one more retail sale outlet is

opened in the district, assuming that all other independent variables remain constant (no change in X_2 and X_3).

2. The net regression coefficient $b_2 = 3.43$ indicates that total sales increase by \$3.43 million when the number of vehicles in the district increases by one million, assuming that variables X_1 and X_3 remain constant.

3. The net regression coefficient $b_3 = 6.05$ indicates that the district's total sales increase by \$6.05 million when the average age of vehicles increases by 1 year, assuming that X_1 and X_2 remain constant.

We will now use the t-distribution to test the significance of the three net regression coefficients b_1, b_2, and b_3. At a .05 level of significance and with 6 degrees of freedom ($n - k = 10 - 4 = 6$), Table E at the end of the book shows a critical value of $t_{.025} = 2.447$ (a two-sided test). Hence, all three t-ratios, also called observed t-values, that are listed in the MINITAB computer output are compared against this critical value of $t_{.025} = 2.447$. We proceed as follows.

1. The computer output lists a t-ratio of 1.92 for the net regression coefficient b_1 ($t_1 = b_1/\hat{\sigma}_{b_1} = .9916/.5158 = 1.92$). This observed value of $t = 1.92$ is compared against the critical t-value of 2.447 (from Table E). Since the observed t-value is less than the critical t-value (1.92 < 2.447), the net regression $b_1 = .992$ is considered not significant. We can therefore conclude that sales are not affected by the number of outlets in the district.

2. In the same manner, to test the significance of b_2, we compare the observed t-ratio of 2.31 listed in the computer output against the same critical t-value of 2.447. Once again, since the observed t-value is less than the critical t-value (2.31 < 2.447), the net regression coefficient $b_2 = 3.43$ is considered not significant. We can therefore conclude that sales are not affected by the number of vehicles in the district.*

3. Finally, to test the significance of $b_3 = 6.05$, we compare the observed t-ratio of 4.30 listed in the computer output against the critical t-value of 2.447 given in Table E. Since the observed t-value is greater than the critical t-value (4.30 > 2.447), the net regression coefficient $b_3 = 6.05$ is considered significant. We can therefore conclude that sales are indeed affected by the average age of vehicles in the district.

---

*You may wonder why the coefficients b_1 and b_2 (number of outlets and number of vehicles) are not significant. Remember that the test of the net regression coefficient determines whether changes in the independent variable result in significant changes in the dependent variable in the presence of the other independent variables. If the number of outlets is correlated with the number of vehicles, each coefficient may be found not significant in the presence of the other independent variables even though the overall regression is significant.

c) The MINITAB computer program output does not list the actual F-ratio as does STATPACK. However, we can easily determine this actual F-ratio from the information contained in the computer output, as follows:

$$F = \frac{MS \text{ (regression)}}{MS \text{ (residual)}} = \frac{211.476}{5.742} = 36.83.$$

To determine whether the regression is significant at the .05 level, this actual F-ratio of 36.83 is compared against the critical $F_{.05}$-ratio from Table B. For a combination of 3 degrees of freedom for the numerator and 6 degrees of freedom for the denominator (see the output column labeled DF), Table B lists a critical $F_{.05}$-ratio of 4.76. Since the actual F-ratio is greater than the critical $F_{.05}$-ratio (36.83 > 4.76), the regression, as a whole, is significant at the .05 level.

EXERCISES

13.1 A supermarket chain wishes to introduce a new product. Management, however, is not sure at what price the product should be sold and how much shelf space should be allocated to it. To study the relationships among sales, price, and shelf space, the company introduced the product into ten similar stores and monitored sales for 12 weeks. The following data show sales, price, and shelf space for the ten stores during the testing period.

Store	Average Weekly Sales (thousands of dollars)	Linear Shelf Space (inches)	Price Per Unit (dollars)
1	218	17	2.75
2	253	20	2.45
3	232	19	2.95
4	260	21	2.75
5	258	20	2.25
6	235	19	2.85
7	234	18	2.45
8	269	22	2.65
9	262	21	2.55
10	288	23	2.35

a) Determine the linear regression equation using average weekly sales as the dependent variable.

b) What is the average increase in weekly sales associated with an additional 1 inch of shelf space?

c) What is the average increase in weekly sales when the price is reduced by $1 per unit?

d) Compute the standard error of the estimate.

e) What are the predicted weekly sales for a store that allocates 24 inches of shelf space to the new product, with a retail price of $2.75 per unit?

f) Compute the coefficient of multiple correlation.

13.2   The marketing research director of a winery wishes to study the relationship between sales and advertising expenditures. The winery advertising outlay is allocated to two media: magazines and television. The director collected the following data from ten randomly selected sales periods.

Sales (millions of dollars)	Magazine Advertising (millions of dollars)	TV Advertising (millions of dollars)
183	2	9
229	4	12
172	2	8
188	3	9
211	3	11
219	4	11
152	1	7
172	2	8
230	4	12
244	5	13

a) Determine the multiple linear regression equation using sales as the dependent variable.

b) What is the meaning of the two net regression coefficients?

c) Use a level of significance of .01 to test the significance of the net regression coefficients.

d) Test the overall significance of correlation using the .05 level of significance.

e) Predict total sales for a period in which magazine and television advertising expenditures are $4 million and $11 million respectively.

13.3   A textile mill utilizes several hundreds of similar machines, called fly frames, in its production of cloth. Management wishes to develop a method to predict the annual repair and maintenance cost of these machines. The cost is believed to be related to the machine's age and its annual usage. To carry out the study, management randomly selected 15 machine records, which show the following information.

Annual Repair and Maintenance Cost (dollars)	*Annual Usage (thousands of hours)*	*Machine Age*
1712	12	6
1920	20	4
1810	10	8
1607	12	5
1703	18	3
1562	19	1
1168	11	1
1619	14	4
1661	13	5
1903	12	8
1808	16	5
1602	16	3
1613	20	1
1754	17	4
1458	15	2

a) Determine the multiple linear regression equation using cost as the dependent variable.

b) What is the meaning of the two net regression coefficients?

c) Compute the standard error of the estimate.

d) Use a level of significance of .05 to test the significance of the net regression coefficients.

e) Compute the coefficient of multiple correlation.

f) Estimate the annual repair and maintenance cost of a five-year-old machine. The machine is used for 18,000 hours during the year.

13.4   It is theorized that the rate of return on common equity depends on the growth rates of common equity and earnings per share. To investigate this notion, ten firms are randomly selected from the chemical industry, and the following information is collected about these firms.

		10-Year Growth	
Firm	*Return on Common Equity (%)* Y	*Common Equity (%)* X_1	*Earnings per Share (%)* X_2
A	12.2	8	14
B	10.9	8	10
C	14.9	13	10

(Continued)

| | | 10-Year Growth | |
Firm	Return on Common Equity (%) Y	Common Equity (%) X_1	Earnings per Share (%) X_2
D	19.8	9	22
E	15.7	12	16
F	19.9	16	24
G	12.5	11	8
H	7.3	8	5
I	10.2	6	10
J	7.6	6	9

A multiple linear regression was carried out, and the computer output yielded the following data.

```
THE REGRESSION EQUATION IS
Y = 1.79 + 0.490 X1 + 0.512 X2
                                    ST. DEV.      T-RATIO =
           COLUMN    COEFFICIENT    OF COEF.      COEF/SD
           ──        1.7886         1.7179        1.04
X1         C2         .4899          .1971        2.49
X2         C3         .5124          .1031        4.97
THE ST. DEV. OF Y ABOUT REGRESSION LINE IS
S = 1.614
WITH (10 − 3) = 7 DEGREES OF FREEDOM

R-SQUARED = 89.8 PERCENT

ANALYSIS OF VARIANCE
DUE TO              DF          SS            MS=SS/DF
REGRESSION         2           161.214       80.607
RESIDUAL           7            18.226        2.604
```

a) What is the effect of growth in earnings per share on the rate of return on common equity?

b) What is the effect of growth in common equity on the rate of return?

c) Use a .05 level of significance to test the hypothesis that the growth rates of common equity and earnings per share have no effect on rate of return on common equity.

d) At a .01 level of significance, is the regression significant as a whole?

e) Predict the rate of return of a firm with a ten-year growth rate of 8% in common equity and 10% in earnings per share.

13.5 During 1984, the Bureau of Continuing Education at California's Southridge University offered several weekend seminars especially designed for individual life insurance salespersons. The Metro Insurance Company encourages its salespersons to attend some or all of these seminars, and the company pays all training expenses. To assess the effectiveness of its training, the bureau selected a random sample of 20 Metro salespersons who attended the seminars and requested that the insurance company provide the following data.

Salesperson	Average Number of Policies Sold per Month, 1984 Y	Number of Seminars Attended X_1	Average Number of Calls Made per Month, 1984 X_2	Selling Experience (years) X_3
1	89	7	71	1
2	71	1	61	2
3	103	6	80	3
4	98	8	62	5
5	95	8	66	3
6	97	4	71	5
7	103	4	74	7
8	99	7	61	7
9	94	4	82	1
10	65	1	55	1
11	84	2	69	3
12	113	7	75	7
13	111	9	80	4
14	86	5	54	6
15	95	8	59	6
16	104	5	64	9
17	105	9	64	6
18	101	2	74	5
19	131	20	72	6
20	86	3	66	3

A multiple linear regression was carried out, and the computer output yielded the following data.

```
THE REGRESSION EQUATION IS
Y = 8.80 + 1.88 X1 + 0.920 X2
    + 3.08 X3
                                    ST. DEV.    T-RATIO =
             COLUMN   COEFFICIENT   OF COEF.    COEF/SD
             ——       8.8012        3.9172      2.25
     X1      C2       1.8773        .1117      16.80
     X2      C3        .9201        .0550      16.74
     X3      C4       3.0813        .2030      15.18
```

```
THE ST. DEV. OF Y ABOUT REGRESSION LINE IS
S = 1.885
WITH (20 - 4) = 16 DEGREES OF FREEDOM
R-SQUARED = 98.6 PERCENT
ANALYSIS OF VARIANCE
DUE TO              DF          SS          MS=SS/DF
REGRESSION          3        3944.146      1314.715
RESIDUAL           16          56.852         3.553
```

a) Predict the average number of policies sold by a salesperson who has 5 years of selling experience, makes 60 sales calls a month, and attends 15 weekend seminars during the year.

b) What is the meaning of each net regression coefficient? Which of these coefficients is significant at a .01 level?

c) At a .01 level of significance, is the regression as a whole significant?

13.6 The objective of this problem is to predict the number of business failures in the United States by means of multiple regression using the following four independent variables:

$$X_1 = \text{Percentage of labor force, unemployed.}$$

$$X_2 = \text{Index of labor cost (1967} = \text{100).}$$

$$X_3 = \text{Average prime interest rate.}$$

$$X_4 = \text{Commercial and industrial loans outstanding.}$$

The *Statistical Abstract of the United States* shows the following data for the years 1970–1981.

Year	Number of Business Failures (thousands) Y	Unemploy- ment Rate X_1	Index of Labor Cost X_2	Average Prime Rate X_3	Loans Outstanding (billions of dollars) X_4
1970	10.7	4.9	112.5	7.9	85
1971	10.3	5.9	113.1	5.7	84
1972	9.6	5.6	113.4	5.2	80
1973	9.3	4.9	117.4	8.0	97
1974	7.9	5.6	127.9	10.8	116
1975	11.4	8.5	143.6	7.9	118
1976	9.6	7.7	145.2	6.8	109
1977	7.9	7.0	154.1	6.8	113
1978	6.6	6.0	164.2	9.1	126
1979	7.6	5.8	175.8	12.7	147
1980	11.8	7.1	195.1	15.3	164
1981	16.9	7.6	212.2	18.9	182

The multiple regression analysis was carried out, and the computer output yielded the following data.

```
THE REGRESSION EQUATION IS
Y =     2.23 + 2.42 X1 + .123 X2
      + 2.24 X3 - .400 X4
                                         ST. DEV.        T-RATIO =
          COLUMN       COEFFICIENT       OF COEF.        COEF/SD
            -            2.2344           1.9088           1.17
  X1        C1           2.4168            .4057           5.96
  X2        C2            .1226            .0511           2.40
  X3        C3           2.2424            .3361           6.67
  X4        C4           -.3997            .0852          -4.69
THE ST. DEV. OF Y ABOUT REGRESSION LINE IS
S = 1.038
WITH (12 - 5) = 7 DEGREES OF FREEDOM
R-SQUARED = 90.6 PERCENT
ANALYSIS OF VARIANCE
DUE TO              DF          SS           MS=SS/DF
REGRESSION          4         72.786         18.196
RESIDUAL            7          7.541          1.077
```

a) Use a .01 level of significance to test the following hypotheses:
   1) The unemployment rate has no effect on number of business failures.
   2) Labor cost has no effect on the number of business failures.
   3) The prime interest rate has no effect on the number of business failures.

b) How can you justify that the net regression coefficient $b_4 = -.4$ is negative? Test the significance of this coefficient using a .01 level of significance.

c) Predict the number of business failures in a year where $X_1 = 9.2$, $X_2 = 230.1$, $X_3 = 12.5$, and $X_4 = 190$.

d) At a .01 level of significance, is the regression as a whole significant?

KEY TERMS

multiple regression   The regression of a dependent variable Y on two or more independent variables.

net regression coefficient   The increase in Y associated with a 1-unit increase in an independent variable, assuming all the other independent variables remain unchanged.

explained variation   The amount of the variation in the dependent variable Y that can be explained by changes in the independent variables. The explained variation is sometimes called the variation due to regression or the sum of squares for regression.

unexplained variation   The amount of the variation in the dependent variable Y that cannot be explained by changes in the independent variables. The unexplained variation is sometimes called the residual variation, variation due to error, or residual sum of squares.

coefficient of determination (R^2)   A measure of the strength of the relationship between the dependent variable and the independent variables taken collectively. R^2 is the fraction of the variation in Y that is explained by the X's collectively.

mean square   The ratio of a sum of squares or variation divided by its degrees of freedom. The mean square for regression is the sum of squares for regression (explained variation) divided by $k - 1$, the degrees of freedom for regression.

SUMMARY OF FORMULAS

normal equations

$$\sum yx_1 = b_1\sum x_1^2 + b_2\sum x_1 x_2$$
$$\sum yx_2 = b_1\sum x_1 x_2 + b_2\sum x_2^2$$
$$a = \bar{Y} - b_1\bar{X}_1 - b_2\bar{X}_2$$

total variation

$$\sum (Y - \bar{Y})^2$$

explained variation

$$\sum (Y' - \bar{Y})^2, \text{ for } k = 3,$$
$$\sum (Y - \bar{Y})^2 = b_1\sum yx_1 + b_2\sum yx_2$$

unexplained variation

$$\sum (Y - Y')^2, \text{ for } k = 3,$$
$$\sum (Y - Y')^2 = \sum y^2 - b_1\sum yx_1 - b_2\sum yx_2$$

standard error of the estimate

$$S_{y \cdot 123\ldots} = \sqrt{\frac{\sum (Y - Y')^2}{n - k}}$$

$$= \sqrt{\frac{\text{Unexplained variation}}{\text{Number of degrees of freedom}}}$$

coefficient of determination

$$R^2 = \frac{\text{Explained variation}}{\text{Total variation}}$$

F-ratio

$$F = \frac{\text{Explained variance}}{\text{Unexplained variance}}$$

$$= \frac{\sum(Y' - \overline{Y})^2 \div (k - 1)}{\sum(Y - Y')^2 \div (n - k)}$$

correlation coefficient

$$r_{12} = \frac{\sum x_1 x_2}{\sqrt{\sum x_1^2 \sum x_2^2}}$$

standard error of the
net regression coefficient

$$\hat{\sigma}_{b_1} = \frac{S_{y \cdot 12}}{\sqrt{\sum x_1^2 (1 - r_{12}^2)}}$$

t-value for testing net
regression coefficient
(null hypothesis)

$$t = \frac{b - 0}{\hat{\sigma}_b} = \frac{b}{\hat{\sigma}_b}$$

TIME SERIES

14

A time series is a set of measured observations made at regular periods over time. The monthly sales of a department store over many months, the U.S. gross national product over several years, and annual wheat exports over time are all examples of economic or business time series. In this chapter we describe the general nature of time series and explain the reasons for variations. We also discuss the various methods used in the graphical representation of time series. The use of time series in forecasting is considered in Chapter 15.

Many companies are faced with the challenging problem of forecasting the future level of business activity. Forecasts of sales, employment, income, population, and many other economic factors are essential elements in planning future business operations. In public utilities, for example, management concerned with capital investment requires an accurate forecast of such factors as income, population, and commercial and industrial activity of the area in which the public utility operates. Such forecasts may extend 20 to 30 years into the future.

We can readily understand the complexity of forecasting if we consider the problem of planning the development of a tourist center such as Honolulu, Hawaii. The present investment in such facilities as hotels, restaurants, transportation, and recreational facilities depends, to a large extent, on the future influx of tourists. The expected volume of tourists in turn depends on the income and population of the regions supplying the tourists as well as on future developments in the field of transportation.

The need for forecasting is by no means confined to large companies. A small retailer is just as interested in knowing future demand as is a public utility. Although the retailer's plans are more flexible than those of a public utility, a good estimate of future sales is nonetheless essential to inventory control as well as to the formulation of future expansion plans.

How are forecasts made? Forecasts are based on past and present facts. These facts are often represented by a set of observations made at consecutive time periods. Such a set of observations is called a **time series.**

Let us consider the time series given in Table 14.1, which is a historical record of U.S. disposable income for the years 1960–1981. The first observation in the series, 350, measures the purchasing power in the United States in 1960, that is, the income at the disposal of consumers that they may either spend or save. Similarly, 364, the second number in the series, is the income at the disposal of U.S. consumers in 1961. Based on this historical record, the future level of disposable income in the United States can be predicted. The time periods over which a set of observations are made can be days,

TABLE 14.1   U.S. DISPOSABLE PERSONAL INCOME, 1960–1981

Year	Disposable Income (billions of dollars)	Year	Disposable Income (billions of dollars)	Year	Disposable Income (billions of dollars)
1960	350	1968	591	1976	1156
1961	364	1969	634	1977	1322
1962	384	1970	690	1978	1463
1963	404	1971	744	1979	1642
1964	436	1972	795	1980	1822
1965	465	1973	903	1981	2016
1966	512	1974	979		
1967	546	1975	1084		

TABLE 14.2 **U.S. CURRENCY IN CIRCULATION, 1979–1981**

End of Month	Currency in Circulation (billions), 1979	Currency in Circulation (billions), 1980	Currency in Circulation (billions), 1981
January	97.4	106.5	115.8
February	97.6	106.9	115.9
March	98.6	107.9	116.8
April	99.9	108.7	118.4
May	100.6	109.9	119.3
June	101.8	111.1	119.9
July	103.2	112.7	121.4
August	103.9	113.7	121.5
September	104.5	113.7	120.8
October	105.2	114.9	121.1
November	106.6	116.6	122.9
December	108.0	118.5	125.4

weeks, months, or years. The time series in Table 14.2 represents the currency in circulation at the end of each month for the years 1979–1981.

Although the data given cover only the years 1979–1981, similar data are available for the past 20 or 30 years, and these are used to predict currency in circulation at the end of a future month, such as May 1988.

GRAPHIC REPRESENTATION OF TIME SERIES

Two kinds of charts are used in representing a time series: the arithmetic line chart and the logarithmic line chart. We can best illustrate the difference between the two by considering an actual time series such as the one given in Table 14.3.

TABLE 14.3 **ABC COMPANY ANNUAL SALES, 1977–1983**

Year	Sales (millions of dollars)
1977	2.4
1978	3.3
1979	4.2
1980	5.2
1981	8.3
1982	15.6
1983	17.1

In constructing both types of charts, the years are always measured along the horizontal axis and sales are measured along the vertical axis. The sales for each year, furthermore, are plotted at the midpoint of the year. The seven points in each chart are connected by straight lines. The arithmetic and logarithmic line charts of the sales series from Table 14.3 are shown in Figs. 14.1 and 14.2.

You may have already observed that the vertical scales of the two charts are entirely different. The vertical scale of the arithmetic line chart is an ordinary scale whose intervals are of *equal* length; each interval represents the same amount of sales ($2 million in this case). Consequently a sales volume of $4 million is represented by a point that is twice as high as the point representing $2 million; a sales volume of $6 million is represented by a point three times as high, and so on. When equal intervals on the vertical scale represent the same amounts of sales, the scale is called an *arithmetic scale* and the resulting chart is called an **arithmetic line chart.** Such a chart reveals the *absolute* yearly change in the amount of sales.

When you examine the logarithmic line chart, you may be bewildered by its vertical scale. Not only are the intervals on this scale different in length, but

Figure 14.1 Arithmetic line chart for ABC Company annual sales, 1977–1983

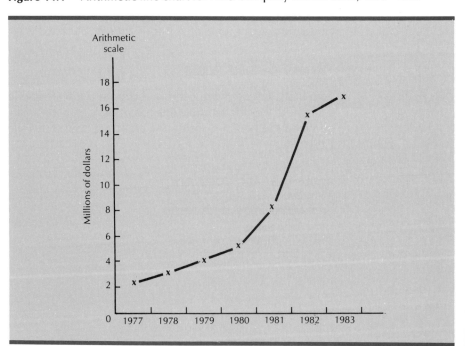

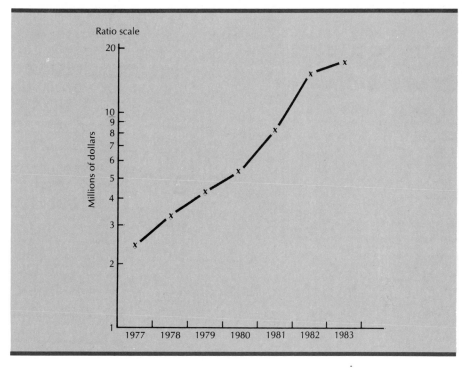

Figure 14.2   Logarithmic line chart for ABC Company annual sales, 1977–1983

the lengths of intervals diminish as we move away from the origin. Thus the distance between 3 and 4 is smaller than the distance between 2 and 3, which in turn is smaller than the distance between 1 and 2.

The intervals on a logarithmic scale are indeed not equal. The scale is constructed such that equal distances represent equal percentage changes. Thus the distances between 1 and 2, 2 and 4, 4 and 8, and 8 and 16 are exactly the same, each representing a 100% increase in the volume of sales. Similarly, the distance between 4 and 6 is the same as the distance between 6 and 9, since each represents a 50% increase in sales. When equal distances on a scale represent the same percentage change, the scale is called a *logarithmic* or *ratio scale*, and the resulting chart is called a **logarithmic line chart.** Such a chart reveals the yearly percentage changes in a series.

The graph paper used in constructing a logarithmic line chart is available at college bookstores and commercial art supply stores. Known commercially as "semi-log" paper, it is available in various forms: one-cycle, two-cycle, three-cycle, four-cycle, and five-cycle (see Fig. 14.3).

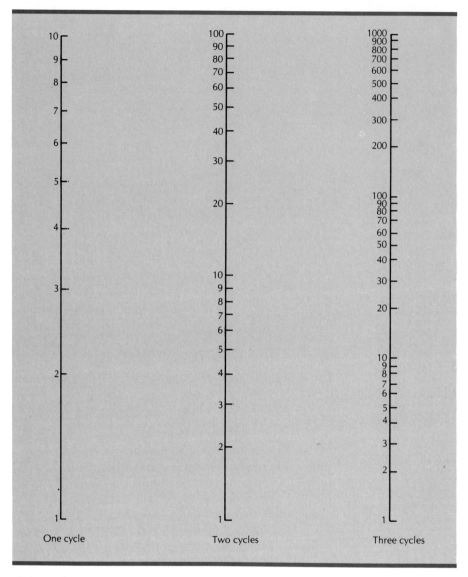

Figure 14.3

The choice among these five forms depends on the range of the data to be plotted along the vertical axis. One-cycle paper is used whenever the maximum value in the series is less than 10 times the minimum value, that is, for a variable that ranges from 1 to 10 or any multiple of this range such

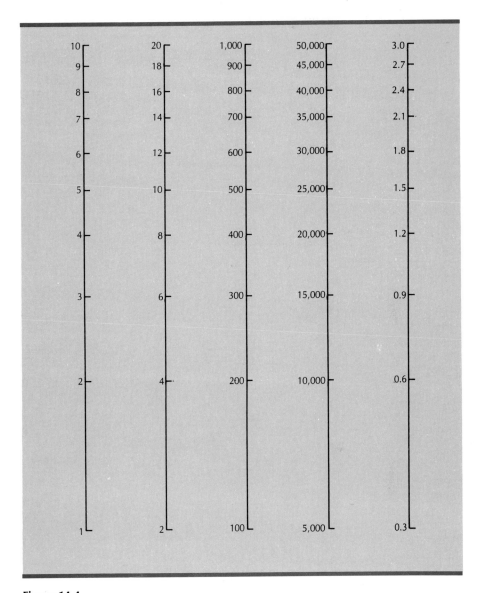

Figure 14.4

as 2 to 20, 100 to 1000, 5000 to 50,000, or .3 to 3. This is illustrated in Fig. 14.4.

Two-cycle paper is suitable for representing a series where the maximum value is not greater than 100 times the minimum value. Thus, two-cycle paper

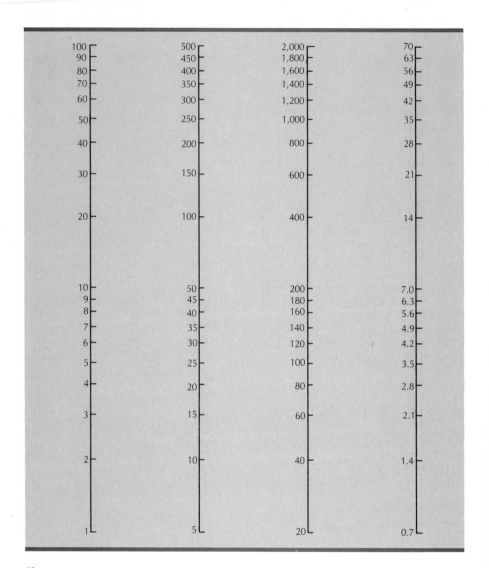

Figure 14.5

is used for a variable that ranges from 1 to 100 or any multiple of this range, such as 5 to 500, 20 to 2000, or .7 to 70 (see Fig. 14.5).

The three-cycle, four-cycle, and five-cycle forms are used to represent variables with a basic range of 1 to 1000, 1 to 10,000, and 1 to 100,000, respectively, or any multiple thereof. Thus, for example, the three-cycle form is suitable not only for a variable with a basic range of 1 to 1000 but also for other

TABLE 14.4   ABC COMPANY ANNUAL PROFIT, 1977–1983

Year	Annual Profit (millions of dollars)
1977	.2
1978	.3
1979	.3
1980	.4
1981	.8
1982	1.8
1983	2.2

TABLE 14.5   VISITORS TO FANTASYLAND, 1969–1983

Year	Visitors (thousands)	Year	Visitors (thousands)
1969	65	1977	280
1970	81	1978	343
1971	95	1979	394
1972	108	1980	440
1973	138	1981	521
1974	167	1982	633
1975	201	1983	768
1976	203		

variables having any multiple of this range, such as 7 to 7000 or .8 to 800.

Before concluding this discussion, we illustrate the use of logarithmic line charts with two or more time series (Tables 14.4 and 14.5, Figs. 14.6 and 14.7).

Figure 14.6   ABC Company annual profits, 1977–1983

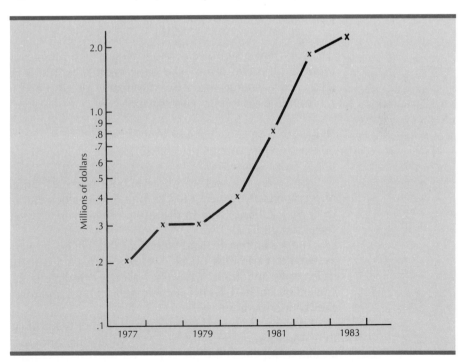

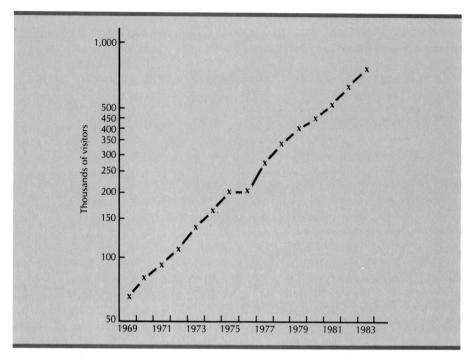

Figure 14.7   Visitors to Fantasyland, 1969–1983

Note that a two-cycle paper with a basic range of 1 to 100 is used to represent the two series. The basic range 1 to 100 is multiplied by .1 in Fig. 14.6, representing the ABC Company profits, and by 50 in Fig. 14.7, representing visitors to Fantasyland.

NATURE OF VARIATIONS IN TIME SERIES

A time series is a set of observations made at various time periods. The observations are represented by numerical values that often vary from period to period. A basic issue in the study of time series is to analyze the nature of these variations.

The variations in time series are classified as systematic and random. **Systematic variations** occur with regularity and can therefore be measured statistically and their future occurrence predicted. **Random variations** are caused by isolated events such as wars, strikes, and tornadoes. Consequently, they cannot be predicted.

Economists have identified three distinct types of systematic variations in time series: secular trend, cyclical variations, and seasonal variations. The **secular trend** describes the general nature of a series over a fairly long period of

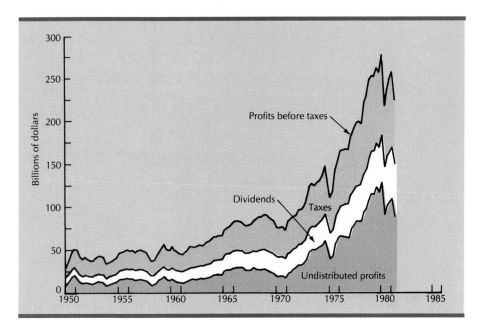

Figure 14.8 Corporate profits, 1950–1980

time. This trend variation is attributed to slowly and gradually moving forces such as population growth, changes in technology, and changes in the habits and tastes of consumers. Depending on the net effect of all these forces, a series may reveal an upward trend, a downward trend, or no trend. Thus, while the corporate profits in the United States have an upward trend, excess reserves of the Federal Reserve member banks have a downward trend (see Figs. 14.8 and 14.9).

When the observations in time series are made at intervals shorter than a year (weekly, monthly, or quarterly), they may exhibit **seasonal variations** that

Figure 14.9 Excess reserves of member banks, 1950–1980

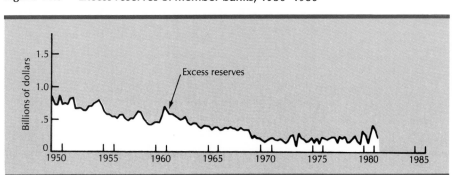

TABLE 14.6 **MONTHLY RETAIL SALES, 1983–1985 (BILLIONS OF DOLLARS)**

	1983	1984	1985
January	18.3	19.2	20.6
February	17.1	18.8	19.6
March	19.7	20.5	21.9
April	20.5	21.2	23.5
May	21.2	22.5	23.8
June	20.7	22.2	23.8
July	20.5	22.1	24.1
August	21.0	21.8	23.0
September	19.2	21.3	22.7
October	21.5	22.6	25.1
November	21.5	21.7	25.2
December	25.1	27.7	30.6

appear in the same fashion and with the same regularity year after year. The variations in total retail sales in the western region of the United States from month to month, for example, appear to be the same each year. While January, February, and September sales are typically low, sales in May, June, October, November, and December are ordinarily high (see Table 14.6 and Fig. 14.10).

Figure 14.10   Monthly retail sales, 1983–1985

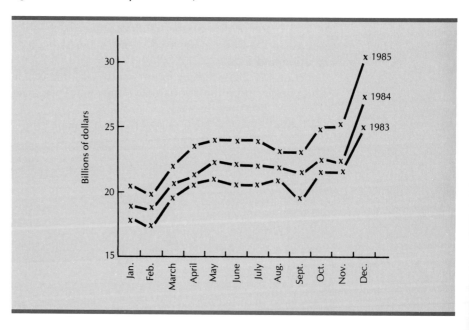

TABLE 14.7   MONTHLY ELECTRIC POWER PRODUCTION, 1982–1984 (BILLIONS OF KILOWATT-HOURS)

	1982	1983	1984
January	90.6	96.6	103.3
February	84.6	88.1	95.0
March	88.0	96.6	101.9
April	84.5	90.3	96.7
May	87.2	93.3	100.6
June	90.6	96.1	105.4
July	95.7	101.6	113.4
August	95.0	103.9	112.3
September	89.5	97.0	102.3
October	89.4	95.7	103.0
November	88.0	95.3	102.7
December	95.7	102.2	109.7

The monthly production of electricity in the western region of the United States also exhibits some considerable seasonal fluctuations; it is typically high in January, July, August, and December. In February and April, production reaches its lowest levels of the year (see Table 14.7 and Fig. 14.11).

Figure 14.11   Monthly electric power production, 1983–1985

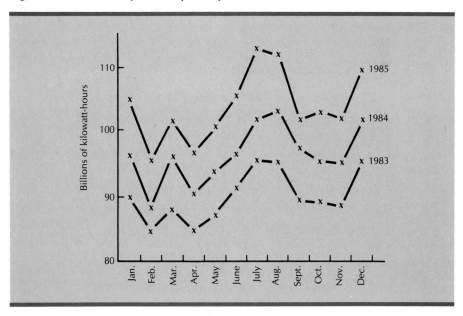

Some other series with marked seasonal variations during the year are currency in circulation, volume of construction, traffic deaths, and automobile sales. Seasonal variations, although largely related to the seasonal changes in nature, are also caused by prevailing customs and habits (Christmas, Easter, Thanksgiving, Fourth of July, Father's Day, Mother's Day, and so on).

The last and least significant type of systematic variation is **cyclical variations.** Some economists believe that business activities undergo some oscillatory movements (peak to trough to peak) every 12 or 15 years. During this period a cycle completes four phases: prosperity, recession, depression, and recovery. The literature on business cycles is voluminous. However, there is no agreement on the nature, causes, or even the existence of such a cycle.

We will study in greater detail the most important types of these variations—secular trends and seasonal variations. Chapter 15 is devoted to the statistical measurement of the secular trend and seasonal variations and to the application of these measures to forecasting.

EXERCISES

14.1 The following data represent the civilian labor force in the United States from 1963 to 1982. Draw an arithmetic line chart of this series.

Civilian Labor Force, 1963–1982					
Year	Labor Force (millions)	Year	Labor Force (millions)	Year	Labor Force (millions)
1963	73.0	1970	82.7	1977	91.4
1964	74.2	1971	84.1	1978	100.4
1965	75.6	1972	86.5	1979	102.9
1966	75.8	1973	88.7	1980	104.7
1967	77.3	1974	91.0	1981	106.9
1968	78.7	1975	92.6	1982	108.9
1969	80.7	1976	94.8		

14.2 The following data represent U.S disposable income from 1960 to 1981. Draw a logarithmic line chart of this series.

	U.S. disposable personal income, 1960–1981				
Year	Disposable Income (billions of dollars)	Year	Disposable Income (billions of dollars)	Year	Disposable Income (billions of dollars)
1960	350	1968	591	1976	1156
1961	364	1969	634	1977	1322
1962	384	1970	690	1978	1463
1963	404	1971	744	1979	1642
1964	436	1972	795	1980	1822
1965	465	1973	903	1981	2016
1966	512	1974	979		
1967	546	1975	1084		

14.3 The following are the numbers (in thousands) of new housing units started each month for three consecutive years. Draw an arithmetic line chart of this series in such a way that it will reveal the seasonal variations of the series.

	New Housing Started (thousands of units)		
	Year 1	Year 2	Year 3
January	69.2	114.8	150.9
February	77.0	102.7	153.6
March	117.8	165.9	205.8
April	130.2	203.6	213.2
May	127.3	203.5	227.9
June	141.6	196.8	226.2
July	143.4	197.0	207.5
August	131.6	205.9	231.0
September	133.4	175.6	204.4
October	143.4	181.7	218.2
November	128.3	176.4	187.1
December	123.9	155.3	152.6

14.4 The following data represent the quantities of commercial fertilizers used in the United States from 1974 to 1981. Draw an arithmetic line chart of this time series.

Year	Quantity of Fertilizer (millions of tons)	Year	Quantity of Fertilizer (millions of tons)
1974	47.1	1978	50.7
1975	48.2	1979	51.5
1976	49.1	1980	52.6
1977	50.2	1981	53.5

14.5 Farm debts outstanding, in billions of dollars, for the years 1974 through 1980 are shown as follows. Draw a logarithmic line chart of this time series.

Year	Farm Debt (billions of dollars)	Year	Farm Debt (billions of dollars)
1974	74.1	1978	119.3
1975	81.8	1979	136.1
1976	90.4	1980	157.9
1977	102.6	1981	174.5

14.6 The following information describes total annual retail sales in the United States, in billions of dollars, for the years 1974–1981. Draw a logarithmic line chart of this time series.

Year	Sales (billions of dollars)	Year	Sales (billions of dollars)
1974	537.7	1978	800.9
1975	580.4	1979	894.3
1976	642.5	1980	956.6
1977	724.0	1981	1045.7

14.7 The following are the monthly sales, in millions of dollars, of apparel and accessory stores for the years 1979–1981. Draw an arithmetic line chart of this time series in such a way that it will reveal the seasonal variations of the series.

	Apparel and Accessory Sales (millions of dollars)		
	1979	*1980*	*1981*
January	2689	3061	3279
February	2416	2796	2911
March	3154	3351	3448
April	3267	3508	3972
May	3204	3608	3755
June	3174	3383	3632
July	3015	3343	3598
August	3628	4010	4126
September	3368	3664	3929
October	3555	4026	4234
November	3886	4262	4256
December	6201	6569	6648

14.8 The following data represent farm employment in the United States from 1970 to 1980. Draw an arithmetic line chart of this time series.

Year	Employment (thousands)	Year	Employment (thousands)
1970	4523	1976	4374
1971	4436	1977	4170
1972	4373	1978	3957
1973	4337	1979	3774
1974	4389		
1975	4342		

14.9 The monthly sales of eating and drinking places, in millions of dollars, for the years 1979–1981 are shown below. Draw an arithmetic line chart of this time series in such a way that it will reveal the seasonal variation of the series.

	Sales, Eating and Drinking Places (millions of dollars)		
	1979	1980	1981
January	5389	6023	7065
February	5339	5871	6742
March	6373	6485	7710
April	6222	6613	7897
May	6472	7022	8344
June	6655	7011	8264
July	6681	7158	8524
August	7006	7428	8588
September	6482	6824	8073
October	6502	7047	8271
November	6351	6590	7702
December	6613	6768	8102

KEY TERMS

time series   A set of observations made at consecutive time periods.

arithmetic line chart   A graph of a time series that uses an arithmetic vertical scale and indicates absolute changes.

logarithmic line chart   A graph of a time series that uses a logarithmic vertical scale and indicates percentage changes.

systematic variations   Changes in the values of a time series that occur with regularity; they can be both measured and predicted.

random variations   Changes in the values of a time series that are caused by isolated events; they cannot be predicted.

secular trend   A long-term trend in a time series that may be either upward or downward.

seasonal variations Variations in a time series that occur regularly in accordance with changes in the calendar. Seasonal variations can be quarterly, monthly, or weekly.

cyclical variations Regular variations that occur over a period of many years.

FORECASTING WITH TIME SERIES

15

In the previous chapter we discussed the nature of time series, the reasons for their variations, and the methods used to represent them graphically. This chapter describes the use of time series in forecasting. We will learn how to measure the secular trend, how to measure seasonal variations, and how to combine these measurements to forecast future business activities.

The secular trend describes the general movement of a time series over a fairly long period of time. For some time series, this general movement is well described by a straight line. For others, it can be described only by one of several standard types of trend curves. The most common and most important of these curves is the exponential or compound interest trend curve. Thus, in addition to the straight-line trend, only the exponential trend curve is discussed here.

STRAIGHT-LINE TREND

The trend of a time series can be described by a **straight-line trend** only when during each time interval the series increases or decreases at a constant or nearly constant absolute amount. The adequacy of the straight line to describe the trend of such a series becomes apparent once the arithmetic line chart of a series is drawn. To illustrate the use of a straight-line trend, let us consider the time series given in Table 15.1.

Since the annual increase in the annual sales is nearly constant, a straight-line trend curve is most appropriate. Its desirability becomes more apparent if we examine the arithmetic line chart of this series in Fig. 15.1.

We determine a straight-line trend, using the least-squares method of regression analysis. The general equation is

$$Y = a + bX,$$

where Y denotes annual sales and X represents time.

TABLE 15.1 STANDARD CORPORATION ANNUAL SALES, 1974–1983

Year X	Sales (millions of dollars) Y	Change in Y
1974	13	
1975	15	2
1976	18	3
1977	20	2
1978	24	4
1979	27	3
1980	30	3
1981	32	2
1982	35	3
1983	36	1

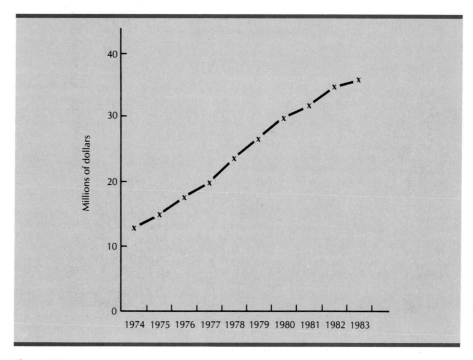

Figure 15.1

There are several ways of using the variable *X* to represent time. One convenient way is to set *X* = 0 for the first year in the series, *X* = 1 for the second year, *X* = 2 for the third year, and so on. For the time series under consideration, the variable *X* assumes the value 0 in 1974, the value 1 in 1975, the value 2 in 1976, and the value 9 in 1983, as shown in the following chart.

Year	74	75	76	77	78	79	80	81	82	83
X	0	1	2	3	4	5	6	7	8	9

The year 1974, for which *X* is set equal to 0, is called the origin.

With 1974 as the origin, we can readily determine the value of *X* in any other year. For example, in 1979, *X* = 5, in 1971, *X* = −3, and in 1959, *X* = −15. Thus, choosing 1974 as the origin, we can present our time series as shown in Table 15.2.

Using the least-squares method to determine the constants *a* and *b* in the trend equation *Y* = *a* + *bX*, we first perform the preliminary computations presented in Table 15.3.

TABLE 15.2

Year	X	Y
1974	0	13
1975	1	15
1976	2	18
1977	3	20
1978	4	24
1979	5	27
1980	6	30
1981	7	32
1982	8	35
1983	9	36

The next step is to convert $\sum X^2$ and $\sum XY$ into $\sum x^2$ and $\sum xy$, respectively. Thus,

$$\sum x^2 = \sum X^2 - n(\bar{X})^2$$
$$= 285 - 10(4.5)^2 = 82.5,$$

and

$$\sum xy = \sum XY - n(\bar{X})(\bar{Y})$$
$$= 1350 - (10)(4.5)(25) = 225.$$

TABLE 15.3

X	Y	X^2	XY
0	13	0	0
1	15	1	15
2	18	4	36
3	20	9	60
4	24	16	96
5	27	25	135
6	30	36	180
7	32	49	224
8	35	64	280
9	36	81	324
$\sum X = 45$	$\sum Y = 250$	$\sum X^2 = 285$	$\sum XY = 1350$
	$\bar{Y} = ^{45}\!/_{10} = 4.5$	$\bar{Y} = ^{250}\!/_{10} = 25$	

Finally, the values of the constants *a* and *b* are determined as follows:

$$b = \frac{\sum xy}{\sum x^2} \qquad a = \bar{Y} - b(\bar{X})$$
$$= \frac{225}{82.5} \qquad = 25 - 2.727(4.5)$$
$$= 25 - 12.271$$
$$= 2.727, \qquad = 12.729.$$

The secular trend equation now becomes

$$Y' = 12.729 + 2.727X,$$

where the origin is 1974; *X*-units are 1 year; and *Y* is annual sales in millions of dollars.

Note that each trend equation must be accompanied by a legend indicating the year of origin and the units in which both variables *X* and *Y* are measured. This legend is an indispensable part of any trend equation.

The above trend equation indicates that the annual sales of the Standard Corporation increase, on average, $2.727 million each year. The value $2.727 million is called the *annual trend increment.* The trend equation, furthermore, enables us to predict the annual sales for any future year. For example, for 1986, annual sales are estimated as

$$Y' = 12.729 + 2.727(12)$$
$$= 12.727 + 32.724$$
$$= \$45.453 \text{ million}$$

and for 1991 as

$$Y' = 12.729 + 2.727(17)$$
$$= 12.729 + 46.359$$
$$= \$59.808 \text{ million}$$

How valid are these forecasts? Forecasts based on the extrapolation of trends are meaningful only if there is reason to believe that the forces that have prevailed in the past will continue to prevail in the future. Even so, forecasts should be considered as benchmarks to be modified by the forecaster's judgment and experience.

Before concluding this discussion we will determine the trend values for each of the years 1974 to 1983 (Table 15.4) and compare them with the actual sales in these years.. The trend values are obtained by substituting 0, 1, 2, . . . , 9 for *X* in the trend equation $Y' = 12.729 + 2.727X$.

TABLE 15.4

Year	Annual Sales Y	Trend Value Y'
1974	13	12.729
1975	15	15.456
1976	18	18.183
1977	20	20.190
1978	24	23.637
1979	27	26.364
1980	30	29.091
1981	32	31.818
1982	35	34.545
1983	36	37.272

Finally, we may want to draw the trend line on the arithmetic line chart of the series. We do this by plotting the trend values for any two years, say 1977 and 1980, and connecting the two points by a straight line (see Fig. 15.2).

Figure 15.2

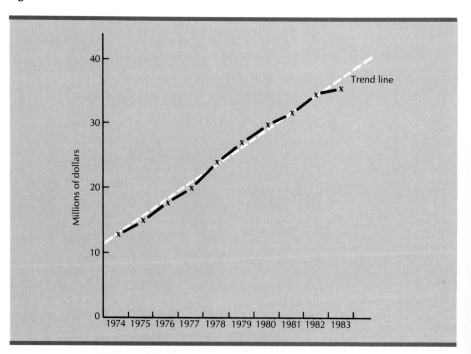

Shifting the Origin of a Trend Equation

For computational purposes it may be convenient to shift the origin of a trend equation to some other period of time. In the trend equation

$$Y' = 12.729 + 2.727X,$$

where the origin is 1974; X-units are 1 year; and Y is annual sales in millions of dollars, it may be convenient, for example, to shift the origin from 1974 to 1980. This means that the variable X assumes the value 0 in 1980, 1 in 1981, 2 in 1982, and so on. To accomplish such a shift, only the constant a in the trend equation has to be changed.

To shift the origin of the trend equation $Y' = 12.729 + 2.727X$ from 1974 to 1980, the constant term a (12.729) of this equation is replaced by the 1980 trend value:

$$Y'_{1980} = 12.729 + 2.727(6)$$
$$= 12.729 + 16.362 = 29.091.$$

The modified trend equation becomes

$$Y' = 29.091 + 2.727X,$$

where the origin is 1980; X-units are 1 year; and Y is annual sales in millions of dollars.

In computing the trend value for any year, say 1981, we must use either the original or the modified trend equation. Using the original trend equation with the 1974 origin, we obtain the 1981 trend value by setting $X = 7$:

$$Y'_{1981} = 12.729 + 2.727(7)$$
$$= 12.729 + 19.089 = \$31.818 \text{ million.}$$

Using the modified trend equation with the 1981 origin, we determine the trend value by setting $X = 1$:

$$Y'_{1981} = 29.091 + 2.727(1)$$
$$= 29.091 + 2.727 = \$31.818 \text{ million.}$$

Thus the 1981 trend values derived from the two equations are identical.

Now let us consider an alternative example. Given the trend equation

$$Y' = 600 + 5X,$$

where the origin is 1980; X-units are 1 year; and Y is annual sales in millions of dollars, we want to shift the origin to 1988. We do this in the following two steps.

Step 1. Compute the 1988 trend value by setting $X = 8$ in the original equation:

$$Y'_{1988} = 600 + 5(8) = 640.$$

Step 2. Use the 1988 trend value as the constant a in the modified equation:

$$Y' = 640 + 5X,$$

where the origin is 1988; X-units are 1 year; and Y is annual sales in millions of dollars.

Converting a Trend Equation from an Annual to a Monthly Basis

Further analysis of a time series may require changing a trend equation from an annual to a monthly basis. Such a conversion is usually required when we analyze the seasonal variations of a time series. To see how this conversion is accomplished, let us consider the time series

$$Y' = 12,000 + 2880X, \qquad (A)$$

where the origin is 1980; X-units are 1 year; and Y is annual sales in dollars.

Using the above trend equation, we compute the trend values for the annual sales for the years 1980, 1981, and 1982 as follows.

Year	X	Annual Sales (Trend Values) Y'
1980	0	$12,000 + 2880(0) = \$12,000$
1981	1	$12,000 + 2880(1) = \$14,880$
1982	2	$12,000 + 2880(2) = \$17,760$

The average monthly sale trend values for any one of these years can now be obtained by dividing the annual sales trend values by 12.

Year	X	Average Monthly Sales (Trend Values) Y'
1980	0	$12,000 \div 12 = \$1000$
1981	1	$14,880 \div 12 = \$1240$
1982	2	$17,760 \div 12 = \$1480$

Alternatively, we can compute the average monthly trend values from a modified trend equation, which we obtain by dividing the constants a and b of the original annual trend equation by 12:

$$Y' = {}^{12000}/_{12} + {}^{2880}/_{12}\, X = 1000 + 240X, \qquad \text{(B)}$$

where the origin is 1980; X-units are 1 year; and Y is the average monthly sales in dollars.

Using the modified trend equation as computed in Eq. (B), we get the average monthly sales trend values for the years 1980, 1981, and 1982 as follows.

Year	X	Average Monthly Sales (Trend Values) Y'
1980	0	$1000 + 240(0) = \$1000$
1981	1	$1000 + 240(1) = \$1240$
1982	2	$1000 + 240(2) = \$1480$

These monthly trend values are the same as the ones we obtained previously.

In examining the modified trend equation

$$Y' = 1000 + 240X, \qquad \text{(B)}$$

where the origin is 1980; X-units are 1 year; and Y is the average monthly sales in dollars, note that while the variable Y represents the average monthly sales, the units in which the variable X is measured are years. Specifically, note that the value of X is 0 in 1980, 1 in 1981, 2 in 1982, and so on. With the value of X measured in years, the equation $Y = 1000 + 240X$ indicates that the average monthly sales increase at the rate of $240 *per year.*

The modified trend equation

$$Y' = 1000 + 240X, \qquad \text{(B)}$$

where the origin is 1980; X-units are 1 year; and Y is the average monthly sales in dollars, gives the trend value for the average month of any given year. For 1980, for example, it is $1000 (obtained by setting $X = 0$ in the equation). But which month is the average month in 1980? With a straight-line trend, the average month is an artificial month consisting of the latter half of June and the first half of July, designated as June–July 1980. The June–July month is the average month of the year regardless of whether the trend of a series is upward, downward, or constant, so long as the trend of the series is a straight line.

Once again, the modified trend equation

$$Y' = 1000 + 240X, \qquad \text{(B)}$$

where the origin is 1980; X-units are 1 year; and Y is the average monthly sales in dollars, indicates that the trend value for June–July 1980 is $1000. Since X is measured in years, it also indicates that the average monthly sales trend value increases at the rate of $240 *per year.* Consequently, the average monthly sales trend value increases at the rate of $240/12, or $20 *per month.*

With a June–July 1980 trend value of $1000 and a trend increment of $20 per month, we are now able to determine the trend value for any month. The trend value for July 1980, for example, is $1000 + 20(1/2) = \$1010$. (The time elapsed between June–July 1980 and July 1980 is only half a month. Thus only half the monthly trend increment is added to the June–July 1980 trend value.) The trend value for January 1980, on the other hand, is

$$1000 - 20(5\frac{1}{2}) = \$890.$$

(The time elapsed between January 1980 and June–July 1980 is $5\frac{1}{2}$. Consequently, $5\frac{1}{2}$ times the monthly trend is subtracted from the June–July 1980 trend value.)

The monthly trend values can also be determined directly from an equation obtained by dividing the coefficient b in the modified equation $Y' = 1000 + 240X$ by 12. This equation is

$$Y' = 1000 + \frac{240X}{12} \tag{C}$$

$$= 1000 + 20X,$$

where the origin is June–July 1980; X-units are 1 *month;* and Y is monthly sales in dollars.

Using Eq. (C), we determine the monthly trend values by setting $X = 0$ for June–July 1980, $X = \frac{1}{2}$ for July 1980, $X = 1\frac{1}{2}$ for August 1980, $X = -4\frac{1}{2}$ for February 1980, $X = 13\frac{1}{2}$ for August 1981, and so on.

However, for ease of computation, it may be convenient to shift the origin of the equation $Y' = 1000 + 20X$ from June–July 1980 to January 1980. This can be accomplished by replacing the constant a in the equation $Y' = 1000 + 20X$ by the January 1980 trend value:

$$Y'_{\text{Jan. 1980}} = 1000 + 20(-5\frac{1}{2})$$

$$= \$890.$$

The final equation is
$$Y' = 890 + 20(X), \tag{D}$$

where the origin is January 1980; X-units are 1 *month;* and Y is monthly sales in dollars.

To summarize our previous discussion, let us repeat that the annual trend equation
$$Y' = 12,000 + 2880X, \tag{A}$$

where the origin is 1980; X-units are 1 year; and Y is annual sales in dollars, can be converted to a monthly basis by dividing the constant a by 12 and the constant b by 144 (the constant b is divided twice by 12):

$$Y' = \frac{12,000}{12} + \frac{2880X}{144} \tag{C}$$
$$= 1000 + 20X,$$

where the origin is June–July 1980; X-units are 1 *month;* and Y is monthly sales in dollars.

To simplify our computations, we shift the origin of this modified equation $5\frac{1}{2}$ months back into January 1980. We do this by computing the January 1980 trend value:

$$Y'_{\text{Jan. 1980}} = 1000 + 20(-5\frac{1}{2})$$
$$= 1000 - 110 = 890.$$

Thus the January 1980 trend value becomes the constant a in the final equation:

$$Y' = 890 + 20X, \tag{D}$$

where the origin is January 1980; X-units are 1 *month;* and Y is monthly sales in dollars.

Using this final equation, let us determine the monthly trend values for all the months in 1980 (see Table 15.5). Note that the total annual trend values for 1980 (computed from the monthly trend values) equal the annual trend values

TABLE 15-5

Month	X	Trend Value Y'	
January	0	$890 + 20(0)$	$=$ 890
February	1	$890 + 20(1)$	$=$ 910
March	2	$890 + 20(2)$	$=$ 930
April	3	$890 + 20(3)$	$=$ 950
May	4	$890 + 20(4)$	$=$ 970
June	5	$890 + 20(5)$	$=$ 990
July	6	$890 + 20(6)$	$=$ 1010
August	7	$890 + 20(7)$	$=$ 1030
September	8	$890 + 20(8)$	$=$ 1050
October	9	$890 + 20(9)$	$=$ 1070
November	10	$890 + 20(10)$	$=$ 1090
December	11	$890 + 20(11)$	$=$ 1110
Total = 1980 annual trend values			$12,000

for 1980 obtained from the annual version of the trend equation

$$Y' = 12,000 + 2880X,$$

where the origin is 1980; X-units are 1 year; and Y is the annual sales in dollars.

Before concluding this discussion, let us consider another annual trend equation:

$$Y' = 12.729 + 2.727X,$$

where the origin is 1974; X-units are 1 year; and Y is annual sales in millions of dollars. To convert this trend equation to a monthly basis, we divide the constant a by 12 and the constant b by 144, obtaining the following modified trend equation:

$$Y' = \frac{2.729}{12} + \frac{2.72X}{144} = 1.0608 + .0189X, \tag{E}$$

where the origin is June–July 1974; X-units are 1 *month;* and Y is monthly sales in millions of dollars.

The origin of Eq. (E) is then shifted 5½ months back to January 1974 by computing the January 1964 trend value:

$$Y'_{\text{Jan. 1974}} = 1.0608 + 0.0189(-5\tfrac{1}{2})$$
$$= 1.0608 - 0.1040 = 0.9568,$$

which becomes the constant a in the equation

$$Y' = .9568 + .0189X,$$

where the origin is January 1974; X-units are 1 *month;* and Y is monthly sales in millions of dollars. This new trend equation can be used to determine the monthly trend value for all the months in 1974 (see Table 15.6).

EXPONENTIAL TREND

An **exponential trend** curve describes the trend of a series that reveals a constant (or nearly constant) *percentage* increase or decrease during each period. If a time series increases 10% per year, for example, its trend can be described exactly by an exponential curve that has the general equation

$$\log Y' = a + bX.*$$

---

*This equation is derived from the compound interest equation

$$Y = Y_0(1 + r)^x,$$

where Y_0 is the present value of money invested at an interest rate r. The value of the investment at the end of X years is Y. Expressed in logarithms this equation becomes

$$\log Y = \log Y_0 + X \log (1 + r).$$

Denoting $\log Y_0$ by a and $\log (1 + r)$ by b, we find that this logarithmic equation becomes

$$\log Y' = a + bX.$$

TABLE 15.6

Month	X	Trend Value (millions of dollars) Y'
January	0	.9568 + .0189(0) = .9568
February	1	.9568 + .0189(1) = .9757
March	2	.9568 + .0189(2) = .9946
April	3	.9568 + .0189(3) = 1.0135
May	4	.9568 + .0189(4) = 1.0324
June	5	.9568 + .0189(5) = 1.0513
July	6	.9568 + .0189(6) = 1.0702
August	7	.9568 + .0189(7) = 1.0891
September	8	.9568 + .0189(8) = 1.1080
October	9	.9568 + .0189(9) = 1.1269
November	10	.9568 + .0189(10) = 1.1458
December	11	.9568 + .0189(11) = 1.1647
Total = 1974 annual trend values		12.729

The constants a and b in this general equation are determined by the least-squares method of regression. The dependent variable in this regression, however, is log Y instead of Y.

To illustrate the use of the exponential trend curve, let us consider the time series shown in Table 15.7. Since in most years, the number of visitors

TABLE 15.7 VISITORS TO FANTASYLAND, 1969–1983

Year X	Number of Visitors Y	Percentage Change in Number of Visitors
1969	64,508	
1970	81,307	26
1971	95,386	17
1972	108,332	14
1973	137,900	27
1974	167,181	21
1975	201,214	20
1976	203,037	1
1977	279,697	38
1978	342,922	23
1979	393,697	15
1980	440,459	13
1981	520,801	17
1982	632,894	22
1983	767,500	21

TABLE 15.8

Y	log Y	Y	log Y
64,508	4.8096	279,697	5.4472
81,307	4.9101	342,922	5.5353
95,386	4.9795	393,697	5.5955
108,332	5.0334	440,459	5.6435
137,900	5.1399	520,801	5.7168
167,181	5.2227	632,894	5.8014
201,214	5.3032	769,500	5.8854
203,037	5.3075		

increases about 20%, an exponential trend curve is appropriate to use in this case.

Using the least-squares method to determine the constants a and b in the equation $\log Y' = a + bX$, we must first obtain the logarithm of Y for each year (see Table 15.8).

Once the conversion of Y into logarithms is completed, we carry out the preliminary computations required by the least-squares method (Table 15.9).

TABLE 15.9

X	log Y	X^2	X log Y
0	4.8096	0	0
1	4.9101	1	4.9101
2	4.9795	4	9.9590
3	5.0334	9	15.1002
4	5.1399	16	20.5596
5	5.2227	25	26.1135
6	5.3032	36	31.8192
7	5.3075	49	37.1525
8	5.4472	64	43.5776
9	5.5353	81	49.8177
10	5.5955	100	55.9550
11	5.6435	121	62.0785
12	5.7168	144	68.6016
13	5.8014	169	75.4182
14	5.8854	196	82.3956
$\sum X = 105$	$\sum \log Y = 80.3310$	$\sum X^2 = 1015$	$\sum X \log Y = 583.4583$

$$\bar{X} = \frac{105}{15} = 7 \qquad \text{Mean log } Y = \frac{80.3310}{15} = 5.3554$$

The next step is to convert $\sum X^2$ and $\sum X \log Y$ into $\sum x^2$ and $\sum x \log y$, respectively. Thus,

$$\sum x^2 = \sum X^2 - n(\bar{X})^2$$
$$= 1015 - 15(7)$$
$$= 1015 - 735 = 280,$$

and

$$\sum x \log y = \sum X \log Y - n(\bar{X})(\text{mean } \log Y)$$
$$= 583.4583 - 15(7)(5.3554)$$
$$= 583.4583 - 562.3170$$
$$= 21.1413.$$

Finally, we determine a and b:

$$b = \frac{\sum x \log y}{\sum x^2} \qquad a = \text{mean } \log Y - b(\bar{X})$$
$$\qquad\qquad\qquad = 5.3554 - .0755(7)$$
$$= \frac{21.1413}{280} \qquad = 4.8269.$$
$$= .0755,$$

Thus the exponential trend equation becomes

$$\log Y' = 4.8269 + .0755X, \qquad\qquad (F)$$

where the origin is 1969; X-units are 1 year; and Y is annual visitors to Fantasyland. The trend equation (F) can be used to estimate the number of visitors to Fantasyland for any future year. For 1988, for example, we compute this estimate by setting $X = 19$ in the trend equation:

$$\log Y'_{1988} = 4.8269 + .0755(19)$$
$$= 4.8269 + 1.4345$$
$$= 6.2614.$$

The expected number of visitors in 1988 is then determined as the antilog of 6.2614, which is 1,830,000.

You may be interested in finding the average annual percentage increase (r) in the number of visitors to Fantasyland:

$$r = (\text{antilog } b) - 1$$
$$= (\text{antilog } .0755) - 1$$
$$= 1.19 - 1 = .19, \quad \text{or } 19\%.$$

You may also be interested in plotting the trend of this series. On a logarithmic line chart, the exponential trend is a straight line that joins the trend values of any two years. Plotted on an arithmetic line chart, it is a curve. To plot our exponential trend, we must first determine the trend values for any two years, such as 1969 and 1979:

$$\log Y'_{1969} = 4.8269 + .0755(0)$$
$$= 4.8269.$$

Therefore,

$$Y'_{1969} = 67,100$$

and

$$\log Y'_{1979} = 4.8269 + .0755(10)$$
$$= 4.8269 + .7550 = 5.5819.$$

Hence,

$$Y'_{1979} = 382,000.$$

When the 1969 and 1979 trend values are plotted on a logarithmic line chart, the straight line joining these two points is the exponential trend of the series (see Fig. 15.3).

Figure 15.3

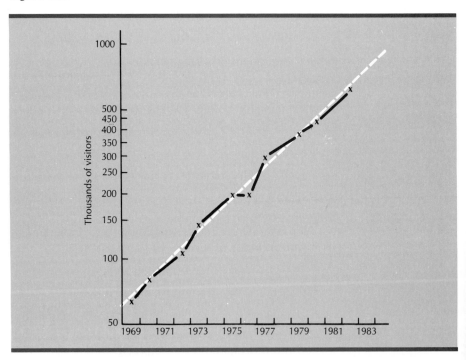

SEASONAL VARIATIONS

Let us consider the time series in Table 15.10 representing monthly retail sales of the XYZ Corporation.

The retail sales series reveals some marked seasonal variations from month to month, which are measured by establishing a **seasonal index** for each month. The index for any given month expresses the sales for the month as a percentage of the average monthly sales. If December's seasonal index is 122%, for example, then the sales in December are typically 122% of those of the average month of the year.

Before constructing the monthly seasonal indexes, however, we must remove the variations due to the trend, as well as any random variations. To do this, we proceed as follows.

Step 1. Determine the annual trend equation for the various years in the series.

Using the least-squares method, we first carry out the preliminary computations shown in Table 15.11.

Next we must convert $\sum X^2$ and $\sum XY$ into $\sum x^2$ and $\sum xy$, respectively. Thus,

$$\sum x^2 = \sum X^2 - n(\bar{X})^2$$
$$= 30 - 5(2)^2 = 10,$$

TABLE 15.10   **MONTHLY RETAIL SALES, 1979–1983 (MILLIONS OF DOLLARS)**

	1979	1980	1981	1982	1983
January	15.8	17.0	18.3	19.2	20.6
February	15.0	16.0	17.1	18.8	19.6
March	17.9	19.0	19.7	20.5	21.9
April	17.4	19.3	20.5	21.2	23.5
May	18.5	20.2	21.2	22.5	23.8
June	18.9	20.3	20.7	22.2	23.8
July	17.9	19.1	20.5	22.1	24.1
August	18.3	19.9	21.0	21.8	23.0
September	18.1	18.9	19.2	21.3	22.7
October	18.8	20.6	21.5	22.6	25.1
November	19.2	20.9	21.5	21.7	25.2
December	22.9	24.1	25.1	27.7	30.6
Total	218.7	235.3	246.3	261.6	283.9

TABLE 15.11

Year	X	Annual Sales Y	X^2	XY
1979	0	218.7	0	0
1980	1	235.3	1	235.3
1981	2	246.3	4	492.6
1982	3	261.6	9	784.8
1983	4	283.9	16	1135.6
	$\sum X = 10$	$\sum Y = 1245.8$	$\sum X^2 = 30$	$\sum XY = 2648.3$

$$\bar{X} = \frac{10}{5} \qquad \bar{Y} = \frac{1245.8}{5}$$

$$= 2 \qquad\qquad = 249.16$$

and

$$\sum xy = \sum XY - n(\bar{X})(\bar{Y})$$
$$= 2648.3 - (5)(2)(249.16)$$
$$= 2648.3 - 2491.6 = 156.7.$$

We then determine the constants a and b of the trend equation:

$$b = \frac{\sum xy}{\sum x^2} \qquad a = \bar{Y} - b\bar{X}$$
$$= 249.16 - (15.67)(2)$$
$$= \frac{156.7}{10} \qquad = 249.16 - 31.34$$
$$= 217.82.$$
$$= 15.67,$$

The annual trend equation thus becomes

$$Y' = 217.82 + 15.67X,$$

where the origin is 1979; X-units are 1 year; and Y is the annual retail sales in millions of dollars.

Step 2. Convert the annual trend equation to a monthly basis.

This conversion is accomplished by dividing the constant a by 12 and the constant b by 144. We obtain the modified trend equation

$$Y' = \frac{217.82}{12} + \frac{15.67}{144} X$$
$$= 18.15167 + .10882X,$$

where the origin is June–July 1979; X-units are 1 month; and Y is monthly retail sales in millions of dollars.

TABLE 15.12 **MONTHLY TREND VALUES**

	1979	1980	1981	1982	1983
January	17.55	18.86	20.16	21.47	22.78
February	17.66	18.97	20.27	21.58	22.89
March	17.77	19.08	20.38	21.69	22.99
April	17.88	19.19	20.49	21.80	23.10
May	17.99	19.29	20.60	21.91	23.21
June	18.10	19.40	20.71	22.01	23.32
July	18.21	19.51	20.82	22.12	23.43
August	18.31	19.62	20.93	22.23	23.54
September	18.42	19.73	21.04	22.34	23.65
October	18.53	19.84	21.14	22.45	23.76
November	18.64	19.95	21.25	22.56	23.86
December	18.75	20.06	21.36	22.67	23.97

To facilitate subsequent computations, the origin of the monthly trend equation is shifted to the first month, January 1979. The final monthly trend equation thus becomes

$$Y' = 17.55316 + .10882X,^*$$

where the origin is January 1979; X-units are 1 month; and Y is monthly retail sales in millions of dollars.

Step 3. Determine the monthly trend value for every month in the series.

Using the final trend equation

$$Y' = 17.55316 + .10882X,$$

where the origin is January 1979; X-units are 1 month; and Y is monthly sales in millions of dollars, we determine the various trend values by setting $X = 0$ for January 1979, $X = 1$ for February 1979, $X = 2$ for March 1979, . . . , $X = 12$ for January 1980, $X = 13$ for February 1980, and so on. The trend values for all the months of the series are shown in Table 15.12.

Step 4. Divide the actual sales in each month by the respective monthly trend value.

To eliminate the trend variation from this series, the actual sales in each month are divided by the respective trend value computed in step 3. In other words, the actual sales in each month are expressed as a percentage of the monthly trend value. These percentages are shown in Table 15.13.

---

*You should verify this equation by shifting the origin of the equation, $Y' = 18.15167 + .10882X$, back 5½ months.

TABLE 15.13

	1979	1980	1981	1982	1983
January	.9003	.9014	.9077	.8943	.9043
February	.8494	.8434	.8436	.8712	.8563
March	1.0073	.9958	.9666	.9451	.9526
April	.9732	1.0057	1.0005	.9725	1.0173
May	1.0283	1.0472	1.0291	1.0269	1.0254
June	1.0442	1.0464	.9995	1.0086	1.0206
July	.9830	.9790	.9846	.9991	1.0286
August	.9995	1.0143	1.0033	.8807	.9771
September	.9826	.9579	.9125	.9534	.9598
October	1.0146	1.0383	1.0170	1.0067	1.0564
November	1.0300	1.0476	1.0118	.9618	1.0562
December	1.2213	1.2014	1.1751	1.2219	1.2766

The first entry in the table, .9003, is obtained by dividing the actual sales in January 1979, which are 15.8, by the trend value of that month, 17.55. The second entry, .8494 is obtained by dividing the actual sales in February 1979, which are 15.0, by the trend value of that month, 17.66. The remaining entries in the table are similarly determined.

Step 5.   Determine the average ratio in each month.

Random variations in the series are eliminated by averaging the five ratios in each month. The arithmetic mean of the five ratios of January, for example, is

$$\frac{.9003 + .9014 + .9077 + .8943 + .9043}{5} = .9016$$

The arithmetic means of the ratios for other months are determined in a similar manner. These means are shown in the first column of Table 15.14. Although the mean ratios recorded in column 1 are satisfactory measures of the seasonal variations in the series, they are modified slightly to agree with the definition of the seasonal index. The index for any given month should express that month's sales as a percentage of the average month's sales. Consequently, the sum of the 12 values of the indexes must be 12.

Since the sum of the mean ratio column is 11.9875, each value in this column should be multiplied by 12/11.9875 to make the sum equal to 12. Thus the January mean ratio of .9016 in column 1 is multiplied by 12/11.9875 to give the January index of .9025 in column 2. Other values of the seasonal indexes in column 2 are obtained in a similar fashion from their corresponding values in column 1. With this modification of the mean ratios, the sum of the seasonal indexes in column 2 is 12.

TABLE 15.14

	(1) Mean Ratio	(2) Seasonal Index
January	.9016	.9025
February	.8528	.8537
March	.9735	.9745
April	.9938	.9948
May	1.0314	1.0325
June	1.0239	1.0205
July	.9949	.9959
August	.9950	.9960
September	.9532	.9542
October	1.0266	1.0277
November	1.0215	1.0226
December	1.2193	1.2206
Total	11.9875	12.0000

Before concluding this discussion, we wish to point out that there are several methods of constructing seasonal indexes. In constructing our seasonal indexes, we have used the ratio-to-trend method. Next we will deal with the various uses of seasonal indexes.

Seasonal Adjustment

When the actual amount in any month is divided by the seasonal index of that particular month, the resulting value is called *deseasonalized* or **seasonally adjusted time series.** The seasonally adjusted sales in January 1983, for example, can be obtained by dividing the actual sales in January 1983 by the January seasonal index:

$$\text{Seasonally adjusted sales} = \text{Actual sales} \div \text{Seasonal index}$$
$$= 20.6 \qquad \div .9025$$
$$= \$22.8 \text{ million.}$$

This January 1983 seasonally adjusted sales figure of $22.8 million can be interpreted as follows: Assuming that the seasonal variations in 1983 conform to the typical pattern described by the seasonal indexes, then the actual sales of $20.6 million in January 1983 imply average monthly sales of $22.8 million for the year 1983. For this reason the result obtained by multiplying the monthly seasonally adjusted sales by 12 is called seasonally adjusted sales at *annual rates.* The seasonally adjusted monthly sales for all the months in 1983, together with their respective annual rates, are shown in Table 15.15.

As explained earlier, each of the actual monthly sales figures in column 1 is divided by the corresponding seasonal index in column 2 and the result is entered in column 3 as the seasonally adjusted monthly sales. The seasonally adjusted sales in column 3 are then multiplied by 12 to give the seasonally adjusted sales at the annual rate in column 4.

The significance of the seasonally adjusted sales becomes clearer if the sales performances in two months are compared. Comparing the sales in February and March, for instance, we notice that the actual sales in March are much higher than those in February. This fact may lead us to believe, at first, that there is a real improvement in the sales activity in March over that in February. However, examination of the seasonal indexes for the two months reveals that the sales level in March is typically higher than that in February. The seasonally adjusted sales for March, furthermore, show a decline from those in February. The reason for this decline is that the increase in actual sales between the two months was much less than the expected normal gain based on the typical seasonal pattern of sales variation.

In comparing the two levels of sales activity, we must therefore conclude that February is a better month than March. While the $19.6 million actual sales in February imply average monthly sales of $23.0 million, the $21.9 million actual sales in March imply average monthly sales of $22.5 million. Expressed on an annual rate basis, the actual sales in February imply total

TABLE 15.15

	(1) Actual Sales	(2) Seasonal Index	(3) Seasonally Adjusted Monthly Sales	(4) Seasonally Adjusted Sales at Annual Rates
January	20.6	.9025	22.8	273.6
February	19.6	.8537	23.0	276.0
March	21.9	.9745	22.5	270.0
April	23.5	.9948	23.6	283.2
May	23.8	1.0325	23.1	277.2
June	23.8	1.0250	23.2	278.4
July	24.1	.9959	24.2	290.4
August	23.0	.9960	23.1	277.2
September	22.7	.9542	23.8	285.6
October	25.1	1.0277	24.4	292.8
November	25.2	1.0226	24.6	295.2
December	30.6	1.2206	25.1	301.2

annual sales of $276 million for 1983. The actual sales in March, on the other hand, imply total annual sales of $270 million for 1983.

The Use of Seasonal Indexes in Forecasting

We can best illustrate the use of seasonal indexes in forecasting by presenting a practical example. Let us consider the following monthly trend equation for retail sales of the XYZ Corporation:

$$Y' = 17.55316 + .1088X,$$

where the origin is January 1979; X-units are 1 month; and Y is monthly retail sales in millions of dollars. The seasonal indexes associated with this equation are listed in Table 15.16.

Using the information in Table 15.16, we determine the sales forecast for any given month as follows:

1. Determine the trend value for the given month.
2. Multiply the trend value by the monthly seasonal index to obtain the sales forecast.

According to this procedure, we determine the January 1988 sales forecast by first computing the trend value for January 1988:

$$Y'_{Jan.\ 1988} = 17.55316 + .10882(108)$$
$$= 17.55316 + 11.75356$$
$$= \$29.30672 \quad \text{million.}$$

We then multiply this trend value by the January seasonal index of .9025 to obtain the forecast. Thus,

$$\text{Forecast} = Y' \cdot \text{index}$$
$$= 29.30672 \cdot .9025$$
$$= \$26.45 \quad \text{million.}$$

TABLE 15.16

	Seasonal Index		Seasonal Index
January	.9025	July	.9959
February	.8537	August	.9960
March	.9745	September	.9542
April	.9948	October	1.0277
May	1.0325	November	1.0226
June	1.0250	December	1.2206

15.1 The following data represent the hourly earnings in a manufacturing industry in Taiwan from 1974 through 1983.

Year	Average Hourly Earnings (dollars)
1974	2.05
1975	2.11
1976	2.19
1977	2.26
1978	2.32
1979	2.39
1980	2.46
1981	2.53
1982	2.61
1983	2.67

a) Determine the linear trend equation for this time series.

b) Estimate the average hourly earnings in 1988.

c) Draw an arithmetic line chart of this time series showing the trend line.

d) Shift the origin of the trend equation from 1974 to 1983.

e) Estimate the average hourly earnings in 1993 using the modified trend equation obtained in part d.

15.2 Machinery, equipment, and supplies sales (wholesale) for the years 1976–1980 in the United States are as follows:

Year	Sales (billions of dollars)
1976	69.2
1977	85.7
1978	99.2
1979	116.0
1980	129.0

a) Determine the linear trend equation for this time series.

b) Draw an arithmetic line chart of this time series showing the trend line.

c) Shift the origin of the trend equation from 1976 to 1980.

d) Estimate annual sales for the year 1988 using the modified trend equation.

15.3 The following information represents U.S. wheat exports, in millions of bushels, for the years 1976–1980.

Year	Exports
1976	950
1977	1124
1978	1194
1979	1375
1980	1525

a) Determine the linear trend equation for this time series.

b) Draw an arithmetic line chart of this time series showing the trend line.

c) Estimate U.S. wheat exports for the year 1990.

15.4 The U.S. imports of automotive vehicles and parts, including engines, for the years 1975–1980, are as follows:

Year	Auto Imports (billions of dollars)
1975	16.2
1976	18.6
1977	21.2
1978	24.2
1979	25.5
1980	27.1

a) Determine the linear trend equation for this time series.

b) Draw an arithmetic line chart of this time series showing the trend line.

c) Shift the origin of the trend equation from 1975 to 1985.

d) Estimate U.S. imports of automotive vehicles and parts for the year 1992 using the modified trend equation.

15.5 Given the following trend equation: $Y' = 48 + 5.76X$, (where the origin is 1983; X-units are 1 year; and Y is annual profits in millions of dollars).

a) Change this trend equation from an annual to a monthly basis, with January 1983 as the origin.

b) Determine the trend for May 1990 profits.

15.6 The following data represent personal income in a certain state from 1969 to 1983.

Year	Personal Income (billions of dollars)	Year	Personal Income (billions of dollars)
1969	22.7	1977	40.9
1970	25.2	1978	42.9
1971	27.0	1979	45.6
1972	27.7	1980	49.0
1973	30.4	1981	52.4
1974	33.1	1982	56.3
1975	35.5	1983	59.5
1976	37.3		

a) Determine the logarithmic trend equation of this time series.

b) Draw the logarithmic line chart of this time series showing the trend line.

c) Estimate personal income in 1993.

d) Determine the average annual growth rate of personal income for the period 1969–1983.

15.7 The U.S. direct investments in developing countries for the years 1976–1980 are as follows:

Year	Investment (billions of dollars)
1976	27.2
1977	31.8
1978	37.6
1979	44.5
1980	52.7

a) Determine the logarithmic trend equation of this time series.

b) Draw the logarithmic line chart of this time series showing the trend line.

c) Estimate U.S. direct investment in developing countries in 1990.

d) What is the average growth rate of U.S. investment in developing countries for the period 1976–1980?

15.8 The median sales price of new one-family houses in the United States for the years 1973–1980 is reported by the Bureau of the Census as follows:

Year	Median Price (thousands of dollars)
1973	32.5
1974	35.9
1975	39.3
1976	44.2
1977	48.8
1978	55.7
1979	62.9
1980	68.5

a) Determine the logarithmic trend equation of this time series.

b) Draw the logarithmic chart of this time series showing the trend line.

c) What is the average increase in the price of homes during the period 1973–1980.

15.9 Direct foreign investments in the United States for the years 1976–1980 are as follows:

Year	Investment (billions of dollars)
1976	27.7
1977	34.5
1978	42.3
1979	54.5
1980	65.5

a) Determine the logarithmic trend equation of this time series.

b) What is the average growth rate of direct foreign investment in the United States during the period 1976–1980?

c) Estimate direct foreign investment in the United States in 1989.

15.10 The domestic wholesale trade volume of nondurable goods for the years 1973–1980 are as follows.

Year	Sales (billions of dollars)
1973	254.1
1974	326.2
1975	329.9
1976	350.9
1977	374.6
1978	422.4
1979	505.1
1980	605.4

a) Determine the logarithmic trend equation of this time series.

b) Draw the logarithmic line chart of this time series showing the trend line.

c) What is the average growth rate of wholesale trade in nondurable goods during the period 1973–1980?

d) Estimate annual sales for the year 1987.

15.11   The monthly automotive sales from 1978 through 1983 are given in the following table. Compute the monthly seasonal indexes for these data.

	Monthly Sales (billions of dollars)					
	1978	1979	1980	1981	1982	1983
January	2.7	3.1	3.5	3.7	4.2	4.3
February	2.6	3.0	3.3	3.7	4.3	4.4
March	3.2	3.8	3.9	4.1	5.0	5.4
April	3.1	3.8	4.3	4.5	5.1	5.1
May	3.4	4.0	4.3	4.6	5.0	4.8
June	3.4	3.9	4.1	4.4	5.1	5.2
July	3.0	3.6	4.0	4.2	4.8	4.8
August	3.0	3.4	3.5	3.9	4.2	4.7
September	2.7	2.8	3.0	3.7	3.8	4.1
October	3.3	4.1	4.4	3.9	5.0	5.1
November	3.4	3.9	3.9	3.7	5.0	4.9
December	3.1	3.4	3.7	4.4	4.8	4.6

15.12   A department store reports the following monthly sales, in thousands of dollars, for the period 1981–1984.

	Monthly Sales (thousands of dollars)			
	1981	1982	1983	1984
January	358	408	467	541
February	352	395	465	505
March	415	461	506	564
April	401	449	504	580
May	423	475	538	597
June	425	482	515	587
July	421	467	527	597
August	436	502	553	601
September	431	478	519	582
October	434	500	570	620
November	460	535	572	620
December	567	651	698	776
Total	5123	5803	6425	7170

a) Determine the linear trend equation for annual sales.

b) Change the trend equation from an annual to a monthly basis, with January 1981 as the origin.

c) Compute the monthly seasonal indexes.

d) Forecast the department store's sales in January 1988.

15.13 Harry T., a haberdasher from Missouri, is interested in forecasting his sales for December 1990. Harry collected the following monthly sales for the past five years:

	Monthly Sales (thousands of dollars)				
	1980	1981	1982	1983	1984
January	19.8	22.2	22.2	26.9	30.6
February	17.7	21.1	20.8	24.2	28.0
March	20.5	25.2	28.5	31.5	33.5
April	23.8	27.5	27.3	32.7	35.5
May	22.0	25.4	28.2	32.0	36.0
June	22.1	25.2	28.0	31.7	33.8
July	22.0	24.7	26.7	30.1	33.4
August	23.1	27.3	31.0	36.3	40.1

(Continued)

	Monthly Sales (thousands of dollars)				
	1980	*1981*	*1982*	*1983*	*1984*
September	23.3	27.0	31.4	33.7	36.6
October	24.8	28.9	31.7	35.6	40.2
November	25.6	31.2	34.8	38.7	42.6
December	40.2	50.1	54.3	62.0	65.7
Total	284.9	310.4	364.9	415.4	456.0

a) Determine the linear trend equation for annual sales.

b) Change the trend equation from an annual to a monthly basis, with January 1980 as the origin.

c) Compute the monthly seasonal indexes.

d) What are the expected sales in December 1990?

15.14   Arnie Bunker's Place, an eating and drinking establishment, reports monthly sales for the years 1980–1984 as follows:

	Monthly Sales (thousands of dollars)				
	1980	*1981*	*1982*	*1983*	*1984*
January	38.9	44.7	48.6	53.9	60.2
February	37.2	45.4	47.6	53.4	58.7
March	40.8	50.7	56.1	63.7	64.9
April	42.1	52.5	57.5	62.2	66.1
May	45.6	54.1	60.6	64.7	70.2
June	45.4	56.1	62.5	66.6	70.1
July	47.9	58.4	64.3	66.8	71.6
August	47.6	59.0	65.6	70.1	74.3
September	44.6	54.9	61.7	64.8	68.2
October	45.3	55.1	60.4	65.0	70.5
November	42.2	53.4	57.4	63.5	65.9
December	45.0	56.1	60.7	66.1	67.7
Total	522.6	640.4	703.0	760.8	808.4

Bunker wishes to forecast his sales for July 1989.

a) Compute the seasonal indexes for the data.

b) Forecast Bunker's sales for July 1989.

15.15 The following information was compiled by the XYZ Corporation for the first six months of 1983:

	Actual Sales	Trend Value	Seasonal Index
January	$45,000	$50,000	.90
February	44,000	54,000	.80
March	48,000	58,000	1.00
April	60,000	62,000	1.05
May	72,000	66,000	1.20
June	66,000	70,000	1.10

a) Determine a monthly trend equation with January 1983 as the origin.

b) What are the expected sales in May 1984?

c) Which is the poorest month in the first half of 1983?

KEY TERMS

straight-line trend The trend of a time series in which the increases (or decreases) are nearly constant in absolute amount. A straight line trend can be fitted using the equation $Y' = a + bX$.

exponential trend The trend of a time series in which the increases (or decreases) are nearly constant in percentage amounts. An exponential trend can be fitted using the equation $\log Y' = a + bX$.

seasonal index An index that indicates the percentage of the average monthly value that can be expected in each month. A seasonal index above 1 indicates that the value for that month should be above the average monthly value.

seasonally adjusted time series The time series obtained by dividing the actual values by the seasonal index.

INDEX NUMBERS

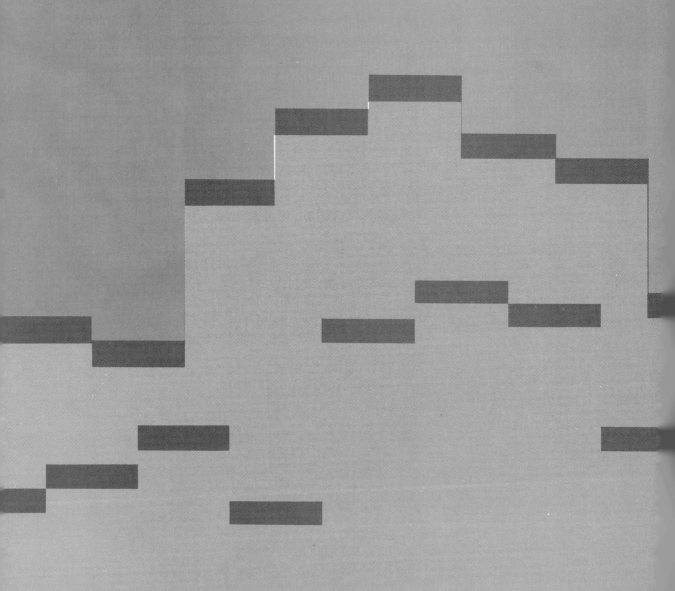

16

Index numbers such as the consumer price index and the Dow Jones industrial average measure the changes in economic and business activity. In this chapter we describe the general nature of index numbers and explain the various methods used in their construction. We examine the consumer price index in some detail as an example.

Once upon a time, such terms as inflation and the consumer price index (CPI) were academic topics, discussed and understood only by economic theorists. However, the sharp and persistent increase in the prices of goods and services in recent years has made these terms an integral part of the average American's vocabulary.

The consumer price index, the Dow Jones average of 30 industrial stocks, and the Federal Reserve Board's index of industrial production are some of the well-known examples of index numbers. These indexes are the barometric indicators of the nation's economic well-being; and in today's world of turbulent global economic conditions and business crises, these economic indicators assume an increasingly important role in shaping our nation's business and public policies.

Our discussion of index numbers in this chapter is organized into two parts. The first part deals with the theoretical and technical aspects of the construction of index numbers, and the latter part is devoted to the roles which some of the indexes play in our economic life.

Index numbers are generally classified into two types: price indexes and quantity indexes. Since most readers are familiar with the consumer price index, we will begin the chapter with price index numbers.

PRICE INDEX

In its simplest form, a price index is a numerical value that measures the change in the price of a *single commodity* over time. If the retail price of chicken is $.89 per pound in 1980 and $1.03 in 1981, we may measure the change in the price of chicken between 1980 and 1981 by computing the following percentage:

$$\frac{1.03}{.89} \cdot 100 = 116\%.$$

This indicates that the 1981 price of chicken is 116% of what it was in 1980. In other words, the 1981 retail price of chicken has increased by 16% relative to the 1980 price. If the retail price of chicken was $1.25 per pound in 1982, we can compare the 1982 price relative to the 1980 price as follows:

$$\frac{1.25}{.89} \cdot 100 = 140\%.$$

Once again, this indicates that the 1982 price of chicken is 140% of what it was in 1980.

Now let P_{80}, P_{81}, and P_{82} denote the retail price of chicken in 1980, 1981, and 1982 respectively ($P_{80} = .89$; $P_{81} = 1.03$; $P_{82} = 1.25$). The 1981 price index relative to 1980 is

$$I = \frac{P_{81}}{P_{80}} \cdot 100 = \frac{1.03}{.89} \cdot 100 = 116\%.$$

Similarly, the 1982 price index relative to 1980 is

$$I = \frac{P_{82}}{P_{80}} \cdot 100 = \frac{1.25}{.89} \cdot 100 = 140\%.$$

Two important concepts must now be clarified in connection with our computation of the price indexes for 1981 and 1982. We have compared the price of chicken in each of the two years relative to the 1980 price. The year 1980 is called the *base year* or *reference year* for the index. In general, the point in time to which the prices are compared is called the *base period.* We must also emphasize that the price index for any given year is a percentage of the price for that year *relative* to the base year price. Hence the price index obtained in this manner is called a **price relative index,** or simply a *price relative.*

The price relative index for any given year is obtained by dividing the price for that year by the base year price and multiplying the resulting ratio by 100 to express the index as a percentage. If we let P_n denote the price of a single commodity in a given year (called *current year*), and P_0 denote the commodity's price for the base year, then the price relative index is defined as

$$I = \frac{P_n}{P_0} \cdot 100.$$

Table 16.1 shows the retail price per pound for round steak during the years 1970–1981 together with the price relative index computations. The base year for the index is 1970. Hence all other prices are compared to the 1970 price. As indicated in Table 16.1, the index for the base year 1970 = 100.

The price relative index computed in Table 16.1 measures the change over time in the price of a single commodity. Such an index is the simplest form of all price indexes. Constructing a price index becomes complicated when an index is designed to measure the overall price changes for a group of commodities. For example, we may wish to construct a price index to monitor the change in food prices. This is accomplished by combining the prices of several food items in such a manner that a single index measures the general price level for the various food items. Similarly, a cost-of-living index is constructed by combining the prices of a variety of goods and services in such a way that a single index measures the change in the cost of living. A price index that measures the overall price changes for several commodities is called a **composite price index.**

We will illustrate the method of constructing a composite index with a simplified example. We consider the case of the Smiths, a family of four in Atlanta, Georgia. The Smith family purchases its food from the local Big Star supermarket. To simplify our analysis let us assume that the family's weekly food purchases are limited to seven food items: rump roast, chicken, milk,

TABLE 16.1   RETAIL PRICE OF ROUND STEAK, 1970–1981

Year	Price (dollars)	Price Relative Index (percent)
1970	1.30	$\frac{1.30}{1.30} \cdot 100 = 100$
1971	1.36	$\frac{1.36}{1.30} \cdot 100 = 105$
1972	1.48	$\frac{1.48}{1.30} \cdot 100 = 114$
1973	1.75	$\frac{1.75}{1.30} \cdot 100 = 135$
1974	1.80	$\frac{1.80}{1.30} \cdot 100 = 138$
1975	1.88	$\frac{1.88}{1.30} \cdot 100 = 145$
1976	1.78	$\frac{1.78}{1.30} \cdot 100 = 137$
1977	1.76	$\frac{1.76}{1.30} \cdot 100 = 135$
1978	1.89	$\frac{1.89}{1.30} \cdot 100 = 145$
1979	1.98	$\frac{1.98}{1.30} \cdot 100 = 152$
1980	2.09	$\frac{2.09}{1.30} \cdot 100 = 161$
1981	2.35	$\frac{2.35}{1.30} \cdot 100 = 181$

oranges, potatoes, eggs, and bread. The retail prices for these items in 1980 and 1981 are shown in Table 16.2.

Using the data in Table 16.2, we will discuss the various methods for measuring the overall price changes from 1980 to 1981 for this group of seven food items.

UNWEIGHTED AGGREGATE PRICE INDEX

The simplest approach to our problem is to construct an *unweighted aggregate price index*. Using the year 1980 as a base period, we define the price index for

TABLE 16.2

Food Commodity	Price, 1980 (dollars) P_{80}	Price, 1981 (dollars) P_{81}
Rump roast (pound)	2.05	2.30
Frying chicken (pound)	.89	.98
Milk (half gallon)	.99	1.15
Oranges, size 200 (dozen)	1.96	1.80
Potatoes (pound)	.39	.45
Eggs, grade A large (dozen)	.93	1.05
Bread (pound)	.49	.59
Total prices	$\sum P_{80} = 7.70$	$\sum P_{81} = 8.32$

1981 as

$$I = \frac{\sum P_{81}}{\sum P_{80}} \cdot 100,$$

where $\sum P_{80}$ = the sum of all seven prices for 1980, that is the price aggregate for 1980, and $\sum P_{81}$ = price aggregate for 1981.

Table 16.2 shows that the price aggregates for 1980 and 1981 equal $7.70 and $8.32 respectively ($\sum P_{80} = 7.70$, $\sum P_{81} = 8.32$). Hence, using 1980 as a base period, we determine the unweighted aggregate price index for 1981 as

$$I = \frac{\sum P_{81}}{\sum P_{80}} \cdot 100 = \frac{8.32}{7.70} \cdot 100 = 108\%.$$

This indicates that the 1981 aggregate price of these food items is 108% of what it was in 1980. Thus the aggregate price has increased by 8% from 1980 to 1981.

In general, denoting a commodity price in the base period by P_0 and its price in period n by P_n, the unweighted aggregate price index is symbolically defined as

$$I = \frac{\sum P_n}{\sum P_0} \cdot 100,$$

where $\sum P_n$ = the sum of the prices paid for commodities in the composite in period n (current period) and $\sum P_0$ = the sum of prices paid for the same commodities in the base period.

The unweighted aggregate price index has a serious disadvantage. The index is affected by, and hence may be seriously distorted by, the choice of units on which prices are based. For example, we have quoted the price of oranges as $1.96 per dozen in 1980 and $1.80 per dozen in 1981. If orange prices are quoted by pound instead ($.49 per pound in 1980 and $.45 in 1981), the unweighted aggregate price index for 1981 becomes

$$\frac{6.97}{6.23} \cdot 100 = 112\%,$$

suggesting a 12% increase in the aggregate price between 1980 and 1981 compared with the 8% increase indicated when we used the price of oranges per dozen.

To avoid such distortion, and to prevent any intentional manipulation of the unweighted aggregate price index, we will assign a proper weight to the price of each commodity. The assigned weights are determined by the purpose for which the price index is constructed. For example, if the purpose of the index is to measure the change in the price of food purchased by the Smith family, then the weight assigned to each food item must reflect the relative importance of that item in the Smith family's food budget. When prices are weighted in some fashion to produce a composite price index, the resulting index is called a *weighted aggregate price index.*

WEIGHTED AGGREGATE PRICE INDEX

A weighted aggregate price index measures the overall price changes for several commodities. There are several methods to construct such an index. All the methods adopt two basic notions: first, that each commodity is assigned a weight that reflects its relative importance in the composite; and second, that the weight assigned to a given commodity is equal to the quantity purchased of that commodity. Adapting these two basic notions, and denoting the quantity purchased by Q, we can symbolically state the general definition of the weighted aggregate price index as

$$I = \frac{\sum P_n Q}{\sum P_0 Q} \cdot 100,$$

where $\sum P_n Q$ = total value of all quantities in the composite when purchased in period n (current period), and $\sum P_0 Q$ = total value of the same quantities in the composite when purchased in the base period.

We will apply this general definition to construct a composite index for *two* of the food items purchased by the Smith family: rump roast and chicken. Assuming that the Smith family purchases 5 pounds of rump roast and 4 pounds of chicken per week, we compute the weighted aggregate price index for these two items as shown in Table 16.3.

In Table 16.3, the base period prices and the current period prices for the elements in the composite are listed in the columns labeled P_0 and P_n respectively. Quantities purchased of the two food items are shown in the column labeled Q. Entries in the column labeled $P_0 Q$ are obtained by multiplying the base period price by the quantity purchased ($P_0 \cdot Q$) to obtain the dollar expenditures for each food item. The sum of these expenditures, $\sum P_0 Q = 13.81$, is the total amount paid to purchase the two elements in the composite when purchased in the base period, 1980. Similarly, the sum of all dollar purchases in the last column of the table, $\sum P_n Q = 15.42$, is the total

TABLE 16.3 WEIGHTED PRICE INDEX (BASE YEAR 1980 = 100)

Food Item in Composite	Price per Pound (dollars)		Quantity (pounds)	Total Value (dollars)	
	1980 P_0	*1981* P_n	Q	*1980* P_0Q	*1981* P_nQ
Roast	2.05	2.30	5	$2.05 \cdot 5 = 10.25$	$2.30 \cdot 5 = 11.50$
Chicken	.89	.98	4	$.89 \cdot 4 = \underline{3.56}$	$.98 \cdot 4 = \underline{3.92}$
				$\sum P_0Q = 13.81$	$\sum P_nQ = 15.42$

$$I = \frac{\sum P_nQ}{\sum P_0Q} \cdot 100$$

$$= \frac{15.42}{13.81} \cdot 100$$

$$= 111.7$$

amount paid to purchase the same quantities of the two food items in the current period, 1981. The weighted aggregate price index is then computed (see Table 16.3) and is equal to 111.7. This figure indicates that the 1981 price of a composite, or market basket (consisting of 5 pounds of rump roast and 4 pounds of chicken), is 111.7% of what it was in 1980, an 11.7% increase between 1980 and 1981.

In constructing the weighted aggregate price index in Table 16.3, we have tacitly assumed that the Smith family (or a consumer in general) purchases the same quantity of each commodity year after year, an assumption that is untenable in the general case. In fact, there has been a radical change in the American family's consumption pattern over the last few years. The high rate of inflation made some food products, especially meat, out of reach for some consumers. At the same time, the rapid change in technology made many new products available to the consumer. Microwave ovens, video recorders, and personal computers are but a few examples of products that consumers did not dream of owning a decade ago.

Since consumption patterns (quantities purchased) change over time, it is no longer clear which quantities should be used to weigh the various elements in the composite. Specifically, there are at least three kinds of quantities that can be used to construct a weighted aggregate price index:

1. Quantities purchased in the *base period,*
2. Quantities purchased in the *current period,* and
3. Quantities purchased in some other period.

Consequently, there are three kinds of weighted aggregate price indexes, each distinguished by the choice of quantities used in constructing the index.

Laspeyres Price Index

Named for the first person who suggested its use, the **Laspeyres price index** uses base year quantities as weights. The formula used in constructing the Laspeyres index is

$$I = \frac{\sum P_n Q_0}{\sum P_0 Q_0} \cdot 100,$$

where

P_n = the commodity's current year price,
P_0 = the commodity's base year price, and
Q_0 = quantity purchased in the base year.

Table 16.4 illustrates the use of the Laspeyres method in constructing a weighted aggregate price index to measure the change in the price of a market basket of seven food items purchased by the Smith family. The index is assumed to measure the overall changes in food prices between 1980 and 1981. The year 1980 is the base period for the index.

TABLE 16.4 **COMPUTATION OF A LASPEYRES PRICE INDEX, BASE PERIOD 1980 = 100**

Food Commodity in Composite	Base Period Price, 1980 (dollars) P_0	Current Period Price, 1981 (dollars) P_n	Base Period Quantity, 1980 Q_0	Total Weekly Expenditures (dollars)	
				1980 $P_0 Q_0$	1981 $P_n Q_0$
Rump roast (pound)	2.05	2.30	5	10.25	11.50
Chicken (pound)	.89	.98	4	3.56	3.92
Milk (half gallon)	.99	1.15	4	3.96	4.60
Oranges (dozen)	1.96	1.80	1	1.96	1.80
Potatoes (pound)	.39	.45	4	1.56	1.80
Eggs (dozen)	.93	1.05	2	1.86	2.10
Bread (pound)	.49	.59	3	1.47	1.77
				$\sum P_0 Q_0 = 24.62$	$\sum P_n Q_0 = 27.49$

$$\text{Laspeyres index} = \frac{\sum P_n Q_0}{\sum P_0 Q_0} \cdot 100$$

$$= \frac{27.49}{24.62} \cdot 100$$

$$= 111.7$$

In Table 16.4, we have listed in the column labeled Q_0 the *average weekly quantities* of seven food items purchased by the Smith family in the base year, 1980. This column shows that in 1980 the Smith family purchased a weekly average of 5 pounds of rump roast, 4 pounds of chicken, 4 half-gallon cartons of milk, and so on. These quantities are the components of a market basket of several foods purchased by the Smiths in the base period, 1980. This market basket is priced at 1980 and 1981 prices (see the last two columns of Table 16.4). With a composite weekly price of $24.62 in 1980 and $27.49 in 1981, the Laspeyres index is computed as

$$\text{Laspeyres index} = \frac{\sum P_n Q_0}{\sum P_0 Q_0} \cdot 100$$

$$= \frac{27.40}{24.62} \cdot 100$$

$$= 111.7$$

which indicates that the price of the market basket in 1981 is 111.7% of what it was in 1980. Assuming that the market basket composition is a representative sample of the food items purchased by the Smith family, we can conclude that the overall increase in the price of food is 11.7% between 1980 and 1981.

There are some advantages to using the base year quantities as weights to construct a price index. One advantage is that the index reflects only changes in prices because we priced the same quantities in all periods. Another advantage is that quantity weights are collected only once (in the base period), and these same quantities are used as weights in every period. In practice, the collection of quantity data is an expensive and time-consuming task. In constructing the Laspeyres index this task is performed only once.

A serious disadvantage of the Laspeyres method is that quantities consumed, or consumption patterns, tend to change from period to period, and the change becomes more pronounced as the time elapsed between the base period and the current period becomes longer. The importance of these issues is more clearly seen when we consider other methods of constructing weighted price indexes.

Paache Index

Like the Laspeyres index, the **Paache index** is named for the statistician who suggested its use. Unlike the Laspeyres index, which uses base period quantities as weights, the Paache index uses current period quantities instead. Hence, we may define the Paache price index symbolically as:

$$I = \frac{\sum P_n Q_n}{\sum P_0 Q_n} \cdot 100,$$

where Q_n is the quantity purchased (consumed or produced) in the current period. We will illustrate the use of the Paache method to construct a weighted price index for the seven food items consumed by the Smith family. Let us now assume that the family purchased the quantities shown in Table 16.5 during 1980 and 1981.

Comparing the family food consumption patterns in 1980 and 1981, we observe that the Smith family purchased less rump roast but more chicken and oranges in 1981 than in 1980. Consumption of other food items remained the same.

Inflation changes family consumption patterns. When prices are rising, families tend to reduce their consumption of high-priced commodities or commodities with most marked price increases, such as steak or beef. The family also buys more low-priced items or commodities with slower price changes. In addition, consumption patterns vary over the year due to changes in consumers' preferences and changes in technology.

Table 16.6 shows how to construct a Paache price index to measure the change in the family's food prices between 1980 and 1981. The base period is 1980, with an index of 100.

In Table 16.6 we have listed current year quantities (quantities purchased in 1981) in the column labeled Q_n. These quantities constitute the components of a new market basket that must now be priced at 1980 and 1981 prices (see last two columns of Table 16.6). For a price of $23.37 in 1980 and $25.67 in 1981, the Paache price index is computed in the table as 109.8 (see Table 16.6), which indicates a 9.8% increase in food prices between 1980 and 1981 (compared with the 11.7% increase shown by the Laspeyres index).

It is useful to compare the two kinds of price indexes used to measure the increase in the Smith family's food costs between 1980 and 1981. The

TABLE 16.5   FOOD PURCHASES, 1980 AND 1981

Food Item	Quantity Purchased per Week	
	1980	*1981*
Rump roast (pound)	5	3
Chicken (pound)	4	5
Milk (half gallon)	4	4
Oranges (dozen)	1	2
Potatoes (pound)	4	4
Eggs (dozen)	2	2
Bread (pound)	3	3

TABLE 16.6   COMPUTATION OF A PAACHE PRICE INDEX, BASE PERIOD 1980 = 100

Food Commodity	Base Period Price, 1980 (dollars) P_0	Current Period Price, 1981 (dollars) P_n	Current Period Quantity, 1981 Q_n	Total Expenditures (dollars)	
				1980 $P_0 Q_n$	1981 $P_n Q_n$
Rump roast (pound)	2.05	2.30	3	6.15	6.90
Chicken (pound)	.89	.98	5	4.45	4.90
Milk (half gallon)	.99	1.15	4	3.96	4.60
Oranges (dozen)	1.96	1.80	2	3.92	3.60
Potatoes (pound)	.39	.45	4	1.56	1.80
Eggs (dozen)	.93	1.05	2	1.86	2.10
Bread (pound)	.49	.59	3	1.47	1.77
				$\sum P_0 Q_n = 23.37$	$\sum P_n Q_n = 25.67$

$$\text{Paache index} = \frac{\sum P_n Q_n}{\sum P_0 Q_n} \cdot 100$$

$$= \frac{25.67}{23.37} \cdot 100$$

$$= 109.8$$

Laspeyres index, which uses quantities purchased in 1980 as weights, shows that the family's food cost in 1981 is 111.7% of what it was in 1980. The Paache method, which uses quantities purchased in 1981 as weights, shows the lower price index, 109.8, or 9.8% increase in cost between 1980 and 1981. The difference between the two indexes can be explained by examining Table 16.5 and Table 16.6. Table 16.5 shows that the Smith family reduced its consumption of roast but increased its consumption of chicken and oranges between 1980 and 1981. Table 16.6 shows that roast is a high-priced item, chicken is a relatively low-priced item, and the price of oranges actually declined between 1980 and 1981 (due perhaps to a large crop in 1981). Thus by reducing the relative importance of roast while increasing the relative importance of chicken and oranges, the Paache index showed a smaller price increase in food prices than the Laspeyres index.

In a period of rising prices, the Laspeyres index tends to overstate the increase in the price level, while the Paache index is expected to show the exact opposite. As mentioned earlier, consumption patterns change in response to inflationary pressures.

The Laspeyres method uses base period quantities as weights, and the Paache method uses current period quantities. A third alternative is to weight the index by quantities that belong to some other period. The period chosen should be a representative period. Quantities in this representative period are called *fixed weights* and the resulting index is called a **fixed-weight aggregate price index.** A fixed weight aggregate price index is symbolically defined as

$$I = \frac{\sum P_n Q_f}{\sum P_0 Q_f} \cdot 100,$$

where

P_n = The current period price of the commodity,
P_0 = The base period price of the commodity, and
Q_f = The quantity purchased in the representative period (quantities that are referred to as fixed weights).

PRICE RELATIVE INDEX

As defined previously, the price relative index for a single commodity is:

$$I = \frac{P_n}{P_0} \cdot 100,$$

where P_n and P_0 are the commodity's prices in the current and base periods, respectively. Let us assume that the price of rump roast is \$2.05 per pound in 1980 and \$2.30 in 1981. With the year 1980 as a base period, the 1981 price relative index for rump roast is determined as

$$I = \frac{P_n}{P_0} \cdot 100$$

$$= \frac{2.30}{2.05} \cdot 100$$

$$= 112.2\%.$$

Hence we can conclude that the 1981 price of rump roast is 112.2% of what it was in 1980.

The price relative concept of an index number may now be extended to measure the overall price changes for a composite of several commodities. The price relative index for a composite can be either a weighted or unweighted index.

The **unweighted price relative index** for a composite of k elements is simply the average of all individual price relative indexes. Symbolically, the unweighted price relative index is defined as:

$$I = \frac{\sum \frac{P_n}{P_0} \cdot 100}{k}.$$

The construction of an unweighted price relative index that measures the overall price changes of the composite of the seven food items consumed by the Smith family is shown in Table 16.7. The year 1980 is the base period for the index. Table 16.7 indicates that the 1981 price of the food composite is 111.2% of what it was in 1980.

The unweighted price relative index has the advantage of being unaffected by the choice of the units in which individual prices are quoted. A major disadvantage of the index is that it gives an equal weight to each element in the composite. This problem can be overcome, however, if one constructs a weighted price relative index.

To construct a **weighted price relative index** for a composite of several commodities, we assign each commodity a weight that reflects its relative importance in the index. The weight assigned to each commodity is equal to the total value of that commodity, and the total value of any commodity is equal to its quantity times the price. Adopting these basic notions, we may now

TABLE 16.7 **COMPUTATION OF UNWEIGHTED PRICE RELATIVE INDEX, BASE PERIOD 1980 = 100**

Food Commodity	Base Period Price, 1980 (dollars) P_0	Current Period Price, 1981 (dollars) P_n	Price Relative Index $(P_n/P_0) \cdot 100$
Roast (pound)	2.05	2.30	$(2.30/2.05)100 = 112.20$
Chicken (pound)	.89	.98	$(.98/.89)100 = 110.11$
Milk (half gallon)	.99	1.15	$(1.15/.99)100 = 116.16$
Oranges (dozen)	1.96	1.80	$(1.80/1.96)100 = 91.84$
Potatoes (pound)	.39	.45	$(.45/.39)100 = 115.38$
Eggs (dozen)	.93	1.05	$(1.05/.93)100 = 112.90$
Bread (pound)	.49	.59	$(.59/.49)100 = 120.41$
			$\sum (P_n/P_0)100 = 779.00$

$$I = \frac{\sum \frac{P_n}{P_0} \cdot 100}{k}$$

$$= \frac{779.00}{7} = 111.3\%$$

state the general definition of a weighted price relative index as

$$I = \frac{\sum \left(\frac{P_n}{P_0} \cdot 100\right) PQ}{\sum PQ},$$

where

$$\frac{P_n}{P_0} \cdot 100 = \text{An individual commodity relative price index,}$$

$$PQ = \text{An individual commodity total value,}$$

$$\sum PQ = \text{Total values of all commodities in the composite.}$$

Although total value equals quantity times price $(Q \cdot P)$, prices and quantities can belong to either the base period or the current period. Consequently, several combinations of P and Q can be used to determine total value. Some of these combinations are $P_0 Q_0$, $P_n Q_n$, $P_0 Q_n$, and $Q_n P_0$. The value $P_0 Q_0$ is the base period value, and $P_n Q_n$ is the current period value. The values $P_0 Q_n$ and $P_n Q_0$ are hybrids of current and base periods values. Of all these possible value weights, the base value, $P_0 Q_0$, is most commonly used.

When the base period value $P_0 Q_0$ is used as a weight, the formula for the weighted price relative index becomes:

$$I = \frac{\sum \left(\frac{P_n}{P_0} \cdot 100\right) P_0 Q_0}{\sum P_0 Q_0}.$$

This formula is used in Table 16.8 to construct a weighted price relative index for the Smith family's food composite, with the year 1980 as a base period. Table 16.8 shows that the 1981 price of the food composite is 111.7% of what it was in 1980.

When base period values are used as weights to construct a weighted price relative index (as in Table 16.8), the resulting index is the same as the Laspeyres index (see Table 16.4). In other words, the price relative index that uses base period values as weights and the Laspeyres index that uses base period quantities as weights produce exactly the same result. Both indexes show that the 1981 price of the food composite is 111.7% of the 1980 price. In fact, the formulas used in the two methods are equivalent, and the choice between the two methods depends on the availability of the data. The Laspeyres method is used when quantity data are more readily available, and the price relative method is used when value data are the easiest to obtain.

QUANTITY INDEX

In comparison with a price index, which measures changes in price over time, a **quantity index** measures changes in physical volume. In its simplest form, a

TABLE 16.8   COMPUTATION OF WEIGHTED PRICE RELATIVE INDEX, BASE PERIOD 1980 = 100

Food Commodity	Price (dollars)		Price Relative Index (percent) $\frac{P_n}{P_0} \cdot 100$	Base Quantity, 1980 Q_0	Base Value (dollars) $P_0 \cdot Q_0$	Weighted Relative Price (dollars) $\left(\frac{P_n}{P_0} \cdot 100\right) P_0 Q_0$
	1980	1981				
Steak (pound)	2.05	2.30	112.20	5	10.25	112.20 · 10.25 = 1150.05
Chicken (pound)	.89	.98	110.11	4	3.56	110.11 · 3.56 = 391.99
Milk (half gallon)	.99	1.15	116.16	4	3.96	116.16 · 3.96 = 459.99
Oranges (dozen)	1.96	1.80	91.84	1	1.96	91.84 · 1.96 = 180.01
Potatoes (pound)	.39	.45	115.38	4	1.56	115.38 · 1.56 179.99
Eggs (dozen)	.93	1.05	112.90	2	1.86	112.90 · 1.86 = 209.99
Bread (pound)	.49	.59	120.41	3	1.47	120.41 · 1.47 = 177.00
					$\sum P_0 Q_0 = 24.62$	2749.02

$$I = \frac{\sum \left(\frac{P_n}{P_0} \cdot 100\right) P_0 Q_0}{\sum P_0 Q_0}$$

$$= \frac{2749.02}{24.62} = 111.7\%$$

quantity index is a numerical value that measures the change in the physical quantity of a single commodity over time. For example, if we assume that the production of corn in the United States was 5.8 billion bushels in 1975 and 7.2 billion bushels in 1981, we can measure the change in the production of corn between 1975 and 1981 by computing a quantity index, as follows:

$$\frac{7.2}{5.8} \cdot 100 = 124.1\%.$$

This index indicates that U.S. production of corn in 1981 was 124.1% of what it was in 1975.

Hence, let Q_n denote the quantity of a single commodity produced in the current period, and let Q_0 denote its quantity in the base period; then the quantity relative index is defined as

$$I = \frac{Q_n}{Q_0} \cdot 100$$

The quantity index for a composite of several commodities can be constructed in a manner similar to that of constructing a price index. A quantity index can be either weighted or unweighted. When a quantity index is weighted, the weight assigned to any element in the composite is equal to the price of that element (or its total value). A weighted quantity index can be constructed with the same methods used in constructing a weighted price index. These methods include the Laspeyres, the Paache, and the weighted relative methods.

We illustrate the construction of a weighted quantity index with two examples. In the first example we use the Laspeyres index, which measures the changes in U.S. production of the four principal crops (corn, wheat, oats, and soybeans) between 1975 and 1981. This index is calculated in Table 16.9 using the following formula:

$$I = \frac{\sum Q_n P_0}{\sum Q_0 P_0} \cdot 100,$$

or, in this case,

$$I = \frac{\sum Q_{81} P_{75}}{\sum Q_{75} P_{75}} \cdot 100.$$

Table 16.9 indicates that the U.S. production of the four principal crops in 1981 was 132.2% of what it was in 1975.

TABLE 16.9   COMPUTATION OF A LASPEYRES QUANTITY INDEX, BASE PERIOD 1975 = 100

Commodity	Base Period Quantity, 1975 (billions of bushels)	Current Period Quantity, 1981 (billions of bushels)	Base Period Price, 1975 (dollars per bushel)	Total Value (billions of dollars)	
				1975	1981
	Q_0	Q_n	P_0	$Q_0 P_0$	$Q_n P_0$
Corn	5.8	7.2	2.54	14.732	18.288
Wheat	2.1	2.4	3.56	7.476	8.544
Oats	1.7	.5	1.46	1.022	.730
Soybeans	1.5	2.5	4.92	7.380	12.300
				$\sum Q_0 P_0 = 30.610$	$\sum Q_n P_0 = 39.862$

$$I = \frac{\sum Q_n P_0}{\sum Q_0 P_0} \cdot 100$$

$$= \frac{39.862}{30.610} \cdot 100$$

$$= 130.2\%$$

TABLE 16.10 COMPUTATIONS OF A PAACHE QUANTITY INDEX BASE PERIOD 1975 = 100

Commodity	Base Period Quantity, 1975 (billions of bushels)	Current Period Quantity, 1981 (billions of bushels)	Current Period Price, 1981 (dollars per bushel)	Total Value (billions of dollars)	
				1975	1981
	Q_0	Q_n	P_n	$Q_0 P_n$	$Q_n P_n$
Corn	5.8	7.2	3.59	20.822	25.848
Wheat	2.1	2.4	4.32	9.072	10.368
Oats	.7	.5	2.04	1.428	1.020
Soybeans	1.5	2.5	7.71	11.565	19.275
				$\sum Q_0 P_n = 42.887$	$\sum Q_n P_n = 56.511$

$$I = \frac{\sum Q_n P_n}{\sum Q_0 P_n} \cdot 100$$

$$= \frac{56.511}{42.887} \cdot 100$$

$$= 131.8\%$$

The Paache method is used in Table 16.10 to construct a weighted quantity index using the formula

$$I = \frac{\sum Q_n P_n}{\sum Q_0 P_n} \cdot 100,$$

or, in this case,

$$I = \frac{\sum Q_{81} P_{81}}{\sum Q_{75} P_{81}} \cdot 100.$$

Using the Paache method, Table 16.10 indicates that U.S. production of the four main crops in 1981 was 131.8% of what it was in 1975.

THE CONSUMER PRICE INDEX (CPI)

Our discussion so far has dealt with the technical aspects of the construction of index numbers. It is important at this point to discuss the economic significance of these indexes which is most apparent in the consumer price index.

Development of the CPI

The U.S. Bureau of Labor Statistics began to publish a national **consumer price index** regularly in February 1917. Over the years, the bureau introduced many changes in what the index covered, how it was constructed, what data were collected, what base periods were used, and how frequently it was published. The index continues to measure the overall price changes of a composite of various goods and services. The composite (called *market basket*) consists of several hundred items typically consumed by an urban American family.

Detailed consumer expenditure surveys, conducted in urban centers, provide the basis for selecting the items to be included in the market basket as well as their relative importance in the index. The items selected represent the major consumer expenditure groups—food, housing, apparel, transportation, entertainment, medical care, and personal care. The prices of items in the market basket are obtained periodically at retail outlets representative of those that consumers patronize.

As has been indicated earlier, consumption expenditure patterns vary over the years, for several reasons. First, consumers adjust their purchases in response to changes in commodities' prices. In a time of rising prices, for instance, consumers substitute commodities with moderate price increases for commodities with sharp price increases. Second, consumers change their consumption patterns as their tastes and preferences change. Third, consumers adjust their purchases as new products and new services become available on the market. To ensure that the CPI reflects changes in spending patterns, the bureau has revised the market basket approximately every 10 years.

In each revision, the market basket is modified on the basis of new data provided by extensive consumer expenditure surveys. The CPI has undergone four major revisions in the past, in 1940, 1953, 1964, and 1978. These revisions were based on consumer expenditure surveys conducted in 1934–36, 1947–48, 1960–61, and 1972–73, respectively. Table 16.11 shows the changing relative importance of each major expenditure group in the total market basket. The most extensive revision of the consumer price index was the 1978

TABLE 16.11   PERCENT DISTRIBUTION OF THE CONSUMER PRICE INDEX MARKET BASKET BY MAJOR EXPENDITURE GROUP, BENCHMARK YEARS

Expenditure Group	1935–39	1952	1963	1972–73
Food and alcoholic beverages	35.4	32.2	25.2	20.4
Housing	33.7	33.5	34.9	39.8
Apparel	11.0	9.4	10.6	7.0
Transportation	8.1	11.3	14.0	19.8
Medical care	4.1	4.8	5.7	4.2
Entertainment	2.8	4.0	3.9	4.3
Personal care	2.5	2.1	2.8	1.8
Other goods and services	2.4	2.7	2.9	2.7

Source: U.S. Bureau of Labor Statistics.

revision, which resulted in a wider coverage and more frequent publication of the CPI.

Prior to the 1978 revision, the Bureau of Labor Statistics published a single price index: the index for wage earners and clerical workers. This index, which the bureau continues to publish, is based on information about a specific segment of the population—wage earners and clerical workers. Since the CPI plays an important role in shaping the country's monetary and fiscal policy, it was felt that a comprehensive consumer price index was needed to represent other segments of the population besides wage earners and clerical workers. Consequently, a new index representing all urban consumers has been published in addition to the index for wage earners and clerical workers. This new index, which represents 80% of the U.S. population, is the index for all urban households.

The 1978 revision resulted not only in wider coverage but also in more frequent publication of the index. Monthly or bimonthly indexes for 28 cities are published now, compared with 24 monthly or quarterly indexes formerly published.

The 1967–1980 values of the consumer price index for urban wage earners and clerical workers, together with values for major expenditure groups, are shown in Table 16.12.

TABLE 16.12 CONSUMER PRICE INDEX FOR URBAN WAGE EARNERS AND CLERICAL WORKERS, ANNUAL AVERAGES 1967–1981 (1967 = 100)

Year	All Items Index	Food and Beverages Index	Housing Index	Apparel and Upkeep Index	Transportation Index	Medical Care Index	Entertainment Index	Other Goods and Services Index
1967	100.0	100.0	100.0	100.0	100.0	100.0	100.0	100.0
1968	104.2	103.6	104.0	105.4	103.2	106.1	105.7	105.2
1969	109.8	108.8	110.4	111.5	107.2	113.4	111.0	110.4
1970	116.3	114.7	118.2	116.1	112.7	120.6	116.7	116.8
1971	121.3	118.3	123.4	119.8	118.6	128.4	122.9	122.4
1972	125.3	123.2	128.1	122.3	119.9	132.5	126.5	127.5
1973	133.1	139.5	133.7	126.8	123.8	137.7	130.0	132.5
1974	147.7	158.7	148.8	136.2	137.7	150.5	139.8	142.0
1975	161.2	172.1	164.5	142.3	150.6	168.6	152.2	153.9
1976	170.5	177.4	174.6	147.6	165.5	184.7	159.8	162.7
1977	181.5	188.0	186.5	154.2	177.2	202.4	167.7	172.2
1978	195.3	206.2	202.6	159.5	185.8	219.4	176.2	183.2
1979	217.7	228.7	227.5	166.4	212.8	240.1	187.6	196.3
1980	233.9	254.6	262.3	178.4	249.7	265.9	205.3	214.5
1981	253.6	274.6	293.5	186.9	280.0	294.5	220.3	232.2

Source: U.S. Department of Labor, Bureau of Labor Statistics

16.1 The U.S. Federal Highway Administration reports the following retail prices of regular gasoline in the United States from 1973 to 1981.

Year	Price per Gallon	Year	Price per Gallon
1973	$.40	1978	$ .63
1974	.55	1979	.86
1975	.57	1980	1.09
1976	.59	1981	1.37
1977	.63		

Calculate price relative indexes for the years indicated, using 1973 as the base year.

16.2 The San Fernando Valley Board of Realtors reports the following average prices for single-family homes sold in the San Fernando Valley from 1976 to 1981.

Year	1976	1977	1978	1979	1980	1981
Price (thousands of dollars)	58.5	74.2	81.3	101.2	126.6	135.8

Calculate price relative indexes for the six years indicated, using 1976 as the base year.

16.3 In a study entitled "Profitability of Insured Commercial Banks," the board of governors of the Federal Reserve system reports net income, in millions of dollars, for all commercial banks, as follows.

Year	Income (millions of dollars)	Year	Income (millions of dollars)
1976	7,849	1979	12,749
1977	8,898	1980	13,950
1978	10,731	1981	14,731

Calculate income relative indexes for the years indicated, using 1980 as the base year.

16.4 A profitability study of federally insured commercial banks shows the following information concerning rate of return on equity for the years 1977 to 1981.

Year	Rate of Return	Year	Rate of Return
1977	11.8	1980	13.7
1978	12.9	1981	13.2
1979	13.9		

Calculate rate of return on equity relative indexes for the years indicated, using 1978 as the base year.

16.5 The U.S. Office of Human Development Services gives the annual maintenance expenditures for mentally retarded patients as follows.

Year	Amount per Patient	Year	Amount per Patient
1960	$ 1,650	1978	$18,360
1965	2,335	1979	20,849
1970	4,635	1980	22,995
1975	11,315		

Calculate price relative indexes for the years indicated, using 1960 as the base year.

16.6 The average price of domestic and imported automobiles for the years 1977–1981 are as follows.

Year	Average Price	Year	Average Price
1977	$5,840	1980	$7,544
1978	6,414	1981	8,804
1979	6,892		

Calculate price relative indexes for the six years indicated, using 1980 as the base period.

16.7 The 1980 International Petroleum Annual gives the average prices of premium gasoline in several major international cities from 1973 to 1979 as follows.

City	Price per U.S. Gallon						
	1973	*1974*	*1975*	*1976*	*1977*	*1978*	*1979*
New York	$ .45	$ .60	$ .65	$ .64	$ .69	$ .71	$ .97
Paris	1.15	1.32	1.56	1.40	1.70	2.15	2.43
Rome	1.05	1.77	1.71	1.81	2.15	2.25	2.53

(Continued)

City	Price per U.S. Gallon						
	1973	1974	1975	1976	1977	1978	1979
London	.81	1.08	1.31	1.05	1.21	1.19	2.21
Bonn	1.31	1.37	1.34	1.48	1.54	1.76	2.19
Ottawa	.53	.62	.67	.72	.75	.73	.78
Mexico City	.36	.61	.91	.92	.66	.67	.67
Tokyo	.98	1.55	1.63	1.51	1.78	2.23	2.46

To monitor the changes in the global price of premium gasoline, calculate the unweighted aggregate price indexes for the years 1973–1979, using 1973 as the base period.

16.8 The following information describes the money market interest rates for the years 1975–1981.

Type	Interest Rate						
	1975	1976	1977	1978	1979	1980	1981
Federal funds	5.82	5.04	5.54	7.93	11.19	13.36	17:18
Commercial paper	6.25	5.24	5.55	7.94	10.97	12.66	15.74
Prime rate	7.86	6.84	6.83	9.06	12.67	15.27	19.07
Eurodollar deposits	7.03	5.58	6.03	8.78	11.96	14.00	17.25
Finance paper	6.15	5.20	5.49	7.80	10.47	11.49	14.24
Bankers' acceptances	6.29	5.19	5.60	8.11	11.04	12.78	15.75
Certificates of deposit	6.44	5.27	5.68	8.22	11.22	13.07	16.33
Treasury bills	5.77	4.97	5.27	7.19	10.07	11.43	14.65

To measure the changes in the money market rate over the period 1975–1981, calculate an unweighted aggregate price index for each of the seven years indicated, using 1980 as the base year.

16.9 The Health Insurance Institute gives the average daily hospital room charge in several major cities as follows.

City	Average Daily Room Charge		
	1976	1980	1981
Atlanta	$ 63	$ 92	$113
Chicago	89	144	166
Los Angeles	109	161	185
New York	92	146	158

To monitor the changes in the average daily hospital room charges in major cities in the United States, calculate the unweighted aggregate price indexes for the years 1980 and 1981, using the year 1976 as the base period.

16.10 To measure the change in college tuition and required fees, the following data are collected for the years 1979–1981.

Institutions of Higher Education	Tuition and Fees			Enrollment (millions)
	1979	1980	1981	1979
Public	$ 554	595	657	9.0
Private	2,793	3,108	3,434	2.1

Construct a Laspeyres price index for 1979, 1980, and 1981, using 1979 as the base year.

16.11 The director of marketing research for a publishing company conducted a study about the pricing of new books and new editions published in selected subjects. The following information was gathered in connection with the study.

Subject	Price per Book			Number of Books Published		
	1978	1979	1980	1978	1979	1980
Business	$19.27	$23.11	$22.45	1258	1362	1185
Education	13.66	15.10	17.01	1063	1121	1011
History	17.20	19.79	22.78	2016	2220	1569
Medicine	25.01	29.27	34.28	2788	3257	3292
Religion	13.04	14.83	17.61	2180	2325	2055
Science	26.20	30.59	37.45	2942	3156	3109
Technology	22.64	27.82	33.64	1896	2391	2337

a) Construct a Laspeyres price index for each of the three years, using 1978 as the base period.

b) Using 1979 as a base period, construct a fixed weight price index with the 1980 quantities as the fixed weights.

16.12 Millionaire oilman Ty Coon has collected the following information about the number and cost of crude petroleum and natural gas wells drilled in the years 1980, 1981, and 1982.

Type of Well	Cost per Well (thousands of dollars)			Wells Drilled (thousands)		
	1980	1981	1982	1980	1981	1982
Oil well	208	243	291	17.8	19.2	21.0
Gas well	347	443	532	13.3	14.0	15.3

a) Construct a Layspeyres cost of drilling index for each year, using 1980 as the base year.

b) Using 1980 as the base period, construct a fixed weight cost index with the 1982 quantities as the fixed weight.

16.13 The following data represent U.S. imports of coffee, tea, and cocoa from 1977 to 1980.

Item	Quantity (millions of pounds)				Average Price (dollars per pound)			
	1977	1978	1979	1980	1977	1978	1979	1980
Coffee	1959	2399	2566	2401	1.97	1.55	1.49	1.61
Tea	203	152	175	185	.86	.75	.71	.70
Cocoa	678	588	501	379	1.39	1.47	1.55	1.39

Calculate a Paache price index for each year, using 1977 as the base period.

16.14 The following data represent the number of public school classroom teachers (elementary and secondary) and their average salaries from 1978 to 1980.

Type of School	Average Salary (thousands of dollars)			Teachers (tens of thousands)		
	1978	1979	1980	1978	1979	1980
Elementary	13.9	14.7	15.6	118	119	120
Secondary	14.6	15.5	16.4	102	102	100

Calculate a Paache salary index for each year, using 1978 as the base year.

16.15 The U.S. Bureau of Labor Statistics reports the following information describing employment and earnings in the mineral industries for the years 1978–1980.

Industry	Average Weekly Earnings (dollars)			Employment (thousands)		
	1978	*1979*	*1980*	*1978*	*1979*	*1980*
Metal	340	382	416	94	101	98
Coal	386	418	435	210	259	248
Oil & gas	315	343	390	429	474	552
Nonmetallic	284	311	328	119	124	123

Calculate a weighted price relative index for each year, using 1978 as the base year. Use the 1980 employment for weight.

16.16 The *Federal Reserve Bulletin* dated February 1982 reports the following number of commercial banks in the United States for the period 1975–1980.

Year	Number
1975	14,459
1976	14,631
1977	14,672
1978	14,704
1979	14,712
1980	14,708

Calculate quantity relative indexes for the years indicated, using 1975 as the base year.

16.17 The Motor Vehicles Manufacturers Association prepared the following data concerning the average number of gallons of fuel consumed and the average number of miles traveled per personal passenger vehicle per year for the years 1977–1981.

Year	Gallons of Fuel Consumed	Miles Traveled
1977	680	9613
1978	688	9812
1979	638	9245
1980	579	8865
1981	557	8758

a) Calculate quantity relative indexes of gallons consumed for the years indicated, using 1977 as the base year.

b) Calculate quantity relative indexes of miles traveled for the same years, using 1981 as the base year.

16.18 The U.S. Department of Agricultural Economics and Statistics Services reports the following data concerning main nutrients available for civilian consumption for the years 1978, 1979, and 1980.

Nutrient	Amount Available per Person per Day (grams)		
	1978	1979	1980
Protein	102	103	103
Fat	160	166	168
Carbohydrate	394	405	406

Construct unweighted quantity relative indexes for the years 1979 and 1980, using 1978 as the base period.

16.19 A national sample of 2044 young adults (18–25 years old) shows the following information concerning drug use in 1975 and 1980.

Type of Drug	Number of Users	
	1975	1980
Marijuana	515	724
Cocaine	51	90
Alcohol	1416	1552

Measure the change in drug use between 1975 and 1980 by constructing an unweighted quantity relative index for 1980, using 1975 as the base year.

16.20 The following data show the number of radios produced and imported, by type, for the years 1977–1980.

Type	Number of Radios (thousands)			
	1977	*1978*	*1979*	*1980*
Table model	1990	1805	1250	938
Portable model	26599	22074	17044	17721
Auto model	12890	12668	12381	9622

Calculate the unweighted average of relative quantity index for each year, using 1980 as the base period.

16.21 The following data show quantities and prices of three nonferrous metals imported by the United States in the years 1977–1980.

Metal	Imports (millions of pounds)				Price (cents per pound)			
	1977	*1978*	*1979*	*1980*	*1977*	*1978*	*1979*	*1980*
Copper	1280	1608	1057	1436	66.8	66.5	93.3	102.4
Aluminum	1484	2065	1687	1360	51.6	54.0	61.0	71.6
Lead	537	513	757	767	30.7	33.7	52.6	42.5

a) Calculate a Laspeyres quantity index, using 1977 as the base year.

b) Calculate a weighted aggregate quantity index, using 1980 prices for weights and 1980 as the base year.

KEY TERMS

price relative index An index of the price of a commodity relative to the price in a base year.

composite price index A price index for a group of commodities.

aggregate price index A price index computed using the total prices of a group of commodities in the current year and the base year.

Laspeyres price index A weighted aggregate price index that uses the quantities purchased in the base year as weights.

Paache index A weighted aggregate price index that uses the quantities purchased in the current year as weights.

fixed-weight aggregate price index A weighted aggregate price index that uses a fixed set of weights from some other period.

unweighted price relative index A price index obtained by averaging the price indexes of a group of commodities.

weighted price relative index A price index obtained by taking a weighted average of the price indexes of a group of commodities.

quantity relative index An index of the quantity of a commodity relative to the quantity in a particular base year.

Laspeyres quantity index A weighted quantity index that uses prices in the base year as weights.

Paache quantity index A weighted quantity index that uses current prices as weights.

Consumer price index A composite index of the prices of several hundred items compiled by the U.S. Bureau of Labor Statistics.

SUMMARY
OF FORMULAS

price relative index

$$I = \frac{P_n}{P_0} \cdot 100$$

unweighted aggregate price index

$$I = \frac{\sum P_n}{\sum P_0} \cdot 100$$

weighted aggregate price index

$$I = \frac{\sum P_n Q}{\sum P_0 Q} \cdot 100$$

Laspeyres price index

$$I = \frac{\sum P_n Q_0}{\sum P_0 Q_0} \cdot 100$$

Paache index

$$I = \frac{\sum P_n Q_n}{\sum P_0 Q_n} \cdot 100$$

fixed-weight aggregate price index

$$I = \frac{\sum P_n Q_f}{\sum P_0 Q_f} \cdot 100$$

unweighted price relative index

$$I = \frac{\sum \frac{P_n}{P_0} \cdot 100}{k}$$

weighted price relative index

$$I = \frac{\sum \left(\frac{P_n}{P_0} \cdot 100\right) PQ}{\sum PQ}$$

quantity relative index

$$I = \frac{Q_n}{Q_0} \cdot 100$$

Laspeyres quantity index

$$I = \frac{\sum Q_n P_0}{\sum Q_0 P_0} \cdot 100$$

Paache quantity index

$$I = \frac{\sum Q_n P_n}{\sum Q_0 P_n} \cdot 100$$

NONPARAMETRIC STATISTICS

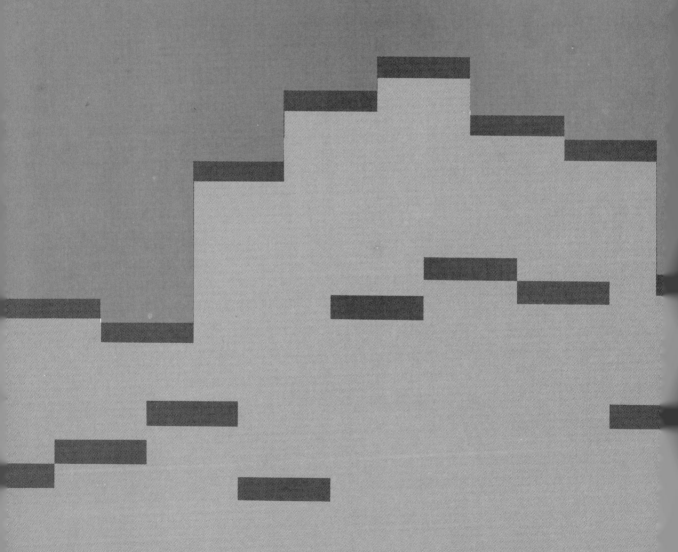

17

We have so far discussed various statistical methods that can be used either in estimating some population parameters or in testing hypotheses concerning these parameters. Statistical methods that deal with population parameters are parametric methods. In contrast to the parametric methods, which involve population parameters, nonparametric methods and tests are concerned with the nature of the population distribution. In this chapter we present some nonparametric statistical methods that are of considerable use nowadays.

In the preceding chapters, we developed various methods for testing hypotheses concerning population parameters. We have used the normal distribution to test the hypothesis that a population parameter such as the arithmetic mean, μ, or the proportion, π, is equal to a specified value. We have also used the normal distribution or the t-distribution to test the hypothesis that two populations have equal means, that is, $\mu_1 = \mu_2$. Finally, we used the F-distribution to test the hypothesis that several populations have equal means, that is, $\mu_1 = \mu_2 = \mu_3 = \cdots = \mu_k$. Tests in which the hypotheses deal with population parameters are called *parametric tests.* Hence, all the tests we have just described are parametric tests.

In contrast to parametric tests, which deal with tests concerning population parameters, nonparametric tests deal with hypotheses concerning population frequency distributions. A nonparametric test is used, for example, to test the hypothesis that two populations have the same frequency distributions.

Parametric tests often require certain assumptions about the population from which the sample is drawn. For example, the use of the t-distribution to test the significance of the difference between the means of two small samples requires that the two samples be independent samples selected from normally distributed populations with equal variances. Similarly, the use of the F-distribution to compare the means of several populations requires that the samples be drawn from normal populations with equal variances. When these stringent assumptions about the distributions of parent populations cannot be met, parametric tests are no longer applicable; and some alternative tests, called "distribution-free" tests, are employed instead. Although the term *nonparametric* originally referred only to tests dealing with hypotheses concerning population frequency distributions, distribution-free tests are also classified now as nonparametric tests.

Nonparametric tests have gained popularity in recent years for two main reasons. First, nonparametric tests require less restricting assumptions than comparable parametric tests and often require very few arithmetic computations. Second, but more important, nonparametric tests are found to be most suitable for analyzing data that consist of observations that can only be rated or ranked. For example, if a consumer panel ranks two products according to personal preference, we will discover that a nonparametric test is the most appropriate means of comparing the ranks received by the two products.

Before concluding this discussion, we must clearly point out that nonparametric tests do not utilize all the information provided by the sample. Consequently, in situations where both parametric and nonparametric tests are applicable, nonparametric tests have the definite disadvantage of allowing a greater risk of accepting a false hypothesis (committing a type II error). Hence, nonparametric tests should be reserved for situations where either the necessary conditions needed for a parametric test cannot be met or the nature of the data is not suitable for a parametric test, as in the case of ranked data.

THE SIGN TEST

We have already mentioned that the use of the t-distribution to test the significance of the difference between the means of two small samples requires that the two samples be independent random samples selected from normally distributed populations with equal variances. If any of these assumptions is not met, the use of the t-test can no longer be justified; an alternative nonparametric test called the **sign test** can be used in this case instead. Another use for the sign test is in the case of ranked data. We will illustrate each of these two cases by an example.

Example The pulse rates of 22 male students are measured before and after smoking. The results are shown in Table 17.1.* In addition, the rightmost column of Table 17.1 indicates whether the pulse rate has increased, decreased, or remained the same after smoking. An increase in pulse rate is indicated by a plus sign and a decrease is indicated by a minus sign. If we ignore the two cases where there are no changes in pulse rate, the sample size is reduced to 20 paired observations in which there are 15 plus signs and 5 minus signs.

Using the information presented in Table 17.1, let us now test the null hypothesis that smoking has no effect on the pulse rate against the alternative hypothesis that the pulse rate increases after smoking. We will use a level of significance of .05.

If the null hypothesis is true (if smoking has no effect on the pulse rate), we would expect an equal number of plus signs and minus signs in the population. Stated in different terms, the null hypothesis states that the probability of getting a plus sign is $\frac{1}{2}$ and the probability of getting a minus sign is $\frac{1}{2}$ also.

If the probability of getting a plus sign is $\frac{1}{2}$, then the number of plus signs in a random sample of size 20 is described by a binomial distribution with $\pi = \frac{1}{2}$ and $n = 20$. The mean and the standard deviation of this binomial distribution are

$$\mu = n\pi = 20 \cdot \frac{1}{2} = 10$$

and

$$\sigma = \sqrt{n\pi(1 - \pi)} = \sqrt{20 \cdot \frac{1}{2} \cdot \frac{1}{2}} = \sqrt{5} = 2.24.$$

Thus, if the null hypothesis is true, the number of plus signs in a random sample of 20 is expected to be 10. By contrast we have observed 15 plus signs in our sample. To test whether such disparity between the expected number of plus signs and the observed number of plus signs could be attributed to chance, we

---

*The t-test is not applicable here because the two samples are not independent.

TABLE 17.1   EFFECT OF SMOKING ON PULSE RATES

Student	Pulse Rate Before Smoking	Pulse Rate After Smoking	Sign of Change
1	72	74	+
2	70	72	+
3	68	69	+
4	67	68	+
5	73	72	−
6	71	72	+
7	72	72	No change
8	70	71	+
9	69	67	−
10	70	73	+
11	68	69	+
12	72	71	−
13	69	68	−
14	66	69	+
15	73	74	+
16	71	73	+
17	70	70	No change
18	72	74	+
19	70	68	−
20	69	71	+
21	72	74	+
22	73	74	+

will use the normal-curve approximation to the binomial distribution to determine the probability of getting 15 or more plus signs.

Hence, using a normal distribution with $\mu = 10$ and $\sigma = 2.24$, we find that the probability of getting 15 or more plus signs is approximated by the area lying to the right of $x = 14.5$ (shaded area in Fig. 17.1).

$$z = \frac{x - \mu}{\sigma} = \frac{14.5 - 10}{2.24} = \frac{4.5}{2.24} = 2.01,$$

$$A = .4778$$

Therefore,

$$P(X \geq 14.5) = .50 - .4778 = .0222.$$

Since the probability of getting 15 or more plus signs is less than .05, we reject the null hypothesis using the .05 level of significance. (The reader may already recall that the decision whether to reject the null hypothesis or to reserve judgment becomes obvious once the z-value is calculated. Using the .05 level

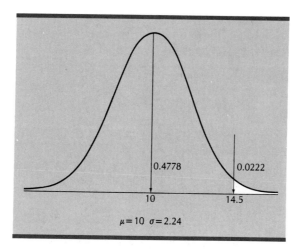

Figure 17.1

of significance, when the test is one-sided, the null hypothesis is rejected when the absolute value of z exceeds 1.64.)

As a final remark, we must note that by using the normal curve we can *approximate* the binomial probability of getting 15 or more plus signs as .0222. Using the cumulative binomial probabilities in Table G instead, we find that the exact probability is .0207. Comparing the approximated probability with the exact probability (.0222 vs. .0207), we see that our approximation indeed seems reasonable. In general, when the value of $\pi = \frac{1}{2}$, as is always the case in the sign test, the normal-curve approximation to the binomial distribution is quite adequate whenever $n \geq 10$.

Example A panel of 12 wine tasters is asked to test two varieties of wine: Cabernet Sauvignon and Pinot Noir. Each member of the panel is instructed to rank the two wines according to personal preference. Rank 2 is to be assigned to the most preferred wine and rank 1 to the least preferred one. Table 17.2 shows the ranks assigned to the two wines by members of the panel. In addition, the rightmost column of the table shows the sign of the difference of the ranks received by the two wines.

Using the information presented in Table 17.2, let us now test the null hypothesis that the two wines are equally preferred by the tasters against the alternative hypothesis that preference for the two wines is not the same. We will use a level of significance of .05.

If the null hypothesis is true (if tasters have equal preference for the two types of wines), we would expect an equal number of plus signs and minus signs in the population; we would consider the probability of getting a plus sign $\frac{1}{2}$ and the probability of getting a minus sign $\frac{1}{2}$.

TABLE 17.2   RANKS RECEIVED BY TWO TYPES OF WINE

Panel Member	Cabernet Sauvignon	Pinot Noir	Sign of Difference
A	2	1	+
B	2	1	+
C	1	2	−
D	2	1	+
E	2	1	+
F	2	1	+
G	1	2	−
H	2	1	+
I	2	1	+
J	1	2	−
K	1	2	−
L	2	1	+

Now, if the probability of getting a plus sign is $\frac{1}{2}$, then the number of plus signs in a random sample of size 12 is described by a binomial distribution with $\pi = \frac{1}{2}$ and $n = 12$. The mean and the standard deviation of this binomial distribution are

$$\mu = n\pi = 12 \cdot \frac{1}{2} = 6$$

and

$$\sigma = \sqrt{n\pi(1 - \pi)} = \sqrt{12 \cdot \frac{1}{2} \cdot \frac{1}{2}} = \sqrt{3} = 1.73.$$

Thus, if the null hypothesis is true, the number of plus signs in a random sample of size 12 is expected to be 6. By contrast, Table 17.2 shows 8 plus signs.

To test whether the disparity between the observed number of plus signs and the expected number of plus signs is significant at the .05 level, we will use the normal-curve approximation to the binomial distribution and determine z as

$$z = \frac{X - \mu}{\sigma} = \frac{7.5 - 6}{1.73} = \frac{1.5}{1.73} = .87.$$

Since the actual value of z is .87, which is less than 1.96, the null hypothesis cannot be rejected using the .05 level of significance (the test is two-sided). Thus we can conclude that the ranks assigned to the two types of wine by members of the board are not enough evidence to reject the hypothesis that consumers have equal preference for the two types of wine.

THE MANN-WHITNEY *U*-TEST

We will once again state that the use of the *t*-distribution to test the significance of the difference between the means of two small samples requires the following assumptions:

1. that the two samples selected are independent random samples, and
2. that the parent populations are normally distributed with equal variances.

We have also learned that the use of the sign test requires no such stringent assumptions.

However, in situations in which the first assumption is satisfied (the two samples are independent) and only the assumptions concerning the parent populations are in doubt, we can use a better nonparametric test, called the **Mann-Whitney *U*-test.** Compared to the sign test, the Mann-Whitney *U*-test utilizes more of the information contained in the sample and hence is more efficient. We will illustrate the Mann-Whitney *U*-test with the following example.

Example   An arithmetic test is administered to a random sample of 10 sixth graders from the Dallas school district. The same test is also administered to a random sample of 11 sixth graders from the Austin school district. The scores achieved by the two groups are as follows.

Dallas	Austin
70	72
68	67
73	74
81	65
66	63
56	77
62	71
75	60
83	76
48	61
	64

Let us now use the Mann-Whitney *U*-test to test the null hypothesis that the performance in arithmetic of all sixth graders in the Dallas school district is the

**TABLE 17.3   RANKING OF SCORES
(MANN-WHITNEY U-TEST)**

Dallas		Austin	
Score	*Rank*	*Score*	*Rank*
70	12	72	14
68	11	67	10
73	15	74	16
81	20	65	8
66	9	63	6
56	2	77	19
62	5	71	13
75	17	60	3
83	21	76	18
48	1	61	4
Rank sum	$R_1 = 113$	64	7
		Rank sum	$R_2 = 118$

same as that of students in the Austin school district. This hypothesis is tested against the alternative hypothesis that the performances are not the same. We will use a level of significance of .05.*

Solution: The Mann-Whitney U-test consists of the following steps:

Step 1.   We assign a rank to every score. Combining the scores of both groups, we assign rank 1 to the lowest score in the combined data, rank 2 to the second-lowest, rank 3 to the third-lowest, and so on. The ranks assigned to the various scores are shown in Table 17.3.

Step 2.   We sum the ranks received by each group. The rank sum is denoted by R. Table 17.3 shows that the sum of the ranks in the Dallas group is 113 and the sum of the ranks in the Austin group is 118. Hence, $R_1 = 113$ and $R_2 = 118$.

Step 3.   We determine the value of the Mann-Whitney U-statistic as

$$U = n_1 n_2 + \frac{n_1 (n_1 + 1)}{2} - R_1,$$

or

$$U = n_1 n_2 + \frac{n_2 (n_2 + 1)}{2} - R_2.$$

---

*The t-test is not applicable here because the Dallas scores show greater variability than the Austin scores.

We will choose the first formula to determine the value of U in our problem. With $n_1 = 10$, $n_2 = 11$, and $R_1 = 113$, the value of U is

$$U = n_1 n_2 + \frac{n_1 (n_1 + 1)}{2} - R_1$$

$$= 10 \cdot 11 + \frac{10(10 + 1)}{2} - 113 = 52.$$

Step 4. We determine the mean and the standard deviation of the statistic U. The mean of the statistic U, denoted by $E(U)$, is

$$E(U) = \frac{n_1 n_2}{2} = \frac{10 \cdot 11}{2} = 55.$$

The standard deviation of U, denoted by σ_U, is

$$\sigma_U = \sqrt{\frac{n_1 n_2 (n_1 + n_2 + 1)}{12}} = \sqrt{\frac{(10)(11)(10 + 11 + 1)}{12}} = 14.2.$$

Step 5. If both n_1 and $n_2 \geq 8$ (as is the case in our problem), the statistic U is approximately normally distributed. Hence, we calculate the value of z as

$$z = \frac{U - E(U)}{\sigma_U} = \frac{52 - 55}{14.2} = -.21.$$

Since the absolute value of z is .21, which is less than 1.96, we cannot reject the null hypothesis using the .05 level of significance. In other words, based on the information contained in the two samples, there is not enough evidence to reject the hypothesis that the arithmetic performance of sixth graders in both school districts is the same.

We will conclude our discussion now with two important remarks.

1. When there are ties between observations, the identical values are assigned the mean of their tied ranks. For example, if the 5th and 6th values are the same, the rank of 5.5 is assigned to each of the two observations, and the next observation in the sequence is assigned the rank 7. Similarly, if there is a tie between the 9th, 10th, and 11th observations, the rank 10 is assigned to each of these three observations and the rank 12 is assigned to the next observation in the sequence.

2. The statistic U is approximately normally distributed only when both n_1 and n_2 are 8 or more. If this condition is not met, the use of the normal distribution is no longer appropriate and special tables are needed to test the significance of U.

THE KRUSKAL-WALLIS *H*-TEST

The **Kruskal-Wallis *H*-test** is an extended version of the Mann-Whitney test. It is used to test the null hypothesis that several independent samples belong to identical populations. As in the Mann-Whitney test, we assign a rank to every observation. Considering the observations of all samples together, we assign rank 1 to the lowest value, rank 2 to the second-lowest value, and so on. After summing the ranks that have been assigned to each sample, we compute the statistic *H* as

$$H = \frac{12}{n(n+1)} \left(\frac{R_1^2}{n_1} + \frac{R_2^2}{n_2} + \cdots + \frac{R_k^2}{n_k} \right) - 3(n+1),$$

where

k = number of samples,
R_1 = sum of ranks assigned to the n_1 observations of the first sample,
R_2 = sum of ranks assigned to the n_2 observations of the second sample,
R_k = sum of ranks assigned to the n_k observations of the kth sample,
$n = n_1 + n_2 + \cdots + n_k$ (total number of observations in all samples).

Assuming that the null hypothesis is true, and assuming that each sample consists of at least five observations, then the statistic *H* has a probability distribution that can be approximated by a chi-square distribution with $k - 1$ degrees of freedom. Hence, the null hypothesis is rejected at the .05 level of significance if the value of $H \geq \chi_{.05}^2$; and it is rejected at the .01 level of significance if the value of $H \geq \chi_{.01}^2$. We will illustrate the Kruskal-Wallis *H*-test with an example.

Example   To compare the effectiveness of three types of weight-reducing diets, a homogeneous group of 22 students was divided into three subgroups, and each subgroup followed one diet plan for a period of two weeks. The weight losses, in pounds, during these two weeks were as follows:

First Plan	Second Plan	Third Plan
5.3	6.3	2.4
4.2	8.4	3.1
3.7	9.3	3.7
7.2	6.5	4.1
6.0	7.7	2.5
4.8	8.2	1.7
	9.5	5.3
		4.5
		1.3

Use the Kruskal-Wallis *H*-test to test the null hypothesis that the effectiveness of the three reducing plans is going to be the same, against the alternative hypothesis that their effectiveness is not going to be the same. Use a level of significance of .01.

Solution: The first step in our solution is to assign a rank to every observation in the combined data. The ranks assigned to the observations and the sum of the ranks received by each sample are shown in Table 17.4. With $n_1 = 6$, $n_2 = 7$, $n_3 = 9$, and $R_1 = 70$, $R_2 = 131$, $R_3 = 52$, we can now determine the value of the statistic *H* as

$$H = \frac{12}{n(n+1)} \left(\frac{R_1^2}{n_1} + \frac{R_2^2}{n_2} + \frac{R_3^2}{n_3} \right) - 3(n+1)$$

$$= \frac{12}{22(22+1)} \left(\frac{70^2}{6} + \frac{131^2}{7} + \frac{52^2}{9} \right) - 3(22+1)$$

$$= 15.633.$$

To test the null hypothesis at the .01 level of significance, we now compare this value of *H* against $\chi^2_{.01}$ with $k - 1$ degrees of freedom. According to Table D, the value of $\chi^2_{.01}$ (d.f. = 2) is 9.210. Hence, since the value of *H* is greater than $\chi^2_{.01}$, the null hypothesis is rejected at the .01 level of significance. In other words, using the information provided by the three samples, we are able to conclude that the effectiveness of the three diet plans is not going to be the same.

TABLE 17.4   ASSIGNMENT OF RANKS (KRUSKAL-WALLIS TEST)

First Plan		Second Plan		Third Plan	
Loss	*Rank*	*Loss*	*Rank*	*Loss*	*Rank*
5.3	12.5	6.3	15	2.4	3
4.2	9	8.4	20	3.1	5
3.7	6.5	9.3	21	3.7	6.5
7.2	17	6.5	16	4.1	8
6.0	14	7.7	18	2.5	4
4.9	11	8.2	19	1.7	2
	$R_1 = 70$	9.5	22	5.3	12.5
			$R_2 = 131$	4.5	10
				1.3	1
					$R_3 = 52$

RANK CORRELATION

The coefficient of rank correlation (also called **Spearman's rank-correlation coefficient**) is used to measure the degree of association between two sets of ranks observations. For example, if the teaching performances of a group of college professors are ranked independently by their dean and by their department chairperson, the coefficient of rank correlation can be used to measure the consistency of the two sets of ranks assigned by the two administrators.

Some observations, such as the teaching abilities of the group of college professors, cannot be measured but can only be ranked; and the coefficient of rank correlations is the best means for measuring the degree of relationship between two sets of ranks. However, the coefficient of rank correlation can also be used to determine the degree of relationship between two sets of measurements once the measurements are converted into ranks. We will illustrate the use of the rank-correlation coefficient with two examples. In the first example, the coefficient of rank correlation is used to determine the consistency of two sets of ratings. In the second example, in addition to computing the coefficient of correlation, we will describe the method used to convert two sets of measurements into two sets of ranks.

Example   The teaching abilities of a group of 10 college professors are ranked independently by their dean and by their department chairperson. Rank 1 is given to the best professor, rank 2 to the second best, . . . , and rank 10 to the professor with the worst teaching performance. The two sets of ranks are as follows:

Professor	Dean's Rating	Chairperson's Rating
A	5	6
B	4	4
C	3	5
D	1	2
E	2	1
F	6	3
G	7	10
H	10	9
I	9	7
J	8	8

Calculate the coefficient of rank correlation as a measure of the consistency of the two ratings.

TABLE 17.5 COMPUTATIONS FOR COEFFICIENT OF RANK CORRELATION

Professor	Dean's Rating	Chairperson's Rating	d	d^2
A	5	6	−1	1
B	4	4	0	0
C	3	5	−2	4
D	1	2	−1	1
E	2	1	+1	1
F	6	3	+3	9
G	7	10	−3	9
H	10	9	+1	1
I	9	7	+2	4
J	8	8	0	0
				$\sum d^2 = 30$

Solution: The Spearman's rank-correlation coefficient, denoted by r_s, is determined as

$$r_s = 1 - \frac{6 \sum d^2}{n(n^2 - 1)},$$

where n is the number of paired observations and d is the difference between each pair of ranks. The preliminary computations for finding r_s are shown in Table 17.5.

Substituting $\sum d^2 = 30$ from Table 17.5 and $n = 10$ into the formula for r_s, we get

$$r_s = 1 - \frac{6 \sum d^2}{n(n^2 - 1)}$$

$$= 1 - \frac{6 \cdot 30}{10(10^2 - 1)} = .82.$$

Example A large automobile agency wishes to determine the relationship between a salesperson's aptitude test score and the number of cars sold by the salesperson during the first year of employment. A random sample of 15 salespersons' files reveals the following information.

Salesperson	Test Score x	Number of Cars y
A	72	341
B	88	422
C	70	322
D	87	440
E	71	287
F	85	415
G	89	463
H	93	497
I	98	510
J	96	512
K	86	432
L	82	390
M	88	453
N	83	374
O	80	385

Calculate the coefficient of rank correlation to measure the degree of relationship between test scores and the number of cars sold.

Solution: The first step in our solution is to replace the two sets of measurements by two sets of ranks. Beginning with the test scores, we assign Rank 1 to the highest score, Rank 2 to the second highest score, . . . , and Rank 15 to the lowest score. The numbers of cars sold are ranked in a similar fashion, giving Rank 1 to the greatest number of cars sold and Rank 15 to the smallest number.

Table 17.6 shows the two sets of measurements and their corresponding sets of ranks, together with the preliminary computations needed to compute r_s.

Substituting $\sum d^2 = 18.5$ (Table 17.6), and $n = 15$ into the formula for r_s, we get

$$r_s = 1 - \frac{6 \sum d^2}{n(n^2 - 1)} = 1 - \frac{(6)(18.5)}{15(15^2 - 1)} = 0.97.$$

Significance of Rank Correlation

To test the significance of the rank-correlation coefficient r_s we begin with the null hypothesis that there is no correlation between the two sets of ranks in the population. Assuming that the null hypothesis is true, and assuming that $n \geq 25$, the statistic r_s is approximately normally distributed, with a mean of 0 and a

TABLE 17.6 COMPUTATIONS FOR COEFFICIENT OF RANK CORRELATION

Score x	Number of Cars y	Rank of x	Rank of y	d	d^2
72	341	13	13	0	0
88	422	5.5	8	−2.5	6.25
70	322	15	14	+1	1
87	440	7	6	+1	1
71	287	14	15	−1	1
85	415	9	9	0	0
89	463	4	4	0	0
93	497	3	3	0	0
98	510	1	2	−1	1
96	512	2	1	+1	1
86	432	8	7	+1	1
82	390	11	10	+1	1
88	453	5.5	5	+0.5	0.25
83	374	10	12	−2	4
80	385	12	11	+1	1
					$\sum d^2 = 18.5$

standard deviation of $1/\sqrt{n-1}$. Hence, to test the significance of r_s, we compute the value of z as

$$z = \frac{r_s - 0}{1/\sqrt{n-1}}$$

$$= r_s \sqrt{n-1}.$$

The coefficient of rank correlation is significant at the .05 level when the absolute value of z is greater than 1.96. It is significant at the .01 level when the value of z is greater than 2.58. Special tables are used to test the significance of r_s when the sample size is small.

Example   Given that $n = 26$ and $r_s = .4$, test the significance of r_s using a .05 level of significance.

Solution: Substituting $r_s = .4$ and $n = 26$ into the formula

$$z = r_s \sqrt{n-1},$$

we get

$$z = .4 \sqrt{26 - 1} = 2.$$

Since the value of z is greater than 1.96, the coefficient of rank correlation is significant at the .05 level of significance.

17.1   Ten viewers selected at random are asked to rate two comedy television programs, X and Y. A rank of 2 is to be assigned to the most preferred program and a rank of 1 to the least preferred one. The ratings received by the two programs are shown below.

Viewer	Program X	Program Y
A	2	1
B	2	1
C	1	2
D	2	1
E	1	2
F	2	1
G	2	1
H	1	2
I	1	2
J	2	1

Perform a sign test to test the hypothesis that programs X and Y are rated the same by television viewers. Use a level of significance of .05.

17.2   An engineering consulting firm is considering moving its main offices to a new location. To assess employees' preferences for the proposed location, a random sample of 16 employees are asked whether they prefer the present or the new location. Employees' responses are shown below.

Employee	Location Preferred	Employee	Location Preferred
A	New	I	New
B	Present	J	New
C	New	K	New
D	New	L	Present
E	New	M	New
F	Present	N	Present
G	Present	O	New
H	New	P	New

Use the sign test to test the hypothesis that the two locations are equally preferred by the company employees. Use a level of significance of .05.

17.3   The play constructiveness of 12 schoolchildren was measured during a free-play period and during play in a frustrating situation. The two ratings are shown below.

Child	Constructiveness Index, Free Play	Constructiveness Index, Frustrating Play
A	3.7	3.1
B	4.2	3.8
C	5.1	4.7
D	6.3	6.1
E	5.3	5.4
F	4.7	3.2
G	6.2	5.3
H	6.3	5.7
I	6.7	4.6
J	7.1	7.6
K	4.2	3.2
L	4.8	3.5

Perform a sign test to test the hypothesis that frustration has no effect on play constructiveness. Use a level of significance of .01.

17.4 An anxiety test was given to a group of 14 male college students while sober. The same test was administered to the same group two hours after each student drank 3 ounces of vodka. The results of the two tests are shown below.

Subject	Anxiety Rating Before Drinking	Anxiety Rating After Drinking
1	97	82
2	81	71
3	72	63
4	63	54
5	92	77
6	63	72
7	81	66
8	73	54
9	63	51
10	82	88
11	54	50
12	88	73
13	93	82
14	68	52

Perform a sign test to test the null hypothesis that alcohol has no effect on anxiety against the alternative hypothesis that alcohol reduces anxiety. Use a level of significance of .01.

17.5 The Army Alpha Test, an intelligence test, was administered to two age groups, a group of 20-year-olds and a group of 40-year-olds. The test scores of the two groups are shown below.

20-Year-Olds	40-Year-Olds
142	122
130	125
132	132
137	127
145	130
143	135
147	124
138	140
141	126
148	133
152	
140	

Perform the Mann-Whitney test to test the hypothesis that the average intelligence of both age groups are the same. Use a level of significance of .05.

17.6 In an experiment concerning dream reporting, 26 healthy female college students were observed for a period of two weeks. According to the number and the detail of the dreams reported in the two weeks, the students were categorized into two groups: recallers and nonrecallers. Among the various personality characteristics of the students observed during the two weeks was time asleep each day. The data below represents the average number of minutes of sleep per day for each student in the two categories.

Dream Recallers	Nonrecallers	Dream Recallers	Nonrecallers
477	430	430	397
432	453	475	424
445	418	463	360
460	392	452	372
480	427	447	438
457	441	431	
422	411	472	

Perform the Mann-Whitney test on the hypothesis that the length of sleep for dream recallers and nonrecallers is the same. Use a level of significance of .05.

17.7 In an investigation concerning the physiological status of schizophrenic patients, 19 patients were classified into three groups according to the severity of their psychosis: (1) remission; (2) moderate; (3) severe. The respiratory rates for individual patients in the three subgroups are shown below.

Remission	Moderate	Severe
16.6	17.8	18.6
16.3	17.2	18.4
17.3	17.7	18.3
16.5	17.5	18.8
17.1	18.2	17.6
16.9	17.4	18.5
	16.8	

Perform the Kruskal-Wallis test of the hypothesis that the respiratory rates of patients in the three stages of schizophrenia are the same. Use a level of significance of .01.

17.8 The social maturity scores received by 39 persons belonging to five occupational groups are shown below.

Dentists	Bankers	Machinists	Military Officers	Research Scientists
56.3	54.3	43.4	50.3	55.7
54.7	56.7	44.3	51.7	55.7
58.2	55.4	47.3	52.6	57.5
53.3	57.4	41.2	49.8	57.3
57.6	56.4	42.7	52.3	58.9
55.1	58.5	45.2	53.7	54.5
56.2		45.7	46.3	
58.4		42.5	54.6	
59.2		46.2		
		40.6		

Use the Kruskal-Wallis test to test the hypothesis that social maturity of the five occupational groups is the same, against the alternative hypothesis that their social maturity is not the same. Use a level of significance of .01.

17.9   Two judges rated the participants of a beauty contest as follows:

Contestant	Rating by First Judge	Rating by Second Judge
A	5	3
B	1	2
C	6	4
D	2	1
E	7	7
F	4	5
G	3	8
H	8	6

Compute the coefficient of rank correlation as a measure of the consistency of ratings assigned by the two judges.

17.10   The following are the scores achieved by a group of sixth graders on tests in arithmetic and reading:

Student	Arithmetic Test Score	Reading Test Score
1	72	75
2	63	68
3	82	85
4	75	82
5	93	95
6	77	79
7	66	63
8	57	60
9	83	88
10	74	86

Compute the coefficient of rank correlation to measure the degree of relationship between the reading ability and the arithmetic performance of a sixth grader.

17.11   A consumer panel rated 10 different models of color television sets according to their overall quality. The quality rank and the average retail price of each set is shown below.

Set	Quality Rank	Average Price (dollars)
A	10	450
B	1	600
C	2	525
D	5	515
E	4	495
F	3	475
G	6	550
H	7	480
I	9	560
J	8	530

Compute the coefficient of rank correlation to measure the degree of relationship between the quality and the price of a color television set.

17.12 Test the significance of the rank-correlation coefficient in each of the following samples.

a) $n = 37$, $r_s = .4$ ($\alpha = .01$)

b) $n = 50$, $r_s = .3$ ($\alpha = .05$)

c) $n = 65$, $r_s = .2$ ($\alpha = .05$)

17.13 Sixteen families are randomly selected in a given community. The sample shows the following information concerning annual family income and monthly housing expenditures.

Family	Annual Income (thousands of dollars)	Monthly Housing Expenditures
A	22	306
B	30	332
C	15	350
D	40	740
E	7	143
F	24	320
G	15	451
H	14	250
I	21	314
J	17	265
K	19	503
L	50	350

(Continued)

Family	Annual Income (thousands of dollars)	Monthly Housing Expenditures
M	25	400
N	19	362
O	7	245
P	13	400

Compute the coefficient of rank correlation to measure the degree of relationship between family annual income and housing expenditures.

KEY TERMS

nonparametric test   A test of a hypothesis about a population that does not depend on strict assumptions about the type of distribution involved.

sign test   A test of the hypothesis that there is no difference between two populations using only the sign ($+$ or $-$) of the change from one population to the next for each observation.

Mann-Whitney U-test   A test of the hypothesis that there is no difference between two independent populations using only the ranks of the values in the two samples.

Kruskal-Wallis H-test   A test of the hypothesis that there is no difference between several independent populations using only the ranks of the values in the samples.

Spearman's rank-correlation coefficient (r_s)   A measure of the association between two sets of rank observations.

SUMMARY OF FORMULAS

Mann-Whitney U-statistic $U = n_1 n_2 + \left(\dfrac{n_1 (n_1 + 1)}{2} \right) - R_1$

mean of Mann-Whitney U-statistic $E(U) = \dfrac{n_1 n_2}{2}$

standard deviation of
Mann-Whitney U-statistic
$$\sigma_U = \sqrt{\frac{n_1 n_2 (n_1 + n_2 + 1)}{12}}$$

Kruskal-Wallis H-statistic
$$H = \frac{12}{n(n + 1)} \left(\frac{R_1^2}{n_1} + \cdots + \frac{R_k^2}{n_k}\right) - 3 (n + 1)$$

Spearman's rank-
correlation coefficient
$$r_s = 1 - \frac{6\sum d^2}{n (n^2 - 1)},$$

where d is the difference
between each pair of ranks.

standard deviation of
rank-correlation
coefficient
$$\sigma_{r_s} = 1/\sqrt{n - 1}$$

DECISION MAKING USING SUBJECTIVE INFORMATION

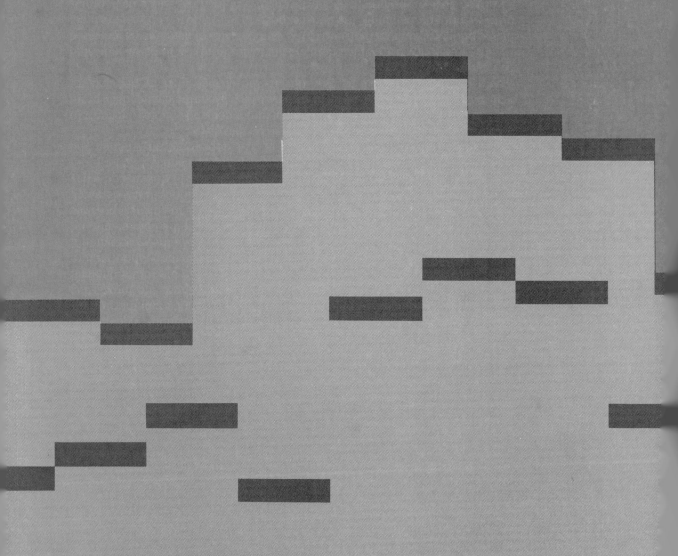

18

The general theme of the preceding chapters has been statistical inference, that is, generalization about the entire population based on sample information. The central issue in this and Chapter 19 is decision making. In this chapter we develop a general model for formulating a decision-making problem and then for solving the decision problem using subjective information. Solutions using both subjective and objective information are reserved for the next chapter.

In the preceding chapters we have dealt primarily with two closely related problems:

1. the problem of estimating some population characteristics such as the population arithmetic mean, μ, and the population proportion, π, and

2. the problem of testing a hypothesis concerning some population characteristic or parameter.

Whether our problem is to estimate some population parameter or to test a hypothesis concerning the value of that parameter, the method we use in solving the problem is one and the same: We select a random sample from the population and use that sample information as the basis for all inferences to be made in regard to the population parameters. Let us assume that the problem at hand is to estimate the proportion of senior students in this college. If a random sample of 100 students selected from this college reveals 10 senior students, we would then estimate the proportion of seniors in the entire college as 10/100 or 10%.*

Two types of information can be used in making an inference about a population characteristic: objective information and subjective information. The information obtained through sampling is **objective information.** The personal opinion of an expert in the field, on the other hand, is **subjective information.** In estimating the proportion of senior students in this college as 10%, we have adopted the traditional or classical method of statistical inference, a method in which inference about the population is based strictly on objective sample information.

In contrast to the classical statistical methods, which can utilize no other information but objective sample information, a new approach in statistics, called *Bayesian statistics,* is capable of utilizing all *relevant* available information, subjective and objective. In Bayesian statistics, an inference about a population parameter can indeed be made on the basis of subjective information exclusively. However, if objective sample information becomes available later, subjective and objective information are combined, and inferences about the population parameter are based on this combined information.

The distinction between classical and Bayesian statistics can be brought into sharp focus by considering the following example. A manufacturing company is considering the purchase of a new machine, called machine A. The decision whether to purchase or not to purchase machine A will be based on the proportion of defective parts turned out by the machine. Based on his past

---

*The sample data can also be used to establish a confidence interval estimate of the parameter. A .95 confidence interval estimate of the proportion of seniors in this college is established as follows:

$$.10 \pm 1.96 \left(\sqrt{\frac{.10 \cdot .90}{100}} \right) = .10 \pm .06,$$

or between 4% and 16%.

experience with similar machines, the company quality-control engineer estimates the proportion of defective parts produced by machine A as follows.

Proportion of Defective parts	Probability
.05	.30
.06	.50
.07	.20

This means that the quality-control engineer is not quite sure of the proportion of defective parts produced by machine A. However, based on his knowledge and experience, the engineer believes that the probability is .30 that the proportion of defective parts produced by machine A is 5%; the probability is .50 that the proportion of defective parts is 6%; and there is a .20 chance that the proportion of defective parts is 7%.

Two important remarks can be made at this stage of our discussion. First, the quality-control engineer's information concerning machine A is personal or *subjective*, since some other engineer might very well give a different estimate of the proportion of defective parts produced by machine A. Second, in contrast to classical statistics, which does not utilize this subjective information at all, Bayesian statistics is specially designed to make the most constructive use of this type of information. In fact, using the quality-control engineer's subjective information, Bayesian statistics would enable the company to decide whether to purchase machine A.

Continuing the case of machine A, let us further assume that in a trial run a random sample of 100 parts produced by machine A reveals 4 defective parts. Now, according to classical statistics, the proportion of defective parts produced by machine A is estimated as 4%. However, using Bayesian statistics, the sample information is combined with the quality-control engineer's subjective information, and an estimate of the proportion of defective parts produced by machine A is made on the basis of this combination of information.

The use of subjective information in statistical inference is but one feature of Bayesian statistics. Recently, Bayesian statistics has been developed into an integrated theory for decision making called *Bayesian decision theory.*

Bayesian decision theory deals with the problem of decision making under conditions of uncertainty. The theory provides decision makers with a rational and systematic procedure that enables them to choose among several alternative courses when the consequence of each course is subject to uncertainty.

As a first step in discussing the role of subjective information in the decision-making process, let us begin with a brief description of some elements common to most decision-making problems. These common characteristics can best be described in relation to a concrete decision problem.

DECISION PROBLEM

A florist orders carnations one day in advance. The cost of carnations is $1 per dozen and the selling price is $3 per dozen. Unsold carnations at the end of each day are worthless. The florist estimates her daily customers' demand for carnations as follows.

Daily Demand (dozens)	Probability of Demand
10	.60
11	.30
12	.10
	1.00

How many dozens of carnations should she stock each day?

Our carnation problem contains all the elements of decision making under uncertainty. First, there is the decision maker, the florist in this case. Second, the decision maker must choose among several alternative courses of actions, called **acts.** The alternative courses open to the florist are act_1—stock 10 dozen carnations each day; act_2—stock 11 dozen carnations each day; and act_3—stock 12 dozen carnations each day. These three acts are the only rational courses of action to be considered by the florist, since she can always sell 10 dozen carnations in a day and can never sell more than 12 dozen. Thus, it is irrational to stock *less than* 10 dozen, or *more than* 12 dozen on any day.

The third element in a decision problem is the various possible **events** that determine the consequences of adopting any act by the decision maker. The events in our problem are represented by the three possible levels of demand for carnations by customers. The first event is that daily demand is 10 dozen; the second event is that daily demand is 11 dozen; and the third event is that daily demand is 12 dozen. The possible events in a decision problem are sometimes called *states of nature* (or states of the world), because it is assumed that these events are beyond the control of the decision maker. The acts and events in our carnation problem are shown in Table 18.1.

The fourth characteristic of a decision problem is the element of uncertainty in regard to the occurrence of the various possible events or states of nature. It is true that these events are beyond the control of the decision maker; however, the decision maker would assign personal or subjective probabilities to the various events, probabilities based on whatever current information is available, together with the decision maker's flair, experience, judgment, and expectations. The subjective probabilities assigned by the decision maker to the various events are called **prior probabilities,** which are to be revised in the light of any additional sample information (the revision of

TABLE 18.1   CARNATION PROBLEM: ACTS AND EVENTS

Events	Acts		
	Act₁: *Stock 10*	*Act₂:* *Stock 11*	*Act₃:* *Stock 12*
E_1: Demand = 10 E_2: Demand = 11 E_3: Demand = 12			

prior probabilities is treated in the next chapter). Thus, the probabilities assigned by the florist to the various levels of customer demand for carnations are subjective prior probabilities. Before we proceed in our discussion, let us summarize the acts, events, and prior probabilities in Table 18.2.

The last and final element in a decision problem is measuring the consequences of the various acts. Frequently, consequences are measured either by the *profit* accrued to the decision maker or by the *cost* incurred by him or her. A consequence, regardless of whether it is a profit or a cost, is called a *payoff*.

Consequences (or payoffs) are displayed in a table called a **payoff table;** such a table shows a payoff for *every possible combination* of acts and events. The payoff table in our carnation problem shows the profit received by the florist under all possible combinations of levels of stock and levels of customer demand for carnations (see Table 18.3).

The nine payoffs in the table were obtained as follows: The first payoff, $20, is the profit obtained when the florist stocks 10 dozen and the demand for carnations by customers is exactly 10 dozen. The second payoff is also $20 because the florist stocked only 10 dozen, although she could have sold 11 dozen; similarly for payoff (3). The fourth payoff in the table, $19, is the profit

TABLE 18.2   CARNATION PROBLEM: ACTS, EVENTS, AND PRIOR PROBABILITIES

Events	Prior Probabilities of Events	Acts		
		Act₁: *Stock 10*	*Act₂:* *Stock 11*	*Act₃:* *Stock 12*
E_1: Demand = 10	.60			
E_2: Demand = 11	.30			
E_3: Demand = 12	.10			

TABLE 18.3   PAYOFF TABLE: CONDITIONAL PROFITS

Events	Prior Probabilities of Events	Acts		
		Act_1: Stock 10	Act_2: Stock 11	Act_3: Stock 12
E_1: Demand = 10	.60	$20 (1)	$19 (4)	$18 (7)
E_2: Demand = 11	.30	$20 (2)	$22 (5)	$21 (8)
E_3: Demand = 12	.10	$20 (3)	$22 (6)	$24 (9)

obtained by stocking 11 dozen and selling only 10 dozen. This profit is computed as follows:

$$\text{Profit} = \text{Total revenue} - \text{total cost}$$
$$(10 \times \$3) \quad - (11 \times \$1) = \$19.$$

All other payoffs are determined in the same manner.

The seventh payoff, $18, is the profit obtained by stocking 12 dozen and selling only 10 dozen:

$$\text{Profit} = \text{Total revenue} - \text{Total cost}$$
$$(10 \times \$3) \quad - (12 \times \$1) = \$18.$$

As designated at the head of Table 18.3, these profits are called *conditional profits* since each is dependent (or conditional) on how much the florist has in stock and how much customers are going to buy.

CHOOSING THE OPTIMAL ACT

Having determined the consequences or payoffs* of each possible course of action, the decision maker must now choose among these acts. The choice can be made using a number of different criteria. Some common criteria of choice are the following.

Maximax Criterion

Using the maximax criterion, the decision maker compares the alternative acts on the basis of their maximum payoff and chooses the act with the highest maximum. In our carnation problem, for example, the maximum payoffs are $20, $22, and $24 for act_1, act_2, and act_3, respectively. Hence, the florist would choose act_3, since this act has the *highest maximum* of all three acts.

---

*Here we assume that payoffs are expressed in terms of profits.

The decision maker who uses the maximax criterion is very optimistic indeed. He or she believes that the most favorable event will occur and consequently chooses the act with the highest possible payoff.

Minimax Criterion

Using the minimax criterion, the decision maker compares alternative acts on the basis of their minimum payoffs and chooses the act with the highest minimum. In the carnation problem, the minimum payoffs are $20, $19, and $18 for act_1, act_2, and act_3, respectively. Hence, the florist would choose act_1 since this act possesses the *highest minimum* of all three acts.

The decision maker here is a pessimistic person who believes that the least favorable event will prevail. Consequently he or she chooses the act that promises the highest payoff under the worst possible event.

Bayesian Decision Criterion*

The maximax and minimax criteria of choice may lead the decision maker to take some irrational actions, because both these criteria fail to take into account the likelihoods (probabilities) of the various events in a problem. The following payoff table demonstrates how unsatisfactory the maximax criterion could become.

	Payoff Table: Conditional Profits		
Events	*Probability of Event*	*Acts*	
		Act₁	*Act₂*
A	.01	$10,000	$9950
B	.99	−$80,000	$9000

Using the maximax rule as a criterion of choice, the decision maker would choose act_1 since, in comparing the two acts on the basis of their maximum payoffs ($10,000 vs. $9,950), he or she would find that act_1 has the *highest maximum*.

Although the minimax rule is satisfactory as a criterion of choice in a certain class of problems (the class called *games* against an intelligent opponent, which will not be treated here), its use may lead to irrational choices in the type of problems we are considering in this chapter. The following payoff table demonstrates how unsatisfactory the minimax criterion could become.

---

*The reader should be warned at the outset that the Bayesian decision criterion to be discussed here is an entirely different concept from Bayes' theorem, discussed in Chapter 3.

Payoff Table: Conditional Profit			
Events	Probability of Event	Acts	
		Act₁	Act₂
A	.01	$0	−$1
B	.99	$0	$10,000

Using the minimax rule as a criterion of choice, the decision maker would select act₁ since, in comparing the two acts on the basis of their minimum payoffs ($0 vs. −$1), he or she finds that act₁ has the *highest minimum* of the two acts.

While the likelihoods of events, or their probabilities, are completely ignored under the maximax and minimax criteria, these probabilities are an integral part of the Bayesian decision criterion.

Using the Bayesian decision criterion, the decision maker compares alternative acts on the basis of their *expected* payoffs and chooses the act with the best expected payoff. Accordingly, the florist must determine the expected profit of each act and select the act with the highest expected profit.

Before we proceed to compute the expected profit of the three possible acts in the carnation problem, we display the payoff table once more.

Payoff Table: Conditional Profits				
Events	Prior Probability	Acts		
		Act₁	Act₂	Act₃
E₁: Demand = 10	.60	$20	$29	$18
E₂: Demand = 11	.30	$20	$22	$21
E₃: Demand = 12	.10	$20	$22	$24

The expected profit of any one act is the sum of the products obtained by multiplying the conditional profits of that act by their corresponding probabilities of occurrence. The computations are carried out in Table 18.4.

Table 18.4 shows that act₂ yields the highest expected profit; it is called the *optimal act.* The expected profit of the optimal act, $20.20, is called **expected profit under uncertainty.** This means that although the florist is uncertain about the level of daily demand for carnations, she expects an average profit of

TABLE 18.4   **CARNATION PROBLEM: DETERMINATION OF EXPECTED PROFITS**

Act$_1$	Act$_2$	Act$_3$
$20 · .60 = $12.00	$19 · .60 = $11.40	$18 · .60 = $10.80
$20 · .30 = $ 6.00	$22 · .30 = $ 6.60	$21 · .30 = $ 6.30
$20 · .10 = $ 2.00	$22 · .10 = $ 2.20	$24 · .10 = $ 2.40
Expected profit $20.00	$20.20	$19.50

$20.20 per day if she continues to stock 11 dozen carnations each and every day.

OTHER CONCEPTS IN DECISION THEORY

Expected Profit with Perfect Information

Let us assume that there exists (at least theoretically) a forecasting service that enables the florist to exactly predict future demand for carnations. With the aid of this perfect predictor, the florist would know in advance whether tomorrow's demand is going to be 10, 11, or 12 dozen. In short, the forecasting service provides the florist with *perfect information* about the future demand for carnations. Under this condition of perfect information about future demand, the florist would order carnations *after* she knows the exact amount demanded by customers. Consequently, she would stock the correct amount of carnations each and every day and hence would realize the highest possible profit each day. In other words, with perfect information about future demand, the florist stocks 10 dozen for the day when demand is 10, 11 dozen for the day when demand is 11, and 12 dozen for the day when demand is 12. Her profit on any given day would be $20, $22, or $24 depending on whether the demand happens to be 10, 11, or 12 dozen on that day.

It is true that perfect information about future demand enables the florist to realize the *highest possible profit* in any given day. Nevertheless her daily profit would fluctuate from day to day, due to the change in daily demand for carnations.

The frequency with which demand fluctuates from day to day is indicated by the prior probabilities assigned to the various states of demand. As indicated by these prior probabilities, the florist expects to sell 10 dozen 60% of the time, 11 dozen 30% of the time, and 12 dozen 10% of the time. Since daily profits fluctuate in the same manner as that of demand, the florist expects a daily profit of $20 60% of the time, a daily profit of $22 30% of the time, and a daily profit of $24 10% of the time; this would result in an expected profit of $21 per day. (See computations below.)

Profit	Prior Probability (frequency)	Profit · Probability
$20	.60	$12.00
$22	.30	$ 6.60
$24	.10	$ 2.40
Expected profit with perfect information		$21.00

Thus, with perfect information about future demand, the florist expects an average profit of $21 per day. This figure is called **expected profit with perfect information.***

It is worthwhile now to contrast the expected profit *under uncertainty*, which is $20.20, and the expected profit *with perfect information*, which is $21.00. When the florist is uncertain about future demand, she stocks 11 dozen carnations each and every day, and she expects an average profit of $20.20 per day. This is her expected profit under uncertainty. Assuming that there is a perfect forecasting service, the florist would place her order after she knows tomorrow's demand. Hence, she would stock the correct amount of carnations each and every day, and she would expect an average profit of $21 per day. This is her expected profit with perfect information.

Before concluding this discussion, we will describe a simple mechanical procedure that enables us to determine the expected profit with perfect information directly from the payoff table.

In the carnation problem, the expected profit with perfect information is determined as follows (see Table 18.5).

1. Identify by an asterisk the *best payoff* for each event. The best payoff for event E_1 (demand = 10) is $20*. For event E_2 (demand = 11) the best payoff is $22*. The best payoff for event E_3 (demand = 12) is $24*.

2. List each event together with its respective prior probability and its best payoff.

Event	Prior Probability of Event	Best Payoff
E_1: Demand = 10	.60	$20*
E_2: Demand = 11	.30	$22*
E_3: Demand = 12	.10	$24*

3. Multiply the best payoff of each event by the prior probability of that event. The total of these products is the expected profit with perfect information.

*Expected profit with perfect information is also called *expected profit under certainty*.

TABLE 18.5　PAYOFF TABLE: CONDITIONAL PROFITS

Events	Prior Probability of Event	Acts		
		Act_1 Stock 10	Act_2 Stock 11	Act_3 Stock 12
E_1:　Demand = 10	.60	$20* 　(1)	$19	$18
E_2:　Demand = 11	.30	$20	$22* 　(2)	$21
E_3:　Demand = 12	.10	$20	$22	$24* 　(3)

Event	Probability	Best Payoff	Payoff · Probability
E_1	.60	$20*	$12.00
E_2	.30	$22*	$ 6.60
E_3	.10	$24*	$ 2.40
		Expected profit with perfect information	$21.00

Example　Given the following payoff table, find the expected profit with perfect information.

Payoff Table: Conditional Profits in Dollars

Event	Prior Probability of Event	Acts			
		Act_1	Act_2	Act_3	Act_4
E_1	.4	9	10*	8	7
E_2	.5	20*	18	16	14
E_3	.1	15	12	28	30*

Solution:

Event	Probability	Best Payoff	Payoff · Probability
E_1	.4	$10	$4
E_2	.5	$20	$10
E_3	.1	$30	$3
		Expected profit with perfect information	$17

Expected Value of Perfect Information (EVPI)

In our carnation problem, we have already concluded that when the florist is uncertain about future demand, she stocks 11 dozen carnations each and every day and expects an average profit of $20.20 per day (expected profit under uncertainty). In comparison, guided by a perfect predictor or with perfect information about future demand, the florist stocks the exact amount demanded by the consumers each and every day, and she expects an average profit of $21.00 per day (expected profit with perfect information). Hence, perfect information about future demand has increased her expected daily profit from $20.20 to $21.00. The difference between expected profit with perfect information and expected profit under uncertainty ($21.00 − $20.20 = $.80) is called the **expected value of perfect information.** Denoted by EVPI, the expected value of perfect information is

$$\text{EVPI} = \begin{pmatrix} \text{Expected profit with} \\ \text{perfect information} \end{pmatrix} - \begin{pmatrix} \text{Expected profit} \\ \text{under uncertainty} \end{pmatrix}$$

$$= 21.00 - \$20.20 = \$.80 \text{ per day.}$$

The EVPI is what a perfect predictor is expected to contribute to daily profit. Hence, *if* such a perfect forecasting service is made available to the florist, she should pay no more than $0.80 per day for this service.

Expected Opportunity Loss (EOL)

Mr. Simons has the option of purchasing either of two baskets containing a mixture of oranges and apples. There are 100 pieces of fruit in each basket. Since Mr. Simons prefers oranges to apples, he would like to purchase the basket with the greater number of oranges. Mr. Simons can make his choice in two ways:

1. count the number of oranges in each basket and select the basket with the greater number of oranges, or
2. count the number of apples and select the basket with the lesser number of apples.

Although it is more straightforward to count oranges, it becomes more convenient to count apples when the proportion of apples is very small. Similarly, when a decision maker uses the Bayesian decision criterion, it is more natural to compare the several acts on the basis of their expected profit and choose the act with the highest expected profit. However, sometimes it is more convenient (the amount of computation is greatly reduced) to compare the various acts on the basis of their **expected opportunity losses** and to select the act with the least expected opportunity loss.

An **opportunity loss** is not a loss in the accounting sense of the word. Instead, it is the profit *missed* for failing to take the best act.* Next, let us see how opportunity losses are determined.

We can construct a conditional opportunity loss table, which is much like a payoff table and intimately related to it. This table shows a conditional opportunity loss, COL, for every possible combination of acts and events. In the carnation problem, the conditional opportunity loss table shows a conditional opportunity loss for *each combination* of levels of stock and levels of demand. Before we proceed to construct the COL table, it is useful to display the payoff table (Table 18.3) once more:

Payoff Table: Conditional Profits

Events	Prior Probability of Events	Act_1: Stock 10	Act_2: Stock 11	Act_3: Stock 12
E_1: Demand = 10	.60	$20 (1)	$19 (4)	$18 (7)
E_2: Demand = 11	.30	$20 (2)	$22 (5)	$21 (8)
E_3: Demand = 12	.10	$20 (3)	$22 (6)	$24 (9)

The conditional opportunity losses can be determined as follows: First, we will assume that the first event E_1 (demand = 10) is *true*. Being able to sell only 10 dozen, the florist will realize the maximum possible profit of $20 only if she adopts act_1 (stock 10). If the florist adopts a wrong act, say act_2 or act_3, she will realize the lesser profits of $19 and $18, respectively (see Table 18.3). Thus, given that demand = 10, no profit is missed by adopting act_1, a profit of $1 ($20 − $19 = $1) is missed by adopting act_2, and a profit of $2 ($20 − $18 = $2) is missed by adopting act_3. Hence, given the event E_1 (demand = 10), the expected opportunity loss is $0 for act_1, $1 for Act_2, and $2 for Act_3. These results are displayed below.

Conditional Opportunity Loss

Event	Act_1	Act_2	Act_3
E_1: Demand = 10	$0	$1	$2

Next, let us assume that the second event E_2 (demand = 11) is true. Being able to sell 11 dozen, therefore, the florist will realize the maximum possible profit of $22 only if she adopts act_2 (stock 11). If she adopts a wrong act, say act_1 or act_3, she realizes the lesser profits of $20 and $21, respectively (see Table 18.3). Hence, given that demand = 11, the conditional opportunity losses

---

*When payoffs are in terms of cost and not profit, an opportunity loss is the additional cost incurred because of *failure* to take the best act.

(profits missed) are

$$\$22 - \$20 = \$2 \text{ for act}_1; \qquad \$22 - \$22 = \$0 \text{ for act}_2;$$
$$\text{and } \$22 - \$21 = \$1 \text{ for act}_3$$

Combining these results with the previously obtained ones, we have

Event	Act₁	Act₂	Act₃
E_1: Demand = 10	$0	$1	$2
E_2: Demand = 11	$2	$0	$1

Finally, let us assume that the third event E_3 (demand = 12) is true. Being able to sell 12 dozen now, the florist will realize the maximum profit of $24 only if she adopts act₃ (stock = 12). If she adopts a wrong act, say act₁ or act₂, she will receive the lesser profit of $20 or $22, respectively (see Table 18.3). Hence, given that the third event E_3 (demand = 12) is true, the conditional opportunity losses are

$$\$24 - \$20 = \$4 \text{ for act}_1; \qquad \$24 - \$22 = \$2 \text{ for act}_2;$$
$$\text{and } \$24 - \$24 = \$0 \text{ for act}_3.$$

These results complete the conditional opportunity loss table (Table 18.6).

Before we proceed to compare the three acts on the basis of their expected opportunity losses, it is desirable to summarize and refine the procedure used in computing conditional opportunity losses. Using the information in Table 18.5, we determine conditional opportunity losses as follows: The best payoff under each event is indicated by an asterisk. Subtract each payoff located in the first row from the asterisked figure in that row to obtain the conditional opportunity losses in the first row. Repeat this operation on each row in the payoff table. Calculations are done in Table 18.7.)

TABLE 18.6 CONDITIONAL OPPORTUNITY LOSS (COL)

Event	Prior Probability of Event	Acts		
		Act₁: Stock 10	Act₂: Stock 11	Act₃: Stock 12
E_1: Demand = 10	.60	$0	$1	$2
E_2: Demand = 11	.30	$2	$0	$1
E_3: Demand = 12	.10	$4	$2	$0

TABLE 18.7 CALCULATION OF CONDITIONAL OPPORTUNITY LOSSES

Event	Prior Probability of Event	Acts		
		Act_1: Stock 10	Act_2: Stock 11	Act_3: Stock 12
E_1: Demand = 10	.60	$20^* - 20^* = 0$	$20^* - 19 = 1$	$20^* - 18 = 2$
E_2: Demand = 11	.30	$22^* - 20 = 2$	$22^* - 22^* = 0$	$22^* - 21 = 1$
E_3: Demand = 12	.10	$24^* - 20 = 4$	$24^* - 22 = 2$	$24^* - 24^* = 0$

After the conditional opportunity losses are determined, our next step is to compute the expected opportunity loss of each of the three acts and compare them on that basis. The expected opportunity loss of any one act is the sum of all products obtained by multiplying the conditional opportunity losses of that act times their corresponding probabilities of occurrence (see computations in Table 18.8).

In comparing the three acts on the basis of their expected opportunity losses, we note that act_2 has the *lowest* expected opportunity loss, $.80. Hence, act_2 (stock 11) is the *optimal act*. This conclusion is no surprise at all, since we have already concluded that act_2 is the optimal act when the three acts were compared on the basis of their expected profit.

As a final remark, we must emphasize that whether we compare the various possible acts on the basis of their expected profits or on the basis of their expected opportunity losses, we find that the *optimal act is one and the same.* The optimal act is the one with the highest expected profit. It is also characterized by the lowest expected opportunity loss. Hence, the optimal act can be determined using either the expected profit method or the expected opportunity loss method. The choice between the two methods depends entirely on the amount of computations involved in each method.

TABLE 18.8 CALCULATION OF EXPECTED OPPORTUNITY LOSS (EOL)

Act_1: Stock 10	Act_2: Stock 11	Act_3: Stock 12
$\$0 \cdot .60 = \$ .00$	$\$1 \cdot .60 = \$ .60$	$\$2 \cdot .60 = \$1.20$
$\$2 \cdot .30 = \$ .60$	$\$0 \cdot .30 = \$ .00$	$\$1 \cdot .30 = \$ .30$
$\$4 \cdot .10 = \$ .40$	$\$2 \cdot .10 = \$ .20$	$\$0 \cdot .10 = \$ .00$
EOL $\$1.00$	EOL $\$0.80$	EOL $\$1.50$

TABLE 18.9   **PRIOR ESTIMATE OF PROPORTION OF STUDENTS WHO WOULD ATTEND CONCERT**

Proportion of Students (π)	Prior Probability
$\pi_1 = .10$	.30
$\pi_2 = .15$	.50
$\pi_3 = .25$	.20

Cost of Uncertainty

The optimal act in our carnation problem is act_2 (stock 11). The expected opportunity loss of this optimal act, which is $.80, is also called the **cost of uncertainty.** With a perfect predictor, the florist would stock the correct amount of carnations each and every day; hence, no profit would be missed and her opportunity losses would be zero. Acting without the benefit of a predictor, or being uncertain about future demand, the florist would stock 11 dozen carnations every day; and her expected opportunity loss is $.80. This $.80 is the price the florist has to pay for *not* having the prefect predictor. It is the cost of making decisions in the face of uncertainty.

Next, we must observe that the cost of uncertainty is equal to the expected value of perfect information (which is $.80). This is not a coincidence, since by removing all uncertainty about future demand, a perfect predictor enables the florist to stock the correct amount each day and reduce her opportunity losses to zero. Thus, we can conclude: The expected opportunity loss of the best act, cost of uncertainty, and the expected value of perfect information are one and the same.

Example   In a college of 20,000 students, the director of the Educational Opportunity Program is considering sponsoring a rock concert as a means of raising funds for his program. The total cost of the concert is $3000 and the price of admission is set at $1 per student.*

On the basis of attendance records at rock concerts given on his campus and other similar campuses, the program director estimates the proportion of students who would attend the concert and assigns probabilities to these events, as shown in Table 18.9.

According to the data shown in Table 18.9, the program director is not certain what proportion of students would attend the concert. However, he believes that there is a .30 chance that only 10% of the students would attend the concert; there is a .50 chance that 15% of the students would attend; and

---

*To simplify our problem we will assume that only students would attend the concert.

TABLE 18.10   PRIOR ESTIMATE OF NUMBER OF STUDENTS WHO WOULD ATTEND CONCERT

Number of Students	Prior Probability
$20,000 \cdot .10 = 2000$	.30
$20,000 \cdot .15 = 3000$	.50
$20,000 \cdot .25 = 5000$	.20

there is only a .20 chance that 25% of all students would attend the concert.

Stated differently, the program director believes that the *number* of students who would attend the concert is either 2000, 3000, or 5000, with a probability of .30, .50, and .20, respectively. (See computations in Table 18.10.)

Tables 18.9 and 18.10 provide us with the same information; both describe the expected concert attendance by students. Table 18.9 describes attendance by the *proportion* of students who would be attending, Table 18.10 describes attendance by the *number* of students expected to attend. For reasons that will become apparent in the next chapter, we will describe attendance as a proportion; that is, we will use the information presented in Table 18.9.

Before we proceed further with our problem, let us define the acts and the various possible events that determine the consequences of the acts.

Acts: Act_1 (Have concert)
Act_2 (No concert)
Events: E_1: $\pi_1 = .10$ (Proportion of students attending is 10%)
E_2: $\pi_2 = .15$ (Proportion of students attending is 15%)
E_3: $\pi_3 = .25$ (Proportion of students attending is 25%)

Acts, events, and prior probabilities of events are summarized in Table 18.11. Prior probabilities are denoted by P_0.

TABLE 18.11   CONCERT PROBLEM: SUMMARY OF ACTS AND EVENTS

Events π	Prior Probability $P_0 (\pi)$	Acts	
		Act_1: Have Concert	*Act_2: No Concert*
E_1: $\pi_1 = .10$	.30		
E_2: $\pi_2 = .15$	.50		
E_3: $\pi_3 = .25$	.20		

TABLE 18.12   **CONCERT PROBLEM: DETERMINATION OF CONDITIONAL PAYOFFS**

Event π	Probability $P_0(\pi)$	Acts	
		Act₁: Have Concert, Conditional Profit	Act₂: No Concert, Conditional Profit
E_1: $\pi_1 = .10$	.30	$20{,}000 \cdot .10 \cdot \$1 - \$3000 = -\$1{,}000$ (1)	\$0 (4)
E_2: $\pi_2 = .15$	.50	$20{,}000 \cdot .15 \cdot \$1 - \$3000 = \$\ \ \ 0$ (2)	\$0 (5)
E_3: $\pi_3 = .25$	.20	$20{,}000 \cdot .25 \cdot \$1 - \$3000 = \$2{,}000$ (3)	\$0 (6)

Next, we determine the optimal act using both the expected payoff approach and the expected opportunity loss approach.

Expected Payoff Approach.   Using the expected payoff approach to identify the optimal act, our first step is to construct a payoff table. The payoff table shows a conditional profit for every possible combination of acts and events, shown in Table 18.12.

The first payoff in Table 18.12, which is −$1,000, is the conditional profit of act₁ (have concert), given that the first event is true (given that 10% of the students would attend). This payoff is determined as follows.

$$20{,}000 \cdot .10 = 2000 \quad \text{(number of students attending)}$$
$$2000 \cdot \$1 = \$2000 \quad \text{(total revenue)}$$
$$\$2000 - \$3000 = -\$1000 \quad \text{(conditional profit)}$$

The second and third payoffs, 0 and $2000, are obtained in the same manner. All payoffs for act₂ (no concert) are clearly zero.

We can compare the two acts on the basis of their expected payoffs. The expected payoff of any one act is the sum of the products obtained by multiplying the conditional payoffs of that act by their corresponding probabilities of occurrence. The computations are shown in Table 18.13. Table 18.13 shows that act₁ has the best expected payoff. Hence, act₁ is the optimal act, and the expected profit under uncertainty is $100.

TABLE 18.13   **CONCERT PROBLEM: DETERMINATION OF CONDITIONAL PROFITS**

Act₁: Have Concert	Act₂: No Concert
$-\$1000 \cdot .3 = -300$	$\$0 \cdot .3 = \$0$
$\$\ \ \ 0 \cdot .5 = \ \ \ \ 0$	$\$0 \cdot .5 = \$0$
$\$2000 \cdot .2 = +400$	$\$0 \cdot .2 = \underline{\$0}$
Expected profit $100	$0

Now we wish to determine the expected profit with perfect information.

1. We identify by an asterisk the best payoff for each event, in Table 18.14.
2. We list each event together with its respective prior probability and its best payoff.

Event (π)	$P_0(\pi)$	Best Payoff
E_1: $\pi_1 = .10$	.30	$ 0*
E_2: $\pi_2 = .15$	.50	$ 0*
E_3: $\pi_3 = .25$	.20	$2000*

3. We multiply the best payoff of each event by the prior probability of that event. The total of these products is the expected profit with perfect information.

Event (π)	$P_0(\pi)$	Best Payoff	Payoff $\cdot$ $P_0(\pi)$
E_1: $\pi_1 = .10$	.30	$ 0*	$ 0
E_2: $\pi_2 = .15$	.50	$ 0*	$ 0
E_3: $\pi_3 = .25$	.20	$2000*	$400
		Expected profit with perfect information: $400	

The expected value of perfect information (EVPI) is computed as follows.

$$\text{EVPI} = \begin{pmatrix} \text{Expected profit with} \\ \text{perfect information} \end{pmatrix} - \begin{pmatrix} \text{Expected profit} \\ \text{under uncertainty} \end{pmatrix}$$

$$= \$400 - \$100$$

$$= \$300.$$

TABLE 18.14   CONCERT PROBLEM: PAYOFF TABLE

Event π	Probability $P_0(\pi)$	Conditional Profit	
		Act_1: Have Concert	Act_2: No Concert
E_1: $\pi_1 = .10$	.30	$-\$1000$	$0*
E_2: $\pi_2 = .15$	.50	$ 0	$0*
E_3: $\pi_3 = .25$	.20	$2000*	$0

TABLE 18.15   CONCERT PROBLEM: PAYOFF TABLE

Event π	Probability $P_0(\pi)$	Conditional Profit	
		Act₁: Have Concert	Act₂: No Concert
E_1: $\pi_1 = .10$	.30	−$1000	$0*
E_2: $\pi_2 = .15$	.50	$ 0*	$0*
E_3: $\pi_3 = .25$	.20	$2000*	$0

Expected Opportunity Loss Approach.   Using the expected opportunity loss approach to identify the optimal act, we first construct a conditional opportunity loss table. We begin with the payoff table.

1. Identify by an asterisk the best payoff under each event (see Table 18.15).

2. Subtract each payoff located in each row from the asterisked figure in that row, to obtain the conditional opportunity losses in the row. (Calculations are done in Table 18.16.)

After the conditional opportunity losses are determined, our next step is to compute the expected opportunity loss of each act and compare the acts on that basis. The expected opportunity loss of any one act is the sum of all products obtained by multiplying the conditional opportunity losses of the act times their corresponding probabilities of occurrence (see Table 18.17).

In comparing the two acts on the basis of their expected opportunity losses, we note from Table 18.17 that act₁ has the lowest expected opportunity loss. Hence, act₁ is the optimal act. The expected opportunity loss of act₁, $300, is the cost of uncertainty or the expected value of perfect information.

The payoffs in the preceding problem and in the carnation problem are

TABLE 18.16   CONCERT PROBLEM: CALCULATION OF CONDITIONAL OPPORTUNITY LOSSES

Event π	Probability $P_0(\pi)$	Conditional Opportunity Losses	
		Act₁: Have Concert	Act₂: No Concert
E_1: $\pi_1 = .10$	.30	$0* − (−$1,000) = $1000	$0* − $0* = $0
E_2: $\pi_2 = .15$	.50	$0* − $0* = $0	$0* − $0 = $0
E_3: $\pi_3 = .25$	.20	$2000* − $2000* = $0	$2000* − $0 = $2000

TABLE 18.17 CONCERT PROBLEM: CALCULATION OF EXPECTED OPPORTUNITY LOSSES

Act$_1$: Have Concert	Act$_2$: No Concert
$1000 · 0.30 = $300	$0 · 0.30 = $ 0
$0 · 0.50 = $ 0	$0 · 0.50 = $ 0
$0 · 0.20 = $ 0	$2000 · 0.20 = $400
EOL $300	EOL $400

expressed in terms of *conditional profit.* It is useful now to present a third problem where payoffs are expressed in terms of *conditional cost.*

Example A television manufacturer uses a special type of electronic component in assembling color television sets. Each television set requires a number of such components. A defective component cannot be detected until a television set has been completely assembled. The cost of detecting, repairing, and replacing a defective component is $20.

The television manufacturer has been purchasing these components in lots of 200 components from supplier A for $220 per lot. Based on past experience, the proportion of defective components in lots purchased from supplier A is estimated as follows.

Proportion of Defective Components (π)	Prior Probability $P_o (\pi)$
.01	.60
.02	.30
.03	.10

A new supplier, supplier B, has offered the television manufacturer a guaranteed quality component for $300 per lot. Supplier B guarantees to refund $20 for each defective component. From which supplier should the television manufacturer purchase electronic components?

Solution: Before we proceed with the solution to this problem, let us define the acts and events.

Acts: Act$_1$ (Buy from A)
Act$_2$ (Buy from B)
Events: E$_1$: $\pi_1 = .01$ (Proportion of defective components from A is 1%)
E$_2$: $\pi_2 = .02$ (Proportion of defective components from A is 2%)
E$_3$: $\pi_3 = .03$ (Proportion of defective components from A is 3%)

Acts, events, and prior probabilities of events are summarized in Table 18.18.

TABLE 18.18   TELEVISION PROBLEM: SUMMARY OF
ACTS AND EVENTS

Event π	Probability $P_0\,(\pi)$	Acts	
		Act$_1$: Buy from A	Act$_2$: Buy from B
E_1: $\pi_1 = .01$	.60		
E_2: $\pi_2 = .02$	.30		
E_3: $\pi_3 = .03$	.10		

Next we will determine the optimal act, using both the expected payoff approach and the expected opportunity loss approach.

Expected payoff approach.   Using the expected payoff approach to identify the optimal act, we first construct a payoff table. The one in this problem, however, is somewhat different from the payoff tables with which we have dealt so far.

We have stated earlier that payoffs can be measured either by the *profits* accrued to the decision maker or by the *cost* incurred by him or her. In our first two problems, the carnation problem and the concert problem, payoffs were expressed in terms of profits. The payoffs of our present problem can be expressed only in terms of the costs incurred by the manufacturer. Consequently, the payoff table in this problem shows a conditional cost for every possible combination of acts and events. Conditional costs are calculated in Table 18.19.

The first payoff in Table 18.19, which is $260, is the conditional cost of act$_1$ (buying from supplier A), given that the first event is true (given that lots purchased from A contain 1% defectives). This payoff is determined as follows.

$$200 \cdot .01 = 2 \quad \text{(Number of defective components per lot)}$$
$$2 \cdot \$20 = \$40 \quad \text{(Cost of replacement per lot)}$$
$$220 + \$40 = \$260 \quad \text{(Purchase cost plus replacement cost)}$$

TABLE 18.19   DETERMINATION OF CONDITIONAL
COSTS (PAYOFFS)

Event π	Probability $P_0\,(\pi)$	Conditional Costs	
		Act$_1$: Buy from A	Act$_2$: Buy from B
E_1: $\pi_1 = .01$	.60	$220 + 200 \cdot .01 \times \$20 = \$260$ (1)	$300 (4)
E_2: $\pi_2 = .02$	.30	$220 + 200 \cdot .02 \times \$20 = \$300$ (2)	$300 (5)
E_3: $\pi_3 = .03$	.10	$220 + 200 \cdot .03 \times \$20 = \$340$ (3)	$300 (6)

TABLE 18.20 **TELEVISION PROBLEM: DETERMINATION OF EXPECTED PAYOFFS (EXPECTED COST)**

Act_1: Buy from A	Act_2: Buy from B
$\$260 \cdot .60 = \$156$	$\$300 \cdot .60 = \$180$
$\$300 \cdot .30 = \$\ 90$	$\$300 \cdot .30 = \$\ 90$
$\$340 \cdot .10 = \$\ 34$	$\$300 \cdot .10 = \$\ 30$
Expected cost $\$280$	Expected cost $\$300$

The second and third payoffs, $300 and $340, are obtained in the same manner. Act_2 (buying from supplier B) has a conditional cost of $300 under all circumstances.

Now we can compare the two acts on the basis of their expected cost to the manufacturer. The expected cost of any one act is the sum obtained by multiplying the conditional costs of that act by the corresponding probabilities of occurrence. The computations are carried out in Table 18.20.

Table 18.20 shows that act_1 has the best payoff (lowest expected cost). Hence, act_1 is the optimal act. The expected cost of the optimal act, which is $280, is the expected cost under uncertainty.

We determine the expected cost with perfect information as follows.

1. Identify by an asterisk the best payoff, that is, lowest cost for each event. See Table 18.21.

2. List each event together with its respective probability and its best payoff.

Event (π)	$P_0(\pi)$	Best Payoff
E_1: $\pi_1 = .01$	.60	$\$260^*$
E_2: $\pi_2 = .02$	.30	$\$300^*$
E_3: $\pi_3 = .03$	.10	$\$300^*$

TABLE 18.21 **TELEVISION PROBLEM: PAYOFF TABLE, CONDITIONAL COST**

Event π	Probability $P_0(\pi)$	Conditional Cost	
		Act_1: Buy from A	Act_2: Buy from B
E_1: $\pi_1 = .01$	.60	$\$260^*$	$\$300$
E_2: $\pi_2 = .02$	.30	$\$300^*$	$\$300^*$
E_3: $\pi_3 = .03$	.10	$\$340$	$\$300^*$

3. Multiply the best payoff of each event by the prior probability of that event. The total of these products is the expected cost with perfect information.

Event (π)	P_0 (π)	Best Payoff	Payoff $\cdot$ P_0 (π)
E_1: $\pi_1 = .01$	.60	$260*	$156
E_2: $\pi_2 = .02$	.30	$300*	$ 90
E_3: $\pi_3 = .03$	.10	$300*	$ 30
		Expected cost with perfect information	$276

The expected value of perfect information (EVPI) is calculated as follows.

$$\text{EVPI} = \begin{pmatrix} \text{Expected cost un-} \\ \text{der uncertainty} \end{pmatrix} - \begin{pmatrix} \text{Expected cost with} \\ \text{perfect information} \end{pmatrix}$$

$$= \$280 - \$276$$

$$= \$4 \text{ per lot}$$

Expected Opportunity Loss Approach. If we wish to use the expected opportunity loss to identify the optimal act, our first step is to determine the conditional opportunity losses for each act. When payoffs are expressed in terms of cost, an opportunity loss is the *additional* cost incurred because of failing to take the best act. Regardless of whether payoffs are expressed in terms of cost or in terms of profit, however, the conditional opportunity losses are determined in the same fashion. Beginning with the payoff table, conditional opportunity losses are determined as follows.

1. Identify by an asterisk the best payoff for each event (see Table 18.22).
2. Subtract the asterisked figure in each row from each payoff located in that row to obtain the conditional opportunity losses in the row. (The calculations are done in Table 18.23.)

TABLE 18.22 TELEVISION PROBLEM: PAYOFF TABLE, CONDITIONAL COST

Event π	Problem P_0 (π)	Conditional Cost	
		Act$_1$: Buy from A	Act$_2$: Buy from B
E_1: $\pi_2 = .01$	.06	$260*	$300
E_2: $\pi_2 = .02$	.03	$300*	$300*
E_3: $\pi_3 = .03$	.10	$340	$300*

TABLE 18.23 CALCULATIONS OF CONDITIONAL OPPORTUNITY LOSSES

Event	Probability $P_0(\pi)$	Conditional Opportunity Losses	
		Act$_1$: Buy from A	Act$_2$: Buy from B
$E_1: \pi_1 = .01$	.60	$260* − $260* = $0	$300 − $260* = $40
$E_2: \pi_2 = .02$	.03	$300* − $300* = $0	$300* − $300* = $ 0
$E_3: \pi_3 = .30$	.10	$340 − $300* = $40	$300* − $300* = $ 0

TABLE 18.24 CALCULATION OF EXPECTED OPPORTUNITY LOSSES

Act$_1$: Buy from A	Act$_2$: Buy from B
$ 0 · .60 = $0	$40 · .60 = $24
$ 0 · .30 = $0	$ 0 · .30 = $ 0
$40 · .10 = $4	$ 0 · .10 = $ 0
EOL $4	EOL $24

After the conditional opportunity losses have been determined, our next step is to compute the expected opportunity loss of each of the two acts and compare the two acts on that basis (see Table 18.24).

In comparing the two acts on the basis of their expected opportunity losses, we see from Table 18.24 that act$_1$ has the lowest expected opportunity loss. Hence, act$_2$ is the optimal act. The expected opportunity loss of act$_1$, $4, is the cost of uncertainty or the expected value of perfect information.

EXERCISES

18.1 Given the following payoff table.

		Payoff Table: Conditional Profits			
Event	Prior Probability	Acts			
		A_1	A_2	A_3	A_4
A	.1	20	0	−20	−40
B	.2	20	40	20	0
C	.5	20	40	60	40
D	.2	20	40	60	80

a) Determine the optimal act using the maximax criterion.

b) Determine the optimal act using the minimax criterion.

c) Determine the optimal act using the Bayesian decision criterion.

d) What is the expected profit under uncertainty?

e) Compute expected profit with perfect information.

f) Determine the expected value of perfect information.

18.2 A grocer estimates daily sales of Slim and Trim bread as follows.

Estimated Daily Sales (loaves)	Probability of Estimated Sales
4	.50
5	.40
6	.10

The cost per loaf is $.25 and the selling price is $.50 per loaf. The bread must be ordered one day in advance, and any bread left unsold at the end of the day is turned over to the Thrift Bakery for a salvage price of $.10 per loaf.

a) Construct a payoff table showing the conditional profits of the three acts.

b) Determine the expected profit under uncertainty.

c) What is the expected profit with perfect information?

d) Compute the expected value of perfect information.

18.3 A newspaper stand specializes in the Sunday editions of several out-of-town newspapers. The Sunday New York Times is the stand's best seller. The stand owner estimates weekly demand for the New York Times Sunday edition as follows.

Demand (Number of Papers)	Prior Probability
40	$\frac{1}{4}$
50	$\frac{1}{2}$
60	$\frac{1}{4}$

The owner buys papers for $.70 each and sells them for $1 per copy. Papers must be ordered one week in advance and papers unsold at the end of the week are worthless.

a) Construct the conditional payoff table for the problem.

b) How many copies of the Sunday New York Times should the owner order each week, and what is the expected profit under uncertainty?

c) What is the EVPI?

d) Construct a conditional opportunity loss table and determine the expected opportunity loss of the best act.

e) What is the cost of uncertainty?

18.4 Given the following payoff table:

Event	Prior Probability	Acts		
		A_1	A_2	A_3
A	.2	20	−10	−40
B	.5	20	40	10
C	.3	20	40	60

a) Construct a conditional opportunity loss table.

b) Compute the expected opportunity loss of each act.

c) What is the expected cost of uncertainty?

18.5 A toy shop has the opportunity to purchase an entire lot of 5000 units of a seasonal toy for $10,000. The toy can be sold during the season for $3. After the season, all remaining toys can be sold by marking the price down to $1. The cost of handling the toy is $.50 per toy (handling cost applies to toys sold during and after the season). Based on similar toys marked previously, the in-season demand for the new toy is estimated by the following probability distribution.

Demand D (units)	Probability $P_0(D)$
3000	.10
4000	.60
5000	.30

a) Construct a conditional profit table.

b) Construct a conditional opportunity loss table and determine the optimal act.

c) What is the expected value of perfect information?

18.6 The publisher of a weekly sports magazine is considering the publication of a special edition to be sold to existing subscribers exclusively. The cost of developing the special edition (fixed cost) is $50,000. The cost of printing and marketing (variable cost) is $.50 per copy. The special edition is to be sold at $1 per copy. The magazine has 1 million subscribers, and the marketing research director estimates the proportion of subscribers who would purchase the magazine as follows.

Proportion of Subscribers	Prior Probability P_0
.09	.30
.10	.50
.12	.20

a) Should the publisher undertake the special edition?

b) What is the expected value of perfect information?

18.7   An appliance manufacturing firm has been purchasing a large number of special parts to be used in manufacturing one of its appliances. The parts can be purchased in any desired quantity from local suppliers for $4 per part. The firm is now considering the production of the parts internally. To produce the parts, the firm must purchase a specialized machine, which can be purchased in three different sizes: small, medium, and large. The purchase prices of the small, medium, and large machines are $1000, $1500, and $2000, respectively; and their annual production capacities are 500, 1000, and 1500 parts, respectively. Variable cost is $1 per part regardless of which machine is used. Each machine has a useful life of one year and has no scrap value at the end of the year. Since the specialized machine must be ordered a considerable time in advance, it is impossible to install additional machines during the year, but this creates no production problem since additional parts can always be purchased from the local suppliers at $4 per part. The firm does not know the exact number of parts needed for the coming year. The following probability distribution provides the best estimate of the number of parts needed next year.

Number of Parts Needed	Probability
500	.25
1000	.50
1500	.25

a) Which machine should the manufacturer order, if any?

b) Determine the expected value of perfect information.

18.8   An automobile manufacturing company uses a special control device in each automobile it produces. Two alternative methods can be used to detect and avoid a faulty device. Under the first method, each device is tested before it is installed, and all faulty devices are discovered before installation. The cost is $2 per test. Alternatively, the control device can be installed without being tested, and a faulty device can be detected and removed after the automobile's final assembly, at a cost of $20 per faulty device. Regardless of which method of inspection is used, faulty devices cannot be repaired and must be discarded. The company has purchased a lot of 10,000 control devices to be used in next month's production. Based on past experience, the manager estimates the proportion of defective devices in the lot as follows.

Proportion of Faulty Devices π	Probability $P_0(\pi)$
.08	.2
.12	.7
.16	.1

a) Which inspection method should the manufacturer adopt?

b) What is the EVPI?

18.9 An international oil company desires to hire a great number of engineers to carry out its future development program. At the present time, a qualified engineer can be recruited at an annual cost of $40,000. Due to this high cost, the company is considering the training of promising high school graduates in colleges in the United States, for a total cost of $60,000 for each student. Since the company assumes all training expense, the student has the obligation to serve with the company for a period of five years after graduation from college, at an annual salary of $20,000. In considering its training program, the company foresees only one problem: Some of the students will not be able to graduate. These students are not hired by the company and their entire cost of training ($60,000 per student) is a total loss to the company. Based on other groups trained in the United States, the company estimates the proportion of students who complete their training successfully and who fulfill their five-year service obligation to the company as follows.

Proportion of Successful Students π	Prior Probability $P_0(\pi)$
.50	$\frac{1}{2}$
.80	$\frac{1}{2}$

a) Compute the expected cost of training and employing an engineer for a five-year period.

b) What is the expected value of perfect information if the company wishes to hire 1000 engineers for a five-year period?

18.10   Fredric Gucci, a Hollywood fashion designer, is planning the production of a new line of ladies' swimwear. Because of its faddish design, Fredric believes that the selling season of the wear is limited to a three-month period. Hence, only one production run is possible, and suits left unsold at the end of the season are worthless. Fredric estimates his sales for the 3-month period as follows.

Sales (thousands of suits)	Probability
20	.2
25	.4
30	.4

If the selling price is $40 per suit and its cost is $25, how many suits should Fredric produce? What is the expected profit under certainty, and what is the expected value of perfect information?

KEY TERMS

objective information   Information that all observers can agree on, such as sample data.

subjective information   Information that is based on someone's personal opinion.

act   One of the courses of action available to a decision maker.

event   One of the states of nature that determine the consequences of a decision maker's act. An event is beyond the control of the decision maker.

prior probabilities   The probabilities assigned to events based on the subjective opinion of the decision maker.

payoff table   A table showing the profits or losses for every possible combination of act and event.

maximax criterion   Choice of an act that maximizes the maximum profit, that is, the act with the highest payoff.

minimax criterion   Choice of an act that minimizes the maximum loss. In a profit problem, the equivalent act maximizes the minimum profit.

Bayesian decision criterion   Choice of an act with the highest expected profit or smallest expected loss.

expected profit under uncertainty   The expected profit of the optimal act, the act with the highest expected profit.

expected profit with perfect information   The expected profit computed using the prior probabilities and assuming that for each event the act with the highest profit is chosen.

expected value of perfect information (EVPI)   The difference between the expected profit with perfect information and the expected profit under uncertainty.

opportunity loss   The difference between the payoff for a particular act-event combination and the payoff for the best act for that same event. A measure of how much the act falls short of being best for the event.

expected opportunity loss   The expected value of the opportunity losses computed using the prior probabilities. The act with the lowest expected opportunity loss is the optimal act as found using the Bayesian decision criterion.

cost of uncertainty   The expected opportunity loss of the optimal act. The cost of uncertainty equals the expected value of perfect information.

BAYESIAN DECISION THEORY WITH SAMPLING

19

The central theme of this chapter, as in the preceding chapter, is decision-making. In the previous chapter we developed the general model of a decision-making problem and used subjective information to find its solution. In this chapter we first learn how to combine subjective and objective information and then how to use the combined information to solve the decision problem.

PRIOR AND POSTERIOR PROBABILITIES

The probabilities assigned by decision makers to the various events in the preceding chapter are called **prior probabilities.** These are personal and initial probabilities based on the current information available to the decision maker together with his or her business flair, experience, judgment, and expectations. When prior probabilities are used in computing expected payoffs, the analysis is called *prior analysis.*

When prior analysis of the problem reveals a high cost of uncertainty (as measured by the expected opportunity loss of the optimal act), it is often desirable to collect some additional information through sampling. The prior probabilities are then adjusted or revised in light of the sample information, and the revised probabilities are called **posterior probabilities.** The revision of prior probabilities into posterior probabilities is accomplished by means of Bayes' theorem. The posterior probabilities are subsequently used to compute new expected payoffs, and the resulting analysis is called *posterior analysis.*

To avoid confusion, it is important at this point to contrast two distinct Bayesian concepts: the Bayesian decision criterion and Bayes' theorem. The Bayesian decision criterion simply means that the decision maker must compare acts on the basis of their expected payoffs. In contrast, Bayes' theorem is the mathematical tool used in blending prior probabilities and sample information into posterior probabilities.

We must also make it clear that the distinction between prior probabilities and posterior probabilities is to some extent relative. The subjective prior probabilities, P_0, are combined with sample information to produce posterior probabilities, P_1. These posterior probabilities, in turn, may be revised through subsequent sampling to obtain a new set of posterior probabilities, P_2, and so on. To demonstrate the use of Bayes' theorem in revising prior probabilities, we will use the concert problem of the last chapter as an illustration.

REVISION OF PRIOR PROBABILITIES

Considering attendance at rock concerts performed on his campus and at other similar colleges, the director of the E.O.P. program estimates the proportion of students who would attend the proposed concert as follows:

Proportion of Students π	Prior Probability $P_0(\pi)$
E_1: $\pi_1 = .10$	.3
E_2: $\pi_2 = .15$	.5
E_3: $\pi_3 = .25$	.2

To facilitate our subsequent analysis, the director's prior estimate of π is represented by Fig. 19.1.

Let us assume the program director selects two students at random and finds out that both students want to attend the concert. How can we now revise the initial prior probabilities in light of this sample information?

The first step in revising prior probabilities is to determine, under *each* event, the probability of getting what we have actually observed in the sample (to determine the probability that both students in a sample of two students would attend, under each possible value of π). Given that the first event is true ($\pi_1 = .10$), the probability that both students would attend, in a random sample of two students, is

$$.10 \cdot .10 = .01.$$

Similarly, given that the second event is true ($\pi_2 = .15$), the probability that both students would attend the concert is

$$.15 \cdot .15 = .0225.$$

Finally, the probability of getting the desired sample outcome, given that the

Figure 19.1

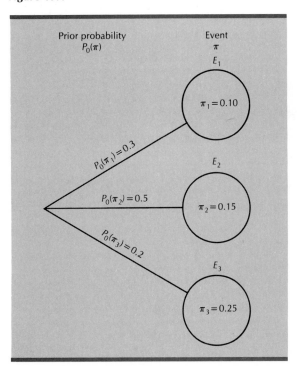

third event is true, is

$$.25 \cdot .25 = .0625.$$

The three probabilities we have just computed are conditional probabilities, since each is conditional on a particular value of π. These three newly computed conditional probabilities, together with other prior information, are displayed in Fig. 19.2.

The second step in revising prior probabilities is to determine the probability of getting the observed sample outcome (both students would attend the concert, in a random sample of size 2) regardless of which event is true.

There are three ways of getting the observed sample result (each is represented by a path in Fig. 19.2). The first way is that event E_1 is true and both students selected would attend. The joint probability of this first path is

$$.3 \cdot .01 = .003$$

The second way is that event E_2 is true and both students selected would attend. The joint probability of this second path is

$$.5 \cdot .0225 = .01125$$

Figure 19.2

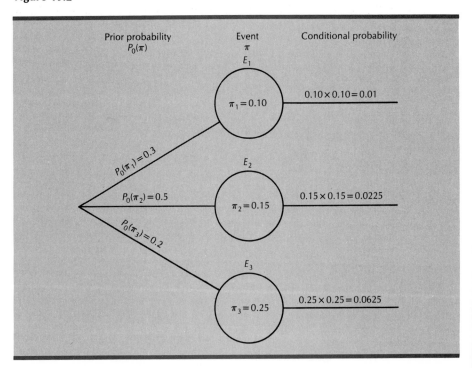

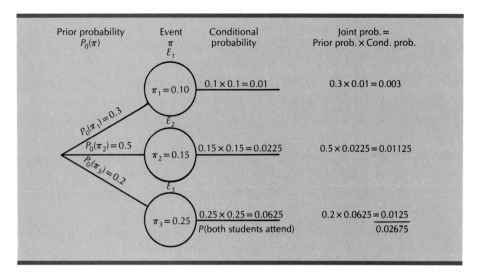

Figure 19.3

The third way is that event E_3 is true and both students would attend. The joint probability of this last path is

$$.2 \cdot .0625 = .0125$$

The probability that both students would attend regardless of which event is true is equal to the sum of joint probabilities for the three mutually exclusive paths. (See Fig. 19.3.)

Finally, according to Bayes' theorem, the probability that event E_1 is true given that both students selected would attend is

$$\frac{.003}{.02675} = .11.$$

This is the revised or posterior probability of π_1 and is denoted by $P_1(\pi_1)$. Similarly, the posterior probability of π_2 is

$$P_1(\pi_2) = \frac{.01125}{.02675}$$

$$= .42,$$

and the posterior probability of π_3 is

$$P_1(\pi_3) = \frac{.0125}{.02675}$$

$$= .47.$$

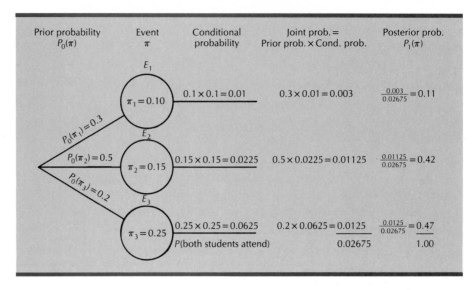

Figure 19.4

TABLE 19.1   REVISION OF PRIOR PROBABILITIES

Event π	Prior Probability $P_0(\pi)$	Conditional Probability	Joint Probability = Prior Prob. · Conditional Prob.	Posterior Probability $P_1(\pi)$
$\pi_1 = .10$	.3	.01	$.3 \cdot .01 = .003$	$.003 \div .02675 = .11$
$\pi_2 = .15$	.5	.0225	$.5 \cdot .0225 = .01125$	$.01125 \div .02675 = .42$
$\pi_3 = .25$	.2	.0625	$.2 \cdot .0625 = .0125$	$.0125 \div .02675 = .47$
	1.0		.02675	1.00

The complete process of revising prior probabilities is displayed in Fig. 19.4 and Table 19.1.

POSTERIOR ANALYSIS

We will perform a posterior analysis using the information we obtained about the concert problem. The prior analysis of this problem, which was discussed in detail in the preceding chapter and is summarized in Table 19.2, shows that act_1 (have concert) has the best expected payoff. Hence, act_1 is the optimal act, and the *prior* expected profit under uncertainty is equal to $+\$100$ (see Table 19.2).

In the prior analysis of the problem, the subjective prior probabilities of the decision maker are used in computing the expected payoffs of the various acts.

TABLE 19.2 CONCERT PROBLEM: SUMMARY OF
PRIOR ANALYSIS

Event π	Prior Probability $P_0(\pi)$	Act$_1$: Have Concert		Act$_2$: No Concert	
		Conditional Profit	Conditional Profit · Prior Probability	Conditional Profit	Conditional Profit · Prior Probability
$\pi_1 = .10$	.3	−$1000	$-1000 \cdot .3 = -300$	$0	$0 \cdot .3 = 0$
$\pi_2 = .15$	.5	$ 0	$0 \cdot .5 = 0$	$0	$0 \cdot .5 = 0$
$\pi_3 = .25$	.2	+$2000	$2000 \cdot .2 = \underline{400}$	$0	$0 \cdot .2 = \underline{0}$
			Prior expected profit +$100		$0

By comparison, the revised or posterior probabilities are used in computing the expected payoffs in the posterior analysis (see Table 19.3).

According to Table 19.3, the posterior expected profits of act$_1$ and act$_2$ are $830 and $0, respectively. Hence act$_1$ (have concert) is the optimal act in the posterior analysis. The expected profit of act$_1$, $830, is the *posterior expected profit under uncertainty*.

We will continue our posterior analysis of the concert problem by computing the posterior expected profit with perfect information (see Table 19.4).

The posterior expected value of perfect information, denoted by EVPI$_1$, is

$$\text{EVPI}_1 = \begin{pmatrix} \text{Posterior expected profit} \\ \text{with perfect information} \end{pmatrix} - \begin{pmatrix} \text{Posterior expected profit} \\ \text{under uncertainty} \end{pmatrix}$$

$$= 940 - 830$$

$$= \$110.$$

TABLE 19.3 CONCERT PROBLEM: DETERMINATION OF
POSTERIOR EXPECTED PAYOFFS

Event π	Posterior Probability $P_1(\pi)$	Act$_1$: Have Concert		Act$_2$: No Concert	
		Conditional Profit	Conditional Profit · Posterior Probability	Conditional Profit	Conditional Profit · Posterior Probability
$\pi_1 = .10$	.11	−$1000	$-1000 \cdot .11 = -110$	$0	$0 \cdot .11 = 0$
$\pi_2 = .15$	.42	$ 0	$0 \cdot .42 = 0$	$0	$0 \cdot .42 = 0$
$\pi_3 = .25$	.47	$2000	$2000 \cdot .47 = \underline{940}$	$0	$0 \cdot .47 = \underline{0}$
			Prior expected profit $830		$0

TABLE 19.4　CONCERT PROBLEM: DETERMINATION OF POSTERIOR EXPECTED PROFIT WITH PERFECT INFORMATION

Event π	Posterior Probability $P_1(\pi)$	Best Payoff	Best Payoff · Posterior Probability
$\pi_1 = .10$	.11	$ 0	$ 0
$\pi_2 = .15$	.42	$ 0	$ 0
$\pi_3 = .25$	.47	$2000	$940
		Posterior expected profit with perfect information	$940

Finally, the posterior expected value of perfect information, $110, can be verified by computing the posterior expected opportunity loss of the best act, since they are one and the same. This is accomplished in Table 19.5. We conclude the material in this chapter with a comprehensive example in which the prior analysis and the posterior analysis are brought into sharp contrast.

Example　A manufacturer of household gadgets sells products exclusively by mail order, using a list of 200,000 customers. The manufacturer contemplates producing a new kitchen gadget. The cost of producing and marketing the new gadget consists of a fixed cost of $10,000 and a variable cost of $3 per unit. The gadget is sold at $5 per unit.

TABLE 19.5　CONCERT PROBLEM: DETERMINATION OF POSTERIOR EXPECTED OPPORTUNITY LOSSES

Event π	Posterior Probability $P_1(\pi)$	Act₁: Have Concert		Act₂: No Concert	
		Conditional Opportunity Loss	Conditional Opportunity Loss · Posterior Probability	Conditional Opportunity Loss	Conditional Opportunity Loss · Posterior Probability
.10	.11	$1000	$1000 · .11 = $110	$ 0	$ 0 · .11 = $ 0
.15	.42	$ 0	$ 0 · .42 = $ 0	$ 0	$ 0 · .42 = $ 0
.25	.47	$ 0	$ 0 · .47 = $ 0	$2000	$2000 · .47 = $940
			Posterior expected opportunity loss $110		$940

Based on similar household gadgets marketed in the past, the manufacturer estimates the proportion of customers who will purchase the new gadget as follows.

Proportion of Customers π	Prior Probability $P_0(\pi)$
.01	.2
.02	.4
.03	.3
.04	.1

a) Based on the manufacturer's prior estimate of the demand for the new gadget, should the manufacturer produce the gadget?

b) If a random sample of 20 customers shows that two customers would purchase the new gadget, should the manufacturer produce it?

Solution:

a) Prior decision. The two courses of action open to the manufacturer are

Act$_1$: Produce the gadget,
Act$_2$: Do not produce the gadget.

The payoffs of these two acts are determined in Table 19.6.

The first payoff in Table 19.6, $-\$6,000$, is the conditional profit of producing the gadget given that only 1% of the customers will purchase it. This payoff is determined as follows.

$$200,000 \cdot .01 = 2000 \quad \text{(Units sold)}$$
$$\$5 - \$3 = \$2 \quad \text{(\emph{Gross} profit per unit sold; excess of selling price over variable cost per unit)}$$
$$2000 \cdot \$2 = \$4000 \quad \text{(Conditional \emph{gross} profit)}$$
$$\$4000 - \$10,000 = -\$6000 \quad \text{(Conditional \emph{net} profit)}$$

TABLE 19.6 PAYOFF TABLE: CONDITIONAL PROFITS

Event π	Prior Probability $P_0(\pi)$	Act$_1$: Produce the Gadget	Act$_2$: Do Not Produce the Gadget
.01	.2	$200,000 \cdot .01 \cdot \$2 - \$10,000 = -\$6,000$	$0
.02	.4	$200,000 \cdot .02 \cdot \$2 - \$10,000 = -\$2,000$	$0
.03	.3	$200,000 \cdot .03 \cdot \$2 - \$10,000 = \$2,000$	$0
.04	.1	$200,000 \cdot .04 \cdot \$2 - \$10,000 = \$6,000$	$0

TABLE 19.7   DETERMINATION OF EXPECTED PAYOFFS

Act$_1$: Produce the Gadget	Act$_2$: Do Not Produce the Gadget
$-\$6000 \cdot .2 = -\$1,200$	$\$0 \cdot .2 = \$0$
$-\$2000 \cdot .4 = -\$\ \ 800$	$\$0 \cdot .4 = \$0$
$\$2000 \cdot .3 = \ \ \ \$\ \ 600$	$\$0 \cdot .3 = \$0$
$\$6000 \cdot .1 = \ \ \ \$\ \ 600$	$\$0 \cdot .1 = \underline{\$0}$
$\underline{-\$\ \ 800}$	$\$0$

Other conditional payoffs of act$_1$ are determined in the same manner. All conditional payoffs of act$_2$ (do not produce the gadget) are clearly $0.

We can compare the two acts on the basis of their expected payoffs. The expected payoff of any one act is the sum of the products obtained by multiplying the conditional payoff of that event by the corresponding prior probabilities of occurrence. The computations are carried out in Table 19.7.

Table 19.7 shows that act$_2$ has the best expected payoff. Hence, according to the prior analysis of the problem, the manufacturer should *not* produce the gadget; and the prior expected profit under uncertainty is $0.

b) Posterior decision. The first step in the posterior analysis of the problem is to revise the prior probabilities assigned by the manufacturer to the various values of π in the light of the information obtained from the sample. The conversion of prior probabilities into posterior probabilities is shown in Fig. 19.5.

Although the computations carried out in Fig. 19.5 are straightforward, it is nevertheless useful to discuss the determination of conditional probabilities. For example, the conditional probability in the upper path of the diagram, .0159, is the probability that 2 out of 20 customers will purchase the gadget, given that only 1% of customers purchase the gadget. This probability is determined by the use of the binomial formula

$$P(X = x) = \frac{n!}{x!\,(n-x)!}\,\pi^x\,(1-\pi)^{n-x}.$$

Substituting the values $n = 20$, $x = 2$, $\pi = .01$ in the formula, we obtain

$$P(X = 2) = \frac{20!}{2!\,18!}\,(.01)^2(.99)^{18}$$

$$= .0159.$$

There is no doubt that the binomial formula in this case involves some lengthy computations. Fortunately, however, these computations can be entirely

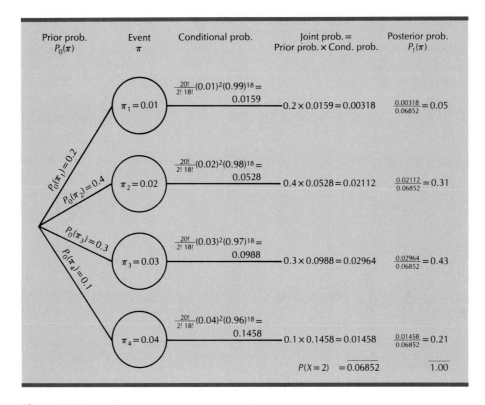

Figure 19.5

avoided, since the results can be easily obtained from the binomial tables. The remaining three conditional probabilities—.0528, .0988, .1458—are determined by changing the value of π in the binomial formula to .02, .03, and .04, respectively. We summarize in Table 19.8 the procedure used in converting prior probabilities into posterior probabilities.

TABLE 19.8   **REVISION OF PRIOR PROBABILITIES**

Event π	Prior Probability $P_0(\pi)$	Conditional Probability	Joint Probability = Prior Probability · Conditional Probability	Posterior Probability $P_1(\pi)$
.01	.2	.0159	$.2 \cdot .0159 = .00318$	$.00318 \div .06852 = .05$
.02	.4	.0528	$.4 \cdot .02112 = .02112$	$.02112 \div .06852 = .31$
.03	.3	.0988	$.3 \cdot .0988 = .02964$	$.02964 \div .06852 = .43$
.04	.1	.1458	$.1 \cdot .1458 = .01458$	$.01458 \div .06852 = .21$
			$\overline{.06852}$	$\overline{1.00}$

TABLE 19.9   DETERMINATION OF POSTERIOR EXPECTED PROFIT

Event π	Posterior Probability $P_1(\pi)$	Act₁: Produce the Gadget		Act₂: Do Not Produce the Gadget	
		Conditional Profit	Conditional Profit · Posterior Probability	Conditional Profit	Conditional Profit · Posterior Probability
.01	.05	−$6000	−$6000 · .05 = −$ 300	$0	$0
.02	.31	−$2000	−$2000 · .31 = −$ 620	$0	$0
.03	.43	+$2000	+$2000 · .43 = $ 860	$0	$0
.04	.21	+$6000	+$6000 · .21 = $1260	$0	$0
	1.00		$1200		$0

Once we have converted prior probabilities into posterior probabilities, our next step in the posterior analysis of the problem is to use the newly derived posterior probabilities to determine the expected profit of each of the two acts. The determination of the posterior expected profits is shown in Table 19.9.

Table 19.9 shows that act₁ has the best expected payoff. Hence, according to the posterior analysis of the problem, the manufacturer should produce and market the gadget, and the posterior expected profit under uncertainty is $1200.

EXERCISES

19.1   The college bookstore manager wishes to publish a student directory. The manager's prior estimate of the proportion of students who would purchase the directory is as follows.

Proportion of Students π	Prior Probability $P_0(\pi)$
.40	.75
.50	.25

In addition, the manager selects a random sample of 20 students. Twelve of these students express their desire to purchase the directory. Revise the manager's prior estimate of π in light of the sample information.

19.2   The faculty senate at San Fernando Valley State College is considering the construction of a private faculty clubhouse. The clubhouse can be constructed and furnished at a total cost of $100,000. The senate would build the clubhouse only if enough faculty members would join the club so that the initial cost of $100,000 could be recovered from an entrance fee of $500 per member. The clubhouse would be completed in five years. At that time the size of the faculty would have reached a stable level of 1000. Based on faculty club memberships on other state college campuses, the executive committee of the senate estimates the proportion of San Fernando Valley State College faculty who would join the club as follows.

Proportion of Faculty π	Prior Probability $P_0(\pi)$
.15	.3
.20	.6
.25	.1

a) Should the faculty senate build the clubhouse?

b) What is the prior expected value of perfect information?

c) A random sample of 10 faculty members shows that 4 would join the club. Taking this information into account, should the senate build the club?

d) What is the posterior expected value of perfect information?

19.3 A labor organization estimates the proportion of its members who will attend its coming annual convention as follows.

Proportion of Members π	Prior Probability $P_0(\pi)$
.20	.3
.30	.5
.40	.2

The organization has 4000 members.

a) Based on the prior estimates, how many members are expected to attend the convention?

b) A random sample of 20 members shows that 10 members will attend the convention. Taking the sample information into account, determine the expected number that will attend the convention.

19.4 A market research agency is considering whether to compile a special mailing list. The list can be compiled and printed at a total cost of $10,000. The agency provides the list to any of its 500 clients for a fixed fee of $100. Based on other mailing lists developed previously, the agency estimates the proportion of its clients who would purchase the new mailing list as follows.

Proportion of Clients π	Prior Probability $P_0(\pi)$
.15	.10
.20	.40
.25	.50

a) Should the agency develop the new mailing list?

b) What is the prior expected value of perfect information?

c) A random sample of 20 clients shows that only 1 client would purchase the new mailing list. Taking sample information into account, should the agency compile the list?

d) What is the posterior expected value of perfect information?

19.5   Machine A produces part 36 and machine B produces part 37. The quality-control engineer believes that the proportion of defective parts turned out by both machines is essentially the same. The following probability distribution is the engineer's prior estimate of the proportion of defective parts turned out by each machine.

Proportion of Defective Parts π	Prior Probability $P_0(\pi)$
.20	.40
.30	.60

a) A random sample of 10 parts produced by machine A showed 2 defective parts. Revise the engineer's prior estimate of the proportion of defective parts turned out by machine A, taking the sample information into account.

b) An additional sample of 10 parts produced by machine A showed 3 defective parts. Revise the posterior estimate of π which you obtained in part a in light of this additional information.

c) A random sample of 20 parts produced by machine B revealed 5 defective parts. Revise the quality-control engineer's prior estimate of the proportion of defective parts turned out by machine B, taking the information provided by this sample into account.

d) Explain why the results of parts b and c are the same.

19.6   As a means of fund raising, the local chapter of the Civil Liberties Defense League is considering the sponsorship of a garden party for its members. Although the food, beverages, and use of the facilities have been donated by some of its members, the league must pay $950 for entertainment. The local chapter has a total membership of 600, and the chapter social director estimates the proportion of members who would attend the party as follows.

Proportion of Members Who Would Attend π	Prior Probability $P_0(\pi)$
.20	.20
.30	.60
.40	.20

Admission to the party is set at a charge of $5 per member.

a) Should the league sponsor the party?

b) What is the prior expected value of perfect information?

c) To obtain a better estimate of those who would attend the party, the social director contacted 20 members at random. Of the members contacted, 8 expressed their desire to attend the party. Taking this information into account, should the league sponsor the party?

d) What is the posterior expected value of perfect information?

19.7 A manufacturer produced a lot of 10,000 units of product X. The entire lot can be sold for $10 per unit. At this price, the manufacturer does not guarantee the quality of the product. If the manufacturer can guarantee the quality of product X, the lot can be sold at $12 per unit. According to the terms of the guarantee, the manufacturer would refund the purchase price of any defective unit. Defective units cannot be repaired and must be discarded. The manufacturer's prior estimate of the proportion of defective units in the lot is as follows.

Proportion of Defective Units π	Prior Probability $P_0(\pi)$
.15	.25
.20	.50
.25	.25

a) Should the manufacturer guarantee the quality of product X?

b) What is the expected value of perfect information?

c) The manufacturer selected a random sample of 20 units and discovered that only 1 unit was defective. Taking the sample information into account, should the manufacturer guarantee the quality of product X?

d) What is the posterior expected value of perfect information?

KEY TERMS

prior probabilities   Probabilities based on current information along with a decision maker's experience, judgment, and expectations.

posterior probabilities   The conditional probabilities of the events given the sample information. The prior probabilities are revised using Bayes' theorem to produce the posterior probabilities.

posterior expected profit under uncertainty   The expected profit of the optimal act when all computations are made using the posterior probabilities.

TABLES

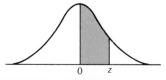

TABLE A   **AREAS UNDER THE NORMAL CURVE**

z	.00	.01	.02	.03	.04	.05	.06	.07	.08	.09
.0	.0000	.0040	.0080	.0120	.0160	.0199	.0239	.0279	.0319	.0359
.1	.0398	.0438	.0478	.0517	.0557	.0596	.0636	.0675	.0714	.0753
.2	.0793	.0832	.0871	.0910	.0948	.0987	.1026	.1064	.1103	.1141
.3	.1179	.1217	.1255	.1293	.1331	.1368	.1406	.1443	.1480	.1517
.4	.1554	.1591	.1628	.1664	.1700	.1736	.1772	.1808	.1844	.1879
.5	.1915	.1950	.1985	.2019	.2054	.2088	.2123	.2157	.2190	.2224
.6	.2257	.2291	.2324	.2357	.2389	.2422	.2454	.2486	.2517	.2549
.7	.2580	.2611	.2642	.2673	.2704	.2734	.2764	.2794	.2823	.2852
.8	.2881	.2910	.2939	.2967	.2995	.3023	.3051	.3078	.3106	.3133
.9	.3159	.3186	.3212	.3238	.3264	.3289	.3315	.3340	.3365	.3389
1.0	.3413	.3438	.3461	.3485	.3508	.3531	.3554	.3577	.3599	.3621
1.1	.3643	.3665	.3686	.3708	.3729	.3749	.3770	.3790	.3810	.3830
1.2	.3849	.3869	.3888	.3907	.3925	.3944	.3962	.3980	.3997	.4015
1.3	.4032	.4049	.4066	.4082	.4099	.4115	.4131	.4147	.4162	.4177
1.4	.4192	.4207	.4222	.4236	.4251	.4265	.4279	.4292	.4306	.4319
1.5	.4332	.4345	.4357	.4370	.4382	.4394	.4406	.4418	.4429	.4441
1.6	.4452	.4463	.4474	.4484	.4495	.4505	.4515	.4525	.4535	.4545
1.7	.4554	.4564	.4573	.4582	.4591	.4599	.4608	.4616	.4625	.4633
1.8	.4641	.4649	.4656	.4664	.4671	.4678	.4686	.4693	.4699	.4706
1.9	.4713	.4719	.4726	.4732	.4738	.4744	.4750	.4756	.4761	.4767
2.0	.4772	.4778	.4783	.4788	.4793	.4798	.4803	.4808	.4812	.4817
2.1	.4821	.4826	.4830	.4834	.4838	.4842	.4846	.4850	.4854	.4857
2.2	.4861	.4864	.4868	.4871	.4875	.4878	.4881	.4884	.4887	.4890
2.3	.4893	.4896	.4898	.4901	.4904	.4906	.4909	.4911	.4913	.4916
2.4	.4918	.4920	.4922	.4925	.4927	.4929	.4931	.4932	.4934	.4936
2.5	.4938	.4940	.4941	.4943	.4945	.4946	.4948	.4949	.4951	.4952
2.6	.4953	.4955	.4956	.4957	.4959	.4960	.4961	.4962	.4963	.4964
2.7	.4965	.4966	.4967	.4968	.4969	.4970	.4971	.4972	.4973	.4974
2.8	.4974	.4975	.4976	.4977	.4977	.4978	.4979	.4979	.4980	.4981
2.9	.4981	.4982	.4982	.4983	.4984	.4984	.4985	.4985	.4986	.4986
3.0	.4987	.4987	.4987	.4988	.4988	.4989	.4989	.4989	.4990	.4990

TABLE B VALUES OF $F_{.05}$

Degrees of Freedom (numerator)

	1	2	3	4	5	6	7	8	9	10	12	15	20	24	30	40	60	120	∞
1	161	200	216	225	230	234	237	239	241	242	244	246	248	249	250	251	252	253	254
2	18.5	19.0	19.2	19.2	19.3	19.3	19.4	19.4	19.4	19.4	19.4	19.4	19.4	19.5	19.5	19.5	19.5	19.5	19.5
3	10.1	9.55	9.28	9.12	9.01	8.94	8.89	8.85	8.81	8.79	8.74	8.70	8.66	8.64	8.62	8.59	8.57	8.55	8.53
4	7.71	6.94	6.59	6.39	6.26	6.16	6.09	6.04	6.00	5.96	5.91	5.86	5.80	5.77	5.75	5.72	5.69	5.66	5.63
5	6.61	5.79	5.41	5.19	5.05	4.95	4.88	4.82	4.77	4.74	4.68	4.62	4.56	4.53	4.50	4.46	4.43	4.40	4.37
6	5.99	5.14	4.76	4.53	4.39	4.28	4.21	4.15	4.10	4.06	4.00	3.94	3.87	3.84	3.81	3.77	3.74	3.70	3.67
7	5.59	4.74	4.35	4.12	3.97	3.87	3.79	3.73	3.68	3.64	3.57	3.51	3.44	3.41	3.38	3.34	3.30	3.27	3.23
8	5.32	4.46	4.07	3.84	3.69	3.58	3.50	3.44	3.39	3.35	3.28	3.22	3.15	3.12	3.08	3.04	3.01	2.97	2.93
9	5.12	4.26	3.86	3.63	3.48	3.37	3.29	3.23	3.18	3.14	3.07	3.01	2.94	2.90	2.86	2.83	2.79	2.75	2.71
10	4.96	4.10	3.71	3.48	3.33	3.22	3.14	3.07	3.02	2.98	2.91	2.85	2.77	2.74	2.70	2.66	2.62	2.58	2.54
11	4.84	3.98	3.59	3.36	3.20	3.09	3.01	2.95	2.90	2.85	2.79	2.72	2.65	2.61	2.57	2.53	2.49	2.45	2.40
12	4.75	3.89	3.49	3.26	3.11	3.00	2.91	2.85	2.80	2.75	2.69	2.62	2.54	2.51	2.47	2.43	2.38	2.34	2.30
13	4.67	3.81	3.41	3.18	3.03	2.92	2.83	2.77	2.71	2.67	2.60	2.53	2.46	2.42	2.38	2.34	2.30	2.25	2.21
14	4.60	3.74	3.34	3.11	2.96	2.85	2.76	2.70	2.65	2.60	2.53	2.46	2.39	2.35	2.31	2.27	2.22	2.18	2.13
15	4.54	3.68	3.29	3.06	2.90	2.79	2.71	2.64	2.59	2.54	2.48	2.40	2.33	2.29	2.25	2.20	2.16	2.11	2.07
16	4.49	3.63	3.24	3.01	2.85	2.74	2.66	2.59	2.54	2.49	2.42	2.35	2.28	2.24	2.19	2.15	2.11	2.06	2.01
17	4.45	3.59	3.20	2.96	2.81	2.70	2.61	2.55	2.49	2.45	2.38	2.31	2.23	2.19	2.15	2.10	2.06	2.01	1.96
18	4.41	3.55	3.16	2.93	2.77	2.66	2.58	2.51	2.46	2.41	2.34	2.27	2.19	2.15	2.11	2.06	2.02	1.97	1.92
19	4.38	3.52	3.13	2.90	2.74	2.63	2.54	2.48	2.42	2.38	2.31	2.23	2.16	2.11	2.07	2.03	1.98	1.93	1.88
20	4.35	3.49	3.10	2.87	2.71	2.60	2.51	2.45	2.39	2.35	2.28	2.20	2.12	2.08	2.04	1.99	1.95	1.90	1.84
21	4.32	3.47	3.07	2.84	2.68	2.57	2.49	2.42	2.37	2.32	2.25	2.18	2.10	2.05	2.01	1.96	1.92	1.87	1.81
22	4.30	3.44	3.05	2.82	2.66	2.55	2.46	2.40	2.34	2.30	2.23	2.15	2.07	2.03	1.98	1.94	1.89	1.84	1.78
23	4.28	3.42	3.03	2.80	2.64	2.53	2.44	2.37	2.32	2.27	2.20	2.13	2.05	2.01	1.96	1.91	1.86	1.81	1.76
24	4.26	3.40	3.01	2.78	2.62	2.51	2.42	2.36	2.30	2.25	2.18	2.11	2.03	1.98	1.94	1.89	1.84	1.79	1.73
25	4.24	3.39	2.99	2.76	2.60	2.49	2.40	2.34	2.28	2.24	2.16	2.09	2.01	1.96	1.92	1.87	1.82	1.77	1.71
30	4.17	3.32	2.92	2.69	2.53	2.42	2.33	2.27	2.21	2.16	2.09	2.01	1.93	1.89	1.84	1.79	1.74	1.68	1.62
40	4.08	3.23	2.84	2.61	2.45	2.34	2.25	2.18	2.12	2.08	2.00	1.92	1.84	1.79	1.74	1.69	1.64	1.58	1.51
60	4.00	3.15	2.76	2.53	2.37	2.25	2.17	2.10	2.04	1.99	1.92	1.84	1.75	1.70	1.65	1.59	1.53	1.47	1.39
120	3.92	3.07	2.68	2.45	2.29	2.18	2.09	2.02	1.96	1.91	1.83	1.75	1.66	1.61	1.55	1.50	1.43	1.35	1.25
∞	3.84	3.00	2.60	2.37	2.21	2.10	2.01	1.94	1.88	1.83	1.75	1.67	1.57	1.52	1.46	1.39	1.32	1.22	1.00

Degrees of Freedom (denominator)

TABLE C   VALUES OF $F_{.01}$

								Degrees of Freedom (numerator)										
	1	2	3	4	5	6	7	8	9	10	12	15	20	24	30	40	60	120	∞
1	4052	5000	5403	5625	5764	5859	5928	5982	6023	6056	6106	6157	6209	6235	6261	6287	6313	6339	6366
2	98.5	99.0	99.2	99.2	99.3	99.3	99.4	99.4	99.4	99.4	99.4	99.4	99.4	99.5	99.5	99.5	99.5	99.5	99.5
3	34.1	30.8	29.5	28.7	28.2	27.9	27.7	27.5	27.3	27.2	27.1	26.9	26.7	26.6	26.5	26.4	26.3	26.2	26.1
4	21.2	18.0	16.7	16.0	15.5	15.2	15.0	14.8	14.7	14.5	14.4	14.2	14.0	13.9	13.8	13.7	13.7	13.6	13.5
5	16.3	13.3	12.1	11.4	11.0	10.7	10.5	10.3	10.2	10.1	9.89	9.72	9.55	9.47	9.38	9.29	9.20	9.11	9.02
6	13.7	10.9	9.78	9.15	8.75	8.47	8.26	8.10	7.98	7.87	7.72	7.56	7.40	7.31	7.23	7.14	7.06	6.97	6.88
7	12.2	9.55	8.45	7.85	7.46	7.19	6.99	6.84	6.72	6.62	6.47	6.31	6.16	6.07	5.99	5.91	5.82	5.74	5.65
8	11.3	8.65	7.59	7.01	6.63	6.37	6.18	6.03	5.91	5.81	5.67	5.52	5.36	5.28	5.20	5.12	5.03	4.95	4.86
9	10.6	8.02	6.99	6.42	6.06	5.80	5.61	5.47	5.35	5.26	5.11	4.96	4.81	4.73	4.65	4.57	4.48	4.40	4.31
10	10.0	7.56	6.55	5.99	5.64	5.39	5.20	5.06	4.94	4.85	4.71	4.56	4.41	4.33	4.25	4.17	4.08	4.00	3.91
11	9.65	7.21	6.22	5.67	5.32	5.07	4.89	4.74	4.63	4.54	4.40	4.25	4.10	4.02	3.94	3.86	3.78	3.69	3.60
12	9.33	6.93	5.95	5.41	5.06	4.82	4.64	4.50	4.39	4.30	4.16	4.01	3.86	3.78	3.70	3.62	3.54	3.45	3.36
13	9.07	6.70	5.74	5.21	4.86	4.62	4.44	4.30	4.19	4.10	3.96	3.82	3.66	3.59	3.51	3.43	3.34	3.25	3.17
14	8.86	6.51	5.56	5.04	4.70	4.46	4.28	4.14	4.03	3.94	3.80	3.66	3.51	3.43	3.35	3.27	3.18	3.09	3.00
15	8.68	6.36	5.42	4.89	4.56	4.32	4.14	4.00	3.89	3.80	3.67	3.52	3.37	3.29	3.21	3.13	3.05	2.96	2.87
16	8.53	6.23	5.29	4.77	4.44	4.20	4.03	3.89	3.78	3.69	3.55	3.41	3.26	3.18	3.10	3.02	2.93	2.84	2.75
17	8.40	6.11	5.19	4.67	4.34	4.10	3.93	3.79	3.68	3.59	3.46	3.31	3.16	3.08	3.00	2.92	2.83	2.75	2.65
18	8.29	6.01	5.09	4.58	4.25	4.01	3.84	3.71	3.60	3.51	3.37	3.23	3.08	3.00	2.92	2.84	2.75	2.66	2.57
19	8.19	5.93	5.01	4.50	4.17	3.94	3.77	3.63	3.52	3.43	3.30	3.15	3.00	2.92	2.84	2.76	2.67	2.58	2.49
20	8.10	5.85	4.94	4.43	4.10	3.87	3.70	3.56	3.46	3.37	3.23	3.09	2.94	2.86	2.78	2.69	2.61	2.52	2.42
21	8.02	5.78	4.87	4.37	4.04	3.81	3.64	3.51	3.40	3.31	3.17	3.03	2.88	2.80	2.72	2.64	2.55	2.46	2.36
22	7.95	5.72	4.82	4.31	3.99	3.76	3.59	3.45	3.35	3.26	3.12	2.98	2.83	2.75	2.67	2.58	2.50	2.40	2.31
23	7.88	5.66	4.76	4.26	3.94	3.71	3.54	3.41	3.30	3.21	3.07	2.93	2.78	2.70	2.62	2.54	2.45	2.35	2.26
24	7.82	5.61	4.72	4.22	3.90	3.67	3.50	3.36	3.26	3.17	3.03	2.89	2.74	2.66	2.58	2.49	2.40	2.31	2.21
25	7.77	5.57	4.68	4.18	3.86	3.63	3.46	3.32	3.22	3.13	2.99	2.85	2.70	2.62	2.53	2.45	2.36	2.27	2.17
30	7.56	5.39	4.51	4.02	3.70	3.47	3.30	3.17	3.07	2.98	2.84	2.70	2.55	2.47	2.39	2.30	2.21	2.11	2.01
40	7.31	5.18	4.31	3.83	3.51	3.29	3.12	2.99	2.89	2.80	2.66	2.52	2.37	2.29	2.20	2.11	2.02	1.92	1.80
60	7.08	4.98	4.13	3.65	3.34	3.12	2.95	2.82	2.72	2.63	2.50	2.35	2.20	2.12	2.03	1.94	1.84	1.73	1.60
120	6.85	4.79	3.95	3.48	3.17	2.96	2.79	2.66	2.56	2.47	2.34	2.19	2.03	1.95	1.86	1.76	1.66	1.53	1.38
∞	6.63	4.61	3.78	3.32	3.02	2.80	2.64	2.51	2.41	2.32	2.18	2.04	1.88	1.79	1.70	1.59	1.47	1.32	1.00

Degrees of Freedom (denominator)

Tables B and C are reproduced from Table 18 of *Biometrika Tables for Statistics*, Vol. 1, 1966.

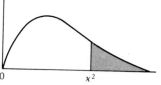

TABLE D χ^2-DISTRIBUTION

df	.10	.05	.025	.01	.005
1	2.706	3.841	5.024	6.635	7.879
2	4.605	5.991	7.378	9.210	10.597
3	6.251	7.815	9.348	11.345	12.838
4	7.779	9.488	11.143	13.277	14.860
5	9.236	11.070	12.832	15.086	16.750
6	10.645	12.592	14.449	16.812	18.548
7	12.017	14.067	16.013	18.475	20.278
8	13.362	15.507	17.535	20.090	21.955
9	14.684	16.919	19.023	21.666	23.589
10	15.987	18.307	20.483	23.209	25.188
11	17.275	19.675	21.920	24.725	26.757
12	18.549	21.026	23.337	26.217	28.300
13	19.812	22.362	24.736	27.688	29.819
14	21.064	23.685	26.119	29.141	31.319
15	22.307	24.996	27.488	30.578	32.801
16	23.542	26.296	28.845	32.000	34.267
17	24.769	27.587	30.191	33.409	35.718
18	25.989	28.869	31.526	34.805	37.156
19	27.204	30.144	32.852	36.191	38.582
20	28.412	31.410	34.170	37.566	39.997
21	29.615	32.671	35.479	38.932	41.401
22	30.813	33.924	36.781	40.289	42.796
23	32.007	35.172	38.076	41.638	44.181
24	33.196	36.415	39.364	42.980	45.558
25	34.382	37.652	40.646	44.314	46.928
26	35.563	38.885	41.923	45.642	48.290
27	36.741	40.113	43.194	46.963	49.645
28	37.916	41.337	44.461	48.278	50.993
29	39.087	42.557	45.722	49.588	52.336
30	40.256	43.773	46.979	50.892	53.672

Abridged with permission of Macmillan Publishing Company from R. A. Fisher, *Statistical Methods for Research Workers.* Copyright © 1970 University of Adelaide.

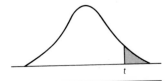

TABLE E   *t*-DISTRIBUTION

df	$t_{.100}$	$t_{.050}$	$t_{.025}$	$t_{.010}$	$t_{.005}$
1	3.078	6.314	12.706	31.821	63.657
2	1.886	2.920	4.303	6.965	9.925
3	1.638	2.353	3.182	4.541	5.841
4	1.533	2.132	2.776	3.747	4.604
5	1.476	2.015	2.571	3.365	4.032
6	1.440	1.943	2.447	3.143	3.707
7	1.415	1.895	2.365	2.998	3.499
8	1.397	1.860	2.306	2.896	3.355
9	1.383	1.833	2.262	2.821	3.250
10	1.372	1.812	2.228	2.764	3.169
11	1.363	1.796	2.201	2.718	3.106
12	1.356	1.782	2.179	2.681	3.055
13	1.350	1.771	2.160	2.650	3.012
14	1.345	1.761	2.145	2.624	2.977
15	1.341	1.753	2.131	2.602	2.947
16	1.337	1.746	2.120	2.583	2.921
17	1.333	1.740	2.110	2.567	2.898
18	1.330	1.734	2.101	2.552	2.878
19	1.328	1.729	2.093	2.539	2.861
20	1.325	1.725	2.086	2.528	2.845
21	1.323	1.721	2.080	2.518	2.831
22	1.321	1.717	2.074	2.508	2.819
23	1.319	1.714	2.069	2.500	2.807
24	1.318	1.711	2.064	2.492	2.797
25	1.316	1.708	2.060	2.485	2.787
26	1.315	1.706	2.056	2.479	2.779
27	1.314	1.703	2.052	2.473	2.771
28	1.313	1.701	2.048	2.467	2.763
29	1.311	1.699	2.045	2.462	2.756
∞	1.282	1.645	1.960	2.326	2.576

Abridged with permission of Macmillan Publishing Company from R. A. Fisher, *Statistical Methods for Research Workers.* Copyright © 1970 University of Adelaide.

TABLE F CRITICAL LEVELS OF *r* AT .05 AND .01 LEVELS
OF SIGNIFICANCE

df	$r_{.05}$	$r_{.01}$	df	$r_{.05}$	$r_{.01}$
1	.997	1.000	24	.388	.496
2	.950	.990	25	.381	.487
3	.878	.959	26	.374	.478
4	.811	.917	27	.367	.470
5	.754	.874	28	.361	.463
6	.707	.834	29	.355	.456
7	.666	.798	30	.349	.449
8	.632	.765	35	.325	.418
9	.602	.735	40	.304	.393
10	.576	.708	45	.288	.372
11	.553	.684	50	.273	.354
12	.532	.661	60	.250	.325
13	.514	.641	70	.232	.302
14	.497	.623	80	.217	.283
15	.482	.606	90	.205	.267
16	.468	.590	100	.195	.254
17	.456	.575	125	.174	.228
18	.444	.561	150	.159	.208
19	.433	.549	200	.138	.181
20	.423	.537	300	.113	.148
21	.413	.526	400	.098	.128
22	.404	.515	500	.088	.115
23	.396	.505	1000	.062	.081

Reprinted by permission from *Statistical Methods,* 7th ed., George W. Snedecor and William G. Cochran. © 1980 by the Iowa State University Press, 2121 South State Avenue, Ames, Iowa 50010.

TABLE G CUMULATIVE BINOMIAL PROBABILITIES

Left $P(X \geq x)$						$n = 1$						Right $P(X \leq x)$
x	$\pi =$	.01	.02	.03	.04	.05	.06	.07	.08	.09	.10	
1		.0100	.0200	.0300	.0400	.0500	.0600	.0700	.0800	.0900	.1000	0
		.99	.98	.97	.96	.95	.94	.93	.92	.91	.90	$= \pi$ x

						$n = 1$						
x	$\pi =$	.11	.12	.13	.14	.15	.16	.17	.18	.19	.20	
1		.1100	.1200	.1300	.1400	.1500	.1600	.1700	.1800	.1900	.2000	0
		.89	.88	.87	.86	.85	.84	.83	.82	.81	.80	$= \pi$ x

						$n = 1$						
x	$\pi =$	.21	.22	.23	.24	.25	.26	.27	.28	.29	.30	
1		.2100	.2200	.2300	.2400	.2500	.2600	.2700	.2800	.2900	.3000	0
		.79	.78	.77	.76	.75	.74	.73	.72	.71	.70	$= \pi$ x

						$n = 1$						
x	$\pi =$	.31	.32	.33	.34	.35	.36	.37	.38	.39	.40	
1		.3100	.3200	.3300	.3400	.3500	.3600	.3700	.3800	.3900	.4000	0
		.69	.68	.67	.66	.65	.64	.63	.62	.61	.60	$= \pi$ x

						$n = 1$						
x	$\pi =$	.41	.42	.43	.44	.45	.46	.47	.48	.49	.50	
1		.4100	.4200	.4300	.4400	.4500	.4600	.4700	.4800	.4900	.5000	0
		.59	.58	.57	.56	.55	.54	.53	.52	.51	.50	$= \pi$ x

						$n = 2$						
x	$\pi =$	.01	.02	.03	.04	.05	.06	.07	.08	.09	.10	
1		.0199	.0396	.0591	.0784	.0975	.1164	.1351	.1536	.1719	.1900	1
2		.0001	.0004	.0009	.0016	.0025	.0036	.0049	.0064	.0081	.0100	0
		.99	.98	.97	.96	.95	.94	.93	.92	.91	.90	$= \pi$ x

						$n = 2$						
x	$\pi =$	.11	.12	.13	.14	.15	.16	.17	.18	.19	.20	
1		.2079	.2256	.2431	.2604	.2775	.2944	.3111	.3276	.3439	.3600	1
2		.0121	.0144	.0169	.0196	.0225	.0256	.0289	.0324	.0361	.0400	0
		.89	.88	.87	.86	.85	.84	.83	.82	.81	.80	$= \pi$ x

						$n = 2$						
x	$\pi =$	.21	.22	.23	.24	.25	.26	.27	.28	.29	.30	
1		.3759	.3916	.4071	.4224	.4375	.4524	.4671	.4816	.4959	.5100	1
2		.0441	.0484	.0529	.0576	.0625	.0676	.0729	.0784	.0841	.0900	0
		.79	.78	.77	.76	.75	.74	.73	.72	.71	.70	$= \pi$ x

TABLE G *(Continued)*

Left $P(X \geq x)$							$n = 2$						Right $P(X \leq x)$
x	$\pi =$	.31	.32	.33	.34	.35	.36	.37	.38	.39	.40		
1		.5239	.5376	.5511	.5644	.5775	.5904	.6031	.6156	.6279	.6400		1
2		.0961	.1024	.1089	.1156	.1225	.1296	.1369	.1444	.1521	.1600		0
		.69	.68	.67	.66	.65	.64	.63	.62	.61	.60	$= \pi$	x

$n = 2$

x	$\pi =$	.41	.42	.43	.44	.45	.46	.47	.48	.49	.50		
1		.6519	.6636	.6751	.6864	.6975	.7084	.7191	.7296	.7399	.7500		1
2		.1681	.1764	.1849	.1936	.2025	.2116	.2209	.2304	.2401	.2500		0
		.59	.58	.57	.56	.55	.54	.53	.52	.51	.50	$= \pi$	x

$n = 3$

x	$\pi =$	.01	.02	.03	.04	.05	.06	.07	.08	.09	.10		
1		.0297	.0588	.0873	.1153	.1426	.1694	.1956	.2213	.2464	.2710		2
2		.0003	.0012	.0026	.0047	.0073	.0104	.0140	.0182	.0228	.0280		1
3					.0001	.0001	.0002	.0003	.0005	.0007	.0010		0
		.99	.98	.97	.96	.95	.94	.93	.92	.91	.90	$= \pi$	x

$n = 3$

x	$\pi =$	.11	.12	.13	.14	.15	.16	.17	.18	.19	.20		
1		.2950	.3185	.3415	.3639	.3859	.4073	.4282	.4486	.4686	.4880		2
2		.0336	.0397	.0463	.0533	.0608	.0686	.0769	.0855	.0946	.1040		1
3		.0013	.0017	.0022	.0027	.0034	.0041	.0049	.0058	.0069	.0080		0
		.89	.88	.87	.86	.85	.84	.83	.82	.81	.80	$= \pi$	x

$n = 3$

x	$\pi =$	.21	.22	.23	.24	.25	.26	.27	.28	.29	.30		
1		.5070	.5254	.5435	.5610	.5781	.5948	.6110	.6268	.6421	.6570		2
2		.1138	.1239	.1344	.1452	.1563	.1676	.1793	.1913	.2035	.2160		1
3		.0093	.0106	.0122	.0138	.0156	.0176	.0197	.0220	.0244	.0270		0
		.79	.78	.77	.76	.75	.74	.73	.72	.71	.70	$= \pi$	x

$n = 3$

x	$\pi =$	.31	.32	.33	.34	.35	.36	.37	.38	.39	.40		
1		.6715	.6856	.6992	.7125	.7254	.7379	.7500	.7617	.7730	.7840		2
2		.2287	.2417	.2548	.2682	.2818	.2955	.3094	.3235	.3377	.3520		1
3		.0298	.0328	.0359	.0393	.0429	.0467	.0507	.0549	.0593	.0640		0
		.69	.68	.67	.66	.65	.64	.63	.62	.61	.60	$= \pi$	x

$n = 3$

x	$\pi =$	.41	.42	.43	.44	.45	.46	.47	.48	.49	.50		
1		.7946	.8049	.8148	.8244	.8336	.8425	.8511	.8594	.8673	.8750		2
2		.3665	.3810	.3957	.4104	.4253	.4401	.4551	.4700	.4850	.5000		1
3		.0689	.0741	.0795	.0852	.0911	.0973	.1038	.1106	.1176	.1250		0
		.59	.58	.57	.56	.55	.54	.53	.52	.51	.50	$= \pi$	x

(Continued)

TABLE G *(Continued)*

Left $P(X \geq x)$						$n = 4$						Right $P(X \leq x)$
x	$\pi =$	.01	.02	.03	.04	.05	.06	.07	.08	.09	.10	
1		.0394	.0776	.1147	.1507	.1855	.2193	.2519	.2836	.3143	.3439	3
2		.0006	.0023	.0052	.0091	.0140	.0199	.0267	.0344	.0430	.0523	2
3				.0001	.0002	.0005	.0008	.0013	.0019	.0027	.0037	1
4										.0001	.0001	0
		.99	.98	.97	.96	.95	.94	.93	.92	.91	.90	$= \pi$ x

						$n = 4$						
x	$\pi =$	.11	.12	.13	.14	.15	.16	.17	.18	.19	.20	
1		.3726	.4003	.4271	.4530	.4780	.5021	.5254	.5479	.5695	.5904	3
2		.0624	.0732	.0847	.0968	.1095	.1228	.1366	.1509	.1656	.1808	2
3		.0049	.0063	.0079	.0098	.0120	.0144	.0171	.0202	.0235	.0272	1
4		.0001	.0002	.0003	.0004	.0005	.0007	.0008	.0010	.0013	.0016	0
		.89	.88	.87	.86	.85	.84	.83	.82	.81	.80	$= \pi$ x

						$n = 4$						
x	$\pi =$	.21	.22	.23	.24	.25	.26	.27	.28	.29	.30	
1		.6105	.6298	.6485	.6664	.6836	.7001	.7160	.7313	.7459	.7599	3
2		.1963	.2122	.2285	.2450	.2617	.2787	.2959	.3132	.3307	.3483	2
3		.0312	.0356	.0403	.0453	.0508	.0566	.0628	.0694	.0763	.0837	1
4		.0019	.0023	.0028	.0033	.0039	.0046	.0053	.0061	.0071	.0081	0
		.79	.78	.77	.76	.75	.74	.73	.72	.71	.70	$= \pi$ x

						$n = 4$						
x	$\pi =$	.31	.32	.33	.34	.35	.36	.37	.38	.39	.40	
1		.7733	.7862	.7985	.8103	.8215	.8322	.8425	.8522	.8615	.8704	3
2		.3660	.3837	.4015	.4193	.4370	.4547	.4724	.4900	.5075	.5248	2
3		.0915	.0996	.1082	.1171	.1265	.1362	.1464	.1569	.1679	.1792	1
4		.0092	.0105	.0119	.0134	.0150	.0168	.0187	.0209	.0231	.0256	0
x		.69	.68	.67	.66	.65	.64	.63	.62	.61	.60	$= \pi$ x

						$n = 4$						
x	$\pi =$	.41	.42	.43	.44	.45	.46	.47	.48	.49	.50	
1		.8788	.8868	.8944	.9017	.9085	.9150	.9211	.9269	.9323	.9375	3
2		.5420	.5590	.5759	.5926	.6090	.6252	.6412	.6569	.6724	.6875	2
3		.1909	.2030	.2155	.2283	.2415	.2550	.2689	.2831	.2977	.3125	1
4		.0283	.0311	.0342	.0375	.0410	.0448	.0488	.0531	.0576	.0625	0
		.59	.58	.57	.56	.55	.54	.53	.52	.51	.50	$= \pi$ x

						$n = 5$						
x	$\pi =$	.01	.02	.03	.04	.05	.06	.07	.08	.09	.10	
1		.0490	.0961	.1413	.1846	.2262	.2661	.3043	.3409	.3760	.4095	4
2		.0010	.0038	.0085	.0148	.0226	.0319	.0425	.0544	.0674	.0815	3
3			.0001	.0003	.0006	.0012	.0020	.0031	.0045	.0063	.0086	2
4							.0001	.0001	.0002	.0003	.0005	1
		.99	.98	.97	.96	.95	.94	.93	.92	.91	.90	$= \pi$ x

TABLE G *(Continued)*

Left $P(X \geq x)$						$n = 5$						Right $P(X \leq x)$
$x \quad \pi =$	.11	.12	.13	.14	.15	.16	.17	.18	.19	.20		
1	.4416	.4723	.5016	.5296	.5563	.5818	.6061	.6293	.6513	.6723		4
2	.0965	.1125	.1292	.1467	.1648	.1835	.2027	.2224	.2424	.2627		3
3	.0112	.0143	.0179	.0220	.0266	.0318	.0375	.0437	.0505	.0579		2
4	.0007	.0009	.0013	.0017	.0022	.0029	.0036	.0045	.0055	.0069		1
5				.0001	.0001	.0001	.0001	.0001	.0002	.0002	.0003	0
	.89	.88	.87	.86	.85	.84	.83	.82	.81	.80	$= \pi$	x

						$n = 5$						
$x \quad \pi =$	.21	.22	.23	.24	.25	.26	.27	.28	.29	.30		
1	.6923	.7113	.7293	.7464	.7627	.7781	.7927	.8065	.8196	.8319		4
2	.2833	.3041	.3251	.3461	.3672	.3883	.4093	.4303	.4511	.4718		3
3	.0659	.0744	.0836	.0933	.1035	.1143	.1257	.1376	.1501	.1631		2
4	.0081	.0097	.0114	.0134	.0156	.0181	.0208	.0238	.0272	.0308		1
5	.0004	.0005	.0006	.0008	.0010	.0012	.0014	.0017	.0021	.0024		0
	.79	.78	.77	.76	.75	.74	.73	.72	.71	.70	$= \pi$	x

						$n = 5$						
$x \quad \pi =$	.31	.32	.33	.34	.35	.36	.37	.38	.39	.40		
1	.8436	.8546	.8650	.8748	.8840	.8926	.9008	.9084	.9155	.9222		4
2	.4923	.5125	.5325	.5522	.5716	.5906	.6093	.6276	.6455	.6630		3
3	.1766	.1905	.2050	.2199	.2352	.2509	.2670	.2835	.3003	.3174		2
4	.0347	.0390	.0436	.0486	.0540	.0598	.0660	.0726	.0796	.0780		1
5	.0029	.0034	.0039	.0045	.0053	.0060	.0069	.0079	.0090	.0102		0
	.69	.68	.67	.66	.65	.64	.63	.62	.61	.60	$= \pi$	x

						$n = 5$						
$x \quad \pi =$	.41	.42	.43	.44	.45	.46	.47	.48	.49	.50		
1	.9285	.9344	.9398	.9449	.9497	.9541	.9582	.9620	.9655	.9688		4
2	.6801	.6967	.7129	.7286	.7438	.7585	.7728	.7865	.7998	.8125		3
3	.3349	.3525	.3705	.3886	.4069	.4253	.4439	.4625	.4813	.5000		2
4	.0949	.1033	.1121	.1214	.1312	.1415	.1522	.1635	.1753	.1875		1
5	.0116	.0131	.0147	.0165	.0185	.0206	.0229	.0255	.0282	.0313		0
	.59	.58	.57	.56	.55	.54	.53	.52	.51	.50	$= \pi$	x

						$n = 6$						
$x \quad \pi =$	.01	.02	.03	.04	.05	.06	.07	.08	.09	.10		
1	.0585	.1142	.1670	.2172	.2649	.3101	.3530	.3936	.4321	.4686		5
2	.0015	.0057	.0125	.0216	.0328	.0459	.0608	.0773	.0952	.1143		4
3		.0002	.0005	.0012	.0022	.0038	.0058	.0085	.0118	.0159		3
4					.0001	.0002	.0003	.0005	.0008	.0013		2
5										.0001		1
	.99	.98	.97	.96	.95	.94	.93	.92	.91	.90	$= \pi$	x

(Continued)

TABLE G *(Continued)*

Left $P(X \geq x)$						$n = 6$						Right $P(X \leq x)$
x $\pi =$	.11	.12	.13	.14	.15	.16	.17	.18	.19	.20		
1	.5030	.5356	.5664	.5954	.6229	.6487	.6731	.6960	.7176	.7379		5
2	.1345	.1556	.1776	.2003	.2235	.2472	.2713	.2956	.3201	.3446		4
3	.0206	.0261	.0324	.0395	.0473	.0560	.0655	.0759	.0870	.0989		3
4	.0018	.0025	.0034	.0045	.0059	.0075	.0094	.0116	.0141	.0170		2
5	.0001	.0001	.0002	.0003	.0004	.0005	.0007	.0010	.0013	.0016		1
6										.0001		0
	.89	.88	.87	.86	.85	.84	.83	.82	.81	.80	$= \pi$	x

						$n = 6$						
x $\pi =$	.21	.22	.23	.24	.25	.26	.27	.28	.29	.30		
1	.7569	.7748	.7916	.8073	.8220	.8358	.8487	.8607	.8719	.8824		5
2	.3692	.3937	.4180	.4422	.4661	.4896	.5128	.5356	.5580	.5798		4
3	.1115	.1250	.1391	.1539	.1694	.1856	.2023	.2196	.2374	.2557		3
4	.0202	.0239	.0280	.0326	.0376	.0431	.0492	.0557	.0628	.0705		2
5	.0020	.0025	.0031	.0038	.0046	.0056	.0067	.0079	.0093	.0109		1
6	.0001	.0001	.0001	.0002	.0002	.0003	.0004	.0005	.0006	.0007		0
	.79	.78	.77	.76	.75	.74	.73	.72	.71	.70	$= \pi$	x

						$n = 6$						
x $\pi =$	.31	.32	.33	.34	.35	.36	.37	.38	.39	.40		
1	.8921	.9011	.9095	.9173	.9246	.9313	.9375	.9432	.9485	.9533		5
2	.6012	.6220	.6422	.6619	.6809	.6994	.7172	.7343	.7508	.7667		4
3	.2744	.2936	.3130	.3328	.3529	.3732	.3937	.4143	.4350	.4557		3
4	.0787	.0875	.0969	.1069	.1174	.1286	.1404	.1527	.1657	.1792		2
5	.0127	.0148	.0170	.0195	.0223	.0254	.0288	.0325	.0365	.0410		1
6	.0009	.0011	.0013	.0015	.0018	.0022	.0026	.0030	.0035	.0041		0
	.69	.68	.67	.66	.65	.64	.63	.62	.61	.60	$= \pi$	x

						$n = 6$						
x $\pi =$	.41	.42	.43	.44	.45	.46	.47	.48	.49	.50		
1	.9578	.9169	.9657	.9692	.9723	.9752	.9778	.9802	.9824	.9844		5
2	.7819	.7965	.8105	.8238	.8364	.8485	.8599	.8707	.8810	.8906		4
3	.4764	.4971	.5177	.5382	.5585	.5786	.5985	.6180	.6373	.6563		3
4	.1938	.2080	.2232	.2390	.2553	.2721	.2893	.3070	.3252	.3438		2
5	.0458	.0510	.0566	.0627	.0692	.0762	.0837	.0917	.1003	.1094		1
6	.0048	.0055	.0063	.0073	.0083	.0095	.0108	.0122	.0138	.0156		0
	.59	.58	.57	.56	.55	.54	.53	.52	.51	.50	$= \pi$	x

						$n = 7$						
x $\pi =$	.01	.02	.03	.04	.05	.06	.07	.08	.09	.10		
1	.0679	.1319	.1920	.2486	.3017	.3515	.3983	.4422	.4832	.5217		6
2	.0020	.0079	.0171	.0294	.0444	.0618	.0813	.1026	.1255	.1497		5
3		.0003	.0009	.0020	.0038	.0063	.0097	.0140	.0193	.0257		4
4				.0001	.0002	.0004	.0007	.0012	.0018	.0027		3
5								.0001	.0001	.0002		2
	.99	.98	.97	.96	.95	.94	.93	.92	.91	.90	$= \pi$	x

TABLE G *(Continued)*

Left $P(X \geq x)$						$n = 7$						Right $P(X \leq x)$
x	$\pi =$	.11	.12	.13	.14	.15	.16	.17	.18	.19	.20	
1		.5577	.5913	.6227	.6521	.6794	.7049	.7286	.7507	.7712	.7903	6
2		.1750	.2012	.2281	.2556	.2834	.3115	.3396	.3677	.3956	.4233	5
3		.0331	.0416	.0513	.0620	.0738	.0866	.1005	.1154	.1313	.1480	4
4		.0039	.0054	.0072	.0094	.0121	.0153	.0189	.0231	.0279	.0333	3
5		.0003	.0004	.0006	.0009	.0012	.0017	.0022	.0029	.0037	.0047	2
6						.0001	.0001	.0001	.0002	.0003	.0004	1
		.89	.88	.87	.86	.85	.84	.83	.82	.81	.80	$= \pi$ x

						$n = 7$						
x	$\pi =$	.21	.22	.23	.24	.25	.26	.27	.28	.29	.30	
1		.8080	.8243	.8395	.8535	.8665	.8785	.8895	.8997	.9090	.9176	6
2		.4506	.4775	.5040	.5298	.5551	.5796	.6035	.6266	.6490	.6706	5
3		.1657	.1841	.2033	.2231	.2436	.2646	.2861	.3081	.3304	.3529	4
4		.0394	.0461	.0536	.0617	.0706	.0802	.0905	.1016	.1134	.1260	3
5		.0058	.0072	.0088	.0107	.0129	.0153	.0181	.0213	.0248	.0288	2
6		.0005	.0006	.0008	.0011	.0013	.0017	.0021	.0026	.0031	.0038	1
7						.0001	.0001	.0001	.0001	.0002	.0002	0
		.79	.78	.77	.76	.75	.74	.73	.72	.71	.70	$= \pi$ x

						$n = 7$						
x	$\pi =$	.31	.32	.33	.34	.35	.36	.37	.38	.39	.40	
1		.9255	.9328	.9394	.9454	.9510	.9560	.9606	.9648	.9686	.9720	6
2		.6914	.7113	.7304	.7487	.7662	.7828	.7987	.8137	.8279	.8414	5
3		.3757	.3987	.4217	.4447	.4677	.4906	.5134	.5359	.5581	.5801	4
4		.1394	.1534	.1682	.1837	.1998	.2167	.2341	.2521	.2707	.2898	3
5		.0332	.0380	.0434	.0492	.0556	.0625	.0701	.0782	.0869	.0963	2
6		.0046	.0055	.0065	.0077	.0090	.0105	.0123	.0142	.0164	.0188	1
7		.0003	.0003	.0004	.0005	.0006	.0008	.0009	.0011	.0014	.0016	0
		.69	.68	.67	.66	.65	.64	.63	.62	.61	.60	$= \pi$ x

						$n = 7$						
x	$\pi =$	.41	.42	.43	.44	.45	.46	.47	.48	.49	.50	
1		.9751	.9779	.9805	.9827	.9848	.9866	.9883	.9897	.9910	.9922	6
2		.8541	.8660	.8772	.8877	.8976	.9068	.9153	.9233	.9307	.9375	5
3		.6017	.6229	.6436	.6638	.6836	.7027	.7213	.7393	.7567	.7734	4
4		.3094	.3294	.3498	.3706	.3917	.4131	.4346	.4563	.4781	.5000	3
5		.1063	.1169	.1282	.1402	.1529	.1663	.1803	.1951	.2105	.2266	2
6		.0216	.0246	.0279	.0316	.0357	.0402	.0451	.0504	.0562	.0625	1
7		.0019	.0023	.0027	.0032	.0037	.0044	.0051	.0059	.0068	.0078	0
		.59	.58	.57	.56	.55	.54	.53	.52	.51	.50	$= \pi$ x

						$n = 8$						
x	$\pi =$	.01	.02	.03	.04	.05	.06	.07	.08	.09	.10	
1		.0773	.1492	.2163	.2786	.3366	.3904	.4404	.4868	.5297	.5695	7
2		.0027	.0103	.0223	.0381	.0572	.0792	.1035	.1298	.1577	.1869	6
3		.0001	.0004	.0013	.0031	.0058	.0096	.0147	.0211	.0289	.0381	5
4				.0001	.0002	.0004	.0007	.0013	.0022	.0034	.0050	4
5								.0001	.0001	.0003	.0004	3
		.99	.98	.97	.96	.95	.94	.93	.92	.91	.90	$= \pi$ x

(Continued)

TABLE G *(Continued)*

Left $P(X \geq x)$						$n = 8$						Right $P(X \leq x)$
x $\pi =$	.11	.12	.13	.14	.15	.16	.17	.18	.19	.20		
1	.6063	.6404	.6718	.7008	.7275	.7521	.7748	.7956	.8147	.8322		7
2	.2171	.2480	.2794	.3111	.3428	.3744	.4057	.4366	.4670	.4967		6
3	.0487	.0608	.0743	.0891	.1052	.1226	.1412	.1608	.1815	.2031		5
4	.0071	.0097	.0129	.0168	.0214	.0267	.0328	.0397	.0476	.0563		4
5	.0007	.0010	.0015	.0021	.0029	.0038	.0050	.0065	.0083	.0104		3
6		.0001	.0001	.0002	.0002	.0003	.0005	.0007	.0009	.0012		2
7									.0001	.0001		1
	.89	.88	.87	.86	.85	.84	.83	.82	.81	.80	$= \pi$	x

$n = 8$

x $\pi =$	.21	.22	.23	.24	.25	.26	.27	.28	.29	.30		
1	.8483	.8630	.8764	.8887	.8999	.9101	.9194	.9278	.9354	.9424		7
2	.5257	.5538	.5811	.6075	.6329	.6573	.6807	.7031	.7244	.7447		6
3	.2255	.2486	.2724	.2967	.3215	.3465	.3718	.3973	.4228	.4482		5
4	.0659	.0765	.0880	.1004	.1138	.1281	.1433	.1594	.1763	.1941		4
5	.0129	.0158	.0191	.0230	.0273	.0322	.0377	.0438	.0505	.0580		3
6	.0016	.0021	.0027	.0034	.0042	.0052	.0064	.0078	.0094	.0113		2
7	.0001	.0002	.0002	.0003	.0004	.0005	.0006	.0008	.0010	.0013		1
8									.0001	.0001		0
	.79	.78	.77	.76	.75	.74	.73	.72	.71	.70	$= \pi$	x

$n = 8$

x $\pi =$	.31	.32	.33	.34	.35	.36	.37	.38	.39	.40		
1	.9486	.9543	.9594	.9640	.9681	.9719	.9752	.9782	.9808	.9832		7
2	.7640	.7822	.7994	.8156	.8309	.8452	.8586	.8711	.8828	.8936		6
3	.4736	.4987	.5236	.5481	.5722	.5958	.6189	.6415	.6634	.6846		5
4	.2126	.2319	.2519	.2724	.2936	.3153	.3374	.3599	.3828	.4059		4
5	.0661	.0750	.0846	.0949	.1061	.1180	.1307	.1443	.1586	.1737		3
6	.0134	.0159	.0187	.0218	.0253	.0293	.0336	.0385	.0439	.0498		2
7	.0016	.0020	.0024	.0030	.0036	.0043	.0051	.0061	.0072	.0085		1
8	.0001	.0001	.0001	.0002	.0002	.0003	.0004	.0004	.0005	.0007		0
	.69	.68	.67	.66	.65	.64	.63	.62	.61	.60	$= \pi$	x

$n = 8$

x $\pi =$	.41	.42	.43	.44	.45	.46	.47	.48	.49	.50		
1	.9853	.9872	.9889	.9903	.9916	.9928	.9938	.9947	.9954	.9961		7
2	.9037	.9130	.9216	.9295	.9368	.9435	.9496	.9552	.9602	.9648		6
3	.7052	.7250	.7440	.7624	.7799	.7966	.8125	.8276	.8419	.8555		5
4	.4292	.4527	.4762	.4996	.5230	.5463	.5694	.5922	.6146	.6367		4
5	.1895	.2062	.2235	.2416	.2604	.2798	.2999	.3205	.3416	.3633		3
6	.0563	.0634	.0711	.0794	.0885	.0982	.1086	.1198	.1318	.1445		2
7	.0100	.0117	.0136	.0157	.0181	.0208	.0239	.0272	.0310	.0352		1
8	.0008	.0010	.0012	.0014	.0017	.0020	.0024	.0028	.0033	.0039		0
	.59	.58	.57	.56	.55	.54	.53	.52	.51	.50	$= \pi$	x

TABLE G *(Continued)*

Left $P(X \geq x)$						$n = 9$						Right $P(X \leq x)$
x	π =	.01	.02	.03	.04	.05	.06	.07	.08	.09	.10	
1		.0865	.1663	.2398	.3075	.3698	.4270	.4796	.5278	.5721	.6126	8
2		.0034	.0131	.0282	.0478	.0712	.0978	.1271	.1583	.1912	.2252	7
3		.0001	.0006	.0020	.0045	.0084	.0138	.0209	.0298	.0405	.0530	6
4				.0001	.0003	.0006	.0013	.0023	.0037	.0057	.0083	5
5							.0001	.0002	.0003	.0005	.0009	4
6											.0001	3
		.99	.98	.97	.96	.95	.94	.93	.92	.91	.90	= π	x

						$n = 9$						
x	π =	.11	.12	.13	.14	.15	.16	.17	.18	.19	.20	
1		.6496	.6835	.7145	.7427	.7684	.7918	.8131	.8324	.8499	.8658	8
2		.2599	.2951	.3304	.3657	.4005	.4348	.4685	.5012	.5330	.5638	7
3		.0672	.0833	.1009	.1202	.1409	.1629	.1861	.2105	.2357	.2618	6
4		.0117	.0158	.0209	.0269	.0339	.0420	.0512	.0615	.0730	.0856	5
5		.0014	.0021	.0030	.0041	.0056	.0075	.0098	.0125	.0158	.0196	4
6		.0001	.0002	.0003	.0004	.0006	.0009	.0013	.0017	.0023	.0031	3
7							.0001	.0001	.0002	.0002	.0003	2
		.89	.88	.87	.86	.85	.84	.83	.82	.81	.80	= π	x

						$n = 9$						
x	π =	.21	.22	.23	.24	.25	.26	.27	.28	.29	.30	
1		.8801	.8931	.9048	.9154	.9249	.9335	.9411	.9480	.9542	.9596	8
2		.5934	.6218	.6491	.6750	.6997	.7230	.7452	.7660	.7856	.8040	7
3		.2885	.3158	.3434	.3713	.3993	.4273	.4552	.4829	.5102	.5372	6
4		.0994	.1144	.1304	.1475	.1657	.1849	.2050	.2260	.2478	.2703	5
5		.0240	.0291	.0350	.0416	.0489	.0571	.0662	.0762	.0870	.0988	4
6		.0040	.0051	.0065	.0081	.0100	.0122	.0149	.0179	.0213	.0253	3
7		.0004	.0006	.0008	.0010	.0013	.0017	.0022	.0028	.0035	.0043	2
8				.0001	.0001	.0001	.0001	.0002	.0003	.0003	.0004	1
		.79	.78	.77	.76	.75	.74	.73	.72	.71	.70	= π	x

						$n = 9$						
x	π =	.31	.32	.33	.34	.35	.36	.37	.38	.39	.40	
1		.9645	.9689	.9728	.9762	.9793	.9820	.9844	.9865	.9883	.9899	8
2		.8212	.8372	.8522	.8661	.8789	.8908	.9017	.9118	.9210	.9295	7
3		.5636	.5894	.6146	.6390	.6627	.6856	.7076	.7287	.7489	.7682	6
4		.2935	.3173	.3415	.3662	.3911	.4163	.4416	.4669	.4922	.5174	5
5		.1115	.1252	.1398	.1553	.1717	.1890	.2072	.2262	.2460	.2666	4
6		.0298	.0348	.0404	.0467	.0536	.0612	.0696	.0787	.0886	.0994	3
7		.0053	.0064	.0078	.0094	.0112	.0133	.0157	.0184	.0215	.0250	2
8		.0006	.0007	.0009	.0011	.0014	.0017	.0021	.0026	.0031	.0038	1
9					.0001	.0001	.0001	.0001	.0002	.0002	.0003	0
		.69	.68	.67	.66	.65	.64	.63	.62	.61	.60	= π	x

(Continued)

TABLE G *(Continued)*

Left P(X ≥ x)						n = 9						Right P(X ≤ x)
x π =	.41	.42	.43	.44	.45	.46	.47	.48	.49	.50		
1	.9913	.9926	.9936	.9946	.9954	.9961	.9967	.9972	.9977	.9980		8
2	.9372	.9442	.9505	.9563	.9615	.9662	.9704	.9741	.9775	.9805		7
3	.7866	.8039	.8204	.8359	.8505	.8642	.8769	.8889	.8999	.9102		6
4	.5424	.5670	.5913	.6152	.6386	.6614	.6836	.7052	.7260	.7461		5
5	.2878	.3097	.3322	.3551	.3786	.4024	.4265	.4509	.4754	.5000		4
6	.1109	.1233	.1366	.1508	.1658	.1817	.1985	.2161	.2346	.2539		3
7	.0290	.0334	.0383	.0437	.0498	.0564	.0637	.0717	.0804	.0898		2
8	.0046	.0055	.0065	.0077	.0091	.0107	.0125	.0145	.0169	.0195		1
9	.0003	.0004	.0005	.0006	.0008	.0009	.0011	.0014	.0016	.0020		0
	.59	.58	.57	.56	.55	.54	.53	.52	.51	.50	= π	x

n = 10

x π =	.01	.02	.03	.04	.05	.06	.07	.08	.09	.10		
1	.0956	.1829	.2626	.3352	.4013	.4614	.5160	.5656	.6106	.6513		9
2	.0043	.0162	.0345	.0582	.0861	.1176	.1517	.1879	.2254	.2639		8
3	.0001	.0009	.0028	.0062	.0115	.0188	.0283	.0401	.0540	.0702		7
4			.0001	.0004	.0010	.0020	.0036	.0058	.0088	.0128		6
5					.0001	.0002	.0003	.0006	.0010	.0016		5
6									.0001	.0001		4
	.99	.98	.97	.96	.95	.94	.93	.92	.91	.90	= π	x

n = 10

x π =	.11	.12	.13	.14	.15	.16	.17	.18	.19	.20		
1	.6882	.7215	.7516	.7787	.8031	.8251	.8448	.8626	.8784	.8926		9
2	.3028	.3417	.3804	.4184	.4557	.4920	.5270	.5608	.5932	.6242		8
3	.0884	.1087	.1308	.1545	.1798	.2064	.2341	.2628	.2922	.3222		7
4	.0178	.0239	.0313	.0400	.0500	.0614	.0741	.0883	.1039	.1209		6
5	.0025	.0037	.0053	.0073	.0099	.0130	.0168	.0213	.0266	.0328		5
6	.0003	.0004	.0006	.0010	.0014	.0020	.0027	.0037	.0049	.0064		4
7			.0001	.0001	.0001	.0002	.0003	.0004	.0006	.0009		3
8									.0001	.0001		2
	.89	.88	.87	.86	.85	.84	.83	.82	.81	.80	= π	x

n = 10

x π =	.21	.22	.23	.24	.25	.26	.27	.28	.29	.30		
1	.9053	.9166	.9267	.9357	.9437	.9508	.9570	.9626	.9674	.9718		9
2	.6536	.6815	.7079	.7327	.7560	.7778	.7981	.8170	.8345	.8507		8
3	.3526	.3831	.4137	.4442	.4744	.5042	.5335	.5622	.5901	.6172		7
4	.1391	.1587	.1794	.2012	.2241	.2479	.2726	.2979	.3239	.3504		6
5	.0399	.0479	.0569	.0670	.0781	.0904	.1037	.1181	.1337	.1503		5
6	.0082	.0104	.0130	.0161	.0197	.0239	.0287	.0342	.0404	.0473		4
7	.0012	.0016	.0021	.0027	.0035	.0045	.0056	.0070	.0087	.0106		3
8	.0001	.0002	.0002	.0003	.0004	.0006	.0007	.0010	.0012	.0016		2
9							.0001	.0001	.0001	.0001		1
	.79	.78	.77	.76	.75	.74	.73	.72	.71	.70	= π	x

TABLE G *(Continued)*

Left $P(X \geq x)$					$n = 10$						Right $P(X \leq x)$
$x \quad \pi =$	.31	.32	.33	.34	.35	.36	.37	.38	.39	.40	
1	.9755	.9789	.9818	.9843	.9865	.9885	.9902	.9916	.9929	.9940	9
2	.8656	.8794	.8920	.9035	.9140	.9236	.9323	.9402	.9473	.9536	8
3	.6434	.6687	.6930	.7162	.7384	.7595	.7794	.7983	.8160	.8327	7
4	.3772	.4044	.4316	.4589	.4862	.5132	.5400	.5664	.5923	.6177	6
5	.1679	.1867	.2064	.2270	.2485	.2708	.2939	.3177	.3420	.3669	5
6	.0551	.0637	.0732	.0836	.0949	.1072	.1205	.1348	.1500	.1662	4
7	.0129	.0155	.0185	.0220	.0260	.0305	.0356	.0413	.0477	.0548	3
8	.0020	.0025	.0032	.0039	.0048	.0059	.0071	.0086	.0103	.0123	2
9	.0002	.0003	.0003	.0004	.0005	.0007	.0009	.0011	.0014	.0017	1
10								.0001	.0001	.0001	0
	.69	.68	.67	.66	.65	.64	.63	.62	.61	.60	$= \pi \quad x$

					$n = 10$						
$x \quad \pi =$	.41	.42	.43	.44	.45	.46	.47	.48	.49	.50	
1	.9949	.9957	.9964	.9970	.9975	.9979	.9983	.9986	.9988	.9990	9
2	.9594	.9645	.9691	.9731	.9767	.9799	.9827	.9852	.9874	.9893	8
3	.8483	.8628	.8764	.8889	.9004	.9111	.9209	.9298	.9379	.9453	7
4	.6425	.6665	.6898	.7123	.7340	.7547	.7745	.7933	.8112	.8281	6
5	.3922	.4178	.4436	.4696	.4956	.5216	.5474	.5730	.5982	.6230	5
6	.1834	.2016	.2207	.2407	.2616	.2832	.3057	.3288	.3526	.3770	4
7	.0626	.0712	.0806	.0908	.1020	.1141	.1271	.1410	.1560	.1719	3
8	.0146	.0172	.0202	.0236	.0274	.0317	.0366	.0420	.0480	.0547	2
9	.0021	.0025	.0031	.0037	.0045	.0054	.0065	.0077	.0091	.0107	1
10	.0001	.0002	.0002	.0003	.0003	.0004	.0005	.0006	.0008	.0010	0
	.59	.58	.57	.56	.55	.54	.53	.52	.51	.50	$= \pi \quad x$

					$n = 20$						
$x \quad \pi =$	.01	.02	.03	.04	.05	.06	.07	.08	.09	.10	
1	.1821	.3324	.4562	.5580	.6415	.7099	.7658	.8113	.8484	.8784	19
2	.0169	.0599	.1198	.1897	.2642	.3395	.4131	.4831	.5484	.6083	18
3	.0010	.0071	.0210	.0439	.0755	.1150	.1610	.2121	.2666	.3231	17
4		.0006	.0027	.0074	.0159	.0290	.0471	.0706	.0993	.1330	16
5			.0003	.0010	.0026	.0056	.0107	.0183	.0290	.0432	15
6				.0001	.0003	.0009	.0019	.0038	.0068	.0113	14
7						.0001	.0003	.0006	.0013	.0024	13
8								.0001	.0002	.0004	12
9										.0001	11
	.99	.98	.97	.96	.95	.94	.93	.92	.91	.90	$= \pi \quad x$

(Continued)

TABLE G *(Continued)*

Left $P(X \geq x)$						$n = 20$						Right $P(X \leq x)$
x	$\pi =$	.11	.12	.13	.14	.15	.16	.17	.18	.19	.20	
1		.9028	.9224	.9383	.9510	.9612	.9694	.9759	.9811	.9852	.9885	19
2		.6624	.7109	.7539	.7916	.8244	.8529	.8773	.8982	.9159	.9308	18
3		.3802	.4369	.4920	.5450	.5951	.6420	.6854	.7252	.7614	.7939	17
4		.1710	.2127	.2573	.3041	.3523	.4010	.4496	.4974	.5439	.5886	16
5		.0610	.0827	.1083	.1375	.1702	.2059	.2443	.2849	.3271	.3704	15
6		.0175	.0260	.0370	.0507	.0673	.0870	.1098	.1356	.1643	.1958	14
7		.0041	.0067	.0103	.0153	.0219	.0304	.0409	.0537	.0689	.0867	13
8		.0008	.0014	.0024	.0038	.0059	.0088	.0127	.0177	.0241	.0321	12
9		.0001	.0002	.0005	.0008	.0013	.0021	.0033	.0049	.0071	.0100	11
10				.0001	.0001	.0002	.0004	.0007	.0011	.0017	.0026	10
11								.0001	.0001	.0002	.0004	.0006	9
12										.0001	.0001	8
		.89	.88	.87	.86	.85	.84	.83	.82	.81	.80	$= \pi$ x

$n = 20$

x	$\pi =$	.21	.22	.23	.24	.25	.26	.27	.28	.29	.30	
1		.9910	.9931	.9946	.9959	.9968	.9976	.9982	.9986	.9989	.9992	19
2		.9434	.9539	.9626	.9698	.9757	.9805	.9845	.9877	.9903	.9924	18
3		.8230	.8488	.8716	.8915	.9087	.9237	.9365	.9474	.9567	.9654	17
4		.6310	.6711	.7085	.7431	.7748	.8038	.8300	.8534	.8744	.8929	16
5		.4142	.4580	.5014	.5439	.5852	.6248	.6625	.6981	.7315	.7625	15
6		.2297	.2657	.3035	.3427	.3828	.4235	.4643	.5048	.5447	.5836	14
7		.1071	.1301	.1557	.1838	.2142	.2467	.2810	.3169	.3540	.3920	13
8		.0419	.0536	.0675	.0835	.1018	.1225	.1455	.1707	.1982	.2277	12
9		.0138	.0186	.0246	.0320	.0409	.0515	.0640	.0784	.0948	.1133	11
10		.0038	.0054	.0075	.0103	.0139	.0183	.0238	.0305	.0385	.0480	10
11		.0009	.0013	.0019	.0028	.0039	.0055	.0074	.0100	.0132	.0171	9
12		.0002	.0003	.0004	.0006	.0009	.0014	.0019	.0027	.0038	.0051	8
13				.0001	.0001	.0002	.0003	.0004	.0006	.0009	.0013	7
14								.0001	.0001	.0002	.0003	6
		.79	.78	.77	.76	.75	.74	.73	.72	.71	.70	$= \pi$ x

$n = 20$

x	$\pi =$	.31	.32	.33	.34	.35	.36	.37	.38	.39	.40	
1		.9994	.9996	.9997	.9998	.9998	.9999	.9999	.9999	.9999	1.0000	19
2		.9940	.9953	.9964	.9972	.9979	.9984	.9988	.9991	.9993	.9995	18
3		.9711	.9765	.9811	.9848	.9879	.9904	.9924	.9940	.9953	.9964	17
4		.9092	.9235	.9358	.9465	.9556	.9634	.9700	.9755	.9802	.9840	16
5		.7911	.8173	.8411	.8626	.8818	.8989	.9141	.9274	.9390	.9490	15
6		.6213	.6574	.6917	.7242	.7546	.7829	.8090	.8329	.8547	.8744	14
7		.4305	.4693	.5079	.5460	.5834	.6197	.6547	.6882	.7200	.7500	13
8		.2591	.2922	.3268	.3624	.3990	.4361	.4735	.5108	.5478	.5841	12
9		.1340	.1568	.1818	.2087	.2376	.2683	.3005	.3341	.3688	.4044	11
10		.0591	.0719	.0866	.1032	.1218	.1424	.1650	.1897	.2163	.2447	10
11		.0220	.0279	.0350	.0434	.0532	.0645	.0775	.0923	.1090	.1275	9
12		.0069	.0091	.0119	.0154	.0196	.0247	.0308	.0381	.0466	.0565	8
13		.0018	.0025	.0034	.0045	.0060	.0079	.0102	.0132	.0167	.0210	7
14		.0004	.0006	.0008	.0011	.0015	.0021	.0028	.0037	.0049	.0065	6
15		.0001	.0001	.0001	.0002	.0003	.0004	.0006	.0009	.0012	.0016	5
16							.0001	.0001	.0002	.0002	.0003	4
		.69	.68	.67	.66	.65	.64	.63	.62	.61	.60	x

TABLE G *(Continued)*

Left $P(X \geq x)$					$n = 20$						**Right** $P(X \leq x)$	
x $\pi =$	.41	.42	.43	.44	.45	.46	.47	.48	.49	.50		
1	1.0000	1.0000	1.0000	1.0000	1.0000	1.0000	1.0000	1.0000	1.0000	1.0000		19
2	.9996	.9997	.9998	.9998	.9999	.9999	.9999	1.0000	1.0000	1.0000		18
3	.9972	.9979	.9984	.9988	.9991	.9993	.9995	.9996	.9997	.9998		17
4	.9872	.9898	.9920	.9937	.9951	.9962	.9971	.9977	.9983	.9987		16
5	.9577	.9651	.9714	.9767	.9811	.9848	.9879	.9904	.9924	.9941		15
6	.8921	.9078	.9217	.9340	.9447	.9539	.9619	.9687	.9745	.9793		14
7	.7780	.8041	.8281	.8501	.8701	.8881	.9042	.9186	.9312	.9423		13
8	.6196	.6539	.6868	.7183	.7480	.7759	.8020	.8261	.8482	.8684		12
9	.4406	.4771	.5136	.5499	.5857	.6207	.6546	.6873	.7186	.7483		11
10	.2748	.3064	.3394	.3736	.4086	.4443	.4804	.5166	.5525	.5881		10
11	.1480	.1705	.1949	.2212	.2493	.2791	.3104	.3432	.3771	.4119		9
12	.0679	.0810	.0958	.1123	.1308	.1511	.1734	.1977	.2238	.2517		8
13	.0262	.0324	.0397	.0482	.0580	.0694	.0823	.0969	.1133	.1316		7
14	.0084	.0107	.0136	.0172	.0214	.0265	.0326	.0397	.0480	.0577		6
15	.0022	.0029	.0038	.0050	.0064	.0083	.0105	.0133	.0166	.0207		5
16	.0004	.0006	.0008	.0011	.0015	.0020	.0027	.0035	.0046	.0059		4
17	.0001	.0001	.0001	.0002	.0003	.0004	.0005	.0007	.0010	.0013		3
18						.0001	.0001	.0001	.0001	.0002		2
	.59	.58	.57	.56	.55	.54	.53	.52	.51	.50	$= \pi$	x

TABLE H CUMULATIVE POISSON PROBABILITIES $P(X \leq x)$

					μ				
x	.1	.2	.3	.4	.5	.6	.7	.8	.9
0	.9048	.8187	.7408	.6730	.6065	.5488	.4966	.4493	.4066
1	.9953	.9825	.9631	.9384	.9098	.8781	.8442	.8088	.7725
2	.9998	.9989	.9964	.9921	.9856	.9769	.9659	.9526	.9371
3	1.0000	.9999	.9997	.9992	.9982	.9966	.9942	.9909	.9865
4		1.0000	1.0000	.9999	.9998	.9996	.9992	.9986	.9977
5				1.0000	1.0000	1.0000	.9999	.9998	.9997
6							1.0000	1.0000	1.0000

					μ				
x	1.0	1.5	2.0	2.5	3.0	3.5	4.0	4.5	5.0
0	.3679	.2231	.1353	.0821	.0498	.0302	.0183	.0111	.0067
1	.7358	.5578	.4060	.2873	.1991	.1359	.0916	.0611	.0404
2	.9197	.8088	.6767	.5438	.4232	.3208	.2381	.1736	.1247
3	.9810	.9344	.8571	.7576	.6472	.5366	.4335	.3423	.2650
4	.9963	.9814	.9473	.8912	.8153	.7254	.6288	.5321	.4405
5	.9994	.9955	.9834	.9580	.9161	.8576	.7851	.7029	.6160
6	.9999	.9991	.9955	.9858	.9665	.9347	.8893	.8311	.7622
7	1.0000	.9998	.9989	.9958	.9881	.9733	.9489	.9134	.8666
8		1.0000	.9998	.9989	.9962	.9901	.9786	.9597	.9319
9			1.0000	.9997	.9989	.9967	.9919	.9829	.9682
10				.9999	.9997	.9990	.9972	.9933	.9863
11				1.0000	.9999	.9997	.9991	.9976	.9945
12					1.0000	.9999	.9997	.9992	.9980
13						1.0000	.9999	.9997	.9993
14							1.0000	.9999	.9998
15								1.0000	.9999
16									1.0000

					μ				
x	5.5	6.0	6.5	7.0	7.5	8.0	8.5	9.0	9.5	10.0
0	.0041	.0025	.0015	.0009	.0006	.0003	.0002	.0001	.0001	.0000
1	.0266	.0174	.0113	.0073	.0047	.0030	.0019	.0012	.0008	.0005
2	.0884	.0620	.0430	.0296	.0203	.0138	.0093	.0062	.0042	.0028
3	.2017	.1512	.1118	.0818	.0591	.0424	.0301	.0212	.0149	.0103
4	.3575	.2851	.2237	.1730	.1321	.0996	.0744	.0550	.0403	.0293
5	.5289	.4457	.3690	.3007	.2414	.1912	.1496	.1157	.0885	.0671
6	.6860	.6063	.5265	.4497	.3782	.3134	.2562	.2068	.1649	.1301
7	.8095	.7440	.6728	.5987	.5246	.4530	.3856	.3239	.2687	.2202
8	.8944	.8472	.7916	.7291	.6620	.5925	.5231	.4557	.3918	.3328
9	.9462	.9161	.8774	.8305	.7764	.7166	.6530	.5874	.5218	.4579
10	.9747	.9574	.9332	.9015	.8622	.8159	.7634	.7060	.6453	.5830
11	.9890	.9799	.9661	.9466	.9208	.8881	.8487	.8030	.7520	.6968
12	.9955	.9912	.9840	.9730	.9573	.9362	.9091	.8758	.8364	.7916
13	.9983	.9964	.9929	.9872	.9784	.9658	.9486	.9261	.8981	.8645
14	.9994	.9986	.9970	.9943	.9897	.9827	.9726	.9585	.9400	.9165
15	.9998	.9995	.9988	.9976	.9954	.9918	.9862	.9780	.9665	.9513
16	.9999	.9998	.9996	.9990	.9980	.9963	.9934	.9889	.9823	.9730
17	1.0000	.9999	.9998	.9996	.9992	.9984	.9970	.9947	.9911	.9857
18		1.0000	.9999	.9999	.9997	.9994	.9987	.9976	.9957	.9928
19			1.0000	1.0000	.9999	.9997	.9995	.9989	.9980	.9965
20					1.0000	.9999	.9998	.9996	.9991	.9984
21						1.0000	.9999	.9998	.9996	.9993
22							1.0000	.9999	.9999	.9997
23								1.0000	.9999	.9999
24									1.0000	1.0000

Reproduced from E. C. Molina, *Poisson's Exponential Binomial Limit.* Copyright 1942, Princeton, N.J.: D. Van Nostrand Company, Inc. Reprinted by permission of Wadsworth Publishing Company, Belmont, CA 94002

SELECTED ANSWERS
TO EXERCISES

Chapter 1

	Class Interval	Lower Boundary	Upper Boundary	Class Width	Class Mark
1.1	10–14	9.5	14.5	5	12
	15–19	14.5	19.5	5	17
	20–24	19.5	24.5	5	22
	25–29	24.5	29.5	5	27

Chapter 2

2.1. a) Mean = 8, mode = 11, median = 9
b) Range = 7, average deviation = 2.8, σ = 2.97
2.2. Mean = 8, median = 8, mode = 8   **2.3.** It is possible.
2.4. Mean = 1, σ = 5.69
2.5. Median = $17,950, mean = $18,600. The median is a better average.
2.6. Median = $18,000, mode = $18,000
2.7. μ and σ must be measured in the same units.
2.8. Annual income: median = $32,750; I.Q.: median = 104; Weight:
mean = 163.4; Hat size: mode = $6\frac{7}{8}$.
2.10. Population A: μ = 11, σ = 3.16, median = 10; Population B: μ = 9, σ = 3.16,
median = 10.

2.11. Population A: mean = 5, $R = 8$, $\sigma = 2.61$; Population B: mean = 5, $R = 8$, $\sigma = 3.16$.

2.12. a) $\mu = 12$, $\sigma = 3$ b) $\mu = 20$, $\sigma = 6$

2.13. $\mu = 65$, $\sigma = 12.19$;   a) 70%   b) 100%   c) 100%

2.15. a) Mean = 32, median = 33, mode = 33
b) Range = 24, average deviation = 5.84, $\sigma = 6.87$
c) (1) 56%   (2) 100%   (3) 100%

Chapter 3

3.1. a) $\{10, 11, 12\}$ b) $\{1, 2, 3, 4, 5, 6, 7, 8\}$ c) $\{3, 6, 9, 12, 15, 18\}$

3.2. a) $\{9, 10, 11, 12\}$ b) $\{10, 11, 12, 13\}$ c) $C = \{-2\}$ d) $D = \{-7, 4\}$

3.3. $\{x, y, 3\}, \{x\}, \{x, y\}, \{y\}, \{x, 3\}, \{3\}, \{y, 3\}, \{\varnothing\}$

3.4. {man, woman, baby, home}, {man, woman, baby}, {man, woman, home}, {man, baby, home}, {woman, baby, home}, {man, woman}, {man, baby}, {man, home}, {woman, baby}, {woman, home}, {baby, home}, {man}, {woman}, {baby}, {home}, {$\varnothing$}

3.5. a) $A \cup B = \{10, 11, 12, 13, 14\}$ b) $(A \cap B) = \{12, 13\}$ c) $A' = \{14, 15\}$

3.6. a) $A \cup B = \{20, 22, 24\}$ b) $(A \cup B)' = \{26\}$ c) $(A \cap B) = \{22\}$
d) $(A \cap B)' = \{20, 24, 26\}$

3.7. a) $(A \cup B) = \{v, w, x, y, z\}$ b) $(A \cup B)' = \{\varnothing\}$ c) $(A \cap B) = \{\varnothing\}$
d) $(A \cap B)' = \{v, w, x, y, z\}$

3.8. $A = \{13, 14, 15, 16, 17, 18, 19\}$; $B = \{18, 19, \ldots, \infty\}$; $(A \cap B) = \{18, 19\}$

3.9. $A \cap B = \{8\}$ **3.10.** a) $(X \cup Y) = \{-4, 2, -2\}$ b) $(X \cap Y) = \{2\}$

3.11. a) $(A \cup B) = U$ b) $(A \cup B)' = \{\varnothing\}$ c) $(A \cap B) = \{\varnothing\}$

3.12. a) $\{1, 2, 3, 4, 5, 6\}$ b) $\{2, 4, 6\}$ c) $\{5, 6\}$

3.13. a) $\{HH, HT, TH, TT\}$ b) $\{HT, TH\}$ c) $\{HH, HT, TH\}$

3.14. a) $S = \{(1, 1), (1, 2), (1, 3), (1, 4), (1, 5), (1, 6),$
$(2, 1), (2, 2), (2, 3), (2, 4), (2, 5), (2, 6),$
$(3, 1), (3, 2), (3, 3), (3, 4), (3, 5), (3, 6),$
$(4, 1), (4, 2), (4, 3), (4, 4), (4, 5), (4, 6),$
$(5, 1), (5, 2), (5, 3), (5, 4), (5, 5), (5, 6),$
$(6, 1), (6, 2), (6, 3), (6, 4), (6, 5), (6, 6)\}$
b) $\{(6, 3), (5, 4), (4, 5), (3, 6)\}$ c) $\{(3, 1), (2, 2), (1, 3), (4, 1), (3, 2), (2, 3), (1, 4)\}$

3.15. a) $S = \{DDD, DDD', DD'D, DD'D', D'DD, D'DD', D'D'D, D'D'D'\}$
b) $\{D'D'D'\}$ c) There are exactly two defective parts.

3.16. $S = \{(H, 1), (H, 2), (H, 3), (H, 4), (H, 5), (H, 6), (T, 1), (T, 2), (T, 3), (T, 4), (T, 5), (T, 6)\}$

3.17. a) $\frac{1}{2}$ b) $\frac{1}{2}$ **3.18.** a) $\frac{1}{2}$ b) $\frac{3}{4}$

3.19. a) $\frac{1}{6}$ b) $\frac{1}{18}$ c) $\frac{2}{9}$ d) $\frac{1}{3}$

3.20. a) $\frac{4}{52}$ b) $\frac{4}{52}$ c) $\frac{8}{52}$ d) $\frac{28}{52}$ e) $\frac{12}{52}$ **3.21.** .12   **3.22.** .85

3.23. .80   **3.24.** .30   **3.25.** a) .95   b) .04   c) .99   **3.26.** .60

3.27. .10   **3.28.** a) $\frac{12}{42}$ b) $\frac{16}{49}$ **3.29.** $\frac{8}{49}$ **3.30.** $\frac{114}{441}$

3.31. a) $\frac{16}{2652}$ b) $\frac{32}{2652}$ c) $\frac{2256}{2652}$ d) $\frac{1892}{2652}$ **3.32.** $\frac{32}{1560}$

3.33. a) $\frac{288}{311,875,200}$ b) $\frac{54,144}{311,875,200}$ c) $\frac{56,448}{311,875,200}$ or $\frac{24}{132,600}$

3.34. a) $\frac{9,024}{132,600}$ b) $\frac{10,200}{132,600}$ or $\frac{1}{13}$

3.35. $\frac{28,824}{132,600}$ **3.36.** a) $\frac{215}{216}$ b) $\frac{6}{216}$ **3.37.** a) $\frac{2}{1296}$ b) $\frac{5}{1296}$ c) $\frac{1}{216}$

3.38. a) $\frac{4}{216}$ b) $\frac{212}{216}$ **3.39.** .9983616   **3.40.** .001999   **3.41.** $\frac{4}{9900}$

3.42. a) $\frac{21984}{24024}$ b) $\frac{576}{2184}$ **3.43.** a) .064   b) .104   **3.44.** a) $\frac{2}{12}$ b) $\frac{10}{12}$

3.45. .002 **3.46.** a) $^{210}/_{380}$ b) $^{30}/_{380}$ c) $^{230}/_{380}$ **3.47.** a) $^{5}/_{24}$ b) $^{1}/_{24}$
3.48. a) .50 b) .65 c) .20 **3.49.** a) .125 b) .957125
3.50. a) .318 b) .976
3.51. a) (1) $^{200}/_{400}$ (2) $^{39,800}/_{159,600}$ b) (1) $^{80}/_{400}$ (2) $^{44,850}/_{159,600}$
3.52. a) $^{6}/_{14}$ b) $^{2}/_{3}$ **3.53.** a) $^{32}/_{252}$ b) $^{3}/_{4}$ **3.54.** a) $^{30}/_{210}$ b) $^{24}/_{30}$
3.55. a) .18 b) $^{10}/_{18}$ **3.56.** a) .56 b) $^{16}/_{56}$ **3.57.** a) .44 b) $^{6}/_{44}$
3.58. a) .62 b) $^{54}/_{62}$ **3.59.** a) .34 b) $^{16}/_{34}$ **3.60.** a) .509 b) $^{192}/_{509}$
3.61. $^{2}/_{65}$ **3.62.** $^{20}/_{31}$ **3.63.** $^{2}/_{3}$, $^{1}/_{3}$ **3.64.** $^{8}/_{14}$ **3.65.** .483 **3.66.** .191
3.67. a) .41 b) $^{27}/_{41}$ **3.68.** -1 **3.69.** 0 **3.70.** $4.20 **3.71.** $4.20
3.72. 37.45 **3.73.** Expected life: A $= 2500$, B $= 2550$
3.74. Expected cost: A $= 137.50, B $= 142.50
3.75. a) $600,000 > $500,000. Wait for rezoning. b) $^{3}/_{8}$
3.76. Order 5: The expected profit is $1.05.
3.77. Expected profit is $1,100. **3.78.** Expected profit is $3,000.
3.79. a) 1.05 b) $120 c) $126 d) .0225 **3.80.** a) .001 b) 10.8
3.81. a) 290,000 b) 325,000 c) $-35,000$ d) .32

Chapter 4

4.1. 20 **4.2.** 16 **4.3.** 5040 **4.4.** 151,200 **4.5.** 35
4.6. a) 17,576 b) 15,600 **4.7.** a) 16 b) 0 **4.8.** a) 10 b) 7
4.9. a) 126 b) 60 **4.10.** 24 **4.11.** a) .2036 b) .2262 **4.12.** $^{64}/_{243}$
4.13. a) .3456 b) .0576 **4.14.** .05853 **4.15.** $^{640}/_{3125}$
4.16. .008333928 **4.17.** a) .1880025 b) .6732 **4.18.** a) $^{3}/_{4}$ b) $^{11}/_{16}$
4.19. a) .3456 b) .0256 c) .8704
4.20. a) .0016 b) .04 c) .1536 d) .5904
4.21. a) x: 0, 1, 2; $P(x)$: $^{4}/_{9}$, $^{4}/_{9}$, $^{1}/_{9}$ b) $\mu = ^{2}/_{3}$, $\sigma = ^{2}/_{3}$
4.22. a) $\mu = 800$, $\sigma = 20$ b) $\mu = 90$, $\sigma = 9$ c) $\mu = 256$, $\sigma = 9.6$
4.23. $\mu = 20$, $\sigma = 4.216$ **4.24.** $\mu = 100$
4.25. a) .5796 b) .3150 c) .0802 d) .0649
4.26. a) .4348 b) .2719 c) .0420 d) .0345
4.27. a) .0248 b) .2815 c) .3811 d) .6626
4.28. a) 0 b) .1144 c) .7723 d) .8867
4.29. .4623 **4.30.** .4242 **4.31.** .4835 **4.32.** .3158 **4.33.** .7049
4.34. a) .8571 b) .1804 **4.35.** .2231 **4.36.** .1493 **4.37.** .1755
4.38. .2424 **4.39.** .1438 **4.40.** .3032
4.41. a) .0668 b) .4772 c) 70.68 inches **4.42.** 456
4.43. a) .1151 b) 51.6 **4.44.** a) 12.616 b) 12.072
4.45. $\sigma = .78$ **4.46.** $\mu = 53$, $\sigma = 2$ **4.47.** 8:31.8 A.M. **4.48.** .4159
4.49. .04782 **4.50.** $\sigma = 23,810$ **4.51.** 7463
4.52. a) .1587, or 159 students b) .2119, or 170 students
4.53. a) .1151 b) .5328 c) .2417 **4.54.** 73,840 miles
4.55. a) .0548 b) 418 hours **4.56.** .1587
4.57. a) .3085 b) .5328 c) 109.6 **4.58.** a) .1056 b) .1620 c) 595.20
4.59. a) .0526 b) .5461 c) $x_1 = 8.176, $x_2 = 10.224
4.60. a) 4134 b) 704 **4.61.** a) .1056 b) .5402 c) $6024
4.62. a) .0918 b) 124,600
4.63. a) .0803 b) .6915 **4.64.** .8531 **4.65.** .7517 **4.66.** $-.5745$

4.67. a) .1056   b) .1251   **4.68.** $-\$.37$
4.69. $z = -4.50$. The claim is untrue.

Cumulative Review Exercises I

1. $\mu = 130, \sigma = 25$ **2.** $A \cap B = \{-4\}$
3. a) $S = \{RRR, RRB, RBR, RBB, BRR, BRB, BBR, BBB\}$ b) $A = \{RBB, BRB, BBR\}$
   c) There are exactly three black cards.
4. a) $\mu = 20, \sigma = 4.2$ b) $^7\!/_{10}$ **5.** a) $^4\!/_{10}$ b) $^{12}\!/_{90}$ c) $^{24}\!/_{90}$ **6.** .006
7. 3 engines   **8.** a) .1296   b) .8704   c) 6 shots   **9.** .960498   **10.** $^{285}\!/_{355}$
11. a) .22   b) $^{14}\!/_{22}$ **12.** $-\$0.27$ **13.** a) $^1\!/_{32}$ b) $^{10}\!/_{32}$
14. a) .16   b) .488   **15.** a) .4096   b) .8
16. a) .3456   b) .9744   c) .0576   **17.** a) .3125   b) .2373
18. a) $^3\!/_8$ b) $^7\!/_8$ c) 4 trials   **19.** $\sigma = 2, \mu = 10$ **20.** .9772
21. a) .0668   b) 10.4   c) 10.4   **22.** 63.6 hours
23. a) .0228   b) $x_1 = 46{,}650, x_2 = 53{,}350$ c) 38,350
24. a) 1097.2 units   b) 1524.4 units   c) $x_1 = 46.65, x_2 = 53.35$
25. a) .2327   b) .0179   **26.** a) .0087   b) .0885
27. a) .1151   b) 69.2 hours   **28.** a) $^2\!/_{12}$ b) $^3\!/_{12}$
29. 88   **30.** a) .25   b) 6.1   **31.** a) .15625   b) .96875
32. a) 3.8   b) $5000   c) $19,000   **33.** a) .3085   b) .140394
34. a) $^1\!/_{16}$ b) $^{270}\!/_{1024}$ c) 40   **35.** a) $^{240}\!/_{720}$ b) $^{1080}\!/_{5040}$
36. a) .40   b) .16   c) .46   **37.** a) .0062   b) 6640
38. a) 131   b) 54   c) .25   d) .20   **39.** $^{18}\!/_{67}$
40. a) $^{15}\!/_{1296}$ b) $^{21}\!/_{1296}$ **41.** a) .3072   b) .8192   **42.** $^{35}\!/_{53}$
43. a) 11.5   b) 26   c) .49   d) .03   **44.** a) .1056   b) .1339

Chapter 5

5.2. $\bar{x} = \$120, s = 30$ **5.3.** $\bar{x} = 21, s = 2$ **5.7.** a) 10   b) 4   c) .56

Chapter 6

6.1. a) $\mu = 5, \sigma = 2.24$ b) 3, 4, 5, 5, 6, 7   c) $E(\bar{x}) = 5, \sigma_{\bar{x}} = \sqrt{5/3}$
6.2. a) Between 68.672 and 69.328   b) Between 68.836 and 69.164
6.3. a) .0228   b) .1587   c) .50   **6.4.** a) .4522   b) .1587   c) .0228
6.5. 16.280   **6.6.** a) .1587   b) .0228   c) $L_1 = 49.18, L_2 = 50.82$
6.7. a) .0793   b) .0384   **6.8.** a) No   b) Yes   **6.9.** .0668
6.10. a) .0174   b) .0571   **6.11.** a) .0014   b) .0367   c) .5
6.12. Between 3.34 and 4.66   **6.13.** a) 97   b) 246
6.14. Between 20.02 and 21.98   **6.15.** a) 1537   b) 385
6.16. a) Between 16.452 and 19.548   b) 1.176
6.17. 239   **6.18.** 54.68%
6.19. a) Between 34.208 and 45.792   b) Between 18.699 and 21.301
   c) Between 65.016 and 74.984
6.20. a) Between $111.80 and $128.20   b) $9.80
6.21. Between 10.30 and 10.70

6.22. Between $5,845,200 and $6,154,800
6.23. Between $73,360,000 and $76,640,000
6.24. a) Between $10,968 and $13,032 b) .8664
6.25. Between 44.448 and 55.552
6.26. a) Between 10.9 and 13.1 b) .9232
6.27. Between 4,632,760 and 5,047,240
6.28. Between 45.90 and 54.10
6.29. a) .99 b) No **6.30.** a) Between 13,376,000 and 16,624,000 b) No

Chapter 7

7.1. $z = .5833$; $.5833 < 1.64$. Reserve judgment.
7.2. $z = -2.25$; $2.25 < 2.33$. Reserve judgment.
7.3. $z = 3$; $3 > 1.64$. Reject H_0. **7.4.** $z = 1.5$; $1.5 < 1.96$. Reserve judgment.
7.5. $z = 3$; $3 > 2.58$. Reject H_0. **7.6.** $z = 6$; $6 > 2.33$. Reject H_0.
7.7. $t = -2$; $2 < 2.492$. Reserve judgment.
7.8. $t = -2$; $2 < 5.841$. Reserve judgment.
7.9. $z = -1$; $1 < 1.96$. Reserve judgment.
7.10. $t = -3.47$; $3.47 > 2.896$. Reject H_0. **7.11.** $z = -3$; $3 > 2.33$. Reject H_0.
7.12. a) $t = 3$; $3 > 1.753$. Reject H_0. b) .95
7.13. $z = 2.2$; $2.2 > 1.64$. Reject H_0.
7.14. $t = 1.42$; $1.42 < 2.132$. Reserve judgment.
7.15. $z = -2.14$; $2.14 > 1.64$. Reject H_0.
7.16. $z = 3.21$; $3.21 > 2.33$. Mean amount has declined.
7.17. $z = 2.68$; $2.68 > 1.64$. Average expenses are exaggerated.
7.18. $z = 5.30$; $5.30 > 2.33$. Big Max should be sold.
7.19. $z = 1.94$; $1.94 > 1.64$. Claim is exaggerated.
7.20. a) .1142 b) .0571 c) .0287
7.21. $n = 63.0436$, or 64; $c^* = \$135.33$
7.22. a) $H_0: \mu = 2$; $H_1: \mu = 1.5$ b) .0228 c) .0013
7.23. a) $H_0: \mu = 502$; $H_1: \mu > 502$ b) .0314 c) .0262
7.24. $n = 35.462$, or 36; $c^* = \$882.62$
7.25. Decision rule: Select a random sample of 64 observations and determine $\bar{x}$. If $\bar{x}$ > 153.28, reject H_0.
7.26. Decision rule: Select a random sample of 49 observations and determine $\bar{x}$. If $\bar{x}$ is not between 59.84 and 70.16, reject H_0.
7.27. Decision rule: Select a random sample of 40 observations and determine $\bar{x}$. If $\bar{x}$ < 86.04, reject H_0.
7.28. $n = 75.064$, $c^* = \$53,277.15$

Chapter 8

8.1. a) .0548 b) .2119 **8.2.** a) .0548 b) .6554
8.3. $z = 1.85$; $1.85 < 1.96$. Not significant.
8.4. $z = -2.4$; $2.4 > 1.96$. Significant.
8.5. $t = .98$; $.98 < 3.169$. Not significant.
8.6. $t = -.242$; $.242 < 2.365$. Not significant.

8.7. $z = 2.02$; $2.02 < 2.58$. Two categories gross equal amounts.
8.8. $z = 5.25$; $5.25 > 1.96$. Degree of aggressiveness is not the same.
8.9. $z = 4.65$; $4.65 > 1.96$. Average family income is not the same.
8.10. $(F = 3.443) < (F_{.050} = 3.89)$. Not significant.
8.11. $(F = 4.8) > (F_{.050} = 4.07)$. Significant.
8.12. $(F = 45.02) > (F_{.01} = 6.36)$. Significant.
8.13. $(F = 4) > (F_{.05} = 3.10)$. Significant.

Cumulative Review Exercises II

1. a) Between 1.9608 and 2.0392 b) Between 1.99804 and 2.00196 c) .0668
2. a) Between 702 and 898 b) Between 787.1 and 812.9 c) .3446 d) Zero
3. a) .6892 b) .2881 **4.** a) .8185 b) 107 **5.** Zero
6. Between \$2.68 and \$3.32
7. a) Between 9.51 and 10.49 b) Between 8.9345 and 11.0655
8. .90 confidence **9.** Between 64,672.5 and 75,327.5
10. $z = 3.33$; $3.33 > 2.33$. Establish a branch.
11. $z = 4$; $4 > 1.64$. Reject H_0.
12. $t = 2.5$; $2.5 < 3.747$. Reserve judgment.
13. a) Between 38.04 and 41.96 b) .90 confidence
c) $z = -3$; $3 > 2.58$. Claim is not valid.
14. $z = -0.75$; $0.75 < 1.64$. Reserve judgment.
15. $z = -3$; $3 > 2.58$. Performance is not the same.
16. $z = 3$; $3 > 2.58$. Seminar is effective.
17. $F = 5$; $5 > 3.10$. Brands are different.
18. a) Between \$78.04 and \$81.96 b) \$2.33 c) $z = 5$. Reject H_0.
19. Between 4,602,000 and 4,798,000 **20.** Between 18.84 and 20.66
21. Between 1,144,560 and 1,255,440 **22.** Between 1.339 and 2.611
23. a) $z = 1.47$; $1.47 < 1.64$. Average price has not declined. b) No
24. a) Between 5.625 and 8.375 b) .95
25. $z = .69$; $.69 < 3.747$. They do allocate 90%.
26. a) Between 8.009 and 8.991 ounces b) Between 78,730 and 91,270 ounces
27. a) No b) Yes **28.** a) Between \$19,020 and \$20,980 b) No
29. a) No b) No c) Yes

Chapter 9

9.1. a) 40% b) .5, 1, .5, .5, .5, 0, 0, .5, .5, 0 c) $E(p) = .40, \sigma_p = .3$ d) $\sigma_p = .3$
9.2. a) .5 b) $\frac{2}{3}, \frac{1}{3}, \frac{2}{3}, \frac{1}{3}, \frac{2}{3}, \frac{3}{3}, \frac{2}{3}, \frac{2}{3}, \frac{1}{3}, \frac{2}{3}, \frac{1}{3}, \frac{2}{3}, \frac{1}{3}, \frac{1}{3}, 0, \frac{1}{3}, \frac{2}{3}, \frac{1}{3}, \frac{2}{3}, \frac{1}{3}$
c) .50 d) .90
9.3. a) .0228 b) .6915 c) .1574 **9.4.** a) .0228 b) .0228 **9.5.** .018
9.6. $p^* = .47, n = 1568.16$ **9.7.** a) .0228 b) $P_1 = .45, P_2 = .55$
9.8. a) .0918 b) .0021 c) .5 **9.9.** .0828 **9.10.** a) .0427 b) .1814
9.11. a) .0427 b) .8944 c) .50 **9.12.** a) .0985 b) .1814
9.13. $n = 161.47, p = .0613$
9.14. Between .1534 and .2466
9.15. a) .0508 to .1492 b) .0588 **9.16.** .8904 **9.17.** a) 246 b) 6147

9.18. 97   **9.19.** Between 2296 and 3204
9.20. Between 10,918 and 14,682
9.21. a) Between .1608 and .2392   b) .9544
9.22. Between 5962 and 8438 accounts
9.23. Between 4569 and 6,231,000   **9.24.** .9544
9.25. a) Between 1660.5 and 2339.5   b) .8502
9.26. a) Between 351 and 1149   b) .7814
9.27. Between 1,521,600 and 1,678,400

Chapter 10

10.1. $z = 1.67; 1.67 > 1.64$. Reject H_0.
10.2. $z = -.824; .824 < 2.33$. Reserve judgment.
10.3. $z = -.7; .7 < 2.58$. Reserve judgment.
10.4. $z = -1.67; 1.67 < 2.33$. Reserve judgment.
10.5. $z = -1; 1 < 1.96$. Reserve judgment.
10.6. $z = 2.5; 2.5 > 1.28$. Reject H_0.
10.7. a) $z = 1.25$. Reserve judgment.   b) $z = 5$. Reject H_0.
10.8. $z = -.75; .75 < 2.33$. Reserve judgment.
10.9 a) Between .7488 and .8512   b) $z = 6; 6 > 1.64$. Reject claim.
10.10. $z = -2.5; 2.5 > 1.64$. Reject H_0.
10.11. $z = 2.24; 2.24 < 2.58$. Claim is valid.
10.12. a) Between .158 and .272   b) $z = 2.62; 2.62 > 2.33$. Claim is exaggerated.
10.13. $z = 4.35; 4.35 > 2.58$. Claim is not valid.
10.14. a) .6331   b) .0869
10.15. $z = -1.74; 1.74 < 2.58$. Not significant.
10.16. $z = 2.198; 2.198 > 1.96$. Significant.
10.17. $z = -.77; .77 < 1.64$. Not significant.
10.18. $z = -3.62; 3.62 > 1.96$. Reject H_0.
10.19. $z = 1.28; 1.28 < 2.58$. Proportions are the same.
10.20. $z = .76; .76 < 2.58$. Vacancy rates are the same.
10.21. $z = 2.03; 2.03 < 2.58$. It is equally preferred.
10.22. $\chi^2 = 5.1875; 5.1875 < 9.488$. Not significant.
10.23. $\chi^2 = 17.28; 17.28 > 9.210$. Significant.
10.24. $\chi^2 = 26.666; 26.666 > 9.210$. Not independent.
10.25. $27.777 > 9.210$. Not independent.
10.26. $\chi^2 = 6.0269; 6.0269 < 9.210$. Independent.
10.27. $\chi^2 = 47.694; 47.694 > 5.991$. They do not prefer the same activities.
10.28. $\chi^2 = 3.5717; 3.5717 < 9.488$. Preference is the same.
10.29. $\chi^2 = 64.28; 64.28 > 5.991$. Television influences performance.

Cumulative Review Exercises III

1. .9525   **2.** a) .1587 b) .1359   **3.** a) .0427 b) $p_1 = .418, p_2 = .582$
4. a) .1335   b) $p_1 = .1933, p_2 = .2067$ c) Between .1488 and .2512
5. a) .8664   b) Between .0608 and .1392   **6.** Between .2935 and .4265
7. a) Between .459 and .541   b) .9544 confidence

8. a) .9544 confidence   b) Several possible answers
9. $z = -3.57; 3.57 > 2.33$; Reject claim.
10. a) $z = -.5$. Reserve judgment.   b) $z = 3.25$. Reject claim.
11. $z = 1.33; 1.33 < 1.64$. No change in quality.
12. a) Between .1752 and .2248   b) $z = 2.96; 2.96 > 2.58$. Claim is not valid.
13. a) Between .1649 and .2351
    b) $z = 3.13; 3.13 > 2.58$. Claim is not valid.
    c) Several possible answers
14. a) Between .7446 and .8554   b) $z = 2; 2 < 2.33$. Reserve judgment.
15. a) Between .198 and .282   b) $z = 2; 2 > 1.64$. Sales have increased.
16. $z = -3.70; 3.70 > 1.96$. Significant.
17. $z = 1.41; 1.41 < 2.58$. Not significant.
18. $\chi^2 = 6.66; 6.66 > 5.991$. Significant.
19. a) .0239   b) .0749   **20.** a) Between 9450 and 13,350   b) .9332
21. a) .1562   b) .0207   **22.** Between .56 and .64

Chapter 11

11.1. b) $Y' = 36 + 13X$; 81.5 heartbeats/minute.
11.2. a) 13   b) 686 heartbeats/minute.
11.3. a) $1750 = 1690 + 60$ b) 3.87   c) $r^2 = .966, r = .983$
11.4. a) $Y' = -.79 + .31X$ b) $293
11.5. a) $Y' = 5.6 + 1.6X$ b) $21,600
    c) Fixed cost = $5600   d) Variable cost per unit = $1600
11.6. a) .7   b) $.7 > .283$. Significant.
11.7. c) For $66 < X < 72$, Y' is always positive.
    d) $r = .51 > .418$. Significant.
11.8. a) $Y' = 4.178 + .901X$ b) $1400.728 billion
    c) $r = .9997 > .487$. Significant.
11.9. a) $Y' = -.518519 + .425926X$ b) $8,851,853   c) $425,926
11.10. a) 20   b) $r = .45; .45 > .449$. Significant.
11.11. $r = .38015; .38015 < .602$. Not significant.
11.12. $r = .9861; .9861 > .765$. Significant.
11.13. a) $r = -.5489; .5489 < .707$. Not significant.

Chapter 12

12.1. a) $Y' = 2.865 + .1372X$ b) $.0845 < B < .1899$
    c) $t = 1.668; 1.668 < 2.998$. Reserve judgment.
12.2. a) $Y' = .0731 + .5688X$ b) $.4187 < B < .7189$
    c) $t = .693; .693 < 1.860$. Reserve judgment.
12.3. a) $Y' = 57.05 + 10.55X$ b) $10,500
    c) $t = .2329; .2329 < 1.812$. Reserve judgment.
    d) Between 188.02 and 242.58
12.4. a) $Y' = 11.824 + 4.696X$
    b) For every additional convention, the hotel expects 470 more customers.
    c) $4.223 < B < 5.169$ d) Between 46,750 and 52,034 customers

12.5. a) $Y' = -37.162 + 116.080X$ b) For $X \geq 1$, Y' is always positive.
c) $116.08   d) $t = -1.738$. $1.738 < 2.650$. Reserve judgment.
e) Between 418.40 and 435.80
12.6. $321.75; between $220.41 and $423.10

Chapter 13

13.1. a) $Y' = 102.230 + 10.230X_1 - 21.615X_2$ b) $10,230   c) $21,615
d) 1.261   e) $288,578   f) .9986
13.2. a) $Y' = 68.75 + 6.25X_1 + 11.25X_2$
c) $t_1 = 4.967$; $4.967 > 3.499$. Significant. $t_2 = 14.730$; $14.730 > 3.499$.
Significant.
d) $F = 2112.5$; $2112.5 > 4.74$. Significant.   e) $217.5 million
13.3. a) $Y' = 517.9982 + 49.7101X_1 + 99.0877X_2$ c) 6.0366
d) $t_1 = 83.297$; $83.297 > 2.179$. Significant. $t_2 = 113.530$; $113.530 > 2.179$.
Significant.   e) .9996   f) $1908.22
13.4. c) $t_1 = 2.49$; $2.49 > 2.365$. Significant. $t_2 = 4.97$; $4.97 > 2.365$. Significant.   d) $F = 30.955$; $30.955 > 9.55$. Significant.   e) 10.83%
13.5. a) 107.6   b) $t_1 = 16.80$; $16.80 > 2.921$. Significant. $t_2 = 16.74$;
$16.74 > 2.921$. Significant. $t_3 = 15.18$; $15.18 > 2.921$. Significant.   c) $F = 370.03$;
$370.03 > 5.29$. Significant.
13.6. a) $t_1 = 5.96$; $5.96 > 3.499$. Significant. $t_2 = 2.40$; $2.40 < 3.499$. Not significant.
$t_3 = 6.67$; $6.67 > 3.499$. Significant.   b) $t_4 = 4.69$; $4.69 > 3.499$. Significant.   c) 4796   d) $F = 16.895$; $16.895 > 7.85$. Significant.

Chapter 14

No answers.

Chapter 15

15.1. a) $Y' = 2.0467 + .0694X$ (origin, 1974; X-units, 1 year; Y, average hourly earnings in dollars)   b) $3.0183   d) $Y' = 2.6713 + .0694X$ e) $3.3653
15.2. a) $Y' = 69.84 + 14.99X$ (origin, 1976; X-units, 1 year; Y, annual sales in billions
of dollars)   c) $Y' = 129.80 + 14.99X$ d) $249.72 billion
15.3. a) $Y' = 953.4 + 140.1X$ (origin, 1976; X-units, 1 year; Y, annual wheat exports
in millions of dollars)   c) $2914.8 million
15.4. a) $Y' = 16.5476 + 2.2343X$ (origin, 1975, X-units, 1 year; Y, annual imports in
billions of dollars)   c) $Y' = 38.8906 + 2.2343X$ d) $54.5307 billion
15.5. a) $Y' = 3.78 + .04X$ b) $7.3 million
15.6. a) $\log Y' = 1.3664 + .0295X$ c) $118.7 billion   d) .0703
15.7. a) $\log Y' = 1.4324 + .0720X$ c) $275.7 billion   d) .1803
15.8. a) $\log Y' = 1.5060 + .0474X$ c) .1153
15.9. a) $\log Y' = 1.4424 + .0946X$ b) .2434   c) $470.1 billion
15.10. a) $\log Y' = 2.4192 + .0469X$ c) .1140   d) $1190.7 billion
15.11. January $= .9323$, February $= .9130$, March $= 1.0828$, April $= 1.0967$,

May = 1.1033, June = 1.0919, July = 1.0120, August = .9362, September = .8171, October = 1.0510, November = 1.0036, December = .9601

15.12. a) $Y' = 5115.8 + 676.3X$ b) $Y' = 400.485763 + 4.696528X$
  c) January = .9137, February = .8774, March = .9880, April = .9697, May = 1.0106, June = .9910, July = .9814, August = 1.0126, September = .9650, October = 1.0012, November = 1.0314, December = 1.2579
d) $726.4 thousands

15.13. a) $Y' = 276.88 + 44.72X$ b) $Y' = 21.365275 + .310556X$
  c) January = .8408, February = .7640, March = .9371, April = .9834, May = .9477, June = .9207, July = .8868, August = 1.0029, September = .9678, October = 1.0090, November = 1.0700, December = 1.6698 d) $103.6 thousand

15.14. a) January = .9034, February = .8803, March = .9929, April = 1.0009, May = 1.0453, June = 1.0565, July = 1.0777, August = 1.0923, September = 1.0070, October = 1.0054, November = .9502, December = .9880
b) $105.5 thousand

15.15. a) $Y' = 50,000 + 4000X$ b) $136,800 c) March

Chapter 16

16.1.
Year	73	74	75	76	77	78
Index	100	137.5	142.5	147.5	157.5	157.5

Year	79	80	81
Index	215.0	272.5	242.5

16.2.
Year	76	77	78	79	80	81
Index	100	126.84	138.97	173.0	216.41	232.14

16.3.
Year	76	77	78	79	80	81
Index	56.27	63.78	76.92	91.39	100.00	105.60

16.4.
Year	1977	1978	1979	1980	1981
Index	91.47	100.00	107.75	106.20	102.33

16.5.
Year	1960	1965	1970	1975	1978	1979	1980
Index	100.00	141.52	280.91	685.76	1112.73	1263.58	1393.64

16.6.
Year	1977	1978	1979	1980	1981	1982
Index	77.41	85.02	91.36	100.00	116.70	130.81

16.7.
Year	73	74	75	76	77	78	79
Index	100	134.34	147.29	143.52	157.83	176.05	214.45

16.8.
Year	1975	1976	1977	1978	1979	1980	1981
Index	49.60	41.64	44.20	62.49	86.09	100.00	125.13

16.9.
Year	1976	1980	1981
Index	100.00	153.82	176.20

16.10.
Year	1979	1980	1981
Index	100.00	109.50	120.95

16.11. a)

Year	1978	1979	1980
Index	100	117.18	137.23

b)

Year	1978	1979	1980
Index	85.16	100	117.46

16.12. a)

Year	1980	1981	1982
Index	100.00	118.38	141.25

b)

Year	1980	1981	1982
Index	100.00	117.75	141.23

16.13.

Year	1977	1978	1979	1980
Index	100	82.78	80.04	83.49

16.14.

Year	1978	1979	1980
Index	100.00	105.95	112.28

16.15.

Year	1978	1979	1980
Index	100.00	109.15	119.77

16.16.

Year	1975	1976	1977	1978	1979	1980
Index	100.00	101.19	101.47	101.69	101.75	101.72

16.17. a)

Year	1977	1978	1979	1980	1981
Index	100.00	101.18	93.82	85.15	81.91

b)

Year	1977	1978	1979	1980	1981
Index	109.76	112.03	105.56	101.22	100.00

16.18.

Year	1978	1979	1980
Index	100.00	102.74	103.20

16.19.

Year	1975	1980
Index	100.00	119.37

16.20.

Year	1977	1978	1979	1980
Index	165.41	149.55	119.37	100

16.21. a)

Year	1977	1978	1979	1980
Index	100	128.65	101.31	106.21

b)

Year	1977	1978	1979	1980
Index	93.91	120.68	94.29	100

Chapter 17

17.1 $z = .32;\ .32 < 1.96$. Reserve judgment.
17.2. $z = 1.25;\ 1.25 < 1.96$. Reserve judgment.
17.3. $z = 2.02;\ 2.02 < 2.33$. Reserve judgment.
17.4. $z = 2.41;\ 2.41 > 2.33$. Reject null hypothesis.
17.5. $z = -3.26;\ 3.26 > 1.96$. Intelligence is not the same.
17.6. $z = -3.37;\ 3.37 > 1.96$. Length of sleep is not the same.
17.7. $H = 13.28;\ 13.28 > 5.99$. Respiratory rate is not the same.
17.8. $H = 30.07;\ 30.07 > 13.277$. Reject H_0.
17.9. $r_s = .524$ **17.10.** $r_s = .903$ **17.11.** $r_s = .212$
17.12. a) $z = 2.4;\ 2.4 < 2.58$. Not significant.
     b) $z = 2.1;\ 2.1 > 1.96$. Significant.   c) $z = 1.6;\ 1.6 < 1.96$. Not significant.
17.13. $r_s = 0.421$

Chapter 18

18.1. a) A_4 b) A_1 c) A_3 d) 44   e) 56   f) 12
18.2. b) \$1.05   c) \$1.15   d) \$0.10
18.3. b) 50, \$12.50   c) EVPI = \$2.50   d) \$2.50   e) \$2.50
18.4.

	A_1	A_2	A_3
b) EOL	22	12	27

     c) 12
18.5.

	Purchase	Not Purchase
b) EOL	\$150	\$1050

     c) \$150
18.6. a) Should undertake.   b) EVPI = \$1500
18.7. a) Purchase medium machine. Expected cost \$2875.   b) EVPI = \$375
18.8. a) Should use first method. Expected cost \$20,000.   b) EVPI = \$800
18.9. a) \$197,500   b) EVPI = \$10,000,000   **18.10.** \$390,000, \$55,000

Chapter 19

19.1. $P_1(\pi = 40) = .47,\ P_1(\pi = 50) = .53$
19.2. a) Should not build.   b) 2500   c) Should build.   d) 3750
19.3. a) 1160   b) 1431.6
19.4. a) Should develop.   b) $EVPI_0 = 250$
     c) Should not develop.   d) $EVPI_1 = 550$
19.5. a) $P_1(\pi = .20) = .46,\ P_1(\pi = .30) = .54$
     b) $P_2(\pi = .20) = .39,\ P_2(\pi = .30) = .61$
     c) $P_1(\pi = .20) = .39,\ P_1(\pi = .30) = .61$
19.6. a) Should not sponsor.   b) $EVPI_0 = \$50$
     c) Should sponsor.   d) $EVPI_1 = \$45.50$
19.7. a) Should not guarantee.   b) $EVPI_0 = \$500$
     c) Should not guarantee.   d) $EVPI_1 = \$1000$

GLOSSARY/INDEX